'Michael Morales has marshalled a breathtaking spectrum of Jewish, Christian and critical perspectives unprecedented in commentary to Numbers – or to any book of the Hebrew Bible. His attention to the ways in which structure, themes and vocabulary create a unified whole within chapters and across the book makes this an indispensable resource.'
Joshua Berman, Bar-Ilan University, Israel, and author of *Inconsistency in the Torah: Ancient Literary Convention and the Limits of Source Criticism*

'With close attention to the text, and deeply informed by classical and modern sources, Michael Morales offers a theologically rich and informative reading of Numbers. By highlighting the importance of Israel's Camp he demonstrates the literary integrity of the book. Far from Numbers being the junk room of the priestly material, he demonstrates that it is a coherent work. This substantial commentary will therefore be a key point of reference for all future work on Numbers.'
David G. Firth, Trinity College Bristol

'Michael Morales's work on Numbers is a breathtaking achievement. It is a rare thing for a work of this scale (or any scale) to marry depth of scholarship, breadth of reading, clarity of expression and an evident commitment to the gospel of Christ, but this book has it all. It's worth having for the introduction alone, which brilliantly outlines a theological approach to Numbers that is both dramatically fresh and yet historically rooted, particularly in the rich Jewish tradition of reading the book as a keystone of the Pentateuch. Morales's careful and thoughtful exegesis is married with a profound commitment to biblical theology. Judicious insights and stimulating suggestions are presented with a beautiful lightness of touch. This deserves to be the standard evangelical work on Numbers for many years to come, and will repay careful study by pastors, scholars and students alike.'
J. Gary Millar, Principal, Queensland Theological College, Brisbane, Australia

'Page-turner and game-changer! I never expected to say that of a book about Numbers. Michael Morales's commentary on Numbers changes everything. No commentary or study opens up Numbers more richly than these two volumes – from the census of the first generation to the second ruling about the inheritance of the daughters of Zelophehad. Every page of Morales's interpretation leads me to re-study Numbers as though I have never read it before. The exciting engagement with rich Judaic interpretative traditions sets every part of Numbers within the entire book and the entire Torah as well as within all of the Christian Scriptures. Pastors, students and scholars will want to set aside the latest paperback in order to take to the beach or to the park Morales's page-turner of a commentary and find out what's next. Morales invites all of us back into the wilderness sojourn of Numbers as though for the very first time.'

Gary Edward Schnittjer, Distinguished Professor of Old Testament, Cairn University, Philadelphia, and author of the award-winning *Old Testament Use of Old Testament: A Book-by-Book Guide*

APOLLOS OLD TESTAMENT
COMMENTARY

4a

NUMBERS 1 – 19

TITLES IN THIS SERIES

EXODUS, T. Desmond Alexander
LEVITICUS, Nobuyoshi Kiuchi
NUMBERS 1 – 19, L. Michael Morales
DEUTERONOMY, J. G. McConville
JOSHUA, Pekka M. A. Pitkänen
RUTH, L. Daniel Hawk
1 & 2 SAMUEL, David G. Firth
1 & 2 KINGS, Lissa Wray Beal
PROVERBS, Paul Overland
ECCLESIASTES & THE SONG OF SONGS,
Daniel C. Fredericks and Daniel J. Estes
DANIEL, Ernest C. Lucas
HOSEA, Joshua N. Moon
OBADIAH, JONAH & MICAH, Elaine A. Phillips
HAGGAI, ZECHARIAH & MALACHI,
Anthony R. Petterson

SERIES EDITORS

Gordon J. Wenham, 2002–23
David W. Baker, 2002–
Beth M. Stovell, 2023–

APOLLOS OLD TESTAMENT
COMMENTARY

4a

NUMBERS
1 – 19

Series Editors
David W. Baker and Beth M. Stovell

L. MICHAEL MORALES

Apollos,
London, England

APOLLOS (an imprint of Inter-Varsity Press)
SPCK Group, Studio 101, The Record Hall, 16–16A Baldwin's Gardens, London
EC1N 7RJ, England
Email: ivp@ivpbooks.com
Website: www.ivpbooks.com

First published 2024

British Library Cataloguing-in-Publication Data
A catalogue record for this book is available from the British Library.

ISBN: 978–1–78974–471–2
eBook ISBN: 978–1–78974–472–9

Typeset in Great Britain by Fakenham Prepress Solutions, Fakenham, Norfolk

For my father, Luis I. Morales, *in memoriam*:
16 February 1944 – 4 February 2023,
and for my mother, Ana, who sows in tears and reaps in joy.

CONTENTS

ILLUSTRATIONS

FIGURES

TABLES

EDITORS' PREFACE

The Apollos Old Testament Commentary takes its name from the Alexandrian Jewish Christian who was able to impart his great learning fervently and powerfully through his teaching (Acts 18:24–25). He ably applied his understanding of past events to his contemporary society. This series seeks to do the same, keeping one foot firmly planted in the universe of the original text and the other in that of the target audience, which is preachers, teachers and students of the Bible. The series editors have selected scholars who are adept in both areas, exhibiting scholarly excellence along with practical insight for application.

Translators need to be at home with the linguistic practices and semantic nuances of both the original and target languages in order to be able to transfer the full impact of the one into the other. Commentators, however, serve as interpreters of the text rather than simply its translators. They also need to adopt a dual stance, though theirs needs to be even more solid and diversely anchored than that of translators. While they also must have the linguistic competence to produce their own excellent translations, they must moreover be fully conversant with the literary conventions, sociological and cultural practices, historical background and understanding, and theological perspectives of those who produced the text as well as those whom it concerned. On the other side, they must also understand their own times and culture, able to see where relevance for the original audience is transferable to that of current readers. For this to be accomplished, it is not only necessary to interpret the text; one must also interpret the audience.

Traditionally, commentators have been content to highlight and expound the ancient text. More recently, the need for an anchor in the present day has also become more evident, and this series self-consciously adopts this approach, combining both. Each author analyses the original text through a new translation, textual notes, a discussion of the literary form, structure and background of the passage, as well as commenting on elements of its exegesis. A study of the passage's interpretational development in Scripture and the church concludes each section, serving to bring the passage home to the modern reader. What we intend, therefore, is to provide not only tools of excellence for the academy, but also tools of function for the pulpit.

David W. Baker
Beth M. Stovell

AUTHOR'S PREFACE

Another commentary on Numbers is fully justified: the book's literary structure remains a matter of debate; its true subject matter (and corresponding theology) has proven elusive; the actual point of transition for Israel's generations, having deep interpretative significance, has with few exceptions been widely mistaken; and Jewish scholarship – ancient, medieval and contemporary – which supplies satisfying solutions to these conundrums, remains an undervalued resource. Perhaps because its purpose and message have not been grasped clearly, Numbers is sorely neglected in the church; and, yet, its narrative is filled with great human drama and adventure and contains possibly the highest vision of the covenant community in the Torah, along with that community's need for an exalted priestly mediator. Indeed, my awe of the LORD God and his mercy, admiration of Moses and insight into the people of God, as well as what true spirituality in the world means, have been reshaped and deepened in inexpressible ways along the nearly ten years of labour on this commentary. May God be pleased to add his blessing, especially in the evangelical preaching and teaching of Numbers; and may the divine light of Numbers shine afresh, and strengthen God's people with hope, joy, holiness and perseverance in the wilderness, as we look to him for that blessed life in the Land.

When I first signed on to this project, Philip Duce was the IVP editor, and the series editors were David W. Baker and Gordon J. Wenham, and I continue to be grateful for their granting me this weighty privilege. Since then Thomas Creedy has become the IVP editor, and I here express my hearty thanksgiving for his Herculean efforts in helping me edit and refine a manuscript that had grown mammoth and unwieldy as I continued the research journey – it has been a joy working with you, Tom. Gordon, who years earlier had served as my thesis supervisor, needed to step down due to declining health; he and his family remain in my heart and prayers, filled with heavenly hope. David offered scrupulous feedback, earning both my gratitude and esteem. Beth Stovell now joins David as series editor and I anticipate gleaning her insight for editing volume 2. Eldo Barkhuizen provided meticulous and skilful copyediting, for which I am deeply grateful. Rima Devereaux was a stellar senior project editor, and a continual source of patient support. Teaching at Greenville Presbyterian Theological Seminary has been a blessing, and I am brimming over with thankfulness for our board of directors, faculty, staff and students, for their support and prayers on this project, and for Jonathan Master, our president, whose friendship has been a kind and constant source of encouragement. Especially as I had endeavoured to read widely for this project, my special thanks go to Jim Higgins for enabling me to secure needed resources. Once more it is a joy to express how grateful I am for Eric Chimenti, who provided the illustrations with patience and skill, and also brotherly encouragement along the way.

The years of commentary labour are most easily tracked by the growth of our sons. I thank God for our family – my wife, Elise, and sons Armando, Augustine, Alejandro and Andres – and, ever dependent on his grace, pray for the strength by his Spirit to pursue the One in whom all glory dwells, the great Shepherd of the sheep (Heb. 13:20), through our wilderness sojourn, until we enter the endless joys of New Jerusalem.

One of my last conversations with my father was on Numbers. From his hospital bed he had asked me about the projected publication date for this commentary. When I replied, he said, 'That's too late for me,' with visible disappointment, even slight annoyance, on his face – he was ever excited to see the beauty and riches of God's Word. These two volumes on Numbers, which are but so much straw compared to what he now sees, are dedicated to my father, who has – by the grace of God in Jesus Christ – joined the camp of the LORD's heavenly hosts.

ABBREVIATIONS

TEXTUAL

1QM	*War Scroll*
4QMMT	*Halakhic Letter*
11Q19, 11QT^a	*Temple Scroll*
Ar.	*Arachin*
b.	Babylonian Talmud
B. Qam.	*Bava Qamma*
Bav. Bat.	*Bava Batra*
Bek.	*Bekhorot*
Ber.	*Berakhot*
CD	Cairo Damascus Document/Rule
Deut.	*Deuteronomy*
Exod. Rab.	*Exodus Rabbah*
Gen. Rab.	*Genesis Rabbah*
Gk	Greek (texts)
HB	Hebrew Bible
Hebr.	Hebrew
Hul.	*Hullin*
Jub.	*Jubilees*
K	Kethibh (the written Hebrew text)
Kel.	*Kelim*
Ket.	*Ketubot*
Lev. Rab.	*Leviticus Rabbah*
LXX	Septuagint
m.	*Mishnah*
Meg.	*Megillah*
Men.	*Menahot*
Mid.	*Middot*
MQ	*Mo'ed Qatan*
MS(s)	manuscript(s)
MT	Masoretic Text
Naz.	*Nazir*
Num. Rab.	*Numbers Rabbah*
Par.	*Parah*
Pes.	*Pesahim*
PesRab.	*Pesiqta Rabbati*

PesRK	*Pesiqta de-Rav Kahana*
Pirk. Av.	*Pirkei Avot*
Q	Qere (the Hebrew text to be read out)
SamP	Samaritan Pentateuch
Sanh.	*Sanhedrin*
Shab.	*Shabbat*
Shev.	*Shevu'ot*
Sif.	*Sifre*
Sif. Deut.	*Sifre Deuteronomy*
Sif. Num.	*Sifre Numbers*
Sif. Zut.	*Sifre Zuta*
Sot.	*Sotah*
Spec. Laws	*Special Laws* (Philo)
Suk.	*Sukkah*
Syr	Syriac Peshitta
T	*Tosefta*
t.	*tractate*
T. Ab.	*Testament of Abraham*
T. Naph.	*Testament of Naphtali*
Tam.	*Tamid*
Tan.	*Tanḥuma*
Tg(s)	Targum(s)
TgNeof	*Targum Neofiti*
TgO	*Targum Onqelos*
TgPal	*Palestinian Targums*
TgPs-J	*Targum Pseudo-Jonathan*
Tos.	*Tosafot*
Vg	Vulgate
Yalk. Reuv.	*Yalkut Reuveni*
Yalk. Shim.	*Yalkut Shim'oni*
Yom.	*Yoma*
Zeb.	*Zebachim*

HEBREW GRAMMAR

abs.	absolute
adj.	adjective, adjectival
art.	article
conj.	conjunction
const.	construct
def. art.	definite article
f.	feminine
gen.	genitive
hiph.	hiphil

hith.	hithpael
hoph.	hophal
imp.	imperative
impf.	imperfect
inf.	infinitive
juss.	jussive
m.	masculine
niph.	niphal
pi.	piel
pl.	plural
pr.	pronoun
prep.	preposition
ptc.	participle, participial
pu.	pual
sg.	singular

MISCELLANEOUS

ad loc.	at the place (passage of a commentary where citation may be found)
Ag. Ap.	Josephus, *Against Apion*
ANE	Ancient Near East(ern)
Ant.	Josephus, *Antiquities of the Jews*
ASV	American Standard Version
AV	Authorized (King James) Version
Barn.	*Barnabas*
c.	circa
Creation	Philo, *On The Creation*
ESV	English Standard Version
Gig.	Philo, *De Gigantibus*
Gk	Greek (texts)
GNT	Good News Translation
JPS	Jewish Publication Society translation
J. W.	Josephus, *Jewish War*
lit.	literally
MishT	Maimonides, *Mishneh Torah*
Moses	Philo, *Life of Moses*
NET	New English Translation (2005 ed.)
NIV	New International Version (1984 ed.)
NJPS	New Jewish Publication Society translation
NKJV	New King James Version
NT	New Testament
Quaest. in Num.	Augustine, *Quaestiones in Numeri* (Questions on Numbers)

SamP	Samaritan Pentateuch
Sir.	Ben Sira, *Sirach* (Ecclesiasticus)

JOURNALS, REFERENCE WORKS, SERIES

AB	Anchor Bible
ABD	D. N. Freedman (ed.), *Anchor Bible Dictionary*, 6 vols., New York: Doubleday, 1992
ABR	*Australian Biblical Review*
ACCS: OT	Ancient Christian Commentary on Scripture, Old Testament
AJT	*American Journal of Theology*
AnBib	Analecta Biblica
AnOr	Analecta Orientalia
AOAT	Alter Orient und Altes Testament
AOTC	Apollos Old Testament Commentary
ArBib	The Aramaic Bible
ATANT	Abhandlungen zur Theologie des Alten und Neuen Testaments
AThR	*Anglican Theological Review*
AUSS	*Andrews University Seminary Studies*
BA	*Biblical Archaeologist*
BAR	*Biblical Archaeology Review*
BASOR	*Bulletin of the American Schools of Oriental Research*
BBR	*Bulletin for Biblical Research*
BBRS	Bulletin for Biblical Research Supplement
BDB	F. Brown, S. R. Driver and C. A. Briggs, *The Brown-Driver-Briggs Hebrew and English Lexicon, with an Appendix Containing the Biblical Aramaic*, Boston: Houghton, Mifflin, 1906; repr. Peabody: Hendrickson, 2012
BETL	Bibliotheca ephemeridum theologicarum lovaniensium
BGBE	Beiträge zur Geschichte der biblischen Exegese
BHS	K. Elliger and W. Rudolph (eds.), *Biblia Hebraica Stuttgartensia*, Stuttgart: Deutsche Bibelgesellschaft, 1983
Bib	*Biblica*
BibInt	*Biblical Interpretation*
BJS	Brown Judaic Studies
BKAT	Biblischer Kommentar, Altes Testament
BN	*Biblische Notizen*
BR	*Biblical Research*

BRev	*Bible Review*
BSac	*Bibliotheca Sacra*
BSC	Bible Student's Commentary
BST	The Bible Speaks Today
BT	*The Bible Translator*
BTB	*Biblical Theology Bulletin*
BZ	*Biblische Zeitschrift*
BZAW	Beihefte zur Zeitschrift für die alttestamentliche Wissenschaft
CAL	Comprehensive Aramaic Lexicon
CBQ	*Catholic Biblical Quarterly*
COT	Commentar op het Oude Testament
CTQ	*Concordia Theological Quarterly*
CV	*Communio viatorum*
DATD	Das Alte Testament Deutsch
DOP	*Dumbarton Oaks Papers*
DSB	Daily Study Bible
DSD	*Dead Sea Discoveries*
EBC	Expositor's Bible Commentary
ECC	Eerdmans Critical Commentary
ETL	*Ephemerides theologicae lovanienses*
EvQ	*Evangelical Quarterly*
ExpTim	*Expository Times*
FAT	Forschungen zum Alten Testament
GKC	*Gesenius Hebrew Grammar*
HALOT	L. Koehler, W. Baumgartner and J. J. Stamm, *The Hebrew and Aramaic Lexicon of the Old Testament*, tr. and ed. under supervision of M. E. J. Richardson, 2 vols., Leiden: Brill, 2001
HAT	Handbuch zum Alten Testament
HBT	*Horizons in Biblical Theology*
HS	*Hebrew Studies*
HSM	Harvard Semitic Monographs
HTR	*Harvard Theological Review*
HUCA	*Hebrew Union College Annual*
IBC	Interpretation: A Bible Commentary for Teaching and Preaching
ICC	International Critical Commentary
IDB	*Interpreter's Dictionary of the Bible*, ed. G. A. Buttrick, 4 vols., Nashville: Abingdon, 1962
Int	*Interpretation*
JAOS	*Journal of the American Oriental Society*
JBL	*Journal of Biblical Literature*
JBQ	*Jewish Bible Quarterly*
JETS	*Journal of the Evangelical Theological Society*

JJS	*Journal of Jewish Studies*
JPT	*Journal of Pentecostal Theology*
JPTSup	Journal of Pentecostal Theology Supplement
JQR	*Jewish Quarterly Review*
JSJ	*Journal for the Study of Judaism in the Persian, Hellenistic, and Roman Period*
JSOT	*Journal for the Study of the Old Testament*
JSOTSup	Journal for the Study of the Old Testament: Supplement
JSQ	*Jewish Studies Quarterly*
LHBOTS	Library of Hebrew Bible / Old Testament Studies
MTZ	*Münchener theologische Zeitschrift*
NAC	The New American Commentary
NCBC	New Century Bible Commentary
NICNT	New International Commentary on the New Testament
NICOT	New International Commentary on the Old Testament
NIDOTTE	W. A. VanGemeren (ed.), *New International Dictionary of Old Testament Theology and Exegesis*, 5 vols., Grand Rapids: Zondervan, 1997
NIGTC	New International Greek Testament Commentary
NIVAC	New International Version Application Commentary
NovT	*Novum Testamentum*
NSBT	New Studies in Biblical Theology
NSKAT	Neuer Stuttgarter Kommentar, Altes Testament
OBO	Orbis biblicus et orientalis
OBT	Overtures to Biblical Theology
Or	*Orientalia*
OTE	*Old Testament Essays*
OTG	Old Testament Guides
OTL	Old Testament Library
OtSt	*Oudtestamentische Studiën*
PBM	Paternoster Biblical Monographs
PEQ	*Palestine Exploration Quarterly*
Presb	*Presbyterion*
RB	*Revue biblique*
ResQ	*Restoration Quarterly*
RevExp	*Review and Expositor*
RTR	*Reformed Theological Review*
SANT	Old Testament Library
SBJT	*Southern Baptist Journal of Theology*
SBL	Society of Biblical Literature
SBLDS	Society of Biblical Literature Dissertation Series

Sem	*Semitica*
SFSHJ	South Florida Studies in the History of Judaism
SJLA	Studies in Judaism in Late Antiquity
SJOT	*Scandinavian Journal of the Old Testament*
SJT	*Scottish Journal of Theology*
SOTSMS	Society for Old Testament Studies Monograph Series
SSN	Studia semitica neerlandica
ST	*Studia theologica*
StOr	Studies in Oriental Religions
TBL	Themes in Biblical Narrative
TDOT	*Theological Dictionary of the Old Testament*, ed. G. J. Botterweck and H. Ringgren, tr. J. T. Willis, G. W. Bromiley and D. E. Green, 8 vols., Grand Rapids, 1974–
THAT	*Theologisches Handwörterbuch zum Alten Testament*, ed. E. Jenni and C. Westermann, Munich, 1971–1976, 2 vols.
TLOT	*Theological Lexicon of the Old Testament*, ed. E. Jenni, with assistance from C. Westermann, tr. M. E. Biddle, 3 vols., Peabody, 1997
TOTC	Tyndale Old Testament Commentaries
TWOT	R. L. Harris, G. L. Archer Jr. and B. K. Waltke (eds.), *Theological Wordbook of the Old Testament*, 2 vols., Chicago: Moody, 1980; repr. as one vol. 2003
TynB	*Tyndale Bulletin*
TZ	*Theologische Zeitschrift*
UF	*Ugarit-Forschungen*
VT	*Vetus Testamentum*
VTSup	Vetus Testamentum Supplements
WBC	Word Biblical Commentary
WTJ	*Westminster Theological Journal*
ZABR	*Zeitschrift für altorientalische und biblische Rechtgeschichte*
ZAH	*Zeitschrift für Althebräistik*
ZAW	*Zeitschrift für die alttestamentliche Wissenschaft*
ZBK	Zürcher Bibelkommentare

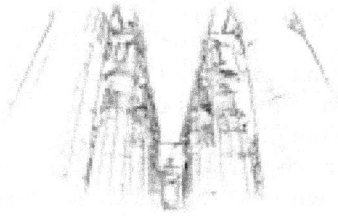

INTRODUCTION

'The LORD is my shepherd, I shall lack nothing.' So begins David's twenty-third psalm, a declaration of faith that expresses the essence of YHWH's character in Numbers. From Mount Sinai to the plains of Moab on the cusp of Canaan, YHWH faithfully led his flock, feeding them manna from heaven and streams of water from the rock, his Cloud shielding them from the heat of the sun by day, and his fire lighting their nights (see Ps. 105:39–41). Indeed, David's 'lack nothing' (*lō' 'eḥsār*) forms an echo of Moses' parting words to Israel in Deuteronomy, where he explains that throughout their long years in the wilderness 'YHWH your God has been with you – you have lacked nothing' (*lō' ḥāsartā*, 2:7).

While the destination, to 'dwell in the house of the LORD for ever' (Ps. 23:6), awaits consummation, Numbers is both compass and map for the journey, revealing both the glory of YHWH and the nature of humanity. 'These things were written for our instruction', wrote Paul of Israel's wilderness experience (1 Cor. 10:11), that we might learn the strength of YHWH's arm, the absolute nature of his holiness and the tenderness of his boundless mercies; that we might forsake unbelief and grumbling, and follow him with simple dependence and songs of gladness. Asaph had made a similar exhortation in Psalm 78, calling on Israel not to be like their fathers in the wilderness, but to remember God's wonderful works with praise and loyalty. This perennial application is built into the shape of Numbers, as the second generation, goaded by the failings of their forebears and by their own yearning for life in the land, steadily matures along their journeys with God. In this way, Israel's second generation serves as a paradigm for God's people in every generation, for Numbers is chiefly an analysis of Israel *as the covenant community* formed at Sinai, structurally expressed as the Camp of Israel.

The English title Numbers derives from the Latin Vulgate *Numeri*, itself a translation of the Greek heading *Arithmoi*, referring to the census lists narrated within. The Talmud preserves a similar name, *Chomesh HaPekudim* as 'that fifth [of the Torah] about countings' (*Yom.* 7.1; *Men.* 4.3; *Sot.* 36b). Both Jerome and Epiphanius knew of another Hebrew title based on the book's first word, *Wayĕdabbēr*, 'And he [YHWH] spoke' (cf. G. B. Gray 1903: xxii). The traditional Jewish ascription, retained in modern Hebrew Bibles, is *Bĕmidbar* or 'In the wilderness', taken from the opening verse. 'In the wilderness' is the preferable title inasmuch as the wilderness describes not only the drama's locale, but also the period in Israel's life encompassed by the book. The wilderness represents more than a place, but a time and a mode of being. With Egypt behind and the hope of the land before, the wilderness is an in-between place for Israel, which characterizes the transitions of *Bĕmidbar*: from Mount Sinai to the plains of Moab, from the first to the second generation of Israel, from Aaron's high priesthood to that of his son Eleazar, from the governance of Moses to the military leadership of Joshua (cf. Wall 2005). The wilderness sojourn was the context for Israel to learn to live as a covenant community, as the multitudes redeemed out of Egypt were organized into a four-square encampment embodying the polity, structure and nature of the Sinai covenant, a community where YHWH dwelled among his people as sovereign.

The 'in the wilderness' journey defines Israel as a flock and YHWH as their Shepherd, whose voice – *torah* – his sheep should recognize and follow. The Hebrew word for wilderness, *midbar*, shares the same root letters for 'word' (*d-b-r*), which, in Aramaic, may also be used of a shepherd leading sheep (CAL; Jastrow 1926: 278; Riskin 2009: 5–6). Ancient Jewish sources associated their roots in wordplay, with the Midrash stating, 'wilderness (*midbar*) is, in essence, but utterance (*dibbur*)' (*Exod. Rab.* 2.5). Kimḥi defined *midbar* as the *maqôm-dĕbar*, the 'place of the word'. As Zornberg writes (2015: 275), 'Both as presence and as absence, *dibbur* courses through the narrative of the *midbar*, the wilderness.' The Marah story (Exod. 15:22–27), the foundation for wilderness theology, sets the path for Israel precisely in terms of 'diligently heeding the voice of YHWH'. In John's Gospel, Jesus made much of the point that sheep respond to and follow their shepherd's voice (10:4, 16, 27). The wilderness thus defines the nature of Israel's covenant relationship with God, prodding the flock to exercise faith and perseverance, trusting daily in YHWH's guidance and provision. Within Numbers, the wilderness era is defined by the Nazirite vow, a period of deprivation unreservedly embraced with the ambition of drawing nearer to YHWH. No less than a trek across geography, then, *Bĕmidbar* narrates a spiritual pilgrimage. It recounts an arduous death to a people's old Egyptian personality and the birth pangs of a new identity as the covenant people of YHWH. This death and rebirth take place literally as the old generation dies out amid the forty years of wandering and a new generation matures to inherit the promise of life with YHWH in the land. As the place where YHWH and Israel were bound together as in marriage by the covenant of Sinai, the wilderness sojourn is later described by prophets as a courtship when YHWH wooed Israel to be his bride (Hos. 2:14; cf. Jer. 2:1–2): 'Therefore – look! – I will allure her, will lead her into the wilderness (*ha-midbār*) and I will speak (*wĕdibbartî*) with her heart' (Zornberg 2015: xxi).

Though Numbers contains a bewildering array of material in various genres, they are all embraced and defined by the wilderness, which arguably becomes the genre. Wilderness literature finds echoes in the literature of exile, and also in journey epics, such as Homer's *Odyssey* and Virgil's *Aeneid*. Ultimately, wilderness literature springs from the longing for home, though the homeward turn is rarely if ever to the home one has left behind. Rather, the journey's end is the eschaton, the eternal city of God where justice flows and righteousness dwells. The journey's end can only be life in the new heavens and earth under Messiah's reign, in the Zion before that will surpass all longings for the Eden behind. Until the final end and new beginning, *bĕmidbar*, 'in the wilderness', will characterize the life of all God's people in every age.

1. THE 'SOUL' OF NUMBERS: LEADERSHIP OF THE COVENANT COMMUNITY

The character and unique perspective of Numbers is illumined by comparison and contrast with Exodus and Leviticus, and with Deuteronomy. While the Torah is set in general chronological order, it is also topically arranged: each book manifests its own angle and personality, its 'soul', as it were. Perhaps the most obvious example of this topical arrangement is in relation to the consecration of the Dwelling, recounted in the three central books, each focusing on a different aspect of the Dwelling and highlighting different persons. After distinguishing the perspective of Numbers in relation to Exodus and Leviticus in relation to the dedication of the Tabernacle, the viewpoint of Numbers will be refined further by contrast with Deuteronomy.

1.1. The consecration of the Dwelling in Exodus, Leviticus and Numbers

Numbers 7 draws the reader back one month before chapter 1, to the consecration of the Dwelling, when the tribal leaders, one prince per day, brought forward their offerings for the transport of the Dwelling and the dedication of the altar. Why narrate these events here, out of chronology? The answer relates to the main thematic interest of Numbers.

The Torah describes the consecration of the Tabernacle, which occurred on the first month of the second year, in three different books: near the end of Exodus, in the early part of Leviticus and in the early part of Numbers (see Rimon 2008; Bick 2014c; cf. also Zweig 1989; Haran 1990; G. A. Anderson 2022; *b. Shabbat* 87b). Each account narrates the event in accord with the general emphasis of its particular book. Exodus 40 recounts Moses' prominent role in the Dwelling's construction, along with how the glory of YHWH filled the Dwelling. Leviticus 8 – 9 narrates the ordination of the priesthood for the Tent of Meeting's inaugural service, which focuses on the altar, an event indicated earlier in Exodus 40:12–15. Numbers 7 – 8 tells how the princes of each tribe brought forth gifts for the transport of the Dwelling by Levites, and for the dedication of the altar, and how the Levites were cleansed for this transport duty. These three perspectives on the Tabernacle's dedication ceremony are consistent with each book's thematic emphasis: Exodus concerns Moses' mediatorial role, while Leviticus deals primarily with the role of the priests, and Numbers with that of the nation of Israel, represented by its tribal leadership, and the Levites' role within the community wherein YHWH sovereignly dwells. The nation of Israel and its leaders are regularly in view throughout Numbers. In theological terms, Numbers is concerned profoundly with *ecclesiology* – it *is* the ecclesiology of the Torah. As such, it is no surprise that over half the occurrences of the word *'ēdâ* (congregation, community) in the HB are found within Numbers (cf. Ashley 1993: 48).

The three separate descriptions of the Tabernacle's consecration also serve as a clue to three different aspects of the Tabernacle developed in each book. Exodus ends with the construction of the Tabernacle as the Dwelling (*miškān*), the anticipated culmination of the book: YHWH God descends to dwell in the Tabernacle, filling the Dwelling with his glory, through the mediatorial role of Moses. The Tabernacle in Exodus is represented in terms of its function as God's abode on earth, reversing his separation from humanity's earthly sphere. The focus of Leviticus is how this Dwelling may also function as the meeting place between YHWH and Israel, as a 'Tent of Meeting' (*'ōhel mô'ēd*): God's Dwelling becomes a meeting place with Israel through a consecrated priesthood within the context of the ordained sacrificial cult. Here the Tabernacle is represented primarily in terms of its role in worship, facilitated by the priests. Once the Dwelling begins to function as a Tent of Meeting, the next concern, taken up by Numbers, is that of establishing the Camp of Israel, the covenant community wherein YHWH dwells. The Tabernacle becomes YHWH's organizing centre for guiding his people in the wilderness, whether encamped or on journey. The book's emphasis on the wilderness journeys of the Camp of Israel coheres with the particular view it offers of the day the Tabernacle was set up and consecrated; namely, of the tribal princes and Levites, including gifts and labour for transporting the Dwelling, as Israel pursues YHWH's Cloud in the wilderness. *Numbers sets forth the Tabernacle primarily in terms of its role in leading and guiding the nation throughout its wilderness journeys.* Israel's role in following him, as led by their tribal chieftains, and the role of Levites to guard and transport his Dwelling, flow out of this emphasis. In Numbers, the central players at the Dwelling, observes Y. Twersky (2007b: 2:125–126), are now the *nesi'im*, the chieftains of the Camp. He further observes that nearly 'every failure in *Sefer Bemidbar* revolves around a failure of leadership', including a *nasi*'s central role in the Baal Peor catastrophe (Y. Twersky 2007b: 2:131, 128).

The results of G. A. Anderson's study (2022) are remarkably close to our own:

> Broadly speaking, the book of Exodus puts its emphasis on the structure of the Tabernacle building (chs. 25–31, 35–40), Leviticus focuses on its altar (chs. 1–10), while Numbers attends to its role in guiding Israel to the promised land (chs. 1–9) . . . The thematic manner of presentation allows our author to give each dimension of the Tabernacle independent development.

Bick's terse summary, related to the person(s) in focus in each book, is insightful: 'Exodus is about God; Leviticus is about Aaron and the priests; Numbers is about Israel and the princes' (2014c: 88). The progress may also be tracked according to time, one to seven to twelve days: Exodus focuses on a single day, New Year's Day, when the Tabernacle was raised and consecrated (40:17); Leviticus underscores the seven days of preparation for the priesthood (8:33–35), seven signifying the cult; and Numbers recounts the twelve-day presentation of gifts for the altar's dedication, one day per each of the twelve tribes, representing all Israel.

To take a second example, the literary centre of each book narrates an ascent of sorts into YHWH's presence: in Exodus 19, Moses alone ascends into YHWH's presence on Sinai; in Leviticus 16, Aaron the high priest alone enters YHWH's presence in the Tent's holy of holies, a ritual entry to cleanse the Tent of Meeting; in Numbers 17, Aaron's rod is brought into the inner sanctum, where it blossoms and bears ripe almonds, a divine demonstration that he alone has been chosen by YHWH for the office of high priest, reaffirming his leadership role, and the hierarchy within the tribe of Levi. Each of these three scenes coordinates perfectly with the perspective and emphases pertaining to its respective book.

1.2. Leviticus and Numbers in relation to the ending of Exodus

The thematic emphasis and perspective of Numbers may be developed further still by looking at the relationship of Leviticus and Numbers to the ending of Exodus more closely, Exodus 40:34–38:

> Then the Cloud covered the Tent of Meeting, and the glory of YHWH filled the Dwelling. And Moses was not able to enter into the Tent of Meeting because the Cloud dwelled upon it and the glory of YHWH filled the Dwelling. And whenever the Cloud ascended from above the Dwelling, the sons of Israel would journey forth in all their journeys. But if the Cloud did not ascend, then they would not journey forth until the day it would ascend. For the Cloud of YHWH was upon the Dwelling by day and there was fire upon it by night, in the eyes of all the house of Israel, in all their journeys.

While verse 34 presents the culmination of Exodus, YHWH's glory dwelling on earth, verse 35 adumbrates the narrative strategy and theme of Leviticus, and verses 36–38 introduce the same for the book of Numbers. Each theme relates to YHWH's presence through his Cloud of glory: in Exodus, the Dwelling is filled with YHWH's glory; in Leviticus, the Dwelling, unapproachable because of YHWH's glory, must come to function as a Tent of Meeting; and in Numbers, YHWH will shepherd his people through the wilderness as Israel follows his Cloud. (See Table 1.)

Leviticus answers Moses' inability to enter the Tent of Meeting, narrating how God's Dwelling came to function as a Tent of Meeting between YHWH and Israel through the divinely ordained sacrifices and consecrated priesthood (see Morales 2015). Correspondingly, Numbers goes on to relate the relationship between YHWH and Israel, in terms of guidance through the wilderness within the context of the newly established Camp of Israel. The same Cloud of YHWH's glory, the *Shekhinah*,

Table 1: The ending of Exodus

Exodus 40:34	40:35 (unapproachable Tent)	→ Leviticus (Tent of Meeting)
	40:36–38 (ascent of Cloud)	→ Numbers (guidance of Camp in wilderness)

which had made entrance into the Tent impossible, now ascends to lead Israel through the wilderness. The phraseology of Exodus 40:36–38 is repeated and expanded with pronounced detail in Numbers 9:15–23, an ideal portrait that culminates with the inaugurating fulfilment, the climactic moment of the glory Cloud's ascent in Numbers 10:11–13.

Table 2: Inclusio with YHWH's Cloud

YHWH's guidance of Israel by his Cloud	The Dwelling becomes a Tent of Meeting between YHWH and Israel			Camp of Israel created around YHWH's Dwelling			YHWH's guidance of Israel by his Cloud
	LEVITICUS (Presence)			NUMBERS (Guidance)			
Exod. 40:34–38 Presence, 34–35 Guidance, 36–38	1–10 Approaching YHWH's Tent of Meeting	11–16 Cleansing YHWH's Tent of Meeting	17–27 Meeting with YHWH at his Tent of Meeting	1–6 Tribes arranged around YHWH's Dwelling	7–8 Dwelling inaugurated for the journey	9:1–14 Passover celebrated	Num. 9:15–23 Presence, 15–16 Guidance, 17–23

The inclusio created by the allusion to Exodus 40 in Numbers 9:15–23 demonstrates that the intervening sections – the entirety of Leviticus and Numbers 1 – 8, along with the Passover account in 9:1–14 – were essential to the fulfilment of the original scene anticipated at the end of Exodus, which portrays the function of the Dwelling primarily in terms of setting out from Mount Sinai. Leviticus 1 to Numbers 8 'catches up' the reader to the events of Exodus 40:36–38, so that with Numbers 9:15–23 the story continues from where it left off. Numbers 9:15–23 and Exodus 40:34–38 are similar structurally, moving from God's presence in the Dwelling, through the Cloud, to his guidance of Israel through the wilderness, also through the Cloud. (See Table 3.)

The presence theme in Exodus 40:34–35 sets up the book of Leviticus, wherein the Dwelling will come to function as a Tent of Meeting, and the portrayal of Israel following YHWH's Cloud in Exodus 40:36–38 anticipates the guidance theme, which incorporates the presence theme, setting up the subject matter of Numbers. The inclusio includes both themes, framing the relevant content of Leviticus and Numbers 1 – 8 as prerequisites to the fulfilment of what will take place after the inclusio; namely, Israel's setting out under the Cloud's guidance (10:11–36),

Table 3: YHWH's Cloud in Leviticus and Numbers

	Exodus	Numbers	
1. YHWH's presence in Dwelling, via Cloud	40:34–35	9:15–16	→ Leviticus
2. YHWH's guidance of Israel, via Cloud	40:36–38	9:17–23	→ Numbers

onward until arriving at the plains of Moab. Numbers 11 – 25 then serves as an exegesis of the dynamic between YHWH's guidance and Israel's response. YHWH's *Shekhinah* presence both in the midst of the Camp and as the ascended, guiding Cloud of glory is integral to Israel's wilderness years. As Grossman writes (2014c: 64), 'The journey is very much a function of the *Mishkan*, since it is the movement of this building which determines the moment that the people are to break camp.' Our observations can be charted as set out here.

Table 4: The tabernacle's three roles

Book	Perspective	Tabernacle role
Exodus	YHWH's mediator, Moses	Dwelling
Leviticus	Aaron's priesthood	Tent of Meeting
Numbers	Israel's princes and Levites	Guidance of the Camp

Needless to say, these are not absolute distinctions but basic emphases; Moses' mediatorial role is evident in all three books.

1.3. Numbers 9:15–23 as reversal of Exodus 33

The resumptive repetition in Numbers 9:15, bringing the reader back to Exodus 40:33–34, reclaims the dramatic momentum of YHWH's filling the Tabernacle before the Camp sets out on the journey to Canaan. Here it is essential to consider Exodus 33, when, after Israel's failure with the golden calf, YHWH had determined *not to accompany Israel*: 'I will not ascend in your midst, lest I consume you on the way' (33:3; cf. Kelly 1970: 487, 488). This statement negates the goal of Israel's following after the ascended Cloud (Exod. 40:36; Num. 9:15–23). The construction of the Tabernacle, filled with his glory and covered by his Cloud (Exod. 40:34), thus signifies *YHWH's renewed determination to accompany his people on the way to Canaan*, a determination requiring the ensuing narrative and legislative movement of Leviticus and Numbers 1 – 10. YHWH's guidance of Israel through the wilderness in Numbers, then, forms a reversal of his original threatened verdict. By YHWH's own prodding, Moses had refused the compromise for Israel to journey to the land and possess it, apart from YHWH's accompanying presence: 'If your presence (*pānîm*) does not go, then do not make us ascend from here' (33:15). Especially significant, Moses declares that YHWH's favour on Israel would be known 'in your going (*bĕlektĕkā*) with us' (33:16), a statement that adds depth and meaning to the wilderness narratives. By his guidance of Israel through the wilderness, in the regular dismantling and setting up of his Dwelling by the Levites, YHWH was manifesting his favour upon Israel, among the nations. YHWH God's contented assent to Moses' intercession unwinds the narrative tension, allowing the Tabernacle plan to progress to its construction and divine infilling. In Numbers, the Tabernacle stands for YHWH's mobile, accompanying presence and, more narrowly, for YHWH's renewed commitment to journey with Israel, to abide among his people. Clines says the Tabernacle 'is precisely the symbol of the *moving* presence of God', that it 'points forward definitively to the journeying that lies ahead' (1997: 28; emphasis original). All the intervening material between Exodus 33 and Numbers 10 forms the outworking of the divine 'yes' to Moses' intercession.

More profoundly, the arrangement of the Camp (Num. 1 – 6) forms a reversal of the estrangement caused by the golden calf incident, as portrayed in the central image of Exodus 33. Set between YHWH's negation of his presence and guidance (33:1–6) and Moses' response (33:12–23), the central section narrates Moses' pitching his own tent 'outside the camp, far from the camp', calling it 'the tent of meeting' (v. 7). While YHWH was pleased to meet with Moses 'face to face', so that Moses' tent constituted a tent for his 'meeting' with YHWH, the dislocation between YHWH and Israel could not be more dramatic. YHWH's renewed promise to accompany his people (33:14, 17), based on Moses' mediation, then leads to the material of Leviticus, which was needed for YHWH's Dwelling to function as a Tent of Meeting for Israel. Beautifully, the Camp of Israel in Numbers, with YHWH's Dwelling forming the community's centre, surrounded by Levites and the twelve tribes of Israel, is the flowering of Moses' plea to YHWH, the resolution to the situation described in Exodus 33:7–11 (cf. Lawlor 2011: 38, 42).

1.4. Numbers and Deuteronomy

Having signalled the differences between Numbers and Exodus and Leviticus, we turn now to Deuteronomy in those places where the material overlaps. Aligning the mission of the scouts in Deuteronomy 1:19–45 with Numbers 13–14 makes the differences obvious: while Deuteronomy focuses on the people en masse, their role and accountability (cf. Y. Kahn 2012: 19–20; Grossman 2012: 44–46), Numbers highlights the role and accountability of leaders. Numbers lists the twelve princely scouts (13:1–16), narrates the debate among them, between the ten scouts and Caleb and Joshua (13:27–31; 14:6–9), describes the particular sin of the scouts in slandering the land (13:32; 14:36–37), and relates their immediate judgement by plague before YHWH, sparing the two faithful leaders (14:36–38). None of these details appears in Deuteronomy, which is concerned only with the people's part in the fiasco, their instigation of the mission (1:22) and how after the original report on the land the people did not believe YHWH, rebelling against his word (1:23–33).

The contrast with Deuteronomy sharpens our understanding of Numbers as a book not merely about the nation of Israel, but especially about the role of its leaders, princes among the tribes, the Levites and priests, within the newly structured covenant community. Frevel similarly perceives that 'leadership is an important and central issue' in Numbers, perhaps even 'the *major* topic in Numbers' (2018: 89, 94; emphasis original), and Pyschny observes, 'Aspects of leadership, guidance, office, authority and legitimacy are addressed almost throughout the whole book' (2018: 115). A leadership focus resonates with one of the book's titles, *Chomesh HaPekudim*. Since related usage for the root *p-k-d* includes not only the idea of counting but leadership roles such as 'commissioner, deputy, overseer', J. M. Cohen urges 'The Book of Leadership' as a translation with broader relevance for the book's content (2000: 125). Even a cursory survey of Numbers' contents shows that nearly every character mentioned holds some status among the people, affirming that Numbers – to an uncanny degree – lays stress on the role of leadership. First, every tribe is represented by its leader in major events so that all Israel is united in taking part. In the book's opening census, YHWH calls for Moses to be helped by 'a man from every tribe, each man a head (*rō'š*) of his father's house . . . leaders (*nāśî'*, 'prince', 'chieftain') of their fathers' houses' (1:4, 16), listing twelve princes (1:5–15). The next chapter delineates a leader for each tribe, according to their encampments around the Tabernacle; for example, 'Nahshon the son of Amminadab shall be the leader of the sons of Judah' (2:3), and the same takes place for the inner, Levitical encampments: 'the leader of the father's house of the clans of the Kohathites was Elizaphan the son of Uzziel' (3:29–30). When the tribal offerings are presented for the work of the Tabernacle, these are brought by 'the leaders of Israel, the heads of their fathers' house, the leaders of the tribes' (7:2), every tribe acknowledged as contributing. Moses' first complaint will be over his own burden of leadership, which God addresses by appointing seventy men of the elders of Israel, men whom Moses knew to be 'elders and officers' (11:16), endowing them with his Spirit. Also, the twelve men selected to survey the land were 'from each tribe of their fathers . . . every one a leader among them' (13:1). Then, for the eventual allocation of the land, YHWH commanded that 'one leader from every tribe' be taken to assist in the division, and each one is delineated by name (34:16–29). As M. Douglas noted, there are precisely seven full listings of the tribal descendants in Numbers (1:1–44; 2; 7:12–84; 10:14–28; 13:1–16; 26:1–62; 34:16–29), a significant repetition that underscores the solidarity and fraternity of the tribes as the covenant community of Israel (2004: 19–21).

Second, Numbers underscores the influence and culpability of leadership. For example, Moses did not send actual 'spies' but influential men of clout, a cross-section of political leaders, each with significant sway over his particular tribe, in order to encourage the tribes with their report (Milgrom 1990: 100; cf. G. J. Wenham 1981b: 131; Beck 2000: 272). Because most of the leaders brought back a negative report, 'all the congregation lifted up their voices and cried, and the people wept at night' and began to complain, wishing they had died in Egypt – even suggesting they 'choose a leader (*rō'š*)' to return to Egypt (14:1–4). The effect of the scouts' slander of the land is described as 'discouraging' (*nw'*) the heart of the people (32:7, 9), the force of which may imply 'to restrain, thwart, forbid, frustrate' (BDB). Moses, therefore, warned the second generation of leaders, saying that if they too turned away in rebellion, YHWH would once again cause the people to remain in the wilderness, adding, 'and you will be the reason for their destruction' (32:15). Similarly, the rebellion of the inner Levitical camp, led by Korah, included 250 'leaders (*nĕśî'ê*) of the congregation, called ones of the assembly, men of name' (Num. 16:2). Finally, for the sin of harlotry with the Moabites, YHWH commands for 'all the heads of the people' to be hanged in judgement for the apostasy (25:4), and then we discover that the principal high-handed culprit was 'Zimri the son of Salu, a leader of a father's house belonging to the Simeonites', and even his consort, Cozbi, was a high-ranking princess, 'the daughter of Zur, who was head of the people of a father's house in Midian' (25:14–15). Contrary to common perceptions, then, the wilderness rebellions in Numbers are seldom generic sins of grumbling, but focused uprisings led by particular leaders with a designated role in the community; nor do they derive from tests on the part of God (as in Exod. 16), but are impulsive and wilful revolts.

Third, Numbers records the transition of leadership. The tribal leaders of the second generation who will divide the land (34:16–29) stand in place of the previous generation's leaders, who forsook the land (13:4–14). And before Aaron dies, YHWH ensures the succession of the high priest by instructing Moses to strip Aaron of his garments and place them on his son Eleazar (20:22–29), and even his successor, Aaron's grandson Phinehas, is later sealed by YHWH (Num. 25:10–13). So, too, when YHWH announces the time for Moses to be gathered to his people in death, Moses' plea is for God to appoint a man over the congregation, to lead them on their way so as not to leave them as sheep without a shepherd. As a result, Joshua is formally ordained as Israel's next leader (27:12–23). While Deuteronomy includes Joshua's induction (31:1–8), Moses addresses the people primarily (vv. 1–6) and, afterward, his address to Joshua is for the sake of the people, 'in the eyes of all Israel' (v. 7). Deuteronomy consistently addresses the people as a whole, instructing them about living devotedly in the land, whereas Numbers focuses on the leadership of the covenant community, embracing YHWH's newly established hierarchy and the need for leaders to fulfil their roles faithfully.

2. THE STORY OF NUMBERS: THE CAMP OF ISRAEL

What is the major theme of Numbers? 'Yahweh's guidance and testing of Israel in the wilderness' (Harrelson 1959: 27) is a popular summary that relates some of the book's contents while missing its theological essence and plot. Stressing that Numbers is 'perhaps the least understood book of the Pentateuch', Sweeney concludes it is 'fundamentally concerned with the character of Israel and its relationship with YHWH during the course of the journey' (2017: 71), which is closer to the mark. Israel's character and relationship with YHWH, however, need to be evaluated more fundamentally within the defining context of the newly forged covenant at Sinai. Accordingly, Magonet proposed that what lends Numbers its 'certain character' across a diversity of material is 'the theme of political and spiritual organization and leadership of the newly emergent people' (1982: 10). Through the covenant at Sinai, Israel had been constituted as a theocracy, a commonwealth governed by YHWH God through his appointed leaders (cf. Shumate 2001: 2), an insight strengthened further by observing *the structure* of the newly organized theocracy, the Camp of Israel. George thus focuses on the social-space of Israel's Camp, underscoring how the wilderness rebellions were not generic acts of unbelief but 'challenges to the social-spatial order established at Sinai', which Israel chafes under and tests 'in most every way possible' throughout the wilderness sojourn (2013: 34; cf. Pyschny 2019: 295–296).

More than anything else, *Numbers is about the covenant community*, Israel's relationship and life with YHWH established at Sinai, divinely arranged as a camp. Numbers explores the wonder of the community's composition and life, its divine nature, and examines the role of tribal leadership, the place of Levites, the function of priestly atonement, all in relation to the organic whole, the covenant community. Each part of the Camp had its own role, leadership, challenges and objectives, and the wilderness sojourn was necessary for Israel to mature as a nation, finally submitting to YHWH's plan and purposes for them as a covenant community. This newly arranged community involved significant changes for the family clans of Israel, requiring adjustment to ways of thinking and decision-making ingrained for centuries in Egypt. While the covenant is ratified in Exodus, and the sacrificial system is legislated in Leviticus, it is not until Numbers, where the covenant community is realized in its archetypal form, that the story of Israel's learning how to submit to YHWH's leadership through his newly appointed offices and institutions is narrated. Before Israel could live the way of blessing in the land, this was the lesson *sine qua non*: submissive, faithful obedience to YHWH's rule as a covenant community. Far from mere semantics, the covenant community *as the Camp of Israel* is at the heart of the book's message – even the drama of Israel's rebellions is mapped out according to the structure of the Camp.

The first major division of Numbers, chapters 1–10, is commonly summarized as 'preparation for departure' (Burns 1989: 214; Ashley 1993: 14). While such a prospective label has some justification, it underrates the material, which actually forms the flowering of YHWH's engagement with Israel at Sinai. What takes place in these chapters, constructively, forms the foundation for the rest of the book, and for Israel's theology of life with God as a covenant community. Israel is not merely preparing to depart: the nation cannot depart Sinai, for the *telos* of YHWH's Sinai revelation has not yet been reached. Before its prospective function, Numbers 1 – 10 presents a culmination, a completion.

Another prevalent summary is 'preparations for the military campaign', again not without justification, especially given the significant use of *ṣābāʾ* throughout the opening chapters, often translated 'war, army', and the like (e.g. Milgrom 1997: 241–242). The problem is one of over-emphasis: the military quality relates primarily to the outer camp of twelve tribes, comprising only the opening two chapters. Even here, while men of fighting age are in focus, all Israel is in view, including wives, children and the elderly – the *ʿēdāh* as a whole (cf. Seebass 2009; Kellermann 1970: 31). The purity laws of Numbers 5 – 6, for example, involve both male and female, and address circumstances within the family and larger society of God's people; these are not the narrow concerns of a military camp as found in Deuteronomy 23:10–14 (cf. Frevel 2013c: 385). Later episodes in the wilderness narratives, having nothing to do with military concerns, do not imply a campaign narrative (Roskop 2011: 152). Further, while it is common for scholars to compare Israel's Camp with the Egyptian military camp of Rameses II (1290–1223 BC), also a square formation with a central royal tent (cf. Yadin 1963a: 1:236–237; Healy 2001: 64–65; Berman 2016), the nature of the sojourn positions the situation of Israel closer to the migratory camps of the Philistines or 'Sea Peoples', whose history remains elusive (cf. Yasur-Landau 2010). The reliefs at Medinet Habu depict Philistines accompanied by herds, flocks, carts pulled by oxen, carrying women, children and possessions (Seevers 2013: 172–173; Yadin 1963b: 2:248–253, 336–338), just like Israel in Numbers (cf. Hieke 2009: 50). Such laden oxcarts may be assumed throughout Israel's wilderness journeys, and in Numbers 7, tribal princes offer six such carts, with twelve oxen for pulling, to the Levites for their duties in transporting the Dwelling.

Throughout the narratives, moreover, there is a concern for 'little ones' (*ṭap*) among the Camp (Num. 14:3, 31; 16:27; 31:9, 17; 32:16, 17, 24, 26), and a reference to 'our little ones, our wives, our livestock, and all our cattle' (32:16). Including the migratory element as well as the Camp's sacral-cultic aspects (cf. Helfmeyer 1986), centred on the sanctuary's role, Numbers has been dubbed 'the saga of the migratory campaign', understood primarily as a 'sanctuary campaign' (Knierim and Coats 2005; W. W. Lee 2003b). Such proposals still fail to appreciate the paradigmatic function of the Camp, which surpasses the necessities of the wilderness sojourn (cf. Leder 2016: 523). The wilderness sojourn (chs. 11–25) functions as an analysis of the Camp of Israel (chs. 1–10), later applied to life in the land (chs. 26–36).

Remaining questions solicit further probing for an alternate principle of coherence (cf. Leibowitz 1982: 5). Why should Israel's departure encompass ten lengthy chapters? What is the purpose of the detailed description of the Camp's organization? Why must the Camp's arrangement be the subject of divine revelation? Why were the purity laws placed here rather than in Leviticus? How does the ordeal for a strayed wife or the Nazirite vow relate to Israel's sojourn? Answers to these questions surface once the Camp of Israel itself, broadly conceived as YHWH's covenant community, is recognized as the organizing principle of Numbers 1 – 10; as Grossman put it (2017), 'The camp is the protagonist of this narrative.' Numbers 1 – 6 concerns the arrangement of the Camp, concluding with the priestly benediction 'YHWH bless you!' (6:22–27), and chapters 7–10 concern the mobility of the Camp, concluding with Moses' liturgical shout 'Arise, O YHWH!' as the uplifted ark marches out, leading the tribes (10:34–36). These chapters solicit a gazing on the wonder of the Camp itself, offering 'a grand vision of God's people' (Seebass 2009: 109).

2.1. The Camp of Israel is created within the context of the Sinai revelation

The Israelites arrive at Mount Sinai in Exodus 19 and remain there through the rest of the book of Exodus, continuing through the entirety of Leviticus, and through the first major section of Numbers, chapters 1–10. Throughout this section, Israel is encamped within the shadow of Mount Sinai as YHWH reveals his constructive torah through Moses. The Sinai revelation found at the heart of the Torah is set apart as constitutional and foundational, having a specific function and character.

Seldom appreciated, there is a logical development, a progression, to the Sinai revelation. In Exodus 19 – 24, YHWH and Israel enter into a covenant, YHWH giving his people the Decalogue as a constitution *in nuce*, claiming Israel as a 'treasured possession' and calling them to be 'a priestly kingdom and holy nation' (Exod. 19:5–6). In Exodus 25 – 40, within the newly established relationship, YHWH gives them himself, his abiding presence, through the Tabernacle, his earthly Dwelling. In Leviticus, YHWH reveals the sacrificial system, including the consecration of Aaron's priesthood and the unveiling of the sacred calendar, enabling the Dwelling to function as a Tent of Meeting between God and Israel. This leaves Numbers 1 – 10 and the arrangement of the Camp. Can it be that when YHWH speaks from within the Tent of Meeting in these chapters, this revelation is somehow less foundational and less constructive than the other elements of the Sinai revelation? Rather, one would assume that Numbers 1 – 10 is integral to the Sinai covenant, and, given the logical progression of the divine speeches, even anticipate this section as forming the fruition of YHWH's agenda for Israel at Sinai.

2.2. The Camp of Israel as the culmination of the Sinai covenant

At the heart of redemptive covenants in Scripture one finds the divine declaration 'I will be your God, you will be my people, and I will dwell in your midst.' This threefold formula recurs, in whole or in part, throughout Israel's history, expressing the prospect of life in fellowship with God, lived before his face, enjoying all his benefits of abundant life, joy and security (see Morales 2015: 103–106; also Rendtorff 1998). Encapsulating the goal of creation and redemption, YHWH's glory in dwelling among his people comprises the great narrative of the Bible.

Within the context of the Sinai covenant, YHWH's dwelling among his people is portrayed as a major goal of the exodus. 'Let them make me a Sanctuary' he instructs in Exodus 25:8, 'that I may dwell in their midst.' Employing covenantal language, the Tabernacle is revealed and constructed for the sake of God's agenda to dwell in the midst of Israel. A fuller development of the formula is given in Exodus 29:45–46, where YHWH declares:

> I will dwell in the midst of the sons of Israel, and I will be their God. And they will know that I am YHWH their God who brought them out of Egypt that I may dwell in their midst – I am YHWH their God.

The question is, *when* is this purpose fulfilled? When do we find God's Dwelling set literally in the midst of his people? When YHWH's fiery glory descends from Sinai's summit on the newly constructed Tabernacle, bringing Exodus to its majestic close, there is a certain allure to assume the covenant promises have been fulfilled. Yet such is not – and could not be – the case. Here the logical progression of the Sinai revelation must be given utmost weight; the sequence is necessary, with every heavenly revealed section having its role and function. Exodus ends with YHWH's

Figure 1: The Mount
Sinai revelation

ISRAEL'S EXODUS
OUT OF EGYPT,
(EXODUS 1 – 18)

YHWH and Israel
enter into Covenant

YHWH's Dwelling
constructed, filled with his Glory

EXODUS 19 – 24

EXODUS 25 – 40

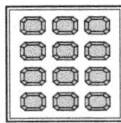

High Priest's
breastplate

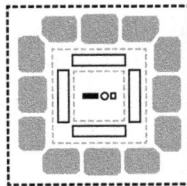

ISRAEL JOURNEYS
FROM MT SINAI
TO THE LAND ...
[NUMBERS 11 – 25]

YHWH's Dwelling
functions as Tent of Meeting

YHWH dwells among his people,
Israel's Camp created

LEVITICUS

NUMBERS 1 – 10

glory filling the Dwelling, and Numbers begins with God's arrangement of Israel, by tribes, around his Dwelling – and the book of Leviticus is the necessary bridge for this movement. Exodus 40:35 reads, 'But Moses was not able to enter the Tent of Meeting,' setting up a dilemma. If Moses, Israel's mediator cannot approach YHWH's Tent, then no other Israelite may do so, and if YHWH's Tent cannot be approached by Israel's tribes, then his Dwelling cannot be set in the midst of his people. Although YHWH's presence has transitioned so that he dwells on earth, he still cannot dwell among the tribes of Israel in life-yielding communion. Such is precisely the goal of Leviticus: for YHWH's Dwelling to function as a Tent of Meeting between God and Israel. Only through the divinely revealed cult is the Dwelling ready to function as a Tent of Meeting between Israel and the Maker of heaven and earth. In Numbers, accordingly, the tribes may now be gathered around the Tent of Meeting, and the covenant promise is finally ready to have its first historical fulfilment outside the gates of Eden. In retrospect, it can be seen that any premature conclusion to the Sinai revelation, ending short of Numbers 1 – 6, would frustrate the *telos* of the revelation, making the previous steps pointless. Not only would YHWH's intention remain incomplete, but the purpose of the covenant, including Israel's vocation as 'a priestly kingdom and holy nation' (Exod. 19:5–6), would be rendered null and void (cf. Exod. 33:16).

By divine revelation, the voice that speaks above the atonement lid from between the golden cherubim in the holy of holies (Num. 7:89; 1:1), YHWH constructs the Camp of Israel in square formation, oriented along the four points of the compass, with three tribes encamped on each side, under the banner of their leading tribe: Judah in the east, Reuben in the south, Ephraim in the west, and Dan in the north. The Camp is laid out in concentric squares according to degrees of holiness. YHWH's Tent establishes the centre, the Levites encamp around his Dwelling, with Aaron's priestly house in the east, and the twelve tribes encamp in the widest square. The tribes are arranged methodically around YHWH's Dwelling, plugged in, as it were, to this *axis mundi*, so that the Camp of Israel becomes connected to the fountain of life in the centre. Fittingly, the section on the Camp's construction ends with the Aaronic benediction shining the light of YHWH's uplifted face to the farthest reaches of the encampment, making it a microcosm filled with the light of God's glory (6:22–27). All of the Sinai revelation was leading up to this moment, for Israel's tribes to dwell with YHWH God in a manner that enables the people to be blessed by him.

The Camp of Israel is, therefore, a *novum*, a sum greater than its parts, a complete cosmos – the first historic expression of the 'covenant community' (*'ēdah*) in all its beautiful bannered array (from a source-critical perspective, see W. P. Wood 1974). (See Fig. 1.)

2.3. The Camp of Israel is the paradigm for the ideal of covenant community

As the divinely orchestrated *form* for the covenant promise's fulfilment, the Camp of Israel becomes the paradigm for the ideal covenant community. If the Camp of Israel is not simply 'preparations for departure', but the culmination of the Sinai revelation, then the Camp's paradigmatic function for future expressions of the covenant relationship is to be expected – and such is indeed the case. In the vision of an eschatological temple-city in Ezekiel, there are significant parallels with the wilderness Camp of Numbers. Within a section on YHWH's renewed covenant with Israel (chs. 36–37), the full threefold covenant formula appears, likely alluding to Exodus 29:45–46 and underscoring the expectation that YHWH's dwelling will be set in the midst of his people (37:26–28). As a visionary fulfilment of this divine declaration, Ezekiel 40 – 48 describes a holy city that is (1) laid out in a square; (2) with four sets of three gates, positioned in the four cardinal directions; (3) each of the twelve gates bearing one of the names of the twelve tribes; (4) and these names representing all Israel are encompassed and unified by the name of the city itself, reflecting YHWH's central presence as its chief attribute: 'YHWH Is There' (*yhwh šāmmā*, 48:30–35). Further, the hierarchical order between priests and Levites is strengthened in Ezekiel, which resonates with their roles in Numbers (e.g. Num. 18; cf. Abba 1978; McConville 1983). Prophesying the future realization of the covenant, Ezekiel's vision is plainly based on the model of the Camp of Israel.

Similarly, in the Dead Sea Scrolls, the Essenes, disillusioned by the corruption of the Jerusalem Temple and its leaders, established their own community in the area of Qumran. In some of their writings, a new Jerusalem is portrayed, which is not so much an eschatological city as it is an idealized city, cleansed and reformed. The Temple Scroll (11Q19) portrays Jerusalem as an idealized temple compound arranged in three concentric courts, resembling the threefold Camp of Israel in the wilderness: the *Shekhinah* is in the centre surrounded by Levites arranged precisely to the pattern of the Levite camps in Numbers 3:14–39, and with the twelve tribes in square formation (cf. Martinez 1996: 164–166; Schiffman 2011; J. A. Davies 1998). Yadin, observing how the Temple Scroll uses the phrase 'outside the city' in a manner such as 'outside the camp' in relation to purity concerns, writes that 'in the judgement of the [Temple] scroll, the Temple city parallels the Pentateuchal *maḥănê* with all its halakhic implications' (1985: 2:199 n. 13). Schiffman elaborates further that the temple plan found in the Temple Scroll presents 'an attempt to recreate within the *temenos* the Israelite camp of the desert period, which surrounded the Tabernacle' (2011: 46; cf. also 1989). The Essenes drew from Numbers because the Camp of Israel is the foundation, the blueprint and paradigm, for the covenant community. As with Ezekiel, the temple plan envisions the tribes encamped around the central temple, dwelling and entering by their respective gates, with YHWH's blessing flowing out to them from the centre (Schiffman 2011: 54–56). Once the Camp's paradigmatic role is perceived, then it follows why 'the primary driving force behind the blueprint described in the Temple Scroll may have been to imitate the arrangement and structure of the Israelite camp in the wilderness under Moses' (Palmer 2012: 269). The Halakhic Letter (4QMMT) displays a similar idea where the temple is equated with the Tent of Meeting, and the city of Jerusalem stands for the holy camp (lines 32–34, 63–64; cf. Martinez 1996: 77–78; Vermes 1997: 224–225). As the following example demonstrates, the analogy between the Camp and Jerusalem was developed in Judaism, especially with reference to purity concerns (cited by Mosser 2004: 317–318; see also Josephus, *Ant.* 3.241–270; Maimonides, *MishT*, *Beit Hebechirah* 7.11–23):

> Just as there were camps in the wilderness, so there was a camp in Jerusalem. From [the walls of] Jerusalem to the Temple Mount was the camp of the Israelites; from the Temple Mount to the Gate of Nicanor was the Levitical camp; beyond that was the camp of the *Shekhinah*. (*b. Zebah* 116b; also *t. B. Qam.* 1:12)

Finally, John's Apocalypse ends with the temple-city of a new creation, New Jerusalem (Rev. 21 – 22). His vision of the holy city is prefaced by the climactic declaration (21:3) 'Behold, the Dwelling of God is with humanity, and he will dwell with them, and they shall be his peoples – God himself will be with them and be their God.' That for the consummating fulfilment of the covenant formula, prefacing his vision of New Jerusalem, John chooses the designation 'the Dwelling' (*hē skēnē*), Tabernacle rather than 'temple', already hints that the wilderness Camp of Israel centred on YHWH God's glorious presence has served as a model for the eschatological City of God (also 20:9). Again we see twelve city gates that had 'names written on them, which are the names of the twelve tribes of Israel: three gates on the east, three gates on the north, three gates on the south, and three gates on the west' (21:13). New Jerusalem's measurements are foursquare, 12 stadia in length, breadth and height (21:15–16). Although the cube form draws on measurements for the holy of holies (cf. Exod. 26; 1 Kgs 6:20; Ezek. 41:4), there is also a parallel with the Palestinian Targum's gloss on Numbers 2, which portrays the wilderness encampment as foursquare, 12 miles in length and breadth. The Apocalypse incorporates another layer of significance from Israel's Camp. The high priest's breast-plate, described in Exodus 28 and 39 as foursquare and having twelve gems with the names of the twelve tribes written on them, appears to have symbolized the Camp, the covenant community, in miniature. John's vision, in addition to the twelve gates of New Jerusalem, describes twelve foundation gems bearing the names of the twelve apostles, imagery that depicts the people of God as a priestly kingdom dwelling in God's sacred presence (21:14, 19–21) – and most commentators trace the twelve gems to the high priest's breastplate (cf. Beale 1999: 1080–1090). In describing the consummation of God's covenant, the *telos* of redemptive history whereby all peoples – Israel and the nations – live with God in paradise, John does so in terms of the ideal paradigm, the Camp of Israel.

In *Antiquities*, Josephus writes that the Camp of Israel 'resembled nothing so much as a city that sometimes was movable, and sometimes fixed' (III.12.5), an insight in accord with later scriptural usage of Numbers. Our brief reception history demonstrates that ancient Jewish authors understood the paradigmatic role of Israel's Camp within the context of the Sinai covenant. Allusions to Numbers in Ezekiel, the Dead Sea Scrolls, and the Apocalypse betray theological comprehension of the wilderness encampment as an ideal portrayal of the covenant community as a temple-city of God. Indeed, the paradigmatic role of Israel's Camp is deeply embedded within Numbers itself, where life with YHWH in the land (chs. 26–36) is modelled after Israel's life with him in the Camp.

2.4. The breastplate of the high priest

The high priest's breastplate, having a fourfold arrangement of twelve gems inscribed with the names of the tribes, invites comparison with the Israel's Camp (cf. Jenson 1992: 127), likely forming a microcosm and anticipation of the latter. Many commentaries on Revelation 21:12–21 correlate the twelve foundation gems of New Jerusalem with those of the high priest's breastplate (Exod. 28:17–20; 39:8–14), unsurprising as the description of the high priest's breastplate in Exodus is the '*locus classicus* of Jewish inventories of twelve precious stones' (Reader 1981: 435). That some of the names for the stones differ or are listed in a differing order is no hindrance, given the uncertainties involved in identifying and translating them – Josephus, moreover, supplies two different orders in his writings (*J. W.* 5.5.7; *Ant.* 3.7.5).

Likely, John's use of the sacred breastplate in Revelation was no innovation, but a discerning appropriation of its function within Exodus itself as symbolizing a foursquare sanctuary-city of God, a symbol for Israel. C. E. Douglas writes that 'the High Priest would bear on his breast a "sanctuary-plan", so to speak, of the tribes' (1936: 55). Although her primary correlation was to the twelve pillars set up at Sinai (Exod. 24:4), the breastplate's prospective symbolism of the established Camp makes more sense. The stones of the breastplate, with the names of the tribes inscribed upon them, make their symbolism for all Israel explicit, for 'they shall be according to the twelve tribes' and 'Aaron will bear the names of the sons of Israel on the breastplate of judgement upon his heart . . . when he enters into the holy place' (28:21,

29). Elsewhere in Scripture there is a play on words between 'son' (*bēn*) and 'stone' (*'eben*), linked to the house/household correlation (*bayit*), as in 2 Samuel 7:1–17 (see Morales 2015: 231–232). The people of God are likened to stones, connected to *the* stone rejected by builders but exalted by God (Ps. 118:22), who form a living temple of God (cf. Eph. 2:19–22; 1 Cor. 3:16–17; 6:19; 1 Peter 2:4–10). Moreover, emphasis on the 'names' of the sons of Israel in Exodus 28:5–14 (on the ephod), 15–30 (on the breastplate), forms a link with the census by 'names' of the sons of Israel in creating the Camp (1:2, 5, 17, 18, 20, 22, etc.). The stones of both the high priest's ephod and his breastplate enable Aaron to 'lift up (*nāśā'*) the names (*šĕmôt*)' of the sons of Israel into YHWH's presence (28:12, 29), just as YHWH instructs Moses to 'lift up' (*nāśā'*) the heads of the community of the sons of Israel by the number of 'names' (*šĕmôt*), to arrange the tribes around YHWH's Dwelling (Num. 1:2).

The precious stones also connect the breastplate to the garden of Eden (Gen. 2:12; Ezek. 28:13; cf. Ellul 1973: 199–206; Beale 1999: 1087–1088), imagery that pervades YHWH's central Dwelling (see Morales 2015: 51–53, 100–103, 175–178). New Jerusalem is described in Edenic terms as well, with a flowing river and tree of life and the absence of the curse (Rev. 22:1–3). In a theologically profound manner, then, the temple-city vision of Revelation forms an exploded-view diagram of the high priest's breastplate, which was a small-scale model of God's city (see the city plans arranged as the high priest's breastplate in C. E. Douglas 1936).

In sum, there are several similarities between Israel's Camp and the high priest's breastplate, which probably explain their correlation in the history of interpretation: (1) arranged in four sets of three (*TgPs-J* has the stones in the quadratic order of Israel's Camp, with three per side); (2) defined by the name of each tribe's patriarch; (3) foursquare in formation; (4) connected to the presence of YHWH; (5) the tribes distinguished by colour (stones; flags) as well as position; (6) arranged by God through divinely revealed instructions. The twelve gems arranged on the sacred breastplate and the twelve tribes arranged around YHWH's Tent share another connection: the twelve signs of the zodiac.

2.5. The Camp of Israel and the signs of the zodiac

Historically, the twelve stones of the high priest's breastplate have been correlated not only with the Camp of Israel, but with the signs of the zodiac as well (for the zodiac in Judaism, see Dobin 1983; Erlanger 2000; Lobel 2013; Jacobus 2015b; 2021). Philo wrote that on the high priest's

> chest there are twelve precious stones of different colours, arranged in four rows of three stones in each row, being fashioned so as an emblem of the zodiac. For the zodiac also consists of twelve animals,

and so divides the four seasons of the year, allotting three animals to each season.

He goes on to ask, what else can the stones 'be emblems of, except of the circle of the zodiac?' (*Spec. Laws* 1.16.84; *Moses* 2.24.124; tr. 1993: 542, 501). In his *Sefer Yesod Mora*, Ibn Ezra describes the breastplate as 'square, corresponding to the four compass points', with the stones of both the ephod and the breastplate alluding to the celestial constellations, placed by Moses in 'the position of the heavenly bodies' (1995: 135–136). Others, too, have connected the twelve stones to the zodiac, linking the breastpiece to the wilderness Camp more deeply, since the arrangement of Israel's Camp has similarly been connected to the twelve constellations of the zodiac (see St. Clair 1907; C. E. Douglas 1936; Dobin 1999, 19–20; also *Num. Rab.* 2.7; *Zohar* 1.173; *Sefer Yetzira* 5–6; *Sefer ha-Zikhronot* of Elazar ben Levi, c. 1325). As summarized by the *Encyclopedia Judaica*, with reference to the aggadic compilation *Yalkut Shim'oni* (Eisenstein 1906: 688; cf. Jacobus 2021: 205–208):

The twelve constellations represent the twelve tribes, while each station of the zodiac has thirty paths, and each path has thirty legions (of stars) (*Ber.* 32b). The standards of the tribes corresponded to the zodiacal signs of the constellations, so that in the east was the standard of Judah, with Issachar and Zebulun beside it, these three being opposite Aries, Taurus, and Gemini; in the south was the standard of Reuben, with Simeon and Gad, opposite Cancer, Leo, and Virgo; in the west was the standard of Ephraim, with Manasseh and Benjamin, opposite Libra, Scorpio, and Sagittarius; and in the north was the standard of Dan, with Asher and Naphtali, opposite Capricornus, Aquarius, and Pisces (*Yalk.*, Num. 418).

In her work *Mazzaroth: or, The Constellations* (1862: 37–61), Rolleston connects the zodiac to the names of Jacob's twelve sons, particularly through the lens of Jacob's blessing of the tribes and Moses' song about the tribes (Gen. 49; Deut. 33), arguing that the signs and names served as prophecies of the coming Messiah – the (sacrificial) bull, for example, signifying Messiah's advent to be a sacrifice for sin. Through the names of the tribes and their corresponding zodiac signs, she connects the banners of the wilderness camp, the stones of the high priest's breastplate, the gates of Ezekiel's city, and the New Jerusalem of the Apocalypse. The first stone mentioned of the high priest's breastplate, *'ōdem* (Exod. 28:17), may be repointed to read 'adam', with reference to Messiah's human nature, and, when connected to the tribal order of encampment, is typified by the Lion of the tribe of Judah (connected to *Leo* of the zodiac), and so on (1862: 44). Further, when Balaam saw the Israelites encamped by their tribes (Num. 24:2), it was the emblems on their standards before his eyes that enabled him by the Spirit to allude to Jacob's prophecies concerning his sons; by way of illustration, his reference to the Messiah's crouching like a lion (v. 9; see Gen. 49:9–10), derived from the lion banner of Judah (1862: 39, 41; also Maunder 1909: 12–13; Burrows 1938: 71–79). Rolleston's work was popularized by Seiss, *The Gospel in the Stars* (1882), and then by Bullinger in *The Witness of the Stars* (1893; also Maunder 1909; Gilbert 1983: 40–46; Bobrick 2005: 1–26). 'The four great signs which thus marked the four sides of the camp, and the four quarters of the Zodiac', writes Bullinger (1893: 19),

> are the same four which form the Cherubim (the Eagle, the Scorpion's enemy, being substituted for the Scorpion). The Cherubim thus form a compendious expression of the hope of Creation, which, from the very first, has been bound up with the Coming One, who alone should cause its groanings to cease.

Such a view takes seriously that Jacob's blessings in Genesis 49 are prophetic and meant to have a programmatic function in the life of Israel, according to the tribes, and that the Camp standards each bore a 'sign' (*'ôt*), with signs first linked to heavenly lights (Gen. 1:14) and bearing witness to God's dealings with humanity (Gen. 4:15; 9:12–17; 17:11; Exod. 3:12, etc.). This view also acknowledges that Jewish tradition offers interpretative insight. In *Jubilees* (12:16–19; c. 150 BC), Abram is portrayed as a skilled Chaldean astrologer before leaving Haran (Jacobus 2021: 192) – historically, Chaldea was a seedbed for astrology. Josephus wrote that the two sardonyx stones of the ephod represented the sun and moon, while the twelve stones of the breastplate may be understood as the twelve months, correlated to the signs of the zodiac (*Ant.* 3.7.7). References to the zodiac occur also in 2 *Enoch* 21:6 and in *Sibylline Oracles* 5.512–531, and 'the zodiac appears on a number of mosaic floors of Jewish synagogues in late antiquity', such as the Beth Alpha synagogue in Galilee (Aune 1998: 52b:681; also Magness 2005). The zodiac is also the subject of later Jewish literature, such as the *Zohar* (I:173) and *Pesikta* (ch. 4). In Scripture, God compares Abraham's vast descendants to the stars of heaven (Gen. 15:5; 22:17) as does Moses (Deut. 1:10), and in Joseph's dream his family is compared to the sun, moon and eleven stars, with Joseph presumably the twelfth (Gen. 37:9; see *Num. Rab.* 2.13; *T. Naph.* 5.1–8; *T. Ab.* B 7.4–16; Philo, *On Dreams* 2.112–113). Connections have also been made to the woman in Revelation 12:1 who is clothed with the sun, having the moon under her feet, and a crown of twelve stars on her head, stars which many commentators interpret in relation to the twelve tribes of Israel (e.g. Beale 1999: 625–627).

The narrative of prophecy some have found in the zodiac signs cannot be linked to Scripture *explicitly*, although arguably 'the Bible is rich with astrological allusion' and that the 'Hebrews knew and revered the zodiac long before the Torah . . . [was] inscribed' (Bobrick 2005: 8, 23). Awareness of the constellations has likely existed as long as human beings have lifted their gaze skyward, and astrology was certainly integral to the cultures of ancient Mesopotamia, with the earliest discovered astrological text dating to the first half of the second millennium BC (Baigent 1994: 1–2), but the twelve zodiacal constellations in their classical form are normally dated to Babylon around 500 BC (J. H. Rogers 1998a; also Koch-Westenholz 1995; J. H. Rogers 1998b). Discussion should include, further, the distinction between astronomy and astrology. Scriptural comparisons of Israel to the stars may simply have the people's vast numerousness in focus (cf. Gen. 15:5; Deut. 1:10), rather than any sort of mythological or prophetic symbolism – although this may be a false either–or scenario. Broadly, some general connection to the zodiac, given the emphasis on the four quadrants of the Camp, accords with the theology that Israel's Camp comprises YHWH's earthly hosts as a parallel to his heavenly hosts. G. J. Wenham, having assessed Barnouin's (1977) correlation of the census figures (Num. 1) with astronomical periods, concludes by reflecting that the celestial bodies are sometimes called God's heavenly host (e.g. Deut. 4:19), and that both God's heavenly and earthly dwellings are attended by the hosts of YHWH: 'the idea that the army of Israel corresponded to the heavenly host was an old one' (1981b: 76; see 74–76). The nature of Israel's wilderness Camp, surrounding the Dwelling of YHWH, is rooted in its reflection of God's heavenly dwelling and hosts, a theological aspect of the Camp's arrangement that is not, ultimately, dependent on any connection between the twelve tribes and the signs of the zodiac, although cosmological symbolism surely pervades both YHWH's Dwelling and Israel's Camp.

2.6. The Camp of Israel as YHWH's earthly hosts

A key for understanding the theology of the Sinai revelation and its object, the Camp of Israel, is vertical typology, whereby the earthly Dwelling of YHWH mirrors the heavenly reality, a dynamic relating chiefly to the instructions for the Dwelling and its furnishings, as in Exodus 25:9, 'According to all that I will show you, the pattern (tabnît) of the Dwelling, and the pattern of all its furnishings, just so you will make it.' That such typology was incorporated into the theology of the Temple is evident in the language of Solomon's dedicatory prayer with its refrain for YHWH to hear the prayers of his people 'toward this place' or 'in this Temple', so that he would 'hear in heaven, the place of your dwelling' (1 Kgs 8:30–53). Following through on this vertical correspondence leads to further insight on the nature of God's covenant community. Since the arrangement of the tribes around the Dwelling is rooted within the context of the heaven–earth analogy of the Dwelling itself, Israel's Camp may be seen to form the earthly counterpart to YHWH's heavenly entourage, which surrounds his heavenly abode.

YHWH's more complete appellation is *yhwh ṣĕbā'ôt*, YHWH of hosts. As an expression of his glory, YHWH is never alone: he is the One surrounded by myriads of angelic hosts, his heavenly entourage, poised to do his bidding. He dwells among the cherubim and travels with and among his heavenly host. Although not mentioned in Exodus, other scriptural passages portray YHWH's presence at Sinai as accompanied by his angelic hosts (on Second Temple traditions, see Najman 2000). Psalm 68:17 reads: 'The chariot of God is double ten thousand, even thousands of thousands. The Lord is among them as in Sinai, the holy place.' A similar understanding of YHWH's advent on Sinai is found in Deuteronomy 33:2, and in the New Testament as well (see Acts 7:53; Gal. 3:19; Heb. 2:2; also the Messiah's return 'with clouds' and/or 'with angels', Matt. 24:30–31; 25:31; 26:64; Rev. 1:7). Just as his heavenly Dwelling is surrounded by heavenly hosts among whom he travels, so YHWH's earthly Dwelling is surrounded by his earthly hosts, the thousands among Israel, among whom he travels. At Mount Sinai he established an earthly Dwelling (Exod. 35 – 40), and part of the progression of Numbers 1 – 6 involves his establishing an earthly host around this earthly Dwelling.

Numbers thus narrates YHWH's divine revelation for the sake of establishing the Camp of Israel as his earthly assembly and entourage so that, as a counterpart to his heavenly hosts, he may travel with and guide Israel through the wilderness. The word 'host' (*ṣābā'*) occurs thirty-six times throughout the opening two chapters of Numbers, portraying the outer camp of Israel's tribes as YHWH's hosts (1:3, 20, 22, etc.) – and there is a sevenfold use of *ṣābā'* with reference to the inner camp of Levites (4:3, 23, 30, 35, 39, 43). Although *ṣābā'* has military overtones (cf. J. R. Spencer 1998), the designation 'host' is preferred over narrower translations such as 'army', 'military', 'battle' and the like since *ṣābā'* 'exhibits a wide range of meanings' (Levine 1993: 134), and may refer to 'the host of cosmic and heavenly powers' or express a 'totality' (Mettinger 1982b: 109–110). The designation YHWH Sabaoth (*ṣĕbā'ôt*) is typically translated 'LORD of hosts', referring to the angelic hosts, which certainly form a vast and powerful militia, but the Name also signifies that YHWH 'dwells among/is enthroned upon the cherubim', surrounded by his heavenly entourage, as evident in the first several uses of the phrase (1 Sam. 1:3, 11; 4:4). While underscoring the might of YHWH's angelic entourage and while YHWH of hosts leads Israel in battle (the context for 1 Sam. 4:4), the emphasis is upon the heavenly host itself – YHWH is the One surrounded by myriads of angels who are ready to do his bidding. The expression YHWH Sabaoth, Mettinger observes (1982b: 117–118), has royal connotations, depicting God as a heavenly king, sitting on his throne, surrounded by his heavenly council – with the divine council being a part of the designation's associative field. More narrowly, since 'God presides over his heavenly council as *yhwh ṣĕbā'ôt*' (Mettinger 1982b: 136), a label that includes cultic connotations, it is best to understand the Israelites as YHWH's earthly hosts – as those who, paralleling the angelic hosts who surround his heavenly throne, have been gathered about his earthly throne. The translation 'host' for *ṣābā'* in Numbers 1 – 2 includes military connotations even while maintaining a deeper significance, the Camp's parallel to the heavenly hosts (see Nachmanides 1975: 6; M. Clark 1999: 211; Hirsch 2007a: 5–6; Samet 2020). Use of *ṣābā'*, rather than more definite military terms such as *ḥayil*, writes Roskop (2011: 172–173; emphasis original), 'may have been a deliberate play on the title *yhwh ṣĕbā'ôt*, an effort to depict *Israelites* as Yahweh's 'hosts' despite the fact that this term usually refers to Yahweh's heavenly entourage' – precisely. We have already observed how the idea that Israel's armies corresponded to the heavenly hosts was established early (see G. J. Wenham 1981b: 76; cf. P. Guillaume 2009: 143).

The arrangement of the tribes around the Dwelling is rooted within the context of the heaven–earth analogy of the Dwelling itself, as an earthly model of the heavenly reality, so the dominant role of the Dwelling in Numbers 1 – 6, to which the tribes are linked, must be given its full significance. YHWH's cherubim-laden throne and footstool, the ark, resided within the holy of holies of the Dwelling, representing the counterpart to his heavenly throne room. The 'temple throne', as Mettinger writes (1982b: 122), 'has heavenly associations', with the cherubim being regarded 'as a tangible representation of God's heavenly chariot of clouds (cf. Deut. 33:26; 2 Sam. 22:11 = Ps. 18:11; Isa. 19:1; Pss 68:5, 34; 104:3)'. YHWH has a heavenly dwelling, surrounded by heavenly hosts; he has now established an earthly dwelling (Exod. 35 – 40), and part of the movement and logic of Numbers' opening chapters are found in YHWH's establishing an earthly host around this earthly Dwelling.

2.7. Traditional Jewish interpretation of the Camp of Israel

The 'glory of the Divine Presence . . . rests in the celestial camp', wrote Nachmanides, 'For the people of Israel comprise God's legions on earth' (1975: 212–213). Among Jewish interpreters, there is a deeply rooted tradition of referring to Israel's Camp as YHWH's divine chariot, that the congregation of Israel 'serves as the chariot of the *Shekhinah*' (Samet 2020; also Grossman 2002; Rimon 2008; Waxman 2014a).

Berlin 'Netziv' describes Israel's wilderness Camp as 'being divided by four directions as a chariot (*merkābā*) for the divine *Shekhinah*', with the original census being the first step toward this goal (1879: 4:1) – the pattern and order of the Camp reflected Israel's new role as the entourage of the *Shekhinah*, the earthly hosts of YHWH. This understanding had already been commonplace among the great Jewish medieval exegetes. Nachmanides wrote that Israel's redemption was not complete *until* the Camp was constituted as 'the chariot of the Holy One', with Israel's Camp forming the culmination of the divine–human relationship begun with the deliverance out of Egypt (1973: 4–5). The interpretation goes further back to the sages of the Midrash. *Numbers Rabbah* 2:6–7 explains that Israel's Camp was organized by YHWH under four standards *because* the tribes formed his hosts, an earthly counterpart to his heavenly hosts (Lehrman 1983: 3:28–30; cf. Ginzberg 1967: 3:230–238). Each tribe's flag was the same colour as its corresponding precious stone in the breastplate of the high priest, as described in Exodus 28:15–30 and 39:8–14, and was decorated with the emblem or sign of the tribal father's house, based on the prophetic blessings for the twelve patriarchs by Jacob in Genesis 49 and on the tribes by Moses in Deuteronomy 33. Reuben's flag had the figure of a Man since of Reuben it is said 'nor let his *men* be few' (Deut. 33:6), and he is also connected to mandrakes presumed to be in the form of a man (Gen. 30:14), as well as to his status as the firstborn son of Israel (Num. 1:20); Judah is described as a 'lion's whelp' who lies down 'as a lion' (Gen. 49:9), so his flag has the emblem of a Lion; Ephraim, under Joseph's blessing, is likened to a 'firstborn bull' whose horns are as those of a 'wild ox' (Deut. 33:17), his banner picturing an Ox; and Dan's emblem is given as an Eagle by Ibn Ezra, perhaps alluding to Deuteronomy 32:11 (1999: 11), whereas *Numbers Rabbah* has a serpent, alluding to Genesis 49:14. Abarbanel held the insignia was of a dragon, a serpent with eagle wings (2015: 37), and other depictions have an eagle clutching a serpent in its talons (on the historical switch from serpent to eagle, see H. J. M. Mason 1818: 108–110). That the tribes were characterized by these prophecies is reflected in Messiah's description as the 'Lion of the tribe of Judah' (Rev. 5:5).

The Midrash, furthermore, also correlates Israel's Camp with Ezekiel's vision of the chariot-throne of God, referring to the four *ḥayyoth* ('living creatures', Ezek. 1:5) that surround YHWH's throne of glory (*Num. Rab.* 2.10). Quoting the Midrash, Ibn Ezra makes the point explicit: the banners appeared as 'the cherubim which the prophet Ezekiel saw' (1999: 11). Just as the cherubim of Ezekiel's vision supported God's throne, so the glory Cloud rested upon Israel's Camp in the wilderness, with his throne in their midst. Nachmanides wrote that 'comparable to the camp on high', Israel comprises 'the hosts of the Eternal on earth', rooting the Camp's significance in the vertical typology related to the Dwelling and its furnishings (1975: 102):

> just as the ark and its cover and the Tabernacle were all made in the likeness of those that minister before Him on high. So also were the four standards made in the image of the Divine Chariot which Ezekiel

saw, in order that the *Shekhinah* should rest upon them on earth as it is present in the heavens.

The Jewish sages were not engaged in manufacturing correspondences, but in making them explicit; rather than fabricating bridges, they fill in gaps intuitively. The Palestinian Targum (*TgPs-J*), dating to the fourth century (Mortensen 2006), with some portions going back perhaps to the first century (McNamara 1966; also Halperin 1982), preserves a similar understanding of Israel's Camp, with a few differing details (e.g. the images of Reuben and Ephraim's standards are reversed), and adding scriptural text for each standard: Judah's eastward standard reads, 'Arise, O Lord, and let Thine adversaries be driven away before Thee'; the southward standard of Reuben has, 'Hear, Israel, the Lord our God is One'; the westward standard of Ephraim has, 'And the Cloud of the Lord was over them, in the going forth of the host'; the northward standard of Dan is inscribed with the words 'Return, O Lord, and dwell in thy glory in the midst of the myriads of Israel' (see Etheridge 1862: 2:342–345). Bachya, the eminent Jewish exegete of Spain, in his commentary marks many connections between YHWH's celestial entourage and Israel's earthly Camp (ad loc., *Bemidbar* 2:2), based on the Midrash and *Ma'aseh Merkabah*. The four main divisions of heavenly camps are led by the archangels Gabriel, Michael, Raphael and Uriel, and correspond to the four main divisions of Israel's Camp, each of which has one leader whose name ends, like the archangels, with *El* (God): Nethanel, Shelumiel, Gamaliel, Pagiel, respectively (see Num. 1:5–15; 2:5, 12, 20, 27). In the midst of the tribes' four camps and surrounding YHWH's Tent are the Levites, numbered at 22,000, corresponding to the 22,000 angels closest to the *Shekhinah*, surrounding his Throne, and who accompanied the *Shekhinah* on Mount Sinai. And just as the four flags in the desert were copies of the four camps of the *Shekhinah*, the same concept is represented by the four *hayyot* in the vision of the divine entourage in Ezekiel. The living creature with the face of a lion corresponds with Gabriel's celestial camp and parallels the camp of Judah's bearing a flag with an image of a lion, and so forth.

   By the Middle Ages this understanding of Israel's Camp as the divine chariot of YHWH was widespread even outside Jewish circles. The Spanish Jesuit scholar de Prado wrote a lengthy summary in his commentary on Ezekiel, describing, for example, Judah's banner as green in colour, matching the emerald of Judah's tribe on the high priest's breastplate, and depicting a lion according to Jacob's blessing (Gen. 49:9; cf. Keil and Delitzsch 1973a: 3:17–18). The French Benedictine Calmet incorporated an even fuller treatment, judiciously averring that while 'we do not pretend to guarantee these descriptions, yet no one can deny they rest upon ancient traditions' (1709: 12). Similarly, my aim is not to validate every aspect of ancient tradition, but to suggest these traditions point to a rich theology of Israel's Camp rooted in the text. Such readings of the Camp of Israel as Chariot of the *Shekhinah*, once widespread, endure among contemporary Jewish scholars, such as Rimon who writes (2008: 5), 'The Camp of Israel is arranged into four forces, corresponding to the four creatures comprising the Chariot of the *Shekhinah* . . . The Camp of Israel represents a chariot for the *Shekhinah*.'

2.8. Ezekiel's vision of the throne-chariot and Israel's Camp

The connection between Israel's Camp and Ezekiel's chariot and/or temple-city has been common in academic circles, largely due to their exegetical links, which we will explore (see G. B. Gray 1903: 18; Ackroyd 1968: 100; Mettinger 1982a). In his inaugural vision, the prophet Ezekiel recounts how the heavens were opened and he saw visions of God, beginning with an enormous Cloud, flashing forth and raging with fire all about. He sees within the Cloud four living creatures, identified later as cherubim (ch. 10), and, above the firmament over their heads, a sapphire throne with the fiery amber appearance of a man high above. Ezekiel 1:10 reads that each cherub had 'the face of a man . . . the face of a lion on the right side . . . of an ox on the left side, and . . . the face of an eagle'. Ezekiel's account may, as traditionally interpreted, be an allusion to Israel's Camp in the wilderness.

Both Ezekiel's language and detail resonate thematically with Israel's Camp. First, Ezekiel 1:4–5, immediately preceding the description of the four living creatures upon which YHWH rides, states:

> I looked and, behold, a stormy wind was coming out of the north, a great Cloud with fire engulfing itself; and a brightness all around it and radiating out of the midst of it like the colour of amber. And out of the midst of it came the likeness of four living creatures.

The manifestation of YHWH through the fiery Cloud hearkens back to the exodus story, as he led his people in the wilderness; and the fiery Cloud envelops not merely the Deity himself but that of his heavenly entourage as well, the heavenly host (cf. Kline 1999).

Second, Israel's camps – aside from the possibility of their standards depicting the four creatures – are organized according to the four cardinal directions, as are the four faces of the four living creatures. Wacholder maintains that the number four is 'the linchpin' for understanding Ezekiel 1 (2004: 23), and Block remarks that the 'entire apparition is dominated by the number *four*: four creatures, with four faces and four wings', and that 'the numbers appear to represent the four winds, viz., the directions of the compass' (1997: 1:97; emphasis original), an observation equally applicable to the arrangement of Israel's tribes around the Dwelling.

Third, the movement of Ezekiel's divine chariot resembles the formulation of the movement of Israel's Camp in the wilderness:

And they went, each one ('*îš*) went before his face: they went there, wherever the spirit would go, they went; they did not turn when they went. (Ezek. 1:12)

The Tent of Meeting will set out with the camp of the Levites in the midst of the camps; as they encamp just so they will set out, each man ('*îš*) by his hand, by their standards. (Num. 2:17)

Beyond their being described at all, the movements themselves are similarly set forth (as they rest, so they move), especially so given their arrangement along the compass points (cf. Grossman 2002).

Fourth, Ezekiel sees that the chariot, as YHWH's heavenly entourage, conveys (the likeness of) the divine throne (*kissē'*, 1:26), the earthly counterpart of which is found in the centre of Israel's wilderness Camp, the Ark of the Covenant (cf. Albright 1938). Here is the most fundamental comparison: both the Camp of Israel and the *ḥayyot* of Ezekiel have the glory of YHWH in their midst, *and travel with him*. Upon the cherubim 'the Deity was borne, as Lord of the four cohorts of the Israelitish hosts' (H. J. M. Mason 1818: 96).

Finally, one more detail from Ezekiel's description is particularly noteworthy:

And I heard the sound of their wings, like the sound of many waters, like the sound of *Shaddai*, as they went; a sound of tumult like the sound of a camp (*maḥăneh*); and when they stood, they let down their wings. (Ezek. 1:24)

It is the prophet Ezekiel himself who compares the divine chariot, in the tumultuous noise of its movement, to a camp; that he has had this analogy in mind particularly with reference to Numbers, as the Torah's most elaborately described camp, is possible, given the other verbal and thematic parallels between the two accounts. Grossman (2002: 5), based on similar observations, elaborates on 'the profound significance' of Israel's Camp:

So long as the *Shekhinah* is on high, it is the holy creatures and wheels that accompany the *Shekhinah* on its journeys, and they comprise its Chariot. But when God chooses to make His *Shekhinah* rest in the world, new escorts – an alternative *Merkava* – are required.

Broader thematic parallels between Numbers and Ezekiel could be mentioned, such as YHWH's presence – its consequences and demands

– being Israel's central problem (e.g. Num. 16 – 17; Ezek. 10), the role of the Spirit in the life of Israel (Num. 11:24–34; Ezek. 2:2; 36:26–27; 37:9–10), the topic of adultery and jealousy (Num. 5:11–31; Ezek. 8:5–6; 16:15–59), emphasis on Israel's princes (e.g. Num. 7; Ezek. 45), the day–year principle of judgement (Num. 14:34; Ezek. 3:25–27; 4:4–6; cf. Block 1997: 1:157), the need for Israel's cleansing before entering the land (Num. 19; Ezek. 36:25, 33–36), the divine agenda to fill the earth with YHWH's glory (Num. 14:20–23; Ezek. 43:1–5), and others such as the regular appearance of the *Shekhinah*. Rather than developing these connections, the meaning of Ezekiel's throne-chariot vision will be probed more deeply for its potential application to the Camp of Israel.

What do the *hayyot* signify? Regarding the faces of Ezekiel 1:10, 'Man' (*'ādom*) is first used in Genesis 1:26 for the creation of humankind; 'Lion' (*'aryê*) is first used in Genesis 49:9, in Jacob's blessing of Judah; 'Ox' (*šôr*) is used in Genesis 49:6, which some take as a reference to Joseph, since otherwise the brothers' offence is unknown – and in Moses' blessing of the tribes, Joseph's glory is likened to a firstborn *šôr* (Deut. 33:17); and 'Eagle' (*nešer*) is first used in Exodus 19:4, YHWH's bearing Israel on eagles' wings (see Deut. 32:11). Terminology and themes such as living creatures (*hayyot*), firmament (*rāqîaʿ*), man (*'ādām*) as the image of God, and the four cardinal directions, suggest that creation theology undergirds the vision (for parallels between Gen. 1 and Ezek. 1, see Wacholder 2004). The Midrash, as with most commentaries, defines the creatures as representative of creation, together comprising its fullness, and particularly as creation in submission to God's sovereign rule, inasmuch as they are stationed beneath the chariot (see *Exod. Rab.* 23.13; M. Greenberg 1983: 56). Chou explains that not only do the four *hayyot* depict the creatures that rule over earth and sky, functioning collectively as a microcosm of creation, but God's throne above them signals his dominion over heaven, earth, and all that is in them, the entire cosmos (2013: 88), thus forming a vivid image for the kingdom of God. As a microcosm, he further observes, the throne-chariot is also an image of the temple and the paradise of Eden (2013: 89, 194; see Morales 2014) – the chariot is a *temple-cosmos* presence. The *hayyot* chariot, more deeply, is automated by the Spirit of God so as to follow the will of God with complete precision (see Num. 9:15–23), further underscoring the idea of divine dominion, but also portraying his presence as being mobile and unhindered, a mobile sanctuary-city. This aspect of the divine chariot communicated that God would be his people's sanctuary throughout their sojourn (see Ezek. 11:16), a theology relevant not only for the exiles of Ezekiel's day, but for the wilderness generation of Israel as well. The throne-chariot represents the cosmos filled with the glory of God, all creation under the dominion of the divine Majesty; as such, it is a picture of the kingdom and heavenly temple of God, associated with Eden and the purity of paradise.

The throne-chariot is, in sum, a foretaste and encapsulation of the divine *goal* – God's agenda in history – for all creation, cleansed and undefiled, to be filled with his glory. The opening vision of Ezekiel, therefore, adumbrates the final vision of the temple-city (Ezek. 40 – 48). As a microcosm of all creation filled with the glorious and sovereign Presence of God, the throne-chariot in Ezekiel 1 is itself the essence of what a temple is, and finds embodiment in the culminating vision of the throne-chariot's return to the (new) Sanctuary where YHWH declares, 'this is the place of my throne and the place of the soles of my feet; there is where I will dwell, in the midst of the sons of Israel for ever' (43:7). The heavenly reality of Ezekiel's chariot finds earthly realization in chapters 40 – 48. The holy city with which the book closes is laid out in a square with four sets of three gates, each having the name of one of the twelve tribes inscribed upon it; and these names, representing all Israel, are encompassed and unified by the name of the city itself, reflecting the divine presence as its chief attribute: 'YHWH is there' (*yhwh šāmmā*) (48:31–34), a vision strikingly similar to the portrayal of Israel's Camp in the wilderness: the sanctuary-city of God adorned in beauty with the presence of the divine Majesty in its midst.

The iconic portrayal of Israel's following the glory Cloud through the wilderness captures the book's story (Num. 9:15–23), as presaged at the end of Exodus (40:36–38). Such divine guidance, along with Israel's need to follow YHWH closely, also appears to be integral to the understanding of the throne-chariot in Ezekiel. *Targum Jonathan* Ezekiel 1:14 explains that 'the living creatures are sent forth' precisely 'to do the will of their Master'. As Chou observes, the *ḥayyot* technically do not propel the throne-chariot: while their wings are for covering and their legs are straight and unmoving, it is the *rûaḥ* that moves and animates the wheels, and the *ḥayyot* seamlessly follow (2013: 88–89). Launderville explains the Spirit's role further (2004: 365–366):

> The spirit (*hārûaḥ*), which can be etymologically associated with the storm wind (*rûaḥ sě'ārâ*) within the thunderhead, provided a more pervasive, elusive, and spiritual form of guidance to the throne-chariot than any of the four faces could offer . . . Each one, left to itself apart from the guidance of the spirit, would be immobilized by the countervailing forces of the four faces. The personal agency of these semidivine creatures would thus be ineffective without the infusion of the spirit.

Far from incidental, the role of the Spirit in the throne-chariot vision is intrinsic to the message of Ezekiel: Israel, like Ezekiel himself, needs direly the animating, life-giving power of the Spirit in order to follow YHWH God and know the blessing of his presence (Ezek. 2:2; 37:9–10; cf. Chou 2013: 91–92). In Numbers, the need for the Spirit's role throughout the wilderness is also emphasized, even precipitating Moses' most profound crisis in the wilderness (Num. 11). And just as the structure of Ezekiel moves from the mobile throne-chariot (chs. 1, 8–10) to the eschatological temple-city (chs. 40–48), so Numbers moves from the mobile Camp of Israel (chs. 1–10) to the prospect of establishing Israel's life in the land with YHWH (chs. 26–36). Structured as a foursquare covenant community around YHWH's central Dwelling, Israel was to exhibit before the nations a portrait of the kingdom of God, redeemed creation in submission to YHWH's kingship and dwelling in the Cloud of his glory.

2.9. Cherubim in the wilderness

Given the importance of the angelic host for understanding the nature of YHWH's entourage, it will be helpful to consider briefly the pervasive representation of angels in relation to the Dwelling. While the terms 'Tabernacle' and 'tent of meeting' conjure images of merely a brown tent, the visual details of YHWH's Dwelling as described in several scriptural texts portray a rich and wondrous celestial abode pervaded by cherubim imagery. The only references outside the gates of Eden (Gen. 3:24) where cherubim (*kĕrubîm*) are mentioned within the Torah – some 18 more times – *all pertain to descriptions of the wilderness Tabernacle*, including 12 uses of cherub/cherubim for the ark as YHWH's throne placed in the holy of holies (see Exod. 25:17–22; 26:1, 31; 36:8, 36; 37:7–9; Num. 7:89). The 18 references can be divided into four sets, each with instruction and fulfilment sections.

Table 5: References to cherub(im)

Set	Instructions	Fulfilment
1. Atonement-lid of Ark	Six uses of *kĕrûb(îm)* (Exod. 25:17–20)	Six uses of *kĕrûb(îm)* (Exod. 37:7–9)
2. Inner covering of Tabernacle	One use of *kĕrubîm* (Exod. 26:1)	One use of *kĕrubîm* (Exod. 36:8)
3. The Veil	One use of *kĕrubîm* (Exod. 26:31)	One use of *kĕrubîm* (Exod. 36:35)
4. Locus of YHWH's Revelation (atonement-lid)	One use of *kĕrubîm* (Exod. 25:21–22)	One use of *kĕrubîm* (Num. 7:89)

(1) *The atonement-lid of the ark.* The cherubim fashioned on the atonement-lid of the ark likely inform the ark's lengthy appellation: 'the Ark of the Covenant of YHWH of hosts (*ṣĕbā'ôt*) dwelling (*yōšēb*) between the cherubim' (1 Sam. 4:4). The ark is precisely a picture of YHWH's enthronement among the cherubim, his heavenly hosts, and

it is this ark that leads the hosts of Israel through the wilderness, as portrayed on its initial setting out from Sinai (10:33–36). Milgrom aptly writes (1997: 252):

> Indeed, that the cherubim are winged means that the divine seat is in reality a chariot. God's dominion is the world, and only when God wishes to be revealed to Israel does God's presence descend upon the Ark-cherubim inside the Holy of Holies.

The ark comprises YHWH's earthly chariot, and by extension Israel's tribes form his earthly hosts. In 1 Chronicles 28:18 the Temple's cherubim are described in the following manner: 'refined gold . . . for the heavenly-pattern (*tabnît*; see Exod. 25:40) of the chariot (*merkābā*), that is, the gold cherubim that spread their wings and covered the Ark of the Covenant of YHWH'. This understanding accords with the ark and its golden cherubim going forth before the camps of Israel in the wilderness (Num. 10:33–36).

(2) *The inner covering*. Inside the Tabernacle, one saw the cherubim-decorated covering, which was considered part of the Sanctuary itself (Biderman 2011: 113). The word used for this covering is simply 'the Dwelling' (*hammiškān*), emphasized by fronting the verb: 'Now as for the Dwelling itself, you will make' (Exod. 26:1). The gloss on this verse by Rashi explains that each side of the covering had a different depiction of cherubim, with lions on one side and eagles on the other, merely two examples of cherubim, with *Minchas Yehudah* and *Sifsei Chachamim* stating the embroidered cherubim were of all four images of YHWH's holy chariot (1994: 2:344; cf. Biderman 2011: 114).

(3) *The veil*. Also containing artistic designs of cherubim woven upon it, the veil marked off the most important division of sacred space, that between the holy place and the holy of holies, where the ark of YHWH resided. The annual entrance into the holiest place through this cherubim-adorned veil conveyed a ritual access to YHWH's Edenic presence (Gen. 3:24; see Morales 2015: 172–178). Throughout the rest of the year, however, it is significant that the veil sectioning off YHWH's heavenly presence continually conveyed that realm as the domain of cherubim, beyond which the golden cherubim formed on the atonement-lid would be found. In addition to this veil, it is widely accepted that the eastern entrance screens of the Tabernacle as well as of the courtyard also contained depictions of cherubim (Biderman 2011: 174–175, 209–212).

(4) *Locus of revelation*. Returning to the atonement-lid, a fourth set of passages focuses particularly on the locale of YHWH's meeting with and speaking to Moses. This divine communication is defined particularly as

proceeding 'from between the two cherubim' (*mibbên šĕnê hakkĕrubîm*), a phrase repeated verbatim in the fulfilment, Numbers 7:89. The source of divine speech, therefore, is YHWH *within the context of his heavenly host*, from between the two cherubim and through the cherubim-embroidered veil to Moses. Here the theophany described in Leviticus 16:2 is relevant. Although the term 'cherubim' does not occur, their presence given the focus on the atonement-lid, which has been associated with – made one piece with – the cherubim who overshadow it (Exod. 25:17–20; 37:7–9), is assumed 'because in the Cloud I will appear above the atonement-lid'. On the most solemn day of Israel's calendar, the Day of Atonement, the high priest entered the inner sanctum of YHWH's throne room to apply sacrificial blood on the atonement-lid of the ark; and there YHWH would appear in the glory Cloud, *with his angelic hosts*, underscoring this locale as the place of divine revelation.

That the Tabernacle should be decorated to portray YHWH's chariot-throne, the heavenly entourage of the glory Cloud, is a sound conclusion, especially as this correlation appears even more plainly in relation to Solomon's Temple. The parallels between Ezekiel's exalted chariot and the furnishings of the Temple are observed regularly in commentaries (see e.g. Zimmerli 1983: 1:21; Israel 2013: 99–100), and seems to be the interpretation of Second Temple contemporaries, onward to medieval rabbis and commentators such as Ralbag and Radak. Elior argues that Ezekiel's vision finds its source in the earthly Temple, demonstrating that many of the concepts noted in the vision are abstractions taken from the ritual objects and symbolism of the Temple (1999: 111–112; also 1993: 23–24; 1997: 236–238). That each of the twelve tribal princes offered an ox on behalf of his tribe, twelve oxen, for the purpose of conveying YHWH's Dwelling (Num. 7:3), and that oxen are equated with cherubim in Ezekiel (1:10; 10:14), the twelve oxen of the Temple's Sea basin form a possible connection to Israel's Camp, especially given their arrangement by groups of three in the four cardinal directions, with 'three facing northward, three facing westward, three facing southward, and three facing eastward' (1 Kgs 7:25), mirroring the arrangement of the twelve tribes – a correlation made by ancient interpreters (cf. Ginzberg 1967: 3:193).

Cherubim, in sum, played a central role in the earliest stage of Israelite religion, and comprise the main motif of the iconography of the Tabernacle and later Temple (Eichler 2015). As one commentator put it, 'What a solemn position these mystic figures had in the Tabernacle; looking down upon it from the roof – over it from the Veil – nay, overshadowing the Mercy Seat itself!' (Cumming 1880: 188). YHWH's earthly abode was made artistically to mirror his heavenly abode, especially with reference to the presence of his angelic hosts, a feature to be kept in mind as the hosts of Israel are gathered about YHWH's Dwelling in Numbers. Several of my connections and conclusions were anticipated in H. J. M. Mason's study 'Essay on the Nature and Symbolical Character of the

Cherubim of the Jewish Tabernacle' (1818). The Israelites, led forth from Mount Sinai by the cherubim of the ark, fittingly formed the hosts of YHWH on earth, as 'The opening of Numbers constitutes another story of God's *tzava*, His host or assembly, the Children of Israel,' writes Waxman (2014a: 78–79), 'the story of His earthly host or assembly, which escorts, accompanies, and bears His presence as earthly counterpart to His heavenly host.' Given the connection between God's Dwelling and his angelic hosts, the psalmist's declaration is fitting: 'How lovely are your dwellings, O YHWH of hosts' (Ps. 84:1), a heavenly parallel to Balaam's pronouncement over Israel's encampment: 'How goodly are your tents, O Jacob, and your dwellings, O Israel!' (Num. 24:5).

2.10. The divine appellation *yhwh ṣĕbā'ôt yōšēb hakkĕrûbîm* and Israel's Camp

The God of Israel is often described in relation to cherubim. He is called *yōšēb (hak)kĕrûbîm*, 'the One dwelling (or enthroned) among the cherubim' (see 2 Kgs 19:15; 1 Chr. 13:6; Pss 80:1; 99:1), and beyond Ezekiel's opening vision is portrayed as riding on a cherub, flying on the wings of the wind (2 Sam. 22:11; Ps. 18:10). Of its seven biblical occurrences (1 Sam. 4:4; 2 Sam. 6:2; 2 Kgs 19:15; 1 Chr. 13:6; Pss 80:1; 99:1; Isa. 37:16), the cherubim formula occurs four times with the epithet *yhwh ṣĕbā'ôt*, 'YHWH of hosts', prompting scholars to make a connection between the two titles (A. Wood 2008: 14). In Isaiah 37:16, Hezekiah prays, 'O YHWH of hosts, God of Israel, who dwells among the cherubim'. As a full title, 'YHWH of hosts who dwells/is-enthroned among the cherubim' appears in 1 Samuel 4:4 and in 2 Samuel 6:2 (cf. Sasson 2011).

Having already discussed the designation *yhwh ṣĕbā'ôt* earlier, it only remains to touch on the fuller appellation in relation to the phrase *yōšēb (hak)kĕrûbîm*. Eichler, after surveying the history of interpretation, and grammatical analysis, determined YHWH's epithet *yōšēb hakkĕrûbîm* should be translated as the one 'who dwells among the cherubim', explaining that it refers to 'the living cherubim in YHWH's heavenly realm', summarizing as follows: 'the representations of cherubim that adorn the sanctuary – both the sculptures above the ark and the two-dimensional figures on the surfaces of the edifice – constitute one of several aspects of the sanctuary that were aimed at reproducing YHWH's heavenly environment in his earthly abode', since 'the conspicuous presence of cherubim' reflect 'those creatures which mark the deity's 'real' home' (2014: 367, 369; also A. Wood 2008: 9–14).

YHWH's angelic entourage, then, is integral to his heavenly abode, affirmed as a basic and central characteristic of Israel's God by the appellation *yōšēb (hak)kĕrûbîm* and reflected in his earthly sanctuary's adornment with cherubim. In arranging Israel's tribes as hosts around

YHWH's sanctuary, the cultic-community forms the earthly counterpart to his heavenly hosts.

2.11. The Sinai theophany and Israel's Camp

Given that cherubim are the dominant image of YHWH's Dwelling and for the cultus in general, pursuing the origin of such imagery leads to Mount Sinai, given the scriptural emphasis on the fiery and thunderous presence – the Advent of YHWH with clouds of glory – upon Sinai as *the* paradigmatic theophany (Exod. 19 – 24). Parallels with Ezekiel's vision are readily discerned:

> And they saw the God of Israel. And under his feet there was like a paved work of sapphire stone, and it was like the very heavens in its clarity. (Exod. 24:10)

> And above the firmament over their heads was – in appearance like a sapphire stone – the likeness of a throne; on the likeness of the throne was a likeness with the appearance of a man high above it . . . This is the living creature I saw under the God of Israel by the River Chebar, and I knew that they were cherubim. (Ezek. 1:26; 10:20)

Scholars have observed the likelihood that Exodus 24:10 serves as the literary prototype for Ezekiel's vision (Zimmerli 1983: 1:95–96). The rare term 'sapphire' (*sappîr*), associating the two accounts, 'may show that the chariot-throne in Ezekiel parallels how God manifested himself on Sinai to give the law' (Chou 2013: 90). Noting the similarity of language for the vision of God in these references, Ibn Ezra indicates that Israel had seen God's throne resting upon the oxlike cherubim, a suggestive point some have pursued further to explain the rationale for Israel's making a molten *calf* in particular – that is, Israel worshipped the golden calf not in spite of the glory they had seen on Sinai, but *because* of it (see e.g. Barth 1984; Halperin 1988: 157–193; Bazak 1997). These conceptual parallels are behind the rationale for the traditional synagogue cycle of readings, where the opening chapters of Numbers are read on the Sabbath before Shavuot (*Tos.* on *Meg.* 31b), for which Ezekiel 1 is the haftarah reading. The Torah reading for Shavuot, correlated with Ezekiel's vision, is YHWH's self-revelation on Mount Sinai and the giving of the law (Exod. 19 – 20).

Numbers Rabbah 2.3 connects the Camp of Israel in Numbers with the angelic host of YHWH's glory Cloud over Mount Sinai: 22,000 angels descended with God as his chariot, arranged by standards (cf. Nachmanides 1975: 102; Lehrman 1983: 3:24–25). The Midrash is working out two analogies, that between Mount Sinai and the Dwelling as a portable mountain of God, and between YHWH's heavenly hosts and his earthly hosts around the Dwelling in the Camp (see also *Num. Rab.* 2.6). Accentuating features implicit in the text, applied from a broader scriptural awareness, the Midrash culls from Moses' blessing in Deuteronomy 33, which recalls YHWH's self-revelation on Mount Sinai, and indeed portrays him as coming with 'ten thousands of holy ones' (v. 2), referring to the heavenly hosts surrounding his throne, and ends by describing him as the one who 'rides the heavens . . . through the skies in his majesty' (v. 26). The plain deduction from this verse, according to Maier (2015: 92), 'is that thousands of angels had been with Yahweh at Sinai'. Psalm 68:17, noted by the Midrash above, affirms a similar understanding:

The chariot of God is ten thousand, even thousands of thousands;
The Lord is among them as in Sinai, in the sacred place.

The Jewish authors of the New Testament, moreover, assume the presence of YHWH's angelic hosts at Sinai (see also *Jub.* 1:27; 2:1; Josephus, *Ant.* 15.136; CD 5.18). Luke writes in Acts 7:53 that Israel had received the law 'as delivered (*diatagas*) by angels' (cf. Acts 7:38). The apostle Paul declares that the law 'was appointed through (*diatageis*) angels' (Gal. 3:19), and Hebrews 2:2 speaks of the message 'declared through (*di'*) angels'. With the sages, they understood that what Scripture elsewhere reveals about YHWH's heavenly entourage may legitimately be assumed as implicit in other passages.

Lastly, we turn to the tassel legislation in Numbers 15:37–41. Aside from serving as a memory device, the tassels also imparted dignity to God's people as 'a priestly kingdom and holy nation' (Exod. 19:6). According to verse 38, the tassels are to be tied to the wings (*kanpê*) of the garment, a blue cord to the tassel of the wing (*kānāp*). The term *kānāp* is also used in the description of the golden cherubim that stretch out their wings (*kĕnāpayim*), overshadowing the atonement-lid with their wings (*kanpê*) (Exod. 25:20; 37:9). While cherubim are variously described in Scripture, what is common to all characterizations is that a cherub is a *winged* hybrid (Staubli 2012: 56). Perhaps the sacred and noble calling bestowed on Israelites by the blue-corded tassels on the wings of their garments affirmed their status as the earthly counterpart to the heavenly hosts of YHWH. There is, in any case, another connection to the Dwelling that is more widely conceded. As commentators observe, the blue thread of the tassels connects the people's garments to the same colour that adorned the high priest (Exod. 39:1, 5, 22, 24, 29, 31) and the Tabernacle coverings (Exod. 25:4; 26:1, 4, 31, 36; 27:16; 28:8, 15, 28, 31, 33, etc.) – the ark itself was wrapped in a cloth entirely of blue when transported (Num. 4:5–6). Rabbinic exegesis connects the tassels' blue colour to the heavenly throne room of God, which is 'sapphire like the very heavens', Exodus 24:10, 'a throne, in appearance like a sapphire stone', Ezekiel 1:26 (cf. *Num. Rab.* 17.5;

on the Jewish exegetical tradition connecting the Sinai theophany with Ezekiel's vision, see Liss 2000: 59).

2.12. The throne-chariot in the book of Revelation and Israel's Camp

In the Apocalypse, John's vision of the heavenly throne room draws on the imagery of Ezekiel 1 (Rev. 4:6–8). The four living creatures, like the *ḥayyot* of Ezekiel, represent *the fullness of creation* (cf. Brütsch 1970: 230–233; Beale 1999: 322–326, 330, 332), even as Israel's Camp represents the firstfruits of the new creation (cf. H. J. M. Mason 1818: 96–101, 116–118). They signify the whole created order ascribing praise to God, submitting to his sovereign will – a new creation and redeemed humanity, the kingdom of God. The theological connections between Ezekiel and Revelation are also structural: just as Ezekiel's vision of YHWH's throne-chariot (ch. 1) functions as a foretaste of his concluding vision of YHWH's temple-city (chs. 40–48), so John's vision of the heavenly throne (ch. 4) looks to his vision of New Jerusalem (chs. 21–22), a pattern found in Numbers, where Israel's Camp (chs. 1–10) forms the paradigm for life in the land of Canaan (chs. 26–36). Such correlations among Numbers, Ezekiel and Revelation, largely absent in current scholarship, have been commonplace historically (e.g. Ainsworth 1619: 704–705, 708; Newton 1733: 259; H. J. M. Mason 1818; Bush 1858: 29–30; C. E. Douglas 1936; Barnes 1973: 184, 186; Jamieson et al. 1973: 3:674).

The theological use of Numbers 1 – 6 in Revelation is evident not only in the description of God's people as 'the camp (*parembolēn*) of the saints, the beloved city' (20:9), but in the use of 'Tabernacle' (*skēnē*) to describe New Jerusalem, a realization of the wilderness Camp's ideal and ultimate fulfilment of the covenant promise 'Behold, the Tabernacle of God is with humanity! He will dwell with them, and they shall be his peoples – God himself will be with them and be their God' (21:3). Steele likewise captured the essence of Israel's Camp, writing that 'its ideal and archetype is "the holy city, the new Jerusalem" . . . This is "the camp of the saints"' (1891: 2:226–227). New Jerusalem – four-square with city-gates arranged along the points of the compass and bearing the names of the twelve tribes of Israel, and studded with the gems of the high priest's breastplate, illumined by the light of God's countenance (Rev. 21) – is the glorious consummation of Israel's Camp.

As with the throne-chariot and temple-city scenes of Ezekiel and Revelation, the Camp of Israel forms a divine portrait of the new creation, the kingdom of God, and temple-city, an earthly chariot mirroring YHWH's heavenly throne and entourage. The divinely structured encampment signifies Israel's spiritual essence and *ecclesiology*, with every Israelite in place in relation to YHWH's majestic throne and one another – the *first* view of Israel as 'a priestly kingdom and holy nation' to YHWH (Exod. 19:6). Numbers thus concerns 'the metaphysical organization of the camp as *tzevaot HaShem*, the earthly assembly bearing and animated by the Divine Presence . . . a microcosm of the divine *Merkava* and resting place of the Divine Presence' (Waxman 2014a: 79), a foretaste of the consummation and firstfruits of the scattered nations that will be gathered from the four corners of the earth for a life suffused by the glorious presence of God.

2.13. Conclusion: Balaam's vision of the Camp of Israel

The Camp of Israel, so I have endeavoured to demonstrate, portrays an ideal city of God, a living symbol of the covenant where YHWH dwells in the midst of his people, blessing them with the light of his uplifted face. My review of the theology of the Camp of Israel justifies Stubbs's assessment (2009: 28; emphasis original), that the Israelites 'are physically structured in a way that is symbolic of who they are; they become a living icon that reveals their *identity* and calling to be a holy and priestly people'. Knierim and Coats, too, regard Numbers 1 – 10 as a carefully crafted theological vision, where 'the newness of Israel as a camp at Sinai in its organization around the Tabernacle' provides a supreme blueprint for the life of God's people, transcending the past since it is linked to Moses' authority and the foundational Sinai event (2005: 22, 25–26). Abarbanel, the Jewish exegete of Portugal, offered a more complete appraisal, drawing out many of the connections we have observed (2015: 37–39):

1. Israel's Camp is the counterpart to YHWH's heavenly hosts.
2. Israel's Camp was a microcosm of all creation, the three camps of the Dwelling, the Levites, and the tribes, representing the spiritual world, the intermediate world of the heavens, stars and constellations, and earthly, physical world, respectively.
3. Israel's Camp was the paradigm for Jerusalem, the city of God, correlating the Dwelling with the Temple, the Levites' camp with Mount Zion, and the twelve tribes with the walled and fortified city of Jerusalem.
4. Israel's Camp was analogous to Israel's stay at Mount Sinai, with the Dwelling representing the *Shekhinah* on top of the mountain, concealed within thick cloud, the camp of Levites representing the positions of Moses and Aaron (Levites) on the mountain, and the camps of the twelve tribes representing Israel at the foot of the mountain.

The theological *vision* of Israel's Camp is emphasized from what is arguably the literary peak of Numbers, during Balaam's climactic, third oracle uttered from the summit of Mount Peor (23:27 – 24:14). The account brings together two points relevant for this study (24:2): (1) that Balaam sees Israel 'encamped according to their tribes', arranged according to the divine revelation of Numbers 1 – 4; and (2) that 'the Spirit of God came upon him', enabling him to discern the spiritual essence of the encampment. Gazing upon the Camp of Israel, the Mesopotamian diviner erupts in exultation, portraying the loveliness of Israel's Camp as the well-watered paradise of YHWH (24:5–6), and then proceeds to describe Israel as a man/king (v. 7), an ox (v. 8), and a lion (v. 9), three of the faces of the *ḥayyot* – perhaps a mere, and auspicious, coincidence. Even so, Balaam's vision functions to invite the reader to discern the theological significance of the divine arrangement of the tribes, a fitting crown to our own study.

3. THE SOJOURN OF ISRAEL'S CAMP (NUM. 11 – 25)

The structural boundaries of the Camp, along with its purity laws, reinforce theological and political boundaries, divinely established lines that are tested during the wilderness sojourn (chs. 11–25). Since, however, Israel's life in the Camp is the model for the nation's life in the land, the community's theological structure and purity laws relate to chapters 26–36 as well. Generally, chapters 11–15 focus on Moses' office of prophet, 16–20 on Aaron's office of priesthood, and 21–25 on YHWH's office of kingship. These three emphases are correlated to the outer camp of the tribes, the inner camp of Levites and the central camp of the *Shekhinah*, respectively. Understanding the goals and challenges for each segment of the Camp unfolds the logic of the sojourn accounts.

Numbers 11 – 15 relates to the outer camp of the twelve tribes, anchored in chapters 1–2 of the Camp's structure. The outer camp is rooted in the book of Genesis, its basis being the twelve sons of Jacob (Gen. 29 – 30) and YHWH's promises to Abraham of many descendants and the possession of Canaan, reaffirmed to Isaac and Jacob (see Gen. 15:1–6, 7–21; 17:1–8; cf. M. Douglas 2004: 18–21). After its basis in Genesis is recalled (Num. 1), the outer camp is constructed as each tribe's encampment locale is divinely revealed (Num. 2). The outer camp of Israel is portrayed idealistically as a bannered militia, since its aim is to possess the land. The authority focus of the twelve tribes is on following YHWH closely through Moses' prophetic office (cf. 14:22, 24). Accordingly, the outer camp's failures are described as sins of speech against God's gifts: the manna is slandered (ch. 11), Moses is slandered (ch. 12), and the land is slandered (chs. 13–14). Moses' crisis in Numbers 11 relates primarily to his prophetic role and is partly alleviated with the addition of seventy elder scribes who, after temporarily prophesying

(11:25), will help spread Moses' divine *torah* through the encampment. In Numbers 12, Moses' prophetic office is slandered by Miriam and Aaron (12:1–3), but vindicated supremely by YHWH (12:4–16). These events partly function as a defence of Moses, clearing him of blame in the outer camp's failure to possess the land, their primary objective (Num. 13–14). Slandering the land in spreading an 'evil report' (13:32; 14:36, 37), not having 'heeded' YHWH's voice (14:21–23, 41), ten of the scouts function in a manner opposite to the elder scribes – denying rather than affirming YHWH's instruction through Moses, repudiating the land promised to the patriarchs. The tribal failure is encapsulated by a disastrous military defeat, the battle being engaged contrary to YHWH's word through Moses (14:30–36). Although the cause is spiritual, the outer camp's failure is *as a militia*, memorably captured by the last word of the narrative, 'Hormah' (14:45). In chapter 15, legislation serves as reassurance to the tribes that YHWH will indeed bring them into the land of Canaan (15:2), capping YHWH's judgement on the tribes with hope for the future, expressed in terms of the Nazirite vow: fulfilling a 'wondrous vow' in the land (15:3), with offerings and accompaniments including 'drink offerings' (15:1–21) and closing with YHWH's exhortation to 'be holy to your God' (15:40). Noticeably, Levites are nowhere mentioned throughout chapters 11–15, and consequently are not implicated in the tribal failure to take the land or in YHWH's judgement against the outer camp; rather, the retribution is phrased precisely in terms of the tribal census: 'all of you who were appointed according to your whole number, from twenty years old and above' (14:29; cf. 1:3, 45).

Numbers 16 – 20 relates to the inner camp of Levites and priests, anchored in chapters 3–4 of the Camp's structure, which establish priestly hierarchy over the Levites (3:1–4, 6; 4:16, 27–28, 33; 8:1–4; cf. Knierim and Coats 2005: 28; Condren 2013: 435, 439). The inner camp is rooted in the book of Exodus, its basis being both (1) the Levitical genealogy, yielding vital background for Korah's rebellion and introducing Phinehas (Exod. 6:16–27), and (2) the Passover deliverance of Israel's firstborn (Exod. 11 – 13; cf. 1:22 – 2:10; 4:22–23). The inner camp's Exodus basis is given in Numbers 3, which begins with Aaron's genealogy (3:1–4) and then narrates YHWH's taking Levites in place of Israel's firstborn (3:5–16, 40–51), along with the encampment assignments for each Levitical house. Numbers 4 details the particular transport labours for each house, and includes a warning that presages Korah's rebellion (4:17–20). The authority focus for the Levitical encampment is Aaron's high-priestly office, which requires the Levitical clans to maintain the hierarchy established by YHWH through Moses. Accordingly, the inner camp's failure relates to a rebellion against Aaron's exclusive rights as high priest (16:8–11), denying YHWH's sanction for Moses' establishment of Aaron's house as Israel's priesthood (16:3). Levites, led by Korah, also gather sons of Reuben, Jacob's firstborn (16:1), along with

250 princes usually assumed to be from Reuben's tribe or firstborn among other tribes by Jewish interpreters (see Rashi), in keeping with the firstborn basis of the inner camp (Num. 3). Contesting the priesthood, with its divinely ordained rites of purification, threatens 'the logic of the cult' (Frevel 2013c: 377), *as mapped out in the Camp's structure*: apart from Aaron's designated priesthood within the divinely revealed cult, YHWH cannot dwell in the midst of the twelve tribes without consuming them. Whereas Moses' prophetic office was vindicated for the outer camp, the focus here is on the vindication of Aaron as YHWH's chosen high priest through his almond-yielding staff (Num. 17). Moses, too, is vindicated as the messenger of YHWH (16:28–30), for the sake of Aaron's priesthood, confirming its divine source. The inner camp's *sacral* failure is captured memorably by the censers used to plate the altar (16:38). YHWH's legislative response in Numbers 18 reinvigorates the offices and roles of priests and Levites. The red heifer ritual of chapter 19, which cleanses from corpse pollution, allowing re-entry into the Camp, functions as the transition between Israel's generations as the second generation is cleansed from the death defilement (and judgement) of the first, marking a new beginning in the nation's relationship with YHWH. Numbers 20 ends with Aaron's death, narrating the transfer of high priesthood from Aaron to his son Eleazar, mirroring the transition to Israel's second generation. Introducing Israel's second generation, chapter 20 is transitional, connected to the next section related to YHWH's kingship (chs. 21–25). Since, however, it is linked to chapter 19 by a water motif, and alludes to chapters 16–17 through Aaron's staff and Moses' words ('rebels'), Numbers 20 is best taken as capping chapters 16–20, an integral narrative unified by the dynamic of holiness and death (cf. Mann 1987).

Numbers 21 – 25 relates to the camp of the Shekhinah, anchored in the book of Leviticus, where the central camp was created: in Numbers 1 – 4, Israelites and Levites are arranged around YHWH's already functioning Tent of Meeting. The purity laws (chs. 5–6) relate the newly created spiritual dynamic, after Israel's Camp has been constructed around YHWH's Dwelling. The authority focus related to the central camp is the kingship of YHWH. Of the book's 28 uses of the root *m-l-k* (king, kingdom), 14 occur within chapters 21–25, and 7 later uses relate directly to this section (31:8; 32:33, 34). Note, however, that Numbers 20 is Janus-faced, concluding the previous section with the death (or judgement) of the first generation's leaders, but also signalling the dawn of Israel's second generation, which must mature under YHWH's kingship, and so introduces chapters 21–25. Accordingly, the nature of Moses' sin was in misrepresenting YHWH's reign (the camp of the *Shekhinah*) to the new generation of Israelites. In supplying abundant waters for his people in the wilderness, however, YHWH vindicates himself; and his judgement on Moses and Aaron accomplishes the same. Chapter 20's central section, verses 14–21, include the book's first two uses of the root *m-l-k* (20:14, 17; the remaining five uses are not pertinent, relating to names, 26:33, 45; 27:1; 36:11). The ensuing chapters not only narrate Israel's encounters with foreign kings (21:1, 21, 33; 22:4), but prophesy of a future Israelite king, the Messiah (24:7, 17), and also recount Israel's dismal failure, being joined to 'Baal' (husband, master) – a rejection of YHWH's reign (25:1–3), which had been adumbrated and remedied in the bronze serpent episode (21:4–9). Cautioning against oversimplification, the Baal Peor account ends with a distinctly priestly image: Phinehas, grandson of Aaron, makes atonement for Israel and receives a covenant of peace. Nevertheless, his action – as with Israel's apostasy – was political in nature, re-establishing Israel's relationship with YHWH as their king. These chapters focus on Israel's relationship to YHWH in a way that reflects the dynamic of the purity laws (Num. 5 – 6).

The wilderness sojourn thus appears to be organized in sync with the Camp's structure. (See Fig. 2.)

Again, chapter 19 is transitional, and chapter 20, narrating the transgression of Moses and Aaron (leaders of the first generation), relates to the kingship of YHWH. The narrative moves from the fringes of the Camp inward, progressing from the outer camp to the inner camp, and

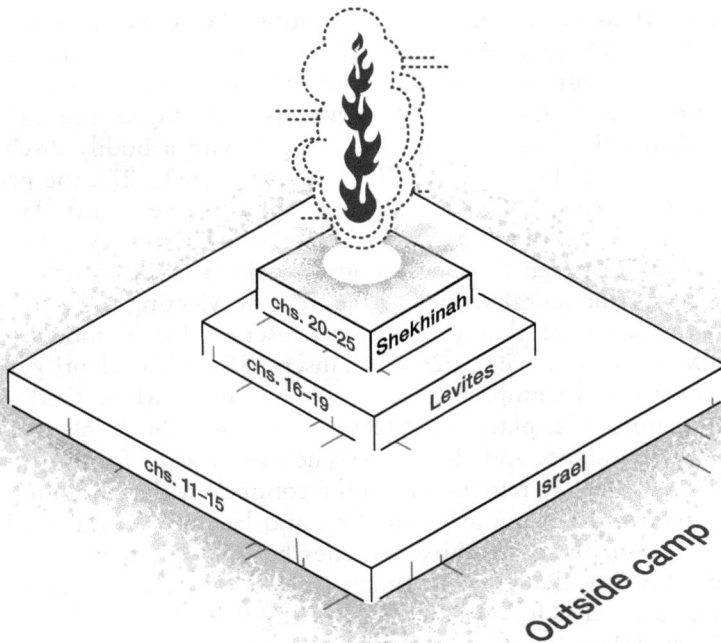

Figure 2: The wilderness sojourn

concludes with the death (or death sentence) of the first generation's leaders. YHWH's judgement falls upon the 'outskirts' or 'edges' of the Camp, representing its 'mixed multitude' in chapter 11, and Miriam is expelled 'from out of the Camp' (*miḥûṣ lammaḥăneh*) in chapter 12 (vv. 14–15), recalling verbatim the language of the purity laws' prologue (see 5:3, 4), as does her 'leprosy' (5:2; 12:10).

4. THE SPIRITUAL NATURE OF ISRAEL'S CAMP: PURITY LAWS (NUM. 5 – 6)

After the physical organization of Israel's Camp around the Dwelling (Num. 1 – 4), the Camp's spiritual essence and community life is set forth through purity laws (Num. 5 – 6), comprised of five speeches by YHWH to Moses. 'If the entire Camp of Israel is a chariot for the *Shekhina*,' writes Rimon (2008: 5), 'then the conduct of this camp is of acute importance'. The placement of the purity laws exhibits the significance of Israel's Camp, upon its creation, as underscored by YHWH's climactic statement (5:3) 'I myself am dwelling (*'ănî šōkēn*)' in the midst of Israel's camps – *signalling the fulfilment of the covenant formula* (Exod. 25:8; 29:45). There is no better way to underscore the nature of the Camp than to insert, as a consequence of its creation, the need to expel unclean persons from its bounds. As Frevel explains, purity is the 'regulative idea' of the Camp, its organization, structure and form (2013c: 384).

The first speech (Num. 5:1–4) serves as a prologue and calls for the expulsion of all (1) who are leprous, (2) with a bodily discharge, and (3) are defiled by a corpse. The last speech (6:22–27), the priestly benediction, forms a conclusion, not only to the purity laws or Numbers 1 – 6, but to the entire Sinai revelation (Exod. 19 – Num. 6). Significantly, although the benediction is widely understood to have concluded the inaugural service of the Tent of Meeting (Lev. 9:22–23), yet the revelation of that blessing was reserved for Numbers 6 (see *Sif. Num.* 39; *b. Tam.* 5:1; 7:2; Wellhausen 1889: 177), identifying the newly constructed Camp of Israel as the one place where God dwells with humanity, *the* place of YHWH's blessing. Such blessings of prosperity, abundance and victory become a motivation for purity, since Israelites will want to remain within the confines of the Camp to enjoy YHWH's favour. Putting aside the first and last speeches as prologue and conclusion, there are three speeches by YHWH, related to oath-breakers (5:5–10), the strayed woman (5:11–31), and the Nazirite vow (6:1–21), outlined as follows (also G. B. Gray 1903: 39; Ingalls 1991: 67; Achenbach 2003b: 499–511; Seebass 2006: 46):

Prologue: Expulsion from Camp wherein YHWH dwells (5:1–4)
  (1) all who are leprous

(2) all with a bodily discharge
(3) all who are defiled by a corpse

Purity laws: Life before YHWH in the Camp (5:5 – 6:21)
(1) the law concerning restitution for oath-breakers (5:5–10)
(2) the law concerning the strayed woman (5:11–31)
(3) the law concerning the Nazirite vow (6:1–21)

Conclusion: Putting YHWH's Name on Israel within the Camp (6:22–27)
(1) YHWH bless you and keep you,
(2) YHWH make his face shine upon you,
(3) YHWH lift up his face to you and give you peace.

The law of restitution (5:5–10) provides resolution to an act of unfaithfulness or treachery against YHWH, in relation to one's *neighbourly* dealings – within the context of a person's interactions with others in Israelite society within the Camp. The law assumes the scenario described in Leviticus 6:1–7, that someone finds or squanders another's deposit or security and in the process swears a false oath in YHWH's Name to cover up the act. Restitution requires the guilty person to (1) confess the sin and offer a sacrifice of atonement, (2) make restitution in full to the offended person, adding a fifth, and (3) in the event the offended party and their kin are no longer living, yield the restitution to the priest as to YHWH.

The law for a strayed woman (5:11–31) deals with a scenario whereby a married woman has strayed into seclusion with another man, and thus involves *familial* dealings. There are no witnesses to what has happened in that seclusion; the law is not about adultery per se, but about purity (see *b. Sot.* 1.2d; Destro 1989; Grushcow 2006; Rosen-Zvi 2012). The term 'adultery' (*nā'ap*) does not appear in the text, precluding the death penalty (cf. Exod. 20:14; Lev. 20:10). The question is whether she has become unclean by another man's seed, and consequently it also relates to the issue of establishing paternity in the event of pregnancy. At the centre of the ritual, the woman must affirm an oath of malediction and drink a concoction that includes the wiped-off Name of YHWH.

The law of the Nazirite vow (6:1–21) allows a man or woman to vow a vow of separation (*nazir*) for a set period of time, to separate him- or herself unto YHWH, thus focusing on one's *individual* relationship with God. During the period designated by the vow, the Nazirite is to abstain from (1) grape products, (2) from cutting his or her hair, and (3) from coming into contact with a corpse. In the event of accidental corpse pollution, the Nazirite undergoes a rite of cleansing, shaves his or her hair, and starts the period all over again. The vow culminates with offerings and accompaniments (including a 'drink offering'), which can be offered only *in the land*, and a ritual whereby the Nazirite's shorn hair is placed on the altar as a sacrifice.

Taken together, the three purity cases solicit purity of living in every sphere of life: within society, within the family and individually with God, each in relation to YHWH's Dwelling at the centre of the Camp (cf. Grossman 2014c: 67–68). Dozeman (1998: 60; also Knierim and Coats 2005: 27), relatedly, outlines chapters 5–6 as a movement toward the Tabernacle, beginning outside the Camp (5:1–4) and moving inward concentrically from defilement in the broadest social relationships (5:5–10), to defilement in marriage relationships (5:11–31), and then to the smallest circle, addressing the human–divine relationship (6:1–21); the movement being completed with YHWH's blessing emanating from the doorway of the Tent of Meeting (6:22–27). The intimate and deeply connected relationship established between Israel and YHWH's Dwelling within the Camp is vivified in the later portrait of Israel's coordinated pursuit of the divine Cloud through the wilderness (Num. 9:15–23).

The Midrash connects the expulsions of Numbers 5:1–4 to the exile, remarking that skin disease, genital discharge and corpse pollution relate to the three defiling sins that lead to expulsion out of the land: idolatry, sexual immorality and bloodshed. As the unclean of Numbers 5:2 cannot re-enter the camp apart from being cleansed with water, so, too, God would sprinkle clean water on the exiles, cleansing them for the return (Ezek. 36:25; *Num. Rab.* 7.10). Minimally, this rabbinical gloss detects what is true of the whole section (Num. 5 – 6); the point is not casuistic legislation per se, but a theological statement about the covenant community, the cases serving to underscore, in exemplary fashion, the spiritual dynamic of Israel's Camp. The fraudulent oath-taker case sets out a path for restoring societal life through confession and recompense, acknowledging that human transactions are ultimately dealings with God; the case of the strayed woman seeks to restore the marriage relationship and ensure a holy seed, with marriage reflecting Israel's covenant relationship with YHWH; the vow of separation opens the way for personal holiness and nearness to God, typifying Israel's calling to live as a 'priestly kingdom and holy nation' to the glory of God (Exod. 19:6).

4.1. The purity laws and the structure of Israel's Camp

Israel's wilderness Camp comprises three concentric squares, each of which may be regarded as its own encampment. In the language and insight of the Midrash (see *Num. Rab.* 7.8; *Sif. Num.* 1), the structure is as follows. First, at the heart of the Camp is YHWH's Tent and courtyard, the central 'camp of the *Shekhinah*'. Second, the encampment of Levites surrounds the courtyard of YHWH's Tent with the priesthood on the east side – this is the inner 'camp of Levites'. Third, the twelve tribes of Israel encamp at a distance from YHWH's Tent, beyond the Levites, with three tribes per side, along the four points of the compass – this is the outer 'camp of the twelve tribes'. Several rabbinic texts preserve this threefold view of Israel's Camp (*b. Zeb.* 116b and *T. Kel. B. Qam.* 1.12; see also *b. Pes.* 67a; *b. Naz.* 45a; *b. Sanh.* 42b; among the Essenes, see *Halakhic Letter*, 4QMMT B 29–33, 58–62). The camps comprise concentric spheres of holiness, beginning with the holy of holies in the camp of the *Shekhinah*, and extending outward by degrees to the inner camp of Levites and then to the outer camp of the twelve tribes. Acknowledging three camps is to trace the unfolding narrative of the Torah, whereby Leviticus focuses on the camp of the *Shekhinah*, Numbers 1 – 2 on the outer camp of the twelve tribes, and Numbers 3 – 4 on the camp of Levites – each division given its own defined boundary and separate treatment. Such a threefold reading of the Camp was once held by 'many distinguished expositors, both Jewish and Christian' (Bush 1858: 68; also Ainsworth 1619: 725).

The threefold structure of Israel's Camp appears to be paralleled by the purity laws structure in Numbers 5 – 6, a correlation found in some Jewish interpretations. The prologue calls for a threefold expulsion (5:1–4): those who are lepers, those with a bodily discharge, and those who become polluted by a corpse. After the prologue, three exemplary cases are set forth: those needing to make restitution (5:5–10), the wayward woman (5:11–31) and the Nazirite (6:1–21). Finally, the section culminates with the priestly blessing (6:22–27), which has a clear threefold structure per a threefold use of the divine Name. Now starting with the prologue, and following this 'three-camp hermeneutic' approach (Mosser 2009: 399), (1) those defiled with **leprosy** are expelled from all three camps, beginning with the centre: the camps of the *Shekhinah*, the Levites, and the twelve tribes of Israel; (2) those defiled with a **bodily discharge** are expelled only from the first two camps, the camps of the *Shekhinah* and of the Levites; and (3) those defiled by a **corpse** are excluded only from the first camp, the camp of the *Shekhinah*. Even if the text calls, rather, for the expulsion from all three camps for each scenario, this suggestive interpretation factors in the purpose clause of 5:3: 'so they do not defile *their camps*' (*maḥănêhem*; cf. Frevel 2013c: 383) – the Greek also reads plural: *tas parembolas autōn*. Further, while Leviticus 13:46 calls for one with skin disease to dwell outside the camp, there is no similar legislation for those with genital discharges (Lev. 15) or corpse pollution (cf. Gane 2004: 520). Corpse pollution in Numbers 19 and 31 appears to involve expulsion from the entire Camp (31:13, 24; see Num. 12:10, 14–15; 19; 31:13, 24), although 9:14 may suggest exclusion from the Tent of Meeting only. On either scenario, the rhetorical place and function of these laws underscore the special status of the newly created Camp along the spectrum of graded holiness – the conceptual link to the various realms is not dependent upon the stratified camp exclusions. (See Fig. 3.)

The three main cases (5:5–10, 11–31; 6:1–21) may also be correlated to the three camps theologically. First, restitution to one's neighbour deals with relationships in the broader community, within the outer camp of the twelve tribes of Israel. Second, the ritual of the wayward woman deals with relationships in the family, which relates to the inner camp of Levites, who represent the firstborn of each household (Num. 3:11–13, 40–51). Third, the Nazirite law deals with personal piety, one's individual relationship with YHWH God, relating to the camp of the *Shekhinah*. The Camp of Israel thus represents three social spheres: (1) the individual's relationship to YHWH God, represented by the central camp, (2) the familial relationship before God, symbolized by the second or inner camp, and, finally, (3) societal relationships before God, symbolized by the third or outer camp. The concentric areas of the Camp relate to each Israelite's concentric commitments: to YHWH God centrally, then to family, then to the nation, with YHWH's presence and will pervading and influencing every sphere. (See Fig. 4.) (Here we will not pursue possible correlation to the authoritative office over each camp: Moses' prophetic office / outer camp of twelve tribes, Aaron's

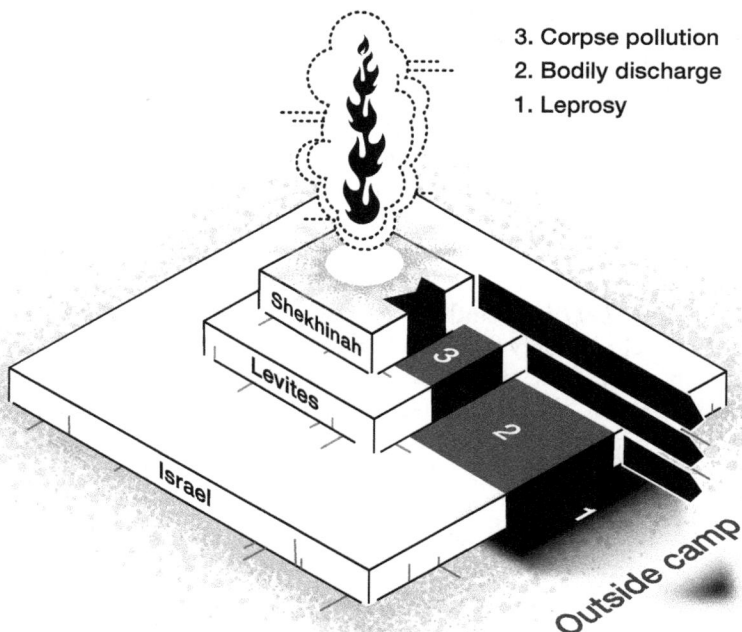

Figure 3: Purity laws: expulsion

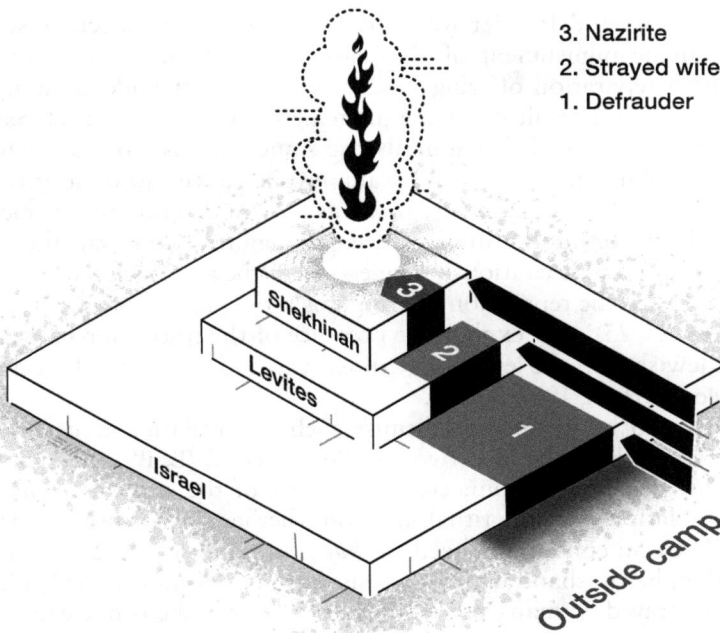

Figure 4: Purity laws: restoration

high-priestly office / inner camp of Levites, and the kingship of YHWH / central camp of the *Shekhinah*.)

More profoundly, this three-camp hermeneutic may also correlate the three expulsions of the prologue with the three main cases that follow. First, the expulsion of lepers is correlated to the case of restitution for false oath-taking (A, A'). Admittedly, it is difficult to perceive a meaningful link here. Jewish sages, however, based on a wordplay whereby 'skin disease' (*metzora*) refers to 'bringing out evil or decay from within' (*motzee ra*), taught that leprosy was divine punishment for an evil tongue (murmuring, lying, gossip, slander), with Miriam's judgement in Numbers 12:10, whose expulsion from the Camp is foreshadowed in 5:2, serving as the prime example (see the Talmud, in *Arachin* 15b; *Lev. Rab.* 16.2; *Num. Rab.* 7.4, 5; *Kli Yakar* on Lev. 13:2; 14:6; *Tan. Metzora* 7, 24a and 22b). Alternate wordplay for leprosy and slander, as Abrams explains (1993: 41), is based on *motzi shem ra* (one who brings forth a bad name). Even Moses' leprous hand in Exodus 4:6 has been understood by some as punishment for speaking ill of Israelites several verses earlier (v. 1), in claiming they would not believe him (see Rashi, ad loc.; Ron 2003: 192). This understanding offers a possible connection between skin disease and fraudulent oath-takers, and may even suggest the defrauder was understood as being especially subject to the divine punishment of skin disease. That the leper's cleansing included a reparation offering (*'āšām*) may support understanding the skin disease as a result of divine judgement (see Lev. 14:12; cf. Saydon 1946). Milgrom noted that skin disease stands out as a prime means of divine punishment, with biblical examples such as the account of Uzziah (2 Chr. 26:18–21; see Num. 12:10; 2 Kgs 5:27) indicating that some sort of 'sacrilege' or 'unfaithfulness' (*ma'al*) against God was the cause (1991: 363–364). He cautiously suggests that 'the association of the leper in verse 2 with the reparation offering, his most important sacrifice (Lev. 14:12–14, 24–25)' may explain the presence of the restitution case (1990: 34). In Jewish lore, the lepers were those who had worshipped the golden calf (see Ginzberg 1967: 3:213).

One would be inclined to dismiss such a correlation if it were not for the strength of the next two parallels. Second (B, B'), the expulsion for bodily discharge is connected to the case of the wayward woman, a firm correlation since the ritual turns on whether she has become defiled (*ṭum'āh*) by an emission of seed (*šikbat-zera'*), a discharge, from a man other than her husband with whom she has been secluded (5:13, 19, 20). She is a 'strayed woman', but it is not certain that she is unclean. Third (C, C'), the expulsion for corpse pollution is correlated to the Nazirite vow, also a firm connection since the main part of the law deals with the remedy for corpse pollution (6:5–12). As a side note, scholars generally surmise that Numbers 5:2 serves as an addendum to Leviticus 11 – 15 (e.g. Kellermann 1970b: 163). In Leviticus 15:31 Moses and Aaron are charged to 'separate' (*hizzartem*) the sons of Israel from their uncleanness lest they defile YHWH's Dwelling, an unexpected use of *nāzar* (cf. Frevel 2013c: 402–403) that forges a link, beyond Numbers 5:2, to the case of the Nazir, who exemplifies Israel's call to be separate from the nations and defilement. Leviticus 15, taken up with bodily discharges, is linked to the strayed woman case as well, which uses similar terms such as *šikbat-zera'* (Lev. 15:16, 17, 18, 32; Num. 5:13). (See Table 6.)

Following the Midrash (*Num. Rab.* 7.8), Hirsch connected the purity laws and their social realms, linking those realms to the concentric three camps, and also made the parallel connections to the expulsions of the prologue (2007a: 62–120).

Table 6: Camp expulsions correlated

Expulsion of unclean persons (Num. 5:1–4)	Three main cases (Num. 5:5–10, 11–31; 6:1–21)	Realms of life in the Camp
A. Leprosy, *ṣārûa'*	A'. Fraudulent oath-breakers?	Society – twelve tribes
B. Discharge, *zāb*	B'. Strayed woman, *šikbat-zera'*	Family – Levites
C. Corpse pollution, *ṭāmē' lānāpeš*	C'. Nazirite, *ṭimmē'/hannāpeš*	Individual – *Shekhinah*

Turning to the priestly benediction, it has been widely observed that the threefold blessing expands incrementally, cascading from 3 words to 5 and then to 7, and from 15 consonants to 20 and then 25 (cf. D. N. Freedman 1975; Milgrom 1990: 51; on the structure, see Stubbs 2009: 74–75; Fishbane 1983: 115; Smoak 2016: 71–72), conveying that YHWH's blessing pours forth increasingly from his central Tent until it reaches the Israelites, encompassing the whole Camp. In keeping with the correlation between the three camps (5:1–4) and the three purity cases that follow (5:5 – 6:21), Hirsch connects the three aspects of the priestly blessing in a reverse manner, accordingly: 'bless you' is realized in the camp of Israel's twelve tribes, 'shine his face upon you' is realized in the camp of the Levites, and 'lift his face upon you' is realized in the camp of the *Shekhinah* (2007a: 129). On this paradigm, while the lines of the benediction increase, their sphere decreases, drawing concentrically closer to YHWH's own face as the source of life and blessing. (See Table 7.)

There is, however, no restriction of the whole blessing from all of God's people, even on Hirsch's correlation. Leibowitz discerns an increasing threefold surge of blessing 'like an ever-flowing spring', from humanity's material needs (24), to spiritual needs (25), and finally to the ultimate blessedness, combining both material and spiritual benefit as directed to the end itself, the supreme good: nearness to God (26; see Pss 73, 28) (1982: 63–73). The priestly benediction is given from the perspective of the *Shekhinah*'s central camp, and is an expression of YHWH's kingship, pouring out blessing to the rest of Israel's Camp much like Eden's river (Gen. 2:10–14). In summary, the threefold nature of the prologue, purity laws and capstone of benediction functions to map out the life-yielding holiness that radiates from YHWH's presence in the central sanctuary, outward to the farthest reaches of the Camp.

4.2. The purity laws as paradigmatic for the life of Israel's Camp

The legislation in Numbers 5 – 6 yields a comprehensive vision for the life of God's newly established covenant community, a life portrayed as *coram deo*, lived before the face of YHWH, whereby YHWH himself is deeply involved in every relationship and dealing. As such, the purity laws function as paradigms for the life of Israel's Camp, setting forth

Table 7: Priestly blessing and Israel's camps

Priestly blessing	*Camps*
(1) 'bless/keep'	⟶ All Israel
(2) 'shine his face / be gracious'	⟶ Levites
(3) 'lift up his face / give peace'	⟶ *Shekhinah*

a theology for life as YHWH's people. Well beyond concerns with ritual defilement, these laws call for behaviour such as confession of sin regarding one's neighbour, fidelity within one's marriage, and selfless, sacrificial devotion to YHWH God (cf. Frevel 2013c: 376). Since the behaviour solicited by the purity laws is paradigmatic for Israel's Camp, failing to live by these ideals makes one unfit for the Camp, leading to expulsion from its bounds.

To demonstrate this paradigmatic function, we will consider the Nazirite vow (6:1–21). The Nazirite, who may be a woman, is to be contrasted with the wayward woman (5:11–31), as two divergent paths set before Israel's wilderness sojourn. As Nachmanides stated, 'a woman who makes the Nazirite vow is the opposite of the *Sotah*' (*ś-ṭ-h*, 'to stray') (1975: 45; cf. MacDonald 2008a: 61–62; Landy 2015: 171–172). The wayward woman and the Nazirite, sharing several aspects that call for comparison, exemplify two ways of responding to YHWH, and should accordingly be interpreted together (cf. Bazak 2014c):

1. Both passages are of comparable length.
2. The strayed woman and the Nazirite are 'brought' (*hiqrîb*) before YHWH (5:15; 6:16).
3. Both scenarios underscore the person's hair as part of the ritual (5:18; 6:5, 18), the woman's hair is 'loosened', using the Hebrew root for *pāra'* in 5:18, also used for the Nazirite's 'locks' of hair in 6:5 – the only two uses of this root in Numbers.
4. Both accounts turn on an oath or vow before YHWH (5:19–22; 6:2).
5. The result of the defilement in both cases is described as a 'falling away' (*nāphal*), of the wayward woman's 'thigh' and the Nazirite's 'days' (5:21–22, 27; 6:12).
6. Both accounts deal with the topic of 'uncleanness' (*ṭāmē'*) (5:13,14; 6:9,12).
7. The priest 'elevates' (*hēnîp*) offerings on behalf of the strayed woman and the Nazirite (5:25; 6:20).
8. Both accounts end with the statement 'This is the Torah . . .' (5:29; 6:21).

'Thus as marriage symbolized the relationship between God and Israel (Num. 5),' G. J. Wenham writes (1981b: 96), 'so the Nazirites epitomized the holy calling of the nation (Num. 6)'. Relatedly, recent studies have emphasized the likeness between the law for the strayed woman and the language used to describe Israel's spiritual harlotries (see e.g. Ezek. 16, 23; Hos. 1 – 4; Jer. 2 – 3). Israel, the bride of YHWH, would prove to be an unfaithful wife, a wife of harlotry, and eventually be made to drink the cup of judgement by the hand of her jealous husband, YHWH God, whose name is 'Jealous' (Exod. 34:14; for allusions to the golden calf apostasy in Exod. 32, see Press 1933: 125; Fishbane 1974: 40; Frymer-Kensky 1984: 640; Bach 1999: 516; R. S. Briggs 2009: 304). MacDonald (2008a) even suggested that the figural interpretation of the strayed woman as Israel *is* the literal reading, an understanding preceded by Douglas (M. Douglas 2001: 160–171).

By contrast, the Nazirite sets before Israel the ideal of self-sacrificing consecration to YHWH (see Gane 2008). Through the Nazirite vow, a male or female Israelite voluntarily aspired to Israel's highest calling as the special possession of YHWH, a priestly kingdom and a holy nation (Exod. 19:5–6). Indeed, the Nazirite's holy status went beyond that of ordinary priests, comparable only to the high priest himself. The Nazirite shares the following commonalities with priests, and with the high priest in particular:

1. Both are regarded as 'holy unto God/YHWH' (Lev. 21:6; Num. 6:8).
2. Both have wine/strong drink restrictions (Lev. 10:9; Num. 6:3).
3. Both have restrictions in relation to their hair (Lev. 10:6; 21:5,10; Num. 6:5).
4. Both have death pollution restrictions even for close family members (Lev. 21:11; Num. 6:6–7).
5. Both the high priest and the Nazirite are said to have a 'crown' or 'consecration' (*nēzer*) upon their heads, signifying their holy status to YHWH – while the priest's crown is engraved with *qōdeš layhwh* ('holy to YHWH'), of the Nazirite we read *qādōš hû' layhwh* ('he is holy to YHWH') (Exod. 29:6–7; 39:30; Lev. 21:12; Num. 6:7).

Whereas the wayward woman strays away from her husband, the Nazirite is a man or woman who voluntarily vows to forsake the pleasures of life to draw nearer to God. Relatedly, the figure of Samson, under a Nazirite vow, is commonly read as representing Israel in the nation's holy calling (e.g. Webb 2008: 162–174), precisely our proposed function for the vow in Numbers.

How is the Nazirite's example relevant within the context of Numbers? The Camp is about to set out on a journey through the wilderness to the land, a journey of limited duration involving a few weeks of deprivation (see Deut. 1:2). How should Israel approach this period in the wilderness, especially given the fact that there are no grapes to be found in the wilderness anyway? The purity law solicits Israel to approach the journey through the wilderness like a Nazirite, gladly forsaking the comforts and pleasures of life for a designated period of time, to follow after YHWH more closely – even as a devoted bride (see Num. 9:15–23; Jer. 2:2; Hos. 2:14; 13:5). As the narrative progresses, it cannot be incidental that the scouts of Israel bring from Canaan a large cluster of grapes carried on a pole, a foretaste of what awaited them in the land *after* their sojourn in the wilderness (see 13:20, 23–27). As I will demonstrate, the Nazirite vow is the pattern for Israel's story in Numbers.

As the story unfolds, Israel will choose the path of spiritual harlotry, the first generation faithlessly refusing to take possession of the land (Num. 13 – 14). In response, YHWH condemns Israel to bear 'your whoredoms' (*zĕnûtêkem*, 14:33), by wandering for forty years until their carcasses 'fall (*yippĕlû*, 14:29, 32) in this wilderness' (cf. Ingalls 1991: 72), a use of *nāpal* linked with its uses in the purity laws, not only in terms of judgement but also in its discounting of days (14:34). Later, the second generation of Israel, too, will fail, committing spiritual harlotry at Baal Peor (Num. 25:1–4; cf. Exod. 32), an incident overcome and atoned for by the young priest Phinehas who was 'jealous' with YHWH's own jealousy as Israel's husband (25:7–18). Remarkably, Hosea appears to have these alternate paths – strayed woman versus Nazirite – in mind, as YHWH declares, 'Like grapes in the wilderness I found Israel . . . but they went to Baal Peor and separated themselves (*wayyinnāzĕrû*) to shame, and became as detestable as what they loved' (9:10). For YHWH, belonging to Israel was like discovering impossibly choice fruit, grapes, in the wilderness, whereas Israel despised him, separating themselves instead to Baal (husband, master). Hosea uses the root *nāzar* (separate), which occurs twenty-four times in Numbers with every reference related to the Nazirite vow. Earlier in Hosea, YHWH speaks of alluring Israel in the wilderness and giving her 'vineyards' so she will desire to return 'to her first husband' and call him 'My Husband', no longer calling him 'My Baal' (*baʿlî*), for he will take away the names of the Baals from her mouth (2:7, 14–17; see Jer. 2:2).

The wilderness era, of limited duration and within the context of privation, presented an opportune moment for Israel to cultivate loyalty to YHWH, temporarily forsaking the pleasures of life – precisely what the Nazirite vow solicits. The threefold outline of the Nazarite vow presents a structural analogy for assessing the wilderness sojourn theologically: (1) period of privation, (2) cleansing from corpse defilement, renewing the period of consecration, and (3) fulfilling the vow in the land, with sacrifices and accompaniments of grain and wine. Israel's wilderness sojourn follows this paradigm, narrating a period of privation (chs. 11–25), which required cleansing from corpse pollution and renewal, transitioning to the second generation (ch. 19), followed by the fulfilment of vows in the land, with sacrifices and accompaniments of grain and wine (chs. 28–30). Within this broad scheme, further connections to the Nazirite vow surface. After the first generation, having refused to embrace any privation during the wilderness sojourn (see 11:4–9), reject the land, with its large clusters of grapes (13:23–24), YHWH's response will renew the promise ('When you come into the land', 15:2) by providing detailed instructions for the accompaniments of grain and wine (15:3–21), portraying life in the land as a fulfilment of the

Nazirite vow (*pallē'-neder*, 15:3). More than this, Numbers 15 ends by donning every Israelite with blue cords, like the high priest, reminding Israel to 'be holy to your God' (vv. 37–41). The tassels not only reinforce the message of the priestly blessing (6:22–27), but encourage Israel to embrace the wilderness period like a Nazirite, holding forth once more their calling to be a 'priestly kingdom and holy nation' (Exod. 19:5–6). After the death of the first generation of Israelites, Numbers 19 provides for waters of purification from corpse pollution. These waters first appear for the Nazirite's cleansing (6:9), but the instructions are placed in the context of cleansing Israel's second generation, portraying them in terms of the Nazirite vow. By no coincidence, when the book anticipates the second generation's life in the land, the first topics addressed, after census-related matters, are sacrifices with their accompaniments of grain and wine (chs. 28–29) and the fulfilment of vows (chs. 30) – these chapters form one unit, framed by references to Moses' death (27:13; 31:1) and bridged by a reference to 'vow offerings' (29:39).

As grapes do not grow in the wilderness, Israel's sojourn would already be marked by a Nazirite's abstention. YHWH later tells the second generation of Israelites, 'I have led you forty years in the wilderness . . . you have not drunk wine or strong drink, that you may know that I am YHWH your God' (Deut. 29:5–6), both the fact and its purpose aligning with the Nazirite vow. In the Torah, the collocation of *lō* + *šātâ* ('not' + 'drink'), with reference to *yayin wĕšēkor* ('wine or strong drink'), occurs only in these two places (Num. 6:3; Deut. 29:6; see Lev. 10:9). Additionally, it cannot be incidental that the featured specimen of the land's fruits was an enormous cluster of grapes, so weighty it was carried on a pole between two men (Num. 13:23). Eshcol is *the* featured locale of Canaan, the only place named by the scouts and the culmination of their expedition before returning (13:23–25) – later, Moses' retelling of the scouts episode reads as if the scouts had *only* ascended up into Eshcol (see 32:9). Note also how the narrator remarks that when Moses sent the scouts, 'it was the days of the first-fruits of grapes' (13:20), anticipating the cluster taken at Wadi Eshcol (v. 23). Portraying the land in terms of bountiful vineyards suggests that YHWH has an abundance of good things, a life of joy abounding with grapes and wine, waiting for his people in the land. In view of inheriting the land, would Israel wholeheartedly embrace the wilderness sojourn, with its deprivations, as a period of self-dedication to YHWH, awaiting their journey's fulfilment when they could render sacrifices with grain and drink offerings, products of the land, to YHWH God? Along these lines, use of *nesek* ('drink offering') in Numbers is revealing, occurring in three clusters of references to drink offerings: twice in the Nazirite vow, four times in Numbers 15, and twenty-seven times in Numbers 28 – 29. Each reference functions in the same way, holding forth the journey's end and *telos*, the prospect of drawing near to YHWH with tokens of the good land's bounty. Worship in the land, including the accompaniments of grain and drink offerings, analogous to the Nazirite's culminating sacrifice, is the goal of the wilderness sojourn, an end that reorients the wilderness period as a time of temporary deprivation embraced willingly out of devotion to YHWH, and in preparation for life in the land.

4.3. The purity laws and Israel's wilderness sojourn

The wilderness sojourn opens in chapter 11 with a sharp contrast, not only to the book's first ten chapters, but especially to the ideal of the Nazirite vow. The mixed multitude craves a craving or 'desires a desire', and their lusting leads Israelites to weep and ask, 'Who will give us flesh to eat?' (v. 4). Israel plunges into the pursuit of pleasure, impatiently demanding the indulgence of their extravagant appetites within the wilderness. Then in Numbers 12 Miriam slanders Moses, and in response YHWH censures her with leprosy. Like leprosy, the evil tongue defiles others (in this case Aaron who joined her in speaking against Moses). Nothing could more plainly declare that such behaviour is unfitting for the covenant community than to punish her with leprosy, since as a leper Miriam must be shut out of the Camp (12:15), as required in the purity section (5:2).

In Numbers 13 – 14, the first generation of Israel, through unbelief and disobedience, refuses to inherit the land. Earlier we had noted that the result of defilement for both the strayed woman and the Nazirite was described by the Hebrew *nāphal*, to 'fall away'. YHWH's judgement of Israel's first generation is similarly phrased, twice: 'the dead bodies of you who complained against me will fall (*nāphal*) in this wilderness' (14:29), and 'but as for you, your dead bodies will fall (*nāphal*) in this wilderness' (14:32). There is, moreover, a good case to be made that the first generation is being likened to the *Sotah* as YHWH condemns Israel to bear 'your harlotries' (*zěnûtêkem*, 14:33).

One of the unique principles underscored in the legislation for those who had taken a false oath in YHWH's Name was that, in the event no kinsman lived to receive the guilty person's restitution, the guilt payment must be restored 'to YHWH, to the priest' (*layheh lakkōhēn*, 5:8; see Lev. 23:20), a system that, as Levine observed, 'is summarized in Numbers 18' (1993: 191). The divine order for life within the covenant community is being re-established at this point in the wilderness sojourn. Numbers 19 presents another area worthy of exploration, with its cleansing from corpse pollution through the red heifer ritual of purification, since the Nazirite's cleansing of death defilement alluded to this ritual (6:9). Why were the details reserved for a later location in the narrative? Perhaps because the second generation, which emerges in chapter 20, is being cleansed from the corpse pollution of the previous generation, signalling a new beginning, a renewed consecration. In this way, the second generation of Israel is characterized as a Nazirite, contrasted against the *Sotah*-like first generation. Keeping in mind both the life versus death framework for purity laws and the analogy between life in the Camp and life in the land, we may observe that the previous generation, defiled, had been condemned to die 'in this wilderness' (14:29, 32), a place that may be interpreted not only as 'outside the land' but 'outside the Camp'; in Numbers 19 the newly risen generation transitions from 'in this wilderness' to life 'within the Camp', cleansed from death's defilement.

In chapter 20, Israel's newly emerged generation contends with Moses because, as the narrator explains, 'there was no water for the community' (20:2). Much like the heavenly benediction poured out to the community from the central camp of the *Shekhinah*, displaying YHWH's generous kingship (6:22–27; see Gen. 2:10–14), Moses was to supply abundant waters for the Israelites and their animals to drink (20:7–8, 11) – yet by his demeanor, words and action, he misrepresented YHWH's kingship. In Numbers 21 the second generation fails by complaining. Yet, like those who make restitution for taking a false oath (Num. 5:5–10), the people of Israel confess their sin, coming before Moses and saying, 'We have sinned, for we have spoken against YHWH and against you' (21:7). With such a confession, rare in the Torah, Israel's second generation begins living the sort of life solicited by the purity laws.

Proceeding to Numbers 22 – 24, the Balaam story turns on whether YHWH can be made to curse Israel. Resolutely, YHWH tells Balaam, 'You will not curse the people for they are blessed' (22:12). Aside from the general truism of Israel's blessedness, if one were to ask, 'How and when is Israel blessed?' the answer, within Numbers, leads to the Aaronic benediction and the theology of Israel's Camp (6:22–27). The benediction that caps the purity laws and pervades the Balaam story are the only two places in Numbers where the language of 'to bless' (*bārak*) is found (17 times: 6:23, 24, 27; 22:6 twice, 12; 23:11 twice, 20 twice, 25 twice; 24:1, 9 twice, 10 twice). Later, Balaam's climactic prophecy occurs as he gazes on the entire encampment around YHWH's Dwelling, divinely arranged with its banners, 'Israel dwelling according to his tribes' (24:2). He sees the substance of Numbers 1 – 6, and, by the *rûaḥ 'ĕlōhîm*'s enabling him to see the community's spiritual essence, describes Israel's Camp as a well-watered Edenic paradise (24:1–6).

Finally, in Numbers 25, many Israelites commit harlotry with the women of Moab, and join themselves to Baal of Peor. Their apostasy is exemplified by Zimri, an Israelite chieftain who brazenly takes Cozbi, a Midianite princess, into the Camp before the eyes of Moses and all the congregation of Israel. In Numbers 5, the resolution for the wayward woman begins with the spirit of 'jealousy' (*qānā'*) coming upon her husband, the root for 'jealously' occurring ten times. At Baal Peor the resolution comes through Aaron's grandson Phinehas, who is commended by YHWH for being 'jealous for my sake among them, so that I did not consume Israel in my jealousy', where forms of *qānā'* occur four times. Israel, the bride of YHWH, had strayed from her nuptial loyalty, committing spiritual harlotry (see Balorda 2002; for literary parallels between Num. 5:11–31 and Num. 25, see Bechara 2012). Phinehas the young priest, filled with the spirit of jealousy on behalf of God, acts to make atonement so as to restore the marriage covenant. Moreover, while different terms are used, the conceptual parallel in the respective retributions experienced by each guilty woman is unmistakable: Phinehas's spear penetrates Cozbi's 'belly' (*qŏbātāh*, 25:8), even as the liquid curse reaches the woman's 'womb' (*beṭen*, 5:21, 22, 27). Later in Numbers Israel's spiritual harlotry with the women of Moab and Midian will be dubbed *ma'al* (treachery, unfaithfulness), the seventh, final and only use of the designation outside the purity laws (four of which relate to *Sot.*: 5.12 [twice], 27 [twice]).

Broadly, and most profoundly, the three defilements of 5:2 – leprosy, bodily discharge and corpse pollution – reappear during the wilderness sojourn in ways that cohere thematically with their respective sections. The wilderness sojourn divides into three sections: (1) chapters 11–15, related to the outer camp of tribes, focusing on Moses' prophetic office; (2) chapters 16–19, related to the inner camp of Levites, focusing on Aaron's priestly office; and (3) chapters (20) 21–25, related to the central camp of the *Shekhinah*, focusing on YHWH's kingship. Beginning with Moses' prophetic office (chs. 11–15), Miriam's leprosy and subsequent expulsion from the Camp occur in 12:10 ('leprosy' occurs only at 5:2; 12:10 twice), a result of her diminishing Moses' prophetic status. Second, in the section concerning Aaron's priesthood (chs. 16–19), the red heifer ritual provides cleansing from corpse pollution (ch. 19), linked also to the Nazirite vow (6:1–21), which indeed solicits Israelites to embrace their calling as a 'priestly kingdom and holy nation' (Exod. 19:6). Lastly, in the section related to YHWH's kingship and the camp of the *Shekhinah* (chs. 20–25), sexual defilement occurs at Baal Peor (ch. 25), which connects to bodily discharge (5:2) and the strayed woman (5:11–31). Phinehas follows an Israelite who has strayed into a secluded place, a tent-shrine, and brings judgement, reaching to his consort's belly. Thematically, marriage thus relates to kingship, with straying after other gods (masters, husbands, 'Baal') being considered spiritual harlotry. Numbers 20, which concludes chapters 16–19 but opens 21–25 with the kingship theme, also resonates with the strayed woman ritual as YHWH directs Moses to 'cause the people and their animals to drink' – the only other use of *šāqâ* (5:24, 26, 27; 20:8). Although the three narrative events of defilement occur in a different order than in 5:2, switching bodily discharge (strayed woman) with corpse pollution (Nazirite vow), they fit precisely with the thematic focus of each section: prophecy, priesthood and kingship. These are some ways in which the purity laws of Numbers 5 – 6 relate to the wilderness sojourn in chapters 11–25.

5. THE STRUCTURE OF NUMBERS

Literary structure has been yet another aspect of Numbers marked by lack of consensus. Dentan's view that 'the material in the book is of the most heterogeneous character' and 'its arrangement, at least as respects the non-narrative elements, is largely fortuitous', not even comprising a book at all (1962a: 568), is shared by many scholars, precluding meaningful efforts toward discerning the book's coherence and structure (e.g. Ska 2014: 102; E. W. Davies 2015: 10–15). Shumate surveyed seventy sources, yielding thirty-four different outlines that differed both as to the number and location of major divisions (2001: 44; cf. Knierim 1995a: 380). Since, however, understanding the plan of a literary text is essential for understanding its message, endeavouring to grasp the structure of Numbers remains profitable.

Rather than rehearsing the variety of proposals – twofold (Olson 1985; Milgrom 1990; B. P. Y. Lee 2003; Knierim and Coats 2005), by geographical indicators, typically threefold (G. B. Gray 1903; Noth 1968; de Vaulx 1972; G. J. Wenham 1981b; Noordtzij 1983; Budd 1984; Ashley 1993; Artus 1997), including chronological indicators (see Ingalls 1991: 34), seven cycles under a threefold and broader twofold structure (Cole 2000), ring-composition (M. Douglas 2001) or chiastic (Currid 2009; cf. G. J. Wenham 1997: 21–22) – and their weaknesses, I will glean from the strengths of previous efforts to suggest Numbers divides naturally into three main sections, structured thematically.

5.1. A threefold literary structure of Numbers

Appreciating that a literary work such as Numbers includes intertextual connections throughout, even crossing major divisions, the outline that captures the book's movement and message most authentically is threefold: chapters 1–10, 11–25 and 26–36. Following Olson's analysis, the census of Numbers 26 is structurally significant (1985; discerned already by Sandys-Wunsch 1961: 194), validating the third section. Tellingly, however, the majority of the parallels he proposed for his twofold structure (chs. 1–25 and 26–36) are limited to those between chapters 1–10 and 26–36. By not restricting his consideration to these two units, moreover, other significant parallels were neglected: there are no Israelite deaths recorded within chapters 1–10 and 26–36, nor are there any rebellions or judgements, whereas the middle section (11–25) contains thousands of deaths as a result of divine judgement for rebellion.

The main question to address in my threefold approach is in relation to the end of the first section: should it end at 10:36, instead of, as a majority of commentators suggest, at 10:10? There is a chiastic parallel between 1:1 (place: 'wilderness of Sinai', date: 'first day of the second month in the second year') and 10:11–12 (date: 'twentieth day of the second month in the second year', place: 'wilderness of Sinai'), which some argue marks the latter passage as a new beginning (e.g. B. P. Y. Lee 2003: 90–100). Granting the chronological notice's function as a new beginning, however, does not determine a major literary break. Within the broader structural pattern, an inclusion for 10:11–36 seems more likely, especially set within the context of broader parallels between these chapters: date (1:1; 10:11), place (1:1; 10:12), listing of the princes by name (1:5–15; 10:14–27) and tribal groupings (1:20–43; 2:1–31; 10:14–27) (Ziegler 2014: 4). Several observations support ending the first section at 10:36. First, Numbers 1 – 10 and 26 – 36 employ a similar literary strategy. After the census in Numbers 26, the rest of the third section is bounded by an inclusio, with Numbers 27 and 36 both narrating legislation related to the daughters of Zelophehad. Similarly, after the census in Numbers 1, the rest of the first section is bounded by an inclusio, with Numbers 2 and 10 narrating the arrangement of the camps for journeying forth. Ingalls also noted these inclusios (1991: 37–38):

Num. 1 First Muster
  Num. 2 Marching order of the camp
  Num. 10 Marching order of the camp

Num. 26 Second Muster
  Num. 27 Inheritance of the daughters of Zelophehad
  Num. 36 Inheritance of the daughters of Zelophehad

Strengthening the case, Numbers 2 and 10 describe the camp arrangements according to each tribe's 'standard' (*degel*). The 13 occurrences of *degel* in Numbers are restricted to this inclusion, used 9 times in the beginning of the first section (1:52; 2:2, 10, 17, 18, 25, 31, 34) and 4 times at its end (10:14, 18, 22, 25). Note that these latter occurrences come *after* 10:11, supporting the argument for concluding the book's first section at 10:36. The same holds true for the noun 'host' (*ṣābā'*), which occurs 36 times in Numbers 1 – 2 (16 and 20 times, respectively) and 17 times in Numbers 10, but only within the unit of 10:11–36 – with not a single instance in chapters 11–25 (Leder 2016: 524–525).

A second observation relates to the literary mood of the text. Even Olson remarks on the drastic change from high optimism in chapters 1–10 to the severe pessimism that begins with the people's complaint in 11:1, referring to the 'major break' and 'the extremely abrupt and wrenching break in the narrative at 11:1' (1985: 121–122). Elsewhere, he writes that 'the reader experiences three dramatic and important movements in tone and character in the shift from chapters 1–10 to chapters 11–25 . . . and then to chapters 26–36' (Olson 1997: 230). Fox, who ends the first section with 10:36, speaks also of the 'narrative mood swings' corresponding to the book's movement from order to chaos, and back to order again (1995: 649), and Gertel refers to the 'radical shift' in tone and mood (2002: 73). The setting forth of Israel recounted in 10:11–36 should thus be read *within* the celebratory atmosphere of chapters 1–10 as whole – it functions as a culmination, anticipated from the beginning. Moreover, while 10:12 states the 'Israelites set out', verses 13–28 do not follow chronologically, but rather describe the actual setting out with expanded detail, tribe by tribe, and verses 34–36 offer an idealized portrayal to cap off the section. In short, the increasing momentum and optimism of the first section would be incomplete without the latter half of chapter 10, yet with it the intensity finds satisfactory resolution. As a unit, Numbers 1 – 10 is *complete* in every sense (cf. Leder 2016).

Furthermore, while the poetic unit segmented in the Hebrew text by inverted nuns, found mysteriously at the end of verses 34 and 36, functions well as a capstone to chapters 1–10; yet when this unit is set in the midst of 10:11 to wherever one ends the second section of Numbers, hardly any rationale for its placement can be discerned. Ashley's commentary exemplifies the point: while he ends the first major section at 10:10, he nevertheless agrees that 10:11–28 'is mostly a recapitulation of material from ch. 2' and that the inverted nuns bracketing off 10:35–36 seem to function not only as a conclusion to the departure, but 'in a sense, to the whole of the Sinai story (Exod. 19–Num. 10)', noting also that references to Jethro and Hobab mark the beginning and end, respectively, of an inclusio from Exodus 18 to Numbers 10 (1993: 190, 199, 197). While the inverted nuns may signal the bracketed text's displacement, they were also understood by ancient rabbis as creating three separate books out of Numbers (*Shab.* 115b–116a), with the song of the ark (10:35–36) serving to separate the ideal portrait of Israel from the dismal reality of Israel's sojourn in the wilderness. As such, 11:1 'marks the central dividing line', a 'dividing line so significant that *Hazal* viewed it as a central cleft which splits the book' (Lichtenstein 2014a: 144). Y. Kahn goes further (2014: 126–127), suggesting the 'books' of Numbers 1:1–10:34 and 10:35–36 offer the first *version* of Israel's story, completing an ideal Pentateuch, since the song of the ark might have been followed by the conquest of Joshua (also Lichtenstein 2014a: 144). Leder also points out that the unit of 10:11–36 contains five wayyiqtol forms (expressing sequential action) of the itinerary verb *nāsaʻ* (to journey), while Numbers 11 – 12 by contrast uses *qatal* forms (non-sequential) of *nāsaʻ*, subordinating Israel's journey under a complaint theme, the thematic shift marked by use of *wayĕhî* in 11:1 (2016: 519–530).

Finally, while the date referenced in 10:11 has led some scholars to begin a major section here, chronological references cannot offer a consistent basis for the book's structure. Moreover, this date notice is intricately connected to the rhetorical shape of the first section, the symmetry being plainly evident:

1:1   2nd year, 2nd month, 1st day
7:1   on the day the Tabernacle was set up (2nd year, 1st month, 1st day)
9:1   2nd year, 1st month, (approx. 14th day) – Passover
9:15 on the day the Tabernacle was set up (2nd year, 1st month, 1st day)
10:11 2nd year, 2nd month, 20th day

Since the date notices in 1:1, 9:1 and 10:11 relate to the *following* material (10:11–36), the complete section should be taken as 1:1 – 10:36. After these orderly and specific notices, characteristic of the first ten chapters as a whole, the chronology becomes vague, with the next referent in 11:18 being simply to 'tomorrow'. So, the date referenced in 10:11, far from signalling a new major division, serves to retain verses 11–36 within the literary structure and character of chapters 1–10 as a complete unit. In this instance, the chapter division – at 11:1 versus 10:11 – manifests sensitivity to the nature and flow of the narrative. Indeed, the chronological reference may be added to the parallels between the beginning and ending of this major section: date, place; leaders, standards (1–2)//place, date; standards, leaders (10:11–28). Perhaps the strongest argument for beginning a new division at 10:11 is the 'wilderness of Paran' inclusion at 10:12 and 12:16; however, 10:12 may simply forecast the next section.

With this one crucial change – ending the first section at 10:36 – our threefold division coincides with that of several others, and incorporates loosely the broad geography of the book as well as the function of the two census accounts (see Naylor 1994: 158; Fox 1995: 647–649; Leder 2010: 152–154). Taking this threefold literary structure as an A–B–A' pattern reflects the similar elements shared between the first and third sections, as well as the general movement from organization (cosmos) to disorganization (chaos) and then to reorganization (new cosmos). Filling in the major theme for each division, we render the outline as follows:

A. 1–10: The Camp of Israel

B. 11–25: The wilderness journeys of Israel

A'. 26–36: The land of Israel

There is an analogous relationship between A and A': the Camp of Israel, an embodiment of the covenant community dwelling with YHWH, serves as a model for Israel's life with YHWH in the land. As soon as the Camp is constructed, therefore, YHWH commands its purity 'in the midst of which I myself am dwelling' (5:3), and later with the prospect of Israel's life in the land YHWH commands his people not to defile the land wherein 'I YHWH am dwelling in the midst of the sons of Israel' (35:34). The wilderness journeys as the Camp of Israel form the training ground for the transition to life in the land. Two-thirds of the book (chs.

1–10, 26–36), then, portrays a happy, fruitful relationship between God and his people, and not necessarily being idealistic either, including give and take on both sides, and marked by Israel's faithful obedience. The negative impressions of Numbers, characterized by Israel's grumbling and rebellions, YHWH's wrath and judgements, and Moses' crises and intercessions, all derive from the central section, the wilderness section proper (chs. 11–25). Although Israelites encamp at the plains of Moab in 22:1, the 'wilderness journeys' as an era, in terms of threats, testing and judgements, is not complete until the census of Numbers 26.

Numbers 1 – 10 narrates the establishment of the Camp by divine revelation as the product of the Sinai covenant, completing the main object of the covenant before setting out for the land. The central wilderness sojourn, Numbers 11 – 25, forms the period whereby YHWH teaches his people, even through their own revolts against the newly formed structure, how to live before his uplifted face as a community, embracing afresh the covenantal offices and institutions as divinely given for their well-being. Learning these lessons, which would require the death and rebirth of Israel in the wilderness, was essential before Israel could be established as a nation in the land. Chapters 26–36 then apply the Camp's covenantal model of life with God to the anticipated context of the land of Canaan.

The organizing principle for *Numbers 1 – 10* is the covenant community, conceived as a mobile encampment around YHWH's central Dwelling, the fruition of the Sinai covenant. Numbers 1 – 6 concerns the arrangement of the Camp, concluding with the priestly benediction 'YHWH bless you!' (6:22–27), and chapters 7–10 concern the mobility of the Camp, concluding with Moses' liturgical shout 'Arise, O YHWH!' as the uplifted ark marches out, leading the tribes (10:34–36). There is a clear break between chapters 6 and 7, inasmuch as the poetic lines conclude the purity laws (chs. 5–6), and chapter 7 begins by going back to the dedication events of the Dwelling, on the first day of the first month. Condren (2013), although limiting the second subsection to 7:1 – 10:10, proposes a threefold parallel structure for these units, moving from the twelve tribes (1:1 – 2:34; 7:1–89) to the Levites (3:1 – 4:49; 8:1–26) to 'community legislation' (5:1 – 6:27; 9:1 – 10:10), which demonstrates shared language between the units and accurately captures the paradigmatic significance of the Camp's structure (cf. Knierim and Coats 2005: 33). The third parallel is better expressed as 'life of the Camp', underscoring its purity and blessedness (5:1 – 6:27) and 'the setting forth of the Camp', underscoring the time and manner of the Camp's departure (9:1 – 10:36) – a movement from the covenant community's encampment to its journeying. With Condren's delimited final subsection, 10:11–36 still functions as an inclusio with chapter 2, capping the major section (chs. 1–10), which conforms with the same separate function of chapter 36: the final scene with the uncles of Zelophehad's daughters is clearly separate from the subsection of chapters 33–35, but caps off the major section (chs. 26–36), as an inclusio with the first half of chapter 27. Grossman (2017) further underscores that the first block of material emphasizes the Camp itself as the context for the tribes, priests and Levites, and legislation (1–6), while the second block has the Dwelling and its altar as the primary context (7–10). The second subdivision focuses on the camp of the *Shekhinah* (chs. 7–10), established in Leviticus and now the centre of the twelve tribes (chs. 1–2) and priests and Levites (chs. 3–4) in the Camp. Going back chronologically enables the progression thematically to the central encampment.

Incorporating the three subsections of the central division into my outline, *Numbers 11 – 25*, the following structure emerges:

A. 1–10: Camp of Israel
B. 11–25: Sojourn of Israel
      11–15: Moses' Prophetic Office: outer camp of 12 tribes
      16–20: Aaron's Priestly Office: inner camp of Levites
      21–25: YHWH's Kingship: central camp of the *Shekhinah*
      (Israel's second generation)
A'. 26–36: Land of Israel

Related to the subsections of chapters 11–25, Mann comes close to my understanding, labelling 11:1 – 14:45 as 'Prophetic Controversies and the Fate of the Wilderness Generation', and 16:1 – 20:13 as 'Priestly Controversies and the Fate of Moses and Aaron' (1987: 190; cf. Cole 1998: 5; 2000: 21), and Artus refers to the 'military project of the Lord' (related to chs. 13–14) and the 'religious project of the Lord' (chs. 16–18) (2013: 373). These insights, while correct, fall short of appreciating the larger narrative logic and purpose, linked to the Camp's structure. Such attention to the divinely designated offices of Israel is in accord with the overarching theme of Numbers as the establishment of YHWH's covenant community, including the probation and vindication of his authorized leadership structure. To function as the special possession and holy nation of YHWH, Israel had to learn to submit to the hierarchical structure of leadership he designated, and, further, to appreciate the need for these offices, rendering honour and obedience.

After a census (ch. 26), the third major section, *Numbers 26 – 36*, is bound by a daughters of Zelophehad inclusio that highlights the theme of inheriting and retaining the land, respectively (chs. 27:1–11; 36). As with the original concern of Zelophehad's daughters, Numbers 27:12–23, whereby Joshua is designated to lead the people for the land's possession, also relates to the census since Moses is not numbered among those to whom the land will be divided. After these post-census matters are resolved, chapters 28–30 form a block related to sacrifices and vows (cf. 29:39), bounded by references to Moses' looming death

(27:12–13; 31:1–2). The next section, the battle and plunder of Midian (ch. 31), along with the distribution of Transjordan to the tribes of Gad, Reuben and the half-tribe of Manasseh (ch. 32), forms a section unified by the pattern of conquest and possession of land, auguring the conquest of Canaan. Taken together, Numbers 28 – 32 present Israelite military victory and possession of land (chs. 31–32) after Israel's Nazirite-like vow fulfilment 'in the land'. After matters pertaining to the east side of the Jordan (chs. 31–32), the final section relates to the land of Canaan – west of the Jordan (chs. 33–36). Chapters 33–35 set forth a summary of Israel's journeys, introducing YHWH's last five speeches, chiastically arranged, pertaining to Israel's life in the land. Israel's life with YHWH in the paradigmatic encampment arrangement is applied to the land, the unit ending with the climactic statement 'I YHWH am dwelling in the midst of the sons of Israel' (35:34), paralleling the similar statement upon the Camp's construction (5:3). Chapter 36, forming an inclusio with chapter 27, emphasizes that the land is a lasting gift from YHWH for each of the tribes. The two literary peaks of the third major section are (1) the Midianite battle, which sets forth the ideal Camp of Israel in action (ch. 31), fulfilling the outer camp's *telos* and potential in a way that alludes to nearly every previous chapter of Numbers, and (2) YHWH's central third speech, designating the ten tribal princes who will divide the land, reversing the failure of the previous generation's ten princes (34:16–29; cf. 13:3–16).

5.2. A twofold division

In terms of the broadest possible outline, a twofold approach to the book is worth exploring for the sake of underscoring the theme of Israel's transition in the wilderness from the old to the new generation. Numbers 1 – 18 rehearses the old generation's failed journey with YHWH, ending with their death in the wilderness, while Numbers 20 – 36 narrates the new generation's successful journey with YHWH, ending on the plains of Moab in anticipation of life in the land; and chapter 19 serves as the transition between the generations, as Israel's second generation is cleansed from the death defilement of the first (cf. Samet 1997; Ziegler 2014). While this general outline flattens the changes that occur between chapters 1–10 and 11–18 for the first generation, and those between 20–25 and 26–36 for the second generation, including thematic shifts, and disconnects chapters 16–20 as a unit, its value is in the clear distinction between generations, dubbed 'obvious' by Abarbanel (2015: 216) yet missed by many interpreters, and in the awareness of chapter 19's centrality. Numbers 19 forms the true transition of generations, even as it narrates the ritual cleansing required for the transition from death defilement to purity: the ritual's position symbolizes the cleansing of the newly emerged second generation of Israel from the death defilement of the first. The stigma and punishment of the former generation's rebellion has been washed away. Brodie (2008), who divides Numbers into nineteen atonement-centred diptychs, identifies chapters 18–19 (beginning at 17:12) as the central and pivotal tenth diptych, and broadly outlines the book as the first half of the journey, from Sinai to Kadesh (Num. 1 – 19) and the second half of the journey, from Kadesh to Moab (Num. 20 – 36). Chapter 18, comprised of legislation whereby YHWH reaffirms the role of the priesthood and Levites, resolves the narrative tensions before chapter 19 signals the transition to the new generation.

6. THE COMPOSITION OF NUMBERS

6.1. Is the book of Numbers a unity?

Discerning any logical relationship across the diverse materials of Numbers, and how they fit within the story of the Pentateuch, has exercised interpreters for millennia. Whereas literary approaches assume a text's unity until proven otherwise (e.g. Sprinkle 1989; Gros Louis 1982: 2:15), those working under the assumptions of source criticism have generally given up attempts to discern literary unity, assuming rather that Numbers comprises a collection of leftover materials of diverse backgrounds, preserved by redactors. Noth's commentary, presuming a long and complicated history, exemplifies this approach, decrying the book's 'confusion and lack of order' (1968: 4). Such sentiments could be multiplied (e.g. Dentan 1962a: 567; Moriarty 1968: 86; Levine 1976b: 634; Riggans 1983: 2), and are commonplace in source criticism (Baentsch 1903; G. B. Gray 1903; Holzinger 1903), form criticism (Gressmann 1922; Binns 1927), and tradition-historical criticism (Noth 1968; Budd 1984), each use a diachronic approach (see Ingalls 1991: 1–8). However, as Frevel discerns (2009: 111), the source-critical model applies in Numbers 'only roughly, and sometimes with violence'.

Taking for granted the presence of varied source material, one still faces the reality that these elements have been brought together into a meaningful composition, a meaning that may remain elusive for any number of reasons, including historical and cultural gaps that exist between the ancient world and our own. Sometimes apparent disorder and confusion signal a unity that lies at a depth too profound for the average contemporary reader to grasp (cf. Brodie 2008: 455). While neither presuming to resolve puzzling features definitively nor reducing them simplistically, wholistic approaches endeavour to discern the literary cohesion and purposeful shaping of Numbers' final form (G. J. Wenham 1981b; Budd 1984: xx; Olson 1985; Harrison 1990: 616–634; Milgrom 1990: xii; M. Douglas 2001; 2007: 43–71; Condren 2005; Caine and Fox 2007: 1250; Carmichael 2012; also Sandys-Wunsch 1961; de Vaulx 1972). While taking source criticism seriously, Stubbs proposes that the juxtaposed materials form beautiful patterns, 'an artfully constructed text in which seemingly disparate parts work together to emphasize central themes' (2009: 21). As I have endeavoured to demonstrate, the map of Israel's Camp forms the pattern that unfolds the logic of both the structure and thematic content of Numbers.

6.2. Who composed the book of Numbers?

We will not enter into the labyrinth of criticism regarding the composition of Numbers, which cannot be considered adequately apart from the Torah as a whole. After many centuries of scholarly enquiry, the historical origins and literary history of the Pentateuch remain intensely debated (e.g. Gertz et al. 2016), with source criticism roundly assessed as 'a failed hypothesis' by Clines (2007), remarking further 'that there are still thousands of people addicted to the four-source theory and whole careers founded upon it'. One's presuppositions and even literary bent will to a large degree determine how persuasive one finds the current versions of critical theories. Whybray questioned the validity of the principles of the documentary hypothesis, along with the various other approaches built upon them (e.g. traditio-critical), since stylistic variation and repetitions in a text may be readily explained without resorting to such a complicated theory, which piles 'one speculation upon another', often in a circular fashion (1987: 194). He surmised there is no reason why the first edition of the Pentateuch (allowing for a few additions) could not have been the final version, composed by a single historian (1987: 240). Other aspects, such as references to Moses in the third person, once used as an argument against Mosaic authorship (G. B. Gray 1903: xxix–xxx), have since been recognized as customary style in the ancient world (Harrison 1990: 23–24). Berman (2017) also critiqued the methods of source criticism, calling for a sober acknowledgement of the limits of historical-critical study for ascertaining the dates and prehistory of biblical texts. This is not the place to address the pillars of source criticism, but Youngblood's assessment still holds true: 'The bankruptcy of the documentary theory is perhaps most glaringly revealed when it is forced to invoke the aid of a redactor to bail it out when its criteria do not fit a passage' (W. H. Green 1978: xvii). Green's earlier critique was equally sharp, and remains justified (Vos 1886: v):

> The critical sundering not only rends apart the most intimately connected paragraphs, but throws out isolated clauses and words *ad libitum*, upon the mere *dictum* of the operator, and to save the consistency of the hypothesis. It is simply and evidently a determined

forcing through of a foregone conclusion in spite of every consideration that stands in the way.

While sound methodological critiques of higher criticism remain unanswered (e.g. Allis 1943; C. H. Gordon 1959; Keil and Delitzsch 1973: 1:17–28; Motyer 1974; W. H. Green 1978; Cassuto 2008; Lawrence 2011), increasing dissatisfaction with its impotence has led to the exploration of new paradigms (e.g. Armgardt et al. 2019; Baker et al. 2020).

Ascription of the Torah's primary authorship to Moses has been, for millennia, the received tradition of both Judaism and Christianity. One could multiply testimonies within the Hebrew Scriptures and the New Testament, as well as from other ancient writers and works, from *Jubilees* (see 1:4–5, 26; 2:1), Ben Sira (*Sir.* 45:2–5), Philo (*Creation* 1.1; *Moses* 2.8) and Josephus (*Ag. Ap.* 1.37–40) to the rabbis (*Bav. Bat.* 14b, 15a). True, questions arose from time to time about certain passages; for example, there was rabbinical discussion over Moses' writing about his own death in Deuteronomy 34:5–12 (*Bav. Bat.* 15a; *Men.* 30a; cf. Dozeman 2017: 33–39). However, as addressing such relatively minor concerns, critical scholarship's wholesale discarding of sound, longstanding traditions can be seen only as an overcompensation of massive proportions. Happily, modern scholarship appears to be maturing away from the extreme scepticism of previous generations and there is a growing appreciation for the historical value of traditions as received, for example, in the Mishnah and Talmud, not to mention as found within Scripture itself. That traditions regarding Mosaic authorship of the Torah developed in terms of post-exilic priests seeking to promote their own political clout neither resolves the matter, for seeking Mosaic validation presumes historical tradition, nor accords with the sublime character of the text itself. Nevertheless, care is wanted to avoid asserting dogmatically what the Bible may not claim, some scholars noting that Mosaic authorship of the Pentateuch (or Numbers) is nowhere explicitly stated within its pages. The Torah's genre, neither prophetic oracle nor epistle, may preclude such an ascription. There is, in any case, a sound basis for the tradition that Moses is the main source of the Pentateuch.

Throughout the Scriptures, Moses is considered the fountain of prophecy, the one to whom and through whom YHWH revealed himself most fully, and the central, incomparable figure of the HB whose royal role encompassed that of every possible office, from deliverer, lawgiver, prophet and judge, to priest, psalmist and sage (cf. Feilchenfeldt 1952: 156; Childs 1989: 109). Passing over his nearly deific place in post-biblical Jewish literature, it is nevertheless not without some merit that the Pentateuch's genre has been regarded by some as a biography of Moses (e.g. Knierim 1995b). As Cornelius observed, although it has been the prevailing opinion since Wellhausen, Moses' persona cannot be attributed to mere legend (1966: 75): the historical reality of YHWH's covenant with Israel attests to the instrumental role of this mediator, the one through whom both Torah and the *Shekhinah* presence of YHWH were brought down from heaven to earth. Israel's most fundamental institutions trace their origins to Moses, institutions which cannot be rent from the sacred writ that gives them life, direction and meaning.

The internal evidence for traditions of Mosaic authorship not only includes his canonical reputation, along with the metonymic references to the Torah by his name in the New Testament (e.g. Luke 16:29, 31; 24:27; Rom. 10:5; etc.), but also his eminent qualification – aside from his Egyptian education and training – as the *primary witness* to the acts and self-revelation of YHWH God. There are, to be sure, some references to Moses' writing activity within the Pentateuch (Exod. 17:4; 24:4, 7; 34:27; Deut. 31:9, 24), Numbers 33:2 stating that 'Moses wrote down the starting points of their journeys at the command of YHWH'. Harrison also suggested Moses might have utilized a class of scribes, the *šōṭĕrîm*, appointed by him first as supervisors (Num. 11:16–17), which later became a guild (Josh. 1:10), who served as record keepers, recording important events and judicial decisions (1990: 15–17). Kitchen has decried the misinformed statements, often parroted, about the dissonance between the Pentateuch's material and its Middle Bronze Age II setting, including writing capability, arguing – from an array of Egyptian, Mesopotamian and Canaanite inscriptions and customs – that the mid-second millennium provides a sound context for Mosaic authorship, he also positing a use of scribes (2006: 304–306). Dating biblical texts is fraught with difficulties, and scholarship has not exercised due caution (cf. Sommer 2011). Knowledge of ancient writing, along with the origins of the Hebrew alphabet, is still incomplete, and there is no sound reason to preclude writing in Moses' era, whether in some form of late Canaanite script or otherwise (Archer 1994: 175–176; Kitchen 2006: 304–306; Goldwasser 2010). Based on the discovery of a sherd from Tel Lachish, dated to the fifteenth century BC, for example, several scholars have asserted (Höflmayer et al. 2021: 717), 'We now can show that early alphabetic writing in the Southern Levant developed independently of, and well before, the Egyptian domination and floruit of hieratic writing during the Nineteenth and Twentieth Dynasties.' As Young observed, there is every reason to believe that, regardless of literacy rates, elite groups such as scribes, priests and government officials such as army officers were literate, and had long existed throughout the biblical era (2016). The biblical witness itself points, and possibly restricts writing, to such elite scribes (also Young 1998a; 1998b). All traditions, biblical or otherwise, portray Moses as having trained under the leading curriculum of the ancient world.

Whatever the manner of inscription, the Pentateuch depicts Moses' mediatorial role as the primary *recipient* of divine revelation, and therefore the instrument through whom Israel received God's word.

The construction of the Dwelling with which Exodus ends is said to have been done 'according to all that YHWH had commanded Moses' (39:42); Leviticus ends with the statement 'These are the commands which YHWH commanded Moses for the sons of Israel in Mount Sinai' (27:34); Numbers ends, similarly, with 'These are the commands and the judgements which YHWH commanded by the hand of Moses to the sons of Israel in the plains of Moab' (36:13); and Deuteronomy ends with a final word on Moses' unsurpassed 'face to face' knowledge of YHWH, prefaced by the notice that the sons of Israel heeded Joshua 'and did just as YHWH had commanded Moses' (34:9–12; also Josh. 22:2, 5). The Torah, moreover, portrays Moses as a scribe (Exod. 24:4, 7; 34:27–28; Deut. 31:9). Moses, then, is not only the recipient of YHWH's comprehensively foundational revelation, but also the one who wrote at least some of it down as Israel's *torah*. Parker (2015: 125) notes, 'the consistent biblical depiction of all written law coming through Moses and all subsequent authority (i.e., Moses' successors) as founded on that written law'. Watts also stresses the Pentateuch's presentation of Moses as having a paradigmatic scribal role, who thus 'exemplifies the ancient scribe who records, teaches, and interprets' so that 'there is no access to divine law except through him' (1998: 417, 422, 425). For those who place themselves under the Torah's divine authority, it is enough to demonstrate clearly the witness of the text itself. Watts concludes his study by stating, 'No wonder the Pentateuch's rhetoric led tradition to claim both divine *and* Mosaic authorship to the whole' (1998: 426; emphasis original). The psalmist declares that YHWH 'made known his ways to Moses' (103:7), a point taken for granted throughout the pages and later eras of Scripture. Indeed, the *instrumentality* of Moses is everywhere asserted in the Hebrew canon (Josh. 22:9; Judg. 3:4; 1 Kgs 2:3; 8:53, 56; 2 Kgs 18:12; 1 Chr. 6:49; 2 Chr. 33:8; 35:6; Neh. 1:7–8; 8:14; 9:14; 10:29; Mal. 4:4). This instrumentality appears to be at the root of the phrase 'Torah of Moses', a designation commonly employed across authors and historical contexts (Josh. 23:6; 13; Ezra 3:2; 7:6; Neh. 8:1; Dan. 9:11; etc.). Any historical reconstruction that wipes away such a tradition, found within the primary sources themselves, may be questioned as suspect.

The rather consistent understanding of Moses' role set forth in the rest of the Hebrew Scriptures accords well with the portrayal found within the Pentateuch. Leaving aside references within Exodus, Leviticus and Deuteronomy, the book of Numbers alone contains sixty-six references to YHWH's communicating to Moses. Narrating YHWH's many speeches to Moses, *the Torah establishes Moses as its own source*, the conduit of revelation. Since YHWH's instruction was revealed primarily – nearly exclusively – to Moses, the Torah could only have been formed *through Moses*. This communication YHWH himself described as unique among the human race, a communication that was 'face to face' (Num. 12:6–8; surpassed only by the Messiah, John 1:17–18). The Hebrew canon acknowledges this primacy, ordering its library by gradations of revelation in a manner not unlike the gradations of sacred space: Torah (face-to-face revelation); Prophets (revelation by dreams and visions); Writings (inspired writing without reference to manner). The entire corpus of the Hebrew canon 'came to be understood as an extension of the Torah', with the Prophets and the Writings 'arranged and presented as works that depend on and expand the books of Moses' (Creach 2008: 137), making Moses' role in the canon foundational in a most fundamental sense. The Torah, as Delitzsch wrote (Keil and Delitzsch 1973: 1:19), 'is as certainly presupposed by the whole of the post-Mosaic history and literature, as the root is by the tree'.

Given the internal witness of Scripture, along with the pivotal function of Moses himself, the traditional view should not be dismissed lightly, in favour of anonymous editors, politically savvy priests or otherwise. As summarized and encompassed by Deuteronomy, the Torah forms Israel's vocational charter, constitution and fundamental instruction (see McBride 1987; P. D. Miller 2004; Berman 2006). The New Testament affirms the 'law was given through (*dia*) Moses', and that the eternal Son and Messiah is the one of whom 'Moses wrote (*egrapse*) in the law' (John 1:17, 45). It also declares that God's breath is the ultimate source of revelation (2 Tim. 3:16), and that the divine means involved holy men of God speaking as they were borne along by the Holy Spirit (2 Peter 2:21), excluding authorship theories that involve impious machinations. Needless to say, this point does not prohibit the role of Spirit-guided servants in updating and/or shaping the Pentateuch into its final form. The historical context for this editorial process remains elusive and need not detract from Moses' principal hand, though the United Kingdom era of David and Solomon (tenth century) has been suggested plausibly (Rendsburg 2001b; Block 2012: 30–33). Luke's account of Stephen's speech opens a window to first-century beliefs regarding Moses as one who 'was learned in all the wisdom of the Egyptians, and was mighty in words and deeds' (Acts 7:22); the Pentateuch's aura and composition cannot be severed from the historical reality and influence of the person of Moses.

7. THE TEXT OF NUMBERS

The Masoretic Text (MT) is the foundation and basis for my translation of and comments on Numbers, while consulting other textual traditions. For simplicity's sake, *all versification throughout follows English translations*. Regarding the Greek text of Numbers, it is widely accepted that the Greek translation 'suffers from all the difficulties involved in translating from one language to another' (Taylor 2010: 26–27), aside from its tendency to harmonize (cf. Tov 2018). Worse, Wevers remarks (1998: ix):

The Greek translation of Numbers . . . is without a doubt by far the weakest volume in the Greek Pentateuch. What makes work on the book so frustrating is that side by side one can find gross failures to follow ordinary rules of grammar, i.e. of apparent incompetence, as well as acute and even subtle distinctions betraying an active mind engaged in the interpretation of sacred scripture, ready not only to clarify obscure passages, but even to correct what might appear to be factual errors or contradictions within the text.

Moreover, attempts to reach an underlying Hebrew text through simple back-translation of the Greek are extremely problematic (Würthwein 1979: 70). Thankfully, the Hebrew text, as Milgrom celebrates (1990: xi), is in an 'excellent state of preservation' with variations in Masoretic manuscripts being 'few and insignificant'.

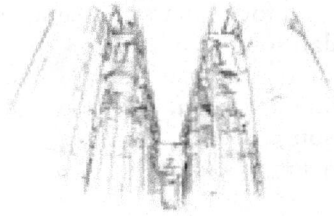

TEXT AND COMMENTARY

NUMBERS 1 – 2: ARRANGING THE TWELVE TRIBES AS THE OUTER CAMP

Translation

¹:¹Now YHWH spoke to Moses in the wilderness of Sinai in the Tent of Meeting on the first of the second month in the second year of their going out from the land of Egypt, saying, ²"Lift up the head of the whole community of the sons of Israel by their clans, by their fathers' house, according to the number of names, all the males according to their skulls. ³From twenty years old and upward, all who go out in the host in Israel, you will appoint them according to their hosts, you and Aaron. ⁴And with you there will be a man from every tribe, each man the head of his fathers' house.

⁵"And these are the names of the men who will stand with you:

for Reuben, Elizur son of Shedeur;
⁶for Simeon, Shelumiel son of Zurishaddai;
⁷for Judah, Nahshon son of Amminadab;
⁸for Issachar, Nethanel son of Zuar;
⁹for Zebulun, Eliab son of Helon;

¹⁰for the sons of Joseph: for Ephraim, Elishama son of Ammihud;
for Manasseh, Gamaliel son of Pedahzur;
¹¹for Benjamin, Abidan son of Gideoni;
¹²for Dan, Ahiezer son of Ammishaddai;
¹³for Asher, Pagiel son of Ochran;
¹⁴for Gad, Eliasaph son of Deuel;
¹⁵for Naphtali, Ahira son of Enan.

¹⁶'These are the ones called from the community, the chieftains of the tribes of their fathers; they are the heads of the thousands of Israel.'

¹⁷Moses, with Aaron, took these men who had been designated by name. ¹⁸And they assembled the whole community on the first of the second month; and they registered their genealogies by their clans, according to their fathers' house, by the number of names, from twenty years old and upward, according to their skulls, ¹⁹just as YHWH had commanded Moses; so he appointed them in the wilderness of Sinai.

²⁰And they were the sons of Reuben the firstborn of Israel, their genealogies according to their clans, according to their fathers' house, by the number of names, according to their skulls, all males from twenty years old and upward, all who go out in the host: ²¹those appointed for the tribe of Reuben, forty-six thousand five hundred.

²²For the sons of Simeon, their genealogies according to their clans, according to their fathers' house, appointed by the number of names, according to their skulls, all males from twenty years old and upward, all who go out in the host: ²³those appointed for the tribe of Simeon, fifty-nine thousand three hundred.

²⁴For the sons of Gad, their genealogies according to their clans, according to their fathers' house, by the number of names, from twenty years old and upward, all who go out in the host: ²⁵those appointed for the tribe of Gad, forty-five thousand six hundred and fifty.

²⁶For the sons of Judah, their genealogies according to their clans, according to their fathers' house, by the number of names, from twenty years old and upward, all who go out in the host: ²⁷those appointed for the tribe of Judah, seventy-four thousand six hundred.

²⁸For the sons of Issachar, their genealogies according to their clans, according to their fathers' house, by the number of names, from twenty years old and upward, all who go out in the host: ²⁹those appointed for the tribe of Issachar, fifty-four thousand four hundred.

³⁰For the sons of Zebulun, their genealogies according to their clans, according to their fathers' house, by the number of names, from twenty years old and upward, all who go out in the host: ³¹those appointed for the tribe of Zebulun, fifty-seven thousand four hundred.

³²For the sons of Joseph: for the sons of Ephraim, their genealogies according to their clans, according to their fathers' house, by the number of names, from twenty years old and upward, all who go out

in the host: ^{33}those appointed for the tribe of Ephraim, forty thousand five hundred; ^{34}for the sons of Manasseh, their genealogies according to their clans, according to their fathers' house, by the number of names, from twenty years old and upward, all who go out in the host: ^{35}those appointed for the tribe of Manasseh, thirty-two thousand two hundred.

^{36}For the sons of Benjamin, their genealogies according to their clans, according to their fathers' house, by the number of names, from twenty years old and upward, all who go out in the host: ^{37}those appointed for the tribe of Benjamin, thirty-five thousand four hundred.

^{38}For the sons of Dan, their genealogies according to their clans, according to their fathers' house, by the number of names, from twenty years old and upward, all who go out in the host: ^{39}those appointed for the tribe of Dan, sixty-two thousand seven hundred.

^{40}For the sons of Asher, their genealogies according to their clans, according to their fathers' house, by the number of names, from twenty years old and upward, all who go out in the host: ^{41}those appointed for the tribe of Asher, forty-one thousand five hundred.

^{42}The sons of Naphtali, their genealogies according to their clans, according to their fathers' house, by the number of names, from twenty years old and upward, all who go out in the host: ^{43}those appointed for the tribe of Naphtali, fifty-three thousand four hundred.

^{44}These are the appointed-ones, whom Moses, with Aaron and with the chieftains of Israel, appointed, twelve men, each one was according to his fathers' house. ^{45}And all who were appointed of the sons of Israel, according to their fathers' house, from twenty years old and upward, all who go out in the host of Israel: ^{46}all who were appointed were six hundred and three thousand five hundred and fifty.

^{47}But the Levites according to the tribe of their fathers were not appointed in their midst. ^{48}And YHWH spoke to Moses, saying, ^{49}'Only the tribe of Levi you will not appoint, and their heads you will not lift up in the midst of the sons of Israel. ^{50}But you will appoint the Levites over the Dwelling of the Testimony and over all its vessels and over all that pertains to it: they will carry the Dwelling and all its vessels, and they will attend to it – and around the Dwelling they will encamp. ^{51}When the Dwelling is to journey out the Levites will take it down, and when the Dwelling is to encamp the Levites will raise it up; but the stranger who draws near will be put to death. ^{52}And the sons of Israel will camp each man with his encampment, each man with his standard according to their hosts. ^{53}But the Levites will camp around the Dwelling of the Testimony, lest there be wrath upon the community of the sons of Israel – the Levites will keep the charge of the Dwelling of the Testimony.'

^{54}And the sons of Israel did all just as YHWH had commanded Moses, just so they did.

2:1And YHWH spoke to Moses and to Aaron, saying, 2'The sons of Israel, each man by his standard with the emblems of their fathers' house, will camp; at a distance around the Tent of Meeting they will camp.

3'And those who will camp eastward, toward the sunrise: the standard of the camp of Judah according to their hosts, and the chieftain for the sons of Judah will be Nahshon son of Amminadab. 4His host and his appointing: seventy-four thousand six hundred. 5And those camping by him will be the tribe of Issachar, and chieftain for the sons of Issachar is Nethanel son of Zuar. 6His host and his appointing: fifty-four thousand four hundred. 7The tribe of Zebulun, and the chieftain for the sons of Zebulun will be Eliab son of Helon. 8His host and his appointing: fifty-seven thousand four hundred. 9All who were appointed for the camp of Judah were one hundred and eighty-six thousand four hundred according to their hosts; these will journey out first.

10'Now the standard of the camp of Reuben will be southward according to their hosts. And the chieftain for the sons of Reuben will be Elizur son of Shedeur. 11His host and his appointing: forty-six thousand five hundred. 12And those camping by him will be the tribe of Simeon, and the chieftain for the sons of Simeon will be Shelumiel son of Zurishaddai. 13His host and their appointing: fifty-nine thousand three hundred. 14And the tribe of Gad, the chieftain for the sons of Gad will be Eliasaph son of Reuel. 15His host and their appointing: forty-five thousand six hundred and fifty. 16All appointed for the camp of Reuben were one hundred and fifty-one thousand four hundred and fifty according to their hosts; these will journey out second.

17'Then the Tent of Meeting will journey out with the camp of the Levites in the midst of the camps; just as they camp so they will journey out, each man at hand according to their standards.

18'The standard of the camp of Ephraim according to their hosts will be westward, and the chieftain for the sons of Ephraim will be Elishama son of Ammihud. 19His host and their appointing: forty thousand five hundred. 20And by him will be the tribe of Manasseh, and the chieftain for the sons of Manasseh will be Gamaliel son of Pedahzur. 21His host and their appointing: thirty-two thousand two hundred. 22And the tribe of Benjamin, the chieftain for the sons of Benjamin will be Abidan son of Gideoni. 23His host and their appointing: thirty-five thousand four hundred. 24All appointed for the camp of Ephraim were one hundred and eight thousand one hundred according to their hosts; these will journey out third.

25The standard of the camp of Dan will be northward according to their hosts, and the chieftain for the sons of Dan will be Ahiezer son of Ammishaddai. 26His hosts and their appointing: sixty-two thousand seven hundred. 27And those camping by him will be the tribe of Asher, and the chieftain for the sons of Asher will be Pagiel son of Ochran. 28His hosts and their appointing: forty-one thousand five hundred.

²⁹Then the tribe of Naphtali, and the chieftain for the sons of Naphtali will be Ahira son of Enan. ³⁰His hosts and their appointing: fifty-three thousand four hundred. ³¹All appointed for the camp of Dan were one hundred and fifty-seven thousand six hundred; they will journey out last according to their standards.

³²These are the appointing of the sons of Israel according to their fathers' house, all the appointing of the camps according to their hosts: six hundred and three thousand five hundred and fifty. ³³But the Levites were not appointed in the midst of the sons of Israel, just as YHWH had commanded Moses.

³⁴And the sons of Israel did according to all that YHWH had commanded Moses; just so they camped according to their standards and just so they journeyed out, each man according to his clan by his fathers' house.

Notes on the text

1:2. 'Lift up': A rare pl. form, likely including Aaron (cf. 26:2).

'skulls': *gll*, in contrast with use of *rō'š* (head); cf. Judg. 9:53; 2 Kgs 9:35; 1 Chr. 10:10.

3. 'twenty years old': lit. 'a son (*mibben*) of twenty years'.

16. 'chieftains': *něśî'ê* from *ns'*, the 'lifted up ones'.

'thousands': *'alpê* from *'elep* means 'thousand' numerically, but may refer to large divisions.

'ones called': Q gives the preferable passive part. form.

18. 'and they registered their genealogies': *wayyityaldû* from *yld* in hith., a hapax legomenon; translated as declarative rather than reflexive: Israelites declared their birth/lineage.

22. 'appointed': *pěqudāyw*. Some MT MSS, LXX, Syr, *TgPs-J* lack this term, which is not present in other tribe summaries.

24–25. LXX has Gad verses at 1:36, 37 between Benjamin and Dan; MT's arrangement reflects the encampment (ch. 2).

42. 'The sons': some MT MSS, LXX, Syr add the prefix *lě* to conform with other tribe listings (e.g. vv. 36, 38, 40). Hirsch, regarding *lě* as a calling 'to' tribal members (to step forward for their count), observes that since Naphtali's tribe was last, it did not need to be called apart from the rest, precluding the need for this preposition (2007a: 12–13).

44. 'appoint' is 3rd sg., *pāqad*, referring to Moses (cf. v. 17).

45. 'their fathers' house': LXX and Syr read *lěṣib'ōtām*, 'by their hosts' (cf. v. 52).

53. 'keep the charge': *wešāměrû* . . . *'et-mišmeret*. Both terms use Heb. *šmr*, Milgrom suggesting 'guard duty' (1970b: 1:8–16).

54. LXX has 'and Aaron' after Moses.

2:2. 'at a distance': *minneged*, 'in front', 'opposite' (BDB 617), possibly 'facing' the Tabernacle (ESV), but probably refers to the safe distance that allows room for Levites to encamp. ASV's 'over against' captures both possibilities.

7. The conjunction should likely be added at the head of the verse, per SamP, LXX and Syr; cf. vv. 14, 22, 29.

14. 'Reuel': With *BHS*, read 'Deuel' as in 1:14; 7:42, 47; 10:20; the letters resh and dalet are easily confused. This change is supported by many MT MSS, although 'Reuel' is preferred throughout by LXX and has some MT support.

17. 'Tent of Meeting' and 'camp of the Levites' may be in apposition; supplying either 'with' or 'and' (as LXX) captures intended meaning of MT (so too Milgrom 1990: 13). *BHS* suggestion to move half the verse has no textual support. 'at hand': idiomatic for his appointed place.

20. The first, second, and fourth encampments include 'And those camping by him', *wĕhaḥōnîm ʿālāw* (5, 12, 27), but the third merely states, 'And by him' (*wĕʿālāyw*), perhaps a case of 'off-balance symmetry' (see McEvenue 1971).

Form and structure

The physical arrangement of the Camp is represented literarily in the structure of chapters 1–2:

> 1:1–46, 54: Twelve tribes appointed for the Camp of YHWH's hosts
> 1:47–53: Levites appointed to camp around, attend and transport the Dwelling
> 2:1–34: Twelve tribes arranged around the Dwelling as the Camp of YHWH's hosts

Chapter 1 divides into three units (vv. 1–19, 20–46, 47–53) with a conclusion statement (54). Lunn notes the central listing of the twelve chieftains centres on Joseph's sons (2010: 169):

> 1. YHWH commands census of Israel with help of twelve tribal chieftains (1–19)
> *YHWH's opening speech, vv. 1–4*
>   A. YHWH spoke to Moses in the wilderness of Sinai, v. 1
>   B. Census by families, vv. 2–3,
>   C. Help of designated men, v. 4
>
> *YHWH's central speech, designating twelve chieftains, vv. 5–16*
>   D. Five tribes: Reuben, Simeon, Judah, Issachar, Zebulun (5b–9)
>   X. Two sons of Joseph: Ephraim and Manasseh (10)
>   D'. Five tribes: Benjamin, Dan, Asher, Gad, Naphtali (11–15)

Moses' follow-through, vv. 17–19
  C'. Help of designated men, v. 17
  B'. Census by families, v. 18
 A'. YHWH commanded Moses in the wilderness of Sinai, v. 19
2. Twelve tribes enumerated (20–46)
3. Levites not counted, but appointed to attend and transport the Dwelling (47–53)
4. Compliance (obedience to YHWH) report (54)

The first unit comprises YHWH's speech (vv. 1–16) and a report of the follow through (17–19). The following similar terms and phrases found in the opening of YHWH's speech (1–4) and in Moses' compliance (17–19) form a concentrically arranged inclusio, bookending the unit's centre, where the twelve chieftains are named: 'YHWH' (1//19), 'wilderness of Sinai' (1//19), 'first of the second month' (1//18), 'appoint' (3//19), 'skull' (2//18), 'Moses, Aaron' (1, 3//17, 19), 'from twenty years old and upward' (3//18), 'clans, fathers' houses' (2//18). At the centre (5–16) is the delineation of the twelve chieftains who will stand with Moses and Aaron to help with the census.

Alternatively, against the MT's paragraph break (v. 20), 1:1–46 may be construed as Table 8.

This outline exhibits the parallels (chronological notice, locale, etc.) between verses 1–4 and 17–19, and aligns the central sections.

Descriptions for each tribe in verses 20–42 are delineated as follows (cf. Knierim and Coats 2005: 47–48):

1. Name of the tribe
 A. Reference to genealogy (corporate)
  i. (*lĕ*) According to clan
  ii. (*lĕ*) According to fathers' house
 B. By the number of names (individual)
  i. (*lĕ*) According to their skulls
   a. (*kol*) All males twenty and upward
   b. (*kōl*) All who go out in the host
2. Summation and tally

Table 8: Panel outline of Numbers 1

Numbers 1:1–46	Panel outline	
Introduction	A. 1:1–4	A'. 1:17–19
Twelve chieftains/tribes	B. 1:5–15	B'. 1:20–43
Summary conclusion	C. 1:16	C'. 1:44–46

This structure is taken up verbatim from YHWH's original command (vv. 2–3), as well as the summary compliance (v. 18).

YHWH's appointment of the tribes around his Tent in Numbers 2 continues the narrative of the previous chapter. The layout of the material reflects that of the Camp itself, with the Tent of Meeting and Levites in the centre surrounded by the other tribes (cf. Ogden 1996: 425):

Introduction:	YHWH's command to Moses and Aaron Sons of Israel to camp around Tent of Meeting	1–2	(two verses)
	Eastward: Judah Judah, Issachar, Zebulun	3–9	(seven verses)
	Southward: Reuben Reuben, Simeon, Gad	10–16	(seven verses)
Tent of Meeting, camp of the Levites		17	(one verse)
	Westward: Ephraim Ephraim, Manasseh, Benjamin	18–24	(seven verses)
	Northward: Dan Dan, Asher, Naphtali	25–31	(seven verses)
Conclusion:	Summary statement Compliance report	32–33 34	(two verses)

The data regarding the four major camps is set out consistently as follows:

Standard of primary tribe, cardinal direction, chieftain of primary tribe (vv. 3, 10, 18, 25)
  Tally for primary tribe (vv. 4, 11, 19, 26)
Second tribe joining primary tribe: the tribe and its chieftain (vv. 5, 12, 20, 27)
  Tally for second tribe (vv. 6, 13, 21, 28)
Third tribe joining primary tribe: the tribe and its chieftain (vv. 7, 14, 22, 29)
  Tally for third tribe (vv. 8, 15, 23, 30)
Final tally for primary tribe's camp; order for journeying out (vv. 9, 16, 24, 31)

The delineation of the Levites' camp differs; since their encampment locale was already given (1:53), only their journey order is explained, verse 17: they journey out as they encamp, 'in the midst of the camps'. The outer camp comprises the four major tribal camps, arranged in the four cardinal directions, each represented by the standard of the lead tribe (Judah, Reuben, Ephraim, Dan), and the inner camp comprises priests and Levites, who surround YHWH's central Dwelling – together, these camps form the earthly hosts of YHWH.

The tribal chieftains listed in Numbers 1:5–16 duplicate those mentioned in the second chapter. Although the order of tribes in 2:1–31 does not correspond precisely to that of the list in Numbers 1, Lunn observes a structural similarity between 1:20–54 and 2:1–34, forming a panel outline (2010: 173). Numbers 2:17, describing the Tent of Meeting and Levites in the centre of the Camp, has no parallel, a rhetorical feature anticipating the subject matter of Numbers 3 – 4 (Lunn 2010: 174).

Comment

1:1–54: Numbering the hosts of Israel's twelve tribes

1. YHWH's opening speech presumes the narrative progression of Exodus and Leviticus, and occurs in 'the wilderness of Sinai', a phrase first used on Israel's arrival at Mount Sinai (Exod. 19:1, 2), occurring once in Leviticus (7:38) and ten times throughout Numbers (1:1, 19; 3:4, 14; 9:1, 5; 10:12; 26:64; 33:15, 16). 'Wilderness' (*běmidbar*), anticipating the broad setting for the journey ahead, refers to a landscape more varied than a desert, with some pasturage for livestock and occasional sources of water.

The locale narrows from 'in (*bě*) the wilderness of Sinai' to 'in (*bě*) the Tent of Meeting'. Whereas Leviticus begins with YHWH's calling to Moses '*from* the Tent of Meeting' (*mē'ōhel*), Numbers opens with YHWH's speaking from '*within* the Tent of Meeting' (*bě'ōhel*), revealing the progress that has taken place through the divine revelation given in Leviticus, the three stages by which the Dwelling began to function as a Tent of Meeting, so that now YHWH speaks to Moses within the Tent. The goal of this divine revelation (Exod. 19 – Num. 6) is the creation of *the covenant community*, the Camp of Israel, with YHWH's dwelling among his people (Exod. 25:8; 29:46). As YHWH's voice from above the atonement lid of the ark, between the cherubim, gathers the tribes, his throne will constitute the political, spiritual and geographic centre of Israel's Camp. A window into this scene is offered in 7:89, a manner of communication that was forecasted as integral to the Tent's function (Exod. 25:22).

The chronological notice, 'the first of the second month in the second year', locates YHWH's speech precisely one month after the construction and consecration of the Tabernacle (Exod. 40:2, 17), and

twenty days before Israel as the Camp of YHWH's hosts journeys forth
(Num. 10:11–13). The phrase 'their going out from the land of Egypt'
not only brings in the theme of redemption (cf. Wijngaards 1965; see
3:11–13, 40–51; 8:13–19; 9:1–14), but presents Israel's Camp as one of
the goals of the exodus, that YHWH 'brought them out of the land of
Egypt in order that I may dwell among them' (Exod. 29:46; cf. 1 Kgs 8:9,
16, 21, 51, 53).

2. With 'Lift up (śĕ'û)' the head, idiomatic for 'count', wordplay on
nāśā' (lift up) begins, including the term 'chieftains' (nĕśî'ê). Levites,
who are not 'lifted up' in this census (1:49), will be 'lifted up' separately
(4:2, 22) and given duties that include 'carrying' (ns') the Tabernacle and
its furnishings (4:15, 25). Numbers 1 – 6 is rounded out by the priestly
benediction, beseeching YHWH to 'lift up' (yiśśā') his face upon Israel
(6:26). The Israelites are being counted in order to be arranged about
YHWH's Dwelling as his people, and from the Dwelling he lifts his face,
reciprocally, that his blessing may flow out to them. Finally, the similar
sounding nāsa' (to journey), its root occurring some ninety-six times
in the book (1:51; 2:9; 2:16; etc.), connects lifting up with journeying.
A related connection is made in 9:15–23: whenever the cloud ascended
('ālā), Israel would journey out (nāsa').

The count is to be of the 'head' (rō'š), singular, referring to God's
people as one body, and that of the 'ēdā (congregation, community) in
particular, portraying the sons of Israel as a cultic community. In this
context, 'ēdā refers to 'the whole people of Israel – men, women and
children' (Ashley 1993: 48), a point that may suggest understanding
the tally as representing all Israel (603, 550), rather than merely the
fighting men. The delineation continues 'by their clans (mišpĕḥōtām),
by their father's house (bêt 'ăbōtām)', terms with a wide semantic
range, displaying seemingly inconsistent use throughout the HB (cf. U.
Wolf 1946). Depending on context, mišpāḥâ may be translated 'family'
or a broadly extended family, 'clan', as here; and there are several
'clans' within a 'father's house', the largest unit in a tribe (Levine 1993:
131–133; cf. Milgrom 1983b: 1–17), sometimes even referring to a tribe
(Num. 17:2). Although Joshua 7:14, presenting tribal units of decreasing
size, lists 'tribe' (šēbeṭ or maṭṭeh), 'clan' (mišpāḥâ), 'household' (bayit),
and 'individual' (geber) (Milgrom 1990: 7), nevertheless, that a 'fathers'
house' – not to be confused with a mere house(hold) – forms a tribe's
largest unit becomes clear by the usage of these terms in Numbers
3, where the tribe of Levi comprises three father's houses (Gershon,
Kohath, Merari), each containing 'clans' (mišpĕḥōt) within them. Thus
each of the twelve patriarchs, Jacob's sons, established a tribe (generation 1), and the direct sons of each patriarch established a 'father's
house' (generation 2), and their sons, in turn, each formed a 'clan'
(generation 3) (cf. Levine 1993: 132–133). There would be a number of
clans within each tribe, and therefore a number of clan chieftains, many

within Israel's Camp (cf. Exod. 6:14–19). Although the leaders listed in Numbers 1 and 3 seem to have pre-eminence above clan chieftains, as chieftains over a father's house, others will later be noted, using language that likely refers to clan chieftains (Num. 13:2; 16:2; 34:18). While Genesis had emphasized the ancestors, and Exodus the role of Moses and Aaron with the Israelites portrayed as a general mass (with some exceptions, Exod. 3:16; 4:29; 6:14; 12:3), Numbers largely fills in the story of Israel's chieftains.

3. The general census of verse 2 is narrowed further in verse 3 to males aged 20 and above. Participation in the community, including responsibilities in warfare, may have begun at this age. The double use of *ṣābā'* (host) anticipates the creation of the Camp as YHWH's earthly hosts. Although the community encompasses all Israelites, including women, children and elderly, use of *ṣābā'* gives the Camp a military association. Shamah offers a helpful summation (2011: 689):

> The word *ṣaba*, by itself, refers to an organized formation of units, whether military or not, such as the array of the components of heaven and earth (Gen. 2:1). But the term *yoṣe ṣaba* ('go forth to the alignment') – the basic locution of our context – invariably appears with reference to military service. With the Levites, who do not participate in military service, *ṣaba* refers to the sanctuary service corps and the attached verb is never *yoṣe* ('go forth'), but usually a form of *ba* ('come').

YHWH's heavenly hosts are not only his armies, but comprise his entourage, even as Israel will comprise his earthly entourage. This new reality – becoming the covenant community around YHWH's central Dwelling, so that Israel sets out from Mount Sinai as YHWH's earthly hosts – is the goal of Numbers 1 – 10, culminating in the Sinai revelation (Exod. 19 – Num. 10).

The term 'appoint' (*tipqĕdû*, from *pqd*, 'record, enroll') is a key word, with 108 occurrences in Numbers. Use of 'appoint' (instead of 'number') reflects its wider usage in designating the Levites' role (1:50), as well as each tribe's position within the Camp. Israelites are being divinely appointed for more than mere pragmatic organization for a wilderness trek. The voice proceeding from between the cherubim (7:89), as with the voice that spoke 'Let there be light' (Gen. 1:3), has begun the creation of a microcosm, the paradigm of the covenant community that would form a symbol for the ideal city of God.

4. The designation *maṭṭeh* (tribe) is synonymous with *šēbeṭ*, both of which may also refer to a rod, staff or sceptre (cf. Num. 17). Sustaining the distinction of each tribe, rather than allowing the tribes to become muddled over time, is a reminder that God's word spoken through Jacob to his twelve sons remains supremely significant, holding prophetic

meaning (Gen. 49). The Torah's first use of the phrase 'head of the house of his fathers' occurs here. Each father's house had a *rō'š* (head), a leader who wielded authority in judicial and military matters

5–16. 'Chieftain' (*nasi'*) may indicate one 'raised' (promoted) to the status of leader, and appears 60 times, out of its 126 occurrences in the HB, in Numbers (Cocco 2020: 132), a book given to leadership thematically (cf. 1:5–16; 2:3–29; 3:1–4; 7:12–83; 13:4–16; 17:1–5; 27:12–23; 31:48–54; 34:16–29). Chieftains represent their respective tribes in a variety of significant events throughout Numbers (see 7; 13:2), including this census, as a function of their role as heads of the subdivisions of the tribes, the 'fathers' houses' (Speiser 1963: 113). That these men are chieftains already recognized and established as such appears evident from their initiative in bringing gifts and offerings for the Tabernacle and altar dedication, which occurred one month earlier – these are the same names as in 7:12–83. Already recognized by the community, the chieftains are divinely confirmed for a sacred task. The designation of these men by name from the voice of YHWH (v. 17) not only confirms their tribal roles in a general manner, assuring the tribes of this necessary hierarchical order, but lends deep significance and solemnity to the particular task at hand: the arrangement of the tribes around God's Dwelling.

The theophoric element of the chieftains' names attests to their antiquity and authenticity (Milgrom 1990: 6); none contains an abbreviated form of YHWH (e.g. 'Elijah'), recently revealed through Moses (Exod. 6:3; see Num. 13:16), and the divine names that are used are among the most ancient: El (*'ēl*, 'god'), Zur (*ṣûr*, 'rock'), and Shaddai (*šadday*, see Gen. 17:1; Exod. 6:3), likely a derivation of the Akkadian *šadû* (mountain), meaning 'God of the mountain' or 'mountain-dweller' (cf. Albright 1935; de Moor 1997: 179–180, 246). 'Zurishaddai' in verse 6, for example, may be translated 'my Rock is Shaddai' (see Ginzberg 1967: 3:220–224; Budd 1984: 5; Cole 2000: 71–72). Given the naming portrayed in Genesis 29:31 – 30:24, along with the theophoric elements in the chieftains' names, the religion and stories of the patriarchs appear to have been passed orally to subsequent generations in Egypt.

Judah and Ephraim's chieftains, as Cole notes, will feature significantly in Israel's later history (2000: 72): Nahshon (serpent) of Judah's tribe, is the ancestor of Boaz, who became the grandfather of David (Ruth 4:20–22; 1 Chr. 2:10–17), through whose seed according to the flesh came the Messiah (Matt. 1:4–16; Luke 3:23–33; Rom. 1:3); and Elishama, of Ephraim's tribe, is the grandfather of Joshua son of Nun, who will be Israel's divinely chosen shepherd after Moses (Num. 27:12–23; 1 Chr. 7:26–27). Nahshon is the *only* chieftain previously mentioned (cf. Frevel 2018: 94): Aaron had married Nahshon's sister, Elisheba, who bore four priestly sons (see Exod. 6:23), linking the priestly house with the tribe of Judah – both encamped on the eastward side of YHWH's Tent (cf.

Galil 1985: 493). The prominence of Judah and Ephraim is not random, but a reflection of divine promise and election. Genesis concludes with a spotlight on their patriarchs (chs. 37–50): Joseph feeds the ancient world under his wise rule, his son Ephraim receiving the firstborn's birthright from Jacob; Judah performs the story's central gesture of atonement (44:18–34) and receives the promise of kingship (49:8–12). There is some question, and even tension, in Israel's early history as to which of the two tribes will lead. The two faithful scouts, Caleb and Joshua, belong to the tribes of Judah and Ephraim. Joshua functions as a faithful ruler in the book that bears his name (compare Josh. 1:7–8 with Deut. 17:14–20), and YHWH's Tabernacle rests for a time in Shiloh, in the hill country of Ephraim. Psalm 78, summarizing the history of Israel (cf. 1–2 Sam.), explains that due to their rebellion and covenant-breaking, Ephraim was rejected, along with Shiloh, YHWH God's choosing David and Zion definitively (vv. 9–12, 60–61, 67–72). When Solomon's kingdom divides, Ephraim leads the larger northern kingdom (ten tribes), although Judah retains the promises of the Davidic covenant, to which prophets direct the northern kingdom (see Amos 9:11; Hos. 3:5). Prophetic expectation fixes hope on the dawning of a new David who would once more unite the twelve tribes, 'all Israel', and the world, under his reign (Jer. 30 – 31; Ezek. 37:15–28; see Luke 6:12–16; Acts 1:15–26).

17–19. Moses' compliance, which repeats notices of both date and locale, forms an inclusio (or panel parallel), completing the circle begun in verses 1–4. The phrase 'registered their genealogies' (*yityaldû*), as with 'their genealogies' (*tôlĕdōtām*) in the delineations of each tribe (vv. 20, 22, 24, etc.), comes from the root *yld* (to bear a child) and, beyond pointing to God's blessing of fecundity, establishes continuity among the Israelites after centuries of life in Egypt – especially so in relation to the patriarchal promises and prophecies (Gen. 49).

20–43. The tribal order here matches the list of chieftains (1:5–16), except for the placement of Gad in the third (rather than eleventh) slot; this change reflects the order of encampment – the arrangement of Israel's Camp, the census goal, takes precedence over genealogy. Reuben's status 'firstborn of Israel' (*bĕkōr yiśrā'ēl*) recurs throughout the Bible (Exod. 6:14; Num. 1:20; 26:5; 1 Chr. 5:1, 3), with 'firstborn of Jacob' used in Genesis (35:23; 46:8). The tribal tallies are listed here.

Table 9: Census totals

Tribal census totals of Numbers 1:20–43 (total: 603,550)			
1. Reuben 46,500	4. Judah 74,600	7. Ephraim 40,500	10. Dan 62,700
2. Simeon 59,300	5. Issachar 54,400	8. Manasseh 32,200	11. Asher 41,500
3. Gad 45,650	6. Zebulun 57,400	9. Benjamin 35,400	12. Naphtali 53,400

Scholars have long noted that, with the exception of Gad, the tribal totals are rounded to the hundredth position. Samet explains the possible logic (2017c, citing Ely Merzbach): when a figure obtained was not in whole tens, it was rounded to the nearest hundred, whereas when it ended in tens, the figure was left without further rounding. In the census of Numbers 26, linking the totals to tribal fidelity to YHWH is possible. Simeon's tribe, for example, suffers a great reduction (cf. 26:14), likely due to divine judgement on the harlotry with Moab (25:9, 14). In Numbers 1, the variation in totals is not so readily explained. All the tribes have enjoyed YHWH's creational blessing and commission to 'be fruitful and multiply' (cf. Gen. 1:28; Exod. 1:7), through YHWH's faithfulness, for he had promised the patriarchs' descendants would be as numerous as the stars of heaven, the sand of the seashore and the dust of the earth (Gen. 15:5; 22:17; 26:4; 28:14). The reality of YHWH's promise-keeping in relation to multiplying the seed of Abraham is acknowledged later by Balaam (Num. 23:10) and proclaimed by Moses (Deut. 1:9–11). Judah's tribe appears singled out especially, having the highest tally. This prominence, in addition to Balaam's messianic prophecy (24:17), which clearly alludes to Jacob's blessing of Judah (Gen. 49:10), augurs the role of Judah's descendants, along with the Davidic covenant that will establish David's dynasty as the primary channel for God's intention to bless the nations (2 Sam. 7; Ps. 89), bringing them under the rule of his Messiah (Ps. 2; Matt. 28:16–20).

Many scholars assume the face-value reading for the tally of those who were appointed, 603,550, includes only Israel's fighting men, increasing the grand total of Israelites in the wilderness to 2 or 3 million people. The tally sum, however, probably represents the whole community, all Israel. Regardless of perceived parallels to Egyptian military encampments, Numbers presents a *migratory* encampment, which included entire households – men with ox carts carrying wives, grandparents, children and possessions, along with flocks. Perhaps the closest comparison would be to the migratory campaigns of the Philistines or 'Sea peoples', which certainly included a militia, as depicted in reliefs of Ramesses III at his mortuary temple in Medinet Habu, but also included entire families, with livestock and other possessions (Yadin 1963b: 2:248–253, 336–338; Seevers 2013: 172–173; cf. Yasur-Landau 2010).

44–53. Emphasis on the 'appointed-ones' justifies applications concerning the blessings and privilege of being numbered among God's chosen people, belonging to the covenant community. Beyond merely being numbered, 'appointed-ones' (*pĕqudîm*) also has in view each tribe's, family's and person's divinely designated place around YHWH's Dwelling.

Verses 48–53 expand verse 47, anticipating the content of chapters 3–4 (Knierim and Coats 2005: 52), and make explicit the Levites' omission from the census. Repetition of their exclusion from 'the midst of the sons of Israel' (47, 49) underscores the point that Levites are set apart from the other tribes. Although Levites will encamp literally in the midst of the sons of Israel, yet their locale is described twice *with reference to the Dwelling only* – they will encamp 'around the Dwelling', *sābîb lĕmiškan* (50, 53). Given the theology of the Camp, Trapp's gloss is fitting, that Levites will pitch round about 'as the living creatures' around God's heavenly throne in Revelation 4 (1650: 3). Verse 51 manifests the close relationship between the Dwelling and Levites: when the Dwelling journeys 'out' (*nāsaʿ*), Levites take it 'down' (*yārad*); when the Dwelling 'encamps' (*ḥānâ*), Levites 'raise' it 'up' (*qām*). Using the typical verbs for movement in Numbers, *nāsaʿ* and *ḥānâ* (Knierim and Coats 2005: 14), the Dwelling itself is portrayed as leading, while the Levites' role is instrumental. When finally journeying out from Sinai, YHWH through his ark and Cloud will lead the tribes onward (10:34–36). Coordinated with the glory Cloud, the Dwelling is dismantled when the Cloud ascends, set up when the Cloud settles, and filled and surrounded by the Cloud when encamped.

While not counted in the tribal census, Levites are nevertheless appointed their place in the Camp (chs. 3–4). Wordplay is evident: Levites will not be 'appointed' (*tipqōd*, as in 'listed') with the tribes, nor have their heads 'lifted up' (*tiśśāʾ*, as in 'counted') (v. 49), yet Moses is commanded to 'appoint' (*hapqēd*, as in 'set') them over the Dwelling, to 'lift up' (*yiśʾû*, as in 'carry') the Dwelling and its vessels (v. 50). YHWH's Tent is called 'Dwelling of the Testimony' (*miškan hāʿēdut*), its primary designation in Numbers. The term *ʿēdut* refers to the Decalogue, 'tablets of the testimony' (Exod. 31:18; 32:15; 34:27–28), set within the ark and thus the 'ark of the Testimony' (Exod. 25:16–22; 26:33–34; 40:3, 20), and its function as a witness or testimony to Israel's covenant relationship with God. The terms *ʿēdut* and *bĕrît* (covenant) are generally synonymous, with 'Dwelling of the Treaty' possibly intended (cf. Hillers 1969: 158–166). A primary nuance of *ʿēdut* is divine testimony (cf. Harrelson 1962), highlighting YHWH's central presence in the Camp and the covenant fidelity Israel owes him.

The Levites' charge over the Dwelling and its equipment is twofold: with respect to the journey (dismantling, carrying and caring for the Dwelling and all of its vessels), and with respect to encampment (assembling, surrounding and guarding the Dwelling). Likely 'attend' (*šārat*, 'minister', 'serve', v. 50) is defined by the next clause as encamping around the Dwelling to guard it, since the latter clause lacks the emphatic pronoun present in the first two injunctions. The movement from journey to encampment is noted twice (50, 51), with the Levites' guard duty, in the light of YHWH's holiness, forming the main stress. Levites are charged to put to death the encroaching stranger (51), 'stranger' (*zār*) here referring to any Israelite not of the tribe of Levi (cf. Camp 2009: 198–200), evident by their distinct encampments (vv. 52–53).

One incentive for discharging this duty faithfully is that executing the encroacher will stay back the threat of God's 'wrath' (*qeṣep*) on the entire community (53). Sparing one presumptuous rebel would bring greater disaster on all the people. Use of the term 'draws near' (*qārēb*, v. 51) may have a cultic context in mind (cf. Lev. 1:2), a dangerous scenario that forms the first of several foreshadowings of the 'inner camp' section of the sojourn (chs. 16–18; see also 4:17–20), where Korah and his band seek the priestly prerogative of approaching the Holy One, and also points to the divinely rewarded act of Phinehas, who turns away God's anger from all Israel by putting to death a prince of Simeon's tribe and his Midianite consort who were committing harlotry, possibly within or nearby the Dwelling's sacred space (25:7–15).

The threat of death upon encroachment of sacred space recalls God's stationing of cherubim at the entryway to Eden's garden (Gen. 3:24). The connection is not incidental: cherubim reappear in only one other context in the Torah, for the decor of YHWH's Dwelling, and particularly in the holy of holies (Berman 1995: 21). The Dwelling is an architectural Eden, marking ritually a return to paradise through Israel's cult (Morales 2015), and with the Camp of Israel itself thereby becoming an emblem of Edenic life with God (cf. Num. 24:5–7). It is unremarkable, then, to find that Adam's tasks when placed in the garden of Eden, 'to serve/worship and guard/obey' (*lěʿobdāh ûlěšāmrāh*, Gen. 2:15), recur in the Torah to describe the duties of Levites pertaining to YHWH's Dwelling within Israel's Camp (Num. 3:7–8; 8:26; 18:5–6), the mobile sanctuary-city of God. A crucial observation follows: Levites are not excluded from the census because they are 'non-military', an oft-asserted angle that reverses the text's focal interest. The heavenly Dwelling of YHWH God forms the Camp's centre, and Levites were divinely chosen to replace Israel's firstborn sons in the aftermath of the golden calf apostasy because they were zealous enough to slay their own rebellious countrymen (Exod. 32:25–29), precisely the criterion *sine qua non* for the role of temple guard, putting to death those who encroach the sanctuary premises (see 25:10–13). The tribe of Levi, 'known as a warlike tribe' (Ashley 1993: 69), will be counted separately to emphasize their separate status as those consecrated for greater nearness to God, in guarding and caring for his Dwelling and its vessels.

Verses 52–53 are a microcosm of chapters 1–4 with the tribes of Israel encamped by their standards, according to their hosts, and Levites encamped around the Dwelling in the centre of the Camp, safeguarding the community from divine wrath. Reference to divine wrath communicates that the greatest threat to the community is not from foreign armies, but from YHWH's holy presence. Failure to grasp YHWH's threatening holiness leads both to Israel's fear of the Canaanites (Num. 13 – 14) and to the fearless presumption of approaching him apart from mediation (Num. 16 – 17). The necessity for the role of both Levites and

Aaron's priesthood becomes obvious under a proper fear of YHWH (cf. 17:12–13).

54. Whereas in 1:19, Moses' obedience is highlighted in the compliance report, here the 'sons of Israel' (*bĕnê yiśrā'ēl*), representing the whole community, are reported as complying with YHWH's command. As a rhetorical device, compliance reports characterize God's people as following YHWH closely through their obedience in the first major section (chs. 1–10; see 1:19, 54; 2:34; etc.), also underscoring Israel's rebellions in the central section (chs. 11–25).

2:1–34: Arranging the twelve tribes as the outer camp around YHWH's Tent

1. After the census, which had distinguished and classified the tribes separately, YHWH reveals to Moses and Aaron the next step for creating the Camp of Israel: arranging the tribes around his Dwelling according to the four points of the compass, yielding cosmic associations. The divine speech formula underscores that the Camp is the result of divine revelation, as well as the mediatorial role and authority of Moses and Aaron in YHWH's newly established priestly theocracy.

2. This general summary is detailed in the verses that follow (vv. 3–31), with two main points regarding Israel's Camp, that it is arranged by four main standards in the four cardinal directions, with every tribe precisely placed, and that YHWH's Tent of Meeting is in their midst, an ideal picture of YHWH's covenant relationship with his people. The implications of this reality remain in focus throughout Numbers. Plainly, the divine Tent is not merely placed in the centre but *constitutes* the centre (cf. W. W. Lee 2008: 481).

Some take *degel* (*diglô*) as a reference to an army division by metonymy, but the text has in mind an actual 'standard', 'banner' or 'flag' under which the group stands. The standards have 'emblems' or 'signs' (*'ōtōt*; pl. of *'ôt*) on them, designating the 'father's house' of the primary tribe of that camp. Presumably the four main standards, each with its sign, were larger than those of the other tribes. Rabbinical tradition assumes correspondence between the Camp of Israel and the high priest's breastplate (Exod. 28:21; 39:14; see *Num. Rab.* 2.7), both laid out in square formation with each of the tribes represented, so that the colours of the standards correspond to the colour of the particular tribe's precious stone, and the emblem on it signifying the tribe drawing from Jacob's blessings of the patriarchal sons (Gen. 49:1–28; e.g. the figure of a lion for Judah). Arguments against Israel's use of images, based on Exodus 20:4 and later Jewish history (e.g. Josephus, *J. W.* 1.33.2–3), are inconclusive, as the concern of the Decalogue pertains to worship (cf. Exod. 20:5), and conflict with use of the divinely mandated bronze serpent (Num. 21:8–9). Far from expressing scruples on this point, Jewish tradition not only details the images (*Num. Rab.*, *TgPs-J* on Num. 2) but suggests that nations derived their use of images on standards from Israelite practice (cf. *Num. Rab.* 2.7), and that Israel's use of standards was derived from the angelic hosts, that the 22,000 angels who descended on Sinai with YHWH (Ps. 68:17) were all arrayed under standards (*Num. Rab.* 2.3; cf. 2.5, 10). Both the Dwelling and the ark were adorned with images of cherubim, a relevant observation as Jewish tradition suggests that each of the four camps' standards depicted one of the four faces of the cherubim (see Introduction), as described in Ezekiel (1:10; 10:14) and Revelation (4:7). The elaborate, symmetrical organization of the tribes, along with their standards and emblems, lend beauty and glory to the Camp, as befits YHWH's earthly entourage and as later acknowledged by the Mesopotamian diviner Balaam (Num. 24:2, 5–7).

'At a distance' (*minneged*; cf. Ps. 38:11) rounds out the summary with a reminder that the Camp's central Dwelling – the earthly throne room of the Holy One who dwells between the cherubim – poses a threat. While the distance provides space for Levites to serve as a buffer between the Dwelling and the tribes (cf. v. 17), the Levites' role is to maintain this distance between YHWH and Israel. That is the point and logic of the arrangement order: the tribes encamp at a distance, not to make room for Levites but out of sheer necessity due to threat of YHWH's holy presence.

2–31. YHWH's instructions continue, delineating the tribal encampments in detail, beginning with the eastward cardinal point, and rotating clockwise to describe the southward, westward and northward encampments. This order displays the Tent of Meeting as the orienting principle of the encampment, determining both the Camp's centre and its eastward priority. Each of the four divisions of three tribes encamps under the one standard of a lead tribe: Judah's standard in the east; Reuben's in the south; Ephraim's in the west; and Dan's in the north. The order in which the encampments are described is the same order of their march: Judah's camp first, Reuben's camp second, and so on. Fittingly, for their lead and rear role on the journey, Judah's camp is the largest by nearly 30,000, totaling at 186,400, and Dan's camp is the second largest at 157,600. Once the duties of Levites are given (Num. 4), the separate departures for their houses (Kohath, Gershon, Merari) will be integrated with this general order, as found in the description of the historic departure in seven movements (Num. 10:11–36): (1) Judah's camp; (2, 3) Levites: Gershon and Merari's camps take down and carry the Dwelling; (4) Reuben's camp; (5) Levites: Kohath's camp carries the sacred vessels of the Dwelling; (6) Ephraim's camp; (7) Dan's camp. YHWH's fiery cloud leads the march, along with the ark, accompanied by Moses and Aaron's house (10:33–36). Presumably, Aaron's sons, the priests, transported the ark, while Kohath's family carried the rest of the sacred vessels separately in their turn (cf. Josh. 3).

The phrases 'And those [pl., the two tribes] camping by him' *wĕhaḥōnîm ʿālāw* (vv. 5, 12, 27) and 'by him' *wĕʿālāyw* (v. 20) imply the two associated tribes encamped each on either side of the primary tribe. The four primary standards were, therefore, cosmologically positioned to correspond precisely to the compass points – directly east, south, west, north, of the Tent of Meeting – situating the four main tribes, with the placement of their associated tribes derived from that position (Knierim and Coats 2005: 56–57). (See Table 10.)

Assuming Leah's sons rank higher than Rachel's, and the handmaids' sons rank lower than those of Jacob's wives, the tribes may be grouped as follows, emphasizing the east–west axis: Leah's sons (east), the disgraced sons (south), Rachel's sons (west), the handmaids' sons (north) (see M. Douglas 2001: 174–178; Schnittjer 2006: 336–338). The 'disgraced sons' category refers to Reuben's having been cursed for sleeping with Jacob's concubine (Gen. 49:4; see Gen. 35:22); and Simeon (along with Levi) was cursed for the Shechem incident (49:5–6; see Gen. 34) – they are joined by the non-ranking Gad, son of Leah's maidservant. In Reuben's camp alone, the lead tribe has a tally that is less than one of its associate tribes. Whether any sense of shame would have been sensed by the original audience, in relation to the position and tally of the tribes, is difficult to discern; all the tribes have been blessed, having increased fruitfully in Egypt, and now listed among YHWH's earthly hosts. Also,

Table 10: Census totals by encampments

EASTWARD STANDARD OF JUDAH: 186,400		
	Issachar	54,400
	JUDAH	74,600
	Zebulun	57,400
SOUTHWARD STANDARD OF REUBEN: 151,450		
	Gad	45,650
	REUBEN	46,500
	Simeon	59,300
CENTRAL CAMP OF LEVITES		
WESTWARD STANDARD OF EPHRAIM: 108,100		
	Manasseh	32,200
	EPHRAIM	40,500
	Benjamin	35,400
NORTHWARD STANDARD OF DAN: 157,600		
	Naphtali	53,400
	DAN	62,700
	Asher	41,500

the southward encampment of Reuben is positioned second in honour after Judah's since, as Milgrom observes, 'the rotation (assuming one is facing east) is always to the right' (1990: 341), so there is need for caution on any assessment of the Camp's figures and places – hierarchy is part of the Creator's orderly design. Judah's eastward position is not only near the entrance to YHWH's encampment and to Aaron's priestly house, honoured among the Levites, but Judah's camp also leads the journey through the wilderness – for it 'was fit the Lion should lead the way' (Trapp 1650: 3). Each tribe of the outer camp – whatever its rank and position – may be regarded as chosen and blessed to be included in the Camp of Israel, *equally distant* to YHWH's Dwelling.

Evident from the two main verbs used, 'they shall encamp' (*haḥōnîm*) and 'they shall journey out' (*yissā'û*) (e.g. 2:3, 9), the journey theme is dominant. Numbers 9:15–23, which offers an ideal portrayal of Israel's following YHWH's Cloud through the wilderness, focuses on precisely the same two movements, and Numbers 10:1–10 gives two main functions for the silver trumpets: gathering Israel and coordinating the journeying out of the tribes.

17. The chapter's arrangement coincides with the Camp: the Tent of Meeting is central, among the descriptions of the four major tribal encampments. Numbers 1:53 had already given the general encampment of Levites as 'around the Dwelling of the Testimony' and more precise details, regarding encampment and the order for setting out, will be supplied in Numbers 3; here only the point that Levites remain connected to YHWH's Tent in transit is communicated. Whether encamped or on journey, the duty of Levites to surround and guard the sacred Tent and its furnishings never relaxes. Explicit attention is given, observes Knierim (1995a: 385), 'to the alternating camp formation: quadrangular for the encampment, linear for the march'.

32–34. With the compliance report, not only is Israel's obedience set forth; a theological statement is made about the essence of the Camp itself, that it is a divine creation, like the cosmos spoken into existence in Genesis 1. Just as the Tabernacle and its cultus 'works' and brings the blessing of atonement and reconciliation because it is revealed and established by God, evident in the compliance reports of its construction, so Israel's Camp is the divine paradigm for YHWH's community. The original divine command (vv. 1–2) and the compliance report (v. 34) form an inclusion, underscoring Israel's encampment by tribal groupings, arranged around the Dwelling (cf. Grossman 2002).

Explanation

What is the purpose of the census? Rashi delightfully remarked that God keeps counting his people 'because of their dearness to him' (1997:

4:2), the way one might continually count a collection of jewels. God had promised Israel that his covenant relationship with them included their becoming his 'treasured possession' (*sĕgullā*), forming them into 'a kingdom of priests and a holy nation' (Exod. 19:5–6; cf. Stubbs 2009: 29). Census-taking in the Torah appears to function as a prequel to assignment, its purpose dictated by that assignment. A census is an act of kingship by YHWH, who sovereignly claims and lifts up his people, individually and by families and tribes, before assigning them to their designated place in his own encampment (that the act implies ownership may explain David's error, 2 Sam. 24). Census-taking is a means of assessment, prior to organization. Israelites are delineated, sorted out and grouped by their tribes in chapter 1 in order to construct the Camp of Israel, the covenant community arranged by tribes around YHWH's Dwelling. As divinely counted and organized, the Camp is a model of orderly cosmos, where every individual part is in its proper place, matters significantly and contributes to the whole (cf. 1 Cor. 12:12–31; Eph. 2:14–22). The tally was for the sake of *sorting out the Israelites according to tribal affiliation*, required before arranging the twelve tribes around YHWH's Dwelling as a unified whole, the Camp of Israel. The disordered mass of Israelites gathered at Sinai are being separated out and clarified, identified and classified according to their ancestral genealogies, an act weighted with definition, a granting of identity, as each individual and family is identified with an individual patriarch whose birth order and history reflect a particular role and prophetic destiny. Those belonging to the tribe of Ephraim, for example, will be placed by divine revelation in their particular space within the Camp, and eventually within the land of Canaan, each tribe's character forged with that of its geographical location. The prophecy of Judah's leadership (Gen. 49:8–12), moreover, is embodied by the tribe's location as head of the eastward tribes (2:3–9), and remains in view (see 24:9). Accordingly, the outer camp's basis is the book of Genesis, especially its account of the twelve sons of Jacob (Gen. 29 – 30; 48 – 49) and YHWH's promises to Abraham of many descendants and the land of Canaan (Gen. 15; 17; cf. M. Douglas 2004: 18–21), which the tribes, portrayed as a sacred militia, are charged to possess.

The chieftains are listed in the general order of tribal priority established by the birth order of their patriarchs (Gen. 29 – 30, excluding Levi), though prioritizing Leah and Rachel's sons before those of their respective maids, whose sons are grouped together in third position (cf. G. B. Gray 1902). In Numbers 1:20–43, the tribal tallies are listed in the same basic order but grouped according to the four cardinal encampments of Israel's Camp, so that Gad (who as firstborn of Leah's maid, Zilpah, appears to rank above the other maid-sons) is moved up. These four encampment groups are maintained throughout Numbers, with one important difference: the list of tribes/chieftains in 2:3–31,

7:12–83 and 10:14–28 begin with the east camp, followed by the south, west and north camps, moving clockwise. Even when the same tribal chieftains are listed in Numbers 7, they are listed according to the new orientation, beginning with the east camp and also with Gad in the sixth slot. The (re)orienting power of YHWH's Dwelling is manifest: the Tent of Meeting's eastward entrance determines the east as the position of prominence, an honour bestowed on Judah. The second census of Numbers 26 follows the order of the census tally here, albeit with Ephraim and Manasseh's order reversed (marked by an asterisk in Table 11 below).

Joseph's sons, Manasseh and Ephraim, form two distinct tribes, a circumstance traced to Genesis 48:5, where Jacob claims the boys directly as his – Jacob's – own. Providentially, the division of Joseph's posterity into two allows the sum of Israel's tribes to remain at twelve, after the Levites, substituting for Israel's firstborn sons in their cultic duties, are removed. The centrality of Joseph's sons (v. 10), with five tribes preceding (vv. 5–9) and following (11–15), is likely due to Joseph's receiving the right of primogeniture from Jacob (Gen. 48; cf. 49:26). Through the daughters of Zelophehad of the tribe of Manasseh (27:1–11; 36:1–13) and Joshua of the tribe of Ephraim (27:12–23) the last major division of Numbers will also highlight Joseph's tribe. As explained in 1 Chronicles 5:1–2, Reuben's 'birthright was given to the sons of Joseph' and though Judah became ruler 'yet the birthright belonged to Joseph' (cf. Lunn 2010: 170). (See Table 11.)

The ordering logic is more difficult for the lists in 13:4–15 and 34:16–29. While Numbers 13 generally maintains priority of matriarch

Table 11: Order of tribal listings

Tribal matriarchs	Order of birth Gen. 29 – 30	Order of chieftains Num. 1:5–15	Order of censuses Num. 1, 26*		Order of camp Num. 2, 7 (chieftains), 10	
Leah	Reuben	Reuben	Reuben		Judah	
Leah	Simeon	Simeon	Simeon	South Camp	Issachar	East Camp
Leah	Levi	(Levi's tribe excluded)	Gad		Zebulun	
Leah	Judah	Judah	Judah		Reuben	
Bilhah (Rachel)	Dan	Issachar	Issachar	East Camp	Simeon	South Camp
Bilhah (Rachel)	Naphtali	Zebulun	Zebulun		Gad	
Zilpah (Leah)	Gad	Joseph: *Ephraim Manasseh*	Ephraim Manasseh*	West Camp	Ephraim Manasseh	West Camp
Zilpah (Leah)	Asher	Benjamin	Benjamin		Benjamin	
Leah	Issachar	Dan	Dan		Dan	
Leah	Zebulun	Asher	Asher	North Camp	Asher	North Camp
Rachel	Joseph	Gad				
Rachel	Benjamin	Naphtali	Naphtali		Naphtali	

and birth order (Zebulun and Manasseh excepted), Numbers 34 is adjusted by removing the tribes of Reuben, Gad and half of Manasseh, since they will inherit on the east side of the Jordan, the list referring to those chieftains who will oversee dividing the land inheritance west of the Jordan.

Numbers 1 – 2 thus recounts the creation of the 'outer camp', comprised of the twelve tribes, cast in a militaristic manner but without reducing the covenant community to a mere militia. While Levites are mentioned in a few limited ways (1:47–51, 53; 2:17, 33), these are exceptions, inserted primarily to indicate that the outer camp could not abide within the Camp of YHWH's earthly hosts apart from the Levitical 'inner camp', an intermediary zone to safeguard the space between the tribes and YHWH's central Dwelling. The literary and structural distinction between the outer tribal camp (chs. 1–2) and the inner Levitical camp (chs. 3–4) is also theological, an architectural embodiment of how the covenant community, with YHWH dwelling in the midst of his people, may function in the light of his holy presence. The drama of the wilderness sojourn will be coordinated precisely along this architectural-theological structure of the covenant community, with chapters 11–15 given entirely to a focus on the outer camp of the tribes (chs. 11–14), along with YHWH's legislative response to their failure (ch. 15) – note how the narrative focus begins with the outer edges of the Camp (11:1). Tellingly, Levites are nowhere mentioned or even in the purview of chapters 11–15. The whole Camp will be comprehended theologically as three camps arranged by gradations of holiness: the outer camp of the twelve tribes, the inner camp of the Levites and the central camp of the *Shekhinah*, YHWH's Dwelling – Aaron's house forming a link between the Levites and the Tent of Meeting. The Camp will be an enclosed *novum*, a threefold entity whereby the life and holiness of YHWH's central presence radiates outward by degree to its outermost edges, so that the tribal encampments comprise an extension of the central Tent.

Numbers opens with Moses' reception of constructive revelation from YHWH from *within* the Tent of Meeting, a significant progression from the opening of Leviticus. The prerequisite transformation of YHWH's Dwelling into a Tent of Meeting that can be approached through Israel's cultic service, including the anointed priesthood, sacrifices and sacred calendar as revealed in Leviticus, means that *only now* may YHWH cause the tribes to approach and surround his Tent of Meeting so as to form the long-anticipated *covenant community*, with YHWH's dwelling literally in the midst of his people (Exod. 25:8; 29:45–46). Israel's arrival at Sinai the previous year (Exod. 19:1) had begun a process of transformation, culminating in Israel's being established as YHWH's Camp, his earthly hosts, before journeying out for life in Canaan. The divinely mandated census was for the sake of creating the Camp of Israel, as Israelites are sorted and enumerated, classified according to tribal affiliations and then given their divinely appointed place in the Camp. The tallying and reconfiguring of Israelites was thus a means of classification, a taxonomy system based on holiness, having the hierarchical, concentrically arranged Camp of Israel in view (cf. George 2013: 25–29). As with Genesis 1, God forms cosmos out of chaos by first making separations – the masses of Israel are first separated and rearranged according to the twelve patriarchal sons of Jacob, a hint that God's expressed purposes in Genesis, as promised to Abraham, Isaac and Jacob, have begun to dawn (esp. Gen. 49). YHWH's call for a census of his people, therefore, formed a *prerequisite* step toward establishing them as his covenant community, whereby the Camp is presented as a portable city of God, the embodiment of an ideal theocracy.

As the covenant community begins to take shape, the Camp's structure forms the silhouette of Israel's theology and ecclesiology. The eschatological vision within the seed of the covenant begins to sprout, orchestrated by the voice of YHWH from between the cherubim within the Tent of Meeting (1:1; cf. 7:89). The relationship between God and humanity, expressed as life lived together, Israel's basking in the radiance of YHWH's glorious face, is the heart of the covenant, as per the formula 'I will be your God, you will be my people and I will dwell in your midst' (see Morales 2015: 103–106; cf. Exod. 29:45–46; Ezek. 37:27; Rev. 21:3). After humanity's expulsion from Eden, Numbers 1 – 2, within the scope of chapters 1–6, *presents the first instance of this covenant reality in the history of redemption, whereby YHWH dwells among his people.* God's promised purpose for his Dwelling, 'Let them build me a Sanctuary so I may dwell in their midst' (25:8) and 'I will dwell in the midst of the sons of Israel and will be their God' (Exod. 29:45), begins to be fulfilled as YHWH himself arranges the tribes around his Dwelling so that he is dwelling literally in the midst of Israel – a foretaste of the covenant's consummation: 'Behold, the Dwelling of God is with humanity, and he will dwell with them, and they shall be his peoples – God himself will be with them and be their God' (Rev. 21:3).

These chapters, therefore, narrate a significant moment in the life of Israel and in redemptive history. The tribes have now been defined *spatially*, according to their cosmic orientation around the central Tent of Meeting, with the Camp serving as a paradigmatic symbol of the Sinai covenant. Whether the sons of Israel will be able to live out this community structure in the sojourn through the wilderness is at the heart of the book's unity and dramatic plot (cf. George 2013: 24–25). Judah's camp is given the primary tribal position, auguring the majestic role of David's house (cf. Gen. 49:10; on the relation of Judah's tribe to Aaron, see Galil 1985). The cardinal points convey the sense of new creation to the Camp that, with YHWH's abiding presence, recalls the paradise of Eden. Eden's garden had been oriented to the east by its entry gate (Gen. 3:24), and the river that flowed through it descended and branched out into four riverheads, watering the four quadrants of the earth (Gen. 2:10–14). Similarly, the Camp is oriented by the entry gate of YHWH's Dwelling, an architectural garden of Eden, facing eastward. Israel, arrayed as four tribal encampments aligned to the compass points, represents a new humanity gathered around the Dwelling of YHWH, whose blessing will flow out to the entire Camp (Num. 6:22–27). Numbers 1 – 2, with their detail and repetition, convey the theological essence of the Camp and should be read through the lens of Balaam's Spirit-infused eyes, as a paradise in the wilderness (see Num. 24:2, 5–7). Ecclesiology *is* the story of Numbers.

The twelve chieftains listed represent and symbolize all Israel construed as the twelve tribes descended from the twelve sons of Jacob (vv. 5–16; cf. 7:12–83). Their honoured role not only sets the focus on the outer camp of tribes, but signals that Numbers is about leadership (cf. Num. 13:4–16, 31–33; 14:36–37; 34:16–29). The Messiah's symbolic act of gathering twelve disciples around him is informed by the same theology, communicating that the prophesied eschatological regathering of all Israel has begun (Matt. 10:2–4; Mark 3:13–19; Luke 6:12–16; cf. Acts 1:15–26).

Adding to the majesty of YHWH's earthly hosts, the tallies list great numbers for each tribe, along with a total sum of Israelites, 603,550 – the vast 'measurements' of God's people akin to the measurements of God's city elsewhere in Scripture (cf. Ezek. 40; Rev. 21:9–27). The methodical, formulaic nature of the figure-reports triumphantly unveils, tribe by tribe, YHWH's accomplishment on behalf of his people during their exile in Egypt, the 'house of bondage' (Exod. 20:2), and underscores his ability to keep the ancestral promises, not only of numerous descendants (Gen. 15:1–6; cf. Exod. 1:7; Gen. 1:28), but also to bring those descendants into the land (Gen. 15:7–21), anticipated now before Israel's wilderness sojourn. The vast number of Israelites looks ultimately to that 'great multitude which no one is able to number, from all nations and tribes and peoples and language', redeemed by the blood of the Lamb of God (Rev. 7:9). What begins here with a divine call to 'lift up the head' of the sons of Israel will come to a conclusion with YHWH's lifting up his own face on the sons of Israel in benediction, within the newly founded Camp of Israel (6:22–27). Psalm 87 praises YHWH for the joy of being counted among his people, declaring the hope that a remnant of all nations will be registered as citizens of Zion, too. In the same manner, the Messiah directed his disciples to find their joy in having their names inscribed in heaven (Luke 10:20). What a blessed joy to be counted among YHWH's beloved people, the sheep of his pasture – 'Glories are spoken of you, O city of God!' (Ps. 87:3).

THE CENSUS FIGURES

In chapters 1 and 26 of Numbers, YHWH commands Moses, along with the high priest (Aaron, then Eleazar), to take a census of the community of Israel, with the resulting tallies reported as 603,550 (1:46) and 601,730 (26:51). Regarding these figures as the total number of fighting men alone has led many interpreters to extrapolate an estimated population upwards of 2.5 million Israelites in the wilderness. Because these large counts raise difficult historical problems (e.g. Colenso 1862: 31–44; G. B. Gray 1903: 10–15), scholars have made a variety of attempts to explain them. The issue, moreover, cannot be reduced merely to conservative versus critical approaches, as if the only stumbling block were over YHWH's ability either to multiply his people or to feed such a multitude in the wilderness – though these points are oft noted (cf. Baentsch 1903: 446; Dillmann 1886: 5–8; countered by Allis 1943: 274–275). Rather, taking seriously the trustworthiness of Scripture is precisely what has led some scholars, who freely confess both the miraculous parting of the sea and the heaven-sent manna, to take seriously as well the problems caused by high census figures and to posit resolutions (e.g. J. W. Wenham 1967). Clearly the numbers are rounded, the tribal totals being divisible by 100 in all but one instance in each of the two counts. That copyists are more likely to err with regard to numbers than to other words, since such errors do not make a statement unintelligible, is simply the case (Baron 1972: 866–867), especially regarding rounded numbers. To illustrate, 2 Samuel 10:18 reads that David killed 700 charioteers, while 1 Chronicles 19:18 has it as 7,000 charioteers. Again, 1 Kings 4:26 mentions 40,000 stalls for Solomon's horses, while 2 Chronicles 9:25 reads 4,000. In the ensuing sections, I will review some of the internal and external challenges related to a face value reading of the large numbers, as well as some of the proposed solutions (cf. E. W. Davies 1995a; Goldstein 2012), before offering my own simple reading.

Challenges for a face value reading of the census figures

Assuming a total of 2.5 million Israelites in the wilderness, based upon a count of some 600,000 military-aged men, raises several issues. First, based on the number of firstborn males as 22,273 (Num. 3:43), the average mother in Israel would have had at least 27 sons, aside from daughters. By contrast, Moses appears to have had two siblings (Aaron and Miriam) and two sons (Gershon and Eliezer), while Aaron had four sons (Nadab and Abihu, Eleazar and Ithamar). Harrison mitigates this statistic by suggesting the firstborn census included only those born as of Passover, which had already served to redeem firstborn sons (1990: 74), a position argued earlier by Keil (1869: 5–6). Nevertheless, Harrison deemed the census figures to be inflated, resting 'on some basis of reality which was quite familiar to the ancients, but which is unknown to modern scholars' (2004: 633).

Second, the logistics for such a throng are perplexing, as Snaith implies, 'When on the march, they would constitute a column twenty-two miles long, marching fifty abreast with one yard between each rank' (1962: 254; also E. Robinson 1856: 57–59) – and this without allowance for accompanying flocks, herds and possessions.

Third, other biblical passages appear to assume a smaller population. In Exodus 23:29–30 and Deuteronomy 7:22, YHWH declares that he will not drive out the Canaanites in one year, but rather allow for Israel to increase steadily in the land, lest the land become desolate and the wild beasts become too numerous for Israel. This point is often taken together with other more modest estimations of the nation that suggest Israel was 'least among the peoples' (Deut. 7:7), and tempted to say, 'these nations are greater than I, how can I dispossess them?' (Deut. 7:17) – indeed, YHWH himself says that no fewer than seven nations (the Hittites, Girgashites, Amorites, Canaanites, Perizzites, Hivites and Jebusites) are each 'greater and mightier than you' (Deut. 7:1). Numerical figures elsewhere in biblical narratives, where battles are referenced, also seem to presume a small tally of armed forces for the tribes. Judges 18:11–17, for example, mentions only 600 fighting men of Dan in subduing Laish, whereas Numbers 26:42–43 lists Dan's hosts at 64,400. Similarly, Joshua 4:12–13 notes a militia of 40,000 from Reuben, Gad and the half tribe of Manasseh, compared to the combined figure of 110,580 from Numbers 26; and Judges 5:8 lists 40,000 fighters from six tribes, versus 301,000 in Numbers 26.

Fourth, other parts of the historical narrative in Scripture seem to make more sense by registering smaller numbers for Israel. Since, for example, it appears that 10–20,000 was a sizeable army in the ancient world, even for a coalition, with Pharaoh's Egyptian army estimated at the latter number (Vasholz 1992: 122; Ashley 1993: 60), Israel's fear of Egypt in Exodus 14 and reluctance to take the land in Numbers 13 – 14, given a militia of some 600,000 fighters, would be incongruous. A smaller appraisal of Israel's forces appears to fit the overall biblical story more consistently. One may argue, however, that Balaam's remark presumes a large throng of Israelites: 'Who can count the dust of Jacob, or number one-fourth of Israel?' (Num. 23:10).

Fifth, demographic analysis of the land of Palestine does not appear to support high census figures for Israel's tribes. Fouts, surveying demographic studies and archaeological data, concludes that 'at no time in the ancient history of Palestine would there have been more than 1,000,000 inhabitants' (2007: 1; 1992; 1997; 2005). He utilizes a variety of methodological approaches, from available water supplies (Wilkinson 1974), to density coefficient calculations (Broshi 1975; Shiloh 1980), which suggest a population rounded to 140,000 in Palestine during the

Middle Bronze (MB) I–II period (c. 2200–1550 BC); and while data for the Late Bronze Age period (c. 1550–1200) – the period in question – is lacking, the total picture, including the Iron Age evidence (c. 1200–586 BC) comports with a population under 1 million (Broshi and Gophna 1986; Gophna and Portugali 1988; Finkelstein and Gophna 1993). Finkelstein estimates the population of Israelites west of the Jordan in the mid-twelfth century at 21,000, some 55,000 during the early monarchy, and 150,000 for the later biblical period (1988: 330–335; cf. Frick 1989; Frendo 2004), around 400,000 for the whole country in the eighth century BC (Broshi and Finkelstein 1992). In short, the estimated populations for ancient civilizations in general, combined with biblical references such as Deuteronomy 7:1, would seem to call for understanding the census figures of Numbers 1 and 26 *differently*.

Having duly noted such internal and external concerns, the simplest resolution may well be to accept the numbers as they stand, as 'given with the utmost care and carefully checked by their use in the construction of the Tabernacle', and finding support in the 'supernaturalism of the narrative' itself (Allis 1943: 274; cf. Gispen 1959: 1:29–34; Davis 1968: 74). There are, however, alternative ways of understanding the large counts that remain faithful to the text, incorporating its genre while appreciating the portrayal of Israel within the larger context of scriptural history.

Census figures reflect the population of David's era

Some scholars see the census figures as accurate but reflecting the later period of the monarchy under David. Noting similarities between the counts of Numbers and those of David (2 Sam. 24:9; 1 Chr. 21:5), Albright (1925) suggested that a post-exilic editor mistook the versions from the era of the united monarchy and inserted them into Numbers, an approach set forth earlier by Dillman (1886: 7). This hypothesis, however, creates its own problems, from overly complicating the text's transmission, to the probability that the figures may still be too large even for the early monarchy (cf. G. J. Wenham 1981b: 62; E. W. Davies 1995a: 454–457). An alternative version of this approach eliminates the editorial blunder, suggesting that the figures from David's era were inserted deliberately to make the theological point that David's kingdom was the goal being realized incipiently through the exodus deliverance.

Census figures are symbolic

Attempting to find real meaning in the figures as they stand, Holzinger used gematria, a cryptograph system giving numerical value to words, and posited different phrases with numerical values that would add up to the census totals (1903). Gematria as a practice, at least in Jewish circles, however, cannot be traced any earlier than to R. Eliezer b. R. Jose, the Galilean (c. AD 200), though Noth suggested the second century BC under Hellenistic influence (1930: 131–132), and its existence in the HB cannot be positively demonstrated (Schechter and Levias 1906). Still, this approach holds potential, assuming a proposal emerged whereby meaning may be shown to apply *consistently* for the figures of each of the twelve tribes, being objectively relevant (e.g. to their compass locale in the Camp, or to their patriarchal prophecy in Gen. 49), along with the sum tally.

Gematria aside, numerical symbolism remains a possible expla- nation. Hill (2003) urges the need to understand the Mesopotamian world view whereby numbers could have either or both numerical and sacred (numerological or symbolic) meaning. Mesopotamians used a sexagesimal system, stressing the number 60, considered a sacred number of perfection, with Anu, the head of their pantheon of gods, being assigned sixty, 'the most perfect number in the hierarchy' (Hill 2003: 241). Hill also offers examples from Scripture, including Moses' lifespan of 120 years (60×2; Deut. 34:7) and Noah's age of 600 years (60×10; Gen. 6:9), symbolic of his perfection (Hill 2003: 243–247; cf. Cavasola 2020). Relevant for the census figures here, the number 600 is also used for the round figure of Israelites who emerged from Egypt (Exod. 12:37), and for the number of Pharaoh's chosen chariots (Exod. 14:7), and appears beyond the Torah as well (Judg. 3:31; 18:11, 16, 17; 20:47; 1 Sam. 13:15; 14:2; 17:7; 23:13; 27:2; 30:9; 2 Sam. 15:18; 1 Kgs 10:14, 16, 29). Relatedly, N. Klein (2017) shows a symbolic use of numbers in Chronicles (2 Chr. 17:14–18). Taking the sum of Jehoshaphat's five military units, 1,160,000, he observes that this figure is precisely double that of the armies of his father Asa, and equals the sum of the armies of the three previous kings of Judah. These figures, he suggests, convey what is said explicitly elsewhere, that Jehoshaphat walked in the ways of David, setting his heart to seek God, and that YHWH was with him (see 2 Chr. 17:3; 19:3–4).

Barnouin, relying on Babylonian astronomy, argues that the counts corresponded to the planetary periods when divided by 100 (1977). The mathematics involved, however, is quite complicated, even requiring several of the recorded numbers to be emended (Goldstein 2012: 103; cf. also G. J. Wenham 1981b: 73–76). Heinzerling, applying quantitative structural analysis to Numbers 1 and 26, developed intriguing statistical data, which he first linked with Gematria (1999), but later abandoned in favour of an astronomical approach (2008), though the inexactness of his final computations (requiring the addition of 5, and subtraction of 7, from the census totals of Num. 1 and 26, respectively) leaves room for doubt. More suggestively, seeking an astronomical significance to the census figures happens to accord well with similar approaches to the arrangement of Israel's Camp, with the twelve tribes organized, it is claimed, in a way related to the zodiac (see St. Clair 1907; C. E. Douglas 1936; Dobin 1999: 19–20; cf. *Sefer ha-Zikhronot* of Elazar ben Levi, c. 1325; *Zohar*, Bemidbar 118), a view similarly taken with regard to the stones of the high priest's breastplate (see Philo, *Moses* II, 24.124). At least, the proposed theology of such astronomical symbolism, to 'represent Israel as Yahweh's terrestrial army, just as the astral bodies were regarded as his celestial host (cf. Gen. 2:1; Deut. 17:3)' (E. W. Davies 1995a: 457–458; cf. G. J. Wenham 1981b: 74–76), accords with the understanding that Israel's Camp represents YHWH's earthly hosts, a counterpart to the heavenly hosts surrounding his celestial abode. Milgrom similarly suggested 'the possibility that the tribal figures were made to correspond to celestial movements', presenting Israel as 'corresponding to the astral bodies, the Lord's celestial armies (Gen. 2:1; Deut. 17:3)' (1990: 338).

Census figures confuse the meaning of *'elef*

Perhaps the most influential approach to refiguring the census numbers, set out first by Petrie (1906: 209–220), is to understand *'elef* (Num. 1:21, 23, 25, 27, etc.) as referring to 'group', 'family' or 'tent', rather than to 'thousand'. In this manner, Manasseh's count of 32,200 becomes 32 families (or tents) of 200 people. Significantly, the numbers fall out with a reasonable average number of persons per tent for both census totals (9 to 10 persons). Also, that there is not a single round thousand in any tribal total aligns with Petrie's system, since a figure such as 32,000 would amount to 32 families of 0 people – patently invalid. Moreover, *'elef* may indeed be taken to mean a group, smaller than a tribe but larger than a father's house, even within Numbers (*NIDOTTE* 1:406–410, 416–418): 'the clans (*'alpî*) of Israel' (10:4; 31:5; also Judg. 6:15; 1 Sam. 10:19).

Several adaptations of Petrie's study have been proposed, leading to a final tally range between 5,500 and 72,000. Mendenhall (1958; supported by Gottwald 1999: 270–276) defined *'elef* as a military fighting unit or contingent, rather than a family or tent, and J. W. Wenham (1967), building on the work of R. E. D. Clark (1955), argued that several occurrences of *'elef* were actually *'alûf* in the original unpointed text, meaning clan chief or military leader (also Humphreys 1998; 2000; Heinzerling 2000; Ziegert 2009; Waite 2010; G. A. Rendsburg 2001a). The Achilles heel for this approach, on any variation, is that it requires a scribal misunderstanding of *'elef*, since the text as it now stands clearly reads the term as 'thousand' for the two census totals and elsewhere. Moreover, the proposed solutions are typically found inconsistent with other references, such as Numbers 3:39, where the number of Levites is

22,000. Also problematic, the troop sizes vary considerably between the census counts: for example, whereas Manasseh has an average of just six men per troop in the first census, there are over thirteen per troop in the second (cf. Budd 1984: 290–291).

Census figures as hyperbolic

The census figures may be deliberately hyperbolic. Rather than a form of crafty deception, such transparent exaggerations merely observe recognized literary convention as attested in the ANE (Hoegger 1984: 9–11). E. W. Davies lists various instances, such as the exaggerated reigns of kings in the ancient Sumerian king-lists (e.g. Alalgar ruled 36,000 years), and bolstered military reports such as Shalmaneser I's blinding 14,400 captives and deporting 28,800 (1995a: 467; cf. Levine 2000: 139). Affirming Davies's position, Rendsburg nevertheless critiqued his sampling of cognate data as not actually fitting the genre of Numbers, which Rendsburg defines as epic literature, and supplied a closer parallel from the Ugarit Kret epic in which a legendary king musters 3,000,000 men (2001a: 393). Fouts defends this approach by offering more ANE parallels of similar genre and arguing that the inflated census numbers are historically based, functioning as a common rhetorical device that does not detract from the legitimacy of the accounts (Fouts 1992; 1997; 2005; 2007). While E. W. Davies disregards the census totals as purely fictitious inventions (1995a: 466), Vasholz (1992) and Allen (2012: 65–69) suggest the figures have been multiplied by ten, a point appealing in its simplicity and also supported by conflicting accounts, between 2 Samuel 10:18 and 1 Chronicles 19:18 (700 vs 7000), and between 1 Kings 4:26 and 2 Chronicles 9:25 (40,000 vs 4,000). Here the Chronicler's differences would not be due to scribal error but to authorial intention. The theological purpose of such hyperbole in Numbers would be to magnify the achievements of YHWH and the invincibility of his people, as well as to emphasize that God's promise to the patriarchs of innumerable descendants was being fulfilled (E. W. Davies 1995a: 468–469; Fouts 1997: 387).

Scolnic (1995), perhaps the most thorough proponent of the hyperbole view, points out that hyperbole is used regularly with regard to Israel's enemies in the Bible, which speaks of the armies of the Canaanites as 'an enormous host, as numerous as the sands on the seashore' (Josh. 11:4), and the Midianites as 'swarming as thick as locusts; they and their camels were innumerable' (Judg. 6:7) and 'as numerous as the sands on the seashore' (Judg. 7:12). The tension or paradox, of course, relates to the actual use of figures, like census totals. Why not simply say the Israelites were 'innumerable like the stars of heaven' – why employ lengthy lists of detailed figures? Scolnic responds (1995: 47), 'One can give a finite number which is, in its impact, at least if not more powerful than an indeterminate indicator of infinitude.' Rather, Scolnic writes (36–37), the census lists 'detail the fulfilment of a theological theme', that 'the promise to the Patriarchs has been fulfilled' and the Israelites are now 'the centre of the world, the chosen of God . . . equal to the hosts of Heaven in terms of their might' – with YHWH in their midst and on their side, 'Israel is the greatest military force possible'.

While for many readers *today* the notion of deliberately inflated census figures comes across as duplicitous, especially in narratives otherwise deemed historically precise, perhaps a wider understanding of epic literature in the ANE context will validate the hyperbolic interpretation as satisfying Harrison's 'basis of reality that was quite familiar to the ancients' (2004: 633). After reviewing the various approaches, Goldstein commends deliberate and purposeful hyperbole as the most adequate understanding of the large census counts, because it is simple, resolves internal inconsistencies, fits better with numerical size references in other biblical books, and does not require a series of emendations (2012: 107–108).

A simple proposal

Questions remain for each of the above approaches; thus, I offer one more possibility, that the census figures represent the counts for *all Israel*. Despite particular language to the contrary (Num. 1:3, 20, etc.), could the totals have been intended as the tally for the community of Israel as a whole? Some of the language resonates: 'Lift up the heads of *the whole community of the sons of Israel* by their clans' (1:2). Possibly, the military-aged men were appointed their duties and placement according to their hosts within the context of a community-wide census, and might even have formed the basis for the total count by their providing genealogical records, as indicated in 1:18.

Some who note the language particular to the whole community have suggested that two censuses were taken and that the results of the first, of all Israel, were left out – but perhaps the reality is the reverse. The following gloss is illustrative: '**By families**: The purpose of counting the Jewish people according to families was in order to add the family tallies together and thus arrive at the sums of the different tribes. The count of the families themselves is not recorded in the Torah' (Schneerson and Wisnefsky 2009: 7; emphasis original). Similar explanations of 'by families' clearly understand its function toward the goal of ascertaining the total number of Israelites (Rashi 1997: 4:2). Incidentally, Petrie's work, in substituting 'families'/'tents' for 'thousands', necessarily assumed the census figures as standing for all Israel (see Petrie 1906: 211), a point noted and subsequently altered by Mendenhall's use of 'troop' for *'elef* (1958). Moreover, when thousands are depicted as destroyed in judgement by YHWH in the wilderness, those figures include women and children, not merely military-aged men, whether the idolaters with the golden calf (Exod. 32:25–35) or the tents of Korah, Dathan and Abiram (Num. 16:20–35). Reducing the figures merely to militia, the encampment assignments raise the question of where everyone else was to be relegated within the Camp. Rather, the text indicates that tribes were arranged by families around the Dwelling, a point likely reflected already in the census figures themselves. Francis Andersen, assessing the census list of Numbers 26, offered the conservative estimate that there must have been about 60 phratries in Israel, each phratry (his understanding of a *mišpāḥāh* as a subtribal group) having at least 10,000 members in populous times (1969: 35). His estimate, which comes to an Israelite total populace of 600,000, could reasonably be the intended portrait of all Israel in Numbers. Ironically, perhaps the rhetorical features of Numbers 1, portraying all Israel as YHWH's hosts, have led to reducing the text's theological vision to merely Israel's militia.

This proposal essentially draws on one important observation, hinted at earlier: the various approaches to refiguring the census numbers are chiefly the result, *not of the figures themselves, but of the 2.5 to 3 million populace extrapolated from those figures.* Yet, the text of Numbers nowhere assumes that such an extrapolation is intended. Some will still regard these figures as too high – Lucas thinks the total number of Israelites could not have been more than ten thousand (1944; cf. Noth 1968: 21). As with the alternative approaches, this understanding resolves problems while creating its own, a unique issue in this case, since it calls for a reinterpretation of the language particular to military-aged men. The simple answer, again, is that the phrases in question may be understood as having the military-aged men form the basis for the total count, in registering their genealogies by their clans and fathers' houses. In relation to Exodus 12:37, Alexander proposes that women are included in the reference to 'men' (*gĕbārîm*), since only infants – small children (*ṭap*) – are excluded from the count (2017: 241–244), which if correct aligns with a general figure of 600,000 for all Israel. Budd had apparently entertained the notion as well, writing (1984: 8):

> There may in fact be a simpler solution to hand. There were texts available to the author in Yahwistic tradition which offered a figure of some six hundred thousand Israelites – presumably the whole community, and not merely fighting men (Exod. 12:37; Num. 11:21).

However tenuous, this proposal is simple, needs no recourse to emendations, nor resort to scribal errors or misunderstandings of *'elef*, it coheres with the picture of Israel in the rest of the Numbers narrative, requires no extrapolation statistics, is more in accord with estimated population levels for ancient Palestine, suffers less in relation to the Levitical census, remains in line with NT references to high numbers in the wilderness (1 Cor. 10:18), retains the purposeful function and theological significance of the census numbers themselves without having to defend hyperbolic language, and it may also be combined readily with other approaches. The proposal does not require any reduction of textual figures – only restraint from making unwarranted extrapolations. To be sure, the question remains open. Nevertheless, 603,550 as the tally for all Israel not only dispels much of the mystery, but also suggests that a large part of the puzzle has been contrived by an early view, assumed by later interpreters.

Not a single passage in Numbers, the Pentateuch or the HB ever explicitly states or presumes that there were upwards of 2.5 million Israelites in the wilderness, an omission all the more striking when compared to the continual touting of this figure in monographs, commentaries and study Bibles. As a case in point, when Moses is overwhelmed by the seeming impossibility of feeding the vast multitudes of Israel with meat in the wilderness, he cries out, 'Six hundred thousand on foot are the people (*hā'ām*) whom I am among, and yet you say to me, I will give them meat and they will eat for a whole month!' (Num. 11:21). Now if Moses were indeed standing among 2.5 to 3 million people, it seems that in precisely this context of incredulity, he would have exclaimed the fuller number of them, rather than reducing it by some 75%. Significantly, the term used, 'the people' (*hā'ām*), clearly has the whole community in its purview, and the people are numbered here at the round figure of 600,000. Taking another example, the men of the tribes of Reuben, Gad and the half tribe of Manasseh, desiring to inherit the land on the east side of the Jordan, vow to send their fighting men across the Jordan to help the other tribes possess their lands, while their own aged folk, women and children remain behind (Num. 32:27, 29). In narrating the fulfilment of their pledge, Joshua alludes to this passage almost verbatim, declaring that some 'forty thousand prepared for war' crossed the Jordan (4:13–14). The 40,000 naturally reads as referring to the fighting men of Reuben, Gad and Manasseh, which would comprise almost 30% of their total population of 136,930 (Num. 26:7, 18, 34), a figure which appears sound. On this angle, then, 136,930 does *not* represent the fighting men of these three tribes, but rather their total population.

Finally, it is worth mentioning once more that efforts to reduce the total number of Israelites in the wilderness era in no way precludes the miraculous activity of YHWH God. When the Gospel authors depict the Messiah's feeding several thousand Israelites in the wilderness, this miraculous event, though involving a fraction of the census figures in Numbers, is nevertheless clearly intended to recall the feeding of Israel in the wilderness and to demonstrate Jesus' divine authority in a powerful way (Matt. 14:13–21; Mark 6:30–44; Luke 9:10–17; John 6:1–14).

NUMBERS 3 – 4: ARRANGING THE LEVITES AND PRIESTS AS THE INNER CAMP

Translation

¹Now these are the generations of Aaron and Moses on the day YHWH spoke with Moses on Mount Sinai. ²And these are the names of the sons of Aaron: Nadab the firstborn and Abihu, Eleazar and Ithamar. ³These are the names of the sons of Aaron the anointed priests who were ordained to serve as priests. ⁴But Nadab and Abihu died before YHWH when they brought near strange fire before YHWH in the wilderness of Sinai, and they had no sons; so Eleazar and Ithamar served as priests in the presence of Aaron their father.

⁵And YHWH spoke to Moses, saying, ⁶'Bring near the tribe of Levi and present them before Aaron the priest that they may minister to him. ⁷And they will keep his guard duty and the guard duty for the whole community before the Tent of Meeting in doing the labour of the Dwelling. ⁸And they will guard all the vessels of the Tent of Meeting – the guard duty for the sons of Israel – for doing the labour of the Dwelling. ⁹You are to give the Levites to Aaron and to his sons; they are wholly given to him from among the sons of Israel. ¹⁰Aaron and his sons you are to appoint, and they will keep charge of their priesthood; but the stranger who draws near will be put to death.'

¹¹And YHWH spoke to Moses, saying, ¹²'Even I – look! – I have taken the Levites from the midst of the sons of Israel in place of all the firstborn who open the womb among the sons of Israel; so the Levites will be mine. ¹³For all the firstborn are mine: in the day I struck down all the firstborn in the land of Egypt, I sanctified to myself all the firstborn in Israel, from man to beast – they will be mine; I am YHWH.'

¹⁴And YHWH spoke to Moses in the wilderness of Sinai, saying, ¹⁵'Appoint the sons of Levi according to their fathers' house, according to their clans, all males a month old and upward you are to appoint.' ¹⁶And Moses appointed them according to the mouth of YHWH just as he was commanded.

¹⁷And these were the sons of Levi by their names: Gershon, Kohath, and Merari. ¹⁸And these were the names of the sons of Gershon according to their clans: Libni and Shimei. ¹⁹And the sons of Kohath according to their clans: Amram, Izhar, Hebron, and Uzziel. ²⁰And the sons of Merari according to their clans: Mahli and Mushi.

These are the clans of the Levites by their fathers' house: ²¹To Gershon belonged the clan of the Libnites and the clan of the Shimeites; these were the clans of the Gershonites. ²²Those appointed in the number of all males from one month and upward – those appointed were seven thousand five hundred. ²³The clans of the Gershonites are to camp behind the Dwelling, westward. ²⁴And the chieftain of the father's house for the Gershonites is Eliasaph son of Lael. ²⁵And the guard duty of the sons of Gershon for the Tent of Meeting included the Dwelling, and the Tent with its covering, and the screen of the doorway of the Tent of Meeting, ²⁶and the hangings of the courtyard, with the screen of the doorway of the courtyard which surrounds the Dwelling and the altar, with its cords, and all the labour related to it.

²⁷To Kohath belonged the clan of the Amramites and the clan of the Izharites, and the clan of the Hebronites, and the clan of the Uzzielites; these were the clans of the Kohathites. ²⁸The number of all the males from one month old and upward was eight thousand six hundred, keeping the guard duty of the sanctuary. ²⁹The clans of the sons of Kohath are to camp by the side of the Dwelling, southward. ³⁰And the chieftain of the father's house of the Kohathites is Elizaphan son of Uzziel. ³¹And their guard duty was the ark and the table and the lampstand and the altars, and the vessels of the sanctuary with which they ministered, and the screen and all the labour related to it. ³²And the chieftain over the chiefs of the Levites is Eleazar son of Aaron the priest, appointed over those who keep the guard duty of the sanctuary.

³³To Merari belonged the clan of the Mahlites and the clan of the Mushites; these were the clans of Merari. ³⁴Those appointed in the number of all males from one month and upward were six thousand two hundred. ³⁵And the chieftain of the father's house according to the clans of Merari is Zuriel son of Abihail; by the side of the Dwelling they are to camp, northward. ³⁶And the sons of Merari are appointed for the guard duty of the frames of the Dwelling, and its bars, and its pillars, and its bases, and all its vessels, and all the labour related to it, ³⁷and all the pillars of the courtyard all around, with their sockets, their pegs, and their cords.

³⁸Those camping before the Dwelling eastward, before the Tent of Meeting toward the sunrise, are Moses and Aaron and his sons, keeping the charge of the sanctuary, according to the charge of the sons of Israel; but the stranger who draws near will be put to death. ³⁹All the appointed Levites, whom Moses, with Aaron, appointed by the mouth of YHWH according to their clans, all males from one month old and upward, were twenty-two thousand.

⁴⁰And YHWH said to Moses, 'Appoint all the firstborn males of the sons of Israel from one month old and upward, and lift up the number of their names. ⁴¹And take the Levites for me – I am YHWH – in place of all the firstborn among the sons of Israel, and the cattle of the Levites in place of all the firstborn among the cattle of the sons of Israel'. ⁴²And Moses appointed just as YHWH had commanded him all the firstborn among the sons of Israel. ⁴³And the number of names of all the firstborn males, from a month old and upward, according to their appointing was twenty-two thousand two hundred and seventy-three.

⁴⁴And YHWH spoke to Moses, saying, ⁴⁵'Take the Levites in place of all the firstborn among the sons of Israel, and the cattle of the Levites in

place of their cattle; and the Levites will be mine – I am YHWH. [46]And for the redemption of the two hundred seventy-three of the firstborn of the sons of Israel in excess of the Levites, [47]take five shekels per skull, by the shekel of the sanctuary you will take, twenty gerahs per shekel, [48]and you will give the silver to Aaron and to his sons for the redemption of those in excess among them.'

[49]So Moses took the silver of the redemption from those in excess of the ones redeemed by the Levites; [50]from the firstborn of the sons of Israel Moses took the silver, one thousand three hundred and sixty-five, by the shekel of the sanctuary. [51]And Moses gave the silver of the redemption to Aaron and to his sons according to the mouth of YHWH, just as YHWH had commanded Moses.

[4:1]And YHWH spoke to Moses and to Aaron, saying, [2]'Lift up each head of the sons of Kohath from among the sons of Levi, according to their clans, according to their fathers' house, [3]from thirty years old and upward to fifty years old, all who come to the host to do the work in the Tent of Meeting. [4]This is the labour of the sons of Kohath for the Tent of Meeting, the holy of holies. [5]Aaron will come, and his sons, when the Camp journeys out, and they will take down the veil of the screen and with it cover the ark of the testimony. [6]And they will put upon it a covering of fine goatskin and spread over it a garment of pure blue and set up its poles. [7]And upon the table of the Presence they will spread a garment of blue, and put upon it the plates and the ladles and the bowls and the libation flagons, and the daily bread will be upon it. [8]And they will spread over them a garment of crimson scarlet, and cover it with a covering of fine goatskin and set up its poles. [9]And they will take a garment of blue and cover the lampstand of the light and its lamps and its tongs and its fire-pans and all the vessels of oil with which they minister for it. [10]And they will put it with all of its vessels in a covering of fine goatskin, and put it on the (carrying) frame. [11]And over the altar of gold they will spread a garment of blue and cover it with a covering of fine goatskin and set up its poles. [12]And they will take all the vessels of the ministry with which they minister in the sanctuary and put them in a garment of blue and cover them with a covering of fine goatskin, and put them on the (carrying) frame. [13]And they will de-ash the altar and spread over it a garment of purple. [14]And they will put upon it all its vessels with which they minister over it, the fire-pans, the meat-hooks, and the shovels and the basins – all the vessels of the altar – and they will spread over it a covering of fine goatskin and set up its poles. [15]When Aaron, with his sons, has finished covering the sanctuary and all the vessels of the sanctuary when the camp journeys out, then afterward the sons of Kohath will come to carry so they do not touch what is holy and die; these are what the sons of Kohath will carry in the Tent of Meeting. [16]The appointed-charge of Eleazar son of Aaron the priest is the oil of the light and the incense of spice and the daily tribute offering and the oil of anointing, with the appointed-charge over all the Dwelling and all that is in it, the sanctuary and its vessels.'

¹⁷And YHWH spoke to Moses and to Aaron, saying, ¹⁸'Do not allow the tribe of the clans of the Kohathites to be cut off from the midst of the Levites. ¹⁹Do this for them so they will not die when they approach the holy of holies: Aaron and his sons will come and set them, each man over his labour and to his carrying-duty, ²⁰so they will not come in to look, even for a moment, at the sanctuary and die.'

²¹And YHWH spoke to Moses, saying, ²²'Lift up the head of the sons of Gershon, them also, according to their fathers' house, according to their clans, ²³from thirty years old and upward to fifty years old appoint them, all who come to wage in the host, to work in the labour for the Tent of Meeting. ²⁴This is the labour of the clans of the Gershonites, as to packing-labour and carrying-duty. ²⁵They will carry the curtains of the Dwelling and the Tent of Meeting with its covering, the covering of goatskin which is over it above, and the screen of the doorway of the Tent of Meeting. ²⁶And the hangings of the courtyard and the screen of the doorway of the gate of the courtyard which is by the Dwelling and by the altar all around, and their cords and all the vessels of their service, and all that is done for them, so they will labour. ²⁷By the mouth of Aaron and his sons will be all the labour of the sons of the Gershonites, according to all their carrying-duty and for all their labour; you will appoint them the charge of all they are to carry. ²⁸This is the labour of the clans of the sons of the Gershonites for the Tent of Meeting, and their guard duty, in the hand of Ithamar son of Aaron the priest.

²⁹'The sons of Merari, according to their clans, according to their fathers' house, you will appoint them, ³⁰from thirty years old and upward to fifty years old you will appoint them, all who come to the host, to work in the labour of the Tent of Meeting. ³¹This is the charge of their carrying-duty, including all their packing-labour, for the Tent of Meeting: the frames of the Dwelling and its bars and its pillars and its bases. ³²And the pillars of the courtyard all around, and their bases and their pegs and their cords, according to all their vessels and according to all their labour, and by name you will appoint the vessels of the guard of what they are to carry. ³³This is the labour of the clans of the sons of Merari, according to all their labour for the Tent of Meeting, which is in the hand of Ithamar son of Aaron the priest.'

³⁴And Moses, along with Aaron and the chieftains of the community, appointed the sons of the Kohathites, according to their clans and according to their fathers' house, ³⁵from thirty years old and upward to fifty years old, all who come to the host to the labour for the Tent of Meeting. ³⁶Those who were appointed according to their clans were two thousand seven hundred and fifty. ³⁷These are the appointed of the clans

of the Kohathites, all who serve in the Tent of Meeting, whom Moses, with Aaron, appointed by the mouth of YHWH by the hand of Moses.

[38]Now those appointed of the sons of Gershon according to their clans and according to their fathers' house, [39]from thirty years old and upward to fifty years old, all who come to the host to the labour for the Tent of Meeting, [40]those who were appointed according to the clans, according to their fathers' house, were two thousand six hundred and thirty. [41]These are the ones appointed of the clans of the sons of Gershon, all who serve in the Tent of Meeting, whom Moses, with Aaron, appointed by the mouth of YHWH.

[42]Those appointed of the clans of the sons of Merari, according to their clans, according to their fathers' house, [43]from thirty years old and upward to fifty years old, all who come to the host to labour for the Tent of Meeting, [44]those who were appointed according to their clans were three thousand two hundred. [45]These are the ones appointed of the clans of the sons Merari whom Moses, with Aaron, appointed by the mouth of YHWH by the hand of Moses.

[46]All the ones appointed whom Moses, along with Aaron and the chieftains of Israel, appointed, the Levites according to their clans and according to their fathers' house, [47]from thirty years old and upward to fifty years old, all who come to do the work of packing-labour, and the labour of carrying-duty for the Tent of Meeting, [48]those who were appointed were eight thousand five hundred and eighty. [49]By the mouth of YHWH they were appointed by the hand of Moses, each man to his packing-labour and to his carrying-duty, so he was appointed, as YHWH had commanded Moses.

Notes on the text

3:1. *BHS* suggestion to remove 'and Moses' has no textual support.

3. 'who were ordained': lit. 'whose hands were filled' (*'ăšer-millē' yādām*).

4. 'before YHWH': the first occurrence is lacking in one MT MS, SamP, Vg, but should be retained (cf. Lev. 10:2).

6. 'present': lit. 'stand', *wĕha'ămadtā*. 'them' is 'him/it', referencing the tribe.

9. 'wholly given': lit. 'given given' *nĕtûnim nĕtûnim*.

'to him': some MT MSS, SamP, LXX read 'to me'. While Levites belong to YHWH (vv. 11–13), context favours Aaron as the referent.

10. LXX contains expansions, related to priestly duties (cf. Num. 18:7).

12. After 'sons of Israel', SamP and LXX read 'and they will be for their redemption' (see vv. 44–51).

16. *BHS* suggests incorporating *wayyihyû* (from v. 17) at the end of v. 16, and reading *yhwh*, along with emending *ṣuwwā*, reading 'as YHWH commanded him', but lacks textual support.

22. 'those appointed': the second occurrence is missing from Syr and Vg, *BHS* suggesting its deletion.

28. While one MT MS, Syr and Vg read the verse's beginning with *pĕqudêhem* (cf. v. 22), such variations are characteristic.

'six hundred': by a simple emendation the text reads 'three hundred', in line with v. 39, supported by the Lucianic recension of LXX.

'the sanctuary': lit. 'the holy', *haqqōdeš* (3:28, 31, 32, 47, 50; 4:15, 20; 7:9, 13, 19, 25, 31, 37, 43, 49, 55, 61, 67, 73, 79, 85, 86; 8:19; 18:3, 5, 16). It may be that *haqqōdeš* is more particular than *miqdāš*, with reference to the holy place of the sanctuary (cf. Exod. 26:33; 28:29, 35).

38. 'before the Tent of Meeting toward the sunrise': omitted by LXX.

39. 'Aaron': lacking in some MT MSS, SamP, and Syr; although the singular verb supports deleting Aaron, this subject–verb disagreement is common when Moses is the primary actor. 'Aaron' has Masoretic dots over it (*punctus extraordinarius*), typically interpreted as suggesting either its deletion or indicating that Aaron was not included in the sum total of Levites (*Bek.* 4a; Greenstone 1948: 29).

'twenty-two thousand': see note for v. 28.

40. 'lift up' (*wĕśā'*): as in 'count' (cf. 1:2).

49. 'redemption': *happidyôm* is a hapax legomenon, and *BHS* suggests transposing two letters; supported by SamP (perhaps harmonizing with addition in v. 12).

4:1. 'and to Aaron': a few MT MSS lack Aaron's inclusion.

6. *tāḥaš*: 'fine goatskin' translated by some as 'porpoise' (also vv. 8, 10, 11, 12, 14, 25); Ezek.16:10 implies rare finery. 'set up its poles' (also in vv. 8, 11, 14). The 'set up' is not identical in each case, since the ark's poles are attached, needing only to be retracted, while poles need to be set in for other furnishings (see Eichler 2016).

13. LXX reads 'and he will place the cover upon the altar' instead of 'they will de-ash the altar'.

14. LXX and SamP have expansions, involving a purple cover for the laver and its base, along with a further covering of skin; Budd suggests this as an addition (1984: 44), while Wevers is likely correct to assume an MT omission due to homoioteleuton (1998: 63).

19. Two MT MSS lack the second *'iš* but it should be retained for the idiom 'each/any/every man'.

20. 'for a moment': lit. *kĕballa'*, 'like a swallow'; presumably an idiom for a brief moment (see 11QT ᵃ 46.9).

26. LXX lacks 'and the screen of the doorway of the gate of the courtyard'; likely a homeoteleuton caused by the double reference to 'the courtyard'.

27. *BHS* suggests adding 'by name' (cf. v. 32), as LXX.

31. LXX expands on the coverings.

32. LXX expands on the curtain. *BHS* suggests *kol* (all) instead of *kĕlî* (vessels) after 'you will appoint', supported by one MT MS, SamP, and *TgPs-J*; LXX reads 'all the vessels'.

41. This verse is rounded off with 'by the hand of Moses' in a few MT MSS, LXX and *TgPs-J*.

49. 'his appointment': *ûpĕqudāyw* is difficult and may be emended to 'and they were appointed', as in LXX, Syr, Tg and Vg (see Num. 1:47; 2:33). However, that each man's 'appointment' was commanded by YHWH is justified by context.

Form and structure

The tribe of Levi receives special prominence in Numbers, with sections relating their appointment, duties and dedication laced throughout its opening chapters (1:47–54; 3:5–10, 11–13, 14–39, 40–51; 4:1–49; 8:5–14, 15–26; also 18:1–32). Frevel points out that the determined plural 'the Levites' (*halwîyyim*), which is absent in Genesis, occurs twice in Exodus, 4 times in Leviticus, and 8 in Deuteronomy, has 55 instances in Numbers (2013b: 142). Levites, Milgrom writes (1997: 242), 'proliferate in Numbers; indeed, they dominate the book'. Why are Levites so significant in Numbers? Mainstream scholarship conjectures that the separation of Levites and priests originated with the exilic prophet Ezekiel, so the details found in Numbers represent a later post-exilic development (see Noth 1968: 33; Levine 1993: 104–105). A unified reading of the Torah, however, suggests a simpler solution.

The two main duties of Levites may be defined as 'guarding' (*mišmeret*) the Tent of Meeting, the focus of Numbers 3, and 'transporting' ('*ăbōdāh*) the Dwelling, the focus of Numbers 4 (cf. Milgrom 1990: 343–344), both of which pertain to the context of Israel's newly created Camp. Levites were not necessary for the purpose or historical setting of Leviticus, which recounts how the Dwelling became a Tent of Meeting between YHWH and Israel by means of the cult – the need for transporting the Dwelling is not in the book's purview. While defilement of the sanctuary forms a major concern (Lev. 11 – 16), nevertheless the Tent of Meeting has not yet been established as the centre of Israel's Camp. Until the twelve tribes are arranged around the Tent (Num. 1 – 2), Levites are not needed to serve as a buffer, encamping between the tribes and the Tent to guard against encroachment. A similar reasoning explains the Levites' role in Deuteronomy as well, which, aside from its context in the plains of Moab *after* the wilderness journey, addresses Israel's life in the land, with the sanctuary established at the place of YHWH's choosing. While the status of Levites, standing in place of Israel's firstborn sons, remains, it is understandable and expected that the tribe's role would change historically, given new settings and different circumstances (cf. 1 Chr. 23). Numbers' emphasis on Levites relates to sections that focus on the inner camp, part of the book's analysis of the covenant community, the Camp of Israel: in chapters 3–4, Levites are established as the inner camp, and chapters 16–18 narrate the failure and reintegration of the inner camp.

Numbers 3 and 4 may be considered jointly, comprised of nine speeches of YHWH and their fulfilment. Though much ink has been shed setting out the complexity of Numbers 3, the material displays logic and purposeful shaping (cf. Budd 1984: 29–33), as YHWH speaks to Moses six times (five *wayiqtols*, one *qatal* in the introduction), his speeches providing a natural division of the content:

Toledot of Aaron and his sons (when YHWH spoke with Moses)		1–4
(locale: *Mount Sinai*)		
Aaron's family by names	2–4	
YHWH spoke to Moses (Levites given to Aaron and his sons)		5–10
YHWH spoke to Moses (Levites claimed by YHWH)		11–13
YHWH spoke to Moses (Levites to be counted)		14–39
(locale: *wilderness of Sinai*)		
Compliance report	16	
Levite family by names	17–20	
Levite census, position, chieftain and duties	21–37	
Gershon	21–26	
Kohath	27–32	
Merari	33–37	
Aaron and his sons, position and duty	38	
Levite census total	39	
YHWH said to Moses (firstborn sons to be counted, replaced by Levites)		40–43
Compliance report	42–43	
YHWH spoke to Moses (redemption of firstborn, given to Aaron and his sons)		44–51
Compliance report	49–51	

The material can be divided into two major sections that correspond, verses 1–13 and 14–51. Kellermann regards verses 11–13 and 40–51 as a frame for 14–39 (1970: 32–49), which Budd extends by adding verses 5–10, noting that the substance of verses 5–10 is developed in 14–39 (note e.g. how the phrase 'the stranger who draws near will be put to death' caps both sections), and that of verses 11–13 in 40–51 (1984: 30). There is nearly verbatim language shared by the instructions to count Levites (vv. 14–16) and the count summary (v. 39), secluding that section (see Table 12).

YHWH's giving the Levites to Aaron is explained first, followed by the basis of that gift, that Levites belong to him as substitutes for Israel's

Table 12: Panel outline of Numbers 3

	I. Numbers 3:1–13	II. Numbers 3:14–51
Levites given to Aaron	vv. 5–10	vv. 14–39
Levites claimed by YHWH	vv. 11–13	vv. 40–51
Locale reference	Mount Sinai	Wilderness of Sinai

firstborn sons, especially emphasized after the Passover deliverance. The general movement from narrow to broad may also be observed in the listing of Aaron's sons by 'names' in verses 2–4, and then the wider listing of the sons of Levi by 'names' in verses 17–20 (expanded out in vv. 21–37), and in the movement from the mountain of Sinai (vv. 1–13) to the wilderness of Sinai (14–51), involving a movement both in space and time.

Aaron's *toledot* serves as prologue indicating that this chapter is oriented toward the priesthood, along with the Levites, as one of the book's storylines. The *toledot* distinguishes the roles between Aaron's priestly line and that of the wider tribe of Levi (cf. Galil 1985: 489–490), Levites themselves being given to Aaron and placed under his authority. After the prologue, the chapter begins with Moses giving the Levites to Aaron and his sons (vv. 5, 9), and ends with Moses giving the redemption silver (for lack of Levites) to Aaron and his sons (v. 51). With the wilderness Camp's creation in focus, this section explains the theology of the Levites' encampment near the Tent of Meeting, their relationship to the Tent and priesthood. A parallel structure is noted by Condren in Numbers 8, where 8:1–4 relates Aaron's tending of the lampstand in the holy place and 8:5–22 recounts the cleansing of Levites; in both Numbers 3 and 8, a priestly prologue contrasts the priesthood from the rest of the Levites, reinforcing the hierarchical structure even while focusing on Levites and their duties (2013: 438–439).

Lunn supplies the following outlines for Numbers 3 (2010, 175–81):

A	Aaron and his sons ordained to serve as priests	1–4
B	The tribe of Levi to be presented to Aaron	5–6
C	Duties of the Levites in the Tent of Meeting	7
C'.	Duties of the Levites in the Tent of Meeting	8
B'.	The Levites to be given to Aaron and his sons	9
A'.	Aaron and his sons appointed to the priesthood	10

Here the role of Levites (C/C') is enveloped within their subordination to Aaron, whereby 'presented' is seen to mean 'given' (B/B'), who have ultimate charge (A/A'), a duty underscored by the death reports for encroachers from within the priesthood and Levites, respectively (4, 10).

A. Replacement of the firstborn by the Levites   12ab
B. Declaration that the Levites will be God's   12c
A'. Reason why the firstborn belong to God   13abc
B'. Declaration that the Levites will be God's   13d

The material in Numbers 3:21–37 is an expansion of the genealogy of the sons of Levi in 3:17–20, and may be construed as a threefold panel outline:

Levitical clan and families	A 21	A' 27	A" 33
Total number of males	B 22	B' 28	B" 34
Camp locale	C 23	C' 29	D" 35a
Leader of camp	D 24	D' 30	C" 35b
Duties detailed	E 25–26	E' 31–32	E" 36–37

Note the reversal of D" and C" elements above, which Lunn suggests is likely a rhetorical device marking the unit's closure (2010: 178–179). Two more panel outlines complete the chapter:

A. Command for Moses to count firstborn   40
B. Command to take Levites in place of firstborn and their
    livestock   41
A'. Moses counted firstborn, as commanded   42–43
B'. Command to take Levites in place of firstborn and their
    livestock   44–45

A. Command to collect redemption money for excess
    among firstborn   46–47a
B. Specification: 'according to the shekel of the sanctuary' 47b
C. Command to give redemption money to Aaron and his
    sons   48
A'. Moses collected the redemption for excess among
    firstborn   49
B'. Total weight of silver 'according to the shekel of the
    sanctuary'   50
C'. Moses gave redemption money to Aaron and his sons,
    as commanded   51

Numbers 4 comprises three speeches of YHWH and their fulfilment, the second a warning (vv. 17–20) that supplements the first (vv. 1–16) – both including Aaron with Moses as recipient inasmuch as they underscore priestly accountability in relation to Kohath's house. The material forms a threefold panel, as seen in Table 13.

Several observations may be made about the first column (4:1–33). The length varies greatly in descending order: Kohath at twenty verses,

Table 13: Panel outline of Numbers 4

Levitical house	Count commanded, duties charged	Compliance report and tally result
Kohath	4:1–16 (17–20) →	4:34–37
Gershon	4:21–28 →	4:38–41
Merari	4:29–33 →	4:42–45
	Summary account and tally: 4:46–49	

Gershon at eight verses, Merari at five. Also, the Kohathite section contains two extra elements not present in the others: the warning from YHWH to Moses and Aaron about guarding the Kohathites against the ever-present threat of being cut off (vv. 17–20) and the role of Eleazar the priest, consistently linked to the house of Kohath (v. 16, cf. 3:32). Moreover, the main Kohathite section (vv. 1–16) is lengthy because it describes the preparatory duties of Aaron and his sons regarding the holy vessels of the Tent prerequisite to the work of the Kohath house. Individual elements of each column in the panel are repeated in order (Lunn 2010: 181–183):

4:1–33	Panel element	Kohath	Gershon	Merari
A.	Command to count	1–2	21–22	29
B.	Age specification	3	23	30
C.	Duties	4–15	24–26	31–32
D.	Supervisory role of priests	16–20	27–28	33

4:34–45				
A.	Counting	34	38	42
B.	Age to serve in the Tent of Meeting	35	39	43
C.	Total count of clans	36	40	44
C'.	'These were those counted'	37a	41a	45a
B'.	'All who serve in Tent of Meeting'	37b	41b	–
A'.	Moses and Aaron counted them	37c	41c	45b

Note that the B' element for Merari is absent, perhaps a signal of closure. The final summary in verses 46–48 repeats many of the elements of the second panel, widening the scope fittingly to 'the Levites' and listing the tribe's total tally at 8,580.

A.	Moses, Aaron, leaders counted	46
B.	All men of age to do service and carrying	47
A'.	Total counted at 8,580	48
A".	Counted by Moses as YHWH commanded	49a

B'.   Each man according to his service and carrying   49b
A'''.   Counted as YHWH commanded Moses   49c

Forms of *pāqad* (to appoint, list, count) occur five times in the summary paragraph alone (46 twice, 48, 49 twice), for the process of counting and the actual figure, emphasizing the solemn duties to which the Levitical houses are called.

Comment

3:1–51: Appointing Levites in place of Israel's firstborn to their encampments for the inner camp

1. The phrase 'these are the generations' is utilized widely in Genesis (2:4; 6:9; 10:1; 11:10, 27; 25:12, 19; 36:1, 9; 37:2), to focus the narrative's progress (cf. R. B. Robinson 1986) from broader humanity (Adam to Noah), to the patriarchs and finally to the twelve sons of Jacob, whose families form the twelve tribes of Israel. There are no literary grounds for excluding Numbers 3:1 from the basic *toledot* scheme of the Torah (Tengström 1981: 55–56; cf. Croatto 1998: 49); on the contrary, there is a logical explanation, consistent with its use in Genesis, for why the formula picks up again in Numbers. Since Exodus was primarily about the redemption of the twelve tribes, and Leviticus largely entails cultic regulations for the workings of the Tent of Meeting, there was no need for a narrower focus until now upon Aaron's house within the hierarchy of the tribe of Levi. By use of the *toledot* formula the Pentateuch's narrative builds a highway from Adam (as archetypal priest) to Aaron the high priest (as cultic Adam), accomplished with Numbers 3:1 as 'the seventh and final narrowing of focus in the Pentateuch' (Thomas 2011: 81), and this twelfth occasion of the formula may intentionally correspond to the number of Israel's tribes (cf. Mathews 1996: 1A:47). Although the vav (and) of *wĕ'ēlleh* (and these) functions to set the genealogy as a substructure and subtheme within the community of Israel rather than as a major heading (Thomas 2011: 124–125; DeRouchie 2013: 232–233), the ensuing narrative will indeed demonstrate the vital roles of Aaron and Moses in their respective cultic and civil leadership for the well-being of Israel (cf. Thomas 2011: 98, 102–103; Sweeney 2017: 71–72). With this new beginning, as Sweeney observes (Sweeney 2012: 128; cf. Dozeman 2017: 9), Numbers 3:1–4

focuses on the foundation of the priestly line of Aaron and Moses as the culminating stage of the Torah's account of the history of creation. Aaron is the primary figure in this presentation insofar as his son, Eleazar, will through his own son Phineas (see Num. 25:10–18) become the founder of the line of high priests that will ultimately serve in the Jerusalem Temple (1 Chr. 5:27–41).

The significance of the Camp of Israel is seen in the Pentateuch's reserving of the priestly *toledot* formula until this point. Rather than placing it earlier at the consecration of the priesthood (Lev. 8) or before the Day of Atonement (Lev. 16), the priestly *toledot* is placed in relation to the construction of Israel's Camp. Whereas in Leviticus, the role of priests is given in terms of their necessity for the operation of the cultus, in Numbers their role is set within their true context – within the life of the community of Israel as architecturally embodied in the Camp, for the sake of Israel's well-being and peace with YHWH (cf. Num. 6:22–27; 25). Moreover, whereas Leviticus, with few exceptions, is static or timeless, Numbers will follow the priestly line from Aaron to his son Eleazar to his grandson Phinehas, a progression signalled by Aaron's genealogy (3:1–4). The *toledot* of Numbers 3 thus serves as a heading that 'introduces the high priest's lineage (3:2–4) and the overview of the Levitical duties' (DeRouchie 2013: 223). Within the context of the newly formed covenant community, *Numbers presents Aaron's priesthood in relation to the nation's survival of the wilderness sojourn, a paradigm for their role in the land.*

That Moses' name comes secondarily (3:1) has led some to question the authenticity of its inclusion here. From the perspective of genealogy, however, it is appropriate to list the younger brother after the firstborn, especially in a chapter concerned with the theology of firstborn sons. As Milgrom observes, among the seventy-eight times Moses and Aaron are listed together, Aaron precedes Moses only and consistently in the genealogical texts (see Exod. 6:20; Num. 3:1; 26:59; 1 Chr. 6:3; 23:13) (1990: 15). The text is focused on the priesthood and its relation to Levites. While the omission of Moses' genealogy emphasizes Aaron's house (cf. Galil 1985: 489–490), his name lends further authority to Aaron, as well as to the wider tribe of Levi.

The timeframe 'on the day YHWH spoke with Moses on Mount Sinai' may function to push back the genealogical details before the death of two of Aaron's sons, explained in verse 4. Day and locale contextualize the speech of verses 5–13, with its setting aside of the Levites, within the day of that tribe's blessing by YHWH. After the sin with the golden calf (Exod. 32), Levites had demonstrated themselves to be zealous for YHWH's honour, carrying out Moses' command to slay all idolaters, even one's own kin, and were subsequently directed by Moses to consecrate themselves to receive a blessing 'this day' from YHWH (32:27–29). Levitical service, though subservient to the priesthood, is seen in terms of divine reward and honour. What was designated at Mount Sinai (vv. 5–13) is worked out and put in place in the wilderness of Sinai (vv. 14–51). 'Mount Sinai' and 'wilderness of Sinai' relate to time as much as to locale: before and after the construction and consecration of YHWH's Dwelling.

The separation between the outer camp (chs. 1–2) and the inner camp (chs. 3–4) is demonstrated by the sharp break between these two sections, the priestly genealogy that precedes the separate census for Levites.

2–4. Repetition of 'these are the names of the sons of Aaron' in verses 2–3 brings their names in parallel with their installation as priests. Their anointing with oil and blood is described in Exodus 29:21 and Leviticus 8:30. The phrase 'who were ordained' reads literally 'whose hands were filled' (*'ăšer-millē' yādām*), likely reflecting some aspect of the ordination ritual (see also Exod. 28:41; Judg. 17:5, 12; 1 Kgs 13:33) rather than the priest's inaugural reception of compensation. Recounting the deaths of Nadab and Abihu (Lev. 10:1–3), serves two purposes. First, it makes way for the role of Eleazar and Ithamar throughout the book, as the closing line of verse 4 suggests. Verses 1–4 relate to the rest of the chapter by clarifying the priesthood's authority over the other Levites even while explaining the Levites' role (Eleazar e.g. is given oversight of Kohathites, v. 32). Second, their deaths echo throughout Numbers as a paradigmatic threat for the inner camp (chs. 16–17; cf. 26:60–61). The point is crucial, unfolding the logic of the book's narrative flow: the chapters on the construction of the outer (chs. 1–2) and inner camps (chs. 3–4) provide the theological foundation for assessing their respective failures in chapters 11–15 and 16–18. The key to the inner camp's failure is both dissected and foreshadowed here in the demise of Nadab and Abihu (v. 4).

Precise understanding of Nadab and Abihu's sin, along with what 'strange fire' means, has proven elusive, generating a variety of theories (see Milgrom 1991: 633–635; Bibb 2001). Given the ensuing order to abstain from intoxicating drink (Lev. 10:8–11), it could be the brothers were drunk and had, consequently, used fire (coal) that had not been taken from the altar of whole burnt offering that had been kindled by YHWH directly (cf. Haran 1985: 232). Intertextually (Lev. 10:1–3 and 16:1–2), it is likely that Aaron's sons had attempted to penetrate into YHWH's Presence within the holy of holies (see Morales 2015: 146–151; also Gradwohl 1963), an act echoed in Korah's rebellion. The surest expression of fearlessness of YHWH is disregard for his commands, even as the surest expression of fearing him is diligent obedience (Gen. 22:12; Jas 2:20–24). Just so, at issue with Nadab and Abihu's presumption is that what(ever) they did was that which YHWH 'had not commanded them' (Lev. 10:1), a phrase underscored by its contrast to the repeated compliance reports leading up to the incident ('as YHWH commanded', Lev. 8:4, 9, 13, 17, 21, 29, 36; 9:7, 10). The need to follow YHWH closely is not incidental, but at the core of Numbers' message (Num. 9:15–23; cf. Exod. 40:36–38).

The remark that Eleazar and Ithamar served 'in the presence' of Aaron their father, draws out the latter's high priestly authority over them in the hierarchical structure, and foreshadows Aaron's death (Num. 20:22–29), after which his grandson Phinehas will serve before the presence of Eleazar the high priest (Num. 25:7–13; 31:6). The opening genealogy signals the developing lineage of Aaron's house as an integral feature of the book's message: the narrative will follow the priestly line as it succeeds from Aaron to Eleazar, and then, by divine declaration, from Eleazar to Phinehas (cf. Frevel 2013b: 145).

5–13. The stratification within the tribe of Levi is a major contribution of Numbers, as its place and function in relation to the priesthood on the one hand and to the twelve tribes on the other is introduced and developed (cf. Levine 1993: 65). While in 1:51 Levites are to guard against the 'stranger' – any Israelite – from approaching God's sacred abode, in 3:10 the 'stranger' includes Levites themselves, as Aaron's priesthood is charged with guarding their sphere of access to YHWH's Dwelling. The stratification is embodied: within the levels of sacred access, Levites are positioned between all Israel and the priesthood.

These verses begin to realize YHWH's previous injunction to Moses concerning the Levites in 1:48–53. Verses 5–10 begin with the result: Levites are to be given *entirely* (*nĕtunim nĕtunîm*) to Aaron's house as manual labourers and helpers. The nature of their service in relation to the Tent will be elaborated according to each Levitical house in verses 21–37. In relation to Israel's participation, Levites are likely to assist them with their offering of sacrifices, even while guarding against their encroachment of sancta. The duty of Levites is twofold, as described in verse 7 (Milgrom 1970a): (1) *guard duty* ('keep his charge', *šāmĕrû 'et-mišmartô*) with *mišmeret* having primary reference to guarding the Tent of Meeting from encroachment, as emphasized in Numbers 3; and (2) *physical labour* ('serving in the service', *la'ăbōd 'et-'ăbōdat*) with *'ăbōdāh* having primary reference to the dismantling, transporting and setting up of the Dwelling, the emphasis in Numbers 4. Their duties relate to the two aspects of the Camp's wilderness sojourn: encamped (Num. 3), on journey (Num. 4). 'Service' (*'ăbōdāh*), then, as Milgrom clarifies (1970a: 132), is not to be construed as *the* 'cultic' service, led only by priests and forbidden to Levites on pain of death (Num. 18:3) – Levites do not assist priests with their officiating of rites. While verse 7 describes the Levites' role while encamped, verse 8 refers to their role in transit, since during the march they are especially tasked with guarding the holy vessels (3:25, 31, 36; Milgrom 1970a: 149). The phrase 'all the labour relating to it (the Dwelling)' (*lĕkōl 'ăbōdātô*) recurs for each of the Levitical clans (vv. 26, 31, 36), although the actual form of the labour will be specified in chapter 4: Kohathites will transport, but not remove or replace the sacred vessels (since that is done by priests alone), while Gershonites and Merarites will dismantle and reassemble their respective parts of the Dwelling and be in charge of transport, utilizing ox carts.

In verses 11–13, the logic of the transaction is explained: Israel's firstborn were claimed by YHWH, set apart to himself, when he had spared them his judgement on Egypt. Although firstborn sons were redeemed by the blood of Passover lambs, this redemption was *by* and thus *unto YHWH* – their lives were to be given entirely to the service of YHWH. Firstborn theology, implicit in the Passover, suggests that firstborn sons had long functioned in a special priestly capacity. Phrases referring to the consecration of firstborn, such as, 'given to YHWH', 'he is YHWH's', 'sanctify to YHWH', express the demand for 'transferring the firstborn to the divine realm . . . to be servants of the cult', writes Brin (1994: 230–231), adding that the consecration of Levites in place of the firstborn implies that, originally, firstborn sons served as priests. As belonging to YHWH in place of the firstborn, Levites are a gift to Aaron and his sons *particularly from YHWH*, though on behalf of Israel. In the Torah's wider context, this life of service at the precincts of YHWH's own Dwelling comes as a reward for the Levites' zeal for him, displayed after the golden calf incident (see Exod. 32:25–29; cf. Hooke 1952: 11–12). Levites thereby represent an ideal for all Israel to follow. The language of verses 11–13 is emphatic regarding YHWH's claim of Levites as 'mine' – the divine speech begins with 'I' (*wa'ănî*, v. 12) and ends with 'I am YHWH' (*'ănî yhwh*, v. 13), a phrase that serves as a divine punctuation (cf. v. 41).

Mention of 'beast' (*běhēmāh*) in verse 13 may recall Exodus 13:12–13, and is not meant to overturn the legislation to sacrifice, destroy or redeem these firstborn male animals (cf. Budd 1984: 32).

14–16. 'And YHWH spoke to Moses in the wilderness of Sinai' repeats verbatim the book's opening (1:1), manifesting a symmetry between the census and arrangement of the twelve tribes (Num. 1 – 2) and that of the Levites (Num. 3 – 4). The need for a separate census for Levites underscores their unique role within Israel's Camp and society. Use of *pĕqōd* (appoint) further relates the count of Levites to that of the twelve tribes (1:3), but also, within the context of its use in verse 10, brings the term into the range of 'appoint' rather than 'count' more clearly. As with the other tribes, Levites are not just counted, but divinely appointed within the Camp. Levites substitute for Israel's firstborn sons, and may therefore be appointed to this status as of a month old. Accordingly, on behalf of Israel's firstborn, Levites serve the priesthood at YHWH's Dwelling, for which they must be between 30 and 50 years of age (4:3). The month requirement for proper Levitical substitution, aside from indicating the infant's survival, coincides with the consecration of the Tabernacle (7:1; cf. 1:1), linking God's Tent and its attendants closely.

17–20. Similar genealogical information is offered in Exodus 6:16–19. Noth suggests identifying Gershon with Moses' son (1968: 35–36; cf. Exod. 2:22; Vg and LXX on Judg. 18:30); Moses, however, might have named his son after an ancestor. The Levitical houses surface again in Chronicles and Ezra/Nehemiah, reviewed by Budd (1984: 35):

> Among the Gershonite functions were music making (the Asaphites belonged to them – 1 Chr. 6:39, 43), and administration of the temple treasuries (1 Chr. 23:7–9; 26:21). Some Kohathites were responsible for the showbread (1 Chr. 9:32). Merarites are depicted as accompanying Ezra on his journey in order to be Temple ministers (Ezra 8:18–19).

Levi's genealogy through Kohath can be mapped as in Figure 5, highlighting priestly succession in Numbers.

This genealogy reveals two relevant points: (1) Korah is first cousins with Aaron and Moses, and (2) Korah had hereditary preference over Elizaphan (son of Uzziel), who was put in charge of the Kohathite house in 3:30. Perhaps this perceived slight contributed to his rebellion (Num. 16), further strengthening the link between Numbers 3 – 4 and 16 – 18. Korah's encampment, moreover, was south of the Dwelling (v. 29), along with the tribe of Reuben, which joins him in rebellion (16:1).

21–26. The Gershonite house is noted first, according to the genealogical order of verse 17, indicating that Gershon was Levi's firstborn son. However, as occurs frequently in the biblical record, another son rises to prominence over the eldest brother – this appears to be the case here inasmuch as Kohath's line supersedes Gershon's in prominence. Both the covenant mediator, Moses, and the priesthood of Aaron's

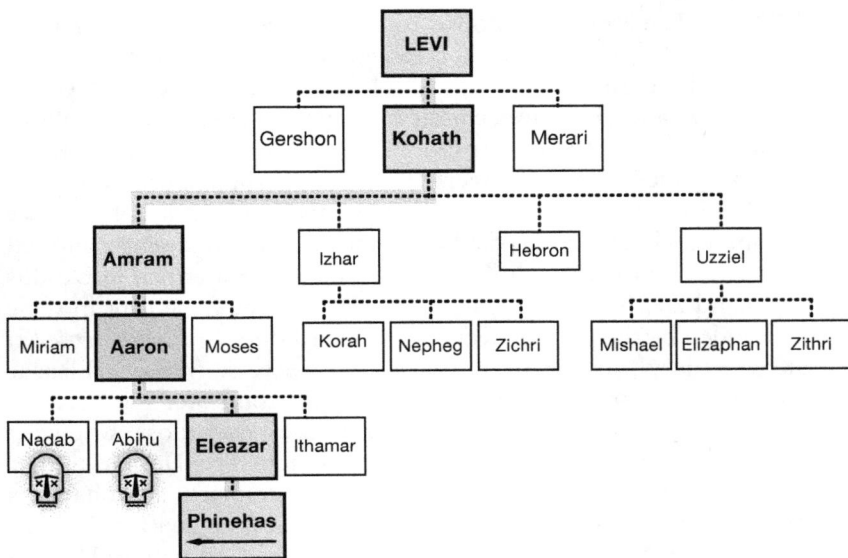

Figure 5: Levi's genealogy

house derive from Kohath. Moreover, Kohath's house is given the noblest duty, having charge over the sacred vessels of the Tent and given the favoured encampments: Aaron and his family, as the priesthood, encamp at the Dwelling's entrance in the east, and the rest of the Kohath house encamp in the south. As reoriented by the central Tent of Meeting, the house of Kohath will be listed first in Numbers 4 – the movement of chapter 3 to 4, from genealogical to sacred order, parallels the transition for the twelve tribes from chapter 1 to 2. Despite variety of role and placement, the whole tribe of Levi is portrayed with dignity, honoured among the tribes of Israel. None of their tasks are menial – rather, their charges are vital for the life of Israel and bring them nearer to YHWH and his Dwelling (cf. Num. 16:8–10).

Details for each Levitical house are delineated according to a set pattern: (1) The Gershon house comprises the Libnite and Shimeite clans, (2) is tallied at 7,500, (3) will encamp 'behind' the Dwelling, westward, (4) have Eliasaph son of Lael as its chieftain, and (5) is given charge over the guarding and physical labour – dismantling, reassembly and transport (on ox carts) – related to the hangings and screens of the Tent and courtyard, along with their cords, which are described in Exodus 26:1–14. The hangings do not include the veil, which is assigned to the Kohathites, after priests have used it to cover the ark (4:5). That the Levitical houses are aligned with reference to the Dwelling is significant, defining their role in accord with their placement in the Camp. The description here, 'behind' the Dwelling (in the west), affirms the theological and spatial priority of the Tent's *eastward* entrance.

27–32. (1) The Kohathite house comprises the Amramite, Izharite, Hebronite and Uzzielite clans, (2) is tallied at 8,600, (3) will encamp 'by the side' of the Dwelling, southward, (4) have Elizaphan son of Uzziel as its chieftain, and (5) is given charge over guarding and physical labour – in their case, restricted to transport – related to the sacred vessels of the sanctuary, including the 'screen' (*hammāsāk*), the veil separating the holy of holies from the holy place (see *pārōket hammāsāk*, 4:5), since the Gershonites have charge of all other curtains and hangings. The veil is of a piece with the other holy objects, which are described in Exodus 25:10–40 and 26:31–35. Two features stand out. The B element in verse 28 is extended by the phrase 'keeping the guard duty (*šōměrê mišmeret*) of the sanctuary', and the paragraph ends in verse 32 with Eleazar son of Aaron the priest being appointed as chieftain over the Levitical chiefs of the Gershon, Kohath and Merari houses, over those 'who keep the guard duty (*šōměrê mišmeret*) of the sanctuary'. Double use of 'sanctuary' (*haqqōdeš*), literally 'the holy', is appropriate as Kohathites will transport especially sacred vessels, normally residing within the Tent and out of Israel's gaze – including the Ark of the Covenant, YHWH's earthly throne.

The same point also accounts for the detail that Levites are under the authority of the Aaronic priesthood, specifically under the charge of Eleazar, for it is the priesthood alone that has been set apart and consecrated to look upon and serve with the holy vessels of YHWH's Dwelling. Both in 3:32 and 4:16, mention of Eleazar the priest is linked specifically to the work of the Kohathites, underscoring the severer gravity and risk of the Kohathites' duty (cf. De Regt 2008: 419; Camp 2009: 204). With Aaron focused on his high priestly duties, and with the death of the older brothers Nadab and Abihu (Lev. 10:1–3), this supervisory role – as chieftain over the Levite leaders and guardian over the sanctuary – falls to Eleazar. Once Eleazar becomes high priest in place of his father Aaron (Num. 20:22–29), then Phinehas, Eleazar's son, will become chief guardian, a role that explains his presence and action in Numbers 25.

33–37. (1) The Merari house comprises the Mahlite and Mushite clans, (2) is tallied at 6,200, (3) has Zuriel son of Abihail as its chieftain, (4) will encamp 'by the side' of the Dwelling, northward, and (5) is given charge over guarding and the physical labour – dismantling and reassembling, and transporting (in ox carts) – related to the structural aspects of the sanctuary and courtyard, its frames, bases and pillars, which are described in Exodus 26:15–37 and 27:9–19.

38–39. Moses and Aaron, along with his priestly sons, encamp at the pre-eminent position of the Dwelling's entrance, eastward 'toward the sunrise' (cf. Judah's position in 2:3), the priestly encampment forming the gateway between the inner camp of Levites and the central camp of the *Shekhinah*. This locale involves the greatest danger but is for the sake of Israel: Moses requires access to YHWH's revelation so as to shepherd the tribes on their journey; Aaron and his sons open communication between Israel and God through the cult. Moreover, their guarding of sacred space – putting to death the 'stranger' who approaches – serves to protect the whole Camp from divine wrath and plague. Priests, like Levites, have 'guard duty', but, unlike the latter, are not charged with the physical labour (*'ăbōdāh*) of dismantling, transporting or setting up the Dwelling (cf. Milgrom 1970a: 134) – only the covering of sacred vessels (4:5–15). The Camp's physical composition is theological: access to the Creator is through his mediator, Moses, who communicates YHWH's *torah*, and his appointed high priest, Aaron, who makes atonement for Israel. The Camp's structure forms a message with central relevance for the narratives related to the outer and inner tribes: the twelve tribes fail with regard to Moses' prophetic word (chs. 11–15) whereas Levites fail with regard to Aaron's high priestly prerogatives (chs. 16–18).

The tally for Levite males a month old and upward is given at 22,000. Problematically, the sum of the previous three tallies is 22,300. The Midrash and Talmud explain this discrepancy in that Levites had to exclude their own firstborn sons from the count, which led to deducting

300 from the tribe's total (*Num. Rab.* 3.14; *Bek.* 5a; Hertz 1988: 577). Others suggest the possibility of a transmission error: the Kohathite sum of 8,600 may originally have been 8,300, *šlš* instead of *šš* in Hebrew (cf. Greenstone 1948: 30).

40–43. After the count of Levite males, YHWH commands a tally of firstborn sons among the other tribes of Israel. Verse 40 presents the book's first of twenty-four uses of *wayyō'mer* (and he said) for YHWH's speech, versus *wayĕdabbēr* (and he spoke). Generally (and with exceptions), *'-m-r* is used when YHWH speaks to momentary concerns, and *d-b-r* for binding law or concerns of lasting significance. The order of these counts is significant, emphasizing the status and role of Levites. YHWH sovereignly elected Levites to replace the firstborn as belonging to him in the service of his Dwelling. Since inclusion of 'the cattle' cannot be understood as annulling Israel's need to sacrifice or redeem firstborn animals (Exod. 13:11–12; Num. 18:15–17), Dillmann's suggestion, that the replacement by Levite animals is limited to unclean cattle, is reasonable (1886: 19–21). There is a strong note of substitution, Levites being claimed by YHWH 'in place of' (*taḥat*) all the firstborn among the sons of Israel.

44–51. While providing an etiology for the redemption price of firstborn sons, which would become regular practice, still observed in Judaism, the focus remains on the substitution of Israel's firstborn sons by Levites. YHWH's command (v. 41) is repeated (vv. 44–45, note the movement of 'I am YHWH'), so that the following redemption price would not be severed from the theology of Levitical substitution. Thus, verse 45 is the controlling thought: every generation of Israel is redeemed by the institution of Levites who belong to YHWH, the Sovereign One.

'Redemption' (*pādāh*) occurs five times (once as a participle) in this paragraph; the root is attested in Akkadian as *padū/pedū*, 'spare, release' (Cazelles, *TDOT* 11:483). As Harrison observes, *pādāh* is the most general of the three Hebrew terms for redemption, the other two being *gā'al* (typically in familial contexts, such as the 'kinsman redeemer') and *kāpar* (ransom price to redeem forfeited life; cf. Num. 35:31–32), and is used only of persons or other living beings (1990: 76; cf. Sklar 2005: 61–67; Dentan, *IDB* 4:21–22). The Passover ceremony links YHWH's exodus deliverance to the 'redemption' (*pādāh*) of Israel's firstborn sons (Exod. 13:14–15). *Pādāh* is used in other contexts of bondage (Exod. 21:8; Lev. 19:20) as well as where the redemption is from death, substituted by another life or other form of payment (Exod. 13:13, 15; 21:30; 34:20; Lev. 27:29), its basic meaning expressed as 'deliverance by payment of price' (cf. Morris 1965: 18–27). The cost of redemption is more narrowly understood as 'ransom'. The exodus deliverance is portrayed with a variety of redemption terms: as YHWH, Kinsman of Israel, redeemed (*gā'al*) his people from Egyptian bondage and their firstborn from death (Exod. 6:6; 15:13), and the same event is declared with *pādāh* (Deut. 7:8;

2 Sam. 7:23; Mic. 6:4). Morris determines that the requisite substitute in lieu of the forfeited life is basic to redemption as *pādāh*, a point relevant for the office of Levites, and suggests that, since there are no familial responsibilities (as with *gā'al*), *pādāh* redemption implies an element of grace (1965: 23).

That such redemption brings one under possession of the redeemer should also be underscored. David, for example, declares YHWH God had redeemed Israel out of bondage 'for yourself' (*lĕkā*) (2 Sam. 7:23). Israel's covenant loyalty, consequently, flows from YHWH's deliverance (Deut. 7:6–12; cf. Exod. 20:2). In the case of Israel's firstborn sons, their forfeit lives were now owed to YHWH utterly, consecrated to service at his Dwelling – it is this obligation Levites take up as substitutes for Israel's firstborn. YHWH's ownership forms the bedrock consideration: any firstborn among clean animals (i.e. suitable for sacrifice) must be offered up; any firstborn among unclean animals (i.e. not suitable for the altar) must be ransomed by sacrificial animals offered in their stead; firstborn sons must be ransomed by Levites – life for life. The five shekels serve as a token for Levitical substitution. Levites are the redemption price or ransom of the firstborn; they belong to YHWH. Use of 'redemption' in relation to the outstanding 273 firstborn sons and their required payment of shekels thus offers a retrospective explanation of the Levites' function.

The count of Israel's firstborn sons comes to 22,273, received as problematic due to its being drastically low by comparison to the total tally of Israelites in the wilderness. One possible explanation is that the figure represents only those firstborn males born after Passover, since the other firstborn sons had already been redeemed by the shed blood of substitute lambs, or simply that the law had no retrospective force (cf. Keil and Delitzsch 1973: 3:9–12). Alternatively, the count may include only firstborn males not yet inducted into participation in the community, under the age of 20 (excluding adult males, fathers and grandfathers). Support for either approach could be found in the redemption laws of Leviticus 27:1–8, where the valuation of a male from a month old up to five years is five shekels of silver (v. 6; also Num. 18:16), a shekel probably weighing just under 4 ounces. Because five shekels equals twenty pieces (gerahs) of silver (Exod. 30:13; Lev. 27:25; Num. 3:47; Ezek. 45:12), rabbinic tradition links this redemption to the sale of Joseph by Judah and his brothers (Gen. 37:28) – a notion not so far-fetched since Numbers 3 has the redemption out of Egypt in its purview, and Joseph's sale into bondage led to Israel's stay in Egypt.

The chapter closes as it began: Levites are given to Aaron's priestly house (vv. 6, 9) and any shortage of Levites is now countered by Israel's giving silver to Aaron and his sons (vv. 48, 51). Aaron's priesthood alone is holy, although Levites are cleansed and dedicated – set apart from the rest of Israel (Num. 8:5–26) – to belong to YHWH, serving at his

Tent under the authority of the priesthood. YHWH's institution of Levites in place of Israel's firstborn sons was no small or inconsequential change, but revolutionary, upsetting long-held traditions and expectations. In part, Numbers' storyline unfolds the drama of challenging the Sinai covenant's reorganization of Israelite society, rebelling against the structure of Israel's Camp, and how the nation ultimately submitted to YHWH's wisdom and work.

4:1–29: Appointing the Levitical transport labours of the inner camp

Numbers 4 offers instructions for the Levite houses regarding their labours in transporting the divine Dwelling. There is a descending priority, a hierarchy, evident in the substance and phraseology of each section (De Regt 2008). Whereas Gershon, the eldest son of Levi (3:17), is listed first in Numbers 3, here Kohath is listed first and linked to Eleazar (4:16; cf. 3:32). The hierarchy flows from Aaron the high priest, himself from the house of Kohath through Amram (see 3:19, 27), and is manifested in the duties assigned to each of the three Levite houses that clearly follow the cult's graded system of holiness: Kohathites carry the holy furnishings, while Gershonites cart the curtains, not including the veil (see 4:5), and Merarites cart the support frames and pillars. The hierarchy is evident in their encampments as well: Aaron's priesthood at the entrance of YHWH's Dwelling in the east, Kohathites at the next place of honour on the south side, followed by Gershonites in the west and Merarites in the north.

1–3. These instructions have many phrases in common with 1:2–4. Since Kohathites will transport sacred vessels for which they have not been sanctified, the priests need to be especially vigilant in their supervision: 4:5–14 focuses on the work of Aaron and his sons. For the phrase 'lift up the head' (*nāśō' 'et-rō'š*), see comments on 1:1. Use of *kol-bā' laṣṣābā'* (all who come to the host) for Levitical work primarily concerns their duties connected to the Tent of Meeting (cf. 4:23, 30, 35, 39, 43; 8:24–25; *haṣṣōb'ôt . . . ṣob'û* (the hosts who served) is used for women's service for the Tent of Meeting, Exod. 38:8; 1 Sam. 2:22). With the military connotations in chapter 1, the stock formula is *yoṣe + ṣaba* ('go forth in the host', whereas for Levitical service, the formula is *ba + ṣaba* (come to the host) (see Shamah 2011: 689). The phrase 'to do the work (*mĕlā'kāh*) of the Tent of Meeting' occurs only for the description of duties for the sons of Kohath (vs *'ăbōdâ*, 'labour', for Gershon and Merari, vv. 23, 30), an indication that the tasks of the other two houses 'is less central' and 'more subordinate' (De Regt 2008: 420).

The age for service at the Tent of Meeting is given seven times as upwards from 30 years old to 50 (vv. 3, 23, 30, 35, 39, 43, 47). In 8:23–25, however, YHWH tells Moses that 25 to 50 years is acceptable. Rabbinic interpreters suggest a five-year apprenticeship (from age 25 to 30), a reasonable explanation (*Hul.* 24a), though some, like Rashbam (ben Meir 2001: 182–183), distinguish between the duties of guarding the Tent (ages 25–30, over 50) and that of lifting and transporting (ages 30 to 50). In 1 Chronicles 23:24–27, Levitical service is stipulated by David as 20 years old and upward (also Ezra 3:8; 2 Chr. 31:17), while earlier in that chapter the age is 30 years old and above (23:3). Since the status of a Levite, as substitute for Israel's firstborn sons, began virtually at birth (one month old), the matter of when a Levite may serve at the Tent and later Temple is treated more practically, according to the nature of the work and time period. Once the Temple was founded in Zion, heavy lifting and transport were no longer concerns, and the age for service could be lowered.

4. The service of the Kohath house opens with a significant description: it involves that which is 'in the Tent of Meeting, the holy of holies' (*bě'ōhel mô'ēd qōdeš haqqŏdāšîm*) – everything that follows, from the covering of the sacred vessels by Aaron and his sons (vv. 5–15) to the sober warning with which the section ends (vv. 17–20), flows from this point, as does the inner camp's narrative conflict in Numbers 16 – 17. The threat of YHWH God's holiness underlies the composition and 'chemistry' of the Camp: while Levites serve as a buffer between YHWH's Tent and the tribes of Israel, yet this role and placement in no wise presumes that Levites themselves are somehow immune to the threat of YHWH's consuming fire. The priesthood itself is not excluded from the need for caution and reverent care in their strictly regulated approach to YHWH on Israel's behalf, as evident in the reminder of Nadab and Abihu's fiery destruction (3:1–4). The twofold duty of Levites is (1) 'keeping the charge', with *mišmeret* having primary reference to guarding the Tent of Meeting from encroachment, the emphasis in Numbers 3, and (2) 'the labour' with *'ăbōdāh* having primary reference to transporting (along with dismantling and setting up) the Dwelling, the emphasis in Numbers 4. 'Labour' recurs in verses 4, 24, 28, 31, 33.

5–15. Verse 4 ends with 'the holy of holies', and verse 5 begins with the entrance of Aaron. The phrase 'when the Camp journeys out' signals the main interest of this chapter on Levitical duties of *transport* during the journey – whereas Numbers 3 focused on the Levitical role of substitutes for Israel's firstborn sons and their encampment locales. Transporting the Dwelling begins with Aaron and his sons, who remove the veil that separates the holy of holies from the holy place, the separation upon which the Dwelling and its cult stand. Akin to God's separation of light from darkness (Gen. 1:4), the cosmos of the Camp derives from the central separation of the holy of holies. With the veil's removal, the rest of the dismantling may proceed. The ark, YHWH's throne and footstool, is immediately covered by the veil, so that even in transport the veil retains its function of veiling YHWH's presence from human gaze. Further coverings of fine goatskin and a 'pure' (*kĕlîl*, as in 'entirely) blue garment cover the ark, and the poles with which it will be carried are 'set up'. While some assume this detail to be a contradiction of Exodus 25:15 (cf. 1 Kgs 8:7–8; 2 Chr. 5:8–9), positing different P strata for each passage (G. B. Gray 1903: 2–3, 34–35; Noth 1968: 41–42), Eichler (2016), noting similar portable chests in the ANE (e.g. the red chest in the tomb of Tutankhamun), shows that the ark was likely fitted with attached poles which would be extended through rings for carrying, a function adequately described by the phrase 'set up its poles' (and broad enough to encompass poles for other furnishings). The blue garment may reflect God's heavenly abode as Creator and his royal status as Israel's Sovereign – and the same for crimson and purple (on the latter, cf. Judg. 8:26). For the other sacred furnishings, the coloured garment (blue, crimson or purple) comes first, followed by the fine goatskin. Perhaps the ark alone is viewed in blue since it is not simply being stored away for transport, but will still function on the journey, going before Israel when they set out from Sinai (see 10:33, 35). The table of the Presence (*šulḥan happānîm*) is distinguished from its vessels (plates, ladles, bowls, flagons and bread), the former alone covered by a blue garment, while the vessels placed atop it are covered in crimson scarlet, before 'it', *'ōtô* (the table), is then covered (along with the vessels on it) with fine goatskin, and its poles are set in place.

In total, the priests prepare six bundles for transport by Kohathites: (1) the ark, (2) the table and its accompanying vessels, (3) the lampstand and its accompanying vessels, (4) the incense altar, (5) the vessels of ministry, and (6) the outer altar and its accompanying vessels. The laver is not mentioned, possibly omitted through scribal error, or perhaps it is included either under 'vessels of ministry' or with the outer altar (since priests would wash before entering the Tent or approaching the altar, Exod. 30:20); although the laver is given its unique and independent value elsewhere (Exod. 30:17–21; 38:8). Since inclusion of the laver would bring the number of bundles to seven, regularly used in cultic matters, and since there is no certain way to account for its absence, a scribal omission seems probable so that one should envisage seven bundles of sacred furnishings and vessels carried by the house of Kohath. The dominant metal and garment colours within the Tent are gold and blue, while outside are bronze (Exod. 27:1–7; 30:18) and purple, allowing for degrees of variation within an overall context of holiness. The lampstand and vessels of ministry are placed on a carrying frame; the other furnishings are carried with poles. As these objects are especially holy, they must be carried by human beings, image-bearers of God – the Levites reflect a renewed humanity.

These details convey God's holiness, requiring further layers of distance from Israel, even as the Camp and cultus comprise bands of holiness. Verse 15 further underscores the holiness of the objects, by reference to Aaron, and threefold use of 'the holy' (*haqqōdeš*), translated here 'sanctuary' (though not the usual *miqdāš*). Kohathites are not to begin their charge until after the priests have finished their task completely, lest they touch 'the holy' and die. This death threat is stated no fewer than three times (vv. 15, 19, 20) exclusively with regard to Kohathites, the last warning heightening the situation to their looking – even 'for a moment' – at 'the holy'. Their work is summarized as *maśśā'* (a nominal form of *nāśā'*, 'to carry'), essentially a transport duty; the same holds true for the houses of Gershon and Merari.

16. Aside from Eleazar's general responsibility and oversight of Levitical transport, he is personally to convey the lampstand's oil, the fragrant incense, the daily tribute offering, and the anointing oil. As these are not implements or 'vessels', perhaps the nature of these items (liquid, powder and grain) made bundling them with the furnishing both impractical and inappropriate for Levitical handling, reiterating the need for priestly hierarchy among Levi's tribe, due to God's holiness.

17–20. Just as Levites serve to safeguard the lives of the tribes from God's threatening presence, so, too, the priests are charged to safeguard the lives of Levites, and of the Kohathites in particular. The penalty of being 'cut off' (*kārat*) refers to a severe form of excommunication, by way of premature death – note the synonymous parallelism in verses 18 and 19 between 'do not cut off' and 'that they may live and not die' (cf. Exod. 31:14). The *kareth* (*kārat*) penalty seems also to involve the extirpation of one's lineage (see 1 Sam. 24:21; Ruth 4:10), either at the hands of YHWH directly or through judicial execution by the covenant community (cf. Sklar 2005: 15–20; cf. Wold 1978; Frymer-Kensky 1983: 404–405). The root *kārat* occurs ten times in Numbers, seven times with reference to the threat of being cut off from the covenant community, 'from among his people' (9:13; 15:30, 31 [twice]) or 'from Israel' (19:13) or 'from among the assembly' (19:20), and, in this case, refers to the Kohathite family branch being cut off 'from among the Levites' (4:18; cf. 11:33; 13:23, 24). Verse 18 thus functions as a grim foreshadowing of the inner camp's central narrative (Num. 16 – 17), even while demonstrating the nearly inconceivable danger of the Kohathite service – the possibility of their extinction is voiced by YHWH. The intensity of danger in turn places a weight of responsibility on the priests, who must ensure that the house of Kohath does not even get a momentary glimpse of the sacred objects in the Dwelling, lest they die. The *kareth* penalty functions as the antithesis to the two census accounts that stand as pillars in the narrative (chs. 1–2; 26): while the highest blessing is to be counted among the covenant community of YHWH, the most dreadful threat is to be cut off from his Camp.

21–28, 29–33. Gershon's head is now 'lifted up' (*nāśō'*) in a tally of all who 'come to wage in the host' (v. 23, *habbā' liṣbō' ṣābā'*). For

Merari 'lift up' is not used, though arguably implied, and his house is said to 'come to the host' (v. 30, *habbā' laṣṣābā'*) as well. The charges of Gershon and Merari are repeated from the previous chapter, with the new element being their duty of transport, using *maśśā'*. While Kohathites are under Eleazar's special supervision, Ithamar oversees the work of Gershon and Merari. Priestly hierarchy within the tribe of Levi is maintained also in the phrases 'by the mouth of Aaron and his sons' (v. 27) and 'by name you will appoint' (v. 32).

34–48. The individual summaries (v. 34) and the total sum of Levites (v. 46) include 'the chieftains of Israel / the community' in line with Numbers' focus on tribal leaders and may also reflect the Levites' role, serving in place of the tribes' firstborn sons. Hierarchy is balanced by communal representation in all major occasions. Kohath is honoured in terms of order, though the Merarites have the largest count (fittingly, for their heavier labour): 2,750 Kohathites, 2,630 Gershonites and 3,200 Merarites, for a sum total of 8,580 Levites appointed to transport duties. The collated summary of Levitical labours is substantial in its description, with repeated use of 'service, labour': *la'ăbōd 'ăbōdat 'ăbōdâ wa'ăbōdat maśśā'*, translated by context as 'to do the work of packing-labour, and the labour of carrying-duty' (cf. Milgrom 1970a: 151).

49. This verse uses an inclusion, beginning (note use of 'mouth' and 'hand) and ending with YHWH's command through Moses' mediation, underscoring that these various duties – down to 'each man' – is by divine ordination. Down to the minutiae, the Camp of Israel is a manifestation of God's will and design, both its composition when encamped and the order and machinations of its movement.

Explanation

Having arranged the twelve tribes into large outer encampments (chs. 1–2), YHWH constructs the inner encampments of Levites and priests (chs. 3–4). Since the Dwelling, along with the Levites and Aaron's priesthood, was already noted as forming the Camp's centre (1:50–53; 2:17), what remained to explain was the institution of Levites as replacing Israel's firstborn sons and then the hierarchical relationship between Levites and Aaron's priesthood. The encampment of the Levites (and priesthood) is described, not only by reference to cardinal points, but especially in relation to the Dwelling (3:23, 29, 35, 38), a feature underscoring their role of guarding and transporting YHWH's Dwelling. In Numbers 2:2, the encampment of twelve tribes was described as 'at a distance' around YHWH's Tent, leaving an area now filled by the Levite encampments. The narrative flow is instructive: placing the tribes at a distance around YHWH's Dwelling first, the Levitical inner camp between them, underscores the Levites' role in maintaining that distance – safeguarding YHWH's Dwelling from defilement, and protecting the tribes from the central threat of God's holiness. The principal space of the Levitical inner camp is that of Moses and Aaron and his sons, described with parallel lines: 'before (*lipnê*) the Dwelling eastward / before (*lipnê*) the Tent of Meeting sunrise-ward', a weighty and exclusive privilege under-scored by threat of execution for encroachers (3:38). As Numbers 3 and 4 tell of the encampment and journeying of Levites, respectively, these chapters convey their two duties: guarding the Dwelling while encamped (Num. 3) and transporting it on journeys (Num. 4).

The genealogy of the Aaronic priesthood signals priestly succession as a major subtheme: Aaron's death and replacement as high priest by Eleazar his son (20:22–29) along with reception of the covenant of priesthood by Phinehas his grandson (25:10–13) are key moments in a book that underscores Israel's need for atonement by YHWH's chosen priesthood (chs. 16–17; 25:13). Within this context, the role of Levites is set forth as YHWH's gift to the priesthood, framed by the giving of Levites (3:5–9) and the redemption money (3:44–51) to Aaron and his sons. Israel is being constructed as YHWH's priestly theocracy, and the testing of (and coming to terms with) new institutions and hierarchy, appreciating the sovereign wisdom and holiness of God, comprises much of the book's story (cf. Shumate 2001), which moves concentrically from the outer (chs. 11–15) to the inner camp (chs. 16–18). As traditionally understood, firstborn sons might have served priestly functions within a father's house, explaining the role by sons of Reuben, Jacob's firstborn, who joined Levites in revolt against the exclusive priesthood of Aaron's house (16:1). After severe and repeated testing of the ordained hierarchy, YHWH will vindicate himself and the structure of his priestly theocracy (ch. 17), reasserting the foundational message of these chapters (ch. 18).

The gift of Levites to Aaron's priesthood is explained through YHWH's sovereign claim on Israel's firstborn sons (3:11–13, 40–51), legitimating the institution of Levites, even while clarifying their theological role as representatives of all Israel. In claiming Levites first as substitutes for the firstborn, and then, secondarily, giving them to the priesthood, YHWH may be claiming Levites *through* their service to the priesthood. A separate tally of Levites follows, appropriate for their particular role (cf. 1:47–50), and the three Levitical houses of Gershon, Kohath and Merari are delineated according to their count, encampment locale, leader, and basic charge of guard duty in relation to the Tent of Meeting. This section ends with the encampment of Moses and Aaron and his sons at the Tent's entrance, nearest YHWH's Presence, underscoring their authority over Levites (3:38–39).

Placing Levites between YHWH's Dwelling and the outer encampment of the twelve tribes entails a comprehensive theological system: due both to YHWH God's holiness and humanity's own condition, pervasively polluted by the effects of sin and death, the distance between Creator and creature cannot be collapsed, even within Israel's covenant bond. Yet in his condescending grace and eternal love, YHWH bridges that distance through the orchestrated mediation of the Sinai revelation, culminating with the creation of the covenant community, wherein YHWH finally dwells among his people (Num. 1 – 6).

The tallies in Numbers 3 were for the sake of the Levitical role of replacing Israel's firstborn sons. Those in chapter 4 relate to their transport labours: carrying frames, hangings and furnishings of YHWH's own Dwelling, whenever his Cloud lifts to break camp and journey forth. This solemn responsibility was for males between 30 and 50 years, requiring a separate count and appointment. With the Camp in view, chapter 3 emphasizes the location of Levites, along with their role of guarding the Dwelling while encamped, and chapter 4 focuses on their transport duties while on journey. Levitical houses and duties are summarized in Table 14 (see Schneerson and Wisnefsky 2009: 19).

Three death threats are laced throughout the material with particular regard to Kohathites (4:15, 19, 20), an ominous augur of Korah's rebellion (Num. 16 – 17). Along with references to priestly supervision, the death threats highlight the need for the cult's system of stratified access to YHWH's presence. Not only are Levites in danger of God's holiness, but the priests are as well, the wider section beginning with the deaths of Nadab and Abihu (Num. 3:1–4). This highlights not only God's supreme holiness, but also that he is completely unchangeable in being and nature – no ritual or role can magically overcome his threat as a consuming fire, for without holiness no one will see God (cf. Matt. 5:29–30; 1 Cor. 9:26–27; Phil. 3:12–21; Heb. 12:14, 28–29; 1 Peter 1:14–16).

Table 14: Levite houses

House	Tallies	Encampment	House and priestly oversight	Duties per house
Gershon *Libni* *Shimei*	7,500 2,630	West, behind the Dwelling	Eliasaph son of Lael *serving under* Ithamar the priest	Dwelling and Tent coverings, entrance screen, hangings and screen of courtyard, cords
Kohath *Amram* *Izhar* *Hebron* *Uzziel*	8,600 2,750	South, by the side of the Dwelling	Elizaphan son of Uzziel, *serving under* Eleazar the priest	Ark, table, lampstand, inner and outer altars, vessels, the screen (veil)
Merari *Mahli* *Mushi*	6,200 3,200	North, by the side of the Dwelling	Zuriel son of Abihail, *serving under* Ithamar the priest	Frames, bars, pillars, bases and vessels of Dwelling; pillars, sockets, pegs, and cords of courtyard
Totals	22,300 8,580	Firstborn sons Men aged 30–50		

Through Numbers 1 – 4, Israel has become an extension of the heavenly patterned Dwelling. God's mobile house has created a mobile society, the Camp of YHWH's earthly hosts. Ensuring that YHWH's Dwelling follows in synch with his Cloud, Levites are like the inner wheel of Ezekiel's divine chariot vision (see Ezek. 1:15–21; 10:6–17) – like the cherubim that transport YHWH's throne as part of his heavenly entourage, Levites transport his earthly throne and Dwelling as part of his earthly entourage.

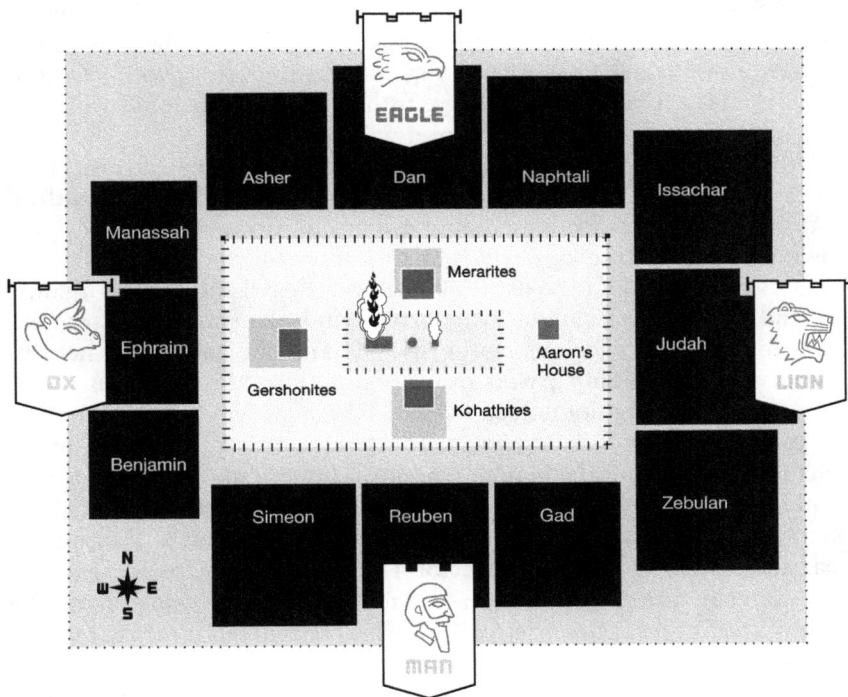

Figure 6: Overview of outer and inner camps

NUMBERS 5 – 6: THE SPIRITUAL NATURE OF THE CAMP

Translation

[1]And YHWH spoke to Moses, saying, [2]"Command the sons of Israel that they send away from the camp all who are leprous, all with a (genital) discharge, and all who are defiled by a corpse. [3]Male and female alike you are to send away, to outside the camp you will send them away, so they do not defile their camps in the midst of which I myself am dwelling.'

[4]Just so did the sons of Israel do: they sent them away to outside the camp; just as YHWH had spoken to Moses, just so the sons of Israel did.

[5]And YHWH spoke to Moses, saying, [6]"Speak to the sons of Israel, "When a man or a woman do any sin of humanity, being unfaithful in unfaithfulness against YHWH, that soul is guilty. [7]And they will confess their sin that they have done; and he will make restoration for his guilt in full, adding a fifth over and above it, and he will give to the one he is guilty against. [8]Now if there is no kinsman for the man, to make restoration of guilt to him, then the guilt-payment will be restored unto YHWH, to the priest, besides the ram of atonement with which atonement is made for him. [9]And every contribution, all the holy things of the sons of Israel which they bring near for the priest, will belong to him. [10]And each man's holy things, to him they will belong; whatever each man gives for the priest to him it will belong."'

[11]And YHWH spoke to Moses, saying, [12]"Speak to the sons of Israel and say to them, "Any man whose wife goes astray, being unfaithful against him in unfaithfulness, [13]and a man lies down with her, a lying down of seed, and the matter is hidden from the eyes of her husband – and it is concealed and she defiled herself but there is no witness against her and she was not caught – [14]and the wind of jealously passes over upon him and he is jealous about his wife and she has defiled herself, or the wind of jealousy passes over upon him and he is jealous about his wife and she has not defiled herself, [15]the man will bring his wife to the priest and he will bring her near-offering for her, one tenth of an ephah of barley flour; he is not to pour oil upon it and he is not to put frankincense upon it, for it is a tribute offering of jealousy, a tribute offering of memorial, remembering iniquity. [16]The priest will bring her near and stand her in the presence of YHWH, [17]and the priest will take holy water in an earthenware vessel and from the dust which is on the floor of the Dwelling the priest will take and he will put it into the water. [18]And the priest will stand the woman in the presence of YHWH and uncover the head of the woman; he will put on her palms the tribute offering of memorial – it is the tribute offering of jealousy – and in the hand of the priest will be the waters of bitterness bringing curses. [19]And the priest will make her swear, and he will say to the woman, If a man did not lie down with you and you did not go astray in uncleanness (with another man) in place of your husband, you will be free from these waters of bitterness bringing curses. [20]But you, if you have gone astray (with another man) in place of your husband so that you are unclean and a man other than your husband has put his lying-down (male organ) in you – [21]the priest will make the woman swear an oath of malediction, and the priest will say to the woman, 'YHWH will put you for a malediction and an oath in the midst of your people when YHWH puts your thigh to fall and your womb to swell. [22]These waters of curses will enter your innards to swell the womb and to fall the thigh.'

And the woman is to say, 'Amen, amen.' ²³And the priest will write these
maledictions on a scroll, and he will wipe them out into the bitter waters.
²⁴And he will make the woman to drink the waters of bitter curses and
the waters of curses will enter into her for bitterness. ²⁵And the priest
will take from the hand of the woman the tribute offering of jealousy,
and he will elevate the tribute offering in the presence of YHWH and
will bring it near to the altar. ²⁶And the priest will take a handful of the
tribute offering, its memorial, and he will turn it into smoke on the altar,
and afterward he will make the woman drink the waters. ²⁷And when
he has made her drink the waters, then it will be that if she is unclean
and was unfaithful in unfaithfulness against her husband, the waters
of curses will enter into her for bitterness, her womb will swell and her
thigh will fall, and the woman will be a malediction within her people.
²⁸And if the woman is not unclean but she is clean, she will be free and
she will be able to conceive seed. ²⁹This is the torah for jealousy, when
a woman has gone astray (with another man) in place of her husband
and has become unclean, ³⁰or for a man when the wind of jealousy has
passed over upon him and he is jealous about his wife: he will stand the
woman in the presence of YHWH and the priest will do for her all this
torah. ³¹Now the man will be free of iniquity and the woman she will
bear her iniquity.'"

^{6:1}And YHWH spoke to Moses, saying, ²"Speak to the sons of Israel
and say to them, "When a man or a woman would make a wondrous
vow, the vow of Nazirite-separation, to separate himself to YHWH,
³from wine and strong drink he will separate himself – he will not
drink fermentation of wine and fermentation of strong drink, and
he will not drink the juice of grapes, and will not eat grapes fresh
or dried. ⁴All the days of his separation, from anything made from
the grapevine, from seeds to skin, he will not eat. ⁵All the days of his
vow of separation a razor will not pass over upon his head; until the
days of his separation unto YHWH are fulfilled, he will be holy – the
loosened-locks of the hair of his head are to grow out. ⁶All the days
of his separation unto YHWH he will not come upon a dead corpse.
⁷For his father and for his mother, for his brother and for his sister, he
will not defile himself for them when they die because the crown-of-
separation to his God is upon his head. ⁸All the days of his separation
he is holy unto YHWH. ⁹And should someone dying die nearby him
all of a sudden and he defiles the head of his separation, then on the
day of his cleansing he will shave his head – on the seventh day he
will shave it. ¹⁰On the eighth day he will bring two turtledoves or two
young pigeons to the priest, to the doorway of the Tent of Meeting.
¹¹And the priest will make one for a purification offering and one
for a whole burnt offering, and atone for him because he went amiss
through the corpse; and he will consecrate his head on that day. ¹²And

he will separate unto YHWH the days of his separation, and he will bring a lamb in its first year for a reparation offering; and the first days will fall away because he had defiled his separation. [13]This is the torah of the Nazirite-separation: when the days of his separation have been fulfilled, he is to be brought to the doorway of the Tent of Meeting. [14]And he will bring near his near-offering unto YHWH: one unblemished lamb in its first year for a whole burnt offering, and one unblemished ewe lamb in her first year for a purification offering, and one unblemished ram for a peace offering; [15]and a basket of unleavened bread of flour, cakes mixed with oil, wafers of unleavened bread anointed with oil, and their tribute offerings and their drink offerings. [16]And the priest will bring (them) near into the presence of YHWH, and will do his purification offering and his whole burnt offering. [17]And the ram he will do as a sacrifice of peace offering unto YHWH, upon the basket of unleavened bread – the priest will do his tribute offerings and his libations. [18]And the Nazirite will shave at the doorway of the Tent of Meeting the head of his separation, and he will take the hair of the head of his separation and will put it upon the fire, which is under the sacrifice of peace offering. [19]And the priest will take the boiled shoulder from the ram and one cake of unleavened bread from the basket and one wafer of unleavened bread, and put them on the palms of the Nazirite, after he has shaved his separated-crown. [20]And the priest will elevate them as an elevation offering in the presence of YHWH; it is holy, for the priest, with the breast of the elevation offering and with the thigh of the contribution; afterward the Nazirite may drink wine. [21]This is the torah for the Nazirite who vows his near-offering unto YHWH upon his separation, aside from what his hand attains; as the vow of his mouth which he vowed, just so he will do, together with the torah of his separation."'

[22]And YHWH spoke to Moses, saying, [23]'Speak to Aaron and to his sons, saying, "Just so you will bless the sons of Israel," saying to them:

[24]YHWH bless you and keep you,
[25]YHWH shine his face to you and favour you,
[26]YHWH lift up his face to you and give you peace.

[27]'So they will put my Name upon the sons of Israel, and I myself will bless them.'

Notes on the text

5:2. 'leprous': ṣārûaʿ refers to a skin ailment with open sores, not to Hansen's Disease. Leprosy was a communicable disease, sometimes a punishment from YHWH (Borowski 2003: 76).

'by a corpse': *lānāpeš*, lit. 'to/according to the soul'; contextually refers to a dead body (cf. Lev. 19:28; 21:1; Num. 9:6, 7, 10). Frevel suggests the soul as the 'personality' of the deceased was not completely detached from corpses (or graves) (2013c: 388–406), but this is uncertain. Hirsch suggests the corpse calls to mind the soul or personality of the person (2007a: 102–103). 'Soul' may be used as a synonym for 'dead' (cf. Lev. 19:28 with Deut. 14:1).

3. 'to outside the camp': GKC §119e presumes each preposition retains full force, 'out in front of the camp'.

6. 'sin of humanity': *hattō't hā'ādām*; possibly alludes to Gen. 2 – 3. 'unfaithful in unfaithfulness': *lim'ōl ma'al*, or 'breaking faith', 'acting treacherously'.

7. 'in full': *běrō'šô*; lit. 'by (or with) its head'.

8. 'kinsman': *gō'ēl*; lit. 'redeemer'; as redemption was performed by the next of kin, the term may refer to a 'kinsman' in a legal sense (cf. Lev. 25:25, 47–52; Num. 35:9–34).

'unto YHWH': LXX, Syr, and Vg retain this phrase while adding a form of the 'to be' verb; this does not justify the *BHS* suggestion to replace *layhwh* with *yihyeh*, 'shall be'. LXX adds 'to the Lord' (*tō kyriō*) before 'to the priest' in v. 9.

9. 'every contribution': *těrûmāh*; lit. 'lifted off, separated'; traditionally rendered 'heave offering', it refers to any gift that goes to priests (by way of dedication to YHWH), always offered 'to YHWH' rather than 'before YHWH' (Milgrom 1983b: 159–172). LXX, one MT MS read 'to the Lord for the priest'; likely an addition.

10. 'they will belong': some MT MSS, SamP, Syr, Tg read a singular verb, perhaps duplicating the sentence's last word.

'to him': two MT MSS read *lō'* of negation rather than possession (*lô*) for the first occurrence – apparently in error.

13, 19. 'with her': the accusative *'ōtāh* should likely be repointed to a prepositional *'ittāh*.

17. 'the Dwelling': LXX reads 'tent of meeting'; Syr reads 'altar'.

18. 'of bitterness': others follow LXX (*tou elegmou*), reading 'of reproof' or 'contention' (cf. G. R. Driver 1956b: 74). Sasson suggests waters 'that curse (or) bless' (1972), Brichto waters 'of portent' (1975: 59) and Snaith waters 'that cause to flow'; i.e. cause an abortion (1967: 202); but Feinstein affirms 'bitter' waters (2012).

27. 'he has made her drink the waters': LXX and Syr lack this phrase, perhaps through homeoteleuton.

6:2. make-a-'wondrous' vow: *yapli'*, hiph. of *pl'* (to be wonderful, surpassing, extraordinary); so Milgrom (1990: 44); *BHS* suggests the vocalization found in Lev. 27:2, which root Levine traces rather to *plh*, 'to set aside', a votive offering (1989: 151, 193). See Num. 15:3, 8; Lev. 22:21; 27:2.

3–4. 'Juice' (*mišrat*), 'seed' (*ḥarṣan*) and 'skin' (*zāg*) are each a hapax legomenon.

5. 'his vow of separation': LXX and a few MT MSS lack 'vow', reading 'days of his separation' (cf. vv. 4, 6, 8); Budd suggests deleting *neder* as dittography (1984: 69), an unlikely error here.

6. 'dead corpse': *nepeš mēt* (lit. 'dying soul'), euphemism for a corpse.

16. 'bring (him) near': there is no object for the priest's action. Given other parallels between the strayed woman and the Nazirite, 'him' seems a stronger possibility than 'them'/the offerings (see 5:6).

21. 'his vow': *nidrô*; a few MT MSS read *nizrô*, an understandable deviation given the latter's frequency in this verse, along with the similar appearance of *d* and *z* in Hebrew.

23. 'saying' (second English occurrence): the singular example of this verb in the inf. abs. form.

24, 25, 26. On jussives here, see GKC §109b.

25, 26. 'upon you': perhaps better rendered 'toward you' (or 'in your direction'), given the prep. *'ēl* (cf. Baentsch 1903: 484; Seebass 2006: 39).

26. 'give you' uses 'put'/'set' (*yāśēm lĕkā*), as granting or appointing. Although the same verb is used with reference to 'name' (v. 27), the prepositions are not parallel (*lĕ* and *'al*), making the intended nuance difficult.

27. This verse completes v. 23 in LXX, and contains 'the Lord' in the last clause (see de Boer 1982: 3–4).

Form and structure

Numbers 5 – 6 comprises a unit, with each subsection being analogous in form (cf. Achenbach 2003b: 499–511; contra van Wolde 2009: 226). There are various helpful approaches (e.g. Ingalls 1991: 67; Seebass 2006, 46; cf. G. B. Gray 1903: 39), but fundamentally the section consists of five speeches by YHWH to Moses concerning the purity of Israel's Camp, featuring three cases related to life within the covenant community (5:5–10, 11–31; 6:1–21), preceded by a prologue (5:1–4) and capped by an epilogue (6:22–27):

Prologue: Expulsion from Camp wherein YHWH dwells (5:1–4)
  (1) all who are leprous
  (2) all with a bodily discharge
  (3) all who are defiled by a corpse

Purity laws: Life before YHWH in the Camp (5:5 – 6:21)
  (1) the law concerning restitution for oath-breakers (5:5–10)
  (2) the law concerning the strayed woman (5:11–31)
  (3) the law concerning the Nazirite vow (6:1–21)

Epilogue: Putting YHWH's Name on Israel within the Camp (6:22–27)
(1) YHWH bless you and keep you,
(2) YHWH make his face shine upon you,
(3) YHWH lift up his face to you and give you peace.

The first speech, a paradigmatic prologue (5:1–4), calls for a threefold expulsion from the Camp, and the last speech as an epilogue (6:22–27), signalling through its threefold priestly benediction that the Camp of Israel – the one place where God dwells with human beings – is the community of YHWH's blessings. Three further speeches relate to oath-breakers (5:5–10), the strayed woman (5:11–31) and the Nazirite vow (6:1–21). All three (1) relate to men and women, (2) require priestly intervention, relating to the Dwelling, (3) deal with a hidden impairment related to purity before God, (4) integrate personal initiative for resolution, and (5) involve at least the prospect of breaching an oath or vow (cf. Frevel 2016: 141–142). Spatially, Numbers 5 – 6 moves from outside the Camp (the expulsions of 5:1–4), inward toward the centre and then, with the priestly blessing, from the centre outward toward the periphery (cf. Dozeman 1998: 60; Knierim and Coats 2005: 27).

Beyond structural organization, the purity laws are also unified by key terms and themes. All five speeches are introduced verbatim with 'And YHWH spoke to Moses saying' (5:1, 5, 11; 6:1, 22). The prologue concerns 'male and female alike' (5:3), and then each of the main purity cases is the same: 'a man or a woman' (5:6), 'a man whose wife goes astray' (5:12), and 'a man or a woman' (6:2). The term *ṭāmē'* (impure, defiled), which appears thirteen times (5:2, 3, 13, 14 [twice], 19, 20, 27, 28, 29; 6:7, 9, 12), links the speeches together – only the law concerning confession and restitution (5:5–10) lacks *ṭāmē'*, but this section is linked to the strayed woman law by the term *mā'al* ('unfaithful, treacherous act', 5:6, 12, 27). Thematically, the laws appear to exhibit a spiritual progression, moving from creational matters pertaining to physical purity (5:1–4), to moral matters among neighbourly relations within Israel (5:5–10), to the need for long-term faithfulness within the marriage covenant (5:11–31), to the voluntary dedication of oneself to YHWH (6:1–21), and, finally, to the bearing of YHWH's holy Name, his presence and blessing, so as to function as a kingdom of priests (6:22–27). Each case is exemplary for Israel's calling and vocation through voluntary and wholehearted separation unto God, soliciting figural readings (Stubbs 2009: 52). After explaining the expulsion of the impure from the Camp (5:1–4), the focus shifts to maintaining persons *within* the Camp by mending relationships and making restoration for purity violations – in concentric relational spheres: neighbourly (5:5–10), marriage (5:11–31) and personally with God (6:1–21) (so, too, Dozeman 1998: 61), each of which involves an oath or vow before YHWH.

There are indicators the strayed wife should be considered alongside the Nazirite, sharing the book's only uses of the term 'uncover' (*pāra'*), both with reference to hair (5:18; 6:5), and both dealing with defilement (*ṭāmē'*, 5:13, 14, 19, 20, 27, 28, 29; 6:7, 9, 12) whereby the result is similarly described with 'fall' (*nāpal*) (5:21, 22; 6:12). Milgrom outlines the strayed woman text in five sections arranged concentrically (1981a; cf. Avishur 1999: 17–18; Cocco 2020: 14–35):

A. The case, 12–14
   B. Preparation of the ritual-ordeal, 15–18
      (1) *minḥāh*, 15
      (2) water, 17
      (3) woman, 18 (16)
         C. The oath-imprecation, 19–24
   B'. Execution of the ritual-ordeal, 25–28
      (1) *minḥāh*, 25–26a
      (2) water, 26b
      (3) woman, effect on, 27–28
A '. The case, 29–30 (postscript, 31)

He also structures the Nazirite vow section concentrically, underscoring the central setback of defilement (Milgrom 1990: 359). Arranged more simply, the Nazirite case follows a threefold movement:

1. A period of separation (6:1–8).
2. A setback requiring cleansing from corpse pollution and a new start (6:9–12).
3. Vow fulfilment: worship in the land with grain and drink offerings (6:13–21).

The priestly blessing is a theological and architectural gem, luminous and radiant from diverse angles. The frame, containing explanatory commentary, is connected chiastically: 'bless'/'sons of Israel' (23), 'sons of Israel'/'bless' (27). The three lines of the blessing (vv. 24, 25, 26) are each a diptych, containing two cola, and progress mathematically, ascending like a cascade from 3 to 5 to 7 words, from 12 to 14 to 16 syllables, and from 15 to 20 to 25 consonants in the Hebrew (cf. D. N. Freedman 1975; Milgrom 1990: 51), conveying the idea that YHWH's blessing pours out increasingly from his central Dwelling, encompassing the farthest reaches of the Camp. The 15 words comprise a threefold use of the divine Name plus 12 remaining words, reflecting YHWH's presence among the twelve tribes of Israel, in a manner not unlike the symbolism of the lampstand shining upon the twelve loaves of bread within the Tent of Meeting (8:1–4; see G. J. Wenham 1981b: 106–107; Morales 2015: 15–17). Perhaps coincidental, the twelve tribes have just formed the outer camp (chs. 1–2) and the three Levitical houses the inner camp (chs. 3–4).

Among the variety of ways in which one may understand the structural logic of the two verbs in each of the three lines, taking lines 2 and 3 as expansions on the verbs 'bless' and 'keep' of line 1, appears most cogent (cf. Stubbs 2009: 74–75). Assuming this structural logic, the two verbs of the first line (v. 24) would be copulative, 'bless and keep', and the two verb pairs of the second and third lines (vv. 25, 26) would be transitional, indicating consequence. The narrative framework is linked to the blessing, with the stem *bārēk* (bless) in verses 23 and 24, and the stem *śîm* (set, place) in verses 26 and 27 (also Fishbane 1983: 115 n. 2; Smoak 2016: 71–72), which may explain the unusual word choice in verse 26 (rather than *nātan*, 'put, give').

Speech formula and introductory frame, vv. 22, 23

Priestly blessing, vv. 24–26:

> 1a YHWH BLESS you → 2a YHWH shine his face to you,
> and favour you, v. 25
> 1b and KEEP you, v. 24 → 3a YHWH lift up his face to you,
> and put for you peace, v. 26

Concluding frame, v. 27

Comment

5:1–4 Prologue: Expulsion from the Camp wherein YHWH dwells

Numbers 5:1–4 calls for the expulsion of those unclean by skin disease, genital discharge and corpse pollution. These are not the concerns of a military camp (as Deuteronomy 23:10–14; cf. Frevel 2013c: 385), but the purity concerns of the newly founded covenant community, Israel's Camp, demonstrating that *YHWH now dwells in the midst of his people*.

1–4. This paragraph contextualizes the rest of Numbers 5 – 6, with its concern about the life and purity of the Camp, which has YHWH dwelling in its midst. Repetition – the terms 'camp' (*maḥăneh*) and 'send away' (*šālaḥ*) are each used four times – is rhetorical and specific (Frevel 2013c: 382). The divine command stipulates (1) the sorts of uncleanness that qualify for being sent away: leprosy, discharge and corpse pollution; (2) those to whom the command applies: male and female alike; (3) where the unclean are sent: outside the Camp, signifying that inside the

Camp is of ultimate concern; (4) the purpose for the expulsion: so the unclean do not defile the Camp; and (5) the rationale: YHWH dwells in the midst of the Camp.

The three defilements for expulsion are leprosy, genital discharge and corpse pollution. 'Leprosy' or 'skin disease' (ṣāra'at), which evidently produced scales of some sort, cannot be related to any known ailment (e.g. Hansen's disease); within the priestly system of purity, it is an aspect of death (Milgrom 1991: 817, 819), arguably true of all defilement. Leprosy is treated more severely than corpse pollution because a person with such skin disease becomes a *source* of defilement while the one polluted by a corpse does not (rather, the corpse itself is a source of pollution). The zāb (discharge) refers to a bodily discharge particularly associated with sexuality (cf. Lev. 15), and foreshadows the strayed woman case (5:11–31). Defilement in relation to human corpses is a feature of Numbers; in Leviticus, human corpse pollution is assumed (21:1, 11), but actual references relate to animal carcasses (Lev. 5:2; 11:24–40). The corpse pollution in 5:2 foreshadows the Nazirite vow (6:6–12), both of which are also connected to the red heifer ritual (Num. 19). Similarities to the purity concerns detailed for Aaron's house (Lev. 22:4–7) portray the covenant community as 'a priestly kingdom and holy nation' (Exod. 19:6). Feldman's thesis 'that *tum'ah* is essentially an absence of life and God, and is thus a metaphor for estrangement and desacralization' (1977: 51) fits the present context, especially as the dichotomy between death and life, with God as absolute life, forms the basis for all purity laws.

YHWH's presence within the Camp (v. 3) underpins the legislation, which announces this wondrous reality, conveying the fulfilment of the covenant formula with the creation of the Camp (cf. Exod. 25:8; 29:45–46). YHWH's presence cannot be thought of such as that of any other occupant of the Camp, having limited impact to its composition – the covenant community as constructed around YHWH's Dwelling, with YHWH God 'in its midst', is transformed completely and reoriented utterly. While the purity legislation of Leviticus had the Tent area primarily in mind (Lev. 11 – 15), Numbers 5 – 6 broadens the focus concentrically to that of the entire Camp, which has just been connected to YHWH's Tent. Concern for defiling the Sanctuary in Leviticus necessarily expands into a concern for defiling God's community in Numbers *because that community is now connected to his Sanctuary* – his Tent is still in focus, but in a new context. As arranged around YHWH's Dwelling, the whole Camp becomes an organism, united to his presence. 'This purification of the *machane*', writes Bick (2017), 'is part of its creation, which is perfectly understandable if we remember that the *machane Yisrael* is the outer receptacle of the Mishkan; in other words, of the Divine Presence. So this *parasha* is actually the last step in the construction of the *machane*.' The command to expel the unclean from the Camp functions rhetorically, then, to underscore the new reality that YHWH God is now dwelling in the midst of his people. The three cases that follow (5:5–10, 11–31; 6:1–21) set forth the ramifications for such a life with God.

The phrase 'in the midst of which I myself am dwelling' (*'ănî šōkēn bětôkām*, v. 3) is fundamental. Emphasizing the reality of YHWH's presence in the Camp, the declaration hearkens back to Exodus 25:8 and 29:45, where YHWH declared 'I will dwell among' (*šākantî bětôk*) them / the sons of Israel – a reality *now* fulfilled. This fulfilment *is* the text's primary lesson – more, *proclamation*. If Leviticus presents YHWH's presence in the Tent of Meeting as a garden of Eden restored, Numbers extends that notion to the Camp of Israel as the land of Eden within which that garden may be found. When an Israelite was sent out of the Camp, the progressive expulsions out of Eden's garden and land may be recalled (Gen. 3:24; 4:16; cf. G. J. Wenham 1979: 201, 213; Wright 1992b: 739; Trevaskis 2011: 93–106, 199–120).

The purity concerns of individuals in Leviticus have in Numbers become the concern of the whole community, the unified Camp. The paragraph concludes optimistically, with Israel's compliance.

5:5–10: Purity in the realm of society

5–10. From defilements requiring banishment (5:1–4), the text moves to broad interrelations within the Camp. Neighbourly interaction among Israelites, 'man or woman', have the fundamental relationship with YHWH at their core – a reality architecturally embodied by his Dwelling at the Camp's centre. The need for restitution, a ram for the sake of atonement, the fivefold use of *'āšam*, and the notion of sacrilege or treachery (*ma'al*) against YHWH, imply the legislation deals with the sorts of offences delineated in the regulations for *'āšam* offerings in Leviticus 6:1–7, which involve finding or squandering another person's deposit or security and, in the process, swearing a false oath in YHWH's Name to cover the act. Numbers adds the requirement of confession and the matter of delivering the restitution to the priest if the wronged person, along with any kinsman, is dead, unable to receive such recompense. Treatment of neighbour is encompassed within the covenant community's relation to God.

The designation 'kinsman' (*gō'ēl*) occurs in Numbers only here and for the 'avenger' in the cities of refuge regulations (35:12, 19, 21, 24, 25, 27 [twice]), possibly pointing to a connection between them. Reasoning that any Israelite would undoubtedly have some remaining relative, Jewish interpretation understands the offended party to be a convert, one of the mixed-rabble that had accompanied the Israelites out of Egypt (see *Num. Rab.* 8.5; Rashi, ad loc.). Inclusive of Israelites with no remaining relatives, YHWH takes up the cause of the destitute. By giving the restitution to the priest, payment is made to YHWH, against whom the unfaithfulness was ultimately committed. The guilty person must (1) confess the particular sin and (2) make restoration in full, adding a fifth, (3) to the offended person (or priest) and (4) offer the prescribed sacrifice of a ram. The law also builds on the admonitions of Leviticus 19, which culminate with the command to 'Love your neighbour as yourself' (Lev. 19:18; cf. Shamah 2011: 706). The first case thus pertains to neighbourly relations among the tribes, and may be correlated to the outer camp of the covenant community.

While what particularly marks the incident as a 'breach of faith' or 'treachery' against YHWH is the false oath sworn in his Name (Lev. 6:2–3; Knohl 2004: 519–520), the legislation here, being supplementary, assumes and does not underscore the false oath. With his central presence in the Camp, YHWH is intimately brought into all of the community's interactions, quite apart from the assumed oath. Thus a sin against another Israelite is also 'unfaithfulness (ma'al) against YHWH'. The phrase lim'ōl ma'al (unfaithful in unfaithfulness) implies an act of sacrilege or treachery that betrays loyalty (cf. BDB 591; TWOT 519–520), hence 'unfaithfulness', portrayed consistently in Scripture as committed against God (cf. 5:12).

The term 'ram of atonement' occurs only here (v. 8), but refers to the 'āšam (reparation offering) ram in Leviticus 6:6–7 with which 'atonement' is made. Milgrom suggests 'ram of atonement' has been substituted for 'āšam with reference to the offering, since the term is already used for 'guilt' and 'restitution' in this section (1990: 35–36). The tĕrûmāh (contribution) offering (rûm, 'to lift up'; hence 'heave' offering) refers to that which is dedicated to YHWH, typically by means of giving it to priests (see Milgrom 1983b: 159–172), as with the priestly portions of peace offerings (Lev. 7:34). The particular priest's ownership of the holy things is emphatic (v. 10).

Life within the Camp is oriented by, around and to YHWH. An act that breaks faith against a fellow Israelite is portrayed as treachery against YHWH himself. Rhetorically, the technical act of ma'al in Leviticus 6:1–7 – a false oath in YHWH's Name – is subdued; while what was likely implicit in Leviticus, the need for confession, is here brought out with emphasis. Taken together, this section stresses the need for just dealings among the Israelites, as before the face of YHWH within the heavenly designed Camp, requiring personal commitment and initiative, even to one's own loss. YHWH's holy presence requires every Israelite to participate in the community's purity, both ritually and morally.

5:11–31: Purity in the realm of marriage and family

It has been well noted that the 'strayed woman' case, the Sotah passage, is 'one of the most perplexing passages in the Bible', regarding its origin, composition and meaning (Jeon 2007: 181; cf. Boer 2006: 87). Whether or not it was ever performed, Friedman underscores the likelihood that the law had not been practised for some six centuries before its earliest rabbinical interpreters (*m. Sot. 9.9* notwithstanding) (2012: 381). Rather than approaching the legislation as a mere historical question, in isolation from its literary context, the strayed woman ordeal is best understood in relation to Numbers 5 – 6 as a whole, which utilizes different scenarios to make a theological point about Israel's Camp and vocation. Given shared creation and Deluge language, such as *'āpor* ('dust', Gen. 2:7; 3:14, 19; Num. 5:17), *rûaḥ* ('wind, spirit', Gen. 1:2; 6:3, 17; 7:15, 22; 8:1; Num. 5:14, 30), *zākar* ('remember', Gen. 8:1; Num. 5:15, 18, 26), *mayim* ('waters', Gen. 6:17, etc.; Num. 5:17), *'arar* ('curse', Gen. 3:14, 17; 4:11; 5:29; Num. 5:18, 19, 22, 24, 27), *māḥâ* ('blot out', Gen. 6:7; 7:4, 23; Num. 23), along with thematic elements such as judgement and cleansing through waters, resolution by *rûaḥ* and the prospect of bearing children (Gen. 1:28; 9:1; Num. 5:28), and the ritual connection between the earth and womb (Whitekettle 1996), the strayed woman ritual takes on cosmic dimensions of judgement and cleansing/rebirth.

The procedure prescribed may suitably be referred to as an ordeal, with some similarities found in other ANE cultures (e.g. de Vaulx 1972: 93; for the ordeal in the ANE, see Cocco 2020: 61–82). A primary difference, according to some, is that ANE ordeals were inherently life-threatening, requiring miraculous intervention in the case of innocence, whereas this procedure is inherently harmless physically, requiring divine intervention for a damaging judgement (cf. Brichto 1975: 64–66). However, it is also possible to understand the 'bitter waters' as naturally poisonous (cf. Exod. 15:23–25), requiring rather God's intervention to make them sweet (Cocco 2020: 97). 'Going astray' (*śāṭah*, vv. 12, 19, 20, 29) is a rare term; its limited use elsewhere implies the metaphor of *turning from* the right path (Prov. 4:15; 7:25; see Cocco 2020: 53), informing our interpretation of the strayed woman as a *path* that Israel, the bride of YHWH, is being warned against before the wilderness sojourn to Canaan. Reading the strayed woman ritual in isolation from its literary context skews the meaning and point of the passage, including the value of women in Israel. As a woman may take the Nazirite vow (see 6:2), it may be the strayed woman is being contrasted with the Nazirite (woman), presented as two divergent paths set before Israel as YHWH's bride. Similarly, Proverbs sets forth the adulteress and Lady Wisdom as two paths (cf. Prov. 7 – 8).

In the immediate context, the woman may or may not have actually made herself unclean when she 'went astray' – there are no witnesses, she was not caught – but when the 'spirit/wind of jealousy (*rûaḥ-qin'āh*) passes over upon him' (mentioned twice verbatim), this becomes the occasion for the ordeal. More is at stake than the vital marriage relationship: since YHWH's presence requires the Camp's purity, the

well-being of the entire community is in view, again bringing the matter
– which could not be dealt with in court, for lack of witnesses – under
the oversight of the priesthood, since priests are charged with making
distinctions between clean and unclean (Lev. 10:10; 11 – 15). Given the
concern with defilement in the Camp, the husband might have been
obligated to resolve the matter of his wife's possible defilement (cf.
Frymer-Kensky 1984: 17–18). Similar to the Levitical duty of guarding
YHWH's Dwelling from encroachment by a 'foreigner', so, too, marriage
is sacrosanct, to be guarded from the encroachment of anyone other
than her husband – a relevant illustration in the light of the Baal Peor
affair (Num. 25).

11–14. The phrase *'îš 'îš* has a distributive value, 'any man', employed
in casuistic law (so Cocco 2020: 37–38). Contemporary approaches to
the legislation often assume the scenario of an innocent woman's plight,
subject to the whims of an unreasonably jealous husband. However,
'spirit/wind of jealousy' does not connote a mere 'whim'. Rather, *rûaḥ*
is used in the Torah for a mighty rushing wind, linked to the Spirit of
God as a means of creation and redemption (see Gen. 1:2; 8:1; Exod.
14:21), connected also to wisdom and skill (Gen. 41:38; Exod. 31:3;
35:31), a significance in accord with its use elsewhere in Numbers (see
11:25, 31). Likewise, 'jealousy' refers to zealousness over one's covenant
relationship, in terms of fidelity, and is frequently used in Scripture for
YHWH God's claim to loyalty from Israel: 'For I, YHWH your God,
am a jealous God' (*'ēl qannā*) (Exod. 20:5) – indeed, YHWH's 'name
is Jealous' (*qannā šĕmô*) (Exod. 34:14). He declares that Israel has
'provoked me to jealousy (*qin'ûnî*)' (Deut. 32:21). These cases occur
within the context of idolatry, commonly dubbed spiritual harlotry
(see Exod. 34:16). Some find in the strayed woman ritual an allusion to
the golden calf apostasy (Exod. 32), noting that the calf was ground to
powder and the people were made to drink it with water; although this
was not an ordeal to determine uncleanness (Press 1933: 125; Fishbane
1974: 40; G. J. Wenham 1981b: 80; Frymer-Kensky 1984: 640; Bach 1999:
516; R. S. Briggs 2009: 304). As Israel's husband, YHWH is neither weak
nor insecure, but zealously guards – for his glory and Israel's blessedness
– his covenantal bond with his people. In Ezekiel, he declares, 'I will
cause you to cease from whoring (*zānâ*) . . . and my jealousy (*qin'ātî*)
will turn aside from you' (16:41–42). And through Zechariah, YHWH
proclaims his jealousy in a threefold manner: 'I am jealous for Zion, with
a great jealousy – with great wrath I am jealous for her' (8:2).

The phrase 'wind/spirit of jealousy' (*rûaḥ-qin'āh*) may also point to
divine action, in line with *rûaḥ 'ĕlōhîm* in the Torah (Gen. 1:2; 41:38;
Exod. 31:3; 35:31; Num. 24:2), as well as the distribution of YHWH's
Spirit that was upon Moses (Num. 11:17, 25, 26, 29) – and *rûaḥ yhwh*
occurs frequently in Scripture, with seven uses in Judges alone (3:10;
6:34; 11:29; 13:25; 14:6, 19; 15:14). Even the description of the strayed

woman's act as 'treachery' (*māʿal*) in verse 12 is a precise designation used almost exclusively elsewhere for covenant unfaithfulness committed against YHWH (cf. 5:6), typically in relation to idolatry (Lev. 26:40; Num. 31:16; Milgrom 1992: 37), wherein 'jealousy' as zealous and holy indignation is the appropriate divine response. The current text is unique in the Pentateuch, where *māʿal* does not have God as its object – however, since the woman likely represents Israel, her unfaithfulness is indeed against YHWH her husband. Such a misdeed, in any case, is understood as 'nonetheless directed also against God' (Cocco 2020: 56). In Numbers 25, significantly, YHWH commends Phinehas *because* of his jealousy, embodying YHWH's own: for Phinehas 'was jealous with my jealousy among them, so that I did not consume the sons of Israel in my jealousy' (25:11; cf. 25:13). The issue in view is not unreasonable male jealousy (cf. Haberman 2000: 16). Ancient audiences would likely have heard the term 'jealous' positively, as zeal for protecting and safeguarding the integrity of an honoured relationship. The prophets portray Israel's harlotry as the height of ingratitude and wickedness (Ezek. 16, 23; Hos. 1 – 4; Jer. 2 – 3; see Fishbane 1974: 40–45). Within an ANE patriarchal society, the parallel to God and Israel would be appreciated since a husband was often *de facto* a woman's primary source of life – of love, shelter, wealth, food and well-being.

Another interpretative challenge is that the strayed woman case 'has partly to be reconstructed by inference' (McKane 1980: 474). The strayed woman has historically been understood as a woman who has secluded herself with a man other than her husband long enough for sexual intercourse to have taken place (cf. e.g. *m. Soṭ.* 1.2d; for rabbinical interpretations, see Destro 1989; Grushcow 2006; Rosen-Zvi 2012). Her guilt or innocence, rendered by the ordeal, relates to whether she has become defiled, made unclean, by another man's seed while in seclusion – this is the point of controversy (contra Boer 2006). Supporting this reading is the underlying tenor of the text, that in some sense the woman is presumed guilty although the ordeal is nevertheless required, and yet her being undefiled is a real possibility: she has strayed into seclusion, but might not have had intercourse. Due to seclusion with another man, her position – like that of Sarah on two occasions (with Abraham's culpability, Gen. 12:10–20; 20:1–17) – has become suspect, requiring divine confirmation of her status, and that of her future child. Moreover, the text's focus is squarely on the possible intercourse of 'seed'. The issue is not one of 'adultery', but of potential impurity ('she had made herself unclean', *niṭmām'āh*, v. 13). Even the terminology for 'being free (from judgement)' (*nāqāh*) in verses 19, 28, 31 conveys the basic notion of 'being clean'. As Milgrom puts it (1990: 351; cf. van Wolde 2009: 228–229), 'the text is cemented together by the sevenfold use of the verb *ṭāmē*', pollute' (5:13, 14 [twice], 20, 27, 28, 29). While often employed when discussing this passage, the text nowhere mentions the word 'adultery' (nā'ap). As a legal term, forbidden by the seventh commandment and requiring the death penalty for both adulterer and adulteress (Exod. 20:14; Lev. 20:10; Deut. 22:22–27; cf. Deut. 17:6; 19:15), 'adultery' is precluded inasmuch as it required two witnesses to the act itself (cf. Milgrom 1981a: 74). The designation 'strayed woman' is therefore preferred over 'suspected adulteress'. Thematically, discussions of adultery elsewhere in the Pentateuch do not include reference to 'seed' – whether the Decalogue (Exod. 20:14), the law against adultery (Lev. 20:10) or the law concerning intercourse with a betrothed woman (Deut. 22:23, 25), while legislation related to clean/unclean concerns *alone*, necessarily involving fluid (blood or semen), do include the topic of seed – for example, the law forbidding sexual relations with a neighbour's wife does not use the term 'adultery' at all, but describes an 'intercourse of seed' with a man's wife and falls within a section that pertains to the topic of impurity (Lev. 18:20; Friedman 2012: 373). The language of her becoming unclean/defiled, with ṭāmē' specifically in the niphal, creating the reflexive sense of defiling herself, is otherwise used *exclusively with Israel as the subject*, another textual clue the strayed woman may represent Israel (Paynter 2022).

The subject of seed also brings the matter of pregnancy into purview, along with questions of establishing paternity, as well as the poetic justice involved in the curse, versus bearing 'seed' in the scenario of blessing (v. 28). Van Wolde points out that all the terms used related to the woman's body construe it with reference to reproduction (2009: 232): mē'eh (v. 22), yārēk (vv. 21, 22, 27), beṭen (vv. 21, 22, 27). As Friedman observes, 'seed' is not a euphemism but mentioned when it matters – it is the concern of the text, in relation to uncleanness, with terms for purity and impurity used nine times in the passage (2012: 373, 376). Language of 'guilt' and 'innocence', therefore, though common among interpreters, is not in accord with the text and leads to misunderstanding. The three places where 'guilt' is not presumed are restricted to the category of purity: she is not unclean/defiled with another man's seed (14b, 19, 28). The woman has 'strayed' (or 'turned', 'become wayward'); the question is, how far – has she become unclean by an intercourse of seed? The parallelism in verse 14 narrows the context clearly:

> the wind of jealousy comes upon him and he is jealous of his wife,
> and she is unclean, or
> the wind of jealousy comes upon him and he is jealous of his wife,
> and she is not unclean.

Both lines assume one situation preceding his jealousy, that she has strayed into seclusion with another man, the question being whether or not she is unclean. Here, 'unclean' refers only to whether or not she has become impure through another man's emission of seed. She has strayed in immodesty, and the husband, desiring to maintain the covenant bond (see Achenbach 2016: 115–116; cf. Ainsworth 1619: 729), requires divine confirmation that he is allowed to continue knowing his wife conjugally. Turning away, as Haberman observes, is not 'tantamount to adultery', but rather, according to the Mishnah, she has 'turned' in having entered a place of seclusion, being 'secretive' (2000: 17, 19, 23–24). Verses 19 and 20 also articulate the quite specific issue of her being either clean or unclean in relation to the seed of another man.

While concern over defilement is set within the context of the community's purity (see Cocco 2020: 59), this section relates to the family sphere of the Camp, cautioning against a public shaming interpretation of the ritual. There are sound reasons to presume a private context for the ordeal, however 'public' the locale of Tabernacle space may seem – only the presence of three involved persons, along with YHWH himself, is taken for granted, the ordeal happening 'at a specifically scheduled performance in private . . . without subsequent public judicial actions' (Knierim and Coats 2005: 83). Her act of treachery and its divine judgement, not the ritual itself, make her 'a curse among her people' (v. 27).

15–28. The response to the wind of jealousy is for the husband to bring his wife to YHWH for his ruling, an undertaking that involves several steps. (1) First, the man brings his wife to the priest, along with a tribute offering for memorial. Since the purpose of the offering is for YHWH to remember the woman's iniquity, if indeed committed, it does not include pleasing elements (oil, frankincense) – this is similar to the purification offering (Lev. 5:11). (2) Second, the priest stands the woman in YHWH's presence, likely near the altar, with the memorial offering placed in her hands, and uncovers her head. She is hereby laid bare before YHWH's searching gaze, her hands holding an offering to solicit his memory upon a particular moment of her life, in which an *act* did or did not take place, 'hidden' from her husband when she strayed into seclusion with another man (v. 13). The loosened hair likely reflects her liminal state (cf. R. Schmitt 2004: 181), perhaps reflective of her presumed seclusion. Loosened hair is also an expression of grief that was forbidden to priests (*rāʾšêkem ʾal-tiprāʿû*, Lev. 10:6; *ʾet-rōʾšô lōʾ yiprāʿ*, Lev. 21:10). Loosened hair or an uncovered head was also required for lepers, so as to be recognizable for keeping separate from the community (Lev. 13:45; Cocco 2020: 94). The root used for the woman's 'loosed' (*pāraʿ*) hair occurs only once more in Numbers, for the Nazirite's 'locks' (*peraʿ*) of hair (5:18; 6:5), one of several connections underscoring the contrast, since the holy Nazirite is likened to the high priest.

(3) Third, holding the vessel of bitter waters, the priest has the woman swear an oath of self-malediction, replying 'Amen, amen'. Although this 'vessel' (*kělî*) is not one of the gold or silver vessels of the Dwelling, yet it is not without significance that in Numbers the term is primarily used

to designate these holy implements (see 1:50; 3:8, 31, 36; 4:9, 10, 12, 14, etc.). The vessel has been compared to God's 'cup of wrath' for Israel's spiritual harlotry (e.g. Ps. 75:8; Isa. 51:17–23; Jer. 8:14; etc.) (McKane 1980), and to the cup of suffering taken by Christ on behalf of his people in Gethsemane (Matt. 26:36–46) (Stubbs 2009: 63; Tedford 2013). The text only mentions the vessel once (5:17), directing attention rather to the water within – for example, the dust is not put into the vessel but 'into the water' (v. 17), and in his hand the priest holds not the vessel but 'the waters of bitterness bringing curses' (v. 18; see vv. 22, 23, 24). The water functions to make the spoken oath physical, so that it is literally internalized as the woman drinks the draught (cf. Kitz 2007b: 453–455). Possibly the earthenware vessel is metonymic for the womb, and the dust-water combination for seed (Bach 1999: 27; cf. G. J. Wenham 1981b: 94). The 'oath of malediction' (*hā'ālāh*) calls down a curse that would, at the least, keep the woman from bearing children if she has been made unclean with another man's seed. An imprecatory oath component is associated with the renewal of the Sinai covenant (Deut. 29:11, 18–19; Cocco 2020: 104), just as her required 'Amen' response to the curse finds a parallel in Israel's 'Amen' response to the covenantal curses recited by Levites (Deut. 27:11–26), further supporting the analogy between the woman's relationship to her husband and Israel's to YHWH. Also, in Deuteronomy, Moses speaks of 'all the curses written on this scroll' (*kol-hā'ālâ hakkĕtûbâ bassēper hazzê*) coming upon Israel (29:19), whereas here the priest is to 'write all these curses on the scroll' (*wĕkātab 'et-hā'ālōt hā'ēllê . . . bassēper*). Although other aspects of the ritual tend to receive greater emphasis in studies, it is the oath that actually dominates the text – this is an 'oath ritual' (cf. Press 1933: 125; Kitz 2007b). Structurally, the oath forms the midpoint and pivot, marking it as centrally important (Milgrom 1981a: 71), and every aspect of the ritual serves to underscore the gravity of the oath; other elements illustrate and vivify the oath given under YHWH.

(4) Fourth, before having the woman drink, the priest takes the offering of jealousy, elevates it before YHWH, and places a handful of it on the altar, turning it into smoke. The two acts of elevating the offering and sending a portion upward in smoke dramatically portray bringing the woman's (mis)deed to YHWH's face. Cocco points out the chiastic scheme of the offering's labels (2020: 94–95): 'tribute offering of jealousy', 'tribute offering of memorial' (15b), then 'tribute offering of memorial', 'tribute offering of jealousy' (18b). Throughout the ritual, the priest's role as mediator is evident: he transfers the woman's offering of remembrance to the sacred realm, and transfers the sacred water to the woman (Milgrom 1981a: 71).

(5) Fifth, the woman drinks the 'waters of bitterness bringing curses', comprised of 'holy water' (*mayim qĕdōšîm*), mixed with dust from the floor of YHWH's Dwelling and with the words of malediction

– including YHWH's own Name – scraped into it from a scroll or parchment. The ritual's threat is clear, given the dichotomy on which the cult is founded: life versus death. Cocco points to the instructions for the bronze laver (Exod. 30:17–21, 29), especially the line 'You shall consecrate these things so that they become most holy: whatever touches them will become holy,' to affirm that 'holy water' in our text almost certainly derives from the laver (2020: 89). Even the dust is from 'the floor of the Dwelling'. Ancient tradition presumed priests and Levites did not wear sandals within the Tabernacle precincts. Elsewhere, sandals are removed from holy ground (Exod. 3:5), and priests are commanded even to wash their feet with water from the laver (Exod. 30:18–21). Conspicuously, the meticulous account of Aaron's priestly garments, including headwear and breeches, lacks any description of footwear (Exod. 28). While, therefore, 'the dust' (*he'āpor*) may recall humanity's origin and end (Gen. 2:7; 3:14, 19), along with God's authority over life and death as Judge (cf. Cocco 2020: 92), here the dust (also) stands as a signifier of holiness. A concoction that is three times holy – holy water from the laver, holy dust from the Dwelling floor, and a divinely revealed curse that includes YHWH's Name scraped from the priest's scroll, and all within the sacred precincts of the Dwelling, 'before the face of YHWH' (vv. 16, 18, 30) – will enter the woman; if she is unclean, having defiled herself with another man's seed, then the drink, bringing her into close contact with holiness, will indeed have bitter, cursed results. The two previous uses of 'before YHWH' (*lipnê yhwh*) in Numbers, both occur at 3:4 with reference to Nadab and Abihu's dreadful fate at the Dwelling (and the notice 'they had no children' also forms a parallel to the strayed woman who, if defiled, will not bear children).

God's holiness, absolute life, must never come into contact with uncleanness, the blotch of death; many of the cult's regulations are intended to prevent such boundary-crossing. The text sets up that deadly dichotomy with a sevenfold use of both 'unclean' and of the divine Name 'YHWH'. Leviticus 7:20–21 warns that eating holy flesh of a sacrifice while in a state of uncleanness results in being 'cut off' (*kārat*) from Israel, a penalty of excommunication associated with premature death and the extirpation of one's lineage, inflicted by YHWH or the covenant community on his behalf (see Sklar 2005: 15–20; cf. Wold 1978; Frymer-Kensky 1983: 404–405). In this instance, if the woman is defiled, coming 'before YHWH', already an event of awe and fear, becomes a foretaste of the Day of Judgement. In the scenario where she has not become unclean with another man, however, YHWH may be seen as a source of refuge. The presence of YHWH, everywhere presupposed (vv. 16, 18, 25, 30), in addition to the language of verse 21, makes clear that it is YHWH who causes the curse or blessing upon her drinking from the vessel, aside from the legislation itself being dictated by him (v. 11). In this sense, that YHWH is an involved character, the idea of 'magic' is precluded (contra D. Miller 2010) however, commentators have also considered some or all of the passage's Yahwistic features as interpolations intended to forestall the allegation that the officiating priest is engaging in magic. The present study argues that if we abandon the outdated view that magic and normative Yahwism were antithetical, Num. 5:11-31 can be interpreted as having been written by a single author who envisions a ritual simultaneously magical and Yahwistic. The ritual is predicated on an incantatory curve in vv. 21-22, and exhibits magic by speech, magic by rite and magic by inherent property (the ancient Egyptian tripartite categorization of magic). Texts related to cultic rites normally use the designation 'Tent of Meeting', whereas here 'Dwelling' is used (v. 17), focusing on YHWH's presence. The summary underscores one vital aspect and controlling thought: the woman is brought to stand before the presence of YHWH (v. 30).

The precise results of the woman's ingestion of the waters of curses is not easy to determine. Some commentators deem the woman, if unclean, would miscarry and have her womb and reproductive organs damaged or cursed so as not to be able to bear children (e.g. Frymer-Kensky 1984; Bach 1999), while others, including Maimonides (*Hilkot Sotah*, 3), believe the ritual merely served to bring about the woman's confession (Eidelberg 1980), or, discounting any supernatural involvement, that it ensured all such women would be found 'innocent' (Milgrom 1981a; cf. Brichto 1975) – as noted, 'clean' is the more correct category. The curse oath structures the result chiastically: 'your thigh to fall and your womb to swell' (v. 21), 'to swell your womb and to fall your thigh' (v. 22; cf. v. 27). As a euphemism for the reproductive organs (cf. Gen. 24:2; 46:26), 'thigh' (*yārēk*), along with 'womb' (*beṭen*), underscores the poetic justice involved in the curse. If the strayed woman is defiled, the other man's seed had entered her 'thigh' to swell the womb in pregnancy; now the bitter waters will also reach her thigh and then cause her womb to swell, but countering the illicit act in judgement.

29–31. The ritual is labelled a 'torah for jealousy', a fitting description as the root for jealousy occurs no fewer than ten times. This torah is employed 'when' (*'ăšer*) a wife has gone astray with another man, or 'when' (*'ăšer*) the wind of jealousy comes upon a husband, and is summarized as standing the woman in YHWH's presence, the torah itself being performed by the priest. Given the connection elsewhere between YHWH and *rûaḥ*, it may be the 'wind'/'Spirit' is God's instrument for bringing the woman into his presence at the Tabernacle.

If the woman is found 'unclean', she will 'bear her iniquity', a phrase that implies a non-expiated sin borne by the sinner as a burden (B. Schwartz 1995), along with a looming punishment of some sort directly from God (see Lev. 5:1,17; 7:18; 17:16; etc.), out of human hands, whether those of her husband or Israel's judicial system (cf. Zimmerli 1954: 8–11; Milgrom 1981a: 73–75). While the woman bears her iniquity, 'the man' is free/clean from (the punishment of) iniquity. Who is this man? Some propose the man is the husband who is free from the guilt of having his wife go through the ordeal. Yet there is nothing in the text to suggest he is to be impugned at all – he is not accusing her falsely, but following YHWH's remedy for answering a question. Others suggest the verse refers to the other man whose seed may have defiled the woman, declaring that he cannot be tried or put to death when she is declared unclean, since there were no witnesses to the sexual act (cf. Friedman 2012). The same, however, remains true for the unclean woman who does 'bear her guilt'. Implying that a guilty man, even while escaping human justice, will not be met with God's judgement – precisely the idea of 'bearing guilt' – would be contrary to the character of God and the message of Scripture. This point also precludes the notion of a principle of 'separation of prosecution' (suggested by Démare-Lafont 1987). The verse declares that *God* will not hold the man accountable for some iniquity. The context of verse 30, along with use of the definite, $h\bar{a}'\hat{\imath}\check{s}$ (vv. 15, 31), favours identifying the man as the husband, and a comparison with Numbers 30 shows that the issue relates to the strayed woman's oath (Shectman 2010: 490–493; cf. Frymer-Kensky 1984: 23–24). A major concern regarding women's oaths in ancient Israel relates to the culpability of either her father, if she is unmarried, or husband, if married, including scenarios requiring that the man 'will bear her iniquity' ($n\bar{a}\acute{s}\bar{a}'$ 'et-'$\check{a}w\bar{o}n\bar{a}h$; see 30:15). As 30:13 makes clear, oaths by a married woman normally involved her husband's accountability. Numbers 5:31 clarifies that, in this scenario, the husband is not culpable in YHWH's sight for the woman's oath – in this case, 'she will bear her iniquity' ($ti\acute{s}\acute{s}\bar{a}'$ 'et-'$\check{a}w\bar{o}n\bar{a}h$). Interestingly, this rare expression is also used in 14:34, where YHWH makes the Israelites 'bear your guilt' for forty years in the wilderness, again connecting the strayed woman and Israel.

The rhetorical function of the strayed wife ritual goes well beyond the actual scenario described. As $m\bar{a}'al$ (treachery, unfaithfulness) elsewhere always refers to an offence against YHWH, the strayed woman has been connected to Israel's infamous spiritual harlotries as an unfaithful wife to YHWH (see Jer. 3:8–15; Ezek. 23:37; Hos. 4:4–22; 5:3; 6:10), with the cup as symbolic of exile and judgement (e.g. Fishbane 1974: 40–45; Milgrom 1990: 37). M. Douglas goes further, stating the legislation makes better sense when the faithless woman is read as Israel 'the mystic bride' in relation to YHWH her husband (2001: 160–171; cf. Isa. 54:5). For spiritual harlotry, Israel is described as being made to drink the dregs of a cup of horror and desolation (Ezek. 23:32–34), becoming a byword and curse among the people (Deut. 28:37; Jer. 42:18) (M. Douglas 2001: 168–169). Her reading of the strayed woman as a symbol for Israel connects Israel's apostasy at Baal Peor (ch. 25) to the legislation on vows (ch. 30) in a meaningful way: Israel 'has made vows to new husbands and defiled herself, but the Lord, her first husband, has heard her vows and made them void at once, so she will not have to bear the consequences, and he is mercifully willing to take her back' (M. Douglas 2001: 171). MacDonald argues the figural interpretation of the strayed woman as Israel *is* the 'literal reading', which incorporates the text's specificity without collapsing into allegory or making the account merely a parable against adultery (2008a). While some see such an approach as 'over-spiritualising' (R. S. Briggs 2009: 304), it is their failure to interpret the *sotah* ritual within the broader context of both the Camp of Israel (Num. 1 – 6) and the wilderness sojourn (chs. 11–25) that leads to a myopic understanding of its function. Seeing the passage within its larger canonical context as 'a description of the relationship between YHWH and Israel in the wilderness, where YHWH is the jealous husband and Israel the wife suspected of unfaithfulness', MacDonald makes the following observations (2008a: 61–62): first, the rare terms *śāṭah* and *māʿal* are used for turning aside from the right paths and for offences particularly against YHWH, respectively, so that the account does not read as a simple case of suspected adultery; second, the waters of 'bitterness' (*hammārim*), whether taken as 'rebellious, contentious' or as 'bitter', are suggestive of stories about water provision during Israel's wilderness experience, such as the paradigmatic Marah incident of bitter waters (Exod. 15:23; cf. Cocco 2020: 97); third, within its immediate context the *Sotah* and Nazirite appear to be juxtaposed as a contrasting pair of two possible responses to YHWH: the *Sotah* representing unfaithfulness, and the Nazirite an ideal Israel who avoids defilement and faithfully fulfils her vow. Landy also presupposes the texts are symbolic, with the strayed woman and Nazirite comprising structural opposites (2015: 171–172). Nachmanides had already noted the contrast, writing: 'a woman who makes the Nazirite vow is the opposite of the *Sotah*' (see 1975: 45).

Reading the *sotah* as signifying Israel accords remarkably well with the portrait of the Camp of Israel, idealized as the paradigmatic expression of the covenant community. Within this context, Numbers 5 – 6 functions as an expression of the Camp's spiritual essence and heavenly character: the forking paths of covenant disloyalty (death) and loyalty (life) set before Israel by way of the strayed woman and the Nazirite vow (see Lev. 26; Deut. 30:11–20). The failures of Israel's first generation, culminating in their refusal to take possession of the land, are thus described by YHWH as 'your whoredoms' (*zĕnûtêkem*, 14:33), and Israel's judgement is described in a similar manner to that of the guilty strayed woman's 'thigh': that generation's carcasses will 'fall' (*yippĕlû*, 14:29, 32), as YHWH makes Israel 'bear your guilt' in the wilderness (Num. 14:34). In Deuteronomy, YHWH declares that Israel's spiritual harlotry with idols, however secret, will result in the burning of his 'jealousy', so that 'every curse' will settle on such an Israelite, and YHWH will 'blot out' his name from under heaven (29:14–29).

6:1–21: Purity as an individual before God

1–2. Becoming a Nazirite is described positively, as a wondrous or extraordinary vow because it involves separation 'unto YHWH' from common living: for a limited period, an Israelite endeavours to live a life of utter dedication to YHWH. The root of Nazirite, *n-z-r*, is first used in the Torah with reference to Joseph: Jacob's blessings 'will be upon the head of Joseph, on the crown of him who was separate (*nĕzîr*) from his brothers' (Gen. 49:26; see Deut. 33:16; cf. de Vaulx 1972: 90, 103). Just as Jacob pronounces 'blessings' (*birkōt*) on the head of Joseph, who was 'separated' from his brothers, so the priestly blessing (6:22–27) follows the Nazirite vow, which stresses the Nazir's head (6:1–21). Several times *n-z-r* refers to the high priest's holy 'crown', inscribed with 'Holiness to YHWH' (Exod. 29:6; 39:30; Lev. 8:9; 21:12), as well as to other crowns (2 Sam. 1:10; 2 Kgs 11:12; 2 Chr. 23:11; Pss 89:39; 132:18; Prov. 27:24; Zech. 9:16). In Leviticus, the priesthood is to 'keep the sons of Israel separate (*n-z-r*) from their uncleanness' for the sake of YHWH's presence among them (15:31; cf. 22:2), just as the Nazirite desires to be separate from all uncleanness, evenly worldly joys, to draw nearer to YHWH individually. Following Bucer, Calvin connected the enigmatic phrase 'He will be called a Nazarene' (Matt. 2:23) to Judges 13:5: 'for the boy will be a Nazirite (*nĕzîr*) to God from the womb', with Joseph, the Nazirite vow, and Samson comprising dim sketches of the Redeemer who was separated from all 'that he might be the firstborn of among many brothers' (Rom. 8:29) (2003a: 1:163–165). It may well be that 'Nazarene' relates rather to the 'preserved of Israel' (Isa. 49:6) or to the Messianic designation 'Branch' (*nēṣer*) who shoots forth from the stump of Jesse (Isa. 11:1; as *ṣemaḥ*, Jer. 23:5; 33:15; Zech. 3:8; 6:12).

Through vow and consecration, the Nazirite becomes holy (Gudme 2009: 76). Nazirite holiness is likened to that of the high priest, a voluntary embrace of YHWH's calling on all Israel to be his special possession, his kingdom of priests and holy nation (Exod. 19:5–6). Sweeney suggests the vow presents 'the Nazir as an ideal human being, like the first humans from creation' (2017: 78), which also coordinates theologically with Adam as archetypal priest within the garden of Eden, the original holy of holies. The individual's experience would be exemplary for fellow Israelites, inspiring a new sense of holiness and devotion in common life. The last phrase in verse 2, 'separate himself unto YHWH', forms an inclusion with verse 8, 'he is holy unto YHWH', underscoring the logic and goal of the instructions. 'Separate one' would be a choice translation, in place of 'Nazirite', bringing out the root's wide use in the text (24 times). The Bible tells of a few lifelong Nazirites, Samson and Samuel (Judg. 13:5; 1 Sam. 1:11), and of Nazirites among Israel's young men raised up by God and honoured akin to prophets (Amos 2:11–12). The limited duration vow appears to have been practised regularly (Acts 18:18; 21:23–24; cf. 1 Macc. 3:49) (see G. B. Gray 1900: 202–204).

Since *'iš* may already designate a man or a woman, it is significant that the text further specifies *'iš 'ô-'iššā*, allowing for contrasting portrayals of Israel as YHWH's bride, two alternate paths: the strayed wife, who forsakes her husband for worldly pleasure (5:11–31) versus the Nazirite woman, who forsakes worldly pleasure to draw closer to YHWH (6:1–21).

3–8. After opening with 'to whom' the Nazirite is separated, these verses describe 'from what' the Nazirite is separated, setting out the double-sided aspect of consecration. The phrase 'all the days of his (vow of) separation' occurs four times, the first three delineating the three abstentions (grape products, hair cutting, death pollution, vv. 4, 5, 6) and the fourth instance summarizing the point of the vow, a Nazirite's status as holy unto YHWH (v. 8). Each of the three abstentions underscores and signifies separation unto YHWH. The first separation is from wine and 'intoxicating drink' (*šēkār*), as well as from any grape product (vv. 3–4). As wine often represents the joys of life (cf. Ps. 104:15), separation from wine and grape products signifies the Nazirite's comprehensively new disposition, endeavouring to seek pleasure in YHWH rather than in the pleasures of this life, sacrificing the latter for a period of time, reorienting those pleasures by prioritizing one's relationship to God. In practical terms, the prohibition creates a spiritual removal from the normal joys of life. Refraining from wine at a wedding, for example, diminished participation in celebration, ensuring a measure of distance – the joys or 'highs' of life were thus measured, set within the broader perspective of being consecrated to YHWH. The Nazirite's prohibition of wine and grape products parallels that of priests, although the former's restriction is more severe since priests were only to abstain from wine and strong drink while officiating at the Tent of Meeting (Lev. 10:8–9). Perhaps, while priests have a designated sacred space of service, the Tent of Meeting, wherein they avoid intoxication, the Nazirite's space is comprehensive, always 'serving' God throughout the period of consecration.

The second abstention is from passing a razor over the head, also phrased positively as allowing the loosened-locks of hair to grow (v. 5). This abstention is central structurally and thematically, as it will become integral to the Nazir's culminating act of worship (v. 18). Once the head is dedicated, then it cannot be shorn during the period of separation as this would be a misappropriation of *sancta*, similar to the prohibition against shearing sheep that have been dedicated to God (Deut. 15:19; Diamond 1997: 5). The language used for the Nazirite's unshorn hair echoes the language used for unpruned grape vines during the land's Sabbatical and Jubilee periods (Lev. 25:5, 11), yielding a helpful analogy: the Nazirite, represented by his or her hair, enters a Sabbath period of dedication to YHWH, the long locks of hair like so many uncut tendrils of a vine. This analogy may also relate to the Nazirite's complete abstention from grape products, since the land's vines were left completely untouched. The nation of Israel is described as God's 'vine' that he brought up out of Egypt and planted in the land (Ps. 80:8–9; Isa. 5:1–2); as such, the Nazirite holds out an ideal for all Israel, one fulfilled ultimately in Jesus Christ, the 'true vine' (John 15:1, 5). The 'head' (rōʾš) in Hebrew stands for the whole (cf. v. 11), even as one's hair represents the whole person (cf. G. B. Gray 1903: 69), and it will eventually be sacrificed to God – a self-sacrifice. The unshorn locks of hair thus signify the Nazirite's period of separation (cf. Kurtz 1863: 445). Noted previously, the strayed woman's 'loosened' (pāraʿ) hair and the Nazir's 'locks' (peraʿ) are the only uses of this root in Numbers (5:18; 6:5), linking the two laws. The phrase 'he is holy' (v. 5) provides the significance of the unshorn hair and purpose of the vow. Later, Israel will be reminded to 'be holy to your God' (15:41), a hint that the Nazirite vow functions as a goal for all Israel.

The third abstention is from any contact with the dead, including close kin – father, mother, or siblings (vv. 6–7). This restriction is more severe than for ordinary priests who were allowed to be defiled for close family members (Lev. 21:1–2), and on par with the requirement for the high priest (Lev. 21:11). Ceremonial law forms a catechism, here teaching that YHWH God is the fountain of life. His holiness being inseparable from his nature as absolute life, one tainted by death cannot approach him without being consumed. As with the distancing from the joys of life effected through the prohibition of grape products, the abstention from contact with the dead effects a distancing from the deep sorrows of life. Grossman captures the individual versus community dynamic involved (2014c: 69): The Nazir 'cannot participate in moments of communal sadness and mourning (being charged to refrain from contact with death), or in moments of communal joy and celebration (since he is prohibited to partake of wine)'. The main reason for avoiding death pollution is given in terms of the unshorn hair, 'the crown-of-separation to his God is upon his head' (v. 7). In the final section (vv. 13–21), it becomes clear the abstentions have in view the vow's fulfilment, that the Nazir's period of consecration was a preparing of his 'hair-sacrifice' (cf. Diamond 1997: 6). As an offering, the Nazirite's hair cannot be defiled or else it will be unfit to offer up to YHWH on the altar.

Even if the declaration of verse 8 forms an integral part of the third abstention (cf. v. 5a for the second abstention), yet being placed at the conclusion it functions as a cap and summation for the whole section (vv. 1–8), before turning to the contingency that follows (vv. 9–12). The Nazirite's three abstentions may reflect the same three concentric spheres comprised by the Camp: wine/grape products (sphere of society), corpse pollution even for father, mother, brother or sister (sphere of family), unshorn hair to be sacrificed (individual sphere). The legislation lists unshorn hair second (v. 5), but this is to make it central and because corpse defilement cannot otherwise be explained (v. 6). Such selfless Godward love in every sphere of life was intended to be inspiring for all Israel. Calvin wrote that 'God's peculiar glory' shone brightly on the Nazirites, who 'shone among the people of God like precious jewels . . . they were as standard-bearers and leaders to awaken zeal amongst the multitude for the service of God' (2003b: 4:486–487).

9–12. Milgrom marks these verses as the centre of a chiastic structure, indicating that ritual impurity is a major concern (1990: 359), in keeping with the general subject matter of Numbers 5 – 6. This section addresses the possible scenario of someone dying unexpectedly in close proximity to the Nazirite, making him unclean. As a result, the previous period of dedication is forfeit, including the growth of locks of hair which are now defiled, and the period vowed to YHWH must be started over. The Nazir is considered unclean until the seventh day, the day of his or her 'cleansing' (ṭohŏrāh), a regulation that depends on and antici-pates the fuller explanation in Numbers 19:11–16. On the eighth day, he brings two turtledoves or pigeons (inexpensive sacrifices; cf. Lev. 5:7; 12:8; 14:30–31), as purification and whole burnt offerings, respec-tively, for the priest to make atonement. The whole burnt offering, in which the entire animal apart from its skin – or, in this case, the whole bird – was consumed on the altar, signified utter consecration to God (Morales 2015: 132–137), a fitting goal in line with the Nazirite vow. These sacrifices were followed by a reparation offering of a yearling male lamb, although previous legislation called for a female lamb (Lev. 5:6), marking out the Nazirite ritual as its own unique case. Whereas purification offerings focused on cleansing (and forgiveness, for moral offences), reparation offerings require some further action on the part of the offeror to make restitution for the previous wrong; in this case, the Nazirite needs to reconsecrate his head.

Probably, 'he sinned' by the corpse (v. 11) should be understood as 'went amiss'. In Deuteronomy 23:21, a delay in fulfilling one's vow to YHWH is considered sin, and it may be the same idea is present in this context since the Nazirite's defilement delays fulfilment. The understanding 'went amiss' seems preferable since statements of being guilty, confessing, and being forgiven, associated with purification and reparation offerings in the context of transgression (vs purity alone), are lacking (cf. Lev. 4:20, 26, 31, 35; 5:10, 13, 16, 18). The reparation offering is required to make restoration for defiled sancta, here the Nazirite, symbolized by his or her hair. Following Milgrom, Gudme suggests the Nazirite is guilty of ma'al, the sin of defiling or misusing a sacred item, with the purification and whole burnt offerings serving to restore cultic order, and the reparation offering serving as an apology (2009: 79; G. A. Anderson 1992b: 880–881). Saydon (1946: 398), however, defined the *'āšām* offering as 'an expiatory offering for sins for which one is accountable though they are unintentional'. In any case, the 'sin' appears to be dealt with by the purification and whole burnt offerings, making atonement for the Nazirite, while the reparation offering is connected to his (re)consecration.

The Nazirite does not shave his head until the seventh day, *after* the period of impurity has passed; otherwise any new growth of hair would still be considered unclean. His shorn head is reconsecrated on the eighth day, the day of new creation, marking a new beginning. The section ends with the notice that the former days 'fall away', since the whole period of the vow, marked by the locks of hair, must be completely undefiled. The judgement for defilement, that the Nazirite's former days 'fall away' (v. 12), marks another parallel with the strayed woman's judgement for defilement, that her thigh 'falls away' (5:21, 22, 27).

13–21. With 'this is the *torah* of the Nazirite', a new section begins that forms the culmination and *telos* for the period of separation. Although offerings are listed in various orders in Scripture, with the whole burnt offering typically heading the list as the cult's summation, the procedural order of sacrifice is as follows: purification offering, whole burnt offering (along with tribute accompaniments), peace offering, in a movement that progresses from expiation to consecration to fellowship (see Morales 2015: 122–124). This lavish set of sacrifices formed a prelude to the offering of the Nazir's hair. Upon fulfilment of the days of separation, the Nazirite is ready to offer up to YHWH the gift of himself, his life of consecration throughout the period of the vow, symbolized by his hair. Among other cultures as well, sacrificing one's hair was understood 'virtually as a sacrifice of oneself' (Robertson Smith 1927: 607). The ceremony, including shearing and sacrifice, served as the culmination of the Nazirite's period of separation. The function of shaving, therefore, is less about the idea of aggregation into normal Israelite society (contra Olyan 1998: 615), but rather its being a means for offering up the consecrated head of hair – the Nazirite is still rising to the culmination of his vow, rather than focusing on a return to mundane life. The phrase 'this is the torah' that frames this section (vv. 13, 21) demonstrates that all that has come before was but preparation for this rite of worship. While every day of consecration was in a sense sacrificial, involving self-denial, yet those days had not been offered up to YHWH *yet*. When the hair, signifying the whole period of separation, is placed on the fire, then that period is finally rendered to God in one supreme act of sacrifice.

The crucial point is that the days of separation and growth of hair locks were for the sake of this ceremony. The hair offering is made possible only by – and would be meaningless without – the previous days of separation. Indeed, this end is the *starting point* of the Nazirite vow: the Nazirite, in response to the goodness and mercies of YHWH, had asked, 'What shall I render unto God?' What can be offered to the One who owns 'the cattle on a thousand hills' (Ps. 50:10), and has 'redeemed your life from destruction' (Ps. 103:4)? The would-be Nazirite determines to offer up his or her *self*, and the period of separation is in view of that culminating offering.

Reference to the tribute (*minḥāh*) and drinking (*nesek*) offerings, usually presented as a pair, is significant (v. 15), as these offerings could only be offered *within the land*, and, more, agriculture and vine-growing would be the characteristic employments and production of the nation in the land (Kurtz 1863: 181) – they signify the good life in the land. The *minḥāh* (also 'grain' or 'cereal offering') required fine flour (Lev. 2; cf. Milgrom 1991: 179), and the *nesek* required viniculture, but no wheat or barley, or grapes were to be found in the wilderness. This point feeds into the theology of the Nazirite vow as a 'path': Israel should face the wilderness sojourn as a Nazirite, a holy nation, anticipating the fulfilment of the vow in the land, where abundant clusters of grapes await (see 13:23–24).

Historically, much puzzlement has been expressed over the Nazirite's need for a purification offering at this point – what sin has the Nazirite committed? While Maimonides regarded the act of becoming a Nazirite, austerely forsaking world and pleasure, to be the sin, for Nachmanides the sin was rather in forsaking the Nazirite vow, so as to return to the world and pleasure (Leibowitz 1982: 56). In this case, however, the purification offering, unlike the one in verse 11, is more general in nature, similar instead to the purification offerings involved in the ordination of priests (Exod. 29:14; Lev. 8:2, 14) and Levites (Num. 8:8, 12) that, within the context of a rite of passage, has the sort of purifying function that is prerequisite for a transition into a state of enhanced intimacy with God. As Gane discerned, the purification offering accomplishes the cleansing needed for being elevated to an exceptional degree of sanctity, one that exceeds the previous status of holiness experienced during the period of the vow, since a purification offering was not needed to become a Nazirite (2008: 11–12, 16). It is crucial to observe, with Grossman (2014c: 70), that the Nazir undertakes 'a dedication ceremony . . . at the completion of his term which resembles the dedication of the *Mishkan*'. Rather than a sort of de-sacralization or a purification from undue asceticism, the Nazirite is rather *being prepared* for his culminating priestly act of (symbolic) self-sacrifice, where he will place (*nātan*) his hair on the fire under the peace offering (v. 18). This placement on the fire, in relation to the peace offering, precludes the notion that this action indicates mere disposal of hair in fire outside the Camp (cf. Keil and Delitzsch 1973: 3:39; Gane 2008: 14–15) – disposal rites use the term śārap consistently (e.g. Lev. 4:12, 21).

The Nazirite thus becomes both offering and officiant – having dedicated himself to YHWH by vow, he now offers himself to YHWH on the altar by means of his hair (Diamond 1997: 5). The long locks of hair, which had grown steadily day by day, encapsulate his daily separation from the world for the sake of God, his daily living for the glory of YHWH throughout the period of his consecration. Culminating in a final act of worship, the Nazirite's Godward sacrificial life is now itself sacrificed. Philo's eloquent statement is justified (*Spec. Laws* 1.248): with nothing else left to offer, Nazirites

> consecrate and offer up themselves, displaying an unspeakable holiness, and most superabundant excess of a God-loving disposition, on which account such a dedication is fitly called the great vow; for every man is his own greatest and most valuable possession, and this even he now gives up and abandons. (Tr. Yonge; Philo 1993: 227)

The Nazirite gift of self-sacrifice is indeed 'as close as the Israelite cult comes to human sacrifice' (Gane 2008: 14). This momentary priestly act, accomplished under heightened sanctity, was the aim of the vow, by which an Israelite aspired to Israel's highest calling as the special possession of YHWH (Exod. 19:5–6). His or her sacrificial act explains why the Nazirite's holiness was even comparable to the high priest's (see Knohl 2007: 160–161; Luzzato 2016: 48). Numbers 6:18 may relate the *only* occasion a non-priestly Israelite was permitted to ascend the altar and place a sacrifice on YHWH's flames – an act forbidden even to the non-priestly Levite on pain of death (cf. Gane 2008: 15). Through the sacrifice of his hair, the Nazirite, as priest and sacrifice, offered himself up to God.

The priest then places parts of the peace offering and an unleavened bread cake and wafer in the hands of the shorn Nazirite, a gesture conjoined with the sacrifice that in a manner draws YHWH's notice on the Nazirite and his offering. The priest's portion of the peace offering is noted, being elevated before YHWH, as happens with all priestly share of sacrifice. The elevation gesture, along with the lifting of the 'contri-bution' (*tĕrûmāh*), was likely intended to put the offering before God for his acceptance (cf. Levine 1989: 46). McNeile suggested the portion was waved or swung toward the altar and back ('wave offering'), signifying the giving of it first to God, and then God returning it for the priest's own use (1911: 36; cf. Budd 1984: 72–73), though Milgrom argues the portions were merely elevated before YHWH (1983b: 133–158). The priest receives a greater portion than is typical for other peace offerings, perhaps due to the exceptional nature of the Nazarite ceremony (cf. Scurlock 2006: 251). See 18:11 for the divine designation of contributions and elevation offerings for priests.

Finally, the Nazirite is allowed to drink wine, portraying his return to common life, and its enjoyments from the hand of God. As the worship-per's portion of meat from the peace offering was typically enjoyed with family and friends, a festive occasion celebrated in the presence of

YHWH, wine was likely a part of this fellowship meal concluding the ceremony (cf. Landy 2015: 189). Having refrained from grape products for a designated period out of devotion to him, the shorn Nazirite now drinks wine anew in a feast with YHWH in the land.

6:22–27: YHWH's presence and blessing throughout Israel's Camp

The priestly blessing, which mediates both the presence and blessing of God, has long been connected to Aaron's blessing at the conclusion of the Tent of Meeting's inaugural service in Leviticus 9:22–23 (*Sif. Num.* 39; cf. Wellhausen 1889: 177), pronounced as the culmination of the morning 'daily' (*tāmîd*) whole burnt offerings (*Tam.* 5.1; 7.2; see J. W. Kleinig 2003: 218–220; Rothkoff 2007: 464; Morales 2015: 141–143). It is all the more remarkable, then, that the divinely revealed script for Israel's benediction was reserved not for Leviticus, the book on Israel's cult, but for Numbers, the book on Israel's covenant community, as the fruition of YHWH's dwelling in the midst of the tribes. Numbers 1 – 6 fittingly ends with divine blessings ushering forth from the central Tent, encompassing the whole Camp and casting the light of his face on every Israelite within its bounds. The purpose of the cult and its culminating blessing by the priesthood (Lev.) is for the sake of the blessed life with YHWH God as a community (Num. 1 – 6) – this life is the *telos* of both cult and covenant. The priestly benediction looks outward to the Camp from the central perspective of the camp of the *Shekhinah*, expressing YHWH's kingship in the form of outpoured blessing.

The form of the priestly benediction has resonances with other divine blessings in the ANE (cf. Awabdy 2018). Such a blessing was particularly relevant within the context of the impending wilderness sojourn. Perhaps the somewhat similar context of the annual journeys to Jerusalem for the pilgrim festivals (Passover, Weeks and Booths), along with the return of the captivity to Zion to stand before YHWH's life-giving face at the Temple (Exod. 23:17; see G. A. Anderson 2008: 15), led to incorporating phrases from the priestly blessing within the Psalms of Ascent (Pss 120 – 134) (see Liebreich 1995; D. Barker 2005; D. C. Mitchell 2015: 7, 17). Just as there are 15 words in the blessing, there are 15 psalms in the Ascent collection (and 15 steps of the Temple stairway on each of which, Jewish tradition indicates, Levites would sing one of the Ascent psalms, *Middot* 2.5; *Sukkah* 5.4). Chavel suggests each of the three lines of the blessing may correspond to the three stages of pilgrimage: greeted and invited to enter upon arrival at Jerusalem, enjoying the pleasure of YHWH's presence when coming before him at the Temple, and being granted safety and bounty upon departing his presence to return home (2012: 19). The entire group of Ascent psalms 'is related, directly or indirectly, to four key words of the Priestly Blessing'; namely *bārak* (bless), *šāmar* (keep), *ḥānan* (be gracious), and *šālôm* (peace), while other psalms allude to YHWH's shining his face upon his people (Pss 31:16; 67:1; 119:135), to the light of his face (Pss 4:6; 44:3; 89:15; 80:3, 7, 19) (Liebreich 1995: 33; cf. Ashley 1993: 151), and to seeking YHWH's face (24:6; 27:8; 105:4). The Ascent psalms are also linked by Zion theology, which has some relevance for the Camp's analogy to the city of God developed earlier; the blessings expressed in relation to Zion in Psalm 147:12–14 are foretasted within Israel's Camp. Seeing God's face is used in the psalms to represent the worshippers' culminating experience in the Temple as an experience of his presence in a restored paradise (M. Smith 1988: 181), a function expressed in the priestly blessing.

As the finale to Israel's cultic ceremonies and festivals, and the summit of the Torah's portrayal of life with God, the priestly benediction expresses the sojourn's end – the goal of creation and salvation history, and the deepest yearning of God's people. In the midst of the dereliction of exile, Daniel's prayer alluded to the priestly blessing when he pleaded with God to 'cause your face to shine upon your sanctuary which is desolate' for 'your city and your people are called by your Name' (Dan. 9:17, 19). As this blessed presence of God had been tasted by Moses, Israel's mediator who knew YHWH 'face to face' and had seen something of the beatific 'form of YHWH' (Num. 12:8) so that his own face radiated with God's glory (Exod. 34:27–35), the Aaronic benediction expresses the hope for all of God's people to share in the glory of God (2 Cor. 3:7–18; cf. D. N. Freedman 1975: 40; Stubbs 2009: 69). The blessing is intrinsic to Israel's calling as Abraham's seed to be a blessing, for as Israel reflects the glory and Name of YHWH, the nations will be blessed (Gen. 12:1–3; 22:18; cf. Num. 14:21). Psalm 67:1–2 captures this reality and calling: 'May God be gracious to us and bless us, may he shine his face upon us, so that your way may be known on the earth, your salvation among all the nations'. God's saving work in history is deeply connected to his work of providential blessing (see P. D. Miller 1975: 248).

With its threefold proclamation of YHWH's Name, linked to his gracious character, the benediction is connected to Exodus 33:12–23, glistening as 'a jewel' of God's self-revelation (Seebass 2006: 43–45). Proclaiming 'my Name YHWH' to Moses, God declares, 'I will be gracious to whom I will be gracious' (Exod. 33:19); now the divine command demonstrates YHWH God's sovereign decision to be gracious to Israel. As the threefold use of the Name is also an invocation, a calling upon YHWH within the context of the cult, the benediction also functions as a verbal theophany, communicating YHWH's commitment to be with Israel, accompanying his people along the wilderness sojourn. On the summit of Sinai, Moses declares, 'If your face (*pānêkā*) does not go with us, do not bring us up from this place' (Exod. 33:15), so the priestly benediction conveys both the weight of Moses' mediation as well as his own comprehension of the utter necessity of God's presence for Israel's beatitude – invoking and communicating the goal of the covenant, YHWH's presence among his people through the cult. The connection between YHWH's *pānîm* (face) and Israel's cult has also led to understanding the priestly blessing as a cultic theophany (Beyerlin 1965: 104–107), the benediction being the 'one passage above all others' where YHWH's blessing is brought together with the cultic theology of his presence, showing that the gift of peace can only be received in his presence (Durham 1970: 286, 292). People err in seeking the benefits of YHWH apart from restoration to his presence.

22–23. 'And YHWH spoke to Moses, saying' opens and unites every section of Numbers 5 – 6 (5:1, 5, 11; 6:1, 22), here serving as the climactic and culminating word from YHWH in the movement of Numbers 1 – 6. Israel's assurance of YHWH's favourable disposition is anchored here, which communicates that the blessing received through Aaron and his sons was not only divinely revealed in substance, but that the act of blessing Israel is itself divinely commanded as an expression of YHWH's established will and determination. 'Just so' (*kō*) indicates a particularity on YHWH's part which, given that he knows precisely the needs of his people better than they, leads to Israel's own prayerful longing after such blessing, and to the jubilant praises of YHWH as their source. The direction 'you (pl.) will bless' (*tĕbārăkû*) marks the priesthood as YHWH's designated channel of blessing. The opening divine speech (v. 22), the threefold use of YHWH within the blessing, and YHWH's emphatic 'I' (*'ănî*, v. 27), make clear, however, that it is not the priests themselves who can bless Israel, nor does their recitation form any sort of magical incantation, but rather the reverse: YHWH uses the priesthood for his own purposes of goodwill toward his people. YHWH's participation establishes priests as the only ones sovereignly designated to pronounce the benediction, who have been set aside to 'bless in his Name' (Deut. 10:8). Aaron's house, moreover, is not simply authorized to pronounce the blessing; rather, the scripted blessing of Israel is their duty, part of their cultic service (cf. Hirsch 2007a: 120).

To 'bless' here comprises a general summary for the whole content of verses 24–26, underscoring God's benevolent plans for Israel. The blessing calls not merely for benefits from YHWH, but rather for YHWH himself to have a favourable disposition toward Israel; the following two lines begin with a general expression of God's favour, such as 'lifting' or 'shining' his face, which, in contrast to the expression for hiding his face (*histîr pānîm*) as a withdrawal of his favour, signals his being favourably disposed (C. W. Mitchell 1987: 96). The benediction's three lines may thus be understood as: 'YHWH's benevolence means protection/ YHWH's benevolence means grace/ YHWH's benevolence means peace'

(Korpel 1989: 7). The blessing invokes, first, God's favourable *movement* and disposition toward Israel, and, second, his *activity* (provision, protection, etc.) on Israel's behalf (P. D. Miller 1975: 243; Milgrom 1990: 51). This twofold aspect explains the logic of verse 27: (1) they will put my Name on the sons of Israel (YHWH's favourable disposition), and so (2) I will bless them (YHWH's gracious action).

24. The opening positions YHWH's Name between 'bless' and 'keep', as the source and centre of Israel's good and help. Psalm 16:1 – 'Keep me (*šāměrēnî*), O God, for in you I take refuge' – is but one example of how Israelites claimed YHWH's blessing, as the revelation of his determined will, for the sake of personal and national deliverance. Bless and keep present the twofold all-encompassing needs of Israel: God's favour and protective care. These two elements are taken up in the blessing's second (v. 25) and third (26) lines, respectively, as his grace and peace. The collocation of 'bless' and 'keep' with YHWH as the subject of both is found elsewhere only in the divine word to Jacob in Genesis 28:14–15 (cf. Korpel 1989: 5) – the link in this passage between God's presence (I am with you) and benefit (and will keep you) is relevant for the message of the priestly blessing as well. YHWH proved faithful in bringing Jacob/'Israel' into Canaan 'in peace', and overflowing with blessings of prosperity and physical fruitfulness, so that the patriarch's return to the land foreshadowed the nation's entry. As in verses 25 and 26, the object of blessing is 'you' in the *singular*, underscoring YHWH's mindfulness and goodwill for every single Israelite in the Camp. Deuteronomy 28:3–14 catalogues what 'bless' means, including fruitfulness regarding children, crops, herds and flocks, with health and well-being in the land, victory over enemies, and is linked to Israel's association with YHWH's Name. As Psalms 91 and 121 show, 'keep' refers to God's watchful care over his people, protecting them from all manner of harm (pestilences, famine, wild beasts, enemy attacks, evil spirits), throughout night and day, whether lying down or rising up, coming or going – that is, 'the help of God in the face of every misfortune and disaster' (Noth 1968: 59). With the wilderness journey ahead, divine 'keeping' of Israel answers the nation's urgent need of guidance and protection. YHWH's benediction forms a deep wellspring for meditation, praise, and prayer. The Lord's prayer, which similarly prescribes recitation ('In this manner' pray, Matt. 6:9//'In this manner' bless, Num. 6:22), includes provisions for daily needs as well as a plea for deliverance from the evil one (Matt. 6:9–13).

While 'bless' certainly includes a life of health and fruitfulness in family and fields, and 'keep' includes guidance while on journey, deliverance from enemies, and protection from pestilence and other dangers, these should not be reduced merely to physical benefits. The priesthood's blessing from YHWH is the culmination of their work of atonement, as the soothing aroma turns YHWH from a posture of wrath against humanity, releasing his blessing (cf. Gen. 8:20–22). The cultic context of the benediction (Lev. 9:22–23; cf. P. D. Miller 1975: 242, 246) is both decisive and defining: the blessing comes to Israel *through a priesthood* at the culmination of cultic rites *based on atonement*. God's benefits begin with his forgiving 'all your iniquities', for as 'far as the east is from the west, so far has he removed our transgressions from us' (Ps. 103:3, 12), integrating spiritual and physical benefits, and blossoming finally into that eternal life of love, peace and joy in New Jerusalem.

25. YHWH's 'blessing' in the first part of verse 24 is elaborated with a portrayal of his face shining upon Israel for the sake of acting graciously toward them. The first part of the verse calls for YHWH's movement and favourable disposition toward Israel, out of which the second part calls for a concrete action, expressing such favour. God is linked to light by his first speech in Scripture, 'Let there be light (*'ôr*)' (Gen. 1:3), a light traditionally understood as uncreated, a manifestation of YHWH's glory (cf. M. Smith 2010: 71–79). Given the Dwelling's eastward orientation, solar imagery is possible here (see M. Smith 1988) – note the description of Judah's encampment: 'eastward, toward the rising of the sun' (Num. 2:3). Psalm 31:16 parallels 'Shine your face upon your servant' with 'save me in your steadfast love'. For YHWH to 'be gracious' to Israel means that his people will experience his loving-kindness and tender mercies in all spheres of life. Ultimately, it is the face of Jesus the Messiah, the light of the world (John 8:12; cf. 1:9), that shines the light of the glory of God upon the redeemed (2 Cor. 4:6). His transfiguration, writes V. Kleinig (1985: 122), fulfils 'many of the expressions in the Aaronic benediction'.

Within the context of the Camp's purity (Num. 5:1 – 6:21), the priestly benediction's portrayal of the Camp as radiant with the shining of YHWH's face marks a logical progression in the ANE worldview. Feder, after examining terms for purity in biblical Hebrew, Akkadian, Hittite, Sumerian and Ugaritic, concluded that in all of these languages purity terms are etymologically related to radiance (brilliance, brightness, shininess), typically used to describe materials – such as gems, precious metals, fine oil – that are associated with the divine (2014). Not only were the Dwelling and its furnishings – many of which were made of precious metals like 'pure gold' (cf. Haran 1985: 163) – anointed with oil, but Aaron and his sons were anointed with oil as well (Exod. 30:30), an act that made one's face radiant, much like Moses' after meeting with YHWH on the summit of Sinai in Exodus 34:29–35 (Ps. 104:15; see Wenkel 2013). That Israelites needed to be 'pure' to approach YHWH's Dwelling may not be unrelated to the 'pure' (*ṭāhôr*) gold that characterized the furnishings of the inner shrine (Exod. 25:11, 17, 24, etc.), the conceptual overlap, again, being that of radiance. The high priest's breastplate portrayed the Camp in miniature, a foursquare arrangement in which each tribe was represented by a precious gem, sparkling with God's luminous glory. These various features portray the Camp as a foretaste of the consummation of the covenant, a paradisal temple-city of God lit up and radiant with divine glory (Ezek. 40 – 48; Rev. 21 – 22; cf. Matt. 5:8).

26. YHWH's uplifted face is a portrait of covenant benefits, based on his pleasurable acceptance of Israel, even as covenant threats are expressed by YHWH's hiding his face (Deut. 31:17–18; 32:20; cf. Lev. 17:10; 20:3–5; Isa. 64:6–7), a summary of the drought and famine, defeat and destruction, and, ultimately, exile, God's people would endure under his displeasure over their apostasy. In Ezekiel 39:23–24, because of Israel's iniquity and unfaithfulness to him, YHWH says 'I hid my face from them,' a gesture that led to Israel's captivity and fall by the sword. Psalm 27, which mentions seeking YHWH's face, parallels YHWH's hiding his face with turning the psalmist away in anger, and with the idea of forsakenness (vv. 8–10), so that turning his face to the psalmist would include the notions of presence, help and salvation. Deuteronomy 28:50 demonstrates that lifting the face was idiomatic for a favourable disposition – YHWH's 'smile' (cf. Gruber 2009: 253). The movement, for both verses 25 and 26, is noteworthy: first, 'may Israel know YHWH's pleasure'; then, as a consequence, or within the context of that relationship, 'may YHWH be gracious to you / give you peace'. As channelled through the priesthood, knowing YHWH's pleasure is supported by the sacrificial cult's provision of reconciliation, making the Aaronic benediction fitting as a conclusion to worship (cf. Lev. 9:22). Seebass suggests a diagonal scheme where 'YHWH bless you' of the first line connects to 'peace', the last word of the last line, as the aim, final point and summary essence of blessing, recalling Psalm 29:11b: 'YHWH bless his people with peace' (2006: 38). Milgrom similarly marks the lines 'May YHWH bless you/ and give you peace' as an envelope around the blessing (1990: 51). 'Peace' is the fundamental goal of 'bless'. From this perspective, 'peace' looks to an Israel that is blessed, guarded and treated graciously by God; an Israel that is doubly in YHWH's presence ('face' in vv. 25, 26); an Israel that is fulfilled and complete (Durham 1970: 292).

While the final word 'peace' serves as a fitting climax, even the goal of Israel's redemptive history, it also retains provision for daily needs. In the Jacob cycle, which also underscores themes of blessing and God's face, Jacob vowed that YHWH would be his God if only YHWH would be 'with me and keep me (*šĕmāranî*) on this way' so that he may return to his father's house 'in peace' (*bĕšālôm*), a condition of well-being which he elaborated as providing bread, clothes and protection (Gen. 28:20–21), the sort of concerns Israel would have along the wilderness trek as well (and both Jacob and the Israelites faced the threat of foes on returning to the land). Nevertheless, 'peace' is here 'used in the widest sense to include every divine blessing, and which now combines the supreme good of fellowship with God with the blessings of earthly life' (Eichrodt 1976a: 2:358). Peace is the comprehensive fullness of life that derives only from the God known as *yhwh-šālôm* (Jud. 6:24), who grants his people peace, through his presence with them (2 Thess. 3:16). The blessing looks to everything the seventh day signifies within the creation account (Gen. 1:1 – 2:3), it *is* Sabbath: abundant life with God, within a creation that abounds with all the pleasures of pure life and goodness. As blessing pours out from YHWH's Dwelling to the farthest reaches of the Camp, the priestly benediction expresses the goal of the Sinai covenant, whose sign is the Sabbath (Exod. 31:12–18).

27. Aside from clarifying that it is YHWH himself (*'ănî*) who will bless Israel, with priests having an instrumental role, this verse closes Numbers 1 – 6 with a deeply profound final statement regarding the newly created covenant community: *the Camp of Israel bears the divine Name*. It has already been noted that the three cases in 5:5–10, 11–31 and 6:1–21 involve (1) an oath in YHWH's Name, and (2) the idea that the holiness of God's Dwelling has been extended by degree to the rest of the Camp. Both notions come together through the priestly benediction, which places YHWH's Name upon the Camp. Y. Twersky, observing similarities with YHWH's previous declaration that 'in every place where I cause my Name to be remembered I will come to you and will bless you' (Exod. 20:24), suggests the priestly benediction not only places the *Shekhinah* on the entire Camp, but serves as a basis for priestly service (2007b: 2:142–143). The significance of YHWH's Name in the benediction should be fully appreciated, as Fishbane makes clear: the 'core of the blessing is not simply the specification of the blessings – central as this is – but rather the ritual use of the sacred divine Name, thrice repeated' (1983: 115). Invoking his Name over Israel, placing it upon them, identifies and links Israel with YHWH, his presence and character, closely. To put the divine Name on Israel pronounces them to be YHWH's possession, renewing Israel's election and vocation (Gispen 1959: 1:120; Seybold 1977: 44); in this sense, the priestly benediction also functions as a means by which YHWH the King claims his property, laying hold of the people he has redeemed – a fitting bookend with the opening census. 'Everyone who is called by my Name', YHWH proclaims, 'is one whom I created for my glory, whom I formed and made' (Isa. 43:7) – a wondrous pronouncement on the newly formed Camp of Israel.

More deeply, the Jerusalem Temple would be known as the place chosen by YHWH for his Name to dwell (Deut. 12:5, 11; 16:6), Solomon declaring that he had built 'the house for the Name of YHWH God of Israel' (1 Kgs 8:20). As such 'name' is the counterpart to the term 'glory' with reference to YHWH's presence in the Dwelling. Achenbach writes, 'Thus the congregation itself seems almost to embody the sanctuary' (2016: 49), since laying his Name on them is like resting his radiant glory on them. Putting YHWH's Name on Israel, therefore, reflects the Camp's new status: pervaded by his presence, the Camp is something of an extended temple even as the blessing itself comprises 'the verbal extension of the temple' (Smoak 2016: 134; see 112–113, 131). YHWH's Name is so sacred, that any desecration of it by an Israelite was subject to the death penalty (Lev. 24:10–23), and here Israel is being clothed, as it were, with his Name. Putting his Name on Israel marks the Camp as the dwelling place of YHWH God. Bearing his Name, the nation of Israel becomes a priestly kingdom, even as the high priest bore YHWH's Name on his brow, inscribed on the golden diadem attached to his turban with a blue cord. Imes writes (2019: 61), 'While Aaron literally bore YHWH's name on his forehead, the people, having been blessed, bore an invisible brand that marked them as belonging to YHWH.' The connection to the high priest's diadem recalls our discussion of the Nazirite vow's function as a path of holiness for all Israel to pursue (cf. Num. 15:37–41). Bearing YHWH's Name was a weighty charge: 'You shall not bear (*tiśśāʾ*) the Name of YHWH your God in vain' (Exod. 20:7; Deut. 5:11; see Bar-Ilan 1989; Imes 2018).

Israel's blessing is portrayed as the *result* of their bearing YHWH's Name (on the Ketef Hinnom amulets, currently the oldest extant biblical text, c. 600 BC, see Bar-Ilan 1989; Smoak 2012; 2016). The closing clause 'I will bless them', one of the rare instances of this verb in the first person with YHWH as its subject, calls to mind the promise to Abraham (Gen. 12:2–3), a connection that, as Smoak observes (2016: 72), links 'the priestly blessing to these theophanies in the narrative of Genesis-Numbers'. With cult sites connected to God's favourable presence (Exod. 20:24), Israel's Camp has become *the* locale of YHWH's Name, presence and blessing. Calling on the Name of YHWH, moreover, defines God's people of every age (cf. Gen. 4:26; 12:8; 13:4; 21:33; 1 Kgs 18:24; etc.), although Levine is correct to emphasize the priesthood's role here, that 'the priests open the door to the granting of the blessings by God' who 'must be invoked by Name' (1993: 228).

Explanation

After the outer camp of twelve tribes is established (Num. 1 – 2), and the inner camp of Levites (Num. 3 – 4), with YHWH's Dwelling in the centre, Numbers 5 – 6 proceeds to set forth the spiritual dynamic of the Camp of YHWH's earthly hosts, in relation to the camp of the *Shekhinah* (cf. Keil and Delitzsch 1973: 3:28). The major function of this section is to underscore that the Camp is a heavenly community, pervaded by YHWH's holy presence, impacting every member and relationship within its bounds. The holiness of the Tent of Meeting as expounded in Leviticus has now extended by degree to the rest of the Camp that has been organized around – and spiritually linked to – YHWH's Dwelling. With YHWH God in its midst, the entire Camp – not merely the Sanctuary area – is to be guarded from the defilement of impurity. Three purity cases are set forth in a concentric progression to the face of YHWH: interrelations in the broader social sphere of neighbours (5:5–10), relationships within the sphere of family (5:11–31), and one's individual relationship with YHWH (6:1–21), followed by YHWH's uplifted face upon them (6:22–27).

The opening expulsions (Num. 5:1–4) are the result and signifier of this new reality, that YHWH God dwells in the midst of his people. Israel's Camp has become the first historical expression of the covenant formula 'I will be your God, you will be my people, and I will dwell in your midst.' YHWH's statement that he is 'dwelling in the midst' (*'ănî šōkēn bĕtôkām*) of the Camp (5:3), forms a clear allusion to his declared intent to dwell among his people in Exodus 25:8 (*šākantî bĕtôkām*) and 29:45 (*šākantî bĕtôk*), signalling fulfilment. As such, the Camp becomes both paradigm and foretaste of the covenant's consummation (as Ezek. 40 – 48; Rev. 21 – 22). Similar to the expulsion from the Camp (Num. 5:1–4), of New Jerusalem it is said 'there shall by no means enter it anything that defiles' (Rev. 21:27). Even as the Camp radiates with the blessing of YHWH's face (Num. 6:22–27), so the city basks in the light of the glory of God and of the Lamb, needing neither sun nor moon (Rev. 21:22–24). And as with the Camp, life in New Jerusalem represents a return to Eden – in the latter, far surpassing the original paradise (Rev. 22:1–5; cf. Num. 24:5–7).

These chapters not only make a theological point about the Camp, exhibiting its heavenly character, but form keys for interpreting Israel's wilderness sojourn. As the strayed woman's plight leads to a curse of bitterness (5:11–31), whereas the Nazirite's to benediction (6:22–27), there are two divergent paths set before Israel regarding her covenant relationship with YHWH: either spiritual unfaithfulness, leading to defilement and judgement, or consecration, leading to holiness and the glory of God (see Diamond 1997: 13–14; also Ps. 11:6–7).

Fittingly, after delineating the path of utter separation unto YHWH through the Nazirite vow, the purity section ends with YHWH's determined intention to bless his people (Num. 6:22–27), a point reasserted dramatically in the Balaam narrative (Num. 22 – 24). YHWH's uplifted face pours out benediction upon Israel through the raised palms of the priest, flowing from the central Dwelling to the farthest reaches of the Camp. Establishing the Camp as a well-watered paradise in the wilderness (Num. 24:1–2, 5–7), the priestly blessing functions like the description of Eden's heavenly river (Gen. 2:10–14; cf. Waltke and Fredricks 2001: 86–87), figured forth in Ezekiel's vision of a river flowing out from the new Temple's holy of holies (Ezek. 47:1–12; see Hurowitz 2007: 81). Within Israel's Camp, YHWH 'is the fountain of life' (Ps. 36:9), even a 'river whose streams make glad the city of God, the sacred Dwelling of the Most High' (Ps. 46:4). In line with the Camp's function as a paradigm for the covenant community, New Jerusalem is portrayed in terms of a fully realized priestly benediction: luminous with the light of divine glory (Rev. 21:11, 23–24; 22:5), a pure river of life flowing forth from the throne of God (22:1–2), his people experiencing abundant blessing and no more curse (22:3), and, greater still, they shall see his face and bear his Name on their foreheads (22:4).

The priestly blessing signifies YHWH's kingship, his sovereign reign characterized by heavenly benediction poured out upon Israel, and demonstrates the life-yielding relation of the *Shekhinah*'s central camp to the rest of the Camp of Israel. The benediction thus forms an appropriate conclusion not only to Numbers 1 – 6, but to the Sinai revelation as a whole (Exod. 19 – Num. 6), the fruition of the Sinai covenant. As capstone and foundation for Israel's life of purity, the priestly blessing puts YHWH's holy Name on his people, claiming them afresh as his treasured possession (cf. Exod. 19:5) and beckoning them to pursue purity and holiness in every sphere of life. Bearing his Name also means Israel has the Maker of heaven and earth as their Shepherd, daily enjoying his provision, compassion, abundant life and protection – perfect benefits for sojourning through a wilderness of pollution and death, enemy threats and sensual enticements. God's people today, baptized into his Name (Matt. 28:19), need the same spiritual provision through life's journey, precisely why historic liturgies conclude with this benediction. Cultivating the highest esteem and even yearning for the benediction, from our exalted High Priest through his ordained minister, calls for a robust doctrine of providence, of God's active presence in and sustaining care of his creation, including his sovereign dealings in human history. Indeed, as 'far as providence is concerned', writes V. Kleinig (1985: 120), 'the Aaronic blessing is the liturgical equivalent of the rainbow'. Every spiritual blessing is assuredly granted through the Son who prayed for his people who are in the world: 'Holy Father, keep through your own Name those you have given me' (John 17:11).

NUMBERS 7 – 8: DEDICATION OF THE DWELLING AND ITS TRANSPORT BY LEVITES

Translation

⁷:¹And it happened on the day Moses finished setting up the Dwelling, that he anointed it and sanctified it and all its vessels, and the altar and all its vessels – he anointed them and he sanctified them. ²Then the chieftains of Israel, the heads of their fathers' house brought near – they are the chieftains of the tribes; they are the ones who stood over the appointing – ³they brought their near-offerings before the presence of YHWH, six covered wagons and twelve oxen, a wagon for every two chieftains and one ox for each one, and they brought them near before

the presence of the Dwelling. ⁴And YHWH said to Moses, saying, ⁵'Take from them and they will be to do the labour of the Tent of Meeting, and you will give them to the Levites, each man according to his labour.'

⁶And Moses took the wagons and the oxen, and he gave them to the Levites. ⁷Two wagons and four oxen he gave to the sons of Gershon, according to their labour; ⁸four wagons and eight oxen he gave to the sons of Merari, according to their labour, which is in the hand of Ithamar, the son of Aaron the priest. ⁹But to the sons of Kohath he did not give, because the labour of the sacred objects is upon them – on the shoulder they will carry.

¹⁰And the chieftains brought near offerings for the dedication of the altar on the day it was anointed, and the chieftains brought near near-offerings before the presence of the altar. ¹¹And YHWH said to Moses, one chieftain per day, one chieftain per day, they will bring near near-offerings for the dedication of the altar.

¹²And the one who brought near the near-offering on the first day was Nahshon son of Amminadab, for the tribe of Judah; ¹³his near-offering: one dish of silver, thirty and a hundred its shekel-weight, one basin of silver, (weighing) seventy shekels by the shekel of the sanctuary, both of them full of flour mixed with oil for a tribute offering, ¹⁴one golden ladle of ten (shekels) filled with incense, ¹⁵one bull, a young of the herd, one ram; one lamb in its first year for a whole burnt offering, ¹⁶one male goat for a purification offering, ¹⁷and for the sacrifice of the peace offering two oxen, five rams, five goats, five lambs in their first year – this was the near-offering of Nahshon son of Amminadab.

¹⁸On the second day, Nethanel son of Zuar, chieftain of Issachar, brought near (his offering), ¹⁹he brought near his near-offering: one dish of silver, thirty and a hundred its shekel-weight, one basin of silver, (weighing) seventy shekels by the shekel of the sanctuary, both of them full of flour mixed with oil for a tribute offering, ²⁰one golden ladle of ten (shekels) filled with incense, ²¹one bull, a young of the herd, one ram; one lamb in its first year for a whole burnt offering, ²²one male goat for a purification offering, ²³and for the sacrifice of the peace offering two oxen, five rams, five goats, five lambs in their first year – this was the near-offering of Nethanel son of Zuar.

²⁴On the third day, the chieftain for the sons of Zebulun, Eliab son of Helon; ²⁵his near-offering: one dish of silver, thirty and a hundred its shekel-weight, one basin of silver, (weighing) seventy shekels by the shekel of the sanctuary, both of them full of flour mixed with oil for a tribute offering, ²⁶one golden ladle of ten (shekels) filled with incense, ²⁷one bull, a young of the herd, one ram; one lamb in its first year for a whole burnt offering, ²⁸one male goat for a purification offering, ²⁹and for the sacrifice of the peace offering two oxen, five rams, five goats, five lambs in their first year – this was the near-offering of Eliab son of Helon.

³⁰On the fourth day, the chieftain for the sons of Reuben, Elizur son of Shedeur; ³¹his near-offering: one dish of silver, thirty and a hundred its shekel-weight, one basin of silver, (weighing) seventy shekels by the shekel of the sanctuary, both of them full of flour mixed with oil for a tribute offering, ³²one golden ladle of ten (shekels) filled with incense, ³³one bull, a young of the herd, one ram; one lamb in its first year for a whole burnt offering, ³⁴one male goat for a purification offering, ³⁵and for the sacrifice of the peace offering two oxen, five rams, five goats, five lambs in their first year – this was the near-offering of Elizur son of Shedeur.

³⁶On the fifth day, the chieftain for the sons of Simeon, Shelumiel son of Zurishaddai; ³⁷his near-offering: one dish of silver, thirty and a hundred its shekel-weight, one basin of silver, (weighing) seventy shekels by the shekel of the sanctuary, both of them full of flour mixed with oil for a tribute offering, ³⁸one golden ladle of ten (shekels) filled with incense, ³⁹one bull, a young of the herd, one ram; one lamb in its first year for a whole burnt offering, ⁴⁰one male goat for a purification offering, ⁴¹and for the sacrifice of the peace offering two oxen, five rams, five goats, five lambs in their first year – this was the near-offering of Shelumiel son of Zurishaddai.

⁴²On the sixth day, the chieftain for the sons of Gad, Eliasaph son of Deuel; ⁴³his near-offering: one dish of silver, thirty and a hundred its shekel-weight, one basin of silver, (weighing) seventy shekels by the shekel of the sanctuary, both of them full of flour mixed with oil for a tribute offering, ⁴⁴one golden ladle of ten (shekels) filled with incense, ⁴⁵one bull, a young of the herd, one ram; one lamb in its first year for a whole burnt offering, ⁴⁶one male goat for a purification offering, ⁴⁷and for the sacrifice of the peace offering two oxen, five rams, five goats, five lambs in their first year – this was the near-offering of Eliasaph son of Deuel.

⁴⁸On the seventh day, the chieftain for the sons of Ephraim, Elishama son of Ammihud; ⁴⁹his near-offering: one dish of silver, thirty and a hundred its shekel-weight, one basin of silver, (weighing) seventy shekels by the shekel of the sanctuary, both of them full of flour mixed with oil for a tribute offering, ⁵⁰one golden ladle of ten (shekels) filled with incense, ⁵¹one bull, a young of the herd, one ram; one lamb in its first year for a whole burnt offering, ⁵²one male goat for a purification offering, ⁵³and for the sacrifice of the peace offering two oxen, five rams, five goats, five lambs in their first year – this was the near-offering of Elishama son of Ammihud.

⁵⁴On the eighth day, the chieftain for the sons of Manasseh, Gamaliel son of Pedahzur; ⁵⁵his near-offering: one dish of silver, thirty and a hundred its shekel-weight, one basin of silver, (weighing) seventy shekels by the shekel of the sanctuary, both of them full of flour mixed with oil for a tribute offering, ⁵⁶one golden ladle of ten (shekels) filled

with incense, ⁵⁷one bull, a young of the herd, one ram; one lamb in its first year for a whole burnt offering, ⁵⁸one male goat for a purification offering, ⁵⁹and for the sacrifice of the peace offering two oxen, five rams, five goats, five lambs in their first year – this was the near-offering of Gamaliel son of Pedahzur.

⁶⁰On the ninth day, the chieftain for the sons of Benjamin, Abidan son of Gideoni; ⁶¹his near-offering: one dish of silver, thirty and a hundred its shekel-weight, one basin of silver, (weighing) seventy shekels by the shekel of the sanctuary, both of them full of flour mixed with oil for a tribute offering, ⁶²one golden ladle of ten (shekels) filled with incense, ⁶³one bull, a young of the herd, one ram; one lamb in its first year for a whole burnt offering, ⁶⁴one male goat for a purification offering, ⁶⁵and for the sacrifice of the peace offering two oxen, five rams, five goats, five lambs in their first year – this was the near-offering of Abidan son of Gideoni.

⁶⁶On the tenth day, the chieftain for the sons of Dan, Ahiezer son of Ammishaddai; ⁶⁷his near-offering: one dish of silver, thirty and a hundred its shekel-weight, one basin of silver, (weighing) seventy shekels by the shekel of the sanctuary, both of them full of flour mixed with oil for a tribute offering, ⁶⁸one golden ladle of ten (shekels) filled with incense, ⁶⁹one bull, a young of the herd, one ram; one lamb in its first year for a whole burnt offering, ⁷⁰one male goat for a purification offering, ⁷¹and for the sacrifice of the peace offering two oxen, five rams, five goats, five lambs in their first year – this was the near-offering of Ahiezer son of Ammishaddai.

⁷²On the eleventh day, the chieftain for the sons of Asher, Pagiel son of Ochran; ⁷³his near-offering: one dish of silver, thirty and a hundred its shekel-weight, one basin of silver, (weighing) seventy shekels by the shekel of the sanctuary, both of them full of flour mixed with oil for a tribute offering, ⁷⁴one golden ladle of ten (shekels) filled with incense, ⁷⁵one bull, a young of the herd, one ram; one lamb in its first year for a whole burnt offering, ⁷⁶one male goat for a purification offering, ⁷⁷and for the sacrifice of the peace offering two oxen, five rams, five goats, five lambs in their first year – this was the near-offering of Pagiel son of Ochran.

⁷⁸On the twelfth day, the chieftain for the sons of Naphtali, Ahira son of Enan; ⁷⁹his near-offering: one dish of silver, thirty and a hundred its shekel-weight, one basin of silver, (weighing) seventy shekels by the shekel of the sanctuary, both of them full of flour mixed with oil for a tribute offering, ⁸⁰one golden ladle of ten (shekels) filled with incense, ⁸¹one bull, a young of the herd, one ram; one lamb in its first year for a whole burnt offering, ⁸²one male goat for a purification offering, ⁸³and for the sacrifice of the peace offering two oxen, five rams, five goats, five lambs in their first year – this was the near-offering of Ahira son of Enan.

⁸⁴This was the dedication of the altar on the day when it was anointed,

from the chieftains of Israel: twelve silver dishes, twelve silver basins, twelve golden ladles, [85]one hundred thirty shekels per silver dish, seventy per basin – all the silver vessels: two thousand four hundred by the shekel of the sanctuary; [86]twelve golden ladles filled with incense, ten (shekels) per ladle by the shekel of the sanctuary – all the gold of the ladles: one hundred twenty shekels; [87]all the cattle for the whole burnt offering: twelve bulls, twelve rams, twelve lambs in their first year and their tribute offerings; twelve male goats for a purification offering; [88]and all the cattle for the sacrifice of peace offering: twenty-four bulls, sixty rams, sixty male goats, sixty lambs in their first year – this was the dedication of the altar after it was anointed.

[89]Now when Moses would come into the Tent of Meeting to speak with him, he would hear the voice speaking to him from above the atonement lid, which was upon the ark of the testimony, from between the two cherubim, and he would speak to him.

[8:1]And YHWH spoke to Moses, saying, [2]'Speak to Aaron and say to him, "When you make the lamps ascend (with burning), make the seven lamps shine to the front, before the face of the lampstand."'

[3]And just so, Aaron did: he made its lamps ascend (with burning) to the front, before the face of the lampstand, just as YHWH had commanded Moses. [4]Now this was the workmanship of the lampstand: hammered work of gold, from its base to its petal it was hammered work, according to the appearance which YHWH showed Moses, just so he made the lampstand.

[5]And YHWH spoke to Moses, saying, [6]'Take the Levites from the midst of the sons of Israel, and cleanse them. [7]And thus you will do to them in order to cleanse them: sprinkle upon them waters of purification and make them pass a razor over all their flesh and they will wash their garments, and so cleanse themselves. [8]And they will take a bull, a young of the herd, and its tribute offering of flour mixed with oil, and a second bull, a young of the herd, you will take for a purification offering. [9]You will bring near the Levites before the presence of the tent of meeting, and you will assemble the whole community of the sons of Israel. [10]And you will bring near the Levites before the presence of YHWH, and the sons of Israel will lean their hands upon the Levites. [11]And Aaron will elevate the Levites as an elevation offering before the presence of YHWH on behalf of the sons of Israel, and they will be for doing the labour of YHWH. [12]The Levites will lean their hands upon the head of the bulls, and you will make the one for a purification offering and the (other) one for an ascension offering before YHWH, to make atonement for the Levites. [13]And you will stand the Levites in the presence of Aaron and in the presence of his sons, and you will elevate them as an elevation offering unto YHWH. [14]And you will separate the Levites from the midst of the sons of Israel, and the Levites will be mine. [15]And so afterward

the Levites will come to labour for the tent of meeting – when you cleanse them and elevate them as an elevation offering. [16]For they are wholly given to me from the midst of the sons of Israel, in place of all those who open the womb, the firstborn from all the sons of Israel – I have taken them for myself. [17]For mine are all the firstborn of the sons of Israel, both man and beast: on the day I struck down all firstborn in the land of Egypt, I consecrated them unto myself. [18]But I will take the Levites in place of all the firstborn of the sons of Israel. [19]And I give the Levites – wholly given – to Aaron and to his sons from the midst of the sons of Israel to work the labour of the sons of Israel for the tent of meeting, and to make atonement for the sons of Israel, so that there will be no plague on the sons of Israel when the sons of Israel approach to the sanctuary.'

[20]And Moses did, along with Aaron and all the community of the sons of Israel, for the Levites all that YHWH had commanded Moses for the Levites – just so the sons of Israel did for them. [21]The Levites underwent purification, and washed their garments, and Aaron elevated them as an elevation offering before the presence of YHWH, and Aaron made atonement for them to cleanse them. [22]And so afterward the Levites came to work their labour for the tent of meeting before the presence of Aaron and before the presence of his sons, just as YHWH had commanded Moses regarding the Levites – just so they did for them.

[23]And YHWH spoke to Moses, saying, [24]'This is what pertains to the Levites: from twenty-five years old and upward, he will come to wage in the host for the labour of the Tent of Meeting; [25]and from fifty years old he will return from the labour of the host, and he will not labour any longer. [26]But he will minister with his brothers for the Tent of Meeting, to keep guard, but he will not work in the labour; just so you will do for the Levites in their charge.'

Notes on the text

7:1, 84. 'on the day': idiomatic for 'when', without implying all events occurred on a single day.

2. 'brought near': *wayyaqrîbû*; BHS proposes reading as qal form; though awkward the hiph. form is sound, with 'near-offerings' supplied from v. 3 as the object.

5, 7, 8. 'according to his labour': lit. 'mouth of his labour'.

12. LXX and Syr include *nāśî'* (chieftain); MT displays variation – other references presume Nahshon is a chieftain (2:3; 7:10–11).

14. 'ladle': lit. 'hand' (throughout chapter).

15. 'young of the herd . . . first year': lit. 'son of the herd . . . son of his year', using *ben* (so also for vv. 21, 27, 33, etc.).

17. 'two oxen': *bāqār*; LXX reads 'heifers' throughout section.

'male goats': *'attûdîm* is nowhere prescribed for sacrifice, though see Pss 50:9, 13; 66:15; Isa. 1:11; 34:6.

42. LXX and Syr have *rĕ'û'ēl*; see note on 1:14.

87. 'tribute offerings': LXX (mis)reads as their 'drink offerings' (*spondai*), which G. B. Gray dubs 'clearly wrong' (1903: 77).

88. 'after it was anointed': LXX reads 'after filling its/his hands and after anointing it/him'.

89. 'the voice': LXX reads 'the voice of the Lord'; likely an explanatory addition.

'speaking': the same hith. form, indicating a reciprocal function (Waltke and O'Connor 1990: 431), occurs in Ezek. 2:2; 43:6; also with the divine voice in a temple context (cf. Gen. 3:8).

8:8. 'second bull': LXX includes that it must be a yearling.

12. 'make': LXX reads 'he will make' instead of imp.; *BHS* suggests an inf. abs.

13. 'presence of Aaron': LXX has 'before the Lord and before Aaron'.

15. LXX adds 'before the Lord' after 'elevation offering'; cf. v. 13.

16. 'all those who open the womb': *BHS* suggests transferring 'all' from before 'womb' to before 'firstborn', while SamP reads 'all firstborn who open the womb'.

Form and structure

Chapters 7:1 – 9:14 entail a flashback to the previous month when the Dwelling had been raised up and consecrated. While chronologically the dedication of the altar belongs after Exodus 40, Numbers 7 presupposes the chieftains of Numbers 1 – 2, the encampment order of Numbers 2 and the separation of Levites to their duties, including transport of the Tabernacle and its furnishings in Numbers 3 – 4 (e.g. Dillmann 1886: 39; G. B. Gray 1903: 74). The presentation of gifts by the twelve chieftains for the altar's dedication fits with Numbers' emphasis on Israel's leadership and on Levites as distinct from both the twelve tribes (representing their firstborn sons) and Aaron's priestly house (set apart to serve them).

Of the Torah's fourteen listings of the tribes, all differ from each other with the exception of those found in Numbers 2 and 7 – deemed by Chinitz 'a radical change' (1996: 36–37, 38). Perhaps the privileged role of the chieftains in Numbers 1 – 2, as well as the camp order of their tribes, can be seen as a *reward* for their exemplary initiative displayed in the previous month (Num. 7). More simply, these passages affirm the already established leadership positions of the chieftains and hierarchy among their tribes – acknowledged but not established in Numbers 2. A third solution understands that the chieftains in Numbers 7, while showing initiative, nevertheless did not dictate their presentation of gifts nor choose the order themselves; these would be under the organizing direction of Moses and Aaron, who chose the same (divine) rubric for ordering the chieftains for the dedication of the altar as they would later use for organizing the camp in Numbers 2. One may understand 7:11 as YHWH dictating the order of tribal presentations to Moses. Given its reference to the census (v. 2), chapter 7 was clearly composed with its present location in mind. Mention of both leaders and census of chapters 1–2 (7:2) brings readers back to the book's beginning and signals a new section (cf. Condren 2005: 171). The granting of gifts to the Levitical houses (vv. 4–9) need not have taken place on the day of the Dwelling's consecration – but since the wagons and oxen were given to YHWH and the priesthood at that time, and since the Levitical clans had already received their assignments (ch. 4), inserting their distribution here makes sense.

The events of the second year after the exodus out of Egypt are shown in Table 15, with the events of Exodus 40 through the end of Leviticus taking place within the first month, and the census of Numbers 1 commencing on the second month (G. J. Wenham 1981b: 103).

Table 15: Second year after the Exodus

Second year	Event	Reference
First month		
Day 1	Tabernacle raised; altar offerings begin	Exod. 40:2; Num. 7:1
	Sacrificial legislation from Tent of Meeting	Lev. 1:1
	Ordination of priesthood begins	Lev. 8:1
Day 8	Ordination of priesthood completed	
Day 12	Altar offerings completed	Num. 7:78
	Levites appointed	Num. 8:5
Day 14	Passover	Num. 9:2
Second month		
Day 1	Census and arrangement of Israel's camp begins	Num. 1:1
Day 14	Delayed Passover	Num. 9:11
Day 20	Cloud moves, camp sets out	Num. 10:11

In the literary arrangement of the material, the delayed Passover is noted prospectively within the section that constitutes a flashback to the first month (7:1–9:14). (See Fig. 7.)

Thus, the departure from Sinai's shadow occurs in conjunction with the (second month's delayed) Passover – and the flashback partly serves to explain this (9:1–2, 11).

The opening verse relates Moses' anointing and sanctification of the Dwelling and the Altar, along with their respective vessels, leading to the chieftains' two separate gifts, for the Dwelling (vv. 2–9) and for the Altar (vv. 10–88). The following is a general outline of Num. 7 – 8:

I.   Israelite chieftains – Gifts for the **Dwelling** and for the **Altar,** 7:1–88
     A. Contextual introduction: Moses anoints and consecrates
        Dwelling and its furnishings, the Altar and its furnishings, 1
     B. Chieftain gifts, 2–88
        1. Chieftain gifts (wagons, oxen) for transport of the Dwelling,
           to the Levites, 2–9
        2. Chieftain gifts for the Altar, 10–88
              Contextual introduction, 10–11
              Day 1 Nahshon (Judah) offering, 12–17
              Day 2 Nethanel (Issachar) offering, 18–23
              Day 3 Eliab (Zebulun) offering, 24–29
              Day 4 Elizur (Reuben) offering, 30–35
              Day 5 Shelumiel (Simeon) offering, 36–41
              Day 6 Eliasaph (Gad) offering, 42–47
              Day 7 Elishama (Ephraim) offering, 48–53
              Day 8 Gamaliel (Manasseh) offering, 54–59
              Day 9 Abidan (Benjamin) offering, 60–65
              Day 10 Ahiezer (Dan) offering, 66–71
              Day 11 Pagiel (Asher) offering, 72–77
              Day 12 Ahira (Naphtali) offering, 78–83
              Summary tally of gifts, 84–88
II. Moses – the **Ark of the Covenant** in the holy of holies, 7:89
     Moses' hears divine voice speaking from above the ark, between
     the cherubim, 89

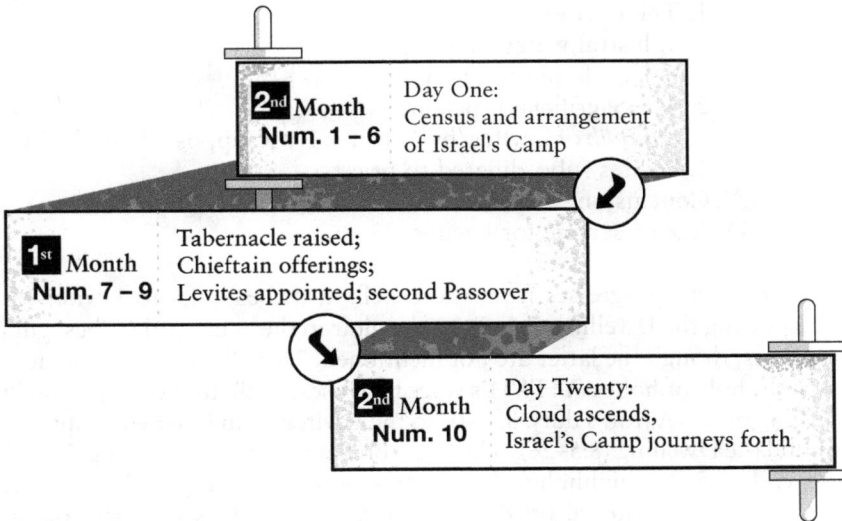

2nd Month
Num. 1 – 6
Day One:
Census and arrangement
of Israel's Camp

1st Month
Num. 7 – 9
Tabernacle raised;
Chieftain offerings;
Levites appointed; second Passover

2nd Month
Num. 10
Day Twenty:
Cloud ascends,
Israel's Camp journeys forth

chs. 1–10

Figure 7: Numbers 7 flashback

III. Aaron's priesthood – the **Lampstand** in the Holy Place, 8:1–4
    A. YHWH speech to Moses formula, 1
    B. Command for Aaron to tend lamps, 2
    C. Compliance report, 3
    D. Workmanship of lampstand, 4
IV. Role of the **Levites** – the Tent of Meeting, 8:5–26 (structure from Milgrom 1987a)
    A. Introduction 5–7a
    B. Prescription for cleansing and dedicating the Levites, 7b–13
        1. The Levites, 7
            a. lustral water
            b. shaving
            c. laundering
            d. bathing
        2. The Sacrificial Procedure, 8–12
            a. Hand-laying by Israel on Levites
            b. *tĕnûpāh* (elevation offering) of Levites
            c. Hand-laying by Levites on bulls
        3. Levites subordinated to priests, 13
    C. The Rationale, 14–19
        1. Separate Levites to God, 14
        2. Qualify Levites for sanctuary labour, 15
        3. Replace firstborn with Levites, 16–18
        4. Ransom Israelites from sacrilege of encroachment, 19
    B'. Summary description of compliance, 20–22a
        1. The Levites
            a. lustral water (shaving)
            b. laundering (bathing)
        2. The Sacrificial Procedure
        tĕnûpāh of Levites (by Aaron, v. 1; presupposes hand-laying)
        3. Levites subordinated to priests
    A'. Conclusion, 22b
    D. Age of service for Levites, 23–26

The movement progresses from the Dwelling (tribes' gifts to Levites for transporting the Dwelling, 7:1–9), to the altar in the courtyard (tribes' gifts to priests, though the latter are not mentioned, 7:10–88), to the atonement lid in the holy of holies (YHWH's voice to Moses, 7:89), to the lampstand in the holy place (Aaron's duty, 8:1–4), to the Levites as an inner encampment around the Dwelling (8:5–26). The focus on Levites at the beginning (7:1–9) and end (8:5–26) highlights their duties of transporting and guarding, and frames the material on the Dwelling, conveying its primary role in Numbers: YHWH's guidance of Israel through the wilderness.

The focus shifts through the tribal leaders (7:1–88), Moses (7:89), and Aaron the high priest (8:1–4), to the Levites (8:5–22), covering the whole

Camp by their roles. More broadly, paralleling the opening subsection (chs. 1–6), this subsection also moves from the twelve tribes represented by twelve chieftains (ch. 7) to the Levites via their dedication ceremony (ch. 8). Grossman (2017) connects the parallels between the two sections (chs. 1–6, 7–10), pointing out that both blocks conclude with laws related to purity, expelling the impure from the Camp (5:1–4) and offering a second celebration of Passover for those who were impure (9:1–14), and with commands applying to priests, to bless the people (6:22–27) and to blow the trumpets (10:1–10). The first section's elements of the Camp are, in the second section, positioned with reference to their connection with the Dwelling, the camp of the *Shekhinah*, so that in Numbers 7 the altar is centre-stage, and in Numbers 8 Levites enter the space of the Dwelling through their dedication ceremony (Grossman 2017). The Dwelling's role within the Camp is no less essential for the logic of the first section, although its place is more implicit, since it follows Leviticus, which is dedicated almost entirely to the camp of the *Shekhinah*. Chronologically moving backward to the dedication of the Dwelling, the narrative progresses to highlight the role of the twelve tribes, via their chieftains, and that of Levites, particularly related to their role of transport (labour). While Numbers 1 – 6 narrates the establishment of YHWH's Camp, chapters 7–10 concern the *mobility* of the Camp.

Numbers 7 – 8 fits within a broader structure (Num. 5 – 8) that repeats in reverse order elements found in Leviticus – the consecration of priests, for example, is mirrored by the cleansing of Levites (see Strauss 1979: 17–19; cf. HaCohen 1997; Seebass 2009: 99–100 n. 3). Aside from lending gravity to the Levites' role, the parallel exhibits the Torah's thematic arrangement: Leviticus concerns the Tent of Meeting as related to the cult officiated by priests, and Numbers concerns the Dwelling as the organizing centre of the Camp, transported by Levites.

Comment

7:1 – 8:4. The first three sections pertain to the three main parts of the *Shekhinah*'s camp and the roles of the participants within each sphere: (1) all Israel, represented by the tribal chieftains, gravitates about the altar in the courtyard (7:1–88); (2) Moses receives guidance from YHWH's voice, speaking from above the atonement lid in the holy of holies (7:89); Aaron the high priest arranges the lamps of the lampstand within the holy place (8:1–4) (cf. Stubbs 2009: 81–82. These areas are coordinated to recall YHWH's promise to meet with and speak to Israel through Moses (Exod. 25:22; 29:42–43), here for the sake of guiding the nation through the wilderness. Levites guard and transport the Dwelling and its furnishings, completing the picture (8:5–26). Since Numbers emphasizes the Tabernacle's function in relation to YHWH's guidance, along with the need for all Israel to follow his Cloud closely, the nation's leaders are given prominence (7:1–88), and the roles of Moses (7:89) and the priesthood (8:1–4) are noted primarily in the context of guiding and blessing Israel, respectively, even while the transport role of Levites is underscored (8:5–26).

7:1–9. The new chronological setting of 7:1, taking readers back to the day YHWH's glory filled the Dwelling (Exod. 40:34–35), is an appropriate context for Numbers 7 – 10 since this section culminates with the Camp's setting out from Sinai, and the glory-filled Dwelling had marked the first transition from Mount Sinai as the glory Cloud moved from the mountain's summit to YHWH's new abode, the Dwelling. References to this day form an inclusio (7:1; 9:15), marking out Numbers 7 – 9 as a flashback (cf. G. J. Wenham 1981b: 103). In contrast to 9:15, which does not mention the altar, 7:1 includes 'and the altar and all its vessels', the twofold reference to Dwelling and altar introducing the subject matter of the chapter: (1) gifts for transporting the Dwelling (vv. 2–9), and gifts for the dedication of the altar (vv. 10–88). Note the dual description 'before the presence of the Dwelling' (v. 3) and 'before the presence of the Altar' (v. 10). Hirsch remarks on the division here of the Sanctuary into its two main parts, with the Dwelling and all its vessels symbolizing the task, and the altar with all its vessels symbolizing the way to accomplish this task (2007a: 131). The second verse specifies that these chieftains are the same as those who assisted in the census, correlating the chieftains' offerings for the altar with the tribes' arrangement about the Dwelling as a Camp. Mention of 'labour', 'service' (*'ăbōdāh*) in verse 5 refers to the Levites' duty of transporting the Tabernacle, relevant for the tribal princes' gifts of wagons and oxen.

Retrospectively coordinated with the Levitical duties in Numbers 4, the tribal chiefs bring offerings useful for transporting the Dwelling. Brought 'before the presence of YHWH', paralleled with 'before the presence of the Dwelling', indicates that the newly consecrated Tent has indeed become YHWH's abode (Exod. 40:34). The detail of six covered wagons, each pulled by two oxen, assumes the transport of heavy material – even excluding the holy furnishings, which will be carried on the shoulders of the sons of Kohath (4:15; 7:9). There is a marked emphasis once more on the unity of the twelve tribes in their contribution, two tribes together giving one of the six wagons, and each tribe giving one of the twelve oxen. The tribal contributions to Levites are fitting, since Levites serve in place of their firstborn sons – the gifts acknowledge that Levites represent the tribes of Israel in their labours. The gifts are distributed by YHWH through Moses (vv. 5–6), according to the need of each Levitical house. While two wagons and four oxen are given to the sons of Gershon (one-third of the gifts), who are charged to carry the coverings and screens of the Dwelling (4:21–28), four wagons and eight oxen are given to the sons of Merari (two thirds of the gifts), since Merarites carry the heavier and bulkier items, the frames, bars, pillars and bases of the Dwelling (4:29–33). Because the holiest objects are to be carried by God's image-bearers alone – even this only by men set apart for the task – the sons of Korah receive none of the transport gifts (see 2 Sam. 6:1–11). Although Kohathites have a privileged role, yet in the phrasing 'But to the sons of Kohath he (Moses) did not give', one may, perhaps, detect the seed of a perceived slight that will come to bitter fruition with Korah's rebellion (Num. 16). The Kohathites' lack of wagons highlights the hierarchical stratification of holiness as displayed in the Camp's structure, emphasizing the privileged role of the sons of Kohath, who 'serve as a sort of chariot and carry the holy to a high and elevated place' (S. Klein 2014). Moses' role as mediator is underscored: the chieftains bring their donations to YHWH's presence at the Dwelling, and Moses, by YHWH's direction, gives them to the Levites. Aaron's son Ithamar is set over the sons of Gershon and Merari in their transport duties (7:8), reiterating Ithamar's charge (4:28, 33), while Eleazar is appointed over the sons of Kohath (4:16).

7:10–88. This section on gifts for the 'dedication' (*ḥănukkat*) of the altar opens with mention, once more, of the altar's dedication and anointing (10, 11; note the inclusion, vv. 84, 88). The altar is described in Exodus 27:1–8. While previous gifts had been brought 'before the presence of YHWH / the Dwelling' (3), here they are brought 'before the presence of the altar', the locale and focus of Israel's encounter with YHWH (see Lev. 9:4–8, 22–24). As with their gifts for the Levites who take Israel's place in serving the priests, the chieftains' gifts for dedicating the altar are fitting; the altar serves Israel's relationship with YHWH, providing a regular means of atonement, forgiveness, and consecration. It appears that all the chieftains were, together, gathered with the gifts of their particular tribe for the altar's dedication (v. 10), but YHWH desired to acknowledge each of the tribes individually, over twelve days (v. 11), a ceremony calculated to display his delight in each tribe and to magnify the place of the altar within the life of Israel.

Nahshon of Judah, Aaron's brother-in-law (Exod. 6:23), is the first to bring contributions. Each tribe, through its chieftain, offers the same gifts: a silver dish, a silver basin, both filled with a tribute offering of flour mixed with oil, a golden ladle filled with incense (also part of tribute offerings, cf. Lev. 2:2); and animals for sacrifices: a bull, ram and lamb for whole burnt offerings; a male goat for a purification offering; and two oxen, five rams, five goats and five lambs for peace offerings. These gifts formed the basis of the altar's dedication, since, likely, the dish, bowl and ladle represent 'the three fundamental procedures' of offerings, performed at the side of the altar (Hirsch 2007a: 137), and the main sacrifices – the purification offering, whole burnt offering, along with its tribute, and the peace offering – are all augured in the princely gifts. The 'bowl' (*mizrāq*) will receive the blood of 'sprinkling' (*zāraq*, cf.

Exod. 24:6, 8); blood, as the life of the soul (Lev. 17:6, 11–14), is integral to atonement in the cult linking this section with the chapter's closing verse and its mention of the 'atonement lid' (7:89).

The 'tabular' (see Levine 1993: 259–260) presentation delineates (1) the day, (2) the chieftain, (3) the vessels offered, (4) the sacrificial animals, and (5) a repeat mention of the chieftain. While large quantities of sacrifices are appropriate during dedication ceremonies (see 1 Kgs 8:63), Milgrom argues these animals were given to supply a stock for later use by the priesthood rather than as sacrifices for the altar's dedication (1992: 362–364). Starting a supply stock would align the animals with the gifts of dishes, basins, and ladles, which were for regular use in the cult, and further communicate that God's people should contribute to the needs of the cult, sustaining its work for the sake of all Israel. The contributions are less about extravagant worship than about Israel's ongoing commitment to maintain the cult's divine service. This under-standing accords with the portrayal of the cult's inaugural service as taking place *after* the consecration of the priesthood on the eighth day of the first month, when YHWH's own fiery glory lit the altar and consumed the daily sacrifices (Lev. 8 – 9) – the chieftains' sacrificial gifts would not have been offered up daily, upon presentation, since seven of the tribes gave their gifts before the priesthood's consecration. The emphasis here falls on their *giving* rather than on the act of offering up sacrifices. The *nature* of the gifts underscores the purpose of atonement; Ezekiel 45:17 lists these same sacrifices with that funda-mental end in mind (and uses 'chieftain', 'prince', *nāśî'*): 'It will be the prince's duty . . . to supply the purification offering, the tribute offering, the whole burnt offering, and the peace offerings, to make atonement on behalf of the house of Israel.' Thematically, atonement is also a focus in 7:89, with mention of 'atonement lid', and in the dedication of Levites (8:19, 21).

Movement begins centripetally, the twelve tribes bringing gifts toward the altar at the centre of the Camp, and then becomes centrifugal, with YHWH's voice emitting outward from the atonement lid (7:89). The procession toward the altar accords with some 35 uses of the root *q-r-b* in the chapter (cf. Cole 2000: 136), communicating the idea of drawing near to YHWH. The order of tribal chieftains follows that of the encampment given (Num. 2), another reflection on the (re)orienting nature of the Dwelling. The account has a liturgical quality, emphasizing the participation of all Israel to the spiritual and theological heart of the community. Rhetorically, the large summary figures of the tribal contri-butions (vv. 84–88) express the ideal of unity in both gratitude and giving among God's people, and this regarding the nation's priority, Israel's relationship with YHWH God as facilitated through the sacrificial cult. The whole burnt offerings signify and solicit Israel's consecration unto God, the purification offerings Israel's atonement (including forgiveness and cleansing from sin), and the peace offerings Israel's fellowship and communion with God, presented here in administrative order, emphasizing the value of the gifts themselves (Morales 2015: 122–141; cf. Rainey 1970). Scolnic discerns *one* as the key number (1995: 49) – we note also the repeated 'one (*'ḥod*) chieftain per day, one chieftain per day' (v. 11). Emphasis on 'one' functions to demonstrate the tribes' unity in their commitment to the sacrificial cult of the Tent of Meeting, YHWH's abode at the centre of the Camp. The twelvefold gift of incense to the priesthood will eventually be used by the high priest to intercede savingly on behalf of the twelve tribes (see 16:46–47).

The altar, with its consuming fire lit by YHWH's glory (Lev. 9:4, 22–24), was a miniature Mount Sinai, whose summit was alight (Exod. 24:17; see Morales 2012: 231–242). While the next two cultic vessels, the atonement lid of the ark (7:89) and the lampstand (8:1–4), were hidden from view, the altar dominated Israel's vision, particularly from the entryway of the courtyard (cf. Berman 1995: 48–52). The altar derives its full designation from Israel's primary sacrifice: 'the altar of the whole burnt offering' (Exod. 30:28; 31:9; 35:16; 38:1; 40:6, 10, 29; Lev. 4:7, 10, 18, 25, 30, 34; 1 Chr. 6:34; 16:40; 21:26, 29; 2 Chr. 29:18). Not only soliciting total surrender and self-dedication, the whole burnt offering, as its name implies (*'ōlāh*, 'ascending one'), visualized humanity's ascent to God as a sweet fragrance, and was typically followed by the 'tribute offering', as fitting upon entrance to YHWH's heavenly abode.

Aaron and the priesthood are absent from the sections dealing with the altar (vv. 10–88) and the holy of holies (v. 89), which accords with Numbers' emphasis on the roles of the tribal leaders and Moses – and which assumes and supplements Leviticus' emphasis on priesthood. Unlike with the gifts of wagons and oxen, which were given to Levites through YHWH and Moses, the altar remains the central focus in this section. The first set of gifts (vv. 2–9) was for the sake of YHWH's guidance, transporting his Dwelling as his fiery Cloud led Israel through the wilderness, and the second set of gifts (vv. 10–88) was for the sake of maintaining YHWH's presence (see Exod. 29:36–46). Inspiringly, the note of Israel's complete accord and unanimity with regard to the nation's relationship with YHWH, through the altar, is struck. It is the blood-smeared altar, from which the fragrant smoke of propitiation ascends, that allows for YHWH God, Maker of heaven and earth, to dwell in the midst of Israel in fellowship and blessing.

The verbatim repetition of each tribe's contribution is itself part of the point: each contribution was, in fact, unique – Judah's young bull and silver dish brought by Nahshon, was not the same young bull and silver dish brought by the sons of Reuben through Elizur. Repetition serves to emphasize what is unique: the name of each tribe and its chieftain, each of which demonstrates his tribe's devotion to the cult's enablement of YHWH's presence in their midst. Priestly service at the altar is supported by every tribe of Israel, who, in turn, receive the blessings both accomplished at and pronounced from the altar (see Lev. 9:22).

7:89. Numbers 7:89 presents an almost verbatim recall of Exodus 25:22, signifying that one of the chief purposes for the whole enterprise of the Tent of Meeting has now come to fruition *within the context of Israel's Camp, and the nation's sojourn through the wilderness* (also Exod. 29:42). Shamah makes two significant observations (2011: 717–718): first, 'an unusual syntactical flourish' in avoiding use of God's name may reflect 'the indescribable status of the new reality', and, secondly, the 'supreme importance of the prophetic function is emphasized by its being highlighted in this manner', even as the high priest's role will be highlighted next (8:1–4). The narrative focus in chapters 11–15 will be on the twelve tribes, the outer camp, in relation to the prophetic word of Moses, while chapters 16–18 focus on Levites, the inner camp, in relation to the priestly ministry of Aaron.

Just as the altar fire continued Israel's experience of YHWH's consuming fire at Mount Sinai, the ark of the testimony continues the 'voice' (*qôl*) of God, central to YHWH's advent on Sinai's summit (Exod. 19:5, 16, 19; 20:18; 23:21–22). In Deuteronomy 5:22–26, Moses recalls the dread with which the 'great voice' (*qôl gādôl*) of God was heard by Israel. Even as Sinai's summit corresponds to the Tabernacle's holy of holies, so, too, the Decalogue received from that summit, and which had resounded from the divine 'voice', was deposited in the holy of holies, in the ark, giving the latter its designation as the 'ark of the testimony'. In Exodus 25:21, Moses was instructed to put within the ark 'the testimony that I (YHWH) will give you', and then, as noted, God continues to declare that the atonement lid above 'the ark of the testimony' would be the new place of his speaking to Moses (v. 22). Berman states the ark and the tablets are 'of testimony' because they witness eternally to the *qôl* uttered at Sinai (1995: 44). The atonement lid, therefore, within the 'summit' (holiest place) of the architectural mountain of God (the Tabernacle), becomes *the* place of divine revelation.

The transition to Moses' entrance into the Tent of Meeting, to hear God's voice of guidance, emphasizes the central role of the altar in relation to YHWH's communication with Moses. There is a dynamic analogical relationship between the altar and the Tent of Meeting, both symbolizing the holy mountain of God. In Exodus 24, twelve pillars surround an altar, reflecting the twelve tribes gathered about Mount Sinai, whose summit, like the central altar, is aflame with a 'consuming fire', linked to the glory of God (24:17), and just as the altar of the whole burnt offering would later be lit by God's glory (Lev. 9:24). Mount Sinai was a grand earthen altar, and the altar itself a miniature Mount Sinai (see Morales 2012: 231–242). At Sinai, Israel witnessed the consuming fire, while Moses entered the thick cloud to hear the instructions of God, out of sight from the people. Similarly, Numbers 7 juxtaposes the tribes of Israel, focused on the altar, with Moses' entrance into the Tent of Meeting to hear instructions from God.

The hithpael form of God's 'speaking' (*middabbēr*) appears again within temple contexts in Ezekiel (2:2; 43:6), and is also used to describe God's walking in temple contexts as well (Gen. 3:8; Lev. 26:12; Deut. 23:15; 2 Sam. 7:6–7). Genesis 3:8, in particular, depicts Adam and the woman within the garden of Eden in a manner that invites comparison with the holy of holies scene: 'they heard the voice (*qôl*) of YHWH God walking (*mithallēk*) in the garden'. The presence of cherubim in both accounts (Gen. 3:24; Num. 7:89) further relates the holy of holies to the garden of Eden – Moses hears the voice of God from the gateway of Eden, emanating from 'between the two cherubim'. The cherubim's duty at the garden of Eden's entry was to guard the way to the tree of life, a function not only relating holiness to abundant life, but which, in the context of Numbers 7:89, relates God's voice to life – hence the wisdom of Torah is regarded as 'a tree of life' (Prov. 3:18; cf. 4:13). The 'ark of the testimony' conveys the idea that all of God's further revelation is founded upon, is in accord with, and, perhaps, marks an expansion of, the Decalogue as the kernel of the covenant relationship. Finally, 'above the atonement lid' cannot but underline the role of the blood of atonement in YHWH's relationship with Israel, including his guidance of his people through revelation to Moses. The atonement lid, singled out as the place where YHWH would speak with Moses (Exod. 25:17–22), becomes the focal point of the high and holy Day of Atonement (Lev. 16:2, 14), the Pentateuch's literary and theological centre (Morales 2015: 27–34). Use of 'atonement lid' (*hakkappōret*) recalls its immediately previous use in the Torah, the Day of Atonement (Lev. 16), where *k-p-r* occurs ten times. Within the holiest place, the atonement lid becomes the crucial *terminus* for the cleansing blood of atonement. With the Dwelling's construction and dedication, the structure's purpose – within the context of Israel's divine guidance through the wilderness – can begin to be fulfilled: YHWH's voice communicates to Moses. Numbers 7:89 functions as a hinge between the sections related to the courtyard, outside the Dwelling (7:1–88) and YHWH's instructions inside the Dwelling (8:1–4) (cf. Dozeman 1998: 77) – the dedicated altar makes YHWH's speech to Moses from within the holy of holies possible, and that opening speech is reflected in the instructions for Aaron's tending of the lampstand. More than this, at the heart and centre of Israel's Camp stands the relationship between YHWH God and the mediator Moses, communicating from above the atonement lid, between the two cherubim – God's *voice*, the Word, is the fountain of life and life-giving Torah at the centre of the cosmos. The voice that had created the cosmos has also created the Camp of Israel, and will guide his people on their sojourn.

When Moses is in company with Aaron or the community of Israel outside the Tent of Meeting, YHWH's glory Cloud appears, the theophany being, as it were, for the benefit of the others. But when YHWH reveals *torah* to Moses, Moses enters the Tent alone as the only one with whom YHWH speaks 'face to face', and, standing before the veil, he alone hears the divine voice – no vision or theophany is needed (cf. Milgrom 1997: 248). Within the story of the outer camp's particular aim of heeding the prophetic office of Moses (chs. 11–15), the divine *qôl* speaking from between the cherubim underscores the gravity of their challenge, and is key to his vindication (12:5–8).

This verse, finally, underscores the gravity of this event as the reversal of the situation in Exodus 33:7–11 where, due to Israel's sin with the golden calf, YHWH would meet with Moses to speak with him outside the camp. Momentously, YHWH's speaking with Moses from the newly constructed Tent of Meeting at the centre of the Camp conveys that Israel has been forgiven, the divine *Shekhinah* has returned, and the nation is ready to journey to the land of Canaan (Leibtag 2023).

8:1–4. From the outer courtyard (7:1–88) and the holy of holies (7:89), the text turns to the holy place (8:1–4), to 'a special service of Aaron for the light in the holy tent as the centre of the march' (Seebass 2009: 107). The juxtaposition with 7:89 adds gravity to these verses, portraying the final instructions for setting up the lampstand's lamps, lighting the holy place, as given when YHWH began speaking with Moses from the atonement lid after the dedication of the altar. Sweeney remarks that the 'placement of this notice indicates that once the sanctuary is dedicated, the lights of the sanctuary will burn to symbolize divine presence' (2012: 130). The Dwelling has become fully functional, 'the lights of Yahweh's home are now turned on' (Condren 2005: 189). The topical progression moves from the Dwelling (7:1–8:4) to the dedication of Levites, who will serve as a buffer between the Dwelling and the encampment of Israel's tribes on the wilderness sojourn (8:5–26). The central camp of the *Shekhinah* was reserved for last topically (chs. 7–8), even though it was the necessary centre chronologically. As a summary of his cultic duty and office, Aaron's lighting the menorah lamps becomes key for the inner camp's story (chs. 16–18), for Aaron's vindication as chosen high priest of YHWH through his almond-budded staff, reflecting the lampstand as an almond tree (Num. 17; cf. Exod. 25:33–34; 37:19–20).

1–3. G. J. Wenham observes that the focus of this legislation is on Aaron's duty of beaming the seven lamps of the lampstand *forward*, shining their light on the bread of the presence on the golden table set directly across from it (1981b: 107; cf. Knierim and Coats 2005: 106). That beaming the lights forward, in front of the lampstand, is an integral purpose for the seven lamps may be discerned from the inclusion of this function within the instructions for making the lampstand (Exod. 25:31–40). Constructed of pure hammered gold, the lampstand was shaped as a stylized tree, comparable to Eden's tree of life (Meyers 1976), and represented the light and life of God's presence. The heaped-up stack of twelve loaves, representing the twelve tribes of Israel, is called the bread of the 'presence' (*pānîm*) because they bask in the light of the lampstand, the light of God's glorious face. Aaron's duty of regularly arranging the lamps so they shine upon the loaves summarizes the role and function of the priesthood to mediate God's blessings to his people. In the symbolism of the cult, Numbers 8:1–4 presents the blessing of God upon the people of God, mediated by the priesthood of God (see Morales 2015: 15–18). As G. J. Wenham notes (1981b: 107), the high priest's daily service of the lamps expresses symbolically what the priestly benediction expresses verbally: God shining the life-giving light of his face upon his people, through the Aaronic priests (note use of *yā'ēr* in 6:25 and *yā'îrû* in 8:2), this within God's house. Instructions for the lampstand have occurred twice already (Exod. 27:20–21; Lev. 24:1–4), but the present text narrates Aaron's fulfilment of this high priestly duty for the first time (Shamah 2011: 719).

4. Based on the heavenly pattern shown Moses on the summit of God's mountain, the original instructions for making the lampstand are found in Exodus 25:31–40, where it is described as a stylized almond tree – alluded to here by its shaft and flowers. Aside from the Dwelling and its furnishings as stated in a general manner in Exodus 25:9, the lampstand is the only piece of furnishing directly said to be made after a 'pattern' (*tabnît*) in Exodus (25:40; *mar'eh*, 'appearance', in Num. 8:4). The central shaft, along with three branches on either side, make for seven lamps, lending the tree a cosmic, Sabbath significance. In Genesis 1:1 – 2:3, the sun, moon, planets and stars are described as 'lamps' (*mā'ôr*) five times in 1:14–16, using the term that elsewhere in the Torah always refers to the lamps of the Tabernacle lampstand (e.g. Exod. 25:6; Lev. 24:2; Num. 4:9, 16; see Vogels 1997; D. J. Rudolph 2003), the cosmos itself forming the original house of God created by him to dwell with humanity (Morales 2015: 39–49). Somewhat mysteriously the lampstand appears in Exodus (25:31–40), Leviticus (24:1–9), and in Numbers (8:1–4). As here, the Exodus reference includes the priestly duty of arranging the lamps before the lampstand without mentioning the bread of the presence explicitly; the Leviticus reference notes Aaron's continual charge of the lamps and is followed by his duty to arrange the loaves every Sabbath. Leviticus 24:1–9, symbolizing Israel's Sabbath day fellowship with God, is framed by two chapters on Israel's feasts days (ch. 23) and jubilee legislation (ch. 25), all of which are founded on the Sabbath (Morales 2015: 197–207).

In Numbers, Aaron's role of tending the lampstand foreshadows the inner camp's dramatic focus: the budding of Aaron's staff in Numbers 17:1–13. Though the detail has drawn little scholarly attention, the description of Aaron's staff as putting forth buds, blooming, and bearing almonds is highly significant (17:8), linking his staff to the lampstand as stylized almond tree, an engrafted branch bearing the fruit of God's life.

Broadly, 7:1 – 8:4 presents the Tent of Meeting at the centre of Israel's Camp, possibly with Eden imagery: the altar (mountain of God), atonement lid (cherubim), and lampstand (tree of life), and does so in a movement reflecting that of Numbers 1 – 6, starting with the twelve tribes arranged around YHWH's Dwelling and ending with his blessing upon Israel mediated by Aaron's priesthood. Finally, the altar's fire and the lampstand's light, tended morning and evening to be kept burning continually (Exod. 29:38–42; 30:7–8; Lev. 24:2–4), represent God's continual presence among Israel – the heart of the covenant relationship. These symbolize God's promise to Israel, as once pronounced to Jacob: 'I will be with you and keep you wherever you go, and will bring you back to this land; for I will not leave you until I have done what I have spoken to you' (Gen. 28:15; see Josh. 1:5; Matt. 28:20).

8:5–26. Numbers 3 relates the genealogy of Aaron's priesthood (vv. 1–4) before turning to the Levites (vv. 5–51). Similarly, Numbers 8 begins with Aaron's duty (vv. 1–4) before turning to the Levites (vv. 5–26). This repeated pattern conveys a hierarchical arrangement, with Levites subordinated to the priesthood – a point brought out in 8:13, as Levites are made to stand before Aaron and his sons. The Levites are now cleansed – unlike priests, who are sanctified – and dedicated to God (cf. Milgrom 1990: 61). Earlier references to Levites noted their status of standing in for firstborn sons of Israel, explaining their practical duties, while chapter 8 'describes their theological function and their induction into office' (G. J. Wenham 1997: 41). This ceremony highlights the status and role of Levites in terms of the *těnûpāh*, 'elevation offering' – given by lay Israelites to YHWH, then from YHWH for the support of the Aaronide priesthood.

5–7. By divine command, Moses is to set apart the Levites for their special service. Before dedicating the Levites to YHWH, two acts are necessary: (1) taking them from the midst of the sons of Israel, separating them out from the other tribes, and (2) 'cleansing them' (*wěṭihartā 'ōtām*), perhaps from possible corpse pollution. The total process of taking, cleansing, and dedicating Levites is summarized in verse 14 as making them 'separate' so as to belong to YHWH, a statement that forms an inclusion with verse 6. The method of cleansing Levites is explained as involving three main elements: (1) sprinkling the 'waters of purification', (2) shaving their bodies, and (3) washing their garments. The first two elements are also required for Nazirites defiled by corpse pollution (6:9). Cleansing is described as something Moses will 'orchestrate' or 'direct', since by compliance Levites are also said to have 'cleansed themselves'. Whereas verse 7 speaks of washing garments and cleansing themselves, verse 21 has 'purifying' (*yiṭḥaṭṭě'û*) themselves and washing garments, and Aaron as having made atonement for them to 'cleanse' them. Though often translated similarly, Numbers 8 speaks of the waters of 'purification' (*ḥaṭṭā't*), while Numbers 19 reads waters of 'separation' (*niddā*) (19:9, 20, 21). The ashes of the red cow are called *ḥaṭṭā't* in 19:9, leading Milgrom to presume the waters of Numbers 8 are the same under an alternate name, noting that if the waters of the laver were meant the designation 'holy water' would be used (1990: 61) – noted by others, too (Wright 1985: 215; Staubli 1996: 233). Otherwise, running or 'living' water is in mind for this cleansing. If the waters of Numbers 19 are in view, the context of cleansing is particularly from death pollution, a detail that, with the redemption of the firstborn in Egypt (v. 17), links this chapter with the following account of the second Passover (9:1–14), where celebration of the redemption out of Egypt is delayed a month for some Israelites who are unclean from death pollution.

Olyan notes the shaving rite (1998: 614) (1) is a component of purification, (2) effects separation, occurring at the beginning of the dedication process whereby Levites are separated from the people and moved into a liminal state to emerge eventually into their new roles as cultic servants, and (3) marks their submission to divine authority.

8–13. Milgrom explains the purification rite has the Levites' removal duties in view, whereas their guard duty is from a distance and for the sake of 'removing wrath', and not mentioned in the text (1970a: 151). This underscores the Levites' function as *replacing* Israelites in the physical labour required for the Tabernacle, rather than on their function of guarding *against* Israelites who would encroach on the Sanctuary. The closing paragraph (vv. 23–26) solidifies this focus: at the age of 50, Levites are discharged from such manual labour, tasked only with 'guard duty' (*mišmeret*). Although there is no reason to exclude guard duty from the significance of their cleansing since such duty required their encampment near the Dwelling, the text indeed emphasizes their transport labours (7:3–9; 8:11, 15, 19, 22, 24), with verse 26 noting an exception to the rule.

After cleansing, the dedication ritual begins. Verse 8 mentions two bulls, specifying the purpose only for the second bull, that it will be for a 'purification offering'. Purification here is general in nature, prerequisite to an elevation in status in view of their future labours. Verse 12 fills in the purpose for the other bull, which will serve as a whole burnt offering. While, as in verse 8, the administrative order of sacrifice typically mentions the whole burnt offering first, the procedural order begins with the purification offering and then proceeds to the whole burnt offering, along with its tribute offering, as in verse 12. In the cult's theology, expiation precedes consecration. The idea of expiation is present in the whole burnt offering's blood rite, which precedes the burning rite, but the purification offering was prefixed to it to underscore that atonement aspect.

Verses 10 and 11 are in parallel; note 'presence of the Tent of Meeting / YHWH' and 'sons of Israel'. Moses is to 'bring near' (*hiqrabtā*) the Levites, language used also for offering sacrifices, or bringing something into YHWH's cultic presence – contrast, for example, the man's 'bringing' (*hēbî'*) his wife to the priest, and the priest's 'bringing' (*hiqrîb*) her before YHWH (Num. 5:15, 16). Having been cleansed, Levites are then dedicated in a solemn ceremony with the whole 'community' (*'ădat*) 'gathered' (*hiqhaltā*). The dedication of Levites involves (1) a hand-leaning rite, and (2) their being offered as an elevation offering. The sons of Israel perform a hand-leaning gesture upon the Levites (v. 10), and then the Levites, standing now in place of the sons of Israel, perform a hand-leaning gesture on the bulls (v. 12), which are then offered up as purification and whole burnt offerings. The 'hand-leaning' (*sĕmikâ*) rite involves pressing down one's hand heavily upon the head of the vicarious substitute, creating a ritual identification between the offeror and the offering (see Morales 2015: 127–129). All Israel is dedicated to serving YHWH, through the nation's firstborn sons, but Levites are 'sacrificed' in their stead; substitute animals, in turn, are sacrificed in the stead of Levites, who will render their lives in service at the Tent of Meeting.

Together, the purification and whole burnt offerings make atonement for the Levites, purifying them. Turning to the elevation offering, which occurs three times (vv. 11, 13, 15), the *tĕnûpāh* (elevation offering) and *tĕrûmāh* ('contribution' or 'gift') designate gifts dedicated to YHWH that were received for use by the priesthood; both refer to the transfer of objects from the offeror's domain to the domain of God, from the profane realm to the sacred (for this section, see G. R. Driver 1956a; von Soden 1970; Milgrom 1983b: 133–170; G. A. Anderson 1987: 133–144). The elevation offering was always performed 'before YHWH', signifying a cultic ritual at the Sanctuary (a dedication rite), while the contribution is 'to YHWH', not requiring a cultic rite. Milgrom suggests the *tĕrûmāh* (setting aside the portion, likely at home) always preceded the *tĕnûpāh* (cultic rite of dedication) at the Sanctuary (1990: 427). Most translations of *tĕnûpāh* follow the rabbinic rendering 'wave offering' (*m. Men.* 5.6), but the Targums consistently translate it as 'raise', 'elevate' (using *r-w-m*), corroborated by most uses of *henif* in the Bible (Isa. 10:15; 11:15; 13:2; 19:16) (Milgrom 1990: 425). While the etymology remains ambiguous for both, *tĕnûpāh* implies the motion of elevating, and *tĕrûmāh* seems to have derived either from 'lifting off' as in 'setting aside' a portion as a gift, or simply from a term for 'gift' itself. Because these dedicated objects were outside the regular set of offerings, they needed to be dedicated separately by a ceremony of elevating the portion within a larger ritual complex for the 'elevation offering', or by a simple act of dedication for the 'gift'. As an added rite at the Sanctuary, the elevation offering may also function to underscore requests made to God. The hand-leaning rite performed on the Levites is cultic in nature and involved one hand, not to be confused with hand-leaning on the blasphemer (Lev. 24:14) or Joshua (Num. 27:18), both of which had other purposes in mind and involved two hands (Peter 1977; Milgrom 1987a: 207).

The goal of the Levites' separation is for them to belong wholly to YHWH, they 'will be mine' (v. 14). Along the spectrum of holiness, with holiness understood as 'belonging to YHWH', Levites stand between Israel (a nation that belongs to YHWH as his special possession) and Aaron's priesthood (which has been especially consecrated to YHWH) – a position brought out in the Levites' central position within the movement of the dual hand-leaning rites, between the sons of Israel and the sacrificial animals (realm of the priests); and also reflected in the Levites' placement in the Camp, between the tribes and YHWH's Tent. Belonging to him, Levites are given by YHWH to the priests as his gift to them (v. 19), for the sake of service at the Tent of Meeting. Major elements in this section are repeated, as follows:

Levites in presence of YHWH (10)	Levites in presence of Aaron and his sons (13)
Hand-leaning rite upon Levites by Israelites (10)	Hand-leaning rite upon bulls by Levites (12)
Levites elevated as elevation offering (11)	Levites elevated as elevation offering (13)
Levites will serve in the service of YHWH (11)	Levites will serve the Tent of Meeting (15)

Milgrom notes that the bulls and the Levites are a means of atonement, in contrast to the priests, who actually make atonement (1990: 369):

The Levites shall lean their hands upon the heads of the bull . . . *lěkappēr 'al* the Levites (12).
Let the Israelites lean their hands upon the Levites . . . *lěkappēr 'al* the Israelites (10, 19).

14–19. These verses, indicating the rationale for the role of Levites, are the focal point of the Levites' dedication, and form the chapter's structural centre (G. J. Wenham 1981b: 108; cf. Milgrom 1990: 368):

A to make atonement for the Levites (12)
  B to do service at the Tent of Meeting (15)
    C given to me (16)
      D instead of all the firstborn (16)
        E redemption of Israel's firstborn in Egypt (17)
      D' instead of all the firstborn (18)
    C' given to Aaron (19)
  B' to do service at the Tent of Meeting (19)
A' to make atonement for the sons of Israel (19)

The verb used for separating the Levites is *bādal* (v. 14), used in Genesis solely regarding the separations God performed in creating the cosmos

(Gen. 1:4, 6, 7, 14, 18). In separating out the Levites, God is creating order, for the Camp will be like a new cosmos (cf. 16:9, 21), even as in Exodus the verb is used for the divisions of the Dwelling as a microcosm (see Exod. 26:33). In Leviticus, the verb is used for the division between holy and profane, clean and unclean, integral for the ritual cosmos (see Lev. 10:10; 11:47; 20:25).

The rationale for the role of Levites had been noted already (Num. 3:9–13). Their role and function is laced throughout the opening section of Numbers (1:47–54; 3:5–51; 4:1–49; 8:5–26), which Cole arranges chiastically (2000: 147–148). They will represent all Israel in service at the Tent of Meeting, in place of the nation's firstborn sons. As the centre of a concentric structure, verses 14–19 set forth the essential element to the rationale for the Levites as their being a *ransom* for Israelites, brought as literal sacrifices by Israel (Milgrom 1987a: 206–207). They function to ransom Israelites from their obligatory life of service. As replacements for the firstborn sons of Israel, Levites are therefore said to belong – 'wholly given' (*nětunîm nětunîm*, v. 16) – to YHWH (16–18). All that open the womb, as well as firstfruits, belong to YHWH and are thus to be sacrificed to him; however, since human beings are not to be sacrificed provision was made for firstborn sons to be redeemed by the sacrifice of substitute animals (Exod. 13:1–2, 11–16), while presumably still owing YHWH a life of service. Levites, redeemed by substitute animals, will render YHWH their lives in service in place of firstborn sons. YHWH's statement regarding the firstborn in Exodus 13:2 'it is mine' (*lî hû'*) is now taken up with reference to Levites: 'the Levites will be mine' (*lî halwîyyim*, v. 14). Note that the Levites' service at the Tent of Meeting is described as the service particularly of 'the sons of Israel' (*'ăbōdat běnê-yiśrā'ēl*, v. 19). The *fivefold* use of 'sons of Israel' in verse 19 is founded on the theology that firstborn sons, whom the Levites have replaced, represent all Israel – in replacing firstborn sons, Levites serve on behalf of all Israel. Repeating 'sons of Israel' five times also reflects God's love for his people, and may even correspond to the five books of Torah (see Rashi, ad loc.; *Lev. Rab.* 2.4). Collectively, Israel stands as God's firstborn son, a status brought out in the nation's deliverance out of Egypt as YHWH declared: 'Israel is my son, my firstborn' (Exod. 4:22).

While their duties include both guarding the Tent of Meeting from encroachment, and transporting the Dwelling, along with dismantling and setting it up, the focus here is on their serving as a buffer to prevent contact between God's holy presence and the rest of the tribes, lest there be any 'plague among the sons of Israel', a role or 'status' that undergirds their duties. As evident in the Camp arrangement, where Levites form a ribbon of separation between the Tent of Meeting and the camps of the tribes, part of the function of Levites is to create a protective layer of separation, serving as 'a lightning rod to attract God's wrath upon themselves whenever an Israelite has encroached upon the sancta' (Milgrom 1990: 371). Levites are 'to make atonement' (*lĕkappēr*, v. 19) for Israel in the sense of serving to 'ransom' firstborn sons of Israel from their duty, and by delivering the nation from the potential plague of YHWH's wrath by standing between the nation and God's Dwelling in their guard-service. While Levites guard against encroachment of the Tent of Meeting, they themselves must not enter the Tent or encroach upon the sacred vessels, upon threat of death (Num. 18:3). In this manner, and likely in other general ways, Levites fulfil their duty to YHWH by serving Aaron's priesthood. YHWH, therefore, takes the Levites as his claim on firstborn sons of Israel, and gives them wholly to the priests for their use. Levites, as sacrifices, are given to the priests inasmuch as all the sacrifices are given to them (see Lev. 7:34; Taggar-Cohen 1998: 82).

The structural centre, element E, rehearses the death of the firstborn in Egypt along with the Passover deliverance by which YHWH 'set apart' Israel's firstborn sons for himself (Exod. 11 – 13). Again, this topic leads into the ensuing Passover celebration (9:1–14), and serves to keep the redemption out of Egypt as the section's broad context. While the Passover deliverance of the firstborn sons of Israel underscores YHWH's claim on them, and becomes the occasion to set forth the principle as a cultic regulation, yet the theology of firstfruits (Exod. 13:1–2, 11–16; 22:29–30; 23:16; Lev. 23:9–14) marks all the 'first issue of the womb' (*piṭrat kol-reḥem*, 16) as already belonging to YHWH, a point made apparent with Isaac, the firstborn son of Sarah, when YHWH called on Abraham to offer Isaac up as a whole burnt offering (Gen. 22). Just as Isaac was substituted by the ram's being offered up as a whole burnt offering in his stead, soliciting total consecration from him, so God provided a lamb as substitute for the firstborn sons of Israel in Egypt (Exod. 12:3–13). Levites now serve as substitutes in place of firstborn sons. Just as Passover lambs had shielded Israel from God's final 'plague' (*negep*) of destruction (Exod. 12:13), so Levites shield Israelites from the 'plague' (*negep*) that would result from encroachment upon the sacred Tent and furnishings (Num. 8:19). Beyond wreaking havoc on Egypt, the plagues had also functioned as a warning for Israel (Hausoul 2018: 87). After 8:19, the root *negep* occurs twelve more times, in three clusters: after Israel's rejection of the land (14:37, 42); after Korah's rebellion (16:46, 47, 48, 49, 50); and after the sin at Baal Peor (25:8, 9, 18, 19; 31:16). This distribution of *negep* forms another instance where the structures and legislation that open Numbers foreshadow the drama to come; both Korah's rebellion (chs. 16–17) at the centre of the wilderness years, as well as the disastrous account of Baal Peor at the end of the wilderness section, where the plague is finally stayed through Phinehas (25:1–9), deal particularly with the situation forewarned of here. 'Both the altar sacrifices (7:11–88) and the Levites as living sacrifices (8:5–22)' serve the sons of Israel by making possible YHWH's Dwelling in the Camp by means of atonement (Condren 2005: 184). The two passages, moreover, may also be united by understanding them as 'gifts in support of the priesthood'.

Whereas the priests had been consecrated (Lev. 8), Levites are cleansed (cf. Jenson 1992: 131). Consecrating the priesthood involved an elevation offering (Lev. 8:27), but here the Levites themselves are an elevation offering. Aaron and his sons had also been washed, but they underwent additional measures, being sprinkled with blood and anointed with oil – the priests were *sanctified* for their holy calling, whereas Levites are simply *cleansed* for their service of guard duty and Tabernacle transport. Levites, not being consecrated like priests, are not permitted to enter the Tent of Meeting nor to officiate at the altar. The contrasts between the installation of priests and Levites are shown in Table 16 (based on D. A. Brueggemann 2005: 278).

There are similarities between the cleansing of Levites and that of lepers (Lev. 14:8) and Nazirites (Num. 6:9, 18).

20–22. Verse 20 begins with Moses' compliance (*ya'aś*, 3ms), inclusive of Aaron and the community of Israel, and ends with that of the sons of Israel (*'āśû*, 3mp). 'Purification' is given in hithpael (*yithạttāē'û*), understood as 'underwent purification' rather than 'purified themselves'. The cleansing and dedication of Levites is summarized (v. 21), and then a report of their beginning to work at the Tent of Meeting is given with emphasis on their subordination to priests: Levites serve in 'the presence' – that is, 'under the supervision' – of Aaron and his sons. The role of Levites, authorized by YHWH through Moses, is affirmed by the community of Israel and the priesthood of Aaron, between which two groups they will serve.

23–26. This new topic of legislation, signalled by the notice of YHWH's speaking to Moses, relates the age limits of service for Levites. In 4:3, 23, 30 the age range for the work of Levite houses is given as 30–50 years of age, while here the range is defined as 25–50. Since Numbers 8 occurred one month earlier than the book's opening, that means the age range was narrowed in chapter 4. Rabbinical tradition dealt with

Table 16: Priests versus Levites

Priests	Levites
Washed (Lev. 8:6)	Sprinkled (Num. 8:7)
Put on new garments (Lev. 8:13)	Washed their clothes (Num. 8:21)
Blood applied to their right ear, thumb and toe (Exod. 29:20; Lev. 8:23; 14:14, 17, 25, 28)	–
Anointed with oil (Exod. 29:7, 21; Lev. 8:30)	–
Consecrated / made 'holy' (Lev. 8:12, 30)	Purified / made 'clean' (Num. 8:6)

the discrepancy by explaining a five-year term of apprenticeship, from age 25–30, a reasonable notion given the gravity of Levitical duties (see comment on 4:3; cf. *Hul.* 24a; Rashi 1997: 4:96). Shamah observes such an apprenticeship is implied in the text (2011: 694): whereas the 30-year citation has 'all who came to the hosts to do work in the Tent of Meeting' (4:3), with Levites reporting for work, plain and simple, the formulation associated with 25 years of age has it that Levites 'should come to congregate in formation around the work going on at the Tent of Meeting' (8:24), consistent with observing and learning. Since Numbers 4 deals particularly with the transport of the Tabernacle, it is possible that the age window there relates only to those duties, while this passage, occurring one month prior, sets the broad service of Levites within a larger time frame (similarly, Keil and Delitzsch 1973: 3:49). David would later lower the age of service-entry to 20 years, reasoning that Levites 'will no longer carry the Dwelling, or any of the vessels for its service' (1 Chr. 23:24–27; cf. Noordtzij 1983: 81; Harrison 1990: 156–157). The focus of this legislation communicates that even after the age of 50, Levites are able to 'minister' (*šērēt*) to or with – to help or support – their fellow Levites to 'keep their charge' (*lišmōr mišmeret*); they may help with guard duty, but are to refrain from doing the main work themselves. The work of Levites is described with similar language as the role of Israelite men in the opening census (cf. 4:1–3). As this section touches on the retirement of Levites from their duties, it makes for a fitting conclusion to their dedication ceremony.

Explanation

The first major section of Numbers (chs. 1–10) continues to follow the path of sacred geography, tracing the layers of the Camp of YHWH's earthly hosts from the outer band comprised of Israel's twelve tribes (1–2), to the inner band of Levites (3–4), to the spiritual dynamic of the community, with YHWH's central Dwelling reorienting not only the physical arrangement of Israel but also their daily lives (5–6), and finally, through a flashback, to the heart of the Camp – the central camp of the *Shekhinah* – where the view narrows on the *altar* in the courtyard, the *atonement lid* in the holy of holies, and the *lampstand* in the holy place, and the corresponding roles of the twelve tribes (chieftains), Moses, and Aaron the high priest, respectively. Attention then turns to the cleansing and dedication of Levites for their transport and guard duties, surrounding the Dwelling (7–8). Once this movement is complete, then the Camp, as a mobile temple-city of God, will set out in the wilderness for the land of promise (9–10). While Numbers 1 – 6 focuses on the structure of the Camp, chapters 7–10 focus on the mobility of the Camp with special reference to the Dwelling, through which YHWH will guide his people: the tribal gifts of wagons and oxen, and the cleansing of Levites who will transport the Dwelling, depict something of the mechanism of mobility for YHWH's Dwelling, akin to the living creatures and wheels of his chariot (cf. Ezek. 1; 10).

While in Exodus, the construction and consecration of the Dwelling emphasizes the historical reality of YHWH's presence on earth, unapproachable in glory (Exod. 40: 34–35), and while Leviticus emphasizes how the Dwelling came to function as a Tent of Meeting between YHWH and Israel, through the priesthood and cult (Lev. 9), Numbers returns to the day of the Dwelling's anointing and consecration to emphasize a third angle: the relationship and conduct of Israel's tribes toward the Dwelling, and YHWH's guidance of the Camp through the Dwelling (cf. Hirsch 2007a: 130). Whereas Exodus generally highlights Moses' role, and Leviticus the role of the priesthood, Numbers highlights the role of the tribes of Israel through their chieftains, as well as the Levites. The lengthy list of contributions from each tribal chieftain underscores their devotion, prioritizing the Camp's sacred centre and wellspring of life – the altar. The dedication of the altar exhibits the ideal of godly leadership, involving sacrificial giving in support of the institutions and hierarchical structure established by YHWH for the good of the whole nation. The list also signals the importance of contributions for maintaining the newly established cult of Israel, conveying the equal stake in the priestly service at the altar shared among the tribes (Friedman 2001: 447). Indeed, the 'equality of offerings symbolizes the equal access each of the tribes, as members of the congregation, has to Tabernacle court space' (George 2013: 33).

The transition between the dedication of the altar (7:10–88) and Aaron's tending of the lampstand (8:1–4) is 7:89, where God's voice is depicted as communicating with Moses from above the atonement lid over the ark of the testimony, between the two cherubim, within the Tent's holy of holies. Although the portrait of Israel's following after God in the wilderness is that of the people following his Cloud of glory (9:15–23), the nature of Israel's religion is auditory, found in heeding the voice of the inscrutable God (Deut. 4:12–20). Here, YHWH's communication with Moses sets forth the mobile Tent of Meeting as the new source of revelation and guidance – the new Sinai summit, as it were – for the wilderness journey ahead.

Juxtaposed with God's opening communication (7:89), in 8:1–4 YHWH through Moses directs Aaron the high priest to set up the lamps of the lampstand so they beam their light in front of it, upon the twelve loaves, representing the tribes of Israel, on the golden table. Whereas the tribes had gravitated to the central altar with gifts, Aaron's ministry now reciprocates. This cultic symbol expresses the substance of the priestly benediction in 6:22–27: the people of God basking in the light of God's blessed presence, through the instrumentality of the priesthood and its cult. As such, 8:1–4 symbolizes the reality of the Camp itself; through dischronology and juxtaposition, it gives expression through the symbolism of the cult of what the movement from Exodus 19 through Numbers 6 has accomplished: the twelve tribes arranged about the Dwelling as a unified Camp, with YHWH's life and blessing shining out upon Israel, illuminating them with his glory. What is symbolized in the holy place is also prospective, since the holy place at the Camp's centre presents a more intense form of communion with God and his people, within the house of God (ultimately, within the 'house' of a new creation, Rev. 21 – 22), foretasted within the bounds of Israel's wilderness Camp. Just as the priestly benediction (6:22–27) followed the ideal of Israel as a holy nation via the Nazirite vow (6:1–21), so here God's light of blessing on his tribes (8:1–4) follows the idealistic portrait of the tribes bringing their gifts for the altar of whole burnt offering (ch. 7). Taken together, Numbers 7 – 8 presents an idealistic portrait of Israel's Camp, each vignette presenting a part in relation to the whole – the twelve tribes for the sake of YHWH's central presence and the duties of Levites (7:1–88), Moses for the sake of the Camp's guidance (7:89), Aaron's intercessory ministry for the sake of blessing the Camp (8:1–4), and the Levites for the sake of the tribes whose firstborn sons they represent (8:5–26). In the first subsection of the wilderness sojourn (chs. 11–15), Moses will be vindicated as YHWH's prophet *par excellence* (12:5–8), which flows out of the scene here (7:89), just as in the following subsection (chs. 16–18) Aaron will be vindicated as YHWH's chosen priest (17:1–12), which flows out of his special duty here (8:1–4).

Having narrowed the focus on the central camp of the *Shekhinah*, on the Dwelling's altar in the courtyard, ark and atonement lid in the holy of holies, and the lampstand in the holy place, the text turns to the middle or inner camp of Levites (8:5–26), who will be dedicated in place of Israel's firstborn sons to transport the Dwelling and serve as a protective encampment around it. Both the section on Aaron's duties within the holy place (8:1–4), and YHWH's declaration in 8:19, that he has given the Levites as a gift to Aaron and his sons, underscore the hierarchy of access to God expressed in the layers of the Camp itself. As with the three purity cases (Num. 5 – 6), the structure of the Camp progresses toward the centre with increased holiness. The dedication of Levites, the inner camp, shows that greater self-dedication is required as one moves toward the Camp's sacred centre. This inward movement of self-dedication corresponds to the outward, expanding movement of holiness from YHWH's presence in the centre – mutual, reciprocal movements that, in an ultimate sense, have the sanctification of the cosmos in view. In the Levites' status as replacement for Israel's firstborn sons, the Passover redemption out of Egypt is recalled in the section's central verse (v. 17), forming a segue into the second Passover account that follows (9:1–14). Numbers 8:5–26 also forms a development of the golden calf episode, where Levites, who demonstrated they were 'on YHWH's side' by wreaking judgement on the idolaters among Israel, had been instructed to consecrate themselves to receive a blessing from YHWH (Exod. 32:25–29). In giving YHWH the Levites as an elevation offering for Aaron's priesthood, in place of their own firstborn sons, Israelites implicitly acknowledge their previous guilt. At the same time, this gift also released the tribe of Levi from other duties and obligations expected by the nation, such as participation in the battles of conquest (cf. Num. 32). The gift of Levites, moreover, is in line with the tribes' other gifts, for transporting the Dwelling (7:1–9) and for the service of the altar (7:10–88); that is, Levites form part of the tribes' efforts to supply the priesthood with all that is necessary for the work of the Tent of Meeting. Both sorts of gifts acknowledge the accountability of all Israel, every tribe, to the work and service of the Sanctuary, and signals the particular perspective of Numbers: not on the cult per se, but on the relationship between Israel and the Sanctuary within the context of the Camp's journey through the wilderness, an angle embodied by Levites as 'lay assistants to the priesthood' (G. J. Wenham 1981b: 109). The Levites' purification took place through water and blood, foreshadowing what would pour out from the Crucified One's side, cleansing his people to be living sacrifices unto God (John 19:34; Rom. 12:1–2; cf. Gane 2009: 37–38).

Numbers 7 – 8 highlights the tribal chieftains as leaders of the outer camp, and Levites, who form the inner camp, furthering the book's focus on the covenant community as embodied by the Camp of Israel. Having reiterated the setting up and consecration of the Dwelling and its altar, along with the installation of Levites, who will transport and guard the Dwelling amid Israel's tribes, the established Camp is now ready to set out from Sinai for the wilderness journey to the land.

NUMBERS 9 – 10: AFTER A SECOND PASSOVER, THE CAMP JOURNEYS FORTH

Translation

[1]And YHWH spoke to Moses in the wilderness of Sinai in the second year after their going out from the land of Egypt, in the first month, saying, [2]'Let the sons of Israel do the Passover offering at its appointed time. [3]On the fourteenth day of this month at twilight you will do it at its appointed time, according to all its statutes and according to all its rules you will do it.'

[4]And Moses spoke to the sons of Israel for them to do the Passover offering. [5]And they did the Passover offering in the first month on the fourteenth day of the month at twilight in the wilderness of Sinai

according to all that YHWH commanded Moses, just so the sons of Israel did.

⁶And it happened that some men were unclean by way of human death, so they were not able to do the Passover offering on that day, and they drew near before the presence of Moses and before the presence of Aaron on that day. ⁷And those men said to him, 'We are unclean by way of human death; why should we be removed from bringing near the near-offering of YHWH at its appointed time in the midst of the sons of Israel?'

⁸And Moses said to them, 'Stand by and I will hear what YHWH will command for you.'

⁹And YHWH spoke to Moses, saying, ¹⁰'Speak to the sons of Israel, saying, "Any man who is unclean by way of human death or on a long journey, among you or among your generations, and he would do the Passover offering: ¹¹In the second month on the fourteenth day at twilight they will do it, with unleavened bread and bitter herbs they will eat it. ¹²They will leave nothing of it until morning, and not a bone of it will they break, according to all the statutes of the Passover offering they will do it. ¹³But the man who is clean and is not on a journey yet fails to do the Passover offering, that soul will be cut off from his people because the near-offering of YHWH he did not bring near at its appointed time – that man will bear his sin. ¹⁴And when a sojourner sojourns with you, and he will do the Passover offering to YHWH, according to the statute of the Passover offering and according to its rule, just so he will do; there will be one statute for you, for the sojourner and for the native of the land."'

¹⁵Now on the day the Dwelling was raised up, the Cloud covered the Dwelling, the Tent of the Testimony; and in the evening it would be upon the Dwelling in appearance as fire until morning. ¹⁶So it was continually: the Cloud would cover it (by day) and the appearance of fire at night. ¹⁷And according to the ascent of the Cloud from over the Tent, so afterward the sons of Israel would journey out; and in the place at which the Cloud would there dwell, there the sons of Israel would camp. ¹⁸According to the mouth of YHWH the sons of Israel would journey out and according to the mouth of YHWH they would camp, all the days during which the Cloud would dwell upon the Dwelling they would camp. ¹⁹And when the Cloud lingered upon the Dwelling many days, the sons of Israel would keep the charge of YHWH, and would not journey out. ²⁰And whenever the Cloud was for a number of days upon the Dwelling, according to the mouth of YHWH they would camp and according to the mouth of YHWH they would journey out. ²¹And whenever the Cloud was from evening until morning and the Cloud ascended in the morning, then they would journey out; whether by day or by night, when the Cloud ascended they would journey out. ²²Whether for a few days or a month or many more days, when the Cloud

was upon the Dwelling to dwell upon it, the sons of Israel camped and would not journey out – but when it ascended they would journey out. [23]According to the mouth of YHWH they camped and according to the mouth of YHWH they journeyed out, the charge of YHWH they kept, according to the mouth of YHWH by the hand of Moses.

[10:1]And YHWH spoke to Moses, saying, [2]'Make for yourself two trumpets of silver, make them of hammered work; they will be for you for the calling together of the community, and for journeying out of the camps. [3]When they sound them, all the community will come to meet with you at the door of the Tent of Meeting. [4]Now if they sound one, the chieftains, the heads of the thousands of Israel, will come to meet with you. [5]And if you sound a trilling blast, the camps that are encamped eastward will journey out; [6]and if you sound a trilling blast a second time, the camps that are encamped southward will journey out; they will sound a trilling blast for them to journey out. [7]And to assemble the assembly you will sound them but not a trilling blast. [8]Now the sons of Aaron the priests will sound the trumpets, and it will be to you for a perpetual statute for your generations. [9]And when you enter into war in your land against the hostile-foe who is being hostile against you, make a trilling blast with the trumpets and you will be remembered before the presence of YHWH your God and you will be saved from your enemies. [10]And in the day of your gladness and at your appointed times and on the first of your months, you will sound the trumpets over your whole burnt offerings and over your sacrifices of peace offerings, and they will be to you for a memorial before the presence of your God – I am YHWH your God.'

[11]Now it happened in the second year in the second month on the twentieth of the month the Cloud ascended from over the Dwelling of the Testimony. [12]And the sons of Israel journeyed out according to their set-journeys from the wilderness of Sinai, and the Cloud dwelled in the wilderness of Paran. [13]And they journeyed out from the first according to the mouth of YHWH by the hand of Moses. [14]The standard of the camp of the sons of Judah journeyed out first according to their hosts, and over his host was Nahshon the son of Amminadab. [15]And over the host of the tribe of the sons of Issachar was Nethanel son of Zuar; [16]and over the host of the tribe of the sons of Zebulun was Eliab son of Helon. [17]And the Dwelling was taken down and the sons of Gershon and the sons of Merari journeyed out, and they were carrying the Dwelling. [18]And the standard of the camp of Reuben according to their hosts journeyed out, and over its host was Elizur son of Shedeur. [19]And over the host of the tribe of the sons of Simeon was Shelumiel son of Zurishaddai. [20]And over the host of the tribe of the sons of Gad was Eliasaph son of Deuel. [21]And the Kohathites journeyed carrying the holy, and they would raise the Dwelling by the time they came. [22]And the standard of the camp of the sons of Ephraim according to their hosts journeyed out, and over its

host was Elishama son of Ammihud. ²³And over the host of the tribe of the sons of Manasseh was Gamaliel son of Pedahzur. ²⁴And over the host of the tribe of the sons of Benjamin was Abidan son of Gideoni. ²⁵And the standard of the camp of the sons of Dan journeyed out, rearguard for all the camps according to their hosts, and over its host was Ahiezer son of Ammishaddai. ²⁶And over the host of the tribe of the sons of Asher was Pagiel son of Ochran. ²⁷And over the host of the tribe of the sons of Naphtali was Ahira son of Enan. ²⁸These are the journeys of the sons of Israel according to their hosts; they journeyed out.

²⁹Now Moses said to Hobab son of Reuel the Midianite, the father-in-law of Moses, 'We are journeying out to the place of which YHWH said I will give it to you; go with us and we will be good to you – for YHWH has spoken good over Israel.'

³⁰And he said to him, 'I will not go but rather to my land and to my birthplace I will go.'

³¹And he said, 'Please do not forsake us, for so you know how we are to camp in the wilderness and you will be for us as eyes. ³²And it will be that when you go with us, from that good which YHWH will be good to us, we will be good to you.'

³³And they journeyed out from the mountain of YHWH a three days' way, with the Ark of the Covenant of YHWH journeying out before their presence (on the) three days' way to search out for them a resting place. ³⁴And the cloud of YHWH was over them by day when they journeyed from the camp. ³⁵And it was that when the ark would journey out, Moses would say:

Arise, O YHWH!
Your enemies be scattered,
And those who hate you flee from before your face!

³⁶And whenever it rested, he would say:

Return, O YHWH!
To the myriad thousands of Israel!

Notes on the text

9:2. LXX begins here with *Eipon*, also suggested by *BHS*; Dillmann reads an originally historical tense, *waya'ăśû* (1886: 46).

'time': SamP reads pl. here and in vv. 3, 7, 13; LXX has pl. for v. 3.

3. 'this month': LXX reads 'first month' (cf. v. 1).

'you will do it': SamP, Syr have *ya'ăśû*, but MT is the stronger reading.

'at twilight': lit. 'between evenings' (*bên hā'ărbayim*; i.e. between sundown and dark).

5. LXX lacks 'and they did the Passover offering' and 'at twilight', the former possibly an elision from v. 4.

10. The hey of *rĕḥōqāh* has a dot over it; Nachmanides, following Akiba, suggests this may imply the 'long' journey is too distant to bring the Passover offering even if not actually distant per se – any distance longer than 15 miles (see 1975: 85).

13. 'journey': LXX reads 'long journey', the intent of MT.

14. 'its rule': SamP, Syr, Vg have pl. here, as in v. 3; however, that verse also has 'statutes' in pl., whereas both are singular in v. 14, perhaps emphasizing the law's singularity – 'one' for sojourner and native.

15. 'it would be': BHS favours a perfect (cf. Paterson 1900: 47); LXX also has imperfect.

16. '(by day)': the sense of the text; LXX, Syr, Vg, *TgPal* read 'by day'. Although MT is the more difficult reading, BHS suggests adding *yômām*.

21. 'when the cloud ascended they would journey out': LXX lacks this concluding phrase; G. B. Gray (1903: 87) suggests a dittographic error in MT, but parallelism is not unusual.

22. 'upon the Dwelling': LXX lacks this phrase; it would appear required by, rather than a gloss for, *'ālāyw*, which follows (although the former replaces the latter in Syr).

'but when it ascended they would journey out': also lacking in LXX.

'many more days': translates *yāmîm* (days); contextually, this indefinite period (BDB 399b) or 'season' (North 1961) refers to a period longer than a month, and may be paralleled with a 'whole year' (Lev. 25:29).

10:3. 'When they sound them': LXX reads second person sg.; MT employs variation (cf. vv. 4, 5).

6. LXX completes the instructions for the westward and northern camps – likely a specimen of gap-filling.

11. SamP contains expansions, including material from Deut. 1:6–8.

17. 'was taken down': LXX, Syr imply *wĕhôridû*, as in 1:51; 4:5.

20. LXX has Reuel (*Ragouēl*) as elsewhere (1:14; 2:14; 7:42, 47); MT reads Deuel everywhere, except at 2:14 reading Reuel – where a copyist's error, confusing dalet and resh, is probable.

31. 'as eyes': LXX reads *presbytēs*, 'aged man' or 'ambassador'.

33. 'three days' way': SamP has 'one day's way' in place of the second occurrence; BHS prefers to omit this second occurrence.

34. LXX places this verse after v. 36.

36. 'to': this prep. is supplied; see GKC §118d, f.

Form and structure

Chapters 9 and 10 are woven together through shared key terms and themes. The journey root *ns'* occurs nine times in Numbers 9 and twenty times in Numbers 10; the Passover is to be celebrated at its 'appointed time' (*mô'ēd*), four times in chapter 9, and the silver trumpets are to be sounded for feasts or 'appointed times' (*mô'ēd*) in 10:10 (cf. 10:3); both Passover and the use of the silver trumpets are declared a 'statute' (*ḥuqqā*, 9:3, 12, 14; 10:8), a term that includes the notion of privilege that is part of YHWH's decree

There is an inclusio between Exodus 40:34–38 and Numbers 9:15–23, both passages relating YHWH's Cloud over the Dwelling and the Cloud's guidance of Israel through the wilderness. The intervening material, Leviticus through Numbers 8, explains how the scenario of Israel's following the Cloud in the wilderness came to be: first, the Dwelling needed to become a functioning Tent of Meeting between YHWH and Israel by means of a consecrated priesthood and cult (Lev.), and then the community of Israel needed to be arranged around YHWH's Tent to form an encampment of his earthly hosts (Num. 1 – 8). The story has now caught up to the end of Exodus (40:36–38), and continues (Num. 9:15–23).

Numbers 9 – 10 relate the Camp's departure from Sinai, a movement that involved celebrating Passover (9:1–14), a portrayal of the wilderness journey ahead (9:15–23), the commissioning of two silver trumpets for orchestrating the Camp's movement (10:1–10), and, finally, the setting out of the Camp of YHWH's earthly hosts, parading tribe by tribe with the Dwelling transported in their midst, and led by his ark (10:11–36). More broadly, Moses' discussion with Hobab in 10:29–32 (and selection of elders in 11:11–17, 25–29) frames the at-Sinai narrative with Moses' discussion with Jethro and selection of judges in Exodus 18 (cf. Lawlor 2011).

I.   Delayed Passover, 9:1–14
     A. Passover commanded and observed, 1–5
     B. Exceptional case, 6–8
     C. YHWH's legislation for contingency, 9–14
II. YHWH's guidance of Israel by Cloud and fire, 9:15–23
     A. YHWH's presence in the Dwelling by means of Cloud, 15–16
     B. Israel follows YHWH's guidance by means of Cloud, 17–23
III. Two silver trumpets, 10:1–10
IV. The camp sets out from Sinai, 10:11–36
     A. The sons of Israel set out by their standards, 11–28
     B. Moses encourages Hobab to journey with Israel, 29–32
     C. Israel led by YHWH's ark, 33–36

The Passover report (9:1–14) has two sections: the original command with its observance in the first month (vv. 1–5), and new legislation allowing for compliance in the second month (6–14). The first part sets the scene for the second, main part (which is twofold: vv. 6–8, 9–14). With its emphasis on the contingency of corpse pollution, the Passover account is related to the Nazirite vow (6:1–21) and red heifer ritual (ch. 19). Through the addendum, allowing for Passover keeping in the second month, the text transitions back from the first to the second month, just before the portrayal of Israel following YHWH's Cloud in the wilderness (9:15–23). Israelites celebrated Passover on the second month, six days before setting out from Sinai (Num. 10:11; cf. G. B. Gray 1903: 82–83). Some propose the second observance law first existed independently of its narrative frame (Holzinger 1903: 35; Kellermann 1970: 129–132; Licht 1985: 1:135–139), or that it reflects Hezekiah's delayed Passover in 2 Chronicles 30 (A. Ehrlich 1899: 1:254; Talmon 1958; against which, see Chavel 2009c). The simplest approach remains that of taking the text at face value and then assessing its theological role within Numbers.

The ideal portrait of Israel following YHWH's guidance by means of his Cloud (9:15–23) is given in almost poetic, elevated prose, with enough rhythmic repetition, that it has been labelled a 'song' or said to have an ancient song as its source (see Cole 2000: 158–160). The text may be divided according to shifts of tense: 15a (perfect) 'YHWH's Presence', 15b–23a (imperfect) 'YHWH's mobility' and 23b 'Israel's faithful obedience', with the central section set out chiastically (W. W. Lee 2003b: 82–83; cf. Ashley 1993: 183):

A. Departure formula, 9:18a
   B. Encampment formula, 9:18bα
      C. Exposition of encampment, 9:18bβ–19
         D. Encamping formula, 9:20a
         D'. Departing formula, 9:20b
      C'. Exposition of departure, 9:21–22
   B'. Encampment formula, 9:23aα
A'. Departure formula, 9:23aβ

Although YHWH's guidance is a dominant concern of the passage, Condren points out that YHWH's activity through the Cloud is usually expressed with clauses grammatically subordinate to Israel's obedient following – for example, 'when the Cloud was lifted, Israel would set out' (vv. 17, 19, 20, 21, 22) – so that both YHWH's guidance and Israel's wholly following after him contribute to the ideal portrait of the Camp's journey through the wilderness (2005: 199). This passage is similar to the twofold structure of Exodus 40:34–38:

| YHWH's presence in the Dwelling, via Cloud | Exod. 40:34–35 | Num. 9:15–16 |
| YHWH's guidance of Israel, via Cloud | Exod. 40:36–38 | Num. 9:17–23 |

The legislation for making two silver trumpets (10:1–10) is set within a narrative context through the introductory speech formula. Verses 2–4 form a direct address to Moses, with use of the second person singular throughout, while vv. 5–10 appear to address all Israel, using second person plural. Following the Cloud's guidance (9:15–23), this section offers a look into how that guidance was coordinated in a practical manner, through use of trumpets. After stating the twofold function of the trumpets, for calling the covenant community and for the camps' journeying out (v. 2), an expansion on the first function, gathering Israel, is given (vv. 3–4), followed by an expansion of the second function, the setting out of the camps (vv. 5–6). A summary statement closes the section, with a remark on the first function, general enough to comprehend both functions of the trumpets (v. 7). The use of trumpets for the wilderness sojourn having been detailed, two new elements are introduced: it is the priesthood, Aaron and his sons, who will blow the trumpets (at Moses' direction), and use of trumpets will continue in the land as a lasting statute (v. 8), this latter point forming the topic for the rest of the section. The next two verses then delineate the trumpets' twofold use in the land (linked by use of *z-k-r*), after the wilderness sojourn, beginning with a role somewhat related to the second function, 'going out' (*bô'*) to war, although the 'journeying out' language of verses 5–6 is not used (v. 9), and then closing with a role related to the first function, Israel's celebration of feasts, although, here too, the language of verses 3–4 is not used (v. 10). (See Table 17.)

Israel's departure (Num. 10:11–28), with its mention of the Cloud and tribal arrangements, is widely deemed a specimen of priestly tradition, while verses 29–36, not being strictly consecutive, is read as an incorporation of J material (cf. Wellhausen 1889: 181, 100–101; G. B. Gray 1903: 90, 92–93; Budd 1984: 109–110, 113–114). Rather than subjecting an ancient composition to modern notions of historical narrative, however, we will glean insight from the text's form as it stands. After a nearly one year stay that began in Exodus 19, Israel's setting out from Sinai, the mountain of God, is fittingly told with splendour and by different angles

Table 17: The silver trumpets

(Introductory speech formula)	1

I. Manufacture and function of two silver trumpets	2

A. For the calling of Israel	B. For the journeying out of camps
i. Meeting of the covenant community 3	i. Eastward camps journey out 5
ii. Meeting of the princes 4	ii. Southward camps journey out 6
iii. Gathering the congregation 7	

II. Trumpets to be sounded by the priests and are a lasting statute	8
	B. At times of war, to be 'remembered' (*zkr*) by YHWH 9
A. At times of sacred gathering, as a 10 'remembrance' (*zkr*) before God	

– an aerial view of the hosts marching out by tribes, and a close-up on Moses' invitation to his brother-in-law, and the liturgy for the ark's setting out and return. Taken together, these vignettes comprise a full theological account of a momentous event in redemptive history.

Comment

9:1–14. The story of the second Passover, as Chavel points out (2009c: 20), caps and summarizes the texts that precede it, dramatizing their themes – sacrifice, impurity, and Camp membership – and, further, 'dramatizes the festival that would have inaugurated' the Camp, whose sacred structure the previous chapters have conveyed by stages. This Passover episode serves as a fitting summary before the idealistic portrait which follows, the Camp's harmonized pursuit of the Cloud through the wilderness.

The precise phrase 'on the first month' (*baḥōdeš hāri'šôn*) occurs four times in Numbers, three with explicit reference to Passover (9:1; 28:16; 33:3) and once, in 20:1, at the dawn of the second generation, where Passover is implicit. Indeed, given the second Passover legislation, it appears likely that the isolated chronological reference in 20:1, bereft of year or context, is intended to express a 'second Passover' in the sense of the second generation's opening journey to the land. This theological message coordinates with the corpse pollution rite of the red heifer (Num. 19), which cleanses the second generation from the first generation's judgement and aligns with the situation here (9:6–7), as well as with the initial setback in the Nazirite vow (6:9–12).

2–5. Without repeating the 'statutes and judgements' set out in Exodus 12:1–28, YHWH's speech (9:2–3) underscores particularly the need to observe the feast 'in its appointed time' (*bĕmô'ădo*), precisely the subject matter that creates the contingency regulation that follows (9:11–13 – note 'appointed time', v. 7). 'Statute' (*ḥuqqâ*) derives from the idea of carving in stone (*ḥāqāh*, *ḥāqaq*) and here (vv. 3, 12, 14), within the context of ritual activity, holds the meaning of an 'established ceremony' (see Ringgren 1986). The 'appointed time' (*mô'ădîm*) is mentioned twice, along with its specification: 'the fourteenth day of this (first) month', a detail also mentioned in the compliance report (v. 5). Israel's cult includes not only the appointed place for meeting with YHWH, a Tent of 'Meeting' (*mô'ēd*), but also the appointed times, using the same root (Exod. 12:6, 14; Lev. 23:5). Hirsch notes the rarity of the shift from third person (v. 2) to second person (v. 3), inclusive of Moses (2007a: 172), perhaps underscoring the feast's importance. With such an emphasis on time, it is ironic that 'at twilight', lit. 'between evenings' (*bên hā'ărbayim*), is now an obscurity. Jewish tradition offers varied interpretation, though settling for the time of the evening *tāmîd* offering, 3 p.m. (Snaith 1967: 152). As the context of Passover, Israel's deliverance out of Egypt in verse 1 forms a natural bridge into the feast's celebration. Not only culminating in the release of Israel out of Egyptian bondage, but also serving to ransom Israel's firstborn sons from death, the Passover ceremony is linked with the dedication of Levites in place of firstborn sons. Passover was *the* national feast, marking the historic deliverance that defined both Israel as a people and YHWH as Israel's deliverer. Alexander brings out the theology of Passover in a threefold manner, according to the ceremony's three distinct elements: slaying the lamb or young goat in place of the firstborn involved the concept of substitutionary atonement; the blood manipulation with hyssop may be understood as a ritual of purification; and eating the lamb, considered sacrificial and therefore sacred meat, conveyed sanctification (Alexander 1995; 2009: 127–135; cf. Morales 2020: 66–76).

After Moses conveys YHWH's command (v. 4), Israel's compliance is noted, with the emphasis falling once more on the timing, the fourteenth day of the first month (v. 5), so that the whole section serves as a transition to the question that arises in verses 6–7.

6–7. Some men, who were 'unclean' (*těmē'îm*) 'by way of human death', literally by a 'soul of a human' (*lěnepeš 'ādām*), faced a problem: the Passover feast was so defining and important that not observing the ceremony meant being cut off from God's people (v. 13; cf. Exod. 12:19), and, yet, to observe the feast in a state of uncleanness risked God's judgement for defiling the sacred Dwelling. Eating the lamb's holy meat while in a state of impurity was a cause for concern (see Lev. 7:20–21), but, evidently, the issue is rather that of defiling the Dwelling since no concern over impurity was registered in the original Passover in Egypt when there was no sanctuary to defile – nor purity laws (Lev. 11 – 15). Leviticus 11 deals only with the impurity caused by animal carcasses, with the phrase *lěnepeš 'ādām* used here specifically to denote the difference (see Frevel 2013c: 392), a phrase that occurs six times in Numbers (9:6, 7; 19:11; 31:35, 40, 46; for avoidance of corpse pollution by priests, see Lev. 21:1–4, 10–12).

The men, zealous to bring the 'offering of YHWH' at its appointed time, are grieved at the thought of being left out of this corporate event at the heart of Israel's identity. Their humble initiative is but one of several examples of the sort of leadership YHWH rewards as exemplary, and may be compared with that of the daughters of Zelophehad (27:1–11) and the chieftains of Manasseh (36:1–12). 'Those men said' is emphatic; likely explained by verse 13, where any who are clean and not on a journey are warned about failing to participate on Passover: it was *only* 'those men' who were enquiring about alternate plans. The allowance by YHWH was not intended to set a precedent for exonerating any excuse for not participating. Failure to bring the required 'offering', the details of which are set forth in Leviticus 23:4–8, is central to the divine judgement expressed in verse 13. Some have suggested that, contextually, the men may be identified as Mishael and Elzaphan, the sons of Aaron's uncle Uzziel who had been directed by Moses to carry the dead bodies of Nadab and Abihu outside the Camp (Lev. 10:4) (cf. M. A. Greenberg 1997: 46).

8–12. Moses takes their question, and their desire to participate, to YHWH. The role of Moses as mediator, as well as the dynamic nature of the Torah while he is still alive, are on display. More narrowly, YHWH's direction through Moses forms a major instance of the guidance of Israel through the wilderness – note 9:23: 'according to the mouth (*pî*) of YHWH by the hand of Moses'. YHWH's speech to Moses is reported in verses 10–14: he commands that the defiled Israelites do the Passover on the fourteenth day of the second month (when clean), strictly observing the stipulations as if being kept in the original month – at twilight, with unleavened bread and bitter herbs, leaving none of the meat until morning, without breaking the lamb's bones, 'according to all the statutes' (Exod. 12). Possibly, absence of the blood ritual (Exod. 12:21–27) is deliberate, perhaps as impractical in the wilderness setting. YHWH's response, moreover, broadens the allowance to those who happen to be away on a journey during the first month, the supplement having continuing application in the land ('among your generations', v. 10). Especially within the context of the wilderness Camp, the unclean person, who is expelled for a time (Num. 5:1–4), and a person away on a distant journey, thus outside the bounds of the covenant community, are in the same predicament (Ashley 1993: 180). The 'bitter herbs' (*mĕrōrîm*) were likely meant to remind Israelites of the hardship of life in Egypt, how taskmasters had 'made their lives bitter (*mārĕrû*) with hard bondage' (Exod. 1:14; 12:8). Faithful participation in Passover should thus have kept Israelites from their almost immediate murmuring in the wilderness, with regard to the delicacies of the land of bondage, Egypt's fish, cucumbers, melons, and leeks (Num. 11:5). Eating bitter things (*mĕrōrîm*) may form an allusion to the purity law for the strayed woman who drinks the 'bitter waters' (5:18, 19, 23, 24, 27).

13. Because, once an allowance is made, it is human nature to slacken strict observance, YHWH attaches a sober warning. For the one who is clean and not away on a journey, and yet thinks he may forgo the first month's Passover (perhaps assuming observation on the second month) – such a person will be 'cut off' from his people, for failing to bring the offering at 'its appointed time'. This verse underscores that no allowance to put off observing Passover in the first month will be made whatsoever for *any* reason other than being unclean or away on journey. While corpse pollution is the sort of uncleanness in focus (6, 7, 10), reference to one 'who is clean' means the stipulation likely covers those also who are unclean by means other than contact with a corpse, such as discharge or skin disease (cf. Num. 5:1).

In the Torah, to be 'cut off from his people' is a punishment for heinous sins, sometimes combined, as here, with the phrase that such a person 'will bear his sin' (e.g. Lev. 20:17; see comments on 5:31), a punishment involving the 'threat of sudden death at the hands of God, and may also hint at punishment in the life to come' (G. J. Wenham 1981b: 112). To be cut off from the people has been understood in a variety of ways (see Keil 1869: 173; Milgrom 1990: 405–408), as excommunication (de Vaulx 1972: 125; Budd 1984: 98), judicial execution (G. B. Gray 1903: 84–85; Noordtzij 1983: 84), or direct divine intervention (McNeile 1911: 48; Wold 1978) – each of which involves premature death. In sum, being 'cut off' is a form of severe excommunication from the covenant community, a definitive exclusion by (premature) death and the extirpation of one's lineage, carried out either directly by YHWH or indirectly as judicial execution by the covenant community (see Sklar 2005: 15–20). Being 'cut off from the people' is fitting since such a person has rejected the observance of the feast that more than any other defined one's inclusion in Israel, reliving the nation's redemptive event. The dominant concern, as Budd observes, is the weighty obligation to celebrate this foundational feast: the 'exceptions enforce the point rather than detract from it' (1984: 99). Also, the ruling, as Frevel explains (2013c: 397), 'shows that the congregation that is constituted by the celebration of the exodus is a pure community that should not be affected by any impurity'.

This second Passover account is one of several occasions where Moses sought guidance from YHWH, the others comprising: the blasphemer (Lev. 24:10–23), the Sabbath gatherer (Num. 15:32–36), and the daughters of Zelophehad (Num. 27:1–11) (cf. e.g. Chavel 2009b). Each story raises the question of being cut off from membership of God's covenant community. Not only does Moses desire a direct word of clarification from YHWH regarding such a sobering prospect of dreadful judgement, but the men, like Zelophehad's daughters who did not want their father's name done away, do not want to be excluded.

14. In the original Passover account, the applicability of the legislation to the sojourner (or 'resident-alien') was communicated, with the instruction that such persons needed first to be circumcised (Exod. 12:19, 48–49). This verse ensures that the same applicability holds for the addendum regarding celebration in the second month. The 'sojourner' (*gēr*) is one who 'sojourns' (*gûr*) with and among Israel, dwelling as a resident-alien, as distinguished from 'temporary resident' (*tôšāb*) or 'hired labourer' (*śākîr*) on the one hand and a foreigner (*nēkār*) on the other – the latter three are forbidden to participate in Passover (Exod. 12:43–45). Abram was a 'sojourner' in the land, the Bible's first use of the term (Gen. 15:13), and confessed to being both a 'sojourner and temporary alien' (*gēr-wĕtôšāb*, Gen. 23:4). Moses, naming his son Gershon, also declared that he had been a sojourner in a foreign land (Exod. 2:22). Because Israelites, too, were sojourners in the foreign land of Egypt, they are expected to treat sojourners among them as natives and to love them (Lev. 19:34) (see J. R. Spencer 1992; Konkel 1997). The refuge found by sojourners within Israel foreshadows the Gentiles' wider inclusion in the new covenant (cf. de Vaulx 1972: 126–127); this text may be connected, then, to Moses' invitation to Hobab (10:29).

9:15–23: Israel follows YHWH's Cloud in the wilderness

Numbers 9:15–23 forms a clear parallel to and expansion of Exodus 40:36–38. Israel's pursuit of the Cloud is placed after the creation of the Camp of Israel (Num. 1 – 6), and a flashback to the dedication of the Tabernacle and Levites (Num. 7 – 8), in such a way as to continue the narrative line with which Exodus had ended. Seebass captures the intent of this ideal portrait, Israel's pursuing the Cloud, writing that it offers 'a happy outlook on the following march by praising a complete obedience of the people to the leadership of the heavenly cloud' (2010: 269–270; cf. W. W. Lee 2008: 486–487). Numbers 9:17, translated as 'whenever' the Cloud ascended, reads more literally as 'according to the mouth' (*ûlĕpî*) of the ascended Cloud. Numbers 9:15–23 is interested in 'the exact obedience of the *'ēdāh* . . . according to the signs of God's cloud' (Seebass 2009: 107; cf. Jensen 1964: 46). The wilderness was thus a place for Israel to learn obedience to YHWH, a school in following him closely.

15–16. The focus returns to the first day of the first month of the second year (see Exod. 40:17, 34–38). The relationship between the Dwelling and the Cloud (*'ānān*), a theophany manifesting YHWH's presence, is akin to body and soul. Numbers, as here particularly, emphasizes the Cloud's guidance of Israel through the wilderness – foregoing mention of how the glory filled the Dwelling (Exod. 40:34) retains focus on the transition from the Cloud's original settling over the Dwelling (9:15–16) to its movements in guidance (9:17–23). Though some translate the second occurrence of 'Dwelling' in construct with 'Tent of the Testimony', the absolute form of Dwelling as well as the Masoretic *zaqef qaton* over it, favour reading the names in apposition. The subtext of Exodus 40:34–38 clarifies the distinction and dynamic between YHWH's Cloud and his glory. While his Cloud 'covered' the Tent of Meeting, his glory 'filled' the Dwelling (v. 34). His indwelling glory makes the Tabernacle the Dwelling; the shielding Cloud forbad any approach until, through the consecrated priesthood and cultic legislation, the Tabernacle could function as a Tent of Meeting. The Cloud, then, serves as a veil for YHWH's fiery glory; thus, by day only the Cloud is seen while in the dark the fire shines through the Cloud, illumining the night (Exod. 40:38; Num. 9:16). At times, the flame of his glory may break through the Cloud (Lev. 9:24; 10:2).

   Here the Dwelling is not contrasted with the more cultic term 'Tent of Meeting' (as in Exod. 40:34), the subject of Leviticus, but with 'Tent of the Testimony' (*hā'ēdut*), a designation fitting with the themes in Numbers of the Camp as covenant community and its guidance through God's voice and word. 'Testimony' appears to be used synonymously with 'covenant' (cf. 1:50; 10:33). The verbal shift from qatal (past tense, 15a) to yiqtol (future tense, 15b–23a) marks the transition from the Cloud's covering the Dwelling as a historic event, linked with the date notice, to the Cloud's regular appearance and movement (cf. Waltke and O'Connor 1990: 502) – 'thus it was continually' (*tāmîd*) (16). There is synonymous parallelism in verses 15 and 16: the Cloud covered 'the Dwelling' / 'it' (understood as its function by day), and the appearance of fire 'in the evening' / 'at night'. These verses focus on the great theophany, YHWH's manifest presence, throughout the wilderness sojourn: a majestic, covering Cloud by day, and a visible, fiery glory by night.

17–23. Expanding on Exod. 40:36–38, this section's elevated prose reflects the poetic language of prophecy and possibly derives from an ancient song. Alter, referencing Avishur, notes the 'studied use of numerically formulaic repetitions': 'the mouth of YHWH' occurs seven times – three times in conjunction with 'they would journey onward', three times with 'they would encamp', and once in the last summary line; 'Dwelling' also occurs seven times, its root *š-k-n* ten times (and 'Cloud' occurs ten times if one follows LXX) (2004: 728). While verses 15–16 underscored YHWH's presence, the theme of this section is on Israel's obedient following of YHWH's guidance (via his Cloud). Paralleled, verses 17–18 explain the manner of the Cloud's guidance of the camp, while verses 19–22 focus on the timing of the Cloud's movements and Israel's reciprocal responses, and verse 23 concludes with a summary statement on Israel's obedience (Condren 2005: 200). Similarity of expression equates the Cloud's movement (*ûlĕpî hē'ālōt he'ānān*, v. 17) with YHWH's command (*'al-pî yhwh*, v. 18) – the Cloud 'speaks', as it were, by its movement (note use of *pî* 'mouth' for Cloud), which movement has the authority of the words of YHWH. Milgrom reasonably translates *pî* as the 'sign' of YHWH – the Cloud's movement is YHWH's sign to Israel, whether to stay encamped or depart (1990: 71).

Table 18: The Cloud and command of YHWH

Verse 17: the Cloud's movement	Verse 18: YHWH's command
(17a) According to the Cloud's ascent from the Tent / → then the sons of Israel departed.	(18a) According to the command of YHWH / → the sons of Israel departed;
(17b) And in the place where the Cloud dwelled / → there the sons of Israel encamped.	(18b) And according to the command of YHWH/ → they encamped.
(18c) All the days in which the Cloud was sitting over the Dwelling / → they encamped.	

The formula 'according to the command of YHWH' (*'al-pî yhwh*) is repeated with various expansions (vv. 18, 20, 23a, 23b), leaving the strong impression of Israel's exacting obedience (cf. Ashley 1993: 183), even as Israel's precise response to the movements of the Cloud are repeated some nine instances.

Double use of 'there' (*šām*) in verse 17 highlights both Israel's precise obedience and the precise nature of the Camp during Israel's encampments, since God's Cloud-canopied Tent formed its centre. The phrase 'keep the charge' (*mišmeret*, vv. 19, 23), has already been used for the Levites' duty to guard the Dwelling (Num. 1:53; 3:7, 8, 25, 28, 31, 32, 38; 4:27, 28, 31, 32; 8:26) and, given that verse 19 links keeping YHWH's charge to Israel's encampment (vs departure), the same general idea may apply here – perhaps with reference to guarding the Camp from impurity (cf. 5:1–4). Israel would not depart while YHWH's Cloud remained descended on the Dwelling, which also meant he had taken his residence in the Dwelling by filling it with his glory (Exod. 40:34). The Cloud's ascent is noted four times (17, 21 [twice], 22), while the Cloud's encampment mode, 'dwell' (*šākan*, 17, 18, 22), 'remain' (*'ārāk*, 19, 22), or simply 'was (upon)' (*yihyeh*, 20, 21), is noted seven times. The Cloud's ascent is correlated with Israel's 'journeying out' (*nāsaʻ*, 17), and the Cloud's abiding with Israel's 'encamping' (*ḥānāh*, 17) – both used in response to YHWH's command (v. 18). The following formula is set up, combining the Cloud's vertical movement with Israel's horizontal movement: the Cloud's ascent equals Israel's departure, while the Cloud's dwelling equals Israel's encampment. Use of *šākan* (to dwell) for the Cloud, instead of 'descent' (*yārad*) and the like, underscores its role in 'the Dwelling' (*hammiškān*), and goes back to YHWH's dwelling on Mount Sinai (Exod. 24:16), typical language for YHWH's presence among his people that led to the rabbinical designation *Shekhinah*. Israel's need to perform the two movements of the Camp are foreshadowed in Numbers 1 – 2, where the creation of the Camp has these two aspects primarily in mind: the order of encampment and the order of journeying out. The image that emerges from 9:15–23 (along with Exod. 40:36–37 and Num. 10:11–12), writes Frankel (1998: 31), 'is the conception of a cloud resting permanently on top of the Tabernacle', visible to the people as a sort of 'sustained theophany'.

Verses 19–22 centre on the timing of the Cloud's movements, with Israel faithfully following after: verses 19–20 address the timing in general terms and 21–22 in more specific periods, with a total of seven time periods underscoring the full 'variety of scenarios in which Israel followed the Cloud' (Condren 2005: 203–204). Jewish interpretation typically offers a sympathetic reading of the unpredictable aspect of the Cloud's movements, pointing out the labour involved in setting up camp, with the need for unloading wagons, building pens for livestock, etc., so that it would have been quite trying not knowing whether the

Cloud's lingering would last merely a night, a few days, or longer (cf. Nachmanides 1975: 87–88). However incomprehensible to them as sheep, Israel needed to learn to follow YHWH as Shepherd with unquestioning trust and wholehearted devotion. While not much is said about long journeys through the wilderness, much space is given regarding the matter of stops, lengthy and otherwise, so that the main challenge to Israel stressed here is on the element of waiting. Israel's 'keeping the charge' of YHWH, then, includes encampment, and needing to wait for the Cloud's ascent before journeying out. The sevenfold use of both 'al-pî yhwh and hammiškān make clear that Israelites are not journeying to Canaan with God in tow, the Dwelling as some sort of talisman; no, the wilderness journey is as much led by YHWH as the exodus out of Egypt was led by him through Moses. Moreover, the divine Presence among Israelites when encamped is the same Cloud that guides and leads them through the wilderness. Derivatively, the various timeframes noted take for granted the wondrous reality of YHWH's continuing presence with Israel in the wilderness – neither leaving nor forsaking, but abiding and guiding, an aspect made explicit in other passages (e.g. Exod. 13:20–21; Neh. 9:19).

The summary statement in verse 23 contains a threefold repetition of 'al-pî yhwh, along with Israel's obedient response, concluding the passage with emphasis on the nature of Israel's journey through the wilderness: YHWH is the guiding Shepherd, through his Cloud, and the Israelites are his sheep, obediently following his lead. A new element is added with the closing words 'by the hand of Moses' (bĕyad-mōšeh), underscoring Moses' mediatorial role, as well as his mission: Moses is in the wilderness to facilitate Israel's faithful following of YHWH. Elsewhere in Numbers, 'al-pî yhwh and bĕyad-mōšeh are linked specifically with YHWH's delivering verbal commands to Israel through Moses (see Num. 4:37, 45, 49; 10:13; 15:23; 17:5; 27:23; 36:13), a feature that links Israel's following the Cloud with Torah observance (cf. Hauge 2001: 210–211) – and vice versa, to obey Torah is to follow YHWH closely. Numbers 10:13 in particular portrays Israel's setting out by YHWH's command through the hand of Moses. The passage bookended by 9:23 and 10:11–13 gives one example of how YHWH commanded through Moses, by the use of two silver trumpets (10:1–10).

The elevated prose, along with use of yiqtol verbs (customary imperfects), mark this passage as proleptic and ideal (akin to Hos. 2:16–17), a figure for YHWH's marriage-like relationship with Israel. The actual setting out is recounted in 10:11–36, and while the subsequent narratives are less than ideal, nevertheless the precise dynamic described in 9:15–23, with YHWH and his people *together*, is maintained with few exceptions (cf. 14:39–45) throughout the wilderness sojourn between Sinai and Canaan. However much the people grumbled and rebelled along the way, the Camp did remain wed to the Cloud's guidance.

THE CLOUD OF YHWH

The significance of the Cloud cannot be overly stressed. In Israel's literature, the Cloud is the major expression of theophany, the visible manifestation of the presence of YHWH (see Luzarraga 1973: 37–38). Of the seven terms for 'cloud' in the HB, five are used to describe theophanies: *'ānān, 'āb, 'ărāpel, šaḥaq, nāśî'*, with *'ānān* being the most common, especially within the Torah; over half of the nearly eighty occurrences of *'ānān* in the HB are theophanic references (P. A. Smith 1994: 18–19, 26; also Sabourin 1974: 294–295). The theophanic Cloud is marked with a definite article, signalling identity (see Waltke and O'Connor 1990: 236) – it is *the* Cloud (*he'ānān*), linking the Cloud that covered the Dwelling (Exod. 40:34; Num. 9:15–16) with the Cloud that guided Israel through the wilderness (Exod. 40:36; 9:17–23), and, before the Dwelling, linking the pillar of Cloud and fire that led Israel out of Egypt (Exod. 13:22; 14:19–20) with the Cloud that descended upon Mount Sinai (Exod. 19:9; 24:15–18). The images of fire and cloud overlap with and eventually give way to the cult's smoke and fire as symbols for the divine presence (cf. Windsor 1972; C. Walsh 2013: 120–122). In Leviticus, the high priest is warned about entrance into the holy of holies precisely because YHWH would appear 'in the Cloud' (*be'ānān*) above the atonement lid (16:2, 13).

The Cloud, however, conceals no less than it reveals: while YHWH's presence is apparent, the Cloud veils his ineffable glory from the gaze of onlookers (cf. Kelly 1970: 488). Within the veil of the Cloud, his fiery glory resides, visible through the Cloud in the darkness of night. The Cloud thus formed a fitting theophany of the living God amid his people, balancing both immanence and transcendence: comforting Israel by the manifestation of his Presence to shield and guide them, yet also warning Israel of the consuming fires of his dreadful holiness, veiling his glory. Since no one can see God's face and live (Exod. 33:20), the Cloud serves as a 'mask' (Mendenhall 1973: 59) or 'envelope' (Morgenstern 1911: 141–153), and as a 'protecting canopy' over Israel's Camp (Sabourin 1974: 301). Strikingly, in Exodus 19:9, YHWH tells Moses, 'I am coming to you in the cloud (*'āb*) of the Cloud (*he'ānān*)', and then we read, in Exodus 34:15, 'YHWH came down in the Cloud and stood there with him (Moses)' (also Exod. 24:15).

It is possible, moreover, that the original audience understood the inner reality within the Cloud as comprised of more than YHWH alone, but also including his entourage and divine council: YHWH enthroned in glory in the midst of myriads of his heavenly beings (on this, see Kline 1999: 17–18). In Ezekiel's vision, the majestic throne of YHWH, borne upon a chariot of four living creatures, four-faced cherubim (1:5–28), is portrayed as journeying within the 'great Cloud' (*'ānān gādôl*) (1:4, 28; also 10:4). In Deuteronomy 33:2 YHWH's theophany at Sinai, the fiery

Cloud of Exodus (see 19:9–20; 24:15–18), is described as his coming with 'ten thousands of holy ones'. As Maier deduces, 'Thus, God did not descend on Sinai by himself. He came in a cloud with thousands upon thousands of holy angels ' (2015: 92). As part of his majesty, YHWH is always surrounded by his angelic hosts. Whether in Isaiah's vision (Isa. 6) or in Micaiah's, depictions of YHWH's throne include 'all the host (ṣĕbā') of the heavens' gathered by him (1 Kgs 22:19–23) – and the vision of God in Exodus 24 was indeed a throne vision (v. 10). Psalm 68:17 affirms such an understanding of YHWH's Advent on Sinai: 'The chariots of God are twenty thousand, thousands of thousands. The Lord is among them, as at Sinai, in holiness' (cf. Callan 1980: 551).

Though using different terms for 'cloud(s)', YHWH is often described as the One who rides the clouds (likely a polemic against Baal; see Deut. 33:26; Pss 68:33–34; 104:3; Isa. 19:1), and his divine council is portrayed as located 'in the Clouds' (baššaḥaq) (set in parallel with 'among the sons of God', in Ps. 89:6; on this latter point, see Heiser 2012). Riding the clouds appears to be related to YHWH's riding of the cherubim; 2 Samuel 22:11–12 (see Ps. 18:10–11) reads:

He rode upon a cherub and flew; he was seen on the wings of the wind. /
He made darkness around him like a canopy – dark waters, thick clouds of the skies.

When YHWH, riding on a cherub, descends out of heaven to deliver David, he is shrouded with dark clouds, thus connecting cherubim with the clouds in YHWH's transport. Craigie glosses this passage as a description of YHWH as cloud rider, stating that 'cherub' is 'poetically synonymous with cloud' (1983: 174). Indeed, 'he makes the clouds ('ābîm) his chariot' (Ps. 104:3). Just as the outer skin coverings of the Dwelling (Exod. 26:14) covered from view the designs of cherubim woven upon each of the ten curtains (Exod. 26:1) and on the veil (Exod. 26:31), God's Dwelling adorned throughout with cherubim, so the Cloud covered from view the living cherubim with which he travelled.

The Cloud, therefore, (1) manifested YHWH's Presence, even while it (2) veiled and guarded his glory, and (3) served YHWH's mobility, clouds being his means of transport (cf. P. A. Smith 1994: 18–57), either to deliver or lead his people. These roles come together in the Cloud's function (4) as a canopy over the people of God, arguably the idea portrayed in Numbers 9:15–23. In Numbers 14:14, Moses states to YHWH that 'your Cloud stands over them ('ălêhem) and you go before them'. The description of the Cloud upon/above Israel appears to describe a canopy function, when encamped and on journey, with the ark going before the people (see Num. 10:33). The term 'stands' ('ōmēd) here likely has the sense not only of position, but of endurance – the

Cloud did not leave its protective care of Israel. This accords with the portrayal in Nehemiah 9:19, which includes the canopy function of the Cloud while Israel journeyed, describing its role in the sojourn as the Cloud's not 'forsaking' or 'turning aside' (*sār*) 'from being upon them' (*mēʿălêhem*). The summary description of Numbers 10:34 confirms this understanding: 'the Cloud of YHWH was over/upon them (*ʿălêhem*) by day, when they journeyed from the camp'. Bachya preserves a tradition of seven clouds (*Bamidbar* 2.2): four clouds positioned in the four cardinal directions around the Camp, one cloud to march a distance of three days ahead, the *Shekhinah*'s Cloud above the whole Camp, including the Dwelling, and one cloud that served as a buffer between the *Shekhinah* and the people and which would also protect the people from harsh climates, such as the heat of the day. Such a tradition likely emerged from an endeavour to account for the various facets of the one Cloud portrayed in Scripture. When encamped, a possible scenario would be that the pillar of cloud formed a funnel over the Tent of Meeting, rising upwards to form a canopy of 'the Cloud' over the entire encampment of Israel (similarly, Fowler 1978: 99). Within the context of guidance, the Cloud as canopy fits the people's needs in the wilderness, for shelter from the scorching heat by day, and for light and warmth amid the cold darkness by night: 'He spread (*pāraś*) a cloud for a covering (*māsāk*), and fire for light in the night' (Ps. 105:39). This portrait, moreover, fits the theological import of the Camp as the first historical expression of the covenant community, and, as such, the paradigm for the city of God, Jerusalem. Isaiah's vision of the eschatological Jerusalem alludes precisely to this feature of the wilderness Camp (4:5–6; cf. H. Wolf 1980; Ridderbos 1985: 65–67; Maier 2015: 89):

> YHWH will create over the whole place of Mount Zion and upon her assemblies a cloud and smoke by day, and the shining of flaming fire by night; for over all the glory there will be a canopy. And there will be a booth for shade by day from the heat, and for a refuge and for a shelter from the storm and from the rain.

Akin to Isaiah's conception, Zechariah speaks of YHWH being a 'wall of fire around (*sābîb*)' Jerusalem and 'the glory (*kābôd*) in her midst' (2:5), again connoting YHWH's glorious and protective presence, sheltering his people.

10:1–2. After the speech formula (YHWH to Moses), introducing a new section, twofold instructions for making silver trumpets (*ḥăṣōṣěrōt*) are followed by their twofold purpose. First, what is to be made and how: two silver trumpets, and of a hammered work. Like the golden lampstand (8:4), the silver trumpets are divinely commissioned and a 'hammered (*miqšāh*) work', that is, hammered out of a single piece of precious metal. Second, by use of the lamed of purpose, the general twofold function of the trumpets is given as 'for calling' (*lĕmiqrā'*) the community and 'for (the camp's) journeying out' (*lĕmassaʻ*). Verses 3–4 will expand on the first function, of calling God's people together, and verses 5–6 will expand on the second function, of coordinating Israel's departure; verse 7 returns to the first scenario, of calling Israel together, forming an inclusion. Based on the root *ḥṣr*, from which, for example, *ḥāṣēr* (courtyard around a main centre) derives, Hirsch suggested the trumpet blast 'forms a court' around the one who blows it, summoning others to come (2007a: 184). His comment brings out an element of the Camp already observed in previous chapters, the centrifugal and centripetal movements associated with YHWH's central Dwelling. As sounded by the priests at the Camp's centre, the two functions of the trumpets are either to gather God's people toward the centre or to direct their journeying out.

Two previous uses of *lamed* in the same verse, link the trumpets as tools for Moses – 'for you' (*lĕkā*). The silver trumpets, blasted by the priests (cf. 10:8), are a means by which YHWH will guide the camps of Israel through the wilderness 'by the hand of Moses', a phrase which closes the previous section while introducing the present one (9:23). The silver trumpets depicted on the Arch of Titus, as part of the spoils from the destruction of Jerusalem's Temple, somewhat longer than their description by Josephus (*Ant.* 3.12.6), are straight and slender clarions with widened mouths. Possibly, as the Dwelling corresponds to Mount Sinai, the former as an architectural embodiment of the mountain of God, so the trumpets correspond to the shofar sounded at Sinai (see *yōbēl* in Exod. 19:13; *šôpār* in 19:16, 19; 20:18) – that is, the Dwelling and trumpets are manufactured versions of mountain and ram's horn. Whereas the blast of the ram's horn was used for meeting with YHWH at Sinai, the blasts of silver trumpets assemble Israel at the Dwelling (cf. Condren 2005: 196). In Psalm 81:3 and Joel 2:15–16, however, it is a *šôpār* that calls an assembly – perhaps, in Joel at least, this is because it is not the priests who are envisioned as calling the congregation (cf. 2:17). Given the uses for the trumpets in verses 9–10, it may be that, generally, the *šôpār* represents God's call to his people, while the *ḥăṣôṣĕrōt* represent the people's call to God (Hirsch 2007a: 194).

There is no conflict between the guidance of the Cloud (9:15–23) and use of the trumpets (contra E. W. Davies 1995b: 86). Israel follows YHWH's lead through Moses: when the Cloud ascends, it is Moses who causes the trumpets to be blown by the priests. The ascent of the Cloud, signalling the *time* for the camps' departure, does not provide coordination for an orderly departure – the function served by the trumpets. Thus, when the Cloud was seen to ascend, there would likely follow a long period of preparation, dismantling and packing up, as the various camps awaited the trumpet blasts. Given the remark in 10:33, it is possible that a period of three days typically intervened between the

Cloud's ascent and the journeying out of the camps. A fourfold use of the root *ns'* (*nāsa'* and *massa'* 10:2, 5, 6 [twice]) links this passage with 10:11–36, where it occurs sixteen times, and with 9:15–23, where the root occurs nine times.

3–7. There is no consensus on the precise meaning of the terms *tĕqî'āh* and *tĕrû'ah*, with Milgrom following the rabbis who say that *teqî'āh* is a longer blast of the trumpet, equivalent to three *tĕrû'ah* sounds (1990: 73–74), while others, because the verb *tāqa'* has the primary meaning of 'stab' and *tĕrû'ah* means 'shout' elsewhere (Josh. 6:5, 10, 16, 20), suggest an opposite understanding, with *teqî'āh* representing the shorter blast (cf. Alter 2004: 729). Snaith has *tĕrû'ah* as a rapid three-note succession (1967: 221), and Fox translates the term as a 'trilling blast' in contrast to the *tĕqî'āh*'s short blast (1995: 704). What may be said with certainty is that the verb *tāqa'* is the general term for sounding the trumpet and *tĕrû'ah* is the exceptional blast, as illustrated by their use in verse 5; thus, *teqî'āh* is likely a regular blast, and *tĕrû'ah* is exceptional either as longer or shorter/staccato. I have followed Fox's translation, as it conveys the exceptional nature of *tĕrû'ah*, and fits with both the staccato and lengthened conceptions of the term. The *tāqa'* is used for assembly (vv. 3–4), while *tĕrû'ah* for setting out (vv. 5–6); in Leviticus 23:24 and Numbers 29:1, however, *tĕrû'ah* is used for holy convocations. The prophets use *tāqa'*, typically with *šôpār*, to signal theophanies and divine judgement (Isa. 18:3; 27:13; Jer. 4:5; 6:1; 51:27; Hos. 5:8; Amos 3:6; Zech. 9:14) (Zobel 2006).

The two uses of the trumpets are: for convoking an assembly of Israel or its princes and for directing the camps to 'journey out . . . on their journeys' (*wayyis'û . . . lĕmas'êhem*). As related to the previous section, the primary purpose is for following YHWH's Cloud and of convening around his Dwelling. As with Israel's following of the Cloud (9:15–23), encamping upon its descent and journeying out upon its ascent, the two functions of the silver trumpets, gathering Israel together and coordinating Israel's setting out, match the two aspects of the Camp emphasized in Numbers 2: the order of encampment and the order of journey. Manifestly, Numbers 1 – 2 anticipates chapters 9–10, as the two main characteristics of the Camp are accounted for through the Cloud's movements and the sounding of the silver trumpets. Further, there are seven scenarios delineated for the trumpets (vv. 3, 4, 5, 6, 7, 9, 10), similar to the seven scenarios in which Israel is portrayed as following the Cloud (Condren 2005: 206–207). Trumpet blasts are not mentioned for the third and fourth camps. Given the order of march provided in 10:14–21, with the sons Gershon and Merari carting the Dwelling (curtains and frames) in between Judah and Reuben's standards, and with the sons of Kohath carrying the sacred furnishings between Reuben and Ephraim's standards, the real need for coordinated direction relates to the first and second camps alone (cf. Hirsch 2007a: 187).

Verses 3 and 7 form an inclusion, but it is difficult to know whether differences in terminology are merely synonymous parallelism or nuanced distinctions (source critical attempts, e.g. B. Luther 1938, remain unconvincing). In verse 3 there is a threefold use of the root *yʿd*: at the sounding of the trumpets, the 'community' (*ʿēdāh*) will 'come to meet' (*nôʿădû*) with you at the door of the Tent of 'Meeting' (*môʿēd*), whereas in verse 7, it is the 'assembly' (*qāhāl*) that is to 'assemble' (*běhaqhîl*) (cf. Num. 20:10). While the terms 'community' and 'assembly' appear to be synonymous elsewhere in the HB, the poetically consistent usage with other terms in each verse, especially regarding the Tent of Meeting in verse 3, may suggest a nuance here between cultic (*ʿēdāh*) and civic/political (*qāhāl*) gatherings, but this remains conjecture (cf. 16:3). *Qāhāl*, 'assembly' or 'congregation', derives from the notion of the community's being 'called together', 'convoked' or 'gathered'; while used in passages before Sinai, *qāhāl* nevertheless defines Israel particularly with reference to the people's gathering to YHWH at Mount Sinai, entering into covenant with him on the great 'day of assembly' (Deut. 9:10; 10:4; 18:6; *ʿēdāh* is not used in Deut.). Possibly, *ʿēdāh* points to the character of the sons of Israel, perhaps in Numbers with special reference to the Camp, while *qāhāl* remains a more general term (cf. Preuss 1995: 1:54–55).

8. After commanding the manufacture of the trumpets and specifying their functions, YHWH now declares that it is the prerogative of the priesthood to blow them. As set aside for use by the priesthood, the trumpets are thereby categorized as holy, undergirding also the authoritative nature of their blasts. While a shofar may be blown fitly by anyone, only Aaronic priests may blow the trumpets (see Milgrom 1990: 372–373). The whole nation of Israel, called and directed through blasts by Aaron's house, is thereby characterized as a cultic community (cf. B. W. Anderson 1986: 464), 'a priestly kingdom and holy nation' (Exod. 19:6). Moreover, while 9:15–23 rendered the ideal of Israel's following the Cloud of YHWH through the wilderness, this section focuses on the practical matters that make such an ideal possible; namely, the response to God by Israel's leadership, and equally the response to Israel's leadership by the rest of the people (cf. Budd 1984: 107). Obedience within the ranks of YHWH's established hierarchy yields the coordination expressed in Israel's following after the Cloud, and thus serves also as an explanation for the scene of Israel's first journey out from Sinai depicted triumphantly in 10:11–28. Thus, the silver trumpets passage (10:1–10) has been inserted between the portrayal of Israel's following the Cloud's movements (9:15–23) and the Cloud's first ascent (10:11), relaying insight into the dynamics of how the Camp was able to set out in an orderly manner.

Use of the trumpets, along with the authorization of priests to blow them, is declared to be 'for' (*lā*) you (pl.), 'for' (*lě*) a 'perpetual statute' (*ḥuqqat ʿôlām*). Although 'statute' already carries the notion of being fixed, '*ôlām* lends the statute a more absolute quality of permanence – it is unchangeable in character, remaining in force 'for' (*lĕ*) 'your generations' (*dōrōtêkem*) (see Wilch 1969: 17–19; Preuss 1999). Such designations not only establish policy but are forward-looking.

9–10. The first scenario for the trumpets' future use once settled in the land is 'when you enter into war', striking for its *not* being established for the sojourn and conquest. While the phrase 'in your land' (*bĕ'arṣĕkem*) is hopeful, in assuming the conquest and settlement, yet it is also realistic, acknowledging that life in the land will not truly be a return to Eden. There will be 'the hostile-foe' (*haṣṣar*) who is being hostile against you' (*haṣṣōrēr*), perhaps a play on 'trumpets' (*ḥăṣōṣĕrōt*). On such occasions, the trumpets will be sounded by the priesthood as a ministry of prayer by the priesthood on behalf of God's people, that you, Israel, may be 'remembered' (*nizkartem*) before YHWH God. Such remembrance by YHWH is tantamount to deliverance – 'salvation' (*yāša'*) – from Israel's enemies (on the role of the priesthood in battle, see Deut. 20:2–4). Although this scenario is given for life after settlement in Canaan, when Israel takes vengeance on the Midianites in Numbers 31 Moses sends Phinehas the priest with the tribes for battle, and 'the vessels of the sanctuary and the trumpets for the trilling blast (*hattĕrû'āh*) were in his hand' (v. 6) – and in Numbers 25, the root for 'the hostile-foe' (*haṣṣar*) is used twice in relation to the Midianites (25:17, 18). 2 Chronicles 13:12–16 is an apt illustration of the use of these trumpets in battle: although ambushed by Jeroboam, surrounded by his troops, Judah was delivered by YHWH as their cry to him was joined by the blowing of the trumpets by priests. Mention of 'your enemies' (*'ōyĕbêkem*) connects this verse with the song of the ark (v. 35), where Moses calls upon YHWH to rise, that 'your enemies' (*'ōyĕkêkā*) may be scattered.

Fittingly, the second scenario, 'the day of your gladness' follows Israel's salvation from enemies. The various instances – 'day of your gladness' (*yôm śimḥatkem*), 'your appointed times' (or 'feast days', *mô'ădêkem*), the 'first of your months' (*rā'šê ḥādĕšêkem*) – assume the integration of the cult into Israel's everyday life, as each occasion incorporates the regular offering of whole burnt offerings and sacrifices of peace offerings. It is over such offerings and sacrifices that the trumpets are to be blown, within the context of the sacred occasions delineated (see Num. 28 – 29; also 2 Chr. 29:27–28). As a form of prayer, calling on YHWH to 'remember' (*yizkōr*) his people, the trumpet blasts over the offerings show that the cult was not mere externalism – the sacrifices solicited spiritual engagement. The phrases 'before the presence of YHWH your God' (v. 9) and 'before the presence of your God' (10) portray the trumpet blasts as being heard by God in his heavenly Dwelling – the trumpets are a divine gift for the sake of invocation, uniquely heard by YHWH. 'I am YHWH your God' stands not only as an assertion of sovereignty over Israel, but as an authoritative signature and seal upon the function of the trumpets.

There is a curious note of emphasis on Israel's ownership throughout YHWH's speech: 'make for yourself two trumpets . . . they will be yours' (2), 'in your land . . . your enemies' (9), 'day of your gladness . . . your appointed times . . . the first of your months . . . your whole burnt offerings . . . your sacrifices' (10). Invoking him through the priestly use of trumpets, Israel is to seek YHWH's remembrance – his presence, help, and blessing – whether in times of war and danger or in times of gladness and celebration.

11. Having arrived at Sinai on the fourteenth day of the third month, year one (Exod. 19:1), after the exodus out of Egypt (fourteenth day of the first month, Exod. 12), Israel, after nearly a one year stay, now journeys out from Sinai on the twentieth day of the second month, year two. The Dwelling had been raised and consecrated on the first day of the first month, year two (Exod. 40:1), and, on that same day, the princes of Israel's tribes began bringing their gifts for the dedication of the altar (Num. 7:1–88). Passover had been celebrated on the fourteenth day of the first month, year two, and then it was celebrated again a week before departure by those who had previously been unclean (9:1–14). The arrangement of Israel's tribes around the Dwelling to form the Camp of YHWH's earthly hosts had begun twenty days earlier – on the first day of the second month, year two (Num. 1:1–2) – by means of the census. Thus, after a backward look to the first month of year two (Num. 7:1 – 9:23), transitioning to the second month through the legislation for celebrating Passover in the second month (9:1–14) and through the portrayal of the Cloud, the text now narrates the ascent of the Cloud, signalling the start of the Camp's journey. The chronological notice functions to underscore the gravity of the momentous event. Cole (2000: 171) observes an inclusion for this section (10:11–36), by use of the words: *wayĕhî* (11, 35), *wayyisʿû* (12, 28) and *ʿānān* (11, 34).

12. The Cloud's 'dwelling' (*yiškōn*), or 'settling down', in the wilderness of Paran foreshadows by way of summary Israel's first trek rehearsed in Numbers 11 – 12, the end of which reads that the people 'encamped in the wilderness of Paran' (12:16) – with Taberah (11:3), Kibroth Hattaavah (11:35) noted as stations beforehand. Here one finds a striking and profound, though typical, difference of perspective between the idealized portrait of Israel following YHWH's Cloud in the wilderness (Exod. 40:36–38; Num. 9:15–23) and the uglier realities of complaint and rebellion in the historical narrative (Num. 11 – 25). It is the difference between Numbers 10:11–12, which portrays the Cloud's ascent from Sinai and descent upon Paran, with the sons of Israel journeying out to follow, and Numbers 11 – 12, which entails two accounts of murmuring, Moses' leadership crisis, and the dissension against Moses by Miriam, his sister, and Aaron, his brother and high priest of Israel – all taking place between the Cloud's ascent from the wilderness of Sinai and arrival at the wilderness of Paran previously described. Positing a contradiction among sources cannot resolve the matter, and evades the sort of theological reflection solicited by the text. The ideal portrait concerns following YHWH's leadership via the Cloud, and, indeed, the historical narrative testifies to the arrival of the sons of Israel at the wilderness of Paran (12:16) – both agree on this fundamental point. The historical narratives make it clear that Israel's arrival in the wilderness of Paran (and, eventually, into Canaan itself) was due solely to the longsuffering mercy and loving-kindness of the Good Shepherd.

As no cartography from this period remains, identifying various sites of the wilderness route with precision is difficult. Based on the biblical material, the wilderness of Paran appears to be a broadly conceived area. The scouts also set out from and return to 'the wilderness of Paran' (13:3, 26), the latter reference identifying it with Kadesh Barnea. It may be the wilderness of Paran was originally a name for the Sinai peninsula, its southernmost reaches beginning somewhere north of the traditional site of Mount Sinai, Jebel Musa, with the lower part of the peninsula regarded as the wilderness of Sinai (Aharoni 1979: 181–183; cf. Briscoe 1995; Cole 2009: 354).

13. A clue to the theology of Israel's wilderness sojourn is given here by way of reiteration: Israel's journeys, from the first, were by YHWH's command, according to his mouth (*'al-pî yhwh*), and under the authority of Moses, by his hand (*bĕyad-mōšeh*). The 'mouth of YHWH' has already been linked to the instructions for the creation of the Camp (3:16, 39, 51; 4:37, 41, 45, 49) as well as to its guidance by the Cloud (9:18, 20, 23); the same is true for the instrumentality of Moses in creating the Camp (4:37, 45, 49) and in the Cloud's leading of Israel (9:23). The particular reference here, within the context of journeying out, may be in relation to Moses' direction of the priests for sounding the trumpets (10:5–6; Ashley 1993: 193), but the emphasis is on YHWH's shepherding his people in the wilderness *through Moses*: 'You (YHWH) led your people like a flock by the hand of Moses and Aaron' (Ps. 77:20).

14–27. The setting out of the four main camps, under the standards of Judah, Reuben, Ephraim and Dan, along with the Levites in their midst, is described in language recalling Numbers 1 – 4 (on *degel*, 'standard', see comments at 2:2). The order of march (vv. 17, 21) need not be read as disagreeing with the order envisioned in 2:17 but 'as an elaboration of it, in the light of the picture as it has developed in Num. 3–4'; appropriate enough since Numbers 2 concerned the constitution of the Camp primarily, whereas this section is focused on detailing the journey (Budd 1984: 110). The Kohathites, who carry the sacred furnishings – the heart of the cultic service – maintain the arrangement set out earlier, after Reuben's standard, and all Levites nevertheless travel 'in the midst' (*bĕtôk hammaḥănōt*) of the other camps (2:17). The chieftains over each tribe are the same as had been called by YHWH for the census (1:5–16), and who had brought gifts for dedicating the altar (7:1–88), listed here according to the order established by encampment around the Dwelling. Mention of the leaders of Israel's tribes is of a piece with references to Moses and the priesthood, a reminder that YHWH reigns over his newly formed theocracy through a designated hierarchy. As the conclusion to the book's first major division, Numbers 10 forms an inclusio with Numbers 2.

21. Translated here as 'the holy', elsewhere *hammiqdāš* means 'the sanctuary'. Since, however, the Levitical roles have been stipulated clearly (Num. 4), with the Gershonites and Merarites carting the curtains and frames of the Dwelling, the term refers here to the sacred furnishings carried by the Kohathites, called 'most holy things' (*qōdeš haqqŏdāšîm*) in 4:4: the ark, table, lampstand, golden altar and altar (4:4–15). The rest of the verse makes this clear, as the Gershonites and Merarites 'would raise the Dwelling' in advance of the Kohathites' arrival with the furnishings. The ark, however, is described as leading the march in verses 33–36, so, naturally, not included with the rest of the furnishings in the midst of the camps, at least not so for this initial march.

28. A summary statement, echoing verse 12, concludes the section (10:11–28). As will be evident in the next two sections (vv. 29–32, 33–36), the rest of the chapter continues portraying events related to the departure – 10:11–36 forms one grand multifaceted view of Israel's departure from Sinai, which caps the book's first major section (chs. 1–10). The wilderness journey section does not begin properly until 11:1. Somewhat similarly to the optimistic angle on the journey noted in verse 12, 'these are the journeys' has particular reference to the order of march. The focus remains on the theology of the encampment itself, the text ever pointing to the Camp's orderly design and arrangement, and, here, to its divinely orchestrated movement.

29–32. In the structural pattern of the Torah, Israel's arrival and departure from Sinai are framed by encounters with Midianites (Exod. 18; Num. 10); in Numbers, Midianites frame the wilderness journey (Num. 10:29–32; 25:6–18; 31) (Dozeman 2008; Lawlor 2011). Various texts name Jethro (Exod. 3:1; 4:18; 18:1–2, 5–6, 12), Hobab (Num. 10:29; Judg. 4:11), and Reuel (Exod. 2:16–18) as a relative of Moses by marriage. The designation *ḥōtēn* (typically translated 'father-in-law) is ambiguous, and may refer either to Hobab or to Reuel. While it would be simple to take Reuel as the referent, as Moses' father-in-law, with Hobab then as Moses' brother-in-law, yet in Judges 4:11 it is Hobab who is called the *ḥōtēn* of Moses. Jethro is called Moses' *ḥōtēn* in Exodus 18:1, and Reuel is shown to become Moses' father-in-law, though the term *ḥōtēn* is not used (Exod. 2:16–17). This textual diversity has often been addressed by positing different sources, with Hobab assigned to the J source and Jethro to E (S. R. Driver 1906: 22–23; see Cassuto's critique, 2008: 18–49). Others, such as Albright (1963), have contrived complicated solutions, suggesting that Reuel was a clan name and that *ḥōtēn* should be vocalized as *ḥātān* (son-in-law). Morgenstern (1927: 40) suggested the possibility that *ḥōtēn* may also be translated 'brother-in-law', a suggestion affirmed by T. C. Mitchell's study (1969), which argues for a general understanding of the term as 'a relative by marriage'. Verse 29 sheds light on the matter inasmuch as it clearly distinguishes between Hobab and Reuel, and, given that Jethro had already departed (Exod. 18:27), Hobab appears to be distinct from him as well. The simplest solution is thus to equate Jethro with Reuel as Moses' father-in-law, and Hobab as Jethro's son and Moses' brother-in-law, a notion that accords with Albright's observation that Jethro is portrayed as older than Moses, able to offer him wise counsel, and Hobab is portrayed as younger and able to manoeuvre through the wilderness (1963: 7). Therefore, if *ḥōtēn* is deemed to refer to Reuel in 10:29 it should be translated 'father-in-law', but if to Hobab then as 'brother-in-law'.

There is further ambiguity as to Moses' motives for inviting Hobab to join Israel on the sojourn. Some see in Moses' plea for Hobab to be Israel's eyes (v. 31), a lack of faith in the guidance of YHWH, especially amid the text's own emphasis on YHWH's role through the Cloud (9:15–23) and ark (10:33–36) (Salomon 1972; J. S. Ackerman 1987: 80; Condren 2005: 215–218). Kelly, however, saw Hobab as God's answer to Moses' request for an experienced guide in Exodus 33:12 (1970: 487). As already noted with reference to the function of the trumpets (10:1–10) and the 'hand of Moses' (10:13), YHWH's guidance, even by the supernatural Cloud, did not preclude practical human means. Given the mention of Hobab's descendants as living in Israel in Judges 4:11 (cf. Judg. 1:16; 1 Sam. 15:6; 30:29), many commentators assume – likely, rightly – that Hobab was indeed persuaded by Moses to join Israel's sojourn. The omission of Hobab's final response perhaps underscores YHWH's own guidance and de-emphasizes Hobab's role (Mann 1977: 169; Milgrom 1990: 78), but also functions as an open-ended invitation for the audience to join the wilderness sojourn. Moses' second plea to Hobab, in any case, was not the hidden motive for his original request. Rather, Moses' second plea is enveloped by his double emphasis on the prospect of Hobab's enjoying the benefits of Israel's covenant privileges:

29: we are journeying out to the place of which YHWH said I will give it to you; go (*lĕkāh*) with us and we will be good (*hēṭabnû*) to you – for YHWH has spoken good (*ṭôb*) over Israel.

32: And it will be that when you go (*tēlēk*) with us, from that good (*haṭṭôb*) which YHWH will be good (*yêṭîb*) to us, we will be good (*hēṭabnû*) to you.

Here it is seen clearly that Moses' second plea is rounded out by his original encouragement, and that the emphasis is on YHWH's goodness, forms of *ṭôb* occurring five times: twice in verse 29, but three times in his follow-up invitation in verse 32. As Milgrom points out, *dibber* (has spoken) in verse 29 is readily translated 'promised' (1990: 79; cf. Deut. 11:1, 21). When the emphasis on Hobab's good is taken at face value, perhaps addressing a fear on any foreigner's part that if he went along he may experience bad in the company of another people, then the second motivation – relating Hobab's usefulness to Israel – would appear as a gracious assurance to his brother-in-law. Indeed, such a fear is not unfounded given Israel's ensuing negative relations with Midianites (25:6–15; 31:2).

Moses' words (vv. 29, 32) hearken back to the promises God had made to Abraham, in line with the overall function of this vignette as something of a rehearsal of the call of Abraham. His actual plea is merely four words that read lyrically (v. 29; Grossman 2014d: 113):

> *lĕkāh* (go)
> *'ittānû* (with us)
> *wĕhēṭabnû* (and we will be good)
> *lāk* (to you)

God's call to Abraham had been to 'go-get yourself out *(lek-lĕkā)* from your land *(mē'arṣĕkā)* and from your kindred *(immôladtĕkā)*' (Gen. 12:1), echoed in Moses' call to 'go' *(lĕkāh)* and Hobab's response that he would not 'go' *('ēlēk)* except to 'to my land *('arṣî)* and to my kindred *(môladtî)*' (v. 30). In a similar situation, the foreigner Ruth, related to Naomi by marriage, declares that she will accompany her mother-in-law to Canaan, that she will 'go' *('ēlēk)* and not 'abandon' *('ozbēk)* her, claiming Naomi's people, land, and God (Ruth 1:16–17). Ruth thereby revealed she was a true daughter of Abraham, willing to leave kith and kindred and go to a place she had not seen before. Moses asks Hobab not to 'abandon' *(ta'ăzōb)* us, but rather to go with God's people and enjoy the blessings of their favour with YHWH (vv. 31–32). In rehearsing the call of Abraham, Israel's journeying out from Sinai to Canaan is brought full circle to the patriarchal promises, so that the wilderness trek is set within the context of Abraham's journey to the promised land – and of God's faithfulness to his promise. Throughout their journeys, Israel will need to demonstrate Abraham's own trust in God. Whereas Abraham did not look back to the city he had left behind (Heb. 11:8–10, 14–16), Israel will desire a return to the land of their oppression, Egypt (Num. 14:1–4). Like Lot's wife, Israel was ever looking back to what had been left behind (11:5; cf. Gen. 19:26; Luke 17:32); and like Lot's wife, the first generation of Israel would perish en route, in the wilderness with their backs turned away from Canaan. The beginning of verse 33 would otherwise naturally be understood as Hobab's acceptance of Moses' invitation: 'And they journeyed out . . .' While context shows that 'they' refers to all Israel, yet there is no reason to exclude Hobab – only his registering a refusal after Moses' second invitation would justify doing so (cf. Achenbach 2003b: 186–187 n. 23). Again, the biblical tradition presumes Hobab did accompany Israel on the sojourn (Judg. 4:11).

Ambiguity continues regarding the intent of verse 31: 'you know how-we-encamp (*ḥănōtēnû*) in the wilderness'. ESV, for example, reads: 'you know where we should camp in the wilderness', understanding Moses' words as an appeal for guidance, again leading to speculation concerning his lack of faith in YHWH. The adverb 'where', however, is not found in the Hebrew, and 'how' is preferable for capturing the infinitive construct of 'camp' (cf. AV, ASV, NKJV). Young's Literal Translation has 'thou hast known our encamping in the wilderness', which easily reads as an allusion to the theological vision of Numbers 1 – 6. The next line of Moses is equally ambiguous: 'and you are our eyes'. Given the difficulties of understanding the dialogue between Moses and Hobab historically, it could be a double entendre is intended – his pragmatic understanding of Israel's encamping in the wilderness perhaps foreshadows Balaam's vision of the Camp in Numbers 24.

The jubilant tone with which verse 32 precedes Israel's departure is a reminder that the journey from Sinai to Canaan entailed only some eleven days for a typical caravan (cf. Deut. 1:2) – even if, given Israel's multitudes, this period is doubled or tripled, the journey was relatively brief. The careful reader of the Pentateuch, however, would have picked up on the single hint thus far that the reality of the sojourn would be otherwise: 'And the sons of Israel ate the manna forty years until they came to a habitable land; they ate the manna until they came to the border of the land of Canaan' (Exod. 16:35).

33. 'And they journeyed out from the mountain of YHWH' is a striking phrase, marking the monumental departure from Mount Sinai, and blocking the material from Exodus 19 through Numbers 10 as 'Sinai revelation', the central section of the Torah forming the foundation of Israel's covenant relationship with YHWH (even the substance of Deuteronomy derives from this Sinai period, cf. Deut. 5:23–31). As mentioned above, *wayyisʿû* (and they journeyed) connects this summary statement with that of verse 12, the whole section serving as a grand, celebratory portrayal of Israel's departure which belongs, thematically, as the cap for the Sinai revelation, rather than as part of the wilderness sojourn (Num. 11 – 25). The typical designation for Sinai is 'mountain of God' (Exod. 3:1; 4:27; 18:5; 24:13). Although leaving the 'mountain of YHWH', Israel journeys to another holy mountain that will become YHWH's permanent abode (Exod. 15:17; Deut. 12:1–12; 2 Sam. 7; 1 Kgs 8; Pss 48; 132:13–14) – Zion will both succeed and surpass the glories of Sinai (Ps. 68:16–18), and be known as the 'mountain of

YHWH' (Isa. 2:3; 30:29; Mic. 4:2; Ps. 24:3). The 'Ark of the Covenant of YHWH' (along with 'Cloud of YHWH', v. 34) is linked to the 'mountain of YHWH', perhaps conveying the notion that whereas God had communicated with and reigned over his people from Sinai, now in the wilderness he will do so primarily through the ark – both leading them onward in their journeys and as speaking to them through Moses from above the ark (7:89). Whereas the pillar of cloud had led Israel out of Egypt to Mount Sinai (Exod. 13:21–22; 14:19–20, 24–25; 16:10; 33:7–11), the ark's leadership marks the covenantal progression that has taken place at Mount Sinai, including the role of the newly established cult.

The repeated phrase 'three days' way' has led to some confusion, when the second occurrence is read as if the ark had a three day head start on the Camp – in which case, of course, the Camp could not have seen the ark let alone follow it. The purpose of the repetition, aside from an unlikely textual error (see *BHS*), is to underscore the ark's function throughout the three day journey (as our translation clarifies; see GKC §118i, k; R. J. Williams 2007: 56) – its position as 'before' (*lipnê*) the people is temporal: *during* the three days. This point may suggest that the ark only led the way on the first march out of Sinai, and otherwise travelled with the other holy furnishings in the midst of the Camp (cf. 2:17; 4:1–20; 10:21), but need not be so – the emphasis on the ark's role may also function as exemplary for the rest of the sojourn. Moreover, in the same way Jethro (Exod. 18) and Hobab (Num. 10) form an inclusio around the Sinai revelation, so also does the three day journey – there was originally a three day journey to Mount Sinai (Exod. 15:22) and now away from Sinai (noted by Ibn Ezra, ad loc.), perhaps foreshadowing the people's complaints (Enns 2000: 322). Given that the redemption out of Egypt had been for the sake of a three-day journey to worship YHWH (Exod. 3:18; 5:3; 8:27) and that Israel had met with YHWH at Sinai on 'the third day' (Exod. 19:15), it is possible that the repeated phrase here has worship connotations (Dozeman 1998: 96).

The ark has been understood variously as YHWH's throne or footstool, or both, with the cherubim forming his throne and the ark itself serving as a footstool (Mowinckel 1953: 49). The notion of YHWH's leading the march while enthroned is not incongruous (contra Woudstra 1965: 92–95), as Ezekiel's opening vision demonstrates: YHWH's mobility is expressed as a cherubim-driven throne (Ezek. 1:4–28). The connection between YHWH and his ark is forged in an impressive manner, with the ark itself 'journeying out' to 'search' for a resting place. The phrase 'to search out' uses the same term 'to explore' or 'scout out' (*lātûr*) that will be used later with reference to scouting out the land, used twelve times in the story of the twelve scouts in Numbers 13 – 14 (13:2, 16, 17, 21, 25, 32 [twice]; 14:6, 7, 34, 36, 38; cf. also 15:39). The ark, as Windsor writes (1972: 415), is a symbol for and 'an active extension' of YHWH's presence. Verses 35–36 continue the anthropomorphism, speaking again of the ark's journeying out, with Moses' liturgical recital aligning the ark's movements with those of YHWH. Specifically, the ark is searching for a 'resting place' (*mĕnûḥāh*) for Israel (v. 33; note use of 'rest' (*nuḥōh*) in v. 36). 'Rest' forms a rich biblical theme sprouting forth from creation (Gen. 2:15) and recreation (Gen. 8:4) through redemption (Matt. 11:28), and is connected to God's purposes of Sabbath day fellowship with human beings (Gen. 2:1–3; Exod. 20:11; Deut. 5:14; see Morales 2012: 145–146, 185–189), and is especially associated with the land. In Deuteronomy, the promised land is described as 'the resting place' (*hammĕnûḥāh*) of Israel, often with the idea of having rest from enemies and enjoying fullness of peace, including prosperity and health (12:9; cf. 3:20; 12:10; Josh. 1:13). Within Canaan, YHWH would eventually choose Jerusalem/Mount Zion as 'my resting place (*mĕnûḥātî*) for ever' (Ps. 132:14; see Deut. 12:9–10; 25:19; 2 Chr. 6:41).

34. After the description of the ark's role in leading the march, this verse clarifies the function of the Cloud as being over the Camp, demonstrating God's good care as Israel's Shepherd: he both leads them (via the ark) and shelters them (via the Cloud). Since both the ark and the Cloud function on behalf of YHWH, it may be said of either that it leads Israel. The Cloud is a supernatural phenomenon that is temporary, while the ark is a cultic object with a sacramental bond to YHWH's presence. 'The Cloud of YHWH' occurs only here and in Exodus 40:38, forming an inclusion (cf. 9:15–23).

35–36. The MT brackets these verses by inverted nuns (Hebrew letters), generally thought to indicate the verses are misplaced (cf. Roberts 1951: 34; Würthwein 1979: 17; Tov 2001: 54–55; Ska 2016: 574–577; see also their sevenfold occurrence in Ps. 107:20, 21, 22, 23, 24, 25, 39). The Greek version places these verses between verses 33 and 34, an attractive placement since verse 34 forms a summary inclusio with Exodus 40:38 – this the simplest solution (cf. also Ginsburg 1966: 343). Such a change is unnecessary, however, since verses 35–36 form a fitting climax and conclusion. Some disjunctive function seems plausible, with Jewish tradition suggesting that the marks (also called 'dots') divide Numbers into three separate 'books' (Num. 1–10:34; 10:35–36; 11 – 26) or that they serve to separate YHWH's glory from Israel's sinfulness (11:1; *Sif.* 84; *b. Shab.* 115a–116a; on textual-critical concerns, see Leiman 1974; Levine 1976a). At the least, the *nuns* serve to call attention to this section, fittingly so as the conclusion to the Sinai revelation (Exod. 19 – Num. 10) and as the climactic culmination of the creation and setting out of the Camp of YHWH's earthly hosts in particular (Num. 1 – 10).

Lack of a preposition in the Hebrew of verse 36 leads to a syntactical difficulty, overcome in translations by adding 'to' or 'unto' (see textual note). Jewish commentators have interpreted *šûbāh* (return) variously (e.g. with a transitive sense) with reference to YHWH's return of the Israelites (see *Da'at Zekenim*; Ibn Ezra), with due application to the restoration of Israel from exile, inclusive of the nations (see Zech. 2:15). On this reading, there is a parallelism set up: when YHWH arises, his enemies are scattered (35), when he rests, his people are gathered (36). The dissimilarity of the two verses, however, is also strong on this scheme: whereas it is YHWH who arises in verse 35, it would be Israel that is being returned in verse 36, although this return is accomplished by him. Another plausible possibility, following NRSV, is to understand YHWH in construct: 'Return, O YHWH of the myriad thousands of Israel!' In the end, each of these expressions is true: YHWH, as going before Israel, returns to his people, and when he does so, the thousands of Israel gather about him, forming the Camp around his Dwelling; while God's enemies are (and will be) scattered from his face, his people find rest in his presence; by covenant YHWH indeed belongs with and to his people. In Psalm 80 'return' is used with reference to restoring Israel and to restoring God's favour – both accomplished by YHWH God (see vv. 3, 7, 14, 19). For a sobering reflection on the role of the ark in battle, see the negative scenario noted in Numbers 14:44 – here, too, as in verses 35–36, the ark and Moses occur together. Use of the term *'alpê* in 10:36 (the myriad thousands of Israel), triumphantly paralleling the book's opening census whereby the people were counted by their thousands (1:16), yields an inclusio, encapsulating Numbers 1 – 10 (cf. Ingalls 1991: 92). When encamped, the ark guides Israel by way of YHWH's voice to Moses (7:89); when on journey, the ark guides by leading the march (10:33–36).

These verses function in much the same way as the priestly blessing does, capping a major section with a view to God's presence and blessing: Num. 1 – 6 (6:22–27); Num. 7 – 10 (10:35–36) (similarly Ashley 1993: 198). Reflexes of these ancient and majestic lyrics are found in the psalms (see 68:1; 132:8). The passage therefore, including both the function of the ark and the poetic declaration by Moses addressed directly to YHWH, sets the whole departure within a liturgical context, as a cultic procession (similarly, Budd 1984: 116; Olson 1996: 58); the same will be true of the entry and conquest (cf. Josh. 6:6). Led by the ark, the cherubim-throne of YHWH, the 'myriad thousands of Israel' are indeed cast as YHWH's earthly hosts, the presence of the ark signifying 'that Yahweh himself on his throne headed his "hosts"' (Mowinckel 2004: 21). Likewise, D. N. Freedman writes (1975: 41), 'This passage is to be compared with Ps. 68:18 and Deut. 33:2, and seems to combine the heavenly hosts of Yahweh (*rbbwt*) with the earthly armies of Israel.' With the ark's movements forming a microcosm of the Camp that follows, at last Israel, the Chariot of God, sets out from Mount Sinai! (See Fig. 8.)

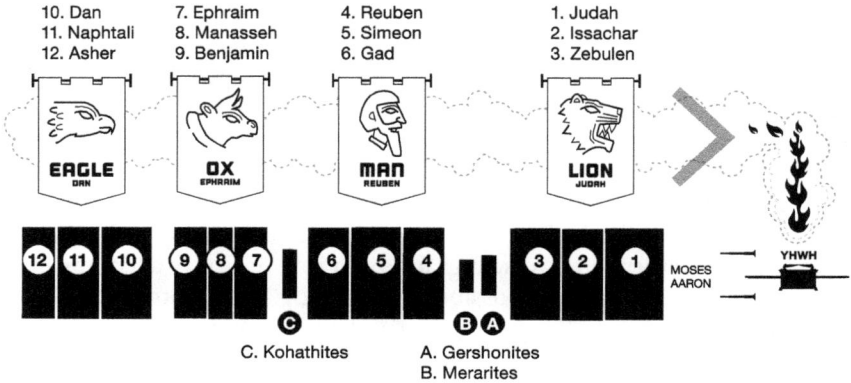

Figure 8: Israel's march from Sinai

Explanation

After celebrating Passover, the feast of departure, every subunit that follows is integrated and unified by the root for the verb for 'journey', *nāsa'*, occurring some twenty-nine times as a verb or noun in chapters 9–10, beginning with 9:17 (Grossman 2014d: 110–111):

1. The Cloud's leading: 'by the mouth of YHWH, the sons of Israel would journey (*yis'û*)' (9:18).
2. The trumpets: 'for the journeying (*lĕmssa'*) of the camps' (10:2).
3. Order of journey: 'sons of Israel journeyed out (*yis'û*) on their journeys (*lĕmas'êhem*)' (10:12).
4. Moses' invitation to Hobab: 'we are journeying (*nōsĕ'îm*) to the place' (10:29).
5. Historic departure: 'they journeyed (*yis'û*) from the mountain of YHWH' (10:33).
6. The song of the Ark: 'when the ark journeyed (*binsōa'*)' (10:35).

As with the installation of Levites (Num. 8), underlining both their cleansing and the redemption out of Egypt, so also with Numbers 9:1–14: the delayed Passover underscores both purity concerns and the redemption out of Egypt. Since some Israelites were barred from observing the feast of Passover due to corpse pollution, YHWH provides an addendum to the previous legislation, allowing for a secondary time (the fourteenth day of the second month) of Passover observation. Such a concession is a *novum* without parallel in the entire Pentateuch (A. Ehrlich 1899: 1:254), underscoring the defining nature of Passover for all Israel – the exodus is to be remembered, relived, annually by every Israelite. Along with other texts concerning corpse pollution (e.g. 5:1–4;

6:9–12; 8:7; 19:1–22), the Passover account continues the general concern for purity that has arisen since the advent of YHWH, first at Sinai, and then especially with his consecrating presence in the newly constructed Dwelling. Having been delivered from Egypt, the place of death, Israel now abides within the abundant life of God's presence, underscoring once more the nature of the Camp.

Observing Passover as a defining feast for every Israelite is so profoundly significant that YHWH makes an allowance for a second observance after cleansing from corpse pollution. The concession echoes the renewal of a Nazirite's vow, after cleansing from corpse pollution (6:9–12) – and seems to foreshadow Israel's wilderness experience, as the second generation is cleansed from the death defilement of the first (Num. 19). The overriding function of the Passover account, however, is in its contribution to the theme of Israel's departure from Sinai, and that in a manner similar to the exodus out of Egypt. Just as, having kept Passover (Exod. 12), Israelites were led out of Egypt by YHWH's Cloud (Exod. 13:21–22), so now, having kept Passover (Num. 9:1–14), the Israelites are led out from Sinai by YHWH's Cloud (9:15–23). Yet there is a significant difference between both journeys, one that encompasses all that has been created between them through YHWH's Sinai revelation. Not only does the delayed observance of Passover mean that it was celebrated just 6 days before Israel's departure, but the delay also means that Israel *as the Camp* of YHWH's earthly hosts, newly created in the second month as the culmination of the Sinai revelation (cf. 1:1), participated in Passover before setting out after YHWH's Cloud.

Numbers 9:15–23, perhaps deriving from an ancient song, portrays Israel ideally, as following YHWH's Cloud through the wilderness. Whether encamping and setting out, Israel awaits the Cloud's sovereign ascent and descents, movements that cannot be predicted or scheduled. Following the Cloud, writes Rimon (2008), is not simply 'a mechanical act', but expresses a meaningful relationship and 'symbolizes the deeper connection' between the nation of Israel and YHWH's *Shekhinah*. The vantage point of this passage appears to encompass all of Israel's sojourns in the wilderness, connecting with the book's summary as found at the end of Exodus (40:36–38). YHWH's guidance through the Cloud is characterized by a sevenfold use of 'by the mouth of YHWH' ('*al-pî yhwh*, vv. 18, 20, 23) and as the 'charge of YHWH by the hand of Moses' (v. 23), thereby likening Israel's following of the Cloud to *torah* obedience. These verses bring out the book's shepherding theme, summarizing Israel's fundamental obligation in a twofold manner: encamping when YHWH's Cloud descends, and journeying out when the Cloud ascends. Although not always given explanations for YHWH's movements, the role of God's people is to wait on him and to follow him with trusting obedience. Through his Cloud, YHWH both led and sheltered his people throughout their sojourn.

While, as a whole, Numbers 9 offered a thematic summary of Israel's departure and sojourn: celebrating a second Passover and following YHWH's Cloud through the wilderness, chapter 10 supplies details of the departure, the use of trumpets (10:1–10) and a description of Israel's historic setting out (10:11–28). The Cloud's ascent and descent served as signals for Israel to set out and to encamp, respectively, but for coordinating the Camp's movements, YHWH commands the manufacture of silver trumpets. Blown only by the priests of Aaron's house, the trumpets are sacred objects used for calling the nation or its leaders to assembly and for coordinating the setting out of Israel upon the Cloud's ascent. Once settled in the land, the trumpets will be blasted over sacrifices at festive gatherings as well as used in times of battle, both scenarios showing that the trumpet blasts function as a kind of prayer to God, that he would remember his people for good in times of joy and threat.

Having just celebrated a second Passover six days earlier and after nearly a year long stay at Mount Sinai, Israel sets out for Canaan on the twentieth day of the second month, the second year after the deliverance out of Egypt. The section of Numbers 7:1 – 9:14 clearly takes place one month prior to the book's beginning, while 9:15–23 offers a timeless and archetypal portrait of Israel's sojourn in the wilderness. Likely, Numbers 10:1–10 should also be taken as occurring one month prior. The chronological notice in 10:11 serves to bring the reader back into the narrative's current time to observe Israel's historic setting out from Mount Sinai, a triumphant procession led tribe by tribe, beginning with Judah's standard, and Levites with YHWH's Dwelling and furnishings (except for the ark) journeying in the midst of the succession. In keeping with the jubilant spirit of Numbers 1 – 10 as a whole and of Israel's historic setting out in particular, the journey from Sinai to the wilderness of Paran is forecasted summarily in verse 12, without any hint of the complaints and difficulties that will be recounted in chapters 11–12 (see 12:16), the conquest of Canaan already in view.

The same celebratory enthusiasm marks Moses' invitation of Hobab, his brother in law, to join God's people so as to have a share in the good he has promised Israel. His further plea that Hobab serve as guide provides assurance that he will not be ill-treated as a foreigner among Israel. Rather than reflecting any distrust in YHWH's guidance, Moses' words allude to the original call of Abram who was willing to leave his country and kindred for the promised land (Gen. 12:1–3). This echo of the patriarch's life colours Israel's departure in terms of Abram's first journey to Canaan. Indeed, the opening and closing episodes of Numbers 9 – 10, before the final cap (10:33–36), bring Israel's departure within the context of redemptive history, with the Passover legislation calling to mind the exodus out of Egypt (Exod. 11 – 13), and Moses' invitation to Hobab echoing the call of Abram (Gen. 12:1–3).

Table 19: Numbers 9 – 10

9:1–14	Passover	→ Exodus out of Egypt
9:15–23	Israel follows the Cloud	
10:1–10	The Trumpets	
10:11–28	Israel sets out	
10:29–32	Hobab's invitation	→ The call of Abraham
	10:33–36 YHWH's ark leads Israel	

By his emphasis on God's promise of good to Israel, it is clear that the 'crux of this section is Moses' great faith in the success of the journey' (Grossman 2014d: 113), hopes which, tragically, will soon be dashed (11:11–15). Combined with the sure prospect of the scattering of YHWH's enemies (v. 35), having immediate reference to the inhabitants of Canaan, the invitation to Hobab underscores the potential blessing awaiting nations who seek refuge with Israel (cf. Josh. 2:12–13). Even as Israel journeys out to conquer in all the glory of the tribal march, arrayed under their banners, the text emphasizes Israel's primary vocation to bring blessing to the nations – the very culminating *telos* of Abram's call (Gen. 12:3).

The procession of the ark before the train of Israel's tribes, along with Moses' liturgical recitations following the ark's movements, serve as a cap both to Numbers 1 – 10 and to the at-Sinai narrative (Exod. 19 – Num. 10). YHWH leads his earthly hosts through his ark, his cherubim-laden throne and footstool, while his Cloud functions as a sheltering canopy over the Israelites. Marching tribe by tribe, according to their banners bearing the emblems of their fathers' houses, and led by YHWH's ark, Israel's departure from the mountain of YHWH is far different from their arrival in the previous year. As a priestly kingdom and holy nation, Israel has become a mobile city of God and paradise in the wilderness, arranged around his earthly, glory-filled Dwelling. Israel marches out as YHWH's earthly entourage, mirroring the heavenly hosts that surround his throne and accompany his movements as he rides the clouds (cf. Ezek. 1). The lyrics recited by Moses in accord with the ark's movements remind Israel that YHWH himself is with them and will bring them into the land, closing the book's first major division in a majestic manner (chs. 1–10). Cherubim, which had once barred humanity from the garden of YHWH (Gen. 3:24), will now lead Israel into YHWH's good land, to enjoy life before his face. In Deuteronomy 1:33, Moses speaks of YHWH God 'who was going before your face in the way to search out for you a place for your encampments, in the fire by night, to show you the way you should go, and in a cloud by day'. Just as myriads of angelic beings surround YHWH's heavenly throne, Israel's wilderness encampment forms the earthly hosts of YHWH – led by his ark, even while his Cloud overshadows and shelters them.

This first journey out from Mt. Sinai, then, is portrayed theologically and serves as a microcosm of the whole wilderness sojourn and entry into Canaan; that is, the summary statement contains an eschatological symbolism – the goal of the journey is Sabbath fellowship with God in the land of Israel's inheritance, ultimately the New Jerusalem. Every respite along the way, is a foretaste of the final rest, even as every Sabbath is a foretaste of the Sabbath that remains (Heb. 4:9–11). Perhaps as wordplay, YHWH's ark seeks *měnûḥāh* (rest) for the *maḥăneh* (camp).

NUMBERS 11 – 12: THE OUTER CAMP AND THE PROPHETIC WORD

Translation

[11:1]And the people became as complainers of evil in the ears of YHWH, and YHWH heard and his fierce anger kindled and the fire of YHWH burned among them and consumed the outskirts of the camp. [2]And the people cried out to Moses and Moses prayed to YHWH and the fire sank down. [3]And he called the name of that place Taberah (Burning) because the fire of YHWH burned among them.

[4]Now the gathered-rabble that was in their midst craved a craving, and the sons of Israel sat and wept also, and they said, 'Who will cause us to consume flesh? [5]We remember the fish that we used to eat in Egypt for no cost, the cucumbers and the melons and the leeks and the onions and the garlic. [6]But now our soul is dried; there is nothing at all – except the manna! – before our eyes.' ([7]Now the manna was like the seed of coriander and its appearance like the appearance of bdellium. [8]The people would roam about and glean it and grind it in millstones or pound it with a pestle, boil it in a pot, and make it into cakes, and the taste of it was like the taste of creamy oil. [9]And when the dew descended upon the camp at night, the manna would descend upon it.)

[10]And Moses heard the people weeping by their clans, each man at the doorway of his tent, and the fierce anger of YHWH kindled greatly, and it was evil in the eyes of Moses. [11]And Moses said to YHWH, 'Why this evil to your servant? Why have I not found favour in your eyes, that you place the burden of all this people upon me? [12]Have I conceived all this people? Did I give birth to them that you should say to me, "Carry them in your bosom," just as a nurse carries a suckling-child, to the land you swore to their fathers? [13]From where do I get flesh to give to all this people? For they weep against me saying, "Give to us flesh and let us eat." [14]I am not able alone to carry all this people, for they are too heavy for me. [15]If this is how you are dealing with me, slay me, please,

slay – if I have found favour in your eyes – and do not let me see this evil to me.'

¹⁶And YHWH said to Moses, 'Gather to me seventy men of the elders of Israel, whom you know that they are elders of the people, and its scribes, and take them to the Tent of Meeting, and stand them there with you. ¹⁷And I will descend and speak with you there, and I will lay aside from the Spirit that is upon you and I will place it upon them, and they will carry with you the burden of the people, and you will not carry the burden yourself alone. ¹⁸Now to the people say, "Sanctify yourselves for tomorrow, and you will consume flesh, for you wept in the ears of YHWH, saying, 'Who will enable us to consume flesh? For it was good for us in Egypt!' So YHWH will give to you flesh and you will consume. ¹⁹You will consume not for one day and not two days and not five days and not ten days and not twenty days; ²⁰but for a month of days, until it comes out of your nostrils and it becomes vomit to you because you have despised YHWH who is in your midst and you have wept before his face, saying 'Why did we ever come out of Egypt?'"

²¹And Moses said, 'Six hundred thousand on foot are the people in whose midst I am, and you, you say I will give them flesh and they will consume for a month of days! ²²Will flock and cattle be slaughtered for them and be found sufficient for them? Or will all the fish of the sea be gathered for them and be found sufficient for them?'

²³And YHWH said to Moses, 'Has the hand of YHWH been shortened? Now you will see if my word happens to you or not.'

²⁴And Moses went out and spoke to the people the words of YHWH, and gathered seventy men from the elders of the people, and stood them round about the Tent. ²⁵And YHWH descended in a cloud and spoke to him, and laid aside from the spirit-wind that was upon him and put it upon the seventy men, the elders; and it happened as the Spirit rested upon them, they prophesied, but they did not again. ²⁶But two of the men were left in the camp: the name of one was Eldad and the name of the second was Medad, and upon them the Spirit rested – they were among those written but had not gone out toward the Tent – and they prophesied in the camp. ²⁷And the lad ran and reported to Moses and said, 'Eldad and Medad are prophesying in the camp!' ²⁸And Joshua son of Nun, the attendant of Moses, from his chosen men, answered and said, 'My lord Moses, restrain them!' ²⁹And Moses said to him, 'Are you jealous for me? Would that all the people of YHWH were prophets, that YHWH would put his Spirit upon them.' ³⁰And Moses gathered to the camp, he and the elders of Israel.

³¹Now the Wind set out from YHWH and swept in quails from the sea and left them by the camp, a day's way here and a day's way there, all around the camp about two cubits thick upon the face of the earth. ³²And the people arose all that day and all night and all the following day, and gathered the quail – the least of them gathered ten homers, and

they spread them out for themselves all around the camp. ³³While the flesh was still between their teeth, before it had yet failed, the fierce anger of YHWH kindled against the people and YHWH struck down the people with a very great striking. ³⁴And he called the name of that place Kibroth-hattaavah (Burial of the Cravers), because there they buried the people who were craving. ³⁵From Kibroth-hattaavah, the people journeyed out to Hazeroth, and they were in Hazeroth.

¹²:¹And Miriam spoke, along with Aaron, against Moses regarding the Cushite woman which he took, because he had taken a Cushite woman. ²And they said, 'Has YHWH spoken only solely with Moses – has he not also spoken with us?' And YHWH heard. ³(Now the man Moses was very bowed down, more than any man on the face of the ground.) ⁴And YHWH said suddenly to Moses, and to Aaron and to Miriam, 'Go out, you three, to the Tent of Meeting,' and the three went out. ⁵And YHWH descended in a pillar of cloud and stood at the doorway of the tent, and called Aaron and Miriam, and the two went forth. ⁶And he said, 'Hear now my words. If there is a prophet of YHWH among you, I make myself known in a vision to him, in a dream I speak with him. ⁷But not so with my servant Moses – he is faithful in all my house. ⁸Mouth to mouth I speak with him, neither in vision nor in riddles; the form of YHWH he beholds – so why did you not fear to speak against my servant – against Moses?' ⁹And the fierce anger of YHWH kindled against them, and he went. ¹⁰And the Cloud turned aside from upon the Tent, and look! Miriam was leprous like snow; and Aaron faced Miriam, and look! she was leprous. ¹¹And Aaron said to Moses, 'Please, my lord, do not lay the sin against us which we have done foolishly and in which we sinned. ¹²Do not let her be as one dead, who comes forth from his mother's womb and half his flesh is consumed.' ¹³And Moses cried out to YHWH, saying, 'Please, God, heal her please!'

¹⁴And YHWH said to Moses, 'If her father but spat in her face would she not be ashamed for seven days? Let her be shut out from the camp for seven days, and afterward be gathered in.' ¹⁵And Miriam was shut out from the camp for seven days, and the people did not journey out until Miriam was gathered in again. ¹⁶And afterward the people journeyed out from Hazeroth and encamped in the wilderness of Paran.

Notes on the text

11:1. BHS suggests *raʿab* (hunger) in place of *raʿ* (evil), neglecting the 'good' versus 'evil' motif linking chs. 10 and 11.

4. 'gathered-rabble': a hapax legomenon, from *ʾsp* (to gather), a key root in Num. 11 – 12 (e.g. 11:16, 30; 12:15).

'sat down': LXX and Vg read 'sat down', *wayyēšbû* instead of *wayyāšubû* ('turned', or 'again') (cf. Beirne 1963; Budd 1984: 123), which corresponds with the people's later 'rising up' (*qām*, v. 32).

12. Suffixes are 3rd m. sg. (him/his).

13. 'against': taking *ʿal* adversatively (cf. R. J. Williams 2007: §288).

15. 'you': a rare form of the pr. in m. *ʾat* (see Deut. 5:27; Ezek. 28:14).

16. 'men': Hebrew has sg. *ʾîš*, a class noun (cf. Waltke and O'Connor 1990: 7.2.2b).

23. 'now': SamP has *ʾattā* (you).

25. 'put': *nātan*, versus 'placed' (*śîm*) in v. 17. 'they did not again': Vg and Tgs read 'they did not stop'; see *BHS*, GKC §120d.

28. 'from his chosen men': a hapax legomenon; for 'young men', see Amos 2:11 and Syr and Tg, read 'from his youth'; LXX and SamP read 'one of his chosen', from the root for *bāḥar*.

29. 'Who wouldn't give': I have employed a negative to capture the 'who' question (cf. v. 4).

33. 'before it had yet failed': understood by LXX, Vg, *TO* as 'before exhausting the supply' (followed by G. B. Gray 1903: 118; Ashley 1993: 206); other translations (e.g. AV) prefer 'before it was chewed', building on previous clause.

12:1. 'Cushite': LXX reads 'Ethiopian'.

5. Some Hebrew MSS read 'the pillar' (see Maier 2015: 87).

6. 'a prophet of YHWH among you': a broken construct chain (D. N. Freedman 1972; Ashley 1993: 220–221), typically emended to *nābî-bākem*.

8. 'in vision': this reading emends MT's *ûmarʾeh* (and a vision) to *bĕmarʾeh*, following SamP, LXX, Syr, Vg, and reads *ʾneither in vision* (see D. N. Freedman 1975: 42–43) for contextual reasons (cf. v. 6).

'the form': *tĕmunat yhwh* is the singular instance in MT; LXX reads *doxan* (glory).

13. 'Please, God': an admittedly unique instance of *nāʾ* following the noun *ʾēl*, the emendation suggested by *BHS* to change to *ʾal* is unnecessary and creates difficulties (see Ashley 1993: 221).

15. LXX adds 'she was cleansed' (*ekatharisthē*).

Form and structure

With good reason, Soloveitchik (1974) referred to this section as one of the most difficult in the entire Pentateuch. Much critical analysis continues to suffer from diversity of date, priority, and background assigned to source layers (e.g. Gray 1903: xxxi; Tunyogi 1962; Newman 1965: 72–101; Coats 1968: 221–224, 251; V. Fritz 1970: 16–18, 122; Seebass 1978; Mettinger 1982a: 81–82; Schart 1990: 165–166; Römer 1997; Achenbach 2003b: 237; Carr 2011: 265–275). In even the simplest reconstruction, positing two sources, Sommer nevertheless suggests such a high level of disparity and tension that the final redaction cannot be called a narrative (1999; cf. also S. R. Driver 1906: 62; G. B. Gray 1903: 101–102). Yet Hymes shows that three key roots (*'-s-p*, 'gather'; *n-ś-'*, 'lift'; and *'-k-l*, 'consume') bridge the supposed fissures of Hymes's two plotlines (2010: 263; cf. Samet 2014a: 131), blurring the line between authorship and redaction (cf. also Aurelius 1988: 178; Blum 1990: 82–84; Van Seters 1994: 228–229). Reis (2005) offers a unified reading filled with insight, even if questions remain. She suggests Moses' complaint was a ruse to distract God from his fierce anger against Israel (vv. 11–15), akin to the sort of distraction displays or 'broken-wing acts' performed among quails, when the parent quails sense a threat near their nests (Reis 2005: 28). It is not readily apparent, however, that Moses' complaint is a ruse, nor is such a reading necessary in order to avoid overly negative portrayals of Moses. When Moses perceives that Israel is threatened with utter destruction by God, he surely does stand in the breach on Israel's behalf through his plea – a *sincere* pleading that he does not want to live to see the day of Israel's annihilation.

Without question, these chapters possess unique features, yet many of the deductions involved in critical reconstructions remain unconvincing or unnecessary from a literary perspective (see A. Berlin 1983: 112). The movements in Numbers 11 and 12, for example, assume the Camp's concentric quadrants, not an *Elohist* Tent pitched outside the camp (see Jobling 1978: 1:50–51; Parker 2015: 232 n. 273). In relation to terms, of the some fifty-six uses of *hā'ām* (the people) in Numbers, fifty-four are confined to the book's central division, chapters 11–25, with the two other uses pointing back to the central section (31:3; 32:15). Clearly, the central division of Numbers marks a change in mood and style as part of the 'creation (order)/de-creation (disorder)/recreation (reorder)' scheme of the book's threefold division. Moreover, a general, if not completely consistent, logic may be discerned in the variegated use of terms for Israelites, with *hā'ām* referring to the people en masse as a populace, while *hā'ēdāh* and *haqqāhāl* refer to them according to their character either in covenant with God or as gathered together for cultic or political occasions (cf. Num. 13:26). Not only use of *hā'ām*, but also key words and phrases such as 'the fierce anger of YHWH kindled' (*yihar*) (11:1, 10; 12:9), 'gathered' (*'āsap*) (11:4, 16, 24, 30, 32; 12:14,15), etiologies for Taberah (11:3), Kibroth-hattaavah (11:34) and possibly Hazeroth (11:35; 12:16; cf. Gressmann 1913: 264–275), and the themes of Spirit and prophecy, along with Moses' status and role, bind the three episodes of Numbers 11 – 12 as a unit (cf. Noth 1968: 128). The story in 11:4–35 in particular shares many similarities with Exodus accounts of quail and manna (Exod. 16; also Pss 78:17–30; 106:14–15), of Moses' burden and need for leadership help (Exod. 18), of the seventy elders and YHWH's presence (Exod. 24), and of Moses' intercession in the midst of Israel's looming punishment (Exod. 32 – 33).

The following outline is Milgrom's (1990: 376–380; cf. 1987b: 49–55), although some wording has been changed, leaving open the interpretation of Moses' character (vv. 11–15), and the nature of God's response (vv. 24b–30):

Complaint 1: Taberah (11:1–3)
a. People complain (1a)
b. God hears, his fierce anger kindles, punishes (1b)
c. People appeal to Moses (2a)
d. Moses intercedes (2bα)
e. Appeal answered (2bβ)
f. March delayed (no travel notice)

Complaint 2: Kibroth-hattaavah (11:4–34)
A. People's complaint: flesh (4–10)
   Gathered-rabble instigate people (4–6)
   God's fierce anger kindled (10b)
    B. Moses' plea: assistance (10b-15)
      Give me assistance or death (11–12, 14–15)
      I cannot supply flesh (13)
      X. God's answer to peoples' complaint and Moses' plea (16–24a)
        God instructs Moses to:
        Choose elders: God will authorize them (16–17)
        Ready the people: *He* will provide flesh (18–20)
        Moses: Where will you get flesh? (21–22)
        God: Wait and see (23)
        Moses tells people to get ready (24a)
    B'. God authorizes elders: distributes spirit on Moses (24b–30)
      Moses chooses and assembles elders (24b–30)
      God distributes Moses' spirit (25)
        Eldad and Medad prophesy (26–27)
        Joshua protests (28)
        Moses acquiesces (29)
      Moses and elders return to camp (30)
A'. God supplies flesh: punishes complainers (31–34)
   Flesh brings death (31–33)
   Dead are buried, giving name to site (34)

Complaint 3: Hazeroth (12:1–16)
a'. Miriam and Aaron complain (1–2a)
b'. God hears, his fierce anger kindles, punishes (2b, 4–5, 9–10)
c'. Aaron appeals to Moses (11–12)
d'. Moses intercedes (13)
e'. Appeal answered (14)
f'. March delayed, travel notice (15–16)

Several literary features, such as key words, unify each episode and link them. First, in the two stories that serve as a frame, YHWH's fierce anger kindles (11:1; 12:9), and in the central story his fierce anger kindles 'greatly' (*me'ōd*, 11:10). In the first two stories, the complaints are 'in the ears' of YHWH, while the third story mentions that 'YHWH heard' (12:2). Numbers 11 – 12 refers to the face (11:20), ears (11:1,18), eyes (11:11, 15), mouth (12:8), and hand (11:23) of YHWH, who descends in a cloud to be active near the Tent (11:25; 12:5) – a reminder of YHWH's Eden-like nearness within Israel's Camp.

Second, the rabble in the second story are a 'gathered-rabble' (*hā'sapsup*) from the root *'-s-p*. The remedy to Moses' complaint, triggered by the gathered-rabble, will be to 'gather' elders (11:16), which resolves with Moses 'gathering' himself, along with the elders, into the Camp (11:30) and the people 'gathering' quails (11:32). In the third story, Miriam will be 'gathered' again after being shut out of the Camp for seven days (12:14, 15). Friedman (2001: 466) suggests a chain of *'-s-p* paronomasia, including *mē'appĕkem* (out of your nostrils) and *kî mĕ'astem* (because you have despised) (11:20), *lō' yāsāpû* ('they did not again', 11:25), and *'ap* ('fierce anger', 11:33; 12:9). Along with the sevenfold use of 'gather', the root for 'burden'/'carry' (*nāśā'*) appears seven times, and Moses asks YHWH seven questions, five in his first plea and two in the second (Reis 2005: 228).

Third, the complaints of the second story are ignited by the gathered-rabble 'in their midst' (from *qereb*, 11:4), but YHWH will remark that the people have despised YHWH who is 'in your midst' (11:20) and then Moses, apparently despairing of providing the people with meat to consume, says that he is 'in the midst' of six hundred thousand of them (11:21).

Fourth, following the previous section's fivefold use of 'good' (*tôb*, 10:29, 32), the people complain in the first story of 'evil' (*ra'*, 11:1), while in the second story the people's weeping and the great kindling of YHWH's fierce anger are 'evil' in the eyes of Moses, who asks YHWH, 'Why this evil to your servant?' and prays to be delivered from seeing 'this evil to me' (11:10, 11, 15) – and, in an ironic twist, the people claim that life was 'good' (*tôb*) in Egypt (11:18).

Fifth, the root *'-k-l* occurs once in the first story, eight times in the second story, and once in the last. In the first story, God's fiery anger 'consumes' (*tō'kal*) the edges of the Camp (11:1), a judgement that adds an ominous note to the eight-fold use of 'consume' found throughout the second story, as the people lust to consume flesh (11:4, 5, 13, 18 [three times], 19, 21). In the third story, Miriam's judgement for defaming Moses is a skin-disease, so that Aaron describes her flesh as being half 'consumed' (12:12), a possible echo of the partly consumed quails in the previous story (11:33) – and Miriam will be sent outside the Camp (12:14–15), where those who lusted went to gather the quails (11:31–33).

Sixth, the consuming of 'flesh' (*bāśār*), which occurs eight times in the second story and once in the third, is contrasted with the work of the 'Spirit/Wind' (*rûaḥ*). The Spirit is distributed among the seventy elders, including Eldad and Medad (11:17, 25 [twice], 26, 29), and a Wind from YHWH brings in the quails from the sea (11:31). The second story associates Moses and God's Spirit with 'prophesying' (*nābā'*), the root of which occurs in 11:25, 26, 27, 29, connecting the account with the third story, which focuses on the supremacy of Moses over any other 'prophet among you' (12:6).

Finally, both motifs of Spirit and prophets flow into the broader concern of God's 'word(s)' (11:23, 24; 12:2, 6). A seven-fold use of the root *d-b-r* (vv. 1, 2 [twice], 6 [twice], 8 [twice]), six times with *bě* (speak 'with/against'), unifies Numbers 12 (cf. also Römer 1997: 492; Winslow 2011: 7), and is thematically linked with chapter 11 inasmuch as twice YHWH is described there as speaking with/to Moses (11:17, 25). In Numbers 11 and 12, YHWH's appearance at the Tent of Meeting is central.

Several of the above connections are noted by Jobling who, in his structural analysis, identifies three topographical codes that further illuminate the dynamic interrelationships among these chapters: I. geographical, II. camp and III. vertical codes, illustrated in Figure 9 (1978: 1:26–62; also Fisch 1986).

The geographical code (I) subsumes a temporal aspect: complaints and rebellions (which are 'counter programmes' to God's 'main programme' of arrival in Canaan) lead to the delay of progress to Canaan. While the manna, in God's design, requires no delays in the sojourn, the gathering and eating of quails would potentially have delayed progress for a month (11:20), and Miriam's rebellion led to a delay of seven days (12:14–15).

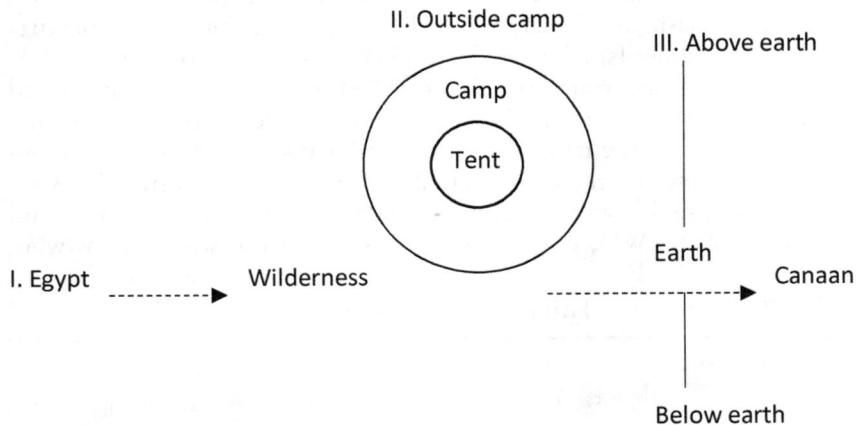

Figure 9: Spatial dynamics in Numbers 11

The camp code (II) structures both authority and purity status. YHWH meets with Moses and the elders (11:16, 24–25) and with Moses, Aaron and Miriam (12:4–5) at the Tent of Meeting, which is clearly set apart from the camp with reference to Eldad and Medad (11:26) and with Moses and the elders' return from the Tent to the camp (11:30). Miriam, shut out of the camp, delays the sojourn until she can be gathered back inside. Interestingly, while the manna descends from heaven within the bounds of the camp (11:9), the quails are gathered 'around the camp' (11:31–32) – and, again, the elders were gathered to the Tent (11:16). With reference to the vertical code (III), YHWH 'descends' (*y-r-d*) in a cloud (11:17, 25; 12:5), just as the manna 'descends' (*y-r-d*) with the dew upon the camp (11:9), but the quail, even as fowl, are said to derive from the sea (11:31), just as the fish, cucumbers, melons, leeks, onions and garlics of Egypt are subearth foods (11:5) (see Lévi-Strauss 1973: 2:468; Jobling 1978: 1:54–55), not to mention that one must *descend* into Egypt, a place that often symbolizes *Sheol* in the Bible (see Morales 2015: 85–86). Jobling also relates a political-hierarchical code to these movements, which includes a unity versus diversity motif (1978: 1:47–49). For example, YHWH and Moses' authority are linked to the centre of the camp, and Miriam may be tracked in the third story in the following manner: from the camp to the Tent (12:4–5), from the Tent to outside the camp (12:12–15), from outside the camp to inside the camp (12:15–16). The parallel relationships may be aligned along a vertical axis, as shown in Table 20.

Among the various literary binaries found in these stories, the following are notable: camp versus outside the camp, Tent versus camp, Canaan versus Egypt, manna versus quail/Egyptian food, progress versus delayed sojourn, Israel versus gathered-rabble, unity versus diversity, Moses versus elders, Moses versus other prophets (whether the seventy elders, Eldad and Medad, Miriam and Aaron, or any 'prophet among you'), spirit versus flesh (also Fisch 1986). The gathered-rabble on the outskirts of the camp draw Israel away from YHWH at the centre (11:4), while the gathered elders around the Tent of Meeting are to draw them toward the centre of the camp (11:16); Moses and the elders later gather to the camp (11:30), but the people's lust for flesh causes them to gather quail on the perimeter of the camp (11:32). Moreover, the contrast between the gathered-rabble and the gathered elders, between lust for flesh and the Spirit of YHWH, may be positioned along the story's two 'who'

Table 20: Spatial correlations in Numbers 11

YHWH/Moses	Heaven	Tent	Canaan
Israel	Earth	Camp	Wilderness
Gathered-rabble	Sea	Outside camp	Egypt

questions: 'Who will cause us to consume flesh?' by the people (11:4), and Moses' urgent plea 'Who wouldn't give for all the people of YHWH to be prophets, that YHWH would put his Spirit upon them?' – the people cry for more flesh for themselves, Moses for more of YHWH's spirit for them.

The Camp stands as a testing ground for Israel's relationship to YHWH/Moses at the centre (Tent), challenged by the gathered-rabble, which represents outside-of-the-camp influences. In the second story, while the gathered-rabble instigate Israel's complaint, the people's complaint, in turn, instigates Moses' complaint (Jobling 1978: 1:40). Moses, manna, and spirit are associated with YHWH/heaven(/Canaan?), while the gathered-rabble and flesh are associated with Egypt/subearth. In Numbers 12, while Miriam had apparently desired to exclude Moses' foreign wife, she herself becomes an outsider, excluded from the Camp (vv. 10–15).

Comment

11:1–3. As an introductory prologue (or 'Vorspiel', Blum 1990: 135; cf. P. J. Johnson 1996: 24; Römer 1997: 487 n. 29), these verses form a microcosm of Israel's wilderness experience, a succinct archetype that will be repeated with little variation throughout chapters 11–25: (1) Israel complains or sins in some fashion, (2) YHWH's fierce anger is kindled in judgement, (3) Moses intercedes on behalf of Israel, (4) YHWH's judgement is mitigated, (5) the place is named so as to remember the episode (or some other memorial is used).

1. This opening may read either as 'the people were as complainers of evil (i.e. misfortune)', or 'the people were as complainers, (and) it was evil in the ears of YHWH'. The stark contrast to the preceding ten chapters is brought out further by the book's first use of *ra'* (evil), which comes on the heels of a fivefold use of *ṭôb* (good) at the end of chapter 10 (vv. 29, 32). These five occurrences of 'good' are matched by four occurrences of 'evil' in Numbers 11 (vv. 1, 10, 11, 15), capped by an ironic use of 'good' in 11:18 (which should be 'evil'). The root for complaining here is not the typical one, 'murmur' (*lûn*), but from the verb *'ānan*, which may include the notion of grief or mourning – the Israelites lament their plight in the wilderness. By comparison to the three-day journey to Sinai, where a complaint over lack of water preceded the supply of (manna and) quail for Israel's hunger (Exod. 15:22–26; 16), some presume the complaint here, followed by the supply of quail in 11:4–35, relates to lack of water. The parallel events, before and after Sinai, however, are more significant by their differences: the people's desire for flesh in Numbers 11 is not out of any actual hunger, and neither should one presume a lack of water. On the contrary, the 'manna has fallen daily for a full year without exception, and the nation knows that God can and will provide them with food' (Lichtenstein 2014a: 145). The non-specificity of the text should be respected, and contextually it is simply the journey itself that stirs the discontent. George adds to Rashbam and Rambam's view that the complaints arise from the march by noting that the 'people complain because this is their first experience marching as the people of YHWH in a prescribed social order (Num. 2)', and even God's judgement is spatial in nature, with the edge of the Camp marking the dividing line between Israel and the world (George 2013: 34–35). The general nature of the complaint allows the focus to remain on the evil of complaining itself, setting forth this instance as paradigmatic.

The anthropomorphism 'in the ears' (bĕ'oznê) of YHWH is followed by the notice that 'YHWH heard', underscoring the flagrant nature of their complaints within the context of the Camp of YHWH's earthly hosts. To complain *within the Camp* is tantamount to speaking contempt into the 'ears' of YHWH. Worse still, the idiom may imply that the people directed their speech to YHWH brazenly (Milgrom 1990: 82). Connecting this episode (11:1–3) with the next (vv. 4–35), the phrase 'in the ears of YHWH' recurs in 11:18. In Numbers 14:28, the judgement upon the first generation will fall after their complaints are spoken 'in my (YHWH's) hearing'. With its threefold use of the divine Name 'YHWH', 11:1 makes for a sharp contrast to the Aaronic benediction, given at the culmination of the Camp's creation (6:22–27). Employing similar anthropomorphism, in Numbers 6 God's favourably disposed face shines, pouring forth blessing throughout the extent of the Camp, whereas in 11:1 his fiery anger consumes the edges of the Camp. Even its outskirts – positioned farthest from the Dwelling – are susceptible to his fire.

In Deuteronomy 4:24, Moses declares to Israel that 'YHWH our God is a consuming fire' (also Heb. 12:29), a reality manifested by his fiery glory, consuming both sacrifices on the altar and those who would draw near to him presumptuously (Lev. 10:1–3). Here in 11:1, YHWH's fierce anger 'kindled' (yiḥar) and his fire burned among his own people – and he 'consumed' (tō'kal) the outskirts of the Camp. One Jewish tradition reads 'in the outskirts' (biqṣêh) of the Camp as a reference to foreigners located at the Camp's fringes (see *Yalk. Shim.*, Num. 11, 732; Y. Kahn 2014: 122). However, the emphasis of the text is on 'the people' (hā'ām), likely including both Israelites and foreigners, whereas the 'gathered-rabble' and the 'sons of Israel' are distinguished in the next story (11:4). Use of 'outskirts of the Camp' is also theological, conveying the problem as beginning with the periphery of the Camp not only in terms of locale and status, but in relation to God's holiness mapped out by the Camp's centre. The word hammaḥăneh ('the camp', v. 1) assumes Numbers 1 – 10. That YHWH's fiery judgement burns the outskirts of the Camp calls to mind 'both the importance and the danger of the boundary' (Camp

2009: 255), a boundary that plays a significant role in chapters 11–12. That YHWH's action is spatial in nature, is also a clue to the function of the Camp structure for the wilderness sojourn. YHWH reasserts the boundary between wilderness and covenant community – abiding in the pure Camp requires entry through his flames of holiness.

The next episode (vv. 4–35) will revolve around the people's base lusting to 'consume' flesh, an ironic defiance and perverse twist to YHWH's consuming of the Camp's fringes.

2. The burning of YHWH's fire causes the people to 'cry' (*yiṣʿaq*) to Moses. The people's crying here, along with their 'weeping' (*bākāh*, v. 4), forms part of their later characterization as a needy infant by Moses (11:12–13), an infant whose flesh is half-consumed through Miriam's leprosy (12:12). Moses intercedes with God on behalf of Israel by 'praying' (*yitpallēl*): the people's cry to Moses leads to Moses' prayer to YHWH on their behalf. All three episodes (11:1–3, 4–35; 12:1–16) centre on the person and role of Moses as prophetic mediator between YHWH and the Camp. Moses' astoundingly effective mediation, based on his unique friendship with YHWH, is highlighted; as soon as he prays to YHWH the fire is quenched. YHWH had called Moses precisely for such prayers and mediation on behalf of his people. Moses' intercessory mediation will reach colossal heights in the next subsection (chs. 13–14).

3. The 'burning' (*tibʿar*) of YHWH's fire leads to naming this incident's locale *Taberah* (Burning), reinforcing the episode's didactic implications for the sojourn: YHWH is to be feared. This paradigmatic account functions as a necessary prologue not only to the wilderness period in general (chs. 11–25), but for the next story in particular: his perception of the escalated repetition of this cycle leads Moses into a profound crisis. Indeed, it is Moses who called the name of that place 'Taberah', on his contemplation of 'the fire of YHWH' that had 'burned among them'. The paradigmatic function of the prologue may account for the absence of a journey report.

11:4–35. This story diverges from the basic pattern found in verses 1–3. While YHWH's fierce anger is kindled greatly (v. 10), Moses' plea to YHWH preempts any judgement (vv. 11–15), so that we do not find the people crying out to Moses for relief. Scholars who berate Moses' character for his lack of intercession have failed to discern the nuances of the pattern's rearrangement, as well as the nature of his plea to YHWH. On this occasion the judgement comes after a new provocation (v. 32). The people's deeply wayward nature is underscored, foreshadowing the first generation's death in the wilderness.

4. The opening vav (and) connects the following story to the previous one (vv. 1–3), even as the x-qatal construction shifts the focus to the 'gathered-rabble', the first of many uses of the key root *ʾ-s-p* in chapters 11–12. As Levine points out (1993: 320), *ʾasapsûp* is a reduplicative form of the verb *ʾ-s-p* (to gather in), captured well in English as 'riffraff'. If the last part of *hā'sapsûp* forms a play on *sûp*, then the name suggests something like 'the end of the gathered ones' or 'the gathered ones consumed', which may allude to their looming judgement. The gathered-rabble is described as 'in the midst' of the people, utilizing merely a pronominal suffix that also depends on the previous story's use of 'the people' (*hā'ām*). The gathered-rabble is distinct from the 'sons of Israel', *'asapsûp* typically being understood as the mixed-multitude that came out of Egypt with Israel (see Exod. 12:38; Lev. 24:10), and their location serves to underscore their influence on Israel. Mixture of the designations 'gathered-rabble' and 'sons of Israel', including the more general 'the people', brings out the identity of the Camp thematically, underscoring the severe gravity of the situation. In being led by the rabble in their midst, Israel came to despise YHWH 'in your midst' (v. 20) – whose Dwelling was located in the midst of the Camp.

The phrase 'craved a craving' or 'lusted a lusting' (*hit'awwû ta'ăwāh*) is forcefully enigmatic. What does the gathered-rabble desire? From verses 5b–6, we discover it is variety of food, particularly meat. The unity of the people is threatened by the mixed-rabble's desire for a mixed menu, rather than being satisfied with YHWH's one provision (Keil and Delitzsch 1973: 3:67; Jobling 1978: 1:53). The people however were not starving, for God's daily provision of manna had never failed. Rather than merely craving sustenance the rabble craved a craving – they have plunged into a *state* of inordinate desire. Defiantly, they lusted for luxury beyond their needs, an important difference with the scenario recounted in Exodus 16, the result of which had been God's provision of manna. Altmann (2011: 66–67) notes that meat was a rare indulgence for most people in the ANE, often reserved for royalty (human and divine), and eaten only at ritual feasts or special occasions. Parker (2012: 3) further suggests that 'meat' is not a neutral category, either in the ancient world or in the biblical text, and should not be reduced simply to another form of diversity in diet – rather, meat-eating may symbolize a feast, entailing intentional cultivation, economic sacrifice, and often special attention to slaughter, blood, and dietary restriction. While the Nazir, Israel's paradigm for the wilderness journey, is willing to forgo the joys of life, symbolized by grape products, for a period of time in order to draw near to YHWH, offering his or her life to him as a free-will act of devotion (cf. 6:1–21), here the people prove themselves unwilling – even for limited period of the wilderness sojourn – to do without meat, a luxuriant and rare feast, and they turn their hearts to Egypt, despising both YHWH and their deliverance out of bondage.

The multifaceted possibilities of the manna, as described in 11:7–9, further underscore the heinous unreasonableness of the complaint. As a result of the rabble's craving, the sons of Israel sit down and 'weep' (*bākāh*), mourning their plight in self-pity as if God were not committed to meeting their daily needs. Beirne (1963) argues persuasively for reading the text, with LXX and Vulgate, as 'sit down' rather than 'again', since sitting down and weeping is a common funeral rite in the ancient world, used for moments of deep sorrow and national disaster, and finds biblical precedent (Neh. 1:4; Job 2:12–13; Lam. 2:10; especially relevant, Ps. 137:1). As a ritual expression of profound lament, the people's weeping reveals the Camp's woeful spiritual condition, having grave implications for Israel's relationship with YHWH, and for the people's journey – implications which Moses discerned only too clearly. The sons of Israel sit down to weep over their provision of manna, but they will 'arise' (qām) all day and night, and the following day, in order to feed their lust by gathering quails (v. 32).

'Who', they cry, 'will cause us to consume (ya'ăkilēnû) flesh (bāśār)?' This is an explicit rejection of YHWH, who provides Israel with manna – they want a different supplier ('Who else . . . ?'), a supplier of flesh implicitly identified as Pharaoh (v. 5). Rather than approach YHWH through Moses regarding their desire, even in complaint, they simply sit and mourn their plight under YHWH's care. That this 'who' is indeed weighed with such significance is evident from YHWH's telling remark that the people have 'despised/rejected (mĕ'astem) YHWH' (v. 20), the same term used for their ultimate despising/rejection of the land in 14:31. In their state of lust their hearts commit apostasy. Ironically, in Deuteronomy 12:20–21 Moses declares that once in the land YHWH would grant the people to 'consume flesh' (tōkal bāśā) to 'your soul's desire' ('awwat). However, for the wilderness journey, which should have taken but weeks (cf. Deut. 1:2), they were called to be both grateful and satisfied with God's provision of manna, to embrace the sort of sacrificial devotion to YHWH exemplified by the Nazir (6:1–21).

5–6. Incongruously, given all they have forgotten, including their harsh labour (cf. Exod. 1:13–14), the people say, 'We remember . . .' Facing hardships in the wilderness, the people's memory of life in Egypt turns subversive (cf. Leveen 2008: 82–83). Fish heads the list of the people's memory of Egyptian cuisine, and, likely, fish counts as 'meat' since Moses will later ask if gathering 'all the fish of the sea' would be sufficient to satisfy the people's lust (11:22). Currid notes the accuracy of Egyptian culinary staples remembered by the Hebrews, quoting from Papyrus Anastasi III, which celebrates the glories of the new capital of Rameses (1997: 145–146; citing ANET, 471):

Its granaries are (so) full of barley and emmer (that) they come near to the sky. Onions and leeks are for food, and lettuce of the garden, pomegranates, apples, and olives, figs of the orchard, . . . red wedj-fish of the canal of the Residence City, which live on lotus-flowers, bedin-fish of the Hari-waters (numerous other types of fish species follow) . . .

Notably, the foods listed from Egypt are all subterranean, in accord with understanding Egypt as a spiritual *Sheol*, the watery grave of the dead, to which one always descends (e.g. Gen. 39:1). Fish, cucumbers, melons, leeks, onions and garlic are from below, as it were, while God's provision of food, the manna, is heavenly, from above – 'the bread of angels' or 'of the mighty', *'abbîrîm* (Ps. 78:25).

Their harsh labour in Egypt notwithstanding, the people declare that their Egyptian menu had been 'without cost' or 'for nothing' (*ḥinnām*), a reality that was only true – and supremely so – of the manna. Again, the people's despising of the provision of manna is understood by YHWH as a despising of the provider himself and of the exodus deliverance, along with the promise of life in the land (11:20) – a clear thematic reversal of Moses' invitation to Hobab (10:29–32). Claiming their soul (or 'throat' – *napšēnû*) is dried up, they disparage the manna that is 'before our eyes'. The expression underscores the lust-aspect of their complaint, not to mention their ingratitude: being fed supernaturally in the wilderness, they complain about what is set before their eyes – perhaps an allusion to humanity's primal sin, as the woman saw that the forbidden fruit was 'desirable' (*ta'ăwāh*) 'for the eyes' (*lā'ênayim*) (Gen. 3:6). The word 'desirable' is the same as translated 'lust' or 'crave' in Numbers 11, and the basis for naming the place Kibroth-*hattaavah*, 'Graves *of Lusting*' (11:34). The outer camp's failure (chs. 11–14) is portrayed according to humanity's first transgression. Moreover, the authorial commentary inserted in verses 7–9 condemns the denigration of the manna as baseless, describing its appearance ('its eye like the eye of', *wĕ'ênô kĕ'ên*) like bdellium, a precious stone associated with Eden (Gen. 2:12). In God's original concession for meat-eating, humanity was forbidden 'flesh with its life (*nepeš*), that is, its blood'; there is, perhaps, some irony then in that the people lust for flesh because their own *nepeš* is dried up.

The people's apostasy may be mapped, with the words 'we remember' consisting of a looking back to Egypt with longing, a reversal of the exodus journey. As with Lot's wife, the backward look in the midst of a gracious deliverance is condemnable, unveiling an apostate heart. J. Z. Smith speaks of a 'narrative reversal' of the exodus: 'Israel wishes to go back to Egypt; the divine feeding results in a plague' (2004: 122). The epic march from Mount Sinai having begun, the only appropriate response would be a looking forward to life in the land with persevering hope. Moreover, YHWH had just caused the people to look back in remembrance of their deliverance from bondage and death before leaving Sinai, through the celebration of Passover (see Num. 9:1–14), a feast that included the eating of meat, unleavened bread, and bitter herbs (9:11). Not only had the people eaten meat recently, but the 'bitter herbs' (*mĕrōrîm*) were intended to recall the bitter treatment of the Israelites by Egyptians, that the latter had 'made their lives bitter' (*wayĕmārĕrû*)

(Exod. 1:14). The people's lusting, therefore, is no mere indication of hunger in the wilderness. Rather, their lusting comprehends a despising and rejection of YHWH and his deliverance, and the desire to return to Egypt. In Numbers 14:3–4, the congregation of Israel will ask, 'Would it not be better for us to return to Egypt?' and then suggest, 'Let us appoint a leader and return to Egypt'. The rumblings of that storm are already heard in this account, and Moses already foresees the bitter end.

7–9. The people's complaint also concerned the monotony of the manna, the lack of variety on their menu, but the commentary in these verses exposes the ingratitude and deceit of their baseless words, since the manna was wondrously flexible as food, open to various ways of preparation. Significantly, while the complaint spans two verses, the narrative description of YHWH's provision of manna takes up three verses. Verses 7, 8a, 8b and 9 set forth the manna as: delightful in appearance, adaptable in preparation, sweet in taste, and regular in its supply. Reis (2005: 210) similarly speaks of how the author extols the manna for its

> attractiveness (like bdellium), versatility (it could be ground like flour, beaten like cream, or boiled like corn), cleanliness (it fell on a protective layer of dew), convenience (it needed only to be picked up), and taste (like that of a cake baked with oil).

The authorial comment steps into the story to defend YHWH's provision, in much the same way as Moses is defended in 12:3. Rhetorically, such comments undermine and delegitimize the complaints, providing the audience with a vantage point that is unmistakable for assessing the heinousness of the people's grievance. The verses function as an indictment against Israel, underscoring their arrogant lack of gratitude, the ludicrous nature of their despondency, and the heinousness of their lust.

In contrast to the subterranean food of Egypt, the manna descended from heaven, and its appearance – like bdellium – links it to humanity's Edenic life with God (Gen. 2:12). Brumberg-Kraus sets forth Bachya's view that meat-eating is God's concession to humanity's animal desires in its fallen state; not only did Adam and Eve not eat meat in Eden, but in the world-to-come the righteous feast only on fine, pure foods created from supernal light (1999: 228–229). Reflecting on the echoes of Genesis 1 in Leviticus 11, he shows that priestly discrimination regarding the flesh of animals was necessary only after God's concession of meat (Gen. 9:3–4), and only with reference to meat since other edible foods (grains, fruit, vegetables) required no discrimination (Gen. 1:29–30; 1999: 240–241), an idea that may underlie the contrast between the people's lust for meat versus God's provision of (Edenic) manna.

In the early twentieth century, Bodenheimer established the prevailing identification of manna, from a scientific approach: manna is now generally thought to come from the excretion of parasites found on tamarisks (Bodenheimer and Theodor 1929: 45–88; 1947). Whether or not God utilized such earthly means, the biblical witness portrays the provision of manna, along with its attendant circumstances (such as an extra, storable provision for Sabbath-keeping in Exod. 16), as supernatural in character, consistently describing manna as 'bread from heaven' (variously as *leḥem min-haššāmāyim*, Exod. 16:4; *leḥem miššāmayim*, Neh. 9:15; and *leḥem šāmayim*, Ps. 105:40), or the 'grain of heaven' and 'bread of angels' (*dĕgan-šāmayim, leḥem 'abbîrîm*, Ps. 78:24–25). Wisdom of Solomon describes manna as the 'bread of angels' that Israelites ate 'without their toil' (16:20; cf. 19:6, 11), alluding to humanity's life in Eden wherein, akin to the wilderness period of Israel, humans experienced an intimate relationship with YHWH God that entailed eating without toil (J. Z. Smith 2004: 122, 124).

10. While in the first and third stories (11:1–3; 12:1–16), we read that 'YHWH heard' (*wayyišma' yhwh*) complaints (11:1; 12:2), this central story declares that 'Moses heard' (*wayyišma' mōšeh*) the people's weeping. The cycle in 11:1–3 with YHWH's hearing a complaint, leading to the kindling of his fierce anger, occurs here as well ('and the fierce anger of YHWH kindled greatly', 10b), except for this replacement of Moses for YHWH with regard to hearing – a significant difference that explains the last clause of this verse, that 'it was evil in the eyes of Moses'. Moses perceives that the cycle has begun again, and that it has done so with escalation. In 11:1 the people were 'as complainers of evil', but here the people have succumbed to weeping en masse, by their clans, and by their individual households, each man at the doorway of his tent, signifying grief-stricken despair. Their weeping undergirds Moses' description of them as a nursing infant (v. 12), but, more importantly, signals the depth of their spiritual bankruptcy – they have despaired not only of their situation but of YHWH their Shepherd (11:4, 20).

Not only has the people's rebellion escalated, but YHWH's fierce anger has consequently been fanned as well: whereas as 11:1 reads that YHWH's 'fierce anger kindled', 11:10 states that the 'fierce anger of YHWH kindled greatly (*mě'ōd*)'. It is at this point in the cycle the text reads 'it was evil in the eyes of Moses'. Some interpret this line as Moses' agreement with YHWH in relation to the people's wickedness (AV, NKJV add 'also': 'Moses also was displeased'), and others understand YHWH's fierce anger as the object of Moses' displeasure, Milgrom even stating that Moses concurred – 'sided' – with Israel against God (1990: 85). The preferable understanding, which accords with his overall portrait in this chapter, is that Moses is deeply displeased with *both* the people's weeping and YHWH's consequent response – not with God's righteous prerogative, but with the pattern that must inevitably lead to the people's annihilation (similarly, Jobling 1978: 1:30; Reis 2005: 211). He has perceived that the cycle of rebellion and consuming anger is being repeated in an escalated manner, and *this reality* – the seemingly unalterable cycle that must surely lead to Israel's utter annihilation – is a calamity in his eyes. The evil in Moses' eyes encompasses the whole substance of verse 10, the people's grievously rebellious weeping and YHWH's compulsory response.

Previously (vv. 1–3), Moses had not feared Israel's destruction, but now, with the people having sunk so low and with YHWH's fierce anger having been kindled greatly, he stares into the face of Israel's threatened demise and sees it now as a certain reality. Rashi, similarly, understands Moses as preferring death to witnessing the destruction of Israel. Moses the singular mediator and prophet of YHWH has discerned that Israel will be annihilated in the wilderness, inescapably, and he does not want to live to see this 'evil' inevitability. No sooner than Israel departs the shadow of Mount Sinai, the wide and dark abyss has opened up before him. YHWH had already consumed the outskirts of the Camp when the people had kindled his fierce anger by their complaints, this judgement abated only by Moses' intercession; what now that their widespread rebellious weeping has kindled his fierce anger 'greatly'? Moses sees the end from the beginning, he knows both the stubborn, wayward heart of the people and the righteousness of YHWH who, while abounding in mercy to those who fear him, will nevertheless not be mocked by a wayward and rebellious people. By no difficult deduction, Moses realizes the people cannot but be consumed by YHWH, and, as his plea to YHWH will convey, he has no heart to follow the trajectory through to its bitter end – 'slay me now' (v. 15). The issue is not even whether YHWH will destroy Israel *now*, on this occasion, but that the cycle will inevitably continue repeating with escalation – there is no way Israel will survive.

The unique nature of Israel's sin in Numbers 11 lies in their lustful pursuit of flesh, of pleasure, a profoundly degraded state that calls for YHWH's judgement and Moses' crisis (Lichtenstein 2014a: 145–146). Using insights from theories of leadership (by Heifetz 1994), Sacks explains two sorts of challenges faced by people, technical challenges and adaptive challenges (2017: 122–124): in technical challenges, someone else provides the solution, while in adaptive challenges the people themselves need to change. Throughout Exodus Moses had exercised technical leadership to a large degree, providing solutions to the people's fears and lack through his access to God; in Numbers, however, he was called to provide adaptive leadership, to help Israel change from a rabble of liberated slaves to mature and loyal followers of YHWH, who feared and trusted God. 'It is precisely because Moses understood this that he was so devastated when he saw that the people *had not changed at all* . . . In a sense they had gotten worse' (Sacks 2017: 124; emphasis original).

Moses could, by God's help, provide for the nation's physical needs and show them the spiritual path they were to follow, but he was helpless to humble their hearts, helpless to change them in their inner being, apart from which their destruction loomed on the horizon. After the people have revealed their base lust and low spiritual estate, he discerns their inevitable failure and destruction in the wilderness, and spirals downward into an abyss of crisis (similarly, Samet 2014a: 134–137). As Soloveitchik (1974) put it, when the people who were craving began to complain and weep, 'Moshe knew: This is the end, he'll never see *Eretz Yisrael*, never!' Given the disastrous results of the scouts' mission (Num. 13 – 14), Moses' vision of the abyss that lay open before Israel was justified, although God would prove well-able both to judge the Israelites and also to fulfil his promises to the patriarchs (with the emergence of a second generation, 14:27–38).

15. Whereas as the people fall to desperate weeping, Moses turns to YHWH. He begins with a twofold use of 'why' (*lāmāh*), the most common interrogative directed at God, typically within laments that raise hard questions concerning relations with God (e.g. Pss 10:1; 22:2; 44:24), the suffering of the righteous (e.g. Jer. 15:18; 20:18; Job 7:20), or the perversion of justice (Hab. 1:3, 13), and one found 'especially on the lips of Moses who, more than any other major character, so interrogates God' (Balentine 1985: 60). Some read these verses critically of Moses, as if he were forsaking his role as mediator. Sommer(1999: 612) refers to Moses as 'not humble but petulant, not beneficent but bitter', displaying 'self-centredness' and 'self-pity'. Cotton (2001: 4) presumes Moses is behaving like the people, complaining. Widmer (2004: 298) claims Moses was overpowered by selfish emotions, contrasting this occasion with his 'surprisingly selfless' prayer in 14:13–19, and suggesting the difference is due to the 'much more serious' situation in Numbers 14. Such remarks betray a common interpretative pitfall, reducing the present situation to mere hunger-induced complaints. Moses, the man on whom YHWH's Spirit rests, who has both tasted and seen more of the divine nature than any other within ancient Israel's history, has rightly judged the situation as a gravely significant crisis – and YHWH's later assessment, that the Israelites have rejected YHWH, fully justifies Moses' desperation.

There is, moreover, no reason why Moses' address to YHWH here should not be taken as an act of intercession on behalf of Israel – especially so, given his intercessory prayers in the two stories that frame this one (11:2; 12:13). Indeed, rather than interceding after YHWH's judgement, here Moses preempts judgement by interposing himself. The plight of Moses comes into sharper focus when this occasion is understood to be as disastrously serious as the unbelief in Numbers 14 – the latter is presaged in the former. Closer to the mark, Hymes (2010: 267) understands 'Moses' daring expostulation as a bold act of intercession', the sort labelled 'loyal opposition' by Coats (1993). Justly, Reis likens

Moses to a wall between God and Israel, as YHWH would seek in Ezekiel's day (2005: 212–213; Ezek. 22:29–31): one who 'would stand in the breach before me in behalf of the land, that I should not destroy it, but I found none'.

Moses' plea is structured chiastically (also G. J. Wenham 1981b: 122; Seebass 1993: 2:49; Römer 1997: 488):

A. why this evil (*ra*') to your servant? (11)
  B. why have I not found (*māṣātî*) favour (*ḥēn*) in your eyes (*bě'ênêkā*)?
    C. the burden (*maśśā'*) of all this people (*kol-hā'ām hazzeh*) upon me (11)

        Did I conceive all this people (*kol-hā'ām hazzeh*) . . . give birth to them
        Carry (*śā'êhû*) them in your bosom as nurse carries (*yiśśā'*)
      X. **. . . to the land you swore to their fathers (12)**
        From where am I to get flesh (*bāśār*) for all this people (*kol-hā'ām hazzeh*)?
        For they weep . . . 'Give to us flesh (*bāśār*) and let us eat' (13)

    C'. to-carry (*lāśē't*) all this people (*kol-hā'ām hazzeh*) . . . too heavy for me (14)
  B'. if I have found (*māṣā'tî*) favour (*ḥēn*) in your eyes (*bě'ênêkā*)
A'. do not let me see this evil (*ra*') to me (15)

With the journey from Sinai having barely begun and yet the cycle of rebellion and judgement underway already for a second, aggravated occasion, the burden of leading a spiritually dissolute people overwhelms Moses (similarly, Waxman 2006b), although not in the petulant manner claimed by some. Moses' character before (11:2), after (12:3, 13), and throughout this story (11:29–30) is consistent with the rest of his life as Israel's mediator, and YHWH deals well with his servant and, further, defends him. Nevertheless, the imminent destruction of the Israelites within sight of experiencing all the good YHWH was ready to pour out on them in the land (10:29, 32) sparks what is, perhaps, the greatest crisis in the life of Moses. All too well, he has come to understand that his constant intercession on behalf of Israel, failing to change the heart of the people, amounts to nothing more than a postponement of their utter destruction. He had just interceded for them, allaying God's righteous anger so that only the outskirts of the Camp had been consumed, and already the people are openly despising YHWH. Moses wants YHWH and Israel's relationship to be transplanted within the land of Canaan in peace, but he cannot square the circle, despite his Herculean efforts: Israel has already proven to be a bride of harlotry, and YHWH cannot change his holy and righteous character. His intercession has become a cog of stubble in the machinery of a repeating cycle of heinous sin and just retribution – so he pleads for YHWH to take ownership over his own agenda, an agenda Moses cannot accomplish if he must do so against YHWH's own resolve and role within the cycle. Clearly, the character of God, who always fulfils his word and who must also judge sin in righteousness, has led to this conundrum in the wilderness.

With the two parties of the covenant having become disunited and antagonistic, repelling one another, and since turning to the Israelites, steeped as they are in defiant mourning, would be utterly futile, Moses turns to YHWH. His plea to YHWH on behalf of the openly rebellious people, beyond a sincere expression of his own tortured soul in crisis, proves strategic upon a careful reading. First, consistent with his intercession on behalf of Israel after the golden calf apostasy, in verse 11 he interposes himself rather than advocating for any merit on the part of the people. In Exodus 32, Moses, in an effort to 'make atonement' (*'ăkappĕrāh*) for Israel's sin (v. 30), had declared that if YHWH would not forgive their sin, then 'blot me out of your book' (v. 32). He understands that he has found favour in the eyes of YHWH, and he consistently uses that favour to procure mercy for Israel. In the present context, while YHWH's fierce anger fumes against the people, Moses redirects YHWH's attention and concern to Moses himself – 'if this is how it will be (i.e. the recurring cycle of rebellion and judgement until the Israelites are utterly destroyed), then slay me now'. His questions are deeply ironic and meant to move YHWH since Moses well knows YHWH intends no evil to his servant, and that he – Moses – has indeed found favour with him. Regular intercession will not break the cycle of inevitable judgement; Moses shifts YHWH's attention to the effect of this rebellion-followed-by-kindled anger pattern on himself: the burden is too great, he needs help beyond his access to YHWH after Israel's presumptuous sins – he needs, rather, help leading the people in the way of YHWH, in *elevating their spiritual condition*. On Israel's side of the relationship, all Moses can do for YHWH's sake is to continue what he has done from the beginning, giving them *torah* instruction, but he is merely one man, merely one channel tasked with irrigating an immense field, a wilderness-like people, spiritually dry and overgrown with thorny weeds – he is alone and needs help if there will ever be a fruitful crop.

Second, in verse 12 Moses, by the same purposeful method of indirection, reminds YHWH of his own responsibility for the people: 'Have I conceived all this people? Did I give birth to them that you should say to me, "Carry them in your bosom, just as a nurse carries a suckling-child, to the land you swore to their fathers?"' His use of the pronoun 'I' in its lengthened form (*'ānōkî*; vv. 12 [twice], 14, 21) is an emphatic expression, pregnant with purpose – communicating that the people are YHWH's responsibility (cf. Beegle 1972: 281; Coats 1987: 164; Reis 2005: 214). Similarly, after the golden calf incident, Moses had called on YHWH to 'see that this nation is your people' (33:13). It is, of course, YHWH God himself who had conceived Israel, a people he had 'redeemed' and 'purchased' (Exod. 15:13, 16), and Moses thus refuses a burden that belongs properly to God alone (Briend 1992: 75) – he pleads for YHWH himself to carry and suckle them, as only he can. The nursing imagery interjects motherly tenderness into the scenario (and may explain the feminine form of 'you' in v. 15): the wicked people are cast as infants, and God Almighty as a gentle mother. But, more than this, Moses wants God to *claim* them – the ones he is prepared to destroy. Already they had been on the brink of utter destruction, averted only through Moses' intercession (Exod. 32:9–10). And yet, eventually, Moses himself will come to acknowledge that these particular Israelites – this first generation – must finally, in their stiff-necked rebellious hearts, succumb to righteous judgement, even as YHWH raises up a new generation in the wilderness that will inherit his divine promises.

Third, just as Moses had called to YHWH's mind his promises to the patriarchs that he would bring their descendants into the land in Exodus 32:13, a reminder framed by two references to YHWH's relenting from 'the evil' (*hārā'āh*, vv. 12, 14) to his people (of destroying them utterly), so here, at the centre of his plea, Moses mentions 'the land you swore to their fathers' (v. 12). The exodus out of Egypt and more recent departure from Mount Sinai had the immediate goal of life in the land, as promised to Abraham, Isaac, and Jacob. Moses, having interposed himself in the light of YHWH God's compassion for him, and having reminded YHWH of his own accountability for the people, now sets God's own promises to, and favour upon, the patriarchs before his face.

From the central focus on Israel's inheritance of the land promised by YHWH to the fathers, Moses' plea unwinds with another reference to his own helplessness in the midst of the people's depravity (vv. 13–14) and with another interposition of himself on their behalf. *Sifre* 91 and *Midrash Leqaḥ Ṭov* understand Moses' plea as on behalf of the people: 'Kill me, lest I witness the suffering you will bring on this people, whom I love' (Sommer 1999: 618). Rashi similarly states that it was because the Holy One had showed Moses the punishments he destined to bring on the people for their rebellion, that Moses responded with 'If that is so, that you will punish them in this manner, then kill me first' (cf. 1997: 4:124). Moses' interposition of his own life – 'slay me, please, slay' – forms the climax of his intercession on behalf of the people, a request for death that may have generated the further issue of Israel's future leadership. Joshua's first appearance in Numbers (11:28) becomes understandable as he will eventually succeed Moses in leadership, bringing them into the land (see Parker 2015: 22) – a point Jewish tradition connects with the assumed content of Eldad and Medad's prophesying (vv. 26–29).

In speaking of the people's lusting for flesh, Moses is addressing their spiritual degradation by its manifestation and symptom. Indeed, when

YHWH later says he will satisfy the people's desire for flesh, Moses implies that all the meat in the world could not appease their insatiable lust (vv. 21–22). YHWH's response to Moses' plea is not founded upon providing the people quail but on providing his servant with help in the spiritual leadership of the people and, then, secondarily, abating the people's immediate concern with flesh. Moses had expressed that he was not 'able alone (*lĕbaddî*) to carry all this people, for they are too heavy for me' (v. 14), a situation he pressed YHWH to redress on the alternative of Moses' own death (v. 15), and YHWH's immediate response will be the gathering of seventy men.

How are we to understand Moses' 'burden' (*maśśā'*, v. 11)? The term derives from the root for lifting or carrying, but what is the nature of Moses' carrying? LXX translates this term with *hormēn*, which includes the idea of 'impulse', translated as such by Dorival (1976: 290, 293; cf. Liddell et al. 1996: 1253; Hymes 2010: 277). Understood this way, Moses' burden is the wayward impulse of the people, demonstrated by their impious and impatient lust, an impulse that only YHWH's Spirit can turn – his Spirit on the people's leaders, but ultimately on the hearts of the people themselves. There may even be a play with *massā*, the term widely used for Israel's 'testing' in the wilderness, in the sense that YHWH's testing of the people's desires is a heavy burden for Moses (see Parker 2015: 227); the root letters *msh* also signify notions of despair and melting, which would similarly fit a play on Moses' crisis. Samet likewise speaks of Israel's 'profound spiritual regression' (2014a: 133). The term *maśśā* is used precisely for a prophet's word from YHWH, a burden understood as an 'oracle' of YHWH (see Isa. 21:1; Jer. 23:33–34, 36, 38; Nah. 1:1; Zech. 12:1; Mal. 1:1) (Parker 2015: 228). YHWH's remedy will thus be to gather seventy elder-scribes, who will share the burden of promulgating divine torah.

16. YHWH responds to Moses' pleas in a twofold manner: (1) he will establish leadership relief for Moses through the spirit-empowerment of seventy men (vv. 16–17), and (2) he will provide flesh for the people to eat (vv. 18–20). It is commonly observed that the seventy elders do not appear again in the wilderness narratives nor aid in providing flesh for the people, making their presumed help dubious (e.g. Wellhausen 1889: 99; Gunneweg 1990: 169). Such views fail to see the divine remedy's wisdom precisely because they fail to diagnose the depth of the people's problem. The mere supply of meat was not the issue at hand, but the people's spiritual shallowness. Psalm 106 has it that the Israelites 'lusted exceedingly' (*wayyit'awwû ta'ăwāh*) in the wilderness, and that even in granting them their desire, YHWH sent 'leanness' (*rāzôn*) into their soul (vv. 14–15). The elders do appear again, in 16:25, taking their stand with Moses against Dathan and Abiram – no insignificant support. Contextually, given the influence of the Egyptian 'gathered-rabble' on the Israelites, more 'localized leadership' serves as a counter-balance (Reis

2005: 218). Given the sevenfold use of the root *n-ś-'* (vv. 11, 12 [twice], 14, 17 [three times]), a key word used throughout the book's opening chapters for the census and the carrying-duties of Levites, this account may manifest Moses' carrying-duty on the sojourn: he carries the burden of all the people – a duty that will soon be shared by the seventy spirit-empowered elder-scribes. While the extra seventy elders do not change the people, they do relieve Moses' burden – both of YHWH's responses are for Moses' sake. Thus, as scribes who have become prophets by a share in Moses' spirit from YHWH, the seventy elders will share Moses' burden in disseminating God's Torah through Moses to the people and by bearing the complaints of the people, responding to them with God's will through Moses.

YHWH's remedy may be understood more deeply by beginning with the qualifications of the seventy men: they are those whom Moses knows *already* serve as 'elders of the people' (*ziqnê hā'ām*) and 'its scribes' (*šōṭĕrāyw*). The Greek version has whom 'you yourself' (*autos sy*) know, stressing YHWH's authorization of Moses to choose personally his co-labourers (cf. Wevers 1998: 169), the sort of prerogative that will later enflame his accusers (see Num. 16:3, 13–14). 'Elders' are primarily understood as office-holders who function as representatives of the people, and the seventy elders likely function as a council (cf. Weinfeld 1977b: 65). They are seen to act collectively, or, more passively, simply to stand as silent representatives of the people collectively, with the word 'head' (*rō'š*) likely used in place of the singular 'elder' (Conrad 1980; Reviv 2014: 15). While there are some similarities to the selection of judges in Exodus 18:13–27 (see Reviv 1982), there are important differences that caution against any conflation of the two accounts (contra Cook 1999) – the role of the seventy elder-scribes is quite apart from, and goes well beyond, the judicial system established in Exodus 18 (on the prophetic and political senses of *rûaḥ*, see *THAT* 2:743–746). Such elders of Israel though referenced infrequently are noted sufficiently to assume their hierarchical role among the tribes (e.g. Exod. 3:18; 4:29). Pentateuchal narratives are focused primarily on Moses' leadership as mediator rather than on the regular function of the elders. The dearth of scriptural specimens of their leadership, therefore, should not be taken as positive proof against their actual role as clan elders. Clearly, 'the point of gathering [the elders] is not to introduce them to the burden of leadership for the first time' (Sommer 1999: 606). The elders, positioned providentially within a tribal hierarchy, are able to influence the people now in a greater capacity. These seventy men taken from a larger body of elders are publicly elevated above the other elders, brought into a more intimate fellowship with Moses, and, partaking of a share in the divine Spirit that is on Moses, are also empowered in a manner that is not so for the other elders. By the albeit temporary gift of prophecy, affirming the Spirit's enabling presence, the elders themselves are renewed as to the spiritual aspect of their position, reinvigorated to govern their spheres of influence according to God's revealed will and words. To be sure, the people's complaints and lusting after flesh was a spiritual problem – having despised YHWH among them (v. 20) – and the remedy must come through the spiritual guidance of their elders. Many leaders, as Nachmanides understood, would now appease the people's rage by speaking to their hearts when they complained; he further explains that since the elders knew what YHWH had commanded for Israel by Moses' hand they could pass on the divine communication each to the people of his own tribe, helping to guide them amid the temporary needs and events in the wilderness (cf. 1975: 100, 106; Hymes 2006: 309–311).

The elders' role is given a new focus: they stand *with Moses* (cf. 16:25), alongside of YHWH's servant and under his authority, for the sake of YHWH's prophecy-driven agenda. Their share in Moses' spirit of YHWH grants them a unity derived from and founded on God's Torah through Moses. From the people's perspective, the elders are set before them in a manner that reaffirms to them not only their authority or political status, but also the spiritual role of these men in their lives, including over the other elders from which they have been gathered. They see how these seventy men stand with Moses, and observe the utterance of prophecy as divine confirmation that their role in ruling bears the authority of God – what was merely political is now prophetic and profoundly spiritual, underscoring the function of God's word and will in Israel's hierarchy. From Moses' perspective, such a renewed commitment and enablement for the seventy men to take up their spiritual calling as leaders among the people would have served as an encouragement. While, therefore, YHWH utilizes a leadership structure already in place for sharing Moses' burden, albeit with a renewed commitment and spiritual enablement to fulfil one's office as directed toward YHWH's own agenda for the people, yet these seventy men take on a status above the rest of the elders that does indeed create a new level within Israel's hierarchy. This text appears foundational to the later establishment of the Sanhedrin (e.g. Lindblom 1973: 100; McKenzie 1959: 406), and, further, there is a strong tradition that these seventy elders were entrusted with, and functioned to establish, the original or 'genuine' Torah (Achenbach 2003b: 274), a tradition encompassing both the Samaritan Pentateuch (M. Gaster 1925: 119) and the Septuagint (Hengel 2002: 26).

The seventy men are not only elders, but also among the class of 'scribes' (*šōṭĕrîm*), translated in LXX as *grammateis*. Noth (1968: 87; cf. BDB) observed that this Hebrew term, often translated as 'officials', 'foremen' and the like, originally meant 'writers' (*šōṭĕrîm*), and this usage underscores their role of prophetic or word-based leadership – implying they will help disseminate among the people God's will revealed to Moses. As the verb *šāṭar* means 'to write', with a parallel in Akkadian *šaṭāru*, Harrison describes the *šōṭĕrîm* as 'literate administrators among the Israelite tribes' who had the charge of recording important events, census lists, judicial decisions, and cultic activities, and, he conjectures, they likely had a role in the compilation of the material in Numbers (1990: 15–21; cf. also de Vaux 1961: 155, 225, 251, 394). Levine also puts forward that the title *šōṭĕrîm* refers to the function of issuing written documents or actually writing them, and notes that in 2 Chronicles 26:11 *šōṭēr* is synonymous with *sôpēr* (scribe) (1993: 323–324). Such men were more than secretaries; they were administrative officials (*HALOT* 2:1441).

Perhaps most significantly, the role of such literate administrators would include the dissemination of rulings and regulations to the masses in their capacity as overseers. Exodus 5:6–17 provides an example (here, LXX uses *grammateis* throughout) in the scene where Pharaoh commanded the taskmasters of the people and their *šōṭĕrîm*, regarding the new regulation that the Hebrew slaves should make the same quota of bricks without any official supply of straw. While Harrison had presumed these *šōṭĕrîm* to be Egyptian, it is more probable that they were, as understood in Jewish interpretation, Israelite. Exodus 5:14–17 reads this way, that Pharaoh's taskmasters used the *šōṭĕrîm* of Israel in order to disseminate instruction to the masses in the Hebrew language, and when the Hebrew slaves failed, it was not the taskmasters who were beaten but the *šōṭĕrîm*. This is precisely the function needed in the wilderness, a role that would be useful to Moses, especially in addressing the spiritual condition of the people with YHWH's guidance. The Midrash identifies the seventy *šōṭĕrîm* of Numbers 11 with those of Exodus 5, declaring that it was *because* they had submitted themselves to beatings for the sake of the Israelites, so as not to exhaust the people, that they are now selected and rewarded with sharing the burden of the people with Moses (*Num. Rab.* 15.20; cf. Slotki 1951: 6:665). On this reading, those who were once beaten under Pharaoh's rule for refusing the taskmaster's instructions to deplete the Israelites physically, will now under YHWH's rule publish Moses' instructions to elevate the Israelites spiritually. Once the *šōṭĕrîm* of Exodus 5 are understood as Israelites, then the connection by the Midrash makes good sense: YHWH directed Moses to choose seventy men whom Moses knew to be *šōṭĕrîm*.

In the ancient world, such scribes comprised an elite class of scholars, indispensable in the religious and political realms (see Pearce 1995: 2265, 73). In contrast to the *sōpĕrîm* who may be thought of as 'transcribers', the *šōṭĕrîm* were part of a highly educated scribal elite akin to magistrates, closely affiliated with centralized authority and granted authority not only to read and interpret law but also to execute it, with the biblical usage portraying them, almost always collectively, as (1) relaying commands, including military orders, (2) settling disputes, (3) representing one segment of national authority structures, and (4) closely engaging and representing either king or priest (Parker 2015: 60–64). The emphasis on the prophetic word in Numbers 11 – 14 in general, and within chapters 11–12 in particular, is therefore consistent both with Moses' needs in guiding the Israelites in the wilderness through the divine word, and with YHWH's qualification that the seventy men must be taken from among the *šōṭĕrîm*. In Deuteronomy 31, as Moses inscribes a song from YHWH to teach the people as a witness against them, the *agency* of elders and scribes is brought to the foreground as Moses says: 'Gather to me all the elders of your tribes and your scribes (*šōṭĕrêkem*), and I will speak in their ears these words' (v. 28), language strikingly similar to YHWH's in Numbers 11:16 (see also their role in Deut. 20:5–9; 29:10; Josh. 1:10; 3:2).

YHWH's 'gather unto me' is paralleled by, and defined as, 'take them (*lāqaḥtā 'ōtām*) to the Tent of Meeting'. One might have expected 'bring them' (*bô'* in the hiph.) – and there is a link with the twofold use of *lāqāḥ* in 12:1 – but *lāqāḥ* is sometimes used for establishing a new status, whether of people (Num. 1:17; 3:12, 41, 45) or objects (3:47, 49, 50), a usage in accord with the nuance of marriage as well (Num. 12:1). The seventy men are to be taken to the Tent of Meeting, the designation for YHWH's Dwelling that typically has the cult in mind – Moses' gathering of the seventy is a ritual of ordination, dramatically portraying and effecting the new role of these men. They are to stand in unity 'with' Moses 'there', a symbolic gesture to be sure, but by no means merely symbolic, given YHWH's action (v. 17). Nevertheless, given that Moses receives divine guidance for the people from the Tent of Meeting (7:89), and that he may now stand there in the place of highest authority with seventy other men together before the people, this display becomes testimony to all not only that Moses is no longer alone but that YHWH himself receives and supports the elders in their new role.

17. YHWH's action is set forth as 'I will descend . . . and I will speak . . . and I will lay aside . . . and I will place', with the result that the men will bear the burden with Moses. There are four points of emphasis: (1) YHWH's 'hands on' activity, (2) the Tent of Meeting as the locale for this activity – 'there' (*šām*), (3) the priority of Moses, to whom alone YHWH speaks and from whom he will distribute the Spirit, and (4) the role of the Spirit in the men's burden-sharing with Moses. Language of placing (*śîm*), that YHWH would *place* the spirit on the elders, echoes Moses' questioning of YHWH, that 'you *place* the burden of all this people on me' (v. 11). Both acts of placing (*śîm*) are by YHWH; the first burdens and the second relieves Moses. Underscored in the next story (Num. 12), Moses is accorded great honour by YHWH, who stresses Moses' superiority to other prophets here by speaking directly to Moses alone (cf. Sommer 1999: 610). The *rûaḥ* is the essential means by which the seventy will share the burden of the people with Moses: the first three points – YHWH's descent, at the Tent of Meeting, and his interaction with Moses there – are all for the sake of the fourth, for distributing the Spirit, who has been upon Moses, to the seventy men. Since Moses cannot distribute out of his own possession of the Spirit, YHWH alone must perform that sovereign act. By paralleling YHWH's declaration and its fulfilment, the *rûaḥ*'s role in enabling the elders to shoulder the burden of the people with Moses is clarified (Hymes 2010: 268–269). (See Table 21.)

While, therefore, in the accomplishment report there is a focus on prophesying (vv. 25–27), that particular manifestation of the Spirit, relevant as it is, should not detract from but feed into the fundamental reality that YHWH's distributing of Moses' Spirit to the seventy – the Spirit himself – is the resolution to *Moses' dilemma*, as they will bear the burden of the people with him. The seventy will share in Moses' authority even while their subjection to him is reaffirmed (cf. Weisman 1981: 231).

YHWH's declaration, 'I will speak with you' (*wĕdibbartî 'immĕkā*) not only reflects the reality of 7:89, but echoes his words at Sinai: 'Look, I will come to you in a thick cloud, so the people may hear when I speak with you (*bĕdabbĕrî 'immāk*) and so believe in you for ever' (Exod. 19:9). Not only does YHWH's display create another Sinai experience, but as at Sinai he orchestrates the distribution of the spirit for the sake of upholding Moses' prophetic role in the experience of the elders and, through them, for all the tribes (cf. Granot 2012: 68). Chapters 11–15, related to the outer camp of tribes, focus on the tribes' need to follow YHWH through Moses' prophetic office.

The term *'āṣal* has been taken by some as a diminution of Moses, since YHWH's giving of the Spirit to the seventy involves 'withdrawing' or 'laying aside' from the Spirit that is on Moses. Such readings, lining up with a negative view of Moses in this chapter, see YHWH's action as a punishment of Moses (so Milgrom 1990: 377; Sommer 1999: 616–617; Calvin 2003b: 4:24–25). However, YHWH clearly desires to relieve some of Moses' burden and the ritual installment of the seventy men serves in many respects to honour Moses himself – and then, in 12:6–9, YHWH vigorously defends him as his singular servant. With the wide consensus

Table 21: Role of the Spirit

11:17	11:25
aα – I will descend and speak with you there	aα – YHWH descended . . . and spoke with him
aβ – I will take some of the spirit which is on you	aβ – he took some of the spirit which was on him
aγ – and I will put it on them;	aγ – and he put it on the seventy men, the elders
bα – and they will *bear the burden of the people* with you	bα – and when *the spirit rested on them*
bβ – so that you will not bear it alone.	bβ – they prophesied but did not continue.

of the history of interpretation, it is better to understand the distribution of Moses' Spirit as the sharing of a torch or candle flame, which loses nothing of its vigour when its flame is used to light another, an analogy used by Philo (*Gig.* 6.24) and the rabbinic tradition (*Num. Rab.* 15.19; *Tan.*, *Be-ha'alotekha* 12; *Sif.* 93), along with other Jewish (e.g. Rashi, Ibn Ezra) and Christian commentators (Origen, *Homilies on Num*bers 6.2.1; Augustine, *De Trinitate* 6.1.1; also Ellicott, Gill and James-Fausset-Brown). The Midrash also recalls how even forty years later, Moses, spiritually undiminished, had imparted much of the Spirit to Joshua (*Tan.*, *Beha'alotcha* 16; cf. Num. 27:18–20; Deut. 34:9).

The *'āṣal* action on the part of YHWH underscores that the Spirit received by the seventy elders (minus Eldad and Medad?) bears the impress of Moses himself: YHWH will lay aside 'from the Spirit that is *upon you*' (*min-hārûaḥ 'ăšer 'ālêkā*). Moses, having received the empowering *rûaḥ* from YHWH, has left his imprint – his selfless life as servant of YHWH on behalf of Israel – upon the Spirit, and it is this particular humanity-in-service-of-YHWH's-agenda that will be 'put upon them' (*śamtî 'ălêhem*), the elder scribes, ensuring that these leaders serve both in accord with Moses' *persona* and as under his authority, as those whose office derives from a share in Moses' authority. Nothing could make YHWH's point more clearly that Israel does not simply need more leadership, but more of Moses' leadership, more of his character to *characterize* the people themselves. The Spirit's role in the Camp – with Israel's spiritual condition in mind – may be summed up with 'more of Moses' and 'less of the gathered-rabble'. More than this, by distributing from the Spirit that is upon Moses, YHWH *safeguards the status and role of Moses* as the singular conduit of mediation between Israel and the Maker of heaven and earth. The theology is profound. First, part of the dismal saga in the wilderness relates to Moses' own confessed inability to raise the people's spiritual nature. A distribution of YHWH's Spirit holds promise for relieving Moses' burden even if, in the end, the remedy will fall short of altering either the character or the fate of the first generation of Israelites. Second, distributing YHWH's Spirit through the mediator is a biblical paradigm observed as well with the Messiah and the people of God in the new covenant. The prophetic promise of the gift of the Spirit is fulfilled *through* Jesus Christ in a manner that renders the gift particularly as the Spirit *of Christ* – the Spirit who has received the impress of Christ's life according to his humanity, his denial of self, his death to sin, and his life of utter devotion and obedience to God, fully loving both the Father and his neighbour, along with his resurrection as a new creation, so as to apply that life to God's people, conforming them to his pattern of humanity (on this topic, see Gaffin 1987: 78–97; Ferguson 1996; Morales 2015: 279–298). The Elijah–Elisha narrative in 2 Kings 2 presents another scenario where the spirit is transferred to a person, having the impress of a previous human character who functions as an archetype, the 'spirit of Elijah' (cf. Weisman 1981; Gertel 2002: 76–77). As YHWH's chosen sieve, Moses's role as the fountainhead of all prophecy and revelation, the Torah, is focus here; ever afterward, a test of new revelation is its conformity to the Torah – the former prophets demonstrate an outworking of Torah, and the latter prophets both stand upon and apply Torah (and, although the new wine of the Messiah must burst the old skin, NT authors are nevertheless burdened to show continuity and conformity with Moses, see John 5:46; Acts 17:11).

YHWH's response aims at strengthening the spiritual dynamic of the twelve tribes, through his word and Spirit, as a counterbalance to the people's fleshly nature. Various scholars have noted that Numbers 11 opposes flesh and spirit in something of a 'quasi Pauline manner' – while the lust for flesh leads to death, YHWH's agenda of life is accomplished through the gift of the Spirit (Römer 1997: 488; 2007: 437; cf. also Seebass 1993: 2:32). Schart explains that flesh is only vivified by spirit (e.g. Gen. 6:17; Job 12:10), but the people lust only for flesh, while Moses yearns for all the people to receive the Spirit – Israel's life is bound up with obedience to those on whom the Spirit rests (1990: 164–165; cf. Hymes 2010: 266). The people's desire (v. 4): 'Who (*mî*) will cause us to consume flesh (*bāśār*)!' will be countered by Moses' desire (v. 29): 'Who (*mî*) will give all the people of YHWH to be prophets, that YHWH will give his Spirit (*rûaḥ*) upon them!' This guiding pair of terms, flesh and spirit, is further coordinated by use of the root '-s-p: The 'gathered-rabble' (*hā'sapsup*; 11:4), influencing the sons of Israel into lusting for flesh, are countered by YHWH's 'gathering' to himself seventy elder-scribes who will serve by the Spirit as an opposing force (11:16) (Samet 2014a: 138–139). While flesh is opposed by spirit, so too, then, the gathered-rabble's influence is opposed by Moses' influence, which is to be strengthened by the seventy spirit-empowered elders. Put this way, the issue of Israel's identity, nature, and end are clarified: gathered-rabble or Moses (YHWH), flesh or spirit, Egypt or land of Canaan?

The gravity of the occasion is brought out in the language of YHWH's descent to the Tent of Meeting, language which had also been used when he descended on Mount Sinai (Exod. 19:11; cf. *Num. Rab.* 15.25). The Dwelling is an architectural embodiment of Mount Sinai, making the parallel stronger – so, too, the presence of seventy elders on the mountain in Exodus 24:9–18. Exodus 19 – 24 highlights the role of Moses as mediator, given his many ascents and descents of the mountain to facilitate communication between YHWH and Israel. Numbers 11, which brings the seventy elders from the Camp to the Tent, and from the Tent back to the Camp, similarly underscores their calling to deepen Moses' mediation among the people in Israel's Camp.

18–20. YHWH, after first addressing the burden of his servant, now addresses the people's lust for flesh. He deals with their denigration of his own honour, including their denial of his ability to spread a table of meat in the wilderness. The supply of meat will both vindicate YHWH and serve as judgement on the people for their ungodly lusting: he will be vindicated to such an extent that the flesh which they longed to consume will itself consume them, coming out of their nostrils. Just as the monotony of manna had made YHWH's provision detestable in their eyes (v. 6), he would now give them a continually abundant supply of meat – not for one, two, five, ten or twenty days, but for a month of days – that their base lust would be unveiled in all of its senseless depravity, for this flesh itself would become loathsome to them, insufficient for their brazen desire and even detestable. The term *zārā'* is a hapax legomenon, perhaps deriving from *zûr* or *zrh*. Hirsch understands the word as 'vomit', having gradational variant and cognate meanings in the realm of 'scatter', 'project outward', and 'erupt' (M. Clark 1999: 70), an understanding that builds on YHWH's previous line (until it comes out of your nostrils). On this reading, the judgement is one of poetic justice: the very flesh they lust insatiably to consume will become that which retches out of their stomachs. Even with the understanding of 'loathsome', judgement is underlined. God's people are regularly warned that in turning to other gods they risked the judgement of receiving what they desire (e.g. Deut. 4:27–28; 32:37–38; Rom. 1:21–26).

Israel's depravity and rebellion in this account cannot be mitigated without skewing the book's message – YHWH is neither capricious nor vengeful. His answer for the people is enclosed with references to Egypt (vv. 18, 20): 'For it was good for us in Egypt' / 'Why did we ever come out of Egypt', remarks which they made while weeping 'in the ears of YHWH' and 'before his face'. The people's implied threat of a return to Egypt, rejecting their deliverance from bondage by YHWH, is part of a larger current building up to Numbers 14:1–4, where the people reject the land in unbelief (Hymes 2010: 262, 266; on the role of Egypt in Numbers, see Greifenhagen 2002: 177–205). They have despised YHWH, along with their deliverance out of Egypt, scorning their redemption, their vocation, their good inheritance in the land. By contrast, Moses' central concern is in bringing the people into the land (v. 12b).

This planned judgement by YHWH nevertheless should not be conflated with the actual turn of events (v. 33), as if God were deceiving his people (contra Milgrom 1990: 380). Rather, it was the people's unfettered frenzied lust that 'kindled' anew YHWH's fierce anger, resulting in a great and immediate smiting of them. Here, however, YHWH has already announced his intended judgement that will serve to discipline the people, teaching them afresh of his ability as their Shepherd to supply a table in the wilderness, but also teaching them to fear him and follow him closely. YHWH's provision was to be a divine demonstration, involving a special manifestation of his presence, for which they were to 'sanctify yourselves' (*hitqaddĕšû*, v. 18), language recalling the command for Moses to sanctify the people for YHWH's advent upon Mount Sinai (Exod. 19:10; cf. Haran 1985: 265–268). Especially when combined with 'tomorrow', such sanctification functions as preparation for a theophanic encounter with God (cf. Milgrom 1990: 384–385). One of the leading theological metaphors for Israel's cult was that of divine hospitality, feasting with God in the house of God (see Morales 2015: 18, 137–138; cf. Pss 23:6; 36:8–9), and YHWH's role as divine host also functions as a motif within the context of the wilderness journeys, with Israel often portrayed as an ungrateful and avaricious guest (see Stallman 1999: 216–270; Ps. 78:19–29). Whether or not meat was considered a sacred meal of commensality, fostering the people's table fellowship with YHWH, the people are to prepare themselves because it is YHWH who will provide the meat – they are to understand the provision as no mere happenstance or bare providence, but as a visit and special manifestation of YHWH himself in response to their having spoken and wept in his ears. Viberg (1992: 9, 75) offers four criteria for biblical covenantal meals, which fulfil a legal function when performed under proper circumstances: (1) the meal's pivotal position in the literary structure of the story, followed by a geographical dislocation, (2) the use of covenantal terminology, (3) the lack of other explicit means for satisfying the covenant, and (4) the mere fact a meal is mentioned. Reis (2005: 227) makes a good case for understanding God's provision of flesh here as a covenantal meal according to Viberg's stipulations, including use of *kārat* ('cut off', v. 33), but there is not enough in the text to affirm that 'God intends to participate in the legality of covenant-sealing', as she suggests. At least *within* Israel's covenant established at Sinai, God's provision of flesh, for which the people were to consecrate themselves, is portrayed as a weighty and set-apart occasion where the people would be confronted by YHWH's holy presence and power. Exodus 16 describes YHWH's arrival for provision of quail and manna as seeing 'the glory of YHWH' (vv. 7, 9), *the first time the nation of Israel beheld YHWH's glory*, and as having the knowledge of him as its primary purpose: 'you will know that I am YHWH your God' (v. 12). Needless to say, the people's ravenous, frenzied behaviour in 11:32 was not in accord with guest ethics on any standard of hospitality, and constituted brazen rebellion before the face of YHWH their host, whose advent required their consecration.

Gunneweg, who considers the elders account to be a secondary and superficial insertion, protests that the seventy elders could not, with or without the Spirit, conjure up meat so as to relieve Moses (Gunneweg 1990: 169–170; cf. Wellhausen 1889: 99; Noth 1968: 89; Fisch 1986: 48). Yet, YHWH's own vision of the people's problem penetrates more deeply, and perceives the spiritual remedy to their lusting. The elder-scribes form a positive divine response, aimed at lifting the spirituality of the people, while the month-long provision of quails formed a negative disciplinary response, aimed at causing the people to despise their craving. Given that the provision of both the elder-scribes and the flesh serves as YHWH's twofold response to Moses' plea, the people's consecration may also have in view the ordination ritual (whether or not it took place the same day), which likewise involved a special manifestation and work of YHWH – a point that further underscores the heinousness of their instant dive into gluttonous frenzy. Upon the heels of such a formal ceremony, a divine demonstration of the community's spiritual nature and vocation, the people – without pause – sink into fleshly lust. Also significant, of the two commands of the chapter, 'gather to me' (v. 16) and 'sanctify yourselves' (v. 18), only the first command, to gather the elders to YHWH, is recounted as fulfilled (v. 24). As the text explains that Moses 'went out and spoke to the people the words of YHWH' (v. 24), their non-fulfilment portrays the people as negligent and even defiant.

21–22. Moses' response brings out the remarkable nature of YHWH's provision: the people number some six hundred thousand on foot, and yet Moses, through YHWH, will provide enough flesh for them to eat for a whole month. As Moses uses the term 'slaughter' (*šāḥēṭ*), it could be his concern includes the special handling of meat in relation to the cultic system, an issue addressed previously in Leviticus 17 and, later, in Deuteronomy 12 (Parker 2012). Moses' language underscores less his incredulity over YHWH's ability to feed such a large number of people; rather, his incredulity concerns any presumed limits to the people's lust for flesh. The repeated use of *māṣā' lāhem* (found for them) suggests that all the flesh on earth would fail to satiate the magnitude of their lust (also Levine 1993: 325). Although it is easy for readers to miss the grave depths of the people's lusting, Moses saw clearly the nature of their spiritual depravity and its implications for the whole agenda of Israel's vocation. The people are insatiable but YHWH had declared he would so provide flesh as to cause them to despise it, to retch it out of their stomachs. Some see Moses' use of the figure 600,000, along with his use of 'the people' (vs *all* the people'), as an intentional exclusion of the 'gathered-rabble' who had instigated the people's rebellion (e.g. Jobling 1978: 1:61 n. 2; Milgrom 1990: 88 n. 21), a suggestive if overly subtle reading. Numbers 11 – 12 deal with non-Israelite relationships, but on either side of this story (10:29–32 and 12:1) Moses shows a proclivity to *include* non-Israelites rather than to exclude them.

23. YHWH's words to Moses render the provision of quails as a demonstration for Moses' sake (cf. Milgrom 1990: 88), no less than the provision of seventy elder-scribes: now 'you' will see if my word happens 'to you'. In addition to setting before Moses the help of seventy spiritual men, YHWH would direct his servant's gaze upon himself, on YHWH's limitless ability, fortifying Moses with the reminder that the 'hand of YHWH' has most emphatically not been shortened. However the people are judged, Moses' vision of the hand – the strength, power, and ability

– of YHWH will be renewed in what 'you will see'. Moreover, as YHWH had already declared what he would do, the demonstration would also renew Moses' utter trust in and reliance upon YHWH's word.

24. Four wayyiqtol's (sequential action verbs) describe Moses' obedience, intertwining YHWH's twofold response: he went out (from YHWH), he spoke (to the people), he gathered and he stood (the seventy elder-scribes). The first two verbs ('went out' and 'spoke') apply YHWH's response to the people's lusting (v. 18), and the second two ('gathered' and 'stood') apply YHWH's response to Moses' leadership crisis (v. 16). While the first two verbs involve a movement away from the central Tent, the second two verbs involve a movement toward the Tent. Moses 'went out' (*yēṣē'*) from YHWH's presence, likely from within the holy place (cf. 7:89), and spoke to the people 'the words of YHWH', which refer primarily to YHWH's planned provision of flesh and the people's need to consecrate themselves. Second, he gathered the seventy men of the elders of the people and stood them round about the Tent. Whether the idea is that the men encircled the Tent within the courtyard or that they encircled the courtyard itself ('Tent' by metonymy) is difficult to determine. Levites had been instructed to 'camp around the Dwelling' (1:50, 53), and the Israelite tribes were warned to camp 'at a distance around the Tent of Meeting' (2:2) – both refer to the camp of the *Shekhinah*, including the courtyard. In the Camp's geography, the elders are placed symbolically on a level between Moses and the twelve tribes. The quail, or 'flesh', will surround the outer rim of the Camp, leading the lusters to continue the centripetal movement away from the centre.

The two sides of God's response are interrelated and deeply unified: the new role of the elder-scribes, who are elders 'of the people', is for the sake of guiding the people spiritually, and the provision of flesh is ultimately for the sake of rebuking the people, both of which should also help with Moses' burden in leading them. YHWH's response has a long-term positive element and a short-term negative element, both of which address the people's low spiritual estate, even while addressing Moses' burden. YHWH had called Moses to 'gather to me seventy elders' (v. 16) and 'say to the people' (v. 18), and this verse reports his compliance (in reverse, logical order) as he 'spoke to the people' and 'gathered seventy men'. Such compliance highlights the lack of any report of obedience for YHWH's other command, that the people consecrate themselves.

25. 'And YHWH descended' (*wayyēred yhwh*) is a rare phrase in the Torah, its last two uses referring to YHWH's Advent upon Sinai, particularly for engagement with Moses (Exod. 19:20; 34:5), and its use here links this story to the one that follows (12:5). The same verb is used of the descent of the manna in 11:9 (Jobling 1978: 1:51–52). While 'the cloud' likely refers to 'the pillar of cloud' (Maier 2015: 87), use of 'the cloud' forms a stronger link with the Sinai theophany – and the phrase 'YHWH descended in a cloud' (*wayyēred yhwh beʿānon*) is verbatim that used in Exodus 34:5 when YHWH proclaimed his Name to Moses, leading the servant to bow his head earthward in worship (see Exod. 34:6–8). In the midst of the apostasy of the golden calf and its consequent judgement, Moses had needed a deeper understanding of God's glory and ways; it may be the seventy elders are receiving a highly mediated form of the same understanding and experience. The parallels with Mount Sinai are especially relevant. There YHWH had planned to speak with Moses, allowing the people to overhear his thunderous voice to him, so as to instill proper reverence and trust in Moses as their mediator (Exod. 19:19). The giving of the Decalogue was, therefore, a theophany, a public revelation to all Israel which had underscored Moses' authoritative role (Dozeman 2000: 33), and there seems to be a similar purpose here, which brings the seventy elders into an authoritative position as well, though under Moses.

The Tent, as Westermann noted (1970: 244), is central to all of YHWH's activity in the wilderness, whether slaking his people's thirst (Num. 20), offering asylum to his faithful followers (Num. 14:10), or manifesting divine judgement (Num. 16). But while the elders are stationed at the Tent of Meeting, the place otherwise reserved for Moses, YHWH nevertheless speaks to Moses alone and the Spirit he distributes to the elders is the Spirit that 'was upon' Moses (cf. Gunneweg 1990: 175). The elders receive the Spirit with the impress of Moses' character and calling, especially for spreading YHWH's will, as revealed to and through Moses, among the people. The verb *'āṣal* was discussed at verse 17, but here we add Reis's observation of a possible three-way pun: *'āṣal* also denotes 'beside', 'joined' and 'chiefs' or 'nobles', so 'the reader understands that the chiefs Moses has selected will work beside him, joined in prophecy' (2005: 222). The Spirit from YHWH is clearly the *sine qua non*, the absolutely essential element, of prophecy (e.g. 2 Sam. 23:2; 2 Peter 1:21), necessary for communication with God to become communication from God. YHWH descends and communicates with Moses – an act that lies at the heart of the exodus redemption, the Sinai covenant and the Torah itself – and the elders now receive of the Spirit that was upon Moses in order to multiply and extend Moses' influence throughout the Camp. They stand as an extension of Moses himself, but not in his place – they do not receive divine revelation directly, and thus do not each become 'another Moses'. Like ministers of the Word today, Dozeman explains, the seventy elders will 'govern by interpreting and applying the revelation received by Moses to Israel's life in the camp' – since preachers 'do not speak with God face to face', their message is authoritative only inasmuch as it is 'authenticated by Scripture' (1998: 112). In conveying his Spirit to the elders *through* Moses, YHWH ensures the elders partake of Moses' authority even while subjecting them to it, maintaining the hierarchy (Weisman 1981: 231).

Bourke (1959: 540) observes that in

> this episode we encounter for the first time the idea of the *ruach* of Yahweh as *charism*, as divine activity working in and through the bodily faculties of men, and it is immensely important to realize how directly and immediately this idea grows out of 'presence theology', the conception of God dwelling in the midst of the community.

Putting the spirit upon the elders is further described as the Spirit 'rested (*nôaḥ*) upon them', which, both here and in verse 26 regarding Eldad and Medad's reception, connotes permanence. By contrast, in Judges (14:6, 19; 15:14) and 1 Samuel (10:6, 10; 11:6; 16:13; 18:10), the Spirit 'rushes' (*ṣālaḥ*), sometimes repeatedly, conveying the idea of temporary, focused empowerment (see Schart 1990: 164; Levine 1993: 340–341). Likely, it is the notion of permanence associated with 'rest' that leads to the final remark that the elders did not prophesy again. Although some translations prefer 'they did not cease' (AV), *wĕlō' yāsāpû* is literally rendered 'they did not add', implying that this moment of prophesying did not continue and was probably meant as a sign to the people of the elders' new spirit-empowered role. The verb *yāsap* (add), a homophone with the key word *'āsap* (gather), may also refer to their not 'adding' to Moses' revelation, as directed in Deuteronomy 4:2 (cf. also 5:22; 12:32): 'Do not add (*yāsap*) to the word that I command you and do not take away from it' (Reis 2005: 223). As a one-time event, moreover, prophesying is secondary to the distribution of the Spirit as YHWH's answer to Moses' need (cf. Hymes 2007: 5).

What does it mean that 'they prophesied'? Scholars commonly assert that *wayyitnabbĕ'û* refers primarily to ecstatic prophecy in terms of frenzied action (e.g. NJPS; Jeremias 1997; Mills 1997). Before the twentieth century, however, most translations (e.g. LXX, TgO, TgNeof and TgPs-J; see *Sif.* 93; *Num. Rab.* 15.19) render the term as 'prophesied' (Parker 2015: 24 n. 1), and shift to 'speaking ecstatically' has been increasingly contested, neither required by the hithpael of *n-b-'* nor reasonable within the context of alleviating Moses' burden (see Wilson 1979: 336; Petersen 1981: 29; Uffenheimer 1988: 263; Levison 2003; Hymes 2010: 260). Rather, the general prophetic behaviour of speaking – prophesying or predicting – such as in 1 Kings 22:8, 18 and Jeremiah 14:14, 29:27, appears to be in view here (Gunneweg 1990: 176). While one-time ecstatic behaviour may be suggested as serving to confirm the reception of the Spirit, no less than one-time prophetic speech, yet nothing within the context of the Torah would lead to such an understanding of prophesying. On the contrary, L. Wood (1966) addresses all the prevalent arguments for ecstatic behaviour, concluding that the basic meaning of prophesy is 'to speak forth a message', and Alden (1966) claims there 'is no evidence whatever in the Bible for the actions usually denoted by ecstasy'. Moreover, the Spirit that rests upon the seventy elders is described as deriving from the Spirit that was upon Moses, and Moses is nowhere portrayed as displaying ecstatic behaviour – but he is every-where portrayed as delivering the speech and will of YHWH. In short, there is no compelling reason for understanding the elders' prophesying as anything other than intelligible, Mosaic speech (Parker 2015: 49). It is specifically as Spirit-inspired scribes who will share in Moses' prophetic ministry that the elders become a source of burden-sharing with Moses.

Using by way of example the previous suggestion of YHWH's self-revelation to Moses in Exodus 34:5–7, the scenario entailed here would be as follows: YHWH speaks to Moses, proclaiming his Name to him, and distributes of the Spirit upon Moses so that the Spirit rests on the seventy elders (perhaps granting a 'word-based' vision of YHWH), who then start declaring the Name of YHWH, that he is 'merciful, gracious, slow to anger, and abounding in loving-kindness and faithfulness' (Exod. 34:6). The elder-scribes will, by spiritual empowerment, continue to spread God's word through Moses to the people, a function displayed dramatically and symbolically in the one-time event of their proph-esying during their appointment. As Gunneweg observes (1990: 177), the account yields an etiology though not of prophetism in general – rather of prophecy *in relation to Moses*. Furthermore, within the wider context, it may be that a correlation is to be drawn with 5:11–31, where the Spirit (of jealousy) comes upon a man, invigorating him to seek the purity of his wife and of the Camp (note use of *hamqannē'* in 11:29).

The elder-scribes will help Moses by way of furthering his *torah* from YHWH among the people, 'instructing and admonishing the people with an authority that was recognized as having its source in God' (Hertz 1988: 616 n. 25; similarly, Reis 2005: 224). While the text offers no explicit description of the content of their prophecy, the Midrash infers from 11:18 that the elders prophesied, saying, 'Sanctify yourselves against tomorrow', while Eldad and Medad prophesied that Moses would die in the wilderness and Joshua would bring Israel into the land of Canaan (*Num. Rab.* 15.19). The distinction is sensible inasmuch as the elders presumably prophesy only of what they hear YHWH speak to Moses (vv. 17, 25), while Eldad and Medad's prophesying is outside of that circumstance. Questions over the content of Eldad and Medad's prophecy even generated what appears to have been a widely known 'book of Eldad and Medad' (prior to the second century AD), now lost though a short sentence of it is quoted in Shepherd of Hermas (*Vision* 2.3.4; see Bauckham 2013).

The public ordination of the elders included not only the elements of YHWH's descent, speaking to Moses, and distribution of the spirit. Emphasis on the locale of the elders, around the Tent, in the midst of a theophany, makes their survival – the simple reflection that they did not die – a testimony about their status (cf. Exod. 24:11), especially given previous warnings about encroachment (Num. 1:51–53; 3:38). Levison (2003), focusing on the terms *'āṣal* and *nûaḥ*, and broadening consideration to Numbers 12:6–8, brings out parallels between the seventy elders of Numbers 11 with the seventy of Exodus 24, and argues for understanding the elders' prophesying as a controlled, communal visionary experience that served to assist Moses in leading Israel. Affinities begin with the description of the elders that ascend Mount Sinai in Exodus 24 as *'ăṣîlê* of the sons of Israel (v. 11), an unusual term probably having the same root as *'āṣal* in Numbers 11:17, 25. Rendered 'nobles' or 'chief men' in standard versions, an *'āṣîl*, Levine suggests, is one who has received the Spirit of YHWH, explaining why the *'ăṣîlîm* were not harmed in God's presence in Exodus 24:11 (1993: 339). The Midrash also connects Numbers 11 with Exodus 24, stating that the original seventy elders of Exodus 24 had been consumed in the Taberah judgement (Num. 11:1–3), necessitating a new set of seventy elders for Moses (*Num. Rab.* 15.24). Admitting that Numbers 11 does not disclose the content of their vision, Levison suggests a vision of God not unlike the one at Sinai, adding: 'The sheer weight of a communal visionary experience underscores that Moses was indeed not alone, that the elders would bear the burden of the people *with* Moses, that Moses need not undertake the responsibility of leadership in isolation' (2003: 515; emphasis original). Noting that the Micaiah ben Imlah story (1 Kgs 22) uses the hithpael of *n-b-'* three times, the account emphasizing YHWH's prophetic word and Micaiah's vision of the heavenly council, Levison musters the prophetic visions of Numbers 12:6 and of the Balaam story (Num. 22 – 24), to make a case for understanding prophesying as including a visionary experience – but not that of frenzied ecstasy. Perhaps the elders' vision was similar to Balaam's, of the Camp of YHWH's hosts as paradise, along with its divinely ordained prospects (24:1–9). This at least is the prophetic vision given to the book's audience through Balaam after 'the Spirit of God came upon him' (24:2), enabling him to see the heavenly nature and future of Israel. Levison also studies the term *nûaḥ*, describing how the Spirit 'rested' on the elders (Num. 11:25), and demonstrates from similar usage in 2 Kings 2:15, where the spirit of Elijah 'rests' on Elisha, and in Isaiah 11:2, where the Spirit of YHWH 'rests' on the Messianic deliverer, that the result of such action is a permanent endowment for leading God's people (2003: 518–519).

Jobling noted many parallels between Exod. 33:7–11, with its depiction of how YHWH and Moses used to communicate, and Numbers 11, with its presentation of the Tent of Meeting as the locale for prophetic utterance, also observing connections more widely between Exodus 32 – 33 and Numbers 11 – 12, including Moses' seeing YHWH (Exod. 33:20–23 // Num. 12:8), Aaron's rebellion (Exod. 32 // Num. 12), and

Moses' readiness for death (Exod. 32:32 // Num. 11:15) (1978: 1:59). Building on Jobling's work, Parker marks comparisons and contrasts (2015: 232):

In precise parallel, the elders of Numbers 11 are described as follows:

1. Coming to the Tent   Exod. 33:8   Num. 11: 24
2. Receiving the descending cloud of presence Exod. 33:9a   Num. 11:25a
3. Listening to YHWH speak with Moses   Exod. 33:9b   Num. 11:25:a
4. With Joshua present at the Tent   Exod. 33:11   Num. 11:28

The distinctions between these accounts are equally precise:

5. In Exod. 33 the people arise and worship, each at the opening of his tent (33:8, 10), whereas in Num. 11 the people are weeping, each at the opening of his tent (11:10).
6. Rather than being allowed inside the Tent as Moses (Exod. 33:9), the elders are set around it, *between* the people and the place where Moses and YHWH meet, a symbolically and ritually rich depiction.

The elders' position around the Tent of Meeting, the locale of God's revelation, grants them authority. As those who hear YHWH speaking to Moses, the elder-scribes are placed in the strategic role of being publishers and teachers of God's communication with Moses, a role that of necessity includes being interpreters of Torah as enabled by Moses' spirit of YHWH who rests on them (see Parker 2015). YHWH's guidance of the Camp through speech to Moses within the Tent of Meeting had already been shown in a wondrous passage (7:89), and now seventy elder-scribes are granted a one-time audience to this mystery.

Given the parallels observed with Exodus 19, 24 and 33 (also Deut. 4:10–11), it seems YHWH is giving the seventy elder-scribes a new Sinai experience, aimed at deepening their consecration to him for the sake of serving alongside and under the authority of Moses.

26–30. Between verses 24b–25 and 30, which together recount the expected fulfilment of YHWH's speech (vv. 16–17), we have an unexpected story of Eldad and Medad, whose names mean something like 'God loved' and 'Beloved', respectively, based on the root *y-d-d* (cf. Levine 1993: 315), though *yādad* has the meaning 'to cast (a lot)' (cf. BDB 391) and may possibly refer to the exceptional nature of their receiving YHWH's Spirit. Although the text describes them as two 'men' (*'ănāšîm*), the context – that they were among those 'written', and that they too received the Spirit – has led to the nearly unanimous understanding that they were among the elders of Israel. Interestingly, while understanding them to be among the chosen elders, Wiesel (1999) portrays them as young, an intuition in accord with their place in the camp and also with the tradition that has them representing leadership for the second generation of Israelites in the wilderness. Similarly, the Midrash identifies Eldad with 'Elidad the son of Chislon' (Num. 34:21) and Medad with 'Kemuel the son of Shiphtan' (34:24), both of whom entered the land (*Num. Rab.* 15.19).

What has been less certain in the history of interpretation is whether or not they are to be numbered among the seventy, or if they bring the tally up to seventy-two. The latter figure yields six elders per tribe, in accord with their representative function. The phrase 'they were left' is a preferable translation to 'they remained', since *wayyiššā'ărû* (in niph.) is used in the Pentateuch for 'remaining' primarily in the sense of being left after an event such as the Flood (Gen. 7:23) or the exile (Deut. 4:27; 28:62), an enigmatic statement that balances the other remark that 'they had not gone out toward the Tent' – in other words, these statements do not imply wilful rebellion on their part, but may just as readily be used in a situation whereby the two men were prevented from attending at the Tent. In isolation, verse 26 may be read straightforwardly as referring to two men among the seventy elder-scribes who were 'written' (as in 'registered' among the seventy) but which for some reason or another had not gone to the Tent, and yet who nevertheless received the Spirit within the locale of the outer camp. Such a reading, however, faces the difficulty of the language in verses 24–25, which refers to Moses gathering 'seventy' men and to YHWH's distributing the Spirit upon 'seventy' elders. The issue may be resolved to a degree by understanding 'seventy' as an idiom for a large or comprehensive group, or in understanding verses 24–25 as a generalized summary, a rhetorical device to set up the Eldad and Medad story as a surprising turn of events. If they were among the seventy, why were they left, or why did they not come? Jewish tradition fills the gap by portraying Eldad and Medad's love for the people, a solidarity with them that was rewarded by YHWH in the Spirit's resting on them even in the Camp. Given the situation in Numbers 9, where certain 'men' ('ănāšîm) were unable to participate in Passover due to corpse pollution, one can only speculate about such a scenario here.

Another question that arises from the story is whether the Spirit received by Eldad and Medad is from the Spirit that was upon Moses, as with the seventy elders around the Tent. Of itself, the phrase 'the Spirit rested on them' does not necessarily imply that the Spirit was not from that of Moses (as per *Tan., Beha'alotcha* 12), any more than does the phrase 'the Spirit rested upon them' (v. 25). Moses' reference to 'his (YHWH's) Spirit' (v. 29) is also not determinative since Moses would understand the Spirit resting on himself in the same manner. Nevertheless, the common scholarly position assumes that since Eldad and Medad were not made to stand with Moses in Moses' locale around the Tent, that the Spirit they received was directly from YHWH, and this may well be the case. While the gift of the Spirit to the seventy elders around the Tent highlights the character and authority of Moses and the Torah, the gift of the Spirit to Eldad and Medad highlights the sovereignty of YHWH to work how he wills (also Artus 2017). (See Fig. 10.) Such surprising activity by the sovereign Spirit may anticipate his use of Balaam later in Numbers (24:2; cf. John 3:8).

What the text emphasizes is not 'Spirit of YHWH' versus 'Spirit of YHWH through Moses', but rather the *locale* of the Spirit's reception and consequent prophesying, 'around the Tent' versus 'in the Camp', a contrast that likely comes to the same point theologically: the Spirit of God is sovereignly able to work outside established channels although this is not the norm. The movement of YHWH's Spirit, from the central Tent (leaders) to the outer camp (the people), already gestures toward Moses' ardent desire for all the people to be given YHWH's Spirit in verse 29 (cf. Cotton 2001: 9). The Tent area represents Moses' position and authority, while the outer camp is the place of the twelve tribes generally, who derive their guidance and life from the central camp of the *Shekhinah* through Moses. Moreover, one function of Moses' response

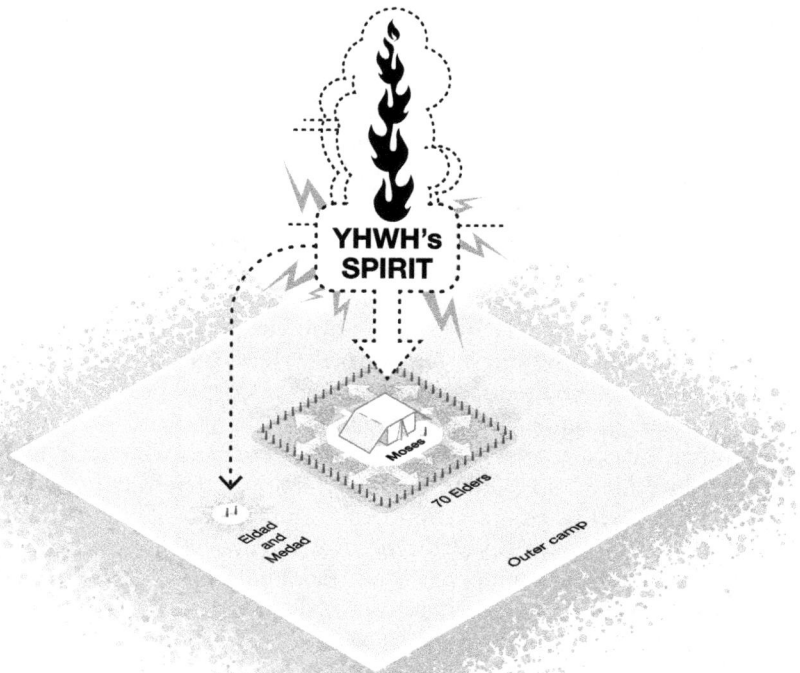

Figure 10: Distributing YHWH's Spirit

to Joshua in 11:29 is precisely to provide Moses' endorsement of such prophesying (cf. Burns 1980: 87–88), which itself asserts the authoritative role of his Torah.

Eldad and Medad prophesied 'in the Camp' (*bammaḥăneh*). Although the additional caveat that they 'did not do so again' is absent here, such is likely to be understood based on the previous verse – and there is certainly no example of their prophesying afterward. However, understanding the reception of the Spirit to be directly from YHWH, rather than through Moses, may lead to interpreting the caveat's absence as pregnant with potential for future prophesying on their part. Furthermore, the text not only says 'they prophesied' (v. 26), but they 'are prophesying' (v. 27), a continuous situation which contrasts with that of the elders at the Tent – and Joshua specifically bids Moses to make them cease (v. 28). Possibly, then, there is a variety of contrasts between the elders on the one hand and Eldad and Medad on the other: (1) the elders are unnamed while Eldad and Medad are named, (2) the elders stand around the Tent while Eldad and Medad are in the Camp, (3) the elders are given of the Spirit that is upon Moses while Eldad and Medad receive the Spirit directly from YHWH, (4) the elders' prophecy is related to what they hear YHWH speak to Moses while Eldad and Medad's prophesying is independent of that circumstance, and (5) the elders prophesy and cease while Eldad and Medad continue prophesying at least on that occasion.

The scene leads to the demonstration of Moses' self-effacing boweddownness, since he is bidden by Joshua to restrain them and he refuses to do so. Once more, the focus is on the locale of the Camp. The lad's report highlights one point alone in a threefold manner, that the men, who 'were left in the Camp' and who 'had not gone out toward the Tent', were now prophesying 'in the Camp' (cf. Lichtenstein 2014a: 148). The issue is not merely their 'prophesying' but *where* they are doing so. In an interesting instance of gap-filling, Jewish tradition depicts Eldad and Medad prophesying about Moses' death in the wilderness and how Joshua would bring the people into the land (*Tan., Beha'alotcha* 12; cf. Soloveitchik 1974). The tradition makes use of two latent aspects of the text: Moses' own request to be slain (v. 15), which raises the issue of the significance of his death for Israel, and the figure of Joshua (v. 28), the first mention of him in Numbers, along with his evident consternation at the prophesying, as if he does not want to hear of his premature succession of Moses. The suggestion is also appealing in terms of Jobling's geographical code since Joshua is cognate with both Canaan and the younger generation that will enter the land, whereas Moses is cognate with the wilderness and the older generation that will die in the wilderness (1978: 1:49). From the text's emphasis on locale, Joshua is likely jealous for Moses' honour inasmuch as Eldad and Medad are not with the other elders who are clearly positioned under Moses' authority. The lad himself appears to share in Joshua's urgent concern, evident by his having run to report their prophesying to Moses. Although 'the lad' (hanna'ar) is definite, we do not know who this young man is, the Midrash suggesting Gershon, Moses' son (Num. Rab. 15.19). If one reads Joshua's 'answer' as a response to the prophesying (rather than to the young man's report), then it would be possible to read verses 27 and 28 as parallel, identifying the young man with Joshua himself, although this is not the most natural reading. In any case, the lad and Joshua underscore the same point: others are prophesying independently of Moses' authority and should be stopped.

Described as 'from his (Moses) chosen men' (mibbĕḥurāyw), Joshua may be one of the seventy whom Moses 'chose' (wayyibḥar) earlier in Exodus 18:25 (Friedman 2001: 464). Joshua responds, 'My lord Moses, restrain them!' (cf. 12:11). The term here, kālā', has the idea of shutting in and withholding, the nominal form kele' referring to confinement or imprisonment. Eldad and Medad, however, will not be shut in or confined for speaking prophecy through YHWH's Spirit. Moses understands that if the Spirit's source is YHWH, then prophesying independently of Moses, who prophesies by the same Spirit, is no threat to the people's guidance – YHWH is one, and his will is one (cf. Mark 9:38–4). Not only does Moses demonstrate humility and a selfless desire to establish YHWH's agenda, his response to Joshua demonstrates what he had already expressed in his plea to YHWH in verse 12: the people belong to YHWH – Moses shepherds them on behalf of YHWH without confusing the difference. Moses, the faithful servant in God's house, cannot be drawn into the envy of fleshly sectarianism – he 'displays withal an almost superhuman generosity and lack of self-importance' (Reis 2005: 208). His leadership crisis had been profound, having seen clearly the depths of the people's spiritual deprivation. Now, as one who understood both the nature and necessity of the remedy, Moses welcomed the distribution of YHWH's Spirit.

One function of the Eldad and Medad scene, then, is that it puts Moses to the test, and, after his selfless response which had prioritized the good of Israel's spiritual condition and the glory of YHWH, vindicates his original plea – his concern over his burden-bearing had not been merely for his own sake but for the cause of Israel. Moses' response to Joshua's zealous words reveals his own understanding of YHWH's remedy, one which has alluded many since: 'God meant to provide not technical assistance but rather a strengthening of the spirit of the entire nation to act as a buffer against the influence of the multitude lusting for meat', a hint of which purpose is also found in the concluding words of verse 30, that 'Moses gathered to the Camp, he and the elders of Israel' – they return to the camp 'to influence, to educate, and to serve as a counterweight' to the gathered-rabble in their midst (Samet 2014a: 139–140; also Lichtenstein 2014a: 147). Moses' response to Joshua, in the face of the myriads of Israel who had sat down to weep over their plight under YHWH's care, not only exonerates him, but serves as a foreshadowing clue to the first generation's ultimate demise in the wilderness, for the only sure remedy to the nation's spiritual degeneracy is a broader outpouring of YHWH's Spirit upon his people.

Are we to understand Eldad and Medad's reception of the Spirit as an *increase* in the Spirit's distribution (from seventy to seventy-two), or as a *variation* of the Spirit's distribution among the seventy elders (with two of the seventy receiving the Spirit, as it were, from under Moses' authority), or both? Even if they are understood as elders, the Camp locale positions Eldad and Medad as being among the people, and this is what seems to make their prophesying of urgent concern. Within the context of the Hebrew Scriptures, the Spirit is given for the sake of leading God's people on his agenda, for ruling, instructing, delivering, mediating divine oracles (e.g. Gen. 41:38; Exod. 31:1–6; Judg. 2:10). In some measure, then, the reception of YHWH's Spirit among the Camp, gestures toward the giving of the Spirit beyond the leadership structure and hierarchy – and this is precisely what Moses understands is direly needed. In an account that plays on the contrast between Spirit and flesh, he knows the true remedy for the people's wayward heart is found in the power of YHWH's Spirit: 'Who wouldn't give for all the people of YHWH to be prophets, that YHWH would put his Spirit on them' (v. 29). 'All the people' may be a deliberate contrast to merely two of the people, again equating Eldad and Medad – whether or not they are elders – with the people. Moses' desire is expressed in a two-fold manner: that all of God's people would be prophets, able to know and communicate God's word personally, and that YHWH would put his Spirit on all his people, the latter being the means of the former. The Spirit not only establishes possession by YHWH in the broad sense of empowerment for his agenda, but the Spirit leads to prophesying, underscoring the role of God's revealed will, his torah, for the people's guidance and spiritual well-being. As Israel will possess YHWH's torah through Moses in written form, Moses' response to Joshua must include the further notion of knowing YHWH more directly and intimately, having YHWH's word inscribed on the heart. There is a sharp contrast between the text's two 'who' questions (vv. 4, 29): the people crying for more flesh for themselves, whereas Moses cries out for more of YHWH's Spirit for them. The people desire anyone to replace YHWH and feed their lust for flesh, whereas Moses cries out for YHWH himself to change their desires by his Spirit. Aside from all other concerns, this episode functions to voice Moses' ardent desire, his urgent plea for the people's only sure remedy: more of the Spirit. In a story of the outer camp's failure (chs. 11–14), Moses discerns the tribes' needed divine provision.

The account resolves with the notice that Moses 'gathered to the Camp', along with the elders of Israel, 'gather' (*'āsap*) being a key word (cf. 12:15). The return of Moses and the elders to the Camp leaves the attention on the status and spiritual guidance of the Camp itself. There is a movement from YHWH's central presence at the Tent to Moses, through Moses to the elders around the Tent, and then from Moses and the elders around the Tent outward into the Camp. As with YHWH's Spirit, who had moved from Moses' place at the central Tent of Meeting outward to the elders and then into the Camp (on Eldad and Medad), so now Moses and the elders, men on whom the Spirit rests, gather to the Camp, to extend YHWH's Spirit-empowered-speech-to-Moses, the Torah, *there* in the Camp. Here, too, the description subordinates the elders to Moses: It is Moses who 'gathered' (3rd. m. sg.) to the Camp, then 'he and the elders'. They are with Moses, but have authority only inasmuch as they first follow Moses.

The next movement will continue outward from the Camp as the people voraciously go after the quails that surround the perimeter, brought there by YHWH's *ruach*. While, however, the Spirit had brought elders to the Camp from the Tent of Meeting, the Spirit/Wind will bring quail to the perimeter of the Camp, outside the Camp, and this from the sea – a place associated in Scripture with anti-creation forces. While the elders are gathered to YHWH in the centre of the Camp, the lusters gather to the flesh outside the Camp. The text uses *sābîb* (around) for Moses' placement of the seventy elders 'around the Tent' (11:24) and for the location of the quails 'around the Camp' (11:31), as well the lusters' spreading of the quails 'around the Camp' (11:32). (See Fig. 11.)

While the Spirit flows out from the centre centrifugally, the *ruach* has a centripetal affect, drawing the life of Israel's Camp toward YHWH and the Tent of Meeting; conversely, while the Spirit/Wind brings quail from the sea toward the Camp centripetally, flesh has a centrifugal affect, drawing the lusters away from the centre to beyond the perimeter and into the wilderness. More simply, YHWH's Mosaic word through the Spirit draws the Camp to himself, while the lusting for flesh draws the Camp away from YHWH out into the wilderness, the place designated for those unfit for life in his presence. While the Spirit, through seventy elders, mediates between the Tent of Meeting and the Camp, the flesh which surrounds the Camp's perimeter draws lusters away. There seems to be a contrast with the manna, which fell 'upon the Camp' (v. 9), just as the people's hording of the flesh is expressed in terms similar to the same sin regarding the manna (cf. Exod. 16:20, 27–29).

31–35. 'Spirit/Wind' is the subject of the verb and, curiously, that verb, 'set out' (*nāsa'*), is the same one employed for Israel's journeys through the wilderness: 'the Spirit/Wind journeyed out from YHWH'. In 12:15, the people 'did not journey out' (*lō' nāsa'*) until Miriam was gathered back to the Camp. YHWH's remedy both for the need of leadership help and for the people's lust for flesh is the same: the activity of his *ruach*. In this case, the Spirit/Wind swept in quails from the sea. The wind was wielded by God in creation (Gen. 1:2), the Deluge (8:1), and

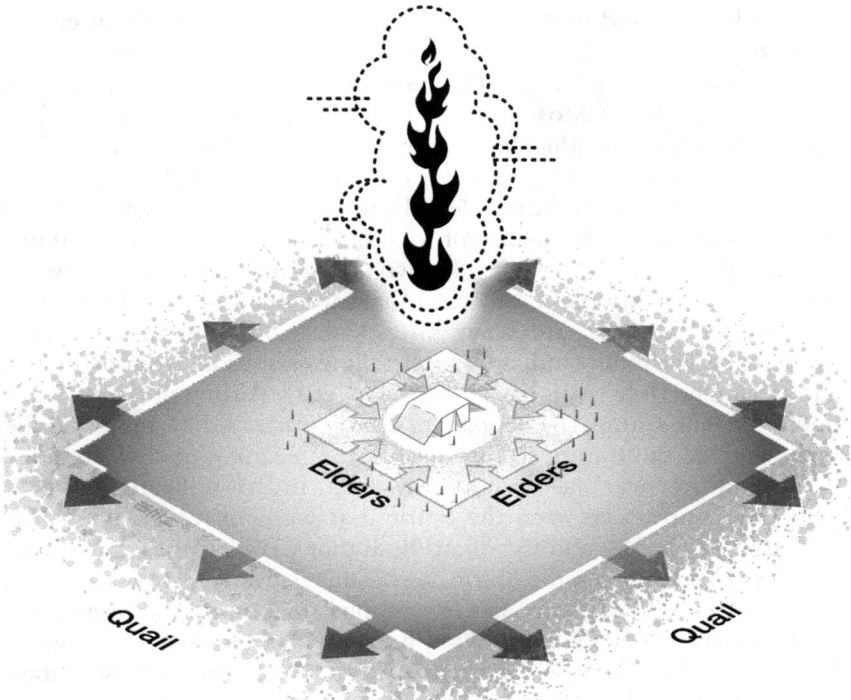

Figure 11: Spirit versus flesh in Israel's Camp

in Israel's sea crossing (Exod. 14:21) for deliverance. For the eighth sign in Egypt, YHWH had used an east wind to bring in locusts, and then afterward a west wind to blow them into the sea, a foreshadowing of the Egyptians' own destruction at sea (Exod. 10:13, 19). By the same mighty *ruach* with which he thrust open the sea for the sons of Israel to escape death at the hand of Pharaoh's Egyptian host, YHWH now drives quails from the sea, in a demonstration of his sovereign power, intended to solicit the trust displayed by Israel after the deliverance at sea (Exod. 14:30–31). Hildebrandt notes that a wind from the east, a scorching sirocco, often hails divine judgement (Jer. 18:17; Ezek. 17:10; 19:12), while a wind from the west may augur deliverance (1993: 9). The east wind of the sea crossing, however, was for the sake of Israel's deliverance, and the Egyptian hosts are only destroyed afterward, when the waters are made to return (Exod. 14:21–22, 26–28). While the wind in 11:31 swept in quails from the sea (from the west), it is sent out from YHWH himself – perhaps as a *third* sending of *ruach* from his Tent (11:25, 26). The broader context indicates a form of judgement by way of his giving Israel their desires in the extreme, to the point of sickness

– not to be confused with the actual immediate judgement that ensues when they incite YHWH's anger afresh by their ravenous consumption and hoarding of flesh (v. 33). The term 'swept in' (*gûz*) is rare, used in Psalm 90, a psalm of Moses, to describe how humanity's brief lifespan is soon 'cut off'. It is difficult to know if any symbolism is intended by reference to the sea (v. 31) – in some instances, things deriving from the sea stand as contrary to heaven (e.g. Dan. 7:3). The *ruach* also 'left' the quail – *nāṭoš* having the nuance of forsake or abandon – on the Camp.

Quail (*Coturnix coturnix*), known to gather in massive waves throughout the Middle East (cf. Johnsgard 1988: 193; Madge and McGowan 2002: 236), are heavy birds with short wings that thereby prefer flying with the wind, and, after falling exhausted from flight, are readily caught (John Wilkinson 1999: 196–201). Although the text has 'upon' (*'al*) the Camp, the people are clearly portrayed as gathering the quails outside the Camp, so that *'al* has the meaning of 'by', 'beside', 'all around' or 'near' (as with AV, ASV, ESV, NET, NIV). There may be a deliberate contrast between the Spirit that was put/rested 'upon' the elders (vv. 17, 25, 26) and the quails/flesh that were left upon the Camp (for aviary imagery for the Spirit, see Gen. 1:2; Matt. 3:16). The basic point about the 'day's way' and 'two cubits thick upon the face of the earth' is that YHWH's Spirit/Wind has provided an excessive – overly abundant in the extreme – amount of flesh for his people. The phrase 'two cubits' may also refer to the low flight, around three feet in the air, of the quail all around the Camp, an interpretation favoured by Jewish commentators (e.g. Rashi) and the Vulgate (cf. John Wilkinson 1999: 199–200). The portrayal serves two purposes: the exorbitant provision of quails demonstrates YHWH's ability to Moses, and it demonstrates the justice of YHWH's judgement on the people by exposing the intensity of their spiritual depravity. Having such an abundant provision from YHWH, and one for which they were to consecrate themselves, the people hurl themselves upon the flesh voraciously, as if starving, presuming the supply would soon expire even though he had avowed to provide for a whole month. They act as if the regular provision of manna had not proven YHWH's faithfulness in daily provision. The people 'arise' all that day (perhaps a play on their having sat down to weep, v. 4) and all night and all the following day – an incessant gathering of quail – the least culpable is described as having gathered excessively, ten homers. Massive amounts of dead quail surround the Camp, spread out for drying in the sun, a common method of preservation. The people thereby plan to store flesh against the prospect of YHWH's failure to provide in the future, despite YHWH's declaration to the contrary (vv. 19–20, 24).

Similarities with the account of quail and manna in Exodus 16, wherein YHWH purposed to see whether Israel would follow his *torah* or not (v. 4), are instructive. In Exodus 16, the people had also looked back longingly to Egypt, where they ate 'pots of flesh' (*sîr habbāśor*) and consumed bread to satiety (v. 3). While employing a different term for 'gather' ('glean', *lāqaṭ*), the story nevertheless describes the gathering in terms of *omers* (vv. 18, 22, 32, 36) – however, and significantly, the provision of quails receives scant attention (v. 13), while the rest of the chapter explores the wonders of the heavenly manna. The Exodus episode mentions no attempt to dry and preserve the meat, and, moreover, faults the Israelites for trying to hoard God's daily provision of manna (v. 20). By contrast, Israelites here spurn the manna and, snubbing YHWH's call for consecration in preparation for his impending act among them, fall upon the flesh and hoard it as if he had not avowed to supply them flesh for a whole month. It is in the light of this unfettered frenzy over the quail that YHWH's consequent judgement must be understood. The original judgement entailed the constant and abundant provision of flesh, such that the people would finally both retch and reject it; but the people, having such a word from YHWH, were to be composed, having been called to consecrate themselves for his provision (v. 18). The new judgement of YHWH in verse 33 is not set forth as a preconceived deception on YHWH's part. Rather, the people's ravenous lust, incessantly gathering quail for a day and a night and another day, oblivious to God's chastisement, this is said to 'kindle YHWH's fierce anger' (also Gertel 2002: 75). Since meat is the most cross-culturally tabooed food item (Rosenblum 2010: 76), the original audience may have discerned some other infringement or crossed boundary by the people's rapaciousness (see Parker 2012: 7) – at the least, failing to offer thanks to God (*TgPs-J* 11.33). Having their want met miraculously, the people were so enslaved to their lust they failed even to acknowledge that YHWH the Maker of heaven and earth had appeared; rather than sanctifying themselves to receive from his hand, they sprang upon the flesh like beasts. In the Bible meals often express the fellowship and communion with God that is the goal of creation and redemption: Israel was redeemed through a meal at Passover (Exod. 12), consummated their relationship with YHWH by a meal at Sinai (Exod. 24:8–11), celebrated their relationship with God in the land by meals (Deut. 12:13–14; 27:17), and their sacrifices typically culminated with the sacred meal of peace offerings (Lev. 3) – meals, in short, displayed the aim of Israel's atonement (Yeung 2018). Avishur marks verse 18, 'sanctify yourselves for tomorrow', as central (1999: 25–26), focusing Israel's consecration for the sake of the feast being prepared for them by YHWH. Without question, Israel's unrestrained falling upon the meat was sacrilegious; the least that may be said is that Israel defied YHWH's presence and work, ignoring the wonder of his supply even while turning his gift into a means for licentiousness. Especially within the context of the induction of the seventy elder-scribes who have prophesied by YHWH's Moses-imparted Spirit, and after Moses' expressed desire that all the people should know YHWH as prophets partaking of his Spirit, the transition to the people's feverish consuming of flesh cannot but cast them as especially base. Rather than sanctifying themselves for a special engagement with God, they threw off all restraint and plunged themselves into a state of lascivious frenzy, inciting the fierce anger of YHWH.

It is difficult to square the days of verse 32 with the onset of judgement described in verse 33, if the common translation is kept: 'while the flesh was still between their teeth, before it had yet been *chewed (yikkārēt)*'. Translating *kārat*, which normally means 'cut off' (and never elsewhere 'chewed'), is difficult (see BDB 504); the idea of 'cutting off' the flesh in terms either of consuming or depleting is likely in view. Although 'chewed' is at best 'a guess' based on the reference to teeth in the previous line (Binns 1927: 74), the translation 'fail' is more than adequate: 'while the flesh was still between their teeth' and before the flesh 'had failed' portrays the onset of YHWH's judgement while the people are in the act of ravenous eating, but also before the depletion of YHWH's abundant provision. In either case, verse 32 offers a panoramic summation of the people's frenzy, while verse 33 zooms in to present idiomatically the people's judgement while they were still engaged in the fleeting pleasures of flesh. Reis sees a pun on *kārat*, conveying the nuances of cutting off the meat supply, cutting of men's lives, and cutting a covenant (2005: 227) – perhaps *kārat* was chosen for its underlying resonance of the severest judgement sanctioned by YHWH, the *kareth* penalty. The threatened judgement in verse 10, when YHWH's fierce anger had kindled greatly, returns in spite of Moses' intervening plea and YHWH's response: YHWH struck down the people with not only a great striking but a 'very great striking' (*makkā rabbā mĕ'ōd*). Verse 31, depicting YHWH's remedy, begins with 'Spirit/Wind', while verse 33, depicting YHWH's kindled anger, begins with 'the flesh' (*habbāśār*). The root for 'to strike' (*nākâ*) and the nominal 'striking' (*makkā*) has so far in Numbers been reserved for God's action against Egypt (see 3:13; 8:17), and may form a measure for measure punishment against those who had remembered Egypt fondly in verse 5 (Leveen 2002: 250–251).

The text does not address nagging questions that remain. Had not YHWH's remedies helped? Had the seventy elder-scribes failed or was it simply too late for their influence? How many died under YHWH's fierce anger? The rhetorical effect seems to place emphasis on the irremediable wickedness of a large portion of the people. The failure of YHWH's planned response serves to vindicate his eventual judgement, proving that the people would not be helped; instead of consecrating themselves, humbling themselves in repentance over his abundant provision, or giving thanks and renewing their trust in him, they gave themselves over to their appetites to the degree that they lost themselves completely. The divine punishment serves as an exclamation point on Moses' profound expression of and plea for the only true remedy (v. 29).

34. The chapter's outward movement from the central Tent continues down into the grave, as the lusters are buried. The place is called Kibroth-hattaavah, 'Burial of the Cravers/Lusters', the name serving as an admonition and warning for God's people concerning the end of any who, forsaking loyalty to YHWH, plunge into unhindered lust. Most significantly, given the theology of the Camp and its purity, the character of the lustful is shown to belong to the sphere of death, *Sheol*, rather than to the Camp of Israel, where YHWH's abundant life wells up from the centre – their burial outside the Camp is both an excommunication and a foreshadowing of the first generation's demise. In poetic justice, after despising the bread of heaven and lusting for the sub-earth foods of Egypt, the lusters themselves are buried in graves. The dichotomy, as G. J. Wenham observes, may be mapped according to the Camp's geography (1981b: 123):

> The spirit was bestowed within the court of the Tabernacle, in the clean and holy area; the quails fell outside the camp, in the zone associated with uncleanness and death. The gift of the spirit drew men towards God; the quails led them away from God.

The term for lusting or 'craving' (*ta'ăwāh*) is used in verse 4, with reference to the gathered-rabble, and in verse 34, where Kibroth-hattaavah is explained by the burial 'of the people who were craving'. This has led some to understand that only the gathered-rabble, who had so negatively influenced the Israelites, fell by YHWH's judgement and were buried – this being the result of Moses' standing in the breach: 'The 600,000 who cried are spared, and the riffraff who lusted have died' (Reis 2005: 227). Jobling (1978: 1:45), similarly, speaks of the people's separation from the rabble by burying them. Thus construed, the story ends with the addition of seventy Spirit-empowered elder-scribes and the elimination of the lusting 'outsiders'. Though an intriguing suggestion, certainty eludes since verse 34 refers to 'the people (*hā'ām*) who were craving', a phrase which would refer to the gathered-rabble only if verse 4 is taken in isolation. Jobling, who takes such a reading, marks a parallel between the punishment of the gathered-rabble and Miriam in the next story (Num. 12:10–15), both being the instigators of rebellion, while the people and Aaron are spared in both cases (1978: 1:40). However, 'the people' is used as the primary descriptor throughout the chapter for the community of Israel broadly (see vv. 2, 8, 10, 11, 12, 13, 14, 16, 17, 18, 21, 24, 32, 35), along with 'sons of Israel' (v. 4), suggesting that those who were buried were the lusters not only among the gathered-rabble, but from among the broader community as well. The story portrays the fleshly nature and impulse of the people en masse, however influenced by the fringe or foreign element, 'the gathered-rabble' (*hā'sapsup*). Psalm 78 preserves the interpretation and tradition that the 'stoutest among them' (*bĕmišmannêhem*) and 'choice men of Israel' (*baḥûrê yiśrā'ēl*) were slain by God (v. 31). As for the name of the place, context makes YHWH the likely subject of 'he called', although Moses may also be understood – in any case, YHWH would name the place through Moses, and Moses would do so on YHWH's behalf.

We noted already how in the archetypal sin in the garden of Eden, the woman 'saw that the tree . . . was desirable (*ta'ăwâ*) to the eyes' (Gen. 3:6), the Bible's first use of 'desire'. Given the interplay between 'good' and 'evil' that pervades both the Eden narrative and Numbers 10 – 11 (cf. Gen. 2:9, 17; 3:5, 6; Num. 10:29–32; 11:1, 10, 11, 15), it seems Israel's sin is being portrayed in similar terms: forsaking YHWH's word and doubting his intentions for them, Israel exchanges good for evil.

35. This journey report shows progress as the people 'journeyed', and there's a transition to the locale of the next story, Hazeroth. However, in an x-qatal construction, the *nāsĕ'û* (journeyed) itself is background information for the people's abiding at Hazeroth, which is narrated with a mainline wayyiqtol. Given the *inclusion* with 12:16, along with the unmarked wayyiqtol verbal sentence that opens 12:1, Abela is likely correct that 11:35 functions to open a new narrative (2008: 523–524). The itinerary reports of 11:35 and 12:16 provide the framework for the narrative of 12:1–15 (Tervanotko 2016: 68–69). One question suggested by 11:35 is why the people stay there, a question answered by the narrative: Miriam's rebellion against Moses. It could be that the name Hazeroth (11:35; 12:16), deriving from *ḥāṣēr* (border, enclosure, courtyard) in the plural (cf. G. J. Wenham 1981b: 124), is meant to characterize chapters 11–12 spatially in terms of the Camp's structure and theology, an idea in accord with the burning of the 'outskirts (*biqṣêh*) of the Camp' (11:1) and Miriam's being shut out of the Camp (12:15). Jobling writes that 'the name means "enclosures", and is identical to the term applied to the courts of the Temple', suggesting the name Hazeroth is a semantic marker for 'separation' between the people (cognate with 'inside the Camp') and the buried gathered-rabble (cognate with 'outside the Camp') (1978: 1:48, 51). The term has already been used six times in Numbers with reference to the courtyard of the Dwelling (see 3:26, 37; 4:26, 32).

12:1 The verb 'spoke' (*wattĕdabbēr*) is feminine which, together with naming her before Aaron, underscores Miriam's lead role in the slander against Moses (cf. Kautzsch 1910: Par. 146g; Trevett 2005: 29; Yoo 2019: 37). Miriam's dominant position is critical for understanding rightly the punishment in verses 10–15 (I. Fischer 2000: 161). Considering his role in the golden calf debacle (cf. Exod. 32:21–35), Aaron's character emerges in the Torah as passive and easily influenced (cf. Buell 2012: 120). Beginning with her leading role (v. 1), and ending with the resolution to her rebellion (v. 15), which concludes on her name, this narrative is the longest passage referring to Miriam in the HB (Abela

2008: 525; Tervanotko 2016: 68). Scripture identifies Miriam in a variety of ways, as a sister to Moses, a prophetess, a poet and musician, a leader of women, and a leper (Exod. 2:4, 7; 15:20–21; Num. 12:1–16; 20:1; 26:59; Deut. 24:8–9) (Pimpinella 2005: 1; Reiss 2010: 183). The speaking of Miriam, along with Aaron, is 'against Moses', setting up Moses' status and role as the chapter's theme. YHWH's defence of Moses' unique status as his servant will serve as a response to, or clarification of, the previous chapter which may have left the impression that others, by virtue of their prophesying, have mitigated Moses' authority. This chapter uses the construction *dbr b-* in wordplay, based on the various meanings of *bet*, referring to Miriam and Aaron's speaking *against* Moses, to YHWH's speaking *with* his prophets, and of the special communication between YHWH and Moses (cf. Winslow 2011: 7; cf. Hymes 2010: 274).

The substance of their speaking against Moses regards 'the Cushite woman which he took', a phrase that has caused no small amount of consternation and gap-filling among interpreters. That the matter is understood as novel is evident by the narratorial affirmation that follows: 'because he had taken a Cushite woman'. This affirmation, moreover, reveals that Miriam and Aaron were not mistaken, and yet they were still blameworthy for speaking against Moses. YHWH's defence of Moses, then, includes implicitly a defence of Moses' marriage to a foreigner. It is slightly possible that Cush represents the idea of an enemy (in Ps. 7 a Benjamite is called 'Cush') or simply that of 'a country lying as far off as possible' (cf. Ezek. 29:10) (J. D. Douglas et al. 2011: 323), notions that underscore the foreignness of Moses' wife. The HB uses the name 'Cush' consistently with reference to the land south of Egypt along the Nile (Westermann 1984: 218), and LXX translates 12:1 as 'Ethiopian', clearly understanding the region south of Egypt (Hays 1996: 398). Genesis 2:10–14 associates Cush with both Eden and Jerusalem, inasmuch as the Gihon head of Eden's river surrounds the land of Cush (and a 'Gihon' spring is located on the east side of the City of David) (cf. Sadler 2009: 23). Cush, a son of Ham, is also associated with Havilah (Gen. 2; 10), as well as with fine gold and precious stones (Sadler 2009: 24–32; cf. Job 28:19). In Genesis 10, Cush is listed first among the sons of Ham, and as the one who begot Nimrod, who began to be a 'warrior on the earth' and 'mighty hunter before YHWH' (Gen. 10:6–9; see Török 1998). Hays notes that during the time of the exodus (which he takes as eighteenth or nineteenth dynasties), Cushites arrived in Egypt in great numbers, and were found at every level of Egyptian society, many of which were likely included in the 'mixed multitude' that joined Israel in departing out of Egypt (Exod. 12:38), the validation of which he sees not only in Moses' Cushite wife but also in the name of Moses' great-nephew and priest 'Phinehas', which means 'the Nubian', a reference to Cush (2003: 68, 81–82).

Who is this Cushite woman? The first option is that 'Cushite' is a variant description of Zipporah the Midianite (for a reception history of Moses' wives, see Winslow 2005). Proponents of this solution point to Habakkuk 3:7: 'I saw the tents of Cushan under affliction, / the curtains of the land of Midian tremble,' and suggest that 'Cushite' could be a synonym for 'Midianite'. Such a conflation between Cushan and Midian, however, cannot be borne out historically, and even the connection of 'Cushite' with 'Cushan' is not a given. Nevertheless, Albright posited that Cushan occurs as two districts or tribes in the second millennium, one of which was in southern Transjordan – though he uses Habakkuk 3:7 to establish this point (1953: 205 n. 49), and Cross, based on Albright, takes Cush as applying originally to an element in the Midianite league, so that there is 'no reason to suppose that the Cushite wife is not also the Zipporah of Yahwistic tradition' (1973: 204). Demetrius the Chronographer (c. third century BC) favoured seeing 'Cushite' as descriptive of Zipporah, an Ethiopian who descended from Abraham's wife Keturah (cf. J. Hanson 1985), and in his dramatization of the exodus, Ezekiel the Tragedian (c. second century BC) also has Zipporah characterized as a North African 'stranger' in Midian, cleverly assigning her two identities (cf. R. G. Robertson 1985). In *Pirke de Rabbi Eliezer* 53, Zipporah is called a Cushite as praise, signifying that by her words and good deeds she was different from other people (as Cushites look different). Numbers 12:1, however, reads as self-consciously providing and affirming new information about Moses (cf. also G. B. Gray 1903: 121–122) – although one may argue it intends new information about Zipporah instead. Zipporah would have been married to Moses for some forty years already – why would Miriam and Aaron bring up the matter now? Perhaps the recent negative impact of foreigners on Israelites in the previous chapter (11:4) supplies a motive, but this would not explain the need for the narratorial comment that follows. Noth, who took Cush as related to the Midian area, nevertheless says that the purpose of the explanatory clause in 12:1 is precisely to distinguish the Cushite woman from Zipporah, Moses' other Midianite wife (1968: 94).

A second strand of interpretation assumes the Cushite woman was Moses' first wife, whom he had married *before* Zipporah, while still living in Egypt. The kingdom of Cush, also known as Nubia (and sometimes conflated with Ethiopia), was located just south of Egypt. In Josephus's account, an Ethiopian princess named Tharbis (alternatively, 'Adoniah') watched Moses leading the Egyptians in a campaign against her city of Meru, and fell in love with him; delivering the city into his hand, Tharbis married Moses and returned with him to Egypt as his Cushite wife (*Ant.* 2.10; cf. Feldman 1993) – a scenario set forth around the third century BC by Artapanus of Alexandria (cf. J. J. Collins 1985). Historically, such a scenario is plausible, as it would not be uncommon for one ensconced in the upper echelons of Egypt to marry another African, as Joseph did (Gen. 41:45–52). Even the narratorial confirmation of such a marriage makes sense though long after the fact, since this information had not been given earlier in Exodus. Less readily answered is why Miriam should only now bring up this marriage as an issue of contention. Perhaps, as with the first scenario, she was incited by the recent destructive influence of foreigners (11:4).

Finally, some interpreters also distinguish the Cushite woman from Zipporah, but suppose Moses had married her more recently, after Zipporah (see Adamo 1989; Hays 1996: 397–401). As the scenario fits the text's details and the historical picture of Cushites in Egypt, Hays judges the case 'extremely strong' that 'Moses married a Black Cushite woman from the Cushite civilization south of Egypt' (2003: 77). Since Egypt ruled over Cush from the sixteenth century BC onward, there were 'thousands of Cushites in Egypt at all levels of society' (Hays 1996: 398). Nevertheless, questions remain, especially concerning the status of Zipporah: Had she died (perhaps in one of the previous judgements recounted), or had she been divorced and left behind in Midian when the Israelites set out from Sinai? Does Moses now have two wives or one? Perhaps in withholding answers to these questions, the text puts the reader in Miriam's position, bidding us simply to trust that such a man as Moses, who lives virtually in a continual state of intense engagement with YHWH God, knowing both the character and will of God profoundly, will have done right by his marriage to a Cushite woman.

Assuming that Moses has recently married a Cushite woman, the next question is why this marriage should so offend Miriam and Aaron. Given the likelihood of the Cushite woman's dark skin (cf. Jer. 13:23), some take the offence as being racist in nature. Such a notion, however, appears anachronistic, reflecting modern European preconceptions rather than those of the ancient world where interracial marriage with Ethiopians was far from unusual (cf. Snowden 1970: 192–193; Felder 1989: 37–46). While not having the deep ebony of the Nubians, most of the peoples of the ancient East, including the Hebrews, were coloured to some degree. Moreover, the black skin of Nubians may have been deemed exotically beautiful (indeed, translated as 'beautiful' by *TgO*, followed by Rashi and Ibn Ezra), and some understand Moses' marriage to the Cushite as a symbol of Moses' elevated authority and status, which in turn led to the jealousy of Miriam and Aaron (R. Bailey 1991: 179). Based on the practice of Egyptian pharaohs, whereby taking Cushite wives provided legitimacy for ruling over Cush, Moses' marriage may readily be taken in royal terms (see Runnalls 1983). Miriam's punishment of leprosy, so that her skin became '(white) as snow', has been taken as poetic justice since Miriam had been offended by the woman with ebony skin (e.g. Cross 1973: 204). Yet caution is needed since 12:10 does not actually use the word 'white'; while the idea of white may be implied, not all concur. Brenner argues that the texture – flakiness – of snow is intended rather than the idea of colour (1982: 42). Use of 'white' (*lābāb*) is especially prominent in Leviticus 13, used some twenty times with reference to leprosy (with only five other occurrences in the Torah), so one may argue the idea of white is assumed in the present story. Withholding the term 'white' may function to focus on 'as snow' (*kaššāleg*), which smacks of wordplay with 'Cushite' (*kušît*), drawing further attention to the poetic justice involved in her punishment (cf. Sadler 2009: 39).

Many modern commentators assume Moses' Cushite wife was merely a pretext for their real concern about his status (v. 2), thus curtailing any further probing into the matter (cf. e.g. G. B. Gray 1903: 121–122; Milgrom 1990: 94; Levine 1993: 328) – and YHWH, after all, defends only Moses' status without addressing the topic of the Cushite woman explicitly. Should the matter of Moses' Cushite wife, then, be dismissed readily? Likely not. The text may be read in an opposite manner, with Moses' status as a pretext for Miriam's disapproval of his marriage: the narrator's insightful comment has it that Moses' marriage is what troubled Miriam and Aaron, while reporting only their actual speech about his status as prophet (Winslow 2011: 3). B. P. Robinson reasons that Miriam was jealous of Moses' new wife and, therefore, prevailed upon Aaron to dispute Moses' unique role (1989: 432). Moreover, while YHWH may only address explicitly Moses' unique status, some form of poetic justice in Miriam's punishment of skin disease appears related to her speech against his Cushite wife. Such an understanding addresses Miriam's original and secondary complaints in reverse order, forming a symmetrical structure: complaint against Cushite wife (v. 1) / complaint against Moses' status (v. 2) → response for Moses' status (vv. 6–8) / response for Cushite wife (vv. 9–10). It is also possible that YHWH's stern warning, over Miriam and Aaron's not fearing 'to speak against' (*lĕdabbēr b-*) Moses (v. 8) refers to verse 1, where Miriam (with Aaron) 'spoke against' (*wattĕdabbēr b-*) Moses specifically with reference to his Cushite wife (also suggested by Sperling 1999: 47). Bazak suggests the same with the following structure (Bazak 2012):

A. Miriam spoke, and Aaron, against Moses concerning the Cushite woman . . .
  B. They said, 'Did God only speak with Moses?'
    C. 'Did he not speak with us also?' And YHWH heard . . .
      D. He said, 'Hear now my words:
    C'. 'If there is a prophet among you, I, YHWH Lord, . . . speak with him in a dream.
  B'. Not so my servant, Moses . . . I speak with him mouth to mouth, clearly, not in riddles . . .
A'. Why then were you not afraid to speak against my servant, against Moses?'

By contrast to much modern scholarship, the history of Jewish and Christian interpretation has both assumed and struggled to understand a relationship between Moses' Cushite wife and the additional issue of his status as prophet (cf. Winslow 2011: 2). A popular rabbinic reading, for example, understands Miriam's speaking against Moses as a defence of his Cushite wife whom he, in a perpetually sanctified state as YHWH's prophet, had been neglecting by abstaining from marital relations (cf. Exod. 19:14–15) (see *MQ* 17b; *Sif. Deut.* 99; *Yalk. Shim. Deut.* 738). An opposite reading is also possible, that Miriam is implying Moses is in a state of impurity, given that 'taking a woman as wife' assumes recent conjugal relations. In the end, given the tenor of novelty in the mention of Moses' marriage to the Cushite (cf. B. P. Robinson 1989: 429–430), along with the probability that a minority of people from Cush resided in Egypt, the soundest scenario is that the Cushite woman left Egypt with Israel as part of the mixed-multitude (Exod. 12:38) and Moses had only recently taken her as wife.

While context leads one to wonder about details, the text is silent about all else except her Cushite identity. What is of import is that the Cushite woman is associated strongly with the foreign or non-Israelite element of the Camp – a key to the text's logic. Whether Zipporah or the Cushite, as the same or two different women, the various traditions concerning Moses' marriage are all connected by the common feature that Moses' wife was a foreigner (Noth 1981: 168–169; Tervanotko 2016: 73). Given the previous chapter's account of the negative influence by foreigners on the sons of Israel (11:4), along with the resulting judgement, Miriam and Aaron are scandalized by Moses' ongoing favour to Gentiles, and their accusation regarding his wife's foreignness likely concerns assumptions over impurity (see Trible 1994: 177). Bekhor Shor took a similar reading, writing that what Miriam and Aaron said was, 'Couldn't Moses find a woman among the daughters of Israel to take for himself as wife, that he had to take himself one of the daughters of the Cushite gentiles?' (1983: 258). As forecasted in Moses' dialogue with Hobab (Num. 10:29–32), Numbers 11 – 12 develops the subject of Israel's relationship to foreigners as a sub-theme. It is Moses' favour to Gentiles that leads to Miriam and Aaron's questioning of his status. As with chapter 11, two themes are intertwined, which must be interpreted together. Reading Numbers 11 – 12 wholistically, two motives for Miriam and Aaron's complaint surface: the negative role of foreigners among Israelites in the Camp, and the fact that the Spirit of prophecy had been distributed among the elder-scribes as a new level of hierarchy, even to Eldad and Medad within the Camp, but *not* given to Miriam (called a prophetess in Exod. 15:20) or to Aaron, causing them enviously to assert such dignity (12:2). The distribution of the Spirit to the seventy involved YHWH's speaking to Moses, but did he not also speak with Aaron and Miriam – should not the seventy be subordinate to them as well? Comparing 11:4–35 with 12:1–16, Miriam, in soliciting Aaron to join in her complaint, resembles the gathered-rabble who sought to have the people of Israel join them in their lust for flesh (cf. Jobling 1978: 1:35). Ironically, in her offence over Moses' foreign wife, Miriam herself acts like the evil faction of foreigners among them, leading a rebellion against Moses, and she ends up outside of the Camp – *a locale that marks her as an outsider*. Moreover, because Miriam is called a prophetess in Exodus 15:20 and Aaron is high priest of Israel, many understand this account as teaching that prophets and priests are subject to Moses – that prophecy and the priesthood are subordinate to the Torah. G. J. Wenham follows this line, seeing 'an alliance of priest and prophet, the two archetypes of Israelite religion, challenging Moses' position as sole mediator between God and Israel' (1981b: 124–125; for Miriam as representing a theo-political position, rather than prophetic, see Rapp 2002; cf. also Burns 1980). Similarly, Gunneweg speaks of the primacy of Moses in terms of the precedence of Torah over priesthood and prophecy, a point which he notes is also the last word of the Torah (1990: 178, 180). Origen, on an allegorical reading, suggested that Moses represents the spiritual law and the Cushite woman the Gentile church, with Miriam and Aaron representing the Jewish nation and priesthood, respectively (*Homilies on Numbers* 6, 7; cf. Kamin 1991: 79–80; Sperling 1999: 47). That Miriam symbolizes Israel is a significant insight that will be relevant when considering her death (20:1).

The audience to whom Miriam and Aaron complained is not stated explicitly in the text. Both the immediate (chs. 11–12) and wider context (chs. 11–14), however, favour Noth's understanding that their voices were made known 'within the Israelite camp' (1968: 95). In the previous chapter, Joshua's jealousy over Moses' unique role was stirred when Eldad and Medad prophesied 'within the camp' (11:27). The issue of prophecy pertains particularly to YHWH's guidance of the twelve tribes, the outer camp. In part, the failure of Israel to inherit the land, the failure of the tribes to embrace YHWH's word with trust and obedience, may already be seen as Miriam and Aaron, casting aspersions on Moses, foster doubt on the supreme channel of that prophetic word.

2. Given the prophesying of seventy elder-scribes, along with Eldad and Medad in the previous account, the question of Moses' unique office is called into question by Miriam and Aaron (cf. Jobling 1978: 1:58; Olson 1996: 70). In a contrast with Joshua, who had been jealous to defend Moses' unique status (11:28–29), Miriam and Aaron jealously deny Moses' status as YHWH's unique prophet (cf. Winslow 2005: 103). 'Has YHWH spoken only solely with Moses?' they ask, 'has he not also spoken with us?' The words 'only solely' are attested only here and, as a collocation of synonyms, are emphatic (Sperling 1999: 43 n. 25), sounding especially abrasive in Hebrew: *hăraq 'ak*. Later, Miriam's judgement is defined as the shame she would experience if her father 'had but *spit* (*yārōq yāraq*) in her face' (12:14), the doubling of the intensive form calling attention to a pun with 12:2, so that her punishment fits the crime (Friedman 2001: 466). The bet of *bĕmōšeh* and *bānû* should be understood as 'with', not 'through'. The capacity to know YHWH's will intimately and authoritatively is what is at stake, and is also what YHWH addresses (vv. 6–8). Miriam was questioning 'that Moses had a monopoly of divine guidance' (B. P. Robinson 1989: 430). Miriam and Aaron's speaking is about Moses, against him, but not to him. Nevertheless, 'YHWH heard', and YHWH is the one who initiates the defence of his servant. The subject of YHWH's singular speaking to Moses flows naturally from the previous account, where YHWH – even in distributing the spirit of prophecy – speaks with Moses alone (11:17, 25), a notion already cultivated (Num. 1:1; 7:89). Moses' leadership of the Camp into the land is at stake: in undercutting Moses' singular access to YHWH and to YHWH's guidance and will, Miriam and Aaron were putting the entire sojourn in peril, inserting a wedge of doubt between YHWH's will and Moses' teaching of the people – the disastrous fruit this seed becomes manifest in Numbers 13 – 14.

3. Not only will YHWH rush to the defence of Moses, but the text itself preempts YHWH's swift response with a narratorial comment about Moses' humility, inserted between 'YHWH heard' (v. 3) and 'YHWH said suddenly' (v. 4). English cannot capture the subtleties of this verse, with Moses described as 'the man' (*hā'îš*), a term that may also connote 'husband' (perhaps coinciding with the Cushite 'woman/ wife', *hā'iššā* in v. 1), contrasted with every 'man' (*hā'ādām*) upon the face of the 'ground' (*hā'ădāmāh*). For *'ānāw*, my translation uses 'bowed down', as the root's core meaning, whether such lowliness is taken as his being meek or as his being afflicted or miserable (C. Rogers 1986; cf. R. Brown 2002: 107). Either sense is true of Moses, even within the present context, and misguided notions of what Moses could write about himself should not tilt the scales away from his humility. G. B. Gray cautions that this is the only instance of the term found in the singular, although in the plural notions of meekness, enduring wrongs, and humility are present (1903: 123; see Zeph. 2:3). Arguably, the notion of 'being oppressed' is present as well (cf. Abbott 1933), Moses' experience among the Israelites likewise qualifying for this designation. Milgrom denies any meaning of meekness, suggesting instead the ideas of devotion and trust, given the synonymous parallel with those 'who seek him (YHWH)' in Psalm 22:26 (1990: 94). Others bring out the quality of tolerance and long-suffering (cf. Harrison 1990: 195), and of being 'modest and non-assertive' (Snaith 1967: 235). Given the weight of leading the myriads of complaining Israelites, described as a heavy burden (Num. 11), C. Rogers argues for understanding Moses' *'ānāw* as misery (1986: 262; cf. Hymes 2007: 14–15). With the accusation against Moses, that he has exalted himself unduly in some way (v. 2), the word on Moses' lowliness, his humility and meekness, stands as a fitting counter-argument. The narratorial defence is akin to that of the despised manna in the previous story (11:7–9). Moreover, given that YHWH himself is about to pronounce on Moses one of the most outstanding divine commendations given in Scripture (vv. 7–8), such a prefatory word is also appropriate, and affirms that God does indeed oppose the proud and exalt the lowly (Ps. 138:6; Prov. 3:34; 29:23; Matt. 23:12; Luke 1:52; Jas 4:6; 1 Peter 5:5). However *'ānāw* is understood, even humility or meekness should not be thought of in terms of passivity; as Coats points out, Moses' leadership is strong and effective, a responsible loyalty and obedience that emerges when he stands boldly face to face with God and intercedes for Israel (1982a: 98). Nevertheless, Moses' own silence, an act of spiritual strength rather than fleshly passivity, is surely a fruit and demonstration of his *'ānāw* character, even a type of the suffering Servant who 'was oppressed and afflicted (*'ānâ*), yet he opened not his mouth' in the face of his accusers (Isa. 53:7; cf. John 19:9–10) – Moses, the first deliverer, was a type of the Messiah, the final deliverer (see Morales 2020: 148–151).

4. There is irony in YHWH's speaking to Moses, Aaron and Miriam, since Miriam and Aaron's ill-speech concerned YHWH's speaking not only with Moses but also with them. 'He has spoken to us, too, no less than to Moses', they claim – so he now speaks to all three, but for the purpose of rebuking Aaron and Miriam. This address is also paradoxically aside from the distinctions of divine revelation in verses 6–9, since YHWH rebukes Aaron and Miriam clearly and not in riddles. The twofold use of 'three' and their summons to the Tent of Meeting, the place where YHWH communicates with Moses (7:89), functions in the same manner, as a temporary and surface-level aligning of Aaron and Miriam with Moses for the sake of underscoring Moses' uniqueness. As with 11:17, 25, the priority is given to Moses – YHWH said 'to Moses' first, and then to the two others, Aaron and Miriam. The adverb 'suddenly' (*pit'ōm*) expresses YHWH's deep concern to defend Moses without delay, and also conveys a swift retribution for Miriam and Aaron, while they were yet speaking (cf. Num. 11:33) – Moses will be divinely vindicated again without hesitation later in the book (see 16:31–33). YHWH's swift response also underscores, by contrast, Moses' non-response to the criticisms, assuming he had heard them (Sperling 1999: 43 n. 28). Use of *yāṣā'* led source critics to equate this Tent with that of Exodus 33:7–11, consigned to the Elohist (E) source. However, the story has in mind the Tent at the centre of the Camp, and chapters 11–12 draw a sharp geographical and theological distinction not only between outside and inside the Camp, but also between the outer camp of the twelve tribes and the central camp of the *Shekhinah*. The last story had left Moses in the outer camp (11:30), and now this event brings Moses back to the Tent of Meeting – and leaves him there, while Miriam is sent first outside the Camp and then back inside (12:15).

5. 'And YHWH descended' parallels God's movement in the previous story (cf. 11:25), except that rather than 'in the cloud', this verse has 'in a pillar of cloud'. Use of 'pillar' (*'ammûd*) combines with 'and he stood' (*wayya'ămōd*) to underscore that YHWH's presence 'at the doorway of the Tent' is anything but ethereal. The elements combine to lend a judicial framework to the scene. Standing at the doorway of his Tent, YHWH, within the standing-pillar of cloud, calls to Aaron and Miriam. The verb *yāṣā'* is used once more to describe their movement, this time from the periphery of the Tabernacle complex, likely the entrance area of the courtyard, toward the doorway of the Tent in the centre. Their gradually increased nearness to YHWH's dangerous holiness is emphasized as the 'two' go forth. In terms of sacred space, the two are now separated from Moses as they draw nearer to the intense holiness of YHWH's standing presence. Having asserted their nearness to YHWH, claiming equal status with Moses, YHWH is granting them their boast, calling them to stand with himself at the place usually reserved for Moses in order finally to put them back in their place. Thus YHWH differentiates them from Moses, by calling them temporarily to stand in Moses' position. The situation presents a reverse image of the previous story where YHWH spoke to Moses at the Tent in the presence of others (11:17, 25), since here Moses is brought to the Tent as YHWH speaks to others. As high priest, anointed to serve YHWH, Aaron is in less danger of such nearness than Miriam who will come away from such access with leprosy (as Uzziah, 2 Chr. 26:19–21).

6–8. 'Hear now my words' continues the ironic judgement: Miriam and Aaron had claimed that YHWH speaks to them no less than with Moses, so YHWH speaks to them exclusively, 'Hear me now,' but this in order to correct and rebuke them for slandering Moses. The following words of YHWH have a poetic quality, and appear to be arranged in an envelope construction (see Cross 1973: 203–204; D. N. Freedman 1975: 42–44; Kselman 1976; Hymes 2007: 15):

[Exhortation] Hear now my words:		
If there is a prophet of YHWH among you,	A '*im-yihyeh nĕbî'ăkem yhwh*	I.
I make myself known in a vision to him,	B *bammar'āh 'ēlāyw 'etwaddā'*	Revelation
in a dream I speak with him.	C *baḥălôm 'ădabber-bô*	to other prophets
But not so with my servant Moses –	D *lō'-kēn 'abdî mōšeh*	
he is faithful in all my house.	D' *bĕkol-bêtî ne'ĕmān hû'*	
Mouth to mouth I speak with him,	C' *peh 'el-peh 'ădabber-bô*	II.
neither in vision nor in riddles;	B' *ûmar'eh wĕlō' bĕḥîdōt*	Revelation
the form of YHWH he beholds –	A' *ûtĕmunat yhwh yabbîṭ*	to Moses

[Rebuke] so why did you not fear to speak against my servant Moses?

Although verses 6a and 8de may be part of the poetic form, they are nevertheless disjoined from the main speech, as an introductory exhortation to heed the speech (6a) and as an applicatory rebuke based on the speech (8de).

Two features bring out Moses' unrivalled status as YHWH's prophet: (1) the contrast between other prophets and Moses in relation to the nature of revelation received (A, B, C versus C', B', A'), and (2) the central commendation of Moses (D, D'). Aaron and Miriam had claimed that YHWH also speaks with them, and YHWH's response serves to distinguish the various ways in which he speaks with prophets: even when he does speak with others, the revelation is not on par with how he speaks with Moses, with the way or *means* of revelation to and through Moses. YHWH's statement also clarifies any misunderstanding regarding the prophesying of the seventy elders, including Eldad and Medad, in the previous chapter, since 'a prophet of YHWH among you' encompasses a wider circle than merely Miriam and Aaron. Both Moses' hearing from YHWH ('mouth to mouth' and clearly vs 'in a dream' and 'in riddles') and Moses' seeing of YHWH ('the form of YHWH' vs 'in a vision') is superior to all other prophets (Jobling 1978: 1:46). Whereas other prophets are removed from God, as it were, by dreams and visions, Moses has direct contact with God, unmediated by mystifying layers that require further interpretation and explanation (cf. Baltzer 1975: 45–46; Pimpinella 2005: 7). YHWH's speech is not intended to negate the authority of those who prophesy from dreams and visions, but to distinguish and subordinate such prophecy to Moses' revelation (see Burns 1980: 84).

The HB is ordered according to levels of revelation, each requiring the person and work of the Holy Spirit: (1) the Torah, revealed plainly and mouth to mouth to Moses, (2) the Prophets, revealed to holy men through dreams and visions, and (3) the Writings, in which revelation seems to come closer to the writer's being divinely 'inspired' to write without necessarily having any sort of experience of God, neither a theophany as with Moses nor a vision as with other prophets. Such a divinely ordained hierarchy of revelation has firm theological repercussions: the Torah is utterly foundational, while the Prophets and Writings, although equally God's word, function as building on Moses' foundation (also Rofé 1994; Hayes 1999: 310; Sperling 1999: 55). Moses' words alone are 'divine Torah', while all 'other inspired speech becomes interpretation of the Torah of Moses' (Dozeman 2000: 30; also B. P. Robinson 1989: 431). Moses and his Torah are the archetype and *criterion* of all true prophecy (Gunneweg 1990: 180).

Although my focus is on revelation and the office of prophecy, it must further be acknowledged that Moses is unique even more comprehensively as a mediator, encompassing the roles of prophet, priest, charismatic leader and judge, as *the* servant and man of God (cf.

Tunyogi 1969: 36–40). The New Testament acknowledges the uniqueness of Moses' revelation, even while exulting in the fuller revelation that has come with the Messiah. While Moses saw only the form and, as it were, 'backside' of YHWH (Exod. 33:18–23; Num. 12:8), the Son comes from the Father's bosom to reveal him more completely (John 1:18; Heb. 1:1–2). The levelling of inscripturation does not take away from the superiority of the revelation that has come through Messiah. Nevertheless, New Testament authors are at pains to demonstrate that the gospel is in accord with Hebrew Scripture (cf. Luke 24:44; Acts 17:11), affirming Moses' significant and otherwise unequalled role (Heb. 3:5), and demonstrating that Moses' own revelation guides to the Messiah (John 5:46). Within the context of Numbers, YHWH's words here affirm the hierarchy manifested in chapter 11, as the seventy elder-scribes partake of the Spirit through and, therefore, under Moses.

Not only does YHWH distinguish Moses' unique status from that of other prophets, but he positively commends and vindicates him before Aaron and Miriam: Moses is YHWH's servant, *faithful* in all YHWH's house. Moses, as Noth remarks (1968: 96), is likened to the chief servant in a household, even the master's confidante and trustee. Hebrews affirms this singular place of Moses within Israel, even while proclaiming the higher place of the Messiah as a son within God's house (see Heb. 3:1–6). With a similar collocation of terms, David is called a 'faithful' (*ne'ĕmān*) 'servant' ('*ăbādêkā*) to Saul, one honoured in the latter's 'house' (*bêtekā*) (1 Sam. 22:14). God's 'house' is his people (Jer. 12:7; Hos. 8:1; on 2 Sam. 7, see Morales 2015: 230–232). In place of 'in all my house', *TgO* reads 'among all my people', *TgNeof* has 'in the entire world I created' and *TgPs-J* has 'among the whole house of Israel, among all my people' (Sperling 1999: 44 n. 33). It may be that *ne'ĕmān* has more to do with the notion of 'loyal' or 'trustworthy' than 'faithful', that Moses is so loyal/trustworthy YHWH entrusts him with greater authority over his house, and deals with him as with a friend (in terms of fuller disclosure and face-to-face revelation).

The phrase *peh 'el-peh* (mouth to mouth) is an abbreviated form of *pānîm 'el-pānîm* (face to face) as found in Exodus 33:11, and is even more intimate, focusing specifically on the mouth. The expression 'mouth to mouth' is utterly unique, occurring nowhere else (apart from the different usage in Ezra 9:11), and, especially as spoken from the mouth of YHWH himself, forms the highest statement concerning the mediatorial role and *torah* of Moses. Aaron and Miriam's accusations of Moses are thus sternly denied. As the apostle Paul would later write: 'Who are you to judge another's servant?' (Rom. 14:4, 12–13). Such accusations are not only illegitimate as outside the purview of Aaron and Miriam, but since Moses belongs to YHWH they should have trembled to speak any word against him. To slander one so claimed and approved by YHWH is to court severe judgement – 'why did you not fear to speak against my servant – against Moses?' The divine double-use of 'against' (*b-*), recalls Miriam and Aaron's sin (v. 1), and forms a strong rebuke as YHWH confronts them in the particularity of their rebellion. The divine agenda is to instil just such fear. Similarly, in Exodus 20:19 Moses' role as God's unique prophet had been embraced with trembling, after the people witnessed YHWH's fearful presence on Mount Sinai, leading them to cry out: 'You (Moses) speak with us and we will hear – but do not let God speak with us lest we die!' In Deuteronomy 18, alluding to the same scene at Sinai, YHWH declares that he will raise up a prophet like Moses whom Israel must heed, but that Israel need not 'dread' (*gûr*) a false prophet – evidently, true prophets of God are to be revered. Not appreciating Moses' nearness to YHWH sufficiently, Aaron and Miriam had referred to him merely as 'Moses', but YHWH twice refers to him as 'my servant' (vv. 7, 8), underscoring their offence against a valued possession of YHWH, but also one who represents his Master – so that YHWH maintains not only Moses' status, but his (YHWH's) own honour. After Moses' vindication by YHWH, Aaron refers to his brother as 'my lord' (v. 11), thereby honouring YHWH as well. As Rashi says, Aaron and Miriam should have known that the King does not love his servant for naught (cf. 1997: 4:140). Also, since Moses has singular access to YHWH God, and therefore knows YHWH's will clearly and profoundly both for Israel and for the nations, Miriam and Aaron should have rather sought to learn the divine will from Moses in relation to his marriage to a Cushite woman.

Some understand YHWH's vindication of Moses in terms of a 'trial by oracle', comparable to the 'trial by sacrifice' used in Numbers 16 to vindicate Aaron against Korah's rebellion (Burns 1980: 101–103; cf. Robertson Smith 1927: 179), an idea in line with – but not necessary to – understanding chapters 11–15 under the subject of 'prophecy', and chapters 16–19 under 'priesthood'.

9. The phrase 'the fierce anger of YHWH kindled', which has by now become gravely common (cf. 11:1, 10, 33), is directed 'against them'. There is a marked similarity between the opening story of Taberah and that of Miriam and Aaron's complaint against Moses: *wayyišma' yhwh wayyiḥar 'appô* ('and YHWH heard and his fierce anger kindled', 11:1), and *wayyišma' yhwh . . . wayiḥar 'ap yhwh* ('and YHWH heard . . . and YHWH's fierce anger kindled', 12:2, 9). Rather than occurring at the point of Miriam and Aaron's sin-of-speech in verses 1–2, YHWH's fierce anger is kindled upon his own reflection of their lack of fear to speak against Moses despite Moses' close relationship to YHWH and his faithfulness toward Israel. The kindling of YHWH's fierce anger leads us to expect a dreadful judgement, but YHWH restrains himself by departing: 'and he went' (*wayyēlak*). The idea is similar to YHWH's earlier refusal to journey in the midst of Israel, lest he consume them on the way (Exod. 33:3), words that have begun to prove prophetic now that the journey has

begun. As the following verses demonstrate, judgement does come, both fitting and mitigated.

10–14. After the report that YHWH 'went', the cloud is depicted as turning aside from over the Tent. Some have read this as the signal for the journey to commence, in accord with 9:17, but the language there is of the cloud's ascent, rather than 'turn aside' (*sār*) as here. One of the lessons is that sin and rebellion suspend the people's journey through the wilderness, delaying their enjoyment of the good land God has promised them. While YHWH's 'cloud' (*'ānān*) is mentioned over a dozen times in Numbers 1 – 10 (cf. 9:15–23; 10:11–12, 34) with reference to YHWH's guidance and protection of the Camp (cf. 14:44), yet within the wilderness journeys of chapters 11–25, the *'ānān* appears only in contexts of YHWH's judgement and dealings with problems (11:25; 12:5, 10; 16:42) (cf. Leder 2016: 524). With YHWH's departure, the effect of such an encounter is now felt heavily: Miriam had become leprous. The text does not describe the onset of the leprosy. Rather, after the cloud departs, the audience is directed to look upon Miriam – 'look!' (*hinnê*) – and discover her leprous condition. After this preview, the audience's attention is shifted to Aaron so as to observe his discovery of Miriam: And Aaron 'turned (his face)' (*yipen*) to Miriam. Again, *hinne* is used, bringing a sense of immediacy (cf. Lambdin 1971: 135), so that we see her leprosy afresh through his eyes. With lepers heading the list of those needing to be expelled from the Camp (5:1–4), Miriam's leprosy is portrayed 'as the ultimate defilement' (M. Douglas 2001: 199). Her skin condition, writes Kitz (2007a: 619), 'indicates divine wrath', and 'publicly marks her as one humiliated by Yahweh'.

Burns points out how the following formal pattern, which appears some twenty-five times in the leprosy legislation of Leviticus 13 – 14, is echoed by Aaron's reaction to Miriam in the present text (1980: 115–119):

(a) The *waw* consecutive plus the verb 'to see' (*wěrā'āh*) is used to refer to an official examination of the skin diseased person;
(b) The subject of the verb is the priest (*hakkōhēn*);
(c) The particle *hinnê* with the *waw* consecutive (*wěhinnê*) then introduces an official statement of the symptom(s) observed by the priest;
(d) An official judgement as to the ritual cleanness or uncleanness of the person is made.

In the language and form of Leviticus, Aaron, acting as 'the priest', examines Miriam and 'it is judged to be a case of ritual uncleanness' (Burns 1980: 116–117), and, as such uncleanness locates and defines one as 'outside the Camp', Miriam temporarily experiences the status of a Gentile – an outsider.

Miriam's leprous condition portrays her 'as snow'. Possibly, the implicit idea is that she has become *white* as snow, poetic justice for offence at the Cushite woman, who had especially dark skin (e.g. J. Williams 2002). While reading racism with regard to skin colour seems anachronistic and implausible, there is an 'Israel versus foreigners' element in the story which allows for an alternative version of poetic justice. Leprosy defines Miriam as one who does not belong in the Camp (i.e. among God's people), based on 5:1. The phrase 'as snow' may simply refer to the flaking scales of skin caused by leprosy (Hulse 1975), imagery of death combined with that of a still-born infant, with the same result that Miriam becomes an outsider at a more fundamental level in relation to purity laws: not in a black versus white dichotomy, but in a life versus death dichotomy, buttressing the Israel versus Gentiles separation (see Morales 2015: 157–159). Leprosy, as the text itself brings out, represents a form of 'death', with the purity laws founded upon a life versus death dichotomy, rooted in the person and nature of YHWH as the fountain of life in the midst of the Camp. Having expressed her disfavour with Moses' marriage to a foreigner as one who in her eyes did not belong among God's people, it is Miriam herself who becomes an outsider, expelled from the Camp for seven days (cf. Robinson 1989: 431–432).

The phrase *mĕṣōraʿat kaššāleg* (leprous as snow) occurs only three times in Scripture, twice in the Torah (Exod. 4:6; Num. 12:10; cf. 2 Kgs 5:27). Abrams (1993) argues that in each instance, the 'leprous as snow' comes as punishment for an unjust challenge of a prophet's power. In the first case, Moses doubts his own ability to perform his duties (see Exod. 4:1, 10, 13). Abrams detects a note of rebuke in YHWH's explanation of the second sign (i.e. '*You* (Moses) did not believe the first sign, so here is the second'), and notes the significance of Moses and Aaron's actual performance of the first sign in Egypt but not the latter (1993: 42). Given other connections between Exodus 4 and Numbers 12, as the only two 'leprous as snow' texts in the Torah, the point of Miriam's leprosy may well be to reaffirm Moses' singular prophetic role to both Miriam and Aaron. Moses' original question in Exodus, 'Look! What if they do not believe me, or listen to my voice? For they will say, YHWH has not appeared to you!' (4:1), appears to be answered by YHWH's response in Numbers 12: 'I speak with him mouth to mouth . . . he beholds the form of YHWH' (v. 8). Moreover, the collocation *bî ʾădōnî* (my Lord), which occurs only five times in the Pentateuch, occurs twice in Exodus 4 with reference to Moses' entreaty of God, whereas in Numbers 12, it is used in Aaron's entreaty of Moses (v. 11). It is surely no coincidence that in Exodus 4, Aaron's role as 'prophet' is defined as Moses' mouthpiece – Aaron is to Moses, as Moses is to God (Exod. 4:14–16), this in the passage where signs, including leprosy, are given as divine confirmation that Moses was sent to speak and deliver as YHWH's agent. Miriam's leprosy and Aaron's entreaty language take the reader back to Exodus 4, an intertextual engagement that discredits Miriam and Aaron's cause, and exonerates Moses.

Leprosy in Scripture appears as a judgement from God on those who have disregarded his holiness, failing to submit to proper authority (see Zakovitch 1985; Sperling 1999: 48; Bazak 2012). Leprosy is thus a punitive demotion, a lowering of place, divinely inflicted on one who has attempted self-promotion. This means that Miriam's judgement concerns more than the Cushite wife, but encompasses her derision of Moses in both forms, against his marriage and his superior status as prophet. Sperling points to further correspondences between Numbers 12 and 2 Kings 5, such as the equation between 'leprosy' and the dead (2 Kgs 5:7), and the association of a leprosy account with prophecy (2 Kgs 5:8) (1999: 48–49). In 2 Chronicles 26 Uzziah took upon himself the priestly prerogative of entering the Temple to burn incense, with the result that leprosy broke out on his forehead – on the place where the high priest's diadem reads 'holy to YHWH' (cf. Exod. 39:30). From a cultic perspective, Miriam's judgement is associated with impurity on multiple levels, as the leprosy, already signifying defilement, is described by Aaron the priest in terms of a corpse and childbirth, sources of impurity (Camp 2009: 253).

YHWH's judgement reasserts a hierarchy, reversing the narrative flow from Miriam (v. 10) to Aaron (v. 11–12) to Moses (v. 13) to YHWH (v. 14). Just as YHWH determined to restore Abimelech only through the mediation of Abraham, establishing Abraham's role among Gentiles (Gen. 20:7, 17), so here Aaron must turn to Moses for help from YHWH. In so doing, Aaron begins to fulfil his priestly duty, interceding for the people of God. The restoration of the status quo is marked by Aaron's penitence, intercession for Miriam, and submission to Moses (Jobling 1978: 1:32), along with the regathering of Miriam into the Camp. In both Numbers 11 and 12, YHWH's presence at the central Tent of Meeting (re)establishes the Camp's structure not only geographically but spiritually and in terms of leadership.

Aaron's speech moves from confession (v. 11) to petition (v. 12) (Coats 1982a: 103). Reverently, Aaron petitions not YHWH but Moses as 'my lord' (*'ădōnî*) and pleads with Moses that Moses himself would not lay the 'sin' (*ḥaṭṭā't*) against 'us' – confessing on behalf of himself and Miriam – adding that they had acted 'foolishly' (*nô'alnû*) and had 'sinned' (*ḥāṭā'nû*). The particle of entreaty, *bî*, often followed by *'ădōnî*, functions as 'craving permission to address a superior' (BDB 106). Aaron's double use of 'please/I pray' (*nā'*), further, adds urgency and a sense of pleading (cf. Kautzsch 1910: 308). The only other time Aaron referred to Moses as 'my lord' was after the golden calf incident (Exod. 32:22). Above we noted that Moses used the same collocation 'my lord' when addressing God in Exodus 4 (vv. 10, 13). The only other uses in the Torah occur when Jacob's sons speak fearfully to Joseph or his steward, addressing the second highest authority in Egypt (Gen. 43:20; 44:18). 'The effect', writes Buell (2012: 138), 'is telling: Aaron is begging Moses.' He has come to acknowledge that his brother, by virtue of the definiteness of his mediation of YHWH's word, stands in a real – though not idolatrous – sense in place of YHWH in relation to the people's obedience of faith. While Miriam stands before him leprous, Aaron includes himself in the culpability: 'the sin upon *us*, wherein *we* have acted foolishly, and wherein *we* have sinned'. In this regard, Aaron's confession and petition are exemplary, and will not be seen in the people until the second generation (cf. Num. 21:7).

Even as high priest, Aaron is powerless to heal Miriam, the priest's role being merely diagnosis. Her cure will come through the intercession of Moses who has incomparable access to YHWH – and not only access, but divine favour. Aaron's plea focuses on help for Miriam, describing her skin disease as making her 'as one dead' with 'flesh half-consumed'. The words 'flesh' (*bāśār*) and 'consume' (*'ākal*) link this story with the previous two (Num. 11). As a unit Numbers 11 – 12 begins with the Camp's outskirts being consumed and ends with Miriam being 'consumed', both due to YHWH's fierce anger (11:1; 12:12), while the central story turns on the people's desire to consume flesh (11:4–35). Miriam's flesh like that of the quails is half eaten (11:33), and she will end up outside the Camp, a space cognate with the quails that fell outside the Camp (11:31) (cf. M. Douglas 2001: 209). Oddly, Aaron's portrait of deathly skin does not turn to an aged corpse, but rather to a still-born infant, coming out of his mother's womb – a jarring contrast between new life and the decay of death. Perhaps, as with Moses in 11:12, he employs motherly imagery for the purpose of garnering sympathy for Miriam. The idea of death is prevalent and more obvious than the notion of 'white' in understanding the theology of leprosy, identifying Miriam as an outsider, one who does not belong in the Camp of YHWH's earthly hosts. In Leviticus, one with leprosy is pronounced 'unclean', which determines that 'he will dwell alone – his dwelling will be outside the Camp' (13:46). Indeed, 'outside the Camp' (*miḥûṣ lammaḥăneh*) in 12:14 echoes the legislation of Leviticus 13:46 and is key for the story's theology. Winslow suggests Miriam's impurity through skin disease is reiterated when she dies in Numbers 20 as there is no water for purification (2011: 11).

Much has been made about the apparent imbalance of justice since only Miriam is punished and not Aaron. On the one hand, the text of 12:1 emphasizes Miriam's more dominant role in the slander, naming her before Aaron, and by using a feminine form of the verb (cf. Graetz 1991: 190). On the other hand, to judge Aaron would be to judge the entire Camp inordinately (beyond a delay of seven days) since, as Israel's high priest, he must live to intercede sacrificially on their behalf – not the least of which is the daily performance of the whole burnt offering liturgy. Apart from these daily sacrifices YHWH's presence amid his people could not be maintained (cf. Exod. 29:42–43; see Morales 2015: 132–137, 141–143). *Pirke de Rabbi Eliezer* 53 offers similar reasoning, adding that part of Aaron's punishment was the distress he experienced in looking at Miriam (brought out by the text's use of 'look!'). Fundamentally, however, the condition of leprosy in particular seems to be the result of unlawful access to YHWH's presence/sacred space. Aaron, as high priest, was anointed and consecrated for such access, even into the holy of holies (Lev. 16), while the same was not true for Miriam – her leprosy was a consequence of her exposure to YHWH's presence, though no less a judgement for that. Aaron, in turn, uses his position immediately to intercede on Miriam's behalf, which leads to her ready healing and mitigated punishment. Aaron's mediation with Moses pleads that 'hers not be a permanent case of ritual uncleanness and hence that she not be cast out of the community permanently' (Burns 1980: 118). Also, Miriam's role appears to be a figuration of Israel (see comments at 20:1). Aaron's description of Miriam, coming out of her mother's womb (12:12), resonates with Moses' words about the conception and begetting of Israel (11:12); and Miriam's leprous condition, like snow and half-consumed (12:10–12), seems to form an ironic judgement for Israel's refusal of the manna, which fell on the dew and was white in colour (11:7–9), fine and flaky like frost (Exod. 16:14). As such, her death-like condition and expulsion from the Camp may augur Israel's judgement in the next section (chs. 13–14), and her re-entry the second generation's cleansing and emergence (chs. 19–20) – the death and rebirth of Israel.

In verse 13, Moses speaks for the first time in the chapter: he 'cried out' (*wayyiṣʿaq*) to YHWH. His response is immediate, without conditions or delay, and filled with urgency. He himself had been healed by YHWH of the same 'leprous as snow' condition (Exod. 4:6–7). While Miriam has repeatedly spoken against him, Moses' only speech in the story is a plea for her deliverance. The particle of petition surrounds his appeal for Miriam's healing (and which sounds like a true cry), forming a concentric structure that centres on the word *rĕpā'*, 'heal' (cf. J. T. Walsh 2001: 15): *'ēl nā' rĕpā' nā' lah*. The particle *nā'* forms an urgent plea best translated as 'please!' (Kaufman 1991). Urgently cried out, the brevity of Moses' plea underscores his pre-eminence all the more for its heroic efficacy – Moses need but speak the word and YHWH will hear and respond so that Miriam's judgement is mitigated greatly. YHWH's response builds on an analogy with a custom that would have presumably been readily understood in the original ANE context: when a father spat upon the face of a child, that daughter or son would be shamed for a week (cf. Deut. 25:9). Such a custom, however strange to modern sensibility, appears to have been a form of chastisement rather low in the spectrum, in that the humiliation was not lasting – this was not any sort of permanent rejection: 'an intense insult soon passing, but with ongoing shame' (Winslow 2011: 6). It is a one-time act with temporary consequence. Based on this analogy, it is clear that YHWH has immediately healed Miriam in answer to Moses' cry, although she must nevertheless carry the shame of her misdeed and rebuke by remaining outside the Camp for seven days. That she was immediately healed is further confirmed as seven days was the holding period for one who had been pronounced healed of leprosy, a period that served to confirm one's cleanness (cf. Lev. 13:4, 26; 14:9; Frymer-Kensky 1983: 399–400). Jobling goes further, suggesting that Miriam's punishment had already been mitigated, that she did not have the 'living' or raw flesh of leprosy which makes one unclean, but had only been judged with the 'dead' flesh which marked a post-leprous condition (cf. Lev. 13:9–17) – a judgement that had marked her without making her unclean (1978: 1:33). Though such a reading is possible, her brothers' pleas for her healing make it unpersuasive. While the verb 'spat' is doubled (*yārōq yāraq*), emphasizing the act of shaming, the use of household imagery in YHWH's response – referring to 'her father' – is also notable, as it acknowledges Miriam as a daughter (cf. Abela 2008: 534), part of YHWH's house over which Moses is faithful (12:7).

YHWH's final word 'and afterward let her be gathered in' (*wĕ'aḥar tē'āsēp*) is just as notable as Miriam's expulsion. However shamed, Miriam's punishment is mitigated. Tervanotko deems Miriam's consequences as surprisingly milder than for other Israelites who stood up to challenge Moses (2016: 89), and E. Brown also alleviates the severity of Miriam's punishment by contrasting it with the death sentences received by her brothers in Numbers 20:2–13 (2011: 49). While such 'mild' judgement on Miriam is true, one misses the theological focus unless it is also understood that only Moses' intercession on Miriam's behalf causes her judgement to be alleviated. Aaron describes his sister as half dead in appearance, as a stillborn infant whose flesh is half consumed – it is this horrific judgement that Moses calls Israel to remember in Deuteronomy 24:9. Only Moses' intervention with YHWH on her behalf allows her deeply dreadful punishment to be mitigated to seven days of shame outside the Camp, after being healed. As such, the story focuses on Moses' role, vindicating him.

The events of Numbers 11 – 12, linked together by the key term 'gather', end with the (re)gathering of God's people within the Camp and the continuation of the people's journey in the wilderness. The three stories have a common message: the well-being and progress of the Camp through the wilderness journey requires submission to YHWH's guidance through Moses' *prophetic ministry* and mediation.

15. Miriam is 'shut out' (*sāgēr*) of the Camp, a term that recurs in the leprosy legislation of Leviticus (13:4, 5, 21, 26, 31, 33, 50, 54; 14:38); the actual usage appears to be 'shut in' with the sense of isolation (also Gen. 2:21; 7:16). Ibn Ezra notes that lepers are shut in so as not to harm others (1999: 100), an appropriate point of instruction, since Miriam's slander had brought Aaron into sin, no less than the gathered-rabble had spurred on the rest of the people to lusting after flesh in the previous story. 'While the Cushite woman becomes part of Moses' family and the people of Israel through marriage, Miriam, through her opposition to Moses, is separated both from the family and the people of Israel' (Hays 2003: 76). Trible similarly writes of the contrast of 'native against foreigner', adding (1994: 177): 'But these opposites merge as the irony folds in upon itself. If the Cushite woman stands outside a system of ritual purity, Miriam belongs with her. She too has become an outcast . . .'. Outside the Camp signifies the place of uncleanness and that of corpses – the place of outsiders, separated from the life of YHWH.

The obedience report communicates that although Miriam was 'gathered in' (*hē'āsēp*) again, such was done at a cost for the rest of the people, after the journey through the wilderness had been stalled for seven days, a significant delay for a relatively brief journey (cf. Deut. 1:2). The phrase 'the people did not journey out' underscores the negative consequence of Miriam's sin, although one may detect a recognition of her honoured status as well in that the people waited for her. The solidarity between Miriam and the people brings us one step closer to understanding not only Miriam's circumstance as a cautionary story with application for Israel, but *Miriam as representing Israel*. Just as she understands the wayward wife of 5:11–31 as a figure for Israel, M. Douglas also interprets Miriam as a symbol for idolatrous Israel (2001: 196–212; cf. 160–171). Camp similarly reads Miriam in terms 'of the prophetic figure of the straying and repentant wife of YHWH' (2009: 234). Miriam never speaks again in Scripture, her silence perhaps being part of the poetic justice not only for speaking against YHWH's servant, but for her presumption of prophetic status on par with Moses. Aaron's mediation on her behalf completes the theological message: Miriam has been marked 'as a major symbol of Israel's broken faith' (M. Douglas 2001: 203), but she is forgiven and restored through the mediation of Aaron's priesthood and Moses.

Since the period of seven days waited out by the community for Miriam, who was described 'as one dead', also happens to be the designated period of mourning the death of a loved one (cf. Gen. 50:10; 1 Sam. 31:13; 1 Chr. 10:12), this episode may foreshadow Miriam's actual death, where the detail of the length of Israel's mourning is omitted (20:1).

16. Since 'the people journeyed' is fronted by 'And afterward' (*wĕ'aḥar*) in an x-qatal construction, the delay rather than the journey is emphasized (cf. Leder 2016: 530). The journey is from 'Hazeroth' which, with the double reference to Hazeroth in 11:35, secludes Numbers 12 as an episode. Hazeroth (ḥăṣērôt) possibly receives its name from the judgement of skin disease on Miriam, described as 'half (ḥăṣî) consumed' by Aaron, and which leads to her temporary separation from the Camp. The two previous place-names derived from YHWH's judgements on his people, 'Taberah' (11:1–4) and 'Kibroth-hattaavah' (11:34–35), and this story resounds with Miriam's judgement (cf. Deut. 24:8–9), so ḥăṣērôt may be a play on ḥăṣî. Locale within theologically structured space being an undercurrent throughout Numbers 11 – 12 (e.g. Jobling 1978: 1:49–51), a double wordplay is possible: Miriam's judgement of leprosy, consuming half (ḥăṣî) her flesh, led to her expulsion from the Camp's enclosures (ḥăṣērôt).

The people then encamp in the wilderness of Paran, setting up the context for the events of chapters 13–14 (just as Hazeroth in 11:35 did for chapter 12). Such journey reports link Numbers 11 – 14 as a subunit, with the legislation of chapter 15 serving as a concluding cap. Numbers 11:35 forms an *inclusion* with 12:16, and the two verses can be read without interruption as a journey report. In the same way a narrative may be inserted into a genealogy (e.g. Gen. 6 – 9, between 5:32 and 10:1), 12:1–15 is inserted within the travelogue to explain the source of the people's delay.

Explanation

Within a subsection that deals with the outer camp of twelve tribes (chs. 11–15), these opening chapters establish Israel's primary objective and challenge in terms of heeding YHWH's word through Moses. The conflict within the outer camp relates entirely to the tribes' relationship to Moses' prophetic office. Although the nation's life is to be shaped and formed by the *torah* YHWH reveals to his servant Moses for Israel's sake, the people, disproportionately influenced by a 'gathered-rabble' and fringes of the Camp (11:1–2, 4), reveal a YHWH-despising fleshly impulse, causing a profound leadership crisis for Moses. YHWH responds to Moses' burden over the people's low spiritual level by gathering seventy elder-scribes to the central camp of the *Shekhinah*. Being 'of Israel' and 'of the people', the seventy elders and scribes are leaders within the outer camp of Israel – perhaps seventy-two (with Eldad and Medad) representing six elders from each of the twelve tribes. Empowering them by his Spirit through Moses, he sends them back with Moses to influence the outer camp (11:30). The exceptional oddity of Eldad and Medad's reception of the spirit *within* the outer camp, along with Moses' plea for YHWH's spirit to be put on the people en masse, serve to portray the outer camp of the twelve tribes as having a critical problem – a tragic flaw underscored as Miriam, likely representing Israel, denigrates Moses the conduit of YHWH's revelation (12:1–16). In both her death-like leprosy and her expulsion from the Camp, Miriam foreshadows the fate of the first generation. The stories form an analysis of Israel and, uncovering the nation's devastating weakness, enable one to foresee the community's end, even as Moses had done. These chapters form a prelude to Numbers 13 – 14, illuminating the nature of the first generation's failure: rejection of the land reflects their refusal to trust YHWH and heed his word – a sin not unlike Adam and the woman's with the Tree of Knowledge.

Whereas the subsection on the inner camp of Levites will relate to the dynamic of its relation to Aaron the high priest (chs. 16–18), the outer camp's focus is the prophetic office of Moses. The three stories of Numbers 11 – 12, as Sommer noted, 'form a unit concerned with Moses' relation to the prophetic office, its roles, and its subsequent history' (1999: 609; cf. Jobling 1978: 1:37). Winslow similarly observes that these narratives focus on the question 'who was a prophet like Moses?' (2011: 10). Among other functions, Numbers 12 responds to chapter 11, clarifying and safeguarding the role – foundational in the fullest sense – of Moses and the Torah (cf. Römer 1997: 492–495), a principal role portrayed symbolically in the ritual installation of the elders, as they derive YHWH's Spirit and authority only as mediated through Moses. The theme of Moses' superiority as servant of YHWH underscores the divine, authoritative nature of God's revealed will through him, the Torah. Integrated into the theme of prophecy, all three stories also deal with evil speech and its influence – a subtheme that finds expression in the scouts' debacle as ten scouts bring a 'bad report' of the land, contradicting God's word through Moses and convincing the tribes to reject YHWH's gift and purposes (13:32–33).

Moses' authority, writes Dozeman, because it does not arise from himself as a profane character, is transcendent – he is one who when he acts, he acts for God, and when he speaks, he speaks for God, so that in effect 'Moses is not even the protagonist of his own story' (2000: 29; quoting from McBride 1990: 229–239). In this way, Dozeman continues, Moses is quite different from any other character in the HB *because* Moses' personality is subsumed in a divine Torah, making him the most authoritative person in the Hebrew canon, his authority arising only from 'his role as a channel for divine teaching' (Dozeman 2000: 29; also Neusner 1985: 374–375). As chief steward of YHWH's house, Moses cannot be co-opted by any narrowly defined social group, for he is 'not simply unique' but '*singularly* unique', so that to 'come into contact with Moses was to come in contact with the very primal form of legitimation itself' (Hutton 1994: 34–35; emphasis original). Miriam's derision of Moses was a rejection of the 'absoluteness' of his prophetic authority (Tunyogi 1969: 48). In preparation for understanding the disastrous rebellion of unbelief in Kadesh Barnea, Numbers 11 – 12 displays the unique role of Moses to whom, although his prophetic authority was undermined by Miriam and Aaron, the people should have heeded – for he alone was YHWH's loyal servant, entrusted with his house and will (Num. 14:4, 39–45; Hymes 1998: 31–32). No less for the people's own sake, in relation to their confidence in the Torah of Moses, YHWH defends Moses' status as the prophet par excellence, who faithfully and clearly reveals YHWH's will for his people. YHWH will not grant face-to-face revelation to every Israelite – they must trust the words that come through Moses, YHWH's faithful servant, and indeed will give an account of how they do so (see Deut. 5:31; Moberly 2006: 6–7). Moses and YHWH's Torah are so deeply united that to defend his word and promote total faith in his word – critical for inheriting the land – YHWH defends the status and role of Moses vigorously. Moses' crisis, addressed by a distribution of the Spirit, and the rebellion of Miriam and Aaron, resolved by YHWH's zealous vindication, highlight Moses' supremely crucial role (also Coats 1982a; B. P. Robinson 1989: 429 n. 2). When the people fail to inherit the land, these stories exonerate him as Israel's shepherd under YHWH. The people will fall in the wilderness by no fault of YHWH's guidance through Moses – rather they failed to enter by their own evil hearts of unbelief, having rebelled against YHWH's word of promise through Moses (cf. Heb. 3:7 – 4:2).

Fittingly, the focus on Moses' prophetic ministry necessarily involves the pervasive role of the *rûaḥ* of YHWH. Indeed, the emphasis on the Spirit/Wind in chapter 11 is both exemplary and extraordinary in the way it weaves together so many of the narrative elements, from Moses' role as mediator and chief prophet, the counterbalance to the people's lust for flesh, the empowerment of the seventy elder-scribes, along with their engagement in prophesying, and Eldad and Medad's unique situation in the Camp, to the gathering of quail – with YHWH himself as the sovereign source and fountain of the *rûaḥ*. With a set of contrasts, the internal struggle for the outer camp's identity, nature, and end unfolds: the gathered-rabble versus Moses and the elder-scribes who represent YHWH's word, flesh versus Spirit, Egypt versus the land of Canaan, and ultimately death in the wilderness versus life in the land. These divergent paths recall the purity laws where the strayed woman (5:11–31) and the Nazirite vow (6:1–21) were presented as opposing ways of approaching the wilderness sojourn. While flesh opposes God's word, the Spirit, who is the source of prophecy, not only empowers divine instruction but enables trusting obedience to his word – a remedy revealed long before its provision.

The way in which YHWH distributes his *rûaḥ* as the Spirit that was upon Moses expresses the point that everything YHWH offered Israel he did so through Moses as conduit, through the agency of his designated mediator. This pattern continues in the New Testament: when on the Feast of Weeks, in fulfilment of Moses' plea (11:29) and the prophetic promise of Joel (2:28–32), God pours out his Spirit on his people, that

Spirit is poured from, through, and with Christ, is so *impressed* with Christ that he is called 'the Spirit of Christ', and his goal is to form Christ within his people (Acts 2:1–33) – he is the Spirit whom God 'poured out upon us through Jesus Christ our Saviour' (Titus 3:5–6). In Numbers 11, Moses is like the rock out of which waters flowed to quench the people's thirst (ch. 20), with seventy streams of living water – the Holy Spirit – flowing from the heart of Israel's Camp within the wilderness, which means that in the moment of his greatest crisis, Moses foreshadowed the Messiah most clearly. In Numbers 12, YHWH vigorously defends his servant as 'faithful in all my house', and proclaims Moses' uniqueness as one to whom he speaks 'mouth to mouth', and who beholds 'the form of YHWH' (12:7–8). Perhaps the only higher commendation given to Moses is in the New Testament's quote of Numbers 12:7, whereby the Son's faithfulness to the Father is set forth by the standard of Moses: 'just as (*hōs*) Moses was faithful in all God's house' (Heb. 3:2). Even the vindication of Moses, however, was aimed at a vindication of the Torah, of YHWH's revelation through him.

In Deuteronomy, Moses will plead with the second generation to labour diligently at internalizing *torah* (6:6–9), explaining how the wilderness testing was meant to teach them the priority of YHWH's word (8:3), and of their ultimate need for YHWH's spiritual circumcision of the heart (30:6). In the Torah, Israel will have YHWH's revealed word, but Moses' expressed desire (Num. 11:29) betrays his understanding that the words of God remain an outward reality. As the ensuing narratives and further history of Israel demonstrate, the distribution of the Spirit from Moses to seventy elders *among* the people will fall short of the only sure remedy, the Spirit *within* the people – the solution for which Moses prayed, and of which the prophets would proclaim. YHWH's Spirit is needed both to communicate *and to receive* his word, and Moses expresses his desire for the people to attain to his own spiritual level, that YHWH would put his Spirit on all his people (11:29). Clearly, he understood the gift of the Spirit as the ultimate remedy for his own burden among the people. Not without justification, Jewish and Christian tradition have connected Moses' desire – indeed, his prayer – to the prophetic expectation of YHWH's Spirit being poured out upon his people within the context of a new covenant (see *Num. Rab.* 15.25). *Midrash Tehillim* 14.6 reads Numbers 11:29 as an expression of Moses' hope for the whole nation's salvation, to be fulfilled in the world to come (Sommer 1999: 610). Moses' desire that 'all the people of YHWH were prophets' (v. 29) corresponds to expressions found in the prophetic corpus, such as Joel 2:28–29, which reads (cf. Römer 1997: 489):

Thus will happen afterward: I will pour out my Spirit upon all flesh, so that your sons and your daughters will prophesy, your elders will dream dreams, your young men will see visions; also upon your servants and upon your maidservants in those days I will pour out my Spirit.

Terms such as YHWH's 'spirit' (*rûaḥ*), 'flesh' (*bāśār*), 'young/choice men' (*bāḥûr*), 'elders' (*zĕqēnîm*) and 'prophet/prophesy' (*nĕbî*') are shared by Numbers 11 and Joel's prophecy, as well as 'dream(s)' (*ḥălôm*), if Numbers 12 is included. Isaiah shares a similarly expectant hope (32:15; 44:3), and Ezekiel's prophecies make clear the relationship between YHWH's Spirit and the place of his word within his people's heart (36:26–27; 39:29). That Moses' words overflow into full prophetic vigour in the exilic era has led some to speculate that his plea was a late addition to the text (e.g. Seebass 1978; Gunneweg 1990: 177). Rather, after the history of Israel had conclusively caught up with Moses' original assessment, demonstrating Israel's desperate and otherwise irremediable situation, all prophetic hope led inescapably back to his original plea, more of YHWH's Spirit for the people themselves. As the first expanded reference to the Spirit of God in the Torah, Numbers 11 is foundational for understanding the Spirit's outpouring on the Feast of Weeks (see Stronstad 1999; Cotton 2001) – the power from on high which the apostles had awaited in Jerusalem (Acts 2; see 1:8). 'Walk in the Spirit', Paul exhorts, 'and you will not fulfil the lust of the flesh,' for those who belong to Christ 'have crucified the flesh with its affections and lusts' (Gal. 5:16, 24).

Numbers 11 – 12 also form a reflection on the complex nature of the covenant community with respect to outsiders, balancing carefully Israel's relationship to foreigners. Narrative references to the 'outskirts' of the Camp (11:1), to the 'gathered-rabble' (11:4), to the 'Cushite' whom Moses married (12:1), along with Miriam's being shut out of the Camp (12:14–15), spur meditation on what makes a covenant community member in terms of insider/outsider categories. After stories narrating the negative influence of foreigners, the third story corrects false notions about Israelite relationships with foreigners. Moses himself will, throughout Deuteronomy (e.g. ch. 7), warn Israel gravely over the influence to apostasy on Israel from foreigners (cf. Num. 25:1–3), but he never loses sight of Israel's vocation to bring blessing on the nations, as clearly expressed to his brother-in-law Hobab just as Israel sets out for the land (Num. 10:29:32), and it should be noted that Moses' marriage to a Cushite was not in violation of any intermarriage prohibition, which referred rather to Canaanites and included exceptions (cf. Exod. 34:11, 16; Josh. 2:9–14; Matt. 1:5). What separates 'the sons of Israel' is as much a theological boundary as an ethnic one (see Rom. 9:6–13; cf. Matt. 3:7–12; John 8:37–47; 2 Cor. 6:11–18) – there is every reason to assume Moses' Cushite wife was a follower of YHWH and perhaps she may even be viewed as a token of God's blessing the peoples of the earth through Abraham's seed (cf. Hays 2003: 66, 79–80). Although an Israelite, Miriam's behaviour, in slandering YHWH's loyal servant, marked her as temporarily unfit for life in the community (cf. 5:1–4). Interestingly, while the challenges for the Camp of the first generation are internal (chs. 11–15, 16–18), those for the second generation will be primarily external, related to Israel's interactions among the nations (chs. 21–25).

In terms of the Camp's structure, the outer camp narrative (chs. 11–15) displays Israel's progressive exile. First, YHWH's fire reasserts the community boundary, blazing the 'outskirts of the Camp', a square-shaped wall of fire separating inside versus outside of the Camp, with 'that place' – the edges of the Camp – being named 'Burning' (11:1, 3). Second, Israelites spread quail 'all around the Camp' where YHWH strikes them, naming 'that place', 'there' where they were buried, 'Grave of Lusters' (11:32–34). The people then journey to 'Hazeroth' ('enclosures', 11:35), perhaps presaging the third story, which concludes with Miriam being 'shut out from the Camp' (12:15). The final story, of the scouts (chs. 13–14), will conclude with Israel's first generation dying 'in the wilderness', dying 'there' (14:35), a designation that signifies 'outside the Camp' theologically, with 'Hormah' (Destruction) serving as a monument.

After the previous section's prospect of a well-coordinated Camp pursuing the divine Cloud through the wilderness, chapters 11–12 introduce the principle of delay on the sojourn due to sin. What was to be a journey of a few weeks is delayed, first for a month due to the people's lusting for flesh (11:19–20), and then for another seven days due to Miriam and Aaron's slander of Moses (12:14–16) (cf. Y. Kahn 2014: 124). This principle of retribution and delay foreshadows the great judgement of forty years in the wilderness, a year for each day the twelve tribal heads scouted the land (14:34), which stalled the sojourn until the bodies of the first generation of Israel had fallen, strewn in the wilderness. Sin – failing to live according to God's Word – always delays spiritual progress. In the church's sojourn, described also as a race to glory, God's people are urged to lay aside the sin that so easily entangles, and to run with patient endurance, looking to Jesus who for the joy set before him endured the cross of agony and shame, and is now enthroned at God's right hand (Heb. 12:1–2).

NUMBERS 13 – 14: THE OUTER CAMP'S REBELLION AND JUDGEMENT

Translation

¹³:¹And YHWH spoke to Moses, saying, ²'Send for yourself men that they may search out the land of Canaan which I am giving to the sons

of Israel; one man for each one of the tribes of his fathers you will send, every one a chieftain among them.' ³And Moses sent them from the wilderness of Paran according to the mouth of YHWH; they were all of them men who were heads of the sons of Israel. ⁴And these are their names:

for the tribe of Reuben, Shammua the son of Zaccur;
⁵for the tribe of Simeon, Shaphat the son of Hori;
⁶for the tribe of Judah, Caleb the son of Jephunneh;
⁷for the tribe of Issachar, Igal the son of Joseph;
⁸for the tribe of Ephraim, Hoshea the son of Nun;
⁹for the tribe of Benjamin, Palti the son of Raphu;
¹⁰for the tribe of Zebulun, Gaddiel the son of Sodi;
¹¹for the tribe of Joseph, the tribe of Manasseh, Gaddi the son of Susi;
¹²for the tribe of Dan, Ammiel the son of Gemalli;
¹³for the tribe of Asher, Sethur the son of Michael;
¹⁴for the tribe of Naphtali, Nahbi the son of Vophsi;
¹⁵for the tribe of Gad, Geuel the son of Machi.

¹⁶These are the names of the men whom Moses sent to search out the land; and Moses called Hoshea the son of Nun Joshua.

¹⁷And Moses sent them to search out the land of Canaan and said to them, 'Ascend this way through the Negeb, and ascend the mountain. ¹⁸And you will see the land – what is it like? and the people who dwell on it – are they strong? weak? are they few or many? ¹⁹And what is the land like in which they dwell – is it good or evil? And what are the cities like wherein they dwell – are they in open-settlements or in fortresses? ²⁰And what is the land like – is it fat or lean, is there a tree within it or not? And you will embolden yourselves and take of the fruit of the land.' Now the days were the days of the firstfruits of grapes.

²¹And they ascended and they searched out the land, from the wilderness of Zin to Rehob, toward Lebo-Hamath. ²²And they ascended into the Negeb and came to Hebron, and Ahiman, Sheshai, and Talmai, the children of the Anak were there. Now Hebron was built seven years before Zoan in Egypt. ²³And they came to Wadi of Eshcol (Grape Cluster), and they cut from there a branch and one cluster of grapes, which they carried on a carrying frame with two men, and of the pomegranates and of the figs. ²⁴That place he called Wadi of Eshcol because of the cluster of grapes which the sons of Israel cut from there. ²⁵And they returned from searching out the land at the end of forty days. ²⁶And they went and came to Moses and to Aaron and to all the community of the sons of Israel, to the wilderness of Paran, to Kadesh; and they brought back word to them and to all the community, and showed them the fruit of the land. ²⁷And they recounted to him and said, 'We came to the land where you sent us, and also it is flowing with milk and honey, and this

is its fruit. ²⁸Nevertheless, the people are mighty who dwell in the land, and the cities are fortified and very huge, and also the children of the Anak we saw there. ²⁹Amalek dwells in the land of the Negeb, and the Hittites and the Jebusites and the Amorites dwell in the mountain, and the Canaanites dwell by the sea and by the hand of the Jordan.'

³⁰And Caleb quieted the people against Moses, and he said, 'Let us surely ascend and possess it, for we are surely able to prevail over it.'

³¹But the men who had ascended with him said, 'We are not able to ascend against the people, for they are stronger than we.' ³²And they spread a bad report of the land which they had searched out to the sons of Israel, saying, 'The land through which we passed to search out is a land that devours its inhabitants, and all the people that we saw in the midst of it were men of great stature. ³³And there we saw the *Nephilim*, the sons of Anak who come from the *Nephilim*, and in our own eyes we were as grasshoppers – and so we were in their eyes!'

¹⁴:¹And the whole community lifted and put forth their voice, and the people wept throughout that night. ²And the sons of Israel grumbled against Moses and against Aaron, and the whole community said to them, 'If only we had died in the land of Egypt, or if only we had died in this wilderness! ³Why did YHWH bring us to this land to fall by the sword, so our wives and our little ones will be for spoil? Would it not be good for us to return to Egypt?' ⁴And they said, each man to his brother, 'Let us appoint a head and let us return to Egypt!'

⁵Then Moses fell, and Aaron, on their faces before the whole assembly of the community of the sons of Israel. ⁶Now Joshua the son of Nun and Caleb the son of Jephunneh, who were among those who searched out the land, tore their garments. ⁷And they said to all the community of the sons of Israel, saying, 'The land through which we passed to search out, is a very, very good land. ⁸If YHWH delights in us he will bring us into this land, and give it to us – a land that is flowing with milk and honey. ⁹Only do not rebel against YHWH; and you, you should not fear the people of the land for they are as our bread: their shade of defence has turned away from them and YHWH is with us – do not fear them!'

¹⁰And the whole community said to stone them with stones, but the glory of YHWH appeared at the Tent of Meeting to all the sons of Israel. ¹¹And YHWH said to Moses, 'How long will this people spurn me, and how long will they not trust in me, by all the signs which I have done in their midst? ¹²Let me strike them down with pestilence and let me dispossess them, and let me make you into a nation greater and mightier than they!'

¹³And Moses said to YHWH, 'The Egyptians will hear, for by your strength you caused this people to ascend from their midst, ¹⁴and they will say to those dwelling in this land – for they have heard that you YHWH are in the midst of this people, that eye to eye you YHWH are

seen, and your Cloud is standing over them, and in a pillar of cloud you are walking before them daily, and in a pillar of fire by night. ¹⁵Now when you kill this people as one man, then the nations who have heard of your fame will speak, saying, ¹⁶"Because YHWH was not able to bring this people into the land which he swore to them, he slaughtered them in the wilderness." ¹⁷But now, please, let the strength of my Lord be great, just as you have spoken, saying, ¹⁸"YHWH is slow to anger and of abundant loving-kindness, forgiving guilt and transgression, but by no means clearing wholly, visiting the guilt of the fathers upon the sons, upon the third and upon the fourth generation," ¹⁹forgive, pray, the guilt of this people according to the greatness of your loving-kindness, just as you have borne with this people from Egypt until now!

²⁰And YHWH said, 'I have forgiven, according to your word. ²¹Yet truly, as I live, the whole earth will be filled with the glory of YHWH. ²²Because all the men who have seen my glory and my signs which I had done in Egypt and in the wilderness, and have tested me these ten times and have not heeded my voice, ²³they will surely not see the land which I have sworn to their fathers, and all who spurned me will not see it. ²⁴But my servant Caleb, because a different spirit is with him, and he has fully followed after me, I will bring him into the land, there where he entered, and his seed will possess it. ²⁵Now the Amalekites and the Canaanites dwell in the valley; tomorrow you (all) will turn and journey out for yourselves into the wilderness, by the way of the Sea of Suph.'

²⁶And YHWH spoke to Moses and to Aaron saying, ²⁷'How long for this evil community, they who grumble against me? The grumblings of the sons of Israel which they grumble against me I have heard. ²⁸Say to them, "As I live – utterance of YHWH – see if not! just as you have spoken in my ears, just so will I do to you. ²⁹In this wilderness your carcasses will fall, even all of you who were appointed according to your whole number, from twenty years old and above, who have grumbled against me. ³⁰You will not be brought into the land of which I lifted my hand (on oath) to have you dwell in it, except for Caleb the son of Jephunneh and Joshua the son of Nun. ³¹And your little ones whom you said would be for spoil, I will bring them in and they will know the land that you have despised. ³²But you, your carcasses will fall in this wilderness. ³³And your sons will be shepherding in the wilderness forty years, and they will bear your whoredoms until your carcasses come to an end in the wilderness. ³⁴By the number of days which you searched out the land – forty days, each day for a year – you will bear your guilt: forty years, and you will know my hostility." ³⁵I YHWH have spoken – will I not do this to this whole evil community, who are gathered together against me? In this wilderness they will come to an end and there they will die.' ³⁶And the men whom Moses had sent to search out the land and returned and caused the whole community to grumble against him,

in spreading a bad report against the land, [37]the men who spread forth an evil bad report of the land died by the plague before YHWH. [38]But Joshua the son of Nun and Caleb the son of Jephunneh, they lived from among the men who went to search out the land.

[39]And Moses spoke these words to all the sons of Israel, and the people mourned greatly. [40]And they rose early in the morning and ascended to the summit of the mountain, saying, 'Here we are; we will ascend to the place that YHWH had said, for we sinned.'

[41]And Moses said, 'Why this, you are transgressing the mouth of YHWH, and it will not succeed? [42]Do not ascend for YHWH is not in your midst, lest you be smashed before your enemies. [43]For the Amalekites and the Canaanites are there before you, and you will fall by sword, because you turned away from following after YHWH; just so, YHWH will not be with you.'

[44]Now they swelled up to ascend to the summit of the mountain, but the Ark of the Covenant of YHWH, and Moses, did not depart from the midst of the Camp. [45]Then the Amalekites and the Canaanites dwelling on that mountain descended and they struck them down and crushed them as far as Hormah.

Notes on the text

13:1. SamP and some Gk texts are preceded by more material here, harmonizing with Deut. 1:20–23.

2. 'you will send': MT has pl., whereas SamP, LXX and Syr have, as context implies, sg. The odd pl. may support the wider background supplied in Deut. 1:20–23.

10–11. *BHS* suggests these verses should follow v. 7, restoring the typical order. While the logic of the present order is allusive, there is no textual support for the change. *BHS* reconstructs v. 11 as 'for the sons of Joseph, for the tribe of Manasseh', which conforms more closely to Num. 1:10.

18. 'strong? weak?': this construction does not have *h-* + *'im* as with the other either/or questions.

19. 'open-settlements': lit. 'camps', *maḥănîm*, as contrasted with walled fortifications.

20. 'a tree': *'ēṣ* sg.; while perhaps intending the collective 'wood', the reference, along with 'take of the fruit' and the previous *tov* or *ra'* (v. 19), suggests a recall of Eden (Gen. 2:9, 17; 3:5–6).

21. SamP and LXX have 'And they went, and came, and toured,' but MT's use of 'ascend' is consistent with use of this key term throughout.

22. 'and came': MT has sg., but there is textual support for pl. As sg., the ref. is to Caleb (see 14:24 with Josh. 14:6–15).

24. 'called': MT has sg.; SamP, LXX, Syr, *TgPs-J* have pl.

29. SamP and LXX add 'and the Hivite' between the Hittite and the Jebusite.

30–31. The adversarial *'el* used in v. 31 (against the people) is an appealing possibility for v. 30 (against Moses), as per translation; see R. J. Williams 2007: §303. SamP has *'al*, fortifying an adversarial interpretation. Both SamP and LXX have 'and said to him' before Caleb's speech, which appears to be the intention of MT.

33. LXX lacks 'the sons of Anak who come from the *Nephilim*', but there is no compelling reason to depart from MT. SamP contains added material, harmonizing the account with Deut. 1:27–33.

14:1. 'wept': MT is pl. (as with 'put forth', while 'lifted' is sg.), but SamP, LXX, Syr, Vg have sg.

5. 'assembly': missing from LXX, *TgPs-J*.

9. LXX has it that 'the time' (of their protection) has departed.

10. LXX has 'in the cloud on the Tabernacle of witness', likely an interpretative gloss.

12. 'will make you': SamP and LXX add 'and the house of your father'.

15. 'your fame': lit. have heard of 'hearing-of-you', *šim'ăkā*; LXX reads 'your name'.

18. 'by no means clearing wholly': lit. 'to clear he will not clear', *naqqê lō' yĕnaqqeh*. SamP, LXX, *TO* add 'and truth' after loving-kindness and 'sin' after transgression, SamP also adding 'and an innocent he will clear him', harmonizing with Exod. 34:6–7.

23. 'sworn to their fathers': SamP adds here 'to give them', and LXX adds a lengthy explanatory gloss anticipating v. 31 (see van der Meer 2008).

24. 'he has fully followed after me': employs a form of *mālē'*.

35. 'gathered together': niph. ptc. of *yā'ad*.

36. 'caused to grumble': following the suggested hiph. Q (versus the niph. K).

44. 'they swelled up': *wayya'pilû*, a picture of presumption.

45. SamP adds 'they chased them as bees', relying on Deut. 1:44; SamP and LXX conclude this verse with 'and they returned to the camp' (cf. Deut. 1:45).

Form and structure

Some scholarship has assessed chapters 13–14 as comprised of two parallel accounts, attributed to J (perhaps with elements of E) and P sources (e.g. G. B. Gray 1903: 128–133; Boorer 1992: 331–338; Achenbach 2003a; Schart 2013; Kislev 2017). Over a century ago, however, W. H. Green ably demonstrated the flaws of this approach to Numbers 13 – 14, demonstrating that the reconstructed sources are inferior to the existing text (1893). Undaunted, critical scholars, in the period from

1860 to 2013, proposed at least seventy-two different hypothetical source allocations for Numbers 13 – 14 (cf. Galbraith 2014: 30). While there are real textual matters with which to grapple, the ancient mind did not likely perceive the level of incongruity ascribed to the text by later scholarship – and features once thought problematic, such as doublets, are now understood as ancient literary artistry (cf. Miles 1981: 28). For interpreting the text as it stands, moreover, source criticism, which seeks to discern the history and politics behind a given text (e.g. Jeon 2020), is of little help. The narrative progresses by use of motifs and wordplays, especially by use of 'ascend' ('ālāh), 'see' (rā'āh) and 'possess' (yāraš) (see Boorer 1992: 342).

Although some of W. W. Lee's critiques of it are valid (2003b: 133–134), Milgrom's proposed literary structure remains useful (1990: 387–388; cf. 1987a: 55–58):

A. The scouts' expedition (13:1–24)
    1. God decides on reconnaissance (and conquest) (vv. 1–2)
    2. Moses chooses and instructs scouts (vv. 3–20)
    3. Expedition fulfilled (vv. 21–24)
        B. The scouts' report (13:25–33)
            1. Majority report: objective (vv. 25–29)
            2. Caleb's counter-report (v. 30)
            3. Majority report: subjective (vv. 31–33)
                X. The people's response (14:1–10a)
                    1. Majority response: abandon project (vv. 1–5)
                    2. Joshua and Caleb's counter-response (vv. 6–9)
                    3. Majority response: stone opposition (v. 10a)
        B'. God's response (14:10b–38)
            1. Destroy Israel except Moses (vv. 10b–12)
            2. Moses intercedes (vv. 13–19)
            3. God mitigates decree (vv. 20–35)
A'. The people's expedition (14:39–45)
    1. People decide on conquest (vv. 39–40)
    2. Moses protests (vv. 41–43)
    3. Expedition aborted (vv. 44–45)

The people's failed 'expedition' (14:39–45) is actually a failed attempt at conquest, but still contrasts with the divinely sanctioned scouting mission that was blessed with no adversity (13:1–24), and while the scouts' majority report is underlined as ultimately culpable (13:31–33), its disastrous effect on the people is central to the story (14:1–10). What may be missed by Milgrom's outline is the poetic justice in God's judgement (14:28–31), matching the people's complaint (14:2–5). Formally, the text is also structured along the divine command and fulfilment scheme, but goes well beyond this order and is positioned, rather, within the rebellion cycle observed since Numbers 11:1–3. The scouts' two-fold report (13:26–33) creates the story's major plot complication, and thus plays a central role in the narrative (S. Schwartz 2020: 583; cf. Condie 2001: 126).

Comment

13:1–3. The account begins with a divine command formula found, with slight variation, some sixty-six times throughout Numbers. The Samaritan Pentateuch harmonizes Numbers with Deuteronomy by inserting Deuteronomy 1:20–23 *before* YHWH's command, so that the command is understood rather as a divine concession. Use of *lĕkā* in verse 2, 'Send *for yourself*', may accord with this understanding, and is Rashi's approach, following *Num. Rab.* 16.7–8, whereby God is saying, 'Send them yourself, if you wish, but I already told them it is a good land' (cf. also Milgrom 1990: 100). However, the notion of God distancing himself from the mission works counter to the text's repeated emphasis on the divine command to send the men. Possibly *lĕkā* functions to recall the Abraham narrative, which begins and ends with a divine *lek-lĕkā* (Gen. 12:1; 22:2). As an ethical dative, *lĕkā* 'indicates a special participation in the action by the agent or speaker, a certain earnestness or zeal with which he acts; but it occurs, as an expression of heartiness' (Ewald 1891: 173), and 'does not detract from the statement's meaning as a command' (Hirsch 2007a: 238). A command phrased in such a manner calls for a special sort of ownership in the follow-through obedience. Moreover, the original request for scouts on the part of the people is not included in Numbers, so emphasis must be allowed to remain on the divinely sanctioned mission. Not only does the account begin with God's command but Moses' fulfilment is also understood as being 'according to the mouth of YHWH' (v. 3). At the least, 'Send for yourself' underscores Moses' authority – the scouts are sent by Moses at YHWH's command, and are to report back to Moses, underscoring their later sedition. YHWH authoritatively commissions the scouts (Knierim and Coats 2005: 185), ensuring that the gift of the land, as every other covenantal gift, will be given through Moses.

The land of Canaan is further defined as the land 'which I [YHWH] am giving to the sons of Israel', a fundamental perspective that will be denied in the majority report. God had long before promised Abraham that he would give this land to his descendants (Gen. 15:18–21), and had reaffirmed his promise to Isaac (Gen. 26:3) and again to Jacob (Gen. 28:13). In calling Moses to lead Israel out of Egypt, YHWH promised the land to this same generation of Israelites directly (see Exod. 3:17) – through Moses, this was God's opening message to Israel in Egypt.

Moreover, YHWH's having sworn to give the land to the patriarchs' descendants is repeatedly mentioned in Moses' intercessions on Israel's behalf (Exod. 33:1; Num. 11:12; 14:16).

The nature of the mission is clear: primarily to have a foretaste of the goodness of the land and, secondarily, for practical purposes related to how the land will be possessed – *not* to determine their ability to take the land YHWH is giving them. The term used to describe the mission's purpose is *tûr*, 'to encircle, traverse' (Levine 1993: 351), used as 'to search out' or 'explore' – not 'to spy' in a military sense. Elsewhere, the term is used in the 'search' for wisdom (Eccl. 1:13; 7:25), and for merchant 'explorers' during Solomon's reign (1 Kgs 10:15). The word is first used in Numbers with reference to the Ark of the Covenant of YHWH, leading forth the Camp in the wilderness 'to search out' (*lātûr*) a resting place (10:33; cf. *Num. Rab.* 16.7). The last use in Numbers is related to the tassels that will remind Israelites not to 'search out' after their own hearts and eyes (15:39), a message that serves as a response to the failed scouting mission. Aside from these two uses framing chapters 11–15 as a unit (along with use of *nātan*), *tûr* is employed another twelve times in the present account (chs. 13–14). In Deuteronomy 1:32–33, Moses summarizes the people's sin of failing to take possession of the land as not believing YHWH God 'who went in the way before you to search out (*tûr*) a place for your encampments'. The people's own request for a mission in Deuteronomy uses the term *ḥāpar*, which also means to search out or explore, though it is closer to the notion of spying. The more typical word used for spies is *mĕraggĕlîm* from *rāgal* (to foot it), used, for example, in Joseph's accusation that his brothers had come to Egypt as spies (Gen. 42). It is used by Moses of the scouts' mission once in Deuteronomy (1:24), although this may be an after-the-fact assessment – the term is not ever used of the scouts or their mission in Numbers. McEvenue rightly concludes that the leaders 'are to know with their own eyes the good thing which Yahweh is about to give them, and they are to evaluate it, giving a favourable evaluation of it to the people' (1971: 118–120). The translation 'to explore' is likely closer to the mark even than 'to scout out', *tûr* used 'in order to describe the purpose of their mission as a theological evaluation of the land' (Dozeman 1998: 122). Ska's on-point assessment is worth quoting in full (2014: 114):

> In Numbers 13–14, the exploration of the land has nothing to do with the sending of spies to prepare for the conquest. The twelve representatives of Israel go through the whole land and take possession of it in a juridical procedure similar to the *ambulatio*. The latter word is a technical term borrowed from Roman Law that describes the way a piece of land becomes somebody's property *de iure*, and not yet *de facto*, when he or she goes walking through this whole piece of land.

The rest of Numbers 13–14 explains the reason why Israel does not take possession of the land *de facto*.

By contrast, in 21:32 we read that Moses sent to 'spy out' (*raggēl*) Jazer, and took its villages and drove out the Amorites who were there'. There, spying out involved no political fanfare as in 13:1–16. Similarly, *měraggělîm* is used throughout Joshua for the two men sent to spy Jericho (2:1; 6:22, 23, 25), as well as later missions (7:2; 14:7). The differences between Joshua's military missions and that of the scouts in Numbers is instructive: Joshua sent only two anonymous men secretly in the night to spy one locale on a mission lasting only a few days (Josh. 2:1–2), whereas Moses sent twelve prominent men – each one a chieftain or 'prince' (*nāśî*) – and he sent them publicly and ceremoniously before the nation of Israel. While Joshua's spies gathered intelligence solely for military attack, Moses' scouts gather economic and demographic-political information (Malamat 1970: 3). As a relative term, 'chieftain' does not necessarily imply that these figures rank as high as the chieftains designated in 1:5–16, or have somehow replaced them, but simply that they are notable leaders with influence. Also, 'men' (*'ănāšîm*) in this context, verses 2, 3, 16, likely signifies 'distinguished men' or 'men of repute' (Cf. *Num. Rab.* 16.5; Rashi 1997: 4:149). Joshua's men did not need to be public figures or 'heads' of their tribes, but young and agile, able to climb through windows and manoeuvre about in the night. Two men are more discreet than twelve. Joshua's spies return to report to him alone (Josh. 2:23), while the tribal leaders return not only to report to Moses but also come before 'all the community of the sons of Israel' (13:26). The two men under the cover of night immediately hid themselves in the house of a harlot, whereas Moses' men encounter the children of Anak and would seem almost to parade about with a large cluster of grapes carried between two men, along with samplings of pomegranates and figs – at the least, there is no indication of an effort to maintain secrecy. As Medan observes (2014: 159; also Grossman 2014b):

> It would appear that there was no great danger involved in sending the princes to tour the country. Canaan was a land full of fruit-merchants, land dealers, and sundry tourists. The group of princes would not look out of place, and their examination of the nature of the land, its climate, and its water would not arouse suspicion. Suspicion arises – as in the case of the spies sent to Jericho – when men come to examine city walls, access and escape routes, city water, sources for siege conditions, etc.

Moses' mission was more political in nature, rather than a strategic military reconnaissance. While Joshua sends trained, anonymous soldiers, Moses sends men who represent one of the tribes of his fathers, 'every one a chieftain among them'. Moses' mission has more similarities with the mission found in Joshua 18, where three representatives from each of the remaining tribes are sent to survey the land for the sake of their tribe's inheritance: 'How long will you tarry to go and possess the land which YHWH God of your fathers has given to you? Bring out for yourselves three men for each tribe and I will send them; and they will arise and walk through the land and write of it according to their inheritance, and they will come to me' (vv. 3–4; cf. Num. 34:16–29). Two other passages bring us to a similar understanding. In Genesis 13:14–17, wherever Abraham walked, all the land he 'saw', was the seal of YHWH's promise to grant the same land to his descendants. Perhaps the mission of the twelve chieftains, representing their tribes, is to be understood as their walking in the footsteps of Abraham. Deuteronomy 11:24–25 portrays a similar fulfilment in Moses' words to the second generation. Given these texts, the mission of the scouts may be understood as serving to claim possession of the land, a seal of YHWH's promise to bring them in. From a source-critical perspective, Schart surmises that in the substantial reworking of the material the 'military character of the mission was eliminated', opting instead for: 'an official delegation of Israel was sent to inspect' (2013: 165), affirming the mission's nature in the text as it stands. Rather than military spies tactically-proficient at reconnoitering, Moses chose 'influential men whose report could sway the community', esteemed men of clout (Beck 2000: 272–273). The twelve princes are 'sent ones', the root šālaḥ (send) employed seven times to define them and their mission (13:2 [twice], 3, 16, 17, 27; 14:36), a designation that even has prophetic dimensions in other contexts, with Moses later being vindicated as 'sent' by YHWH (see 16:28–29; cf. Jer. 23:21). Ironically, the ten scouts' speech will actually contradict the word and will of YHWH through Moses – they are anti-prophets.

The wilderness of Paran is a general locale (v. 3), whereas the scouts' departure is recounted more narrowly as from the wilderness of Zin (and Kadesh-Barnea), a focused area within Paran (v. 21). The wilderness of Paran links the first generation's failed mission (10:12; 12:16; 13:3, 26). Verse 3 reiterates two points: Moses' sending of the scouts was by divine command, and the political status of the scouts, each one a 'head' (rōʾš) of the sons of Israel – their clout will be emphasized further through the listing of their names by tribe (vv. 4–15). Both points serve to underscore these leaders' culpability in the national disaster that is about to ensue. Moses is not to be blamed for sending scouts; the political sway and influence of these men, which should have been used to promote faith in God's promises, served to spread their rebellious unbelief, plunging an entire generation into judgement. Moreover, the emphasis on their being sent by Moses also establishes that they are to report back to Moses rather than to the people – their later behaviour in verse 32 is clearly insubordinate (so, too, Abarbanel 2015: 137).

The scouts' mission was according to 'the mouth of YHWH' (*pî YHWH*), a phrase which forms an inclusio with 14:41, where Moses warns the people of their transgressing 'the mouth of YHWH'. These bookends demonstrate that the first generation's failure was in relation to their disposition toward the word of YHWH – the Israelites did not receive the promise with faith (cf. Heb. 3:19–4:2).

4–16. An oft neglected but crucial point is the fact that the scouting mission, indeed, the entire episode (chs. 13–14), relates only to the twelve tribes – Levites (who will not, in any case, inherit land) are nowhere mentioned, which also includes their omission from culpability in Israel's rebellion and failure to inherit the land. As the narrative flow coordinates with the Camp's structure, the section on Levites, the 'inner camp', occurs in chapters 16–18.

The listing of names adds solemnity to the event of searching out the promised land, paralleling that of the leaders who participated in the census for the construction of the Camp (1:5–16). The twelve scouts are presented 'as a sort of microcosm of the community at large' (Frankel 2014: 194–195). The antiquity of the record is evident not only in the theophoric element of names, using *'ēl* rather than abbreviated forms of YHWH, but in the transcription of Joshua's original name as Hoshea (v. 8) – the scribal record was not changed, but explained (v. 16). That every tribe is represented serves to give all Israel equal dignity in participating in this historic event, which also means equal accountability. The twelve tribal heads search out the land on behalf of their respective tribes who are being given the land by YHWH.

The order of the men listed does not follow that of the Camp as in Numbers 2, 7, 10, but, with a little variation, maintains birth order, as with Numbers 1 and 26. Based on the list in 1:5–15, here Issachar and Zebulun have been separated, with Ephraim and Benjamin inserted between them, and Manasseh following Zebulun; and Naphtali and Gad have been reversed. Likely, the chieftains are younger men of influence among their tribes (as is clear with Joshua and Caleb), more fit for the mission than the senior chieftains who had overseen the census earlier. Only Joshua and Caleb will appear again elsewhere, and are part of the larger thematic movement of Israel's leadership by Ephraim (the northern kingdom of Israel) and Judah (the southern kingdom). Caleb is also dubbed a Kenizzite (Num. 32:12; Josh. 14:6, 14), a clan of Edom descended from Esau (Gen. 36:10–11) and living in Canaan (Gen. 15:19), which apparently had become affiliated with the tribe of Judah (Ashley 1993: 233). The Chronicler links Caleb with Hezron, the son of Perez (1 Chr. 2:1–5, 18), and Kaufmann argues that Kenizzites were attached to the tribe of Judah since patriarchal times (1970: 670–672). Although 'Caleb' means 'dog', Milgrom notes that in the literature of the ANE dogs were praised for loyalty, so that his name, contrary to a derogatory impression, may signify his faithfulness (1990: 101). Attempts have been made to understand the significance of the other names as well (Cole 2000: 1217–1218; Sherwood 2002: 157). (See Table 22.)

'These are the names . . . ' (v. 16) is an instance of resumptive repetition, framing the list of the tribal leaders' names. The explanation of Hoshea's (salvation) name-change to Joshua (YHWH saves) functions in a variety of ways: Joshua is singled out from the list, as is the revelation of YHWH's Name to Moses (3:13–15; 6:2–3), since Joshua is the first name to incorporate YHWH's Name – a custom begun no less by Moses. Perhaps coincidental, Manasseh is linked with Joseph's tribe in the list, while Ephraim is not; Hoshea (Ephraim) is linked instead with Moses in a special way. As of his first textual appearance (Exod. 17:9), he has been called Joshua anachronistically, since that is how he had become known to the original and later audiences. While the new name may have come, possibly, with his inauguration as Israel's new leader (Num. 27:12–23), we are told of that change here, first, to explain the discrepancy with the official recorded list, and, secondly, to undergird the narrative theologically. Moses' act of naming him links Joshua closely with Moses, underscoring his role as Moses' protégé (11:28). Sonnet has it that this change of name ensured that YHWH would be with Joshua (1997: 133; also Hirsch 2007a: 243). Frevel, intriguingly, sees verse 16 as Joshua's being 'elected to lead the spies in his function as military leader (Exod. 17)' (2018: 102). Having been inseparable from Moses since his youth, the presence of Joshua on this mission would embody Moses' presence to some degree, just as his renaming by Moses represents Moses' role in the nation's life, even YHWH's salvation. For the original audience, understood as the second generation of Israelites who would enter the land, mention of Joshua here would gild this otherwise dark account with a reminder of the gracious and merciful redemption

Table 22: Significance of chieftain names

Tribe	Name and significance	Father
Reuben	Shammua – one who has heard (God's report?)	ben Zaccur
Simeon	Shaphat – he judged	ben Hori
Judah	Caleb – dog	ben Jephunneh
Issachar	Igal – he redeems, may he redeem	ben Joseph
Ephraim	Hoshea – salvation	ben Nun
Benjamin	Palti – my safety, deliverance	ben Raphu
Zebulun	Gaddiel – my fortune is God	ben Sodi
Manasseh	Gaddi – my fortune	ben Susi
Dan	Ammiel – God of my people, or God is my kinsman	ben Gemalli
Asher	Sethur – hidden	ben Michael
Naphtali	Nahbi – my hiding place, or fearful	ben Vophsi
Gad	Geuel – loftiness of God	ben Maki

YHWH extended to them in the midst of divine judgement in the wilderness. At the beginning of the account of their darkest hour, Israel is reminded that, indeed, 'YHWH saves', and he was already raising up a saviour before the nation's tragedy. For the mission itself, the list of tribal leaders closes with a reminder that YHWH's role is what matters. The incarnate Son would also be called Joshua, *Jesus* (*Iēsous*) in Greek, for he himself would save his people from their sins (Matt. 1:21; Luke 2:11).

17. This verse's resumptive repetition of verse 3 serves as a summary heading that also begins the details of the account. The mission encompasses the 'land of Canaan', setting out from the southern area, the Negeb, and is characterized as ascending 'the mountain'. While this may technically refer to 'the hill country', the characterization of the promised land as spiritually elevated, as Mt. Zion, to which one always ascends, may also inform the story. 'Ascend' (*'ālāh*) is a key word, used fourteen times in Numbers 13 – 14 with reference to entering or possessing the land (13:17 [twice], 18, 21, 22, 30 [twice], 31 [twice]; 14:13, 40 [twice], 42, 44). At the centre of the story is the decision of whether 'to ascend' or not (13:30–31), a mission that begins with the command 'to ascend' (13:17) and ends disastrously with a presumptuous ascent (14:39–45) (cf. Boorer 1992: 342–343). Within the context of taking the land against enemies, ascent carries the idea of gathering strength and overcoming (cf. Josh. 6:20; 15:14–15; Judg. 1:1–4), reaching beyond merely the notion of physical terrain to the need for inward effort and spiritual motivation (see Samet 2014d). The mountain imagery will be especially striking in the final episode (14:40–45), which twice refers to the summit of the mountain.

18–20. Moses gives the parameters for the mission: the twelve chieftains are to survey the land, bringing a report about its quality as well as the quality of the land's inhabitants – everything has reference to the land: 'You will see the land, what it is like, and the people who dwell on it (the land).' As to the people, the first question(s) 'Are they strong? weak?' has a different construction, so that strong and weak are presented as side by side possibilities rather than as either/or opposites. Historically, the open-settlements (lit. 'encampments') versus fortified cities has been understood in a counterintuitive manner: open-settlements means the inhabitants are strong and courageous, while fortified cities implies they are weak and cowardly (*Num. Rab.* 16.12). Likely, however, fortified cities represent the strength of civilizations, and the idea of impregnability.

Moses' questions move from the land to inhabitants and back to the land, establishing emphasis and priority on the land:

18 You will see **the land** → and the people who dwell on it
(What is it like?)   (Strong? Weak? Few or many?)
19 What is **the land** like → What are the cities like wherein they dwell
(Good or evil?)   (Open-settlements or fortresses?)

20 What is the land like?
(Fat or lean, trees or no trees?)
Embolden yourselves to take the fruit of the land
(days of the firstfruits of grapes)

YHWH's later judgement on the ten scouts is twice expressly stated as
due to their bringing a 'bad report' and an 'evil bad report' against the
land (14:36, 37). Given that the nature of their mission was to confirm
YHWH's promises by their testimony to the tribes, along with the
specimen of fruit, their evil report, which caused the people to reject
the land – as well as the nation's vocation within the land – is especially
heinous. Rashi, following the Midrash (*Num. Rab.* 16.12), limits the
questions about the people by their relation to the land, marking verse
18's vav (and' the people . . .) as explanatory, noting that some lands
produce mighty people and increase population, while other lands
produce weak people and decrease population (1997: 4:150). While not
needing to argue against some tactical reconnaissance, nevertheless the
mission's priority and the account's theological message indeed concerns
the land. 'The people' are mentioned one time in these verses; otherwise,
they are regarded only in relation to the land, as those who 'are dwelling
on it' (three times). This order will be reversed for rhetorical, devious
purposes in the scouts' majority report (vv. 27–29). The land mission,
moreover, is framed by references to searching out the land, the same
frame given for the chieftains listing:

'search out the **land of Canaan**' (v. 2) / the chieftains (vv. 4–16) /
'search out **the land**' (v. 16)

'search out the **land of Canaan**' (v. 17) / land mission (vv. 18–20) /
'searched out **the land**' (v. 21)

Both the scouts and their mission are bracketed by 'the land', and the
nature of the mission, 'to search out' (*lātûr*), has 'the land' as its object
in every use of *tûr* within Numbers (10:33 likely has the land in view as
well). The land's qualities are surveyed as 'good' (*ṭôb*) or 'evil' (*rā'āh*), fat
or lean, trees or not. It is possible to interpret these more particularly as
(v. 18) general, topographical features, such as mountainous or flat, well-
watered and so on; (v. 19) its quality as a dwelling place, able to promote
moral and cultural life; (v. 20) the nature of its soil as a source of food
and prosperity, and the presence of forested regions for industry (Hirsch
2007a: 243–246). Beck takes Moses' guidelines as queries regarding the
land's population density (v. 18), hydrology (v. 19), urban construction
(v. 19) and agricultural quality (v. 20) (Beck 2000: 275–277). The overall
thrust of the expected report of the land as good and fat and having
trees, along with the recurring description of its 'flowing with milk
and honey' throughout the HB, is to portray God's gift to Israel as

paradise. The land as "good" recalls YHWH's description of the land at the burning bush, as both "good" and "flowing with milk and honey" (Exod. 3:8); the scouts' report will include the latter phrase (13:27), while neglecting the land's goodness altogether, which was the focus of Moses' question. Moses' expectation was for the scouts to return, bearing the land's abundant fruit, and declaring the goodness of the land God has promised to give them (cf. Waxman 2017) – regardless of the formidable strength of its inhabitants, since YHWH was with them.

Moses directs the tribal leaders to 'strengthen yourselves' (hith. of *ḥāzaq*) to take of the fruit of the land, a bold gesture of ownership. With foresight, Moses has the encouragement of the community of Israel in mind, wanting the fruit to serve as a foretaste for them of life in the land, a token of God's sure promise to bring them into a good land of abundance. While fruit would be brought back – and perhaps Caleb and Joshua were the two men who had emboldened themselves to take and carry it (v. 23) – ten scouts failed to 'strengthen themselves', claiming that Israel was not able to possess the land since the people are 'stronger (*ḥāzaq*) than we' (v. 31). We are told that it was the days of the firstfruits of grapes (v. 20), which anticipates the cluster of grapes taken at Wadi Eshcol (v. 23). This season places the expedition around late July, some two months after leaving Mount Sinai (G. J. Wenham 1981b: 132). Taking the fruit successfully would be like taking the land in miniature, as given by YHWH but requiring courage. This was Moses' last summary word by which their whole mission is characterized: 'Strengthen yourselves and take of the fruit of the land!' Bringing back that fruit would fortify the rest of the community of Israel to inherit the land. The phrases 'good or evil', 'is there a tree within it' and 'take of the fruit' call to mind the Eden narratives (Gen. 2 – 3), not only portraying the land as Eden but the scouts' sin as the primal transgression (see below).

Understanding the scouts as distinguished leaders, chosen to witness to the people the reality of God's promise by affirming the goodness of the land, the mission was more a test of faith than a military reconnaissance (Milgrom 1990: 100), a point which may explain the question they are asked to answer in verse 19: 'And what is the land like in which they dwell – is it good (*hāṭôbāh*) or evil (*rā'āh*)?' This word-pair takes one back to the Tree of the Knowledge of 'good and evil' in Genesis 2:9 (cf. also Gen. 2:12; 3:5, 22; 24:50; 31:24, 29; 44:4; 50:20; Num. 24:13). The scouts are asked to assess the land, already having God's word that he was bringing his people 'into a land good (*ṭôbāh*) and large, a land flowing with milk and honey' (Exod. 3:8; cf. Exod. 3:17; 13:5; 33:3; Lev. 20:24; Deut. 8:7). 'Good' versus 'evil' was a theme underlined as Israel set out in the wilderness, with Moses employing a fivefold use of 'good' (10:29, 32), only to be met by a fourfold use of 'evil' in chapter 11 (vv. 1, 10, 11, 15) – from beginning to end, the outer camp's challenge is to embrace YHWH's will through Moses. 'Good' was the original divine assessment throughout each stage of creation (Gen. 1:4, 10, 12, 18, 21, 25), God's completed creation being declared 'very good' (Gen. 1:31), linking the Promised Land with the idea of paradise, the place where Israel would dwell with God in harmony and abundance. YHWH's 'good' promise to Israel (10:29) will be exchanged as 'evil' by the scouts – language that resonates with humanity's first sin (Gen. 2 – 3). The damning sin of the ten faithless scouts will be to spread an 'evil' bad report about the land (14:37; cf. 13:32; 14:32), while Joshua and Caleb will exclaim that the land is a 'very, very good land' (*ṭôbāh hā'āreṣ mĕ'ōd mĕ'ōd*, 14:7). The people will cry and determine that it would be 'good' instead to return to Egypt (14:3; cf. Exod. 14:12; Num. 11:5, 20). The assessment of 'good' they withheld from the land, is here proffered to the place of bitter oppression, Egypt – nothing better captures the disposition of the first generation than this statement.

21. This verse stands as a summary heading: the tribal leaders ascended and searched out the land. From the wilderness of Zin to Rehob, toward Lebo-Hamath, designates the 250-mile south-to-north route of the scouts, Zin being just north of Israel's encampment at Kadesh, forming the land's southern border, and Lebo-Hamath marking the northern border of the land (Num. 34:8), where David and Solomon's kingdom would have its northernmost city (1 Kgs 8:65; 1 Chr. 13:5) (Sprinkle 2015: 264–265).

22–25. The objective account of the scouts' obedience is encouraging; although they encountered the children of Anak at first, the scouts still proceeded to take of the fruit of the land successfully, and were able to return from searching out the land after forty days. The text merely states that the children of Anak were there, and then continues onward – the subjective report will come in verse 33. Ahiman, Sheshai and Talmai will be encountered a generation later, driven out and slain by Caleb and his tribe of Judah (Josh. 15:13–14; Judg. 1:10).

In each instance, the text offers details to guide the original audience in making an assessment. First, since 'the Anak' (*hā'ănāq*), meaning 'necklace' or 'people of the neck', likely refers to a tall pre-Israelite tribe, the presence of the Anak's children leads the audience to understand the presence of some giants in Hebron (see 'Anak' in *IDB* 1:123; *ABD* 1:222). Second, rather than saying that Hebron was an ancient, well-fortified city, the account says that it was built seven years before Zoan, the great Egyptian city known as Tanis that served as capital for the Hyksos dynasty (c. 1700 BC). Some believe this note refers to the (re)founding of Israelite Hebron under David, also about seven years before the rebuilding of Tanis (see Bimson 1978: 188–190; Na'aman 1981). Joshua 14:15 reports that the ancient name of Hebron was 'City of Arba', Arba being the greatest among the Anakim; since 'Arba' means 'four', Nachmanides suggests that Arba and his three sons (Ahiman, Sheshai and Talmai) are the four giants for which the city was known (1975:

127). Third, rather than stating that the land is good, having abundant large fruit, we are told that one cluster of grapes was borne between two men on a carrying frame. In Numbers 4:10, the Menorah candelabra, a stylized almond tree, is carried on a 'frame' (*môṭ*), the same unique word used to describe the pole that carried the cluster (cf. also 4:12). As a token of God's gift of the land to his people, the cluster of grapes is carried ceremoniously back to the Camp, underscoring Moses' intended role for this fruit, to encourage the people. Eshcol means '(grape) cluster'. The largeness of the one cluster, needing to be carried by two men, indicates the land's incredible fertility. Aside from an allusion to the Nazirite vow (6:3–4, 20), the sheer abundance of grapes also recalls Jacob's blessing over Judah, whose Messianic descendant would bind his donkey to a sturdy vine and even wash his garments in wine (Gen. 49:11) – an allusion that gains significance in relation to other echoes of the same blessing in the Balaam narrative (24:9; cf. 22:24).

While it is possible that this brook-area (also Num. 32:9; Deut. 1:24) was already called 'Eshcol' after one of its pre-Israelite inhabitants (Gen. 14:13, 24), the name obtained a new significance for the Israelites in the cluster of grapes brought back by the scouts (cf. Moster 2013). The naming of Eshcol is but another way for the text to underscore the great import of the fruit's intended role. Moses had asked: 'Is the land good or bad?' MacDonald notes that of the fruits the Israelites were familiar with, grapes, figs, and pomegranates were the most important (2008b: 62). Twersky interprets verse 24 as the response of Canaanites who named the place after being awed by the Israelite chieftains' bold act, likely a politically charged claim for which Moses had admonished them to 'strengthen themselves' (v. 20; 2007b: 2:162). When Jesus taught about good trees bearing good fruit, his two examples of good fruit were grapes and figs (Matt. 7:16–17), two of the three fruits brought back from the land by the scouts.

The narrative emphasis on Hebron must be given due exegetical weight. As G. J. Wenham observed, Hebron is near where God first promised Abraham that he would inherit the land (Gen. 13:14–18), the area from which Abraham had set out to defeat the coalition of kings (Gen. 14:13), the place in which Abraham owned his one plot of land, a burial site for his wife Sarah, and where all the patriarchs – Abraham, Isaac and Jacob – along with their wives (aside from Rachel) were buried (Gen. 23; 25:9; 35:27–29; 49:29–33; 50:13) (1981b: 133). The scouts' rejection of the land was all the more heinous in the light of this visit to Hebron (Milgrom 1990: 103). Like the cluster of grapes, this site, owned by the patriarchs and where they were buried, served as a token of the full inheritance, a seal of YHWH's promises to Israel. In the oral tradition of Israelites in Egypt, Hebron would have been legendary (and may be the source for the naming of Levi's grandson, one of Kohath's sons, as 'Hebron', Exod. 6:18; Num. 3:19) – visiting this city and even seeking out the graves of the patriarchs should have been an experience full of wonder and encouragement in faith. In later history, David would be anointed king at Hebron (2 Sam. 2:1–3; 5:1–5). Hebron also appears to have been within the special purview of Caleb during the scouting mission, granted to him by YHWH (14:24), so that, under Joshua, he would come to possess it (Josh. 14:6–15). In Jewish tradition, Caleb alone went to seek out the patriarchs' graves in Hebron, an act that had strengthened him against the faithless majority report of the scouts (see *m. Sot.* 34b; Rashi 1997: 4:152). The lore builds on two exegetical points: (1) first, YHWH gives Hebron to Caleb as the place 'there where he entered' (14:24; see Josh. 14:6–15), and (2) the actual wording of 13:22 says, 'And-they-ascended into the Negeb, and-he-came to Hebron.' While the second verb may be understood as collective, yet since Hebron is described by YHWH as the place where 'he entered', using the same verb in singular with reference to Caleb, such gap-filling is not baseless. The singular 'he called' (v. 24) may thus be a reference to Caleb.

26–29. Verse 26 is a summary statement given as a threefold panel:

A they went and came to Moses and to Aaron	B and to all the community of the sons of Israel
A' and brought back word unto them	B' and to all the community
A" and showed them the fruit of the land	B" ——

As a summary statement, we are to understand that the scouts reported first to Moses (and Aaron) alone, as verse 27 demonstrates ('And they recounted to him'), before they turned in rebellion to the people in verse 32. Moreover, the second element of the third parallel (B") is missing: did the scouts not display the fruit before the people? The text's summary, 'they showed *them* the fruit', is ambiguous, possibly referring only to Moses and Aaron, but even if the fruit was (unavoidably) displayed before the rest of the people, the cluster of grapes is completely absent from the scouts' later engagement with the people. Again, verse 27 only narrates their showing the fruit to Moses and Aaron. 'The fruit is a metonymy for the land', S. Schwartz notes (2020: 590), so that 'seeing the fruit is tantamount to seeing the land', making the land present within the wilderness where Israel sojourns. Thus the damning sin of the scouts was their slandering of the land (also Lohfink 1969: 53), in effect, playing the same role as the serpent in Eden, who had slandered God's character to dissuade the woman from clinging to God's word with faith and obedience. Nachmanides also picks up on the difference between the scouts' report to Moses, that the land is good, flowing with milk and honey, and the evil report they spread among the people 'in their tents, in a secretive manner' lest Moses contradict their report openly (1975: 133). In Deuteronomy, Moses speaks of the official report 'brought to us' (i.e.

Moses and Aaron, vs 'you' in v. 26) – the people were accountable for the official report delivered to and passed on by Moses.

As Caleb interrupts them in verse 30, the 'they' of verse 27 clearly refers to the ten scouts who bring the majority report. Whereas Moses' instructions began and ended with the land, emphasizing it throughout, the scouts quickly pass over the land's description with seven words in Hebrew, and end their report with a drawn-out account – thirty-one words – of the formidable strength of the land's inhabitants. S. Schwartz also observes that although their first report is truthful, the scouts' rhetoric remains negative, as seen in the contrast between the narrator's descriptions and the emphases of the scouts' speech (2020: 591–592): the narrator gives little space in describing the inhabitants (v. 22) and much to the land's abundance (vv. 23–24), whereas the scouts devote much space to the land's inhabitants (28–29) and little to the land's abundance (vv. 26b–27). Moses' instructions had ended with questions regarding the land and with its fruit (v. 20) – that was to be the matter of emphasis; but the scouts reverse this order so as to end with the strength of the inhabitants. The whole report is prefaced with the remark that 'We came to the land where you sent us.' While the statement is certainly true (see v. 3), the rhetorical disassociation is manifest – this is not the 'land promised to our fathers', or the land that YHWH is 'giving the sons of Israel' (13:2; 14:16, 23, 30, 40; 15:2), but 'the land' is modified instead by the relative clause 'where you sent us' (similarly, G. J. Wenham 1981b: 134). Then the land is described, again, with merely seven words: 'and also it is flowing with milk and honey, and this is its fruit'. 'Milk and honey' has been a description of the land consistently linked with its being a gift of YHWH to Israel, promised to the patriarchs (see Exod. 3:8, 17; 13:5; 33:3; Lev. 20:24) – the ten scouts downplay the reality of this feature, which confirmed YHWH's promise. As the Talmud explains (*Ket.* 111b), 'milk and honey' refers to the many goats and fig trees that fill the land of Canaan. The description of the land begins with *wĕgam* (and also), which can be taken in different ways – 'and it really does flow', 'moreover, it is flowing' (cf. v. 28). There are other ways to show dramatic emphasis (it is surely flowing), as when Caleb says 'Let us surely ascend' and 'we are surely able', both of which repeat the verb (v. 30). Here, the blank statement, while reporting accurately, seems to function as a subsidiary thought, as does the two-word phrase 'and-this [is] its-fruit', connected by a maqqef (*wĕzeh-piryāh*). Crucially, the scouts neglect Moses' question as to the land's goodness (13:19), which also linked to YHWH's original description of the land as both 'good' and 'flowing with milk and honey' (Exod. 3:8). Indeed, they will assess returning to Egypt as 'good' (14:3), and give an 'evil' report of the land (14:37).

Without any perceptible pause to observe the wondrous specimen of grapes, pomegranates and figs, verse 28 begins with a bold adverb of negation – 'Nevertheless! (*'epes*)', which has 'a harsher nuance than other more common negative expressions' (S. Schwartz 2020: 591). This little two-syllable word *'epes* led to thousands on thousands of corpses strewn about the wilderness over a forty-year period. The rhetorical effect in English is something like 'We went where you told us and, yes, it does flow with milk and honey, here's its fruit – But! Nevertheless!' and then the lengthy description of the inhabitants and their fortified cities ensues. The people are 'mighty', 'fierce' (*'az*) and the cities are fortified and 'very huge' (*gĕdōlōt mĕ'ōd*), and, as subsidiary support (*wĕgam*), they note seeing the children of the Anak 'there' (*šām*) with reference to 'the land' (v. 28), whereas the narrator had restricted their presence to Hebron (v. 22). While their description may be misleading, causing hearers to think that children of Anak pervaded every locale in the land, yet the scouts have stated defensible facts in verse 28 (cf. S. Schwartz 2020: 593). Their subtle deception lies rather in their either/or reporting. Moses had asked about both the land *and* the inhabitants, whereas these scouts report on the land versus the inhabitants. The whole description serves to undergird the negation with which it starts, 'Nevertheless'. The land is unattainable due to its fierce inhabitants – YHWH's terrible presence, power, and promises, in other words, are irrelevant.

In verse 29, the scouts effectually block every path toward entering the land: Amalek dwells in the Negeb, the south; the Hittites, Jebusites, and Amorites dwell on the mountain, north of the Negeb; and the Canaanites dwell by the sea, in the west, and by the hand of the Jordan, in the east (cf. also Sprinkle 2015: 266; Havrelock 2014: 2–3). As long-standing enemies of Israel, the Amalekites, who had already attacked them in the wilderness (Exod. 17:8–16) – repeatedly (Deut. 25:17–19) – heads the scouts' report, likely calculated to strike fear. And yet, significantly, God had already declared, 'I will utterly blot out the memory of Amalek from under heaven,' commanding Moses to write this promise in a scroll and to recite it in the hearing of Joshua (Exod. 17:14). YHWH had promised Abraham that he would bring judgement on the Amorites (used generally for inhabitants of Canaan) and bring his descendants into the land (Gen. 15:16), and now he had warranted the scouting mission with the reminder of his intention to give them the land (Num. 13:2), but the scouts leverage the presence of strong inhabitants against God's promise and sovereign omnipotence. The scouts' more pernicious and blatantly false account, regarding the Nephilim, will be reserved for the Israelite masses (vv. 32–33).

30. Interpreting *'el-mōšeh* is difficult: should the prepositional phrase be taken adverbially (linked to the verb 'quieted') or adjectivally (linked to the noun 'the people')? Most translations render 'to Moses' adverbially, giving the sense of Caleb's action merely as taking place before or in front of Moses, but this does not appear adequate – and *lipnê-mōšeh* would be preferred for this sense. The Greek uses *pros Mōusēn*, which

is as ambiguous as MT, although with the additional phrase 'and said to him'. Brenton's translation of LXX supplies 'from speaking': 'Caleb stayed the people from speaking before [or to] Moses and said to him' (1986: 192). The scouts' official report is directed to Moses, and Caleb is not simply acting in front of Moses, but silencing the other scouts' report to Moses. This understanding is further clarified, again, by use of 'and said to him' (missing from MT). The phrase may also be understood with an adversarial tone as 'against Moses', that Caleb stilled the people (who were) against Moses, as in verse 31: we are not able to ascend 'against (*'el-*) the people'. Caleb not only senses the scouts' rebellion but their mounting agitation against Moses – their report, after all, began with: 'We came to the land to which *you sent us*', presumably blaming him for their threatening encounter with Canaanites. Samaritan Pentateuch preserves the adversarial understanding with *'al-mōšeh*: 'Caleb stilled the people against (*'al*) Moses and said to him'. G. B. Gray reads Caleb as silencing 'the murmurings of the people against Moses' (1903: 150) – in accord with 14:2–4, and with the subsection's focus on the outer camp's relation to Moses' prophetic office.

Context determines that the scouts are reporting to Moses: verse 26 is a general heading and summary statement, while verse 27 clarifies that the scene begins with an official report to Moses directly: 'And they recounted to him (*lô*)'. Part of the significance is that it is not until verse 32 that the scouts, leaders among the people, turn to bring an evil report of the land, directed only then 'to (*'el-*) the sons of Israel'. This will be their damning sin. If 'the people' here refers to the sons of Israel, then the scenario assumes they are listening in as the scouts report to Moses – Caleb quiets the people (the Israelites) who, upon hearing the report to Moses, begin to murmur against him. Otherwise, 'the people' refers to the majority of the scouts. Although little explored, another possibility is that 'the people' refers to the inhabitants of Canaan, the previous and next referents (vv. 28, 31). Caleb's action, in turn, would be understood as 'diminished/belittled the people to Moses, saying . . . we are well able to conquer the land', serving as a counter to the other scouts' emphasis on the might of 'the people'. The term for Caleb's action, *hāsāh*, appears only here, although *hās*, from which it seems to derive (*HALOT* 1:253), appears frequently as an interjection for silencing, hushing or stilling (Judg. 3:19; Neh. 8:11; Amos 6:10; 8:3; Hab. 2:20; Zeph. 1:7; Zech. 2:13), making this last reading unlikely.

Caleb, seeing that the report was turning into an aggressive threat to Moses against taking the land, interrupts and silences the other scouts – that his intuition was correct is proven in verse 31. Caleb's own counsel is urgent, filled with immediacy and phrased emphatically: 'surely ascend' (*ālōh na'āleh*), 'surely able' (*yākōl nûkal*). He wants to curtail the scouts' negativity by proceeding with the divine plan speedily, burning down, as it were, the bridge of retreat before their faithless fear spreads to the people. Doubtless, Caleb assumes YHWH's going before them in power, but it may be significant that he, however innocently, did not mention God's help at this point, since this left the scouts opportunity to respond at the human level alone: 'We are not able . . . for they are stronger than we' (v. 31), rather than imposing a confession of their lack of trust in YHWH. Possibly, as G. J. Wenham points out (1981b: 135), Caleb's use of 'ascend' and 'possess' form keyword allusions to previous divine promises (Exod. 3:8, 17; 33:3; Lev. 20:24).

31–33. Like the serpent in the garden of Eden (Gen. 3:1–5), the ten scouts use rhetoric to influence Israel to doubt God's word, character, and good purposes for them. S. Schwartz (2020) brings out the negative progression from the scouts' first report, a truthful account marked by rhetoric (vv. 26–29), to their second report, a false account marked by demagoguery (including lies, logical fallacies, false evidence, and using the language of magic and myth instead of logic), intended both to undermine the current leadership, striving to breech the trusting relationship between the people and Moses, and to promote anxiety and fear over the land (vv. 31–33) – the shift occurring in reaction to Caleb's central response (v. 30). S. Schwartz observes the following differences concerning their two speeches (2020: 585–586): the second report reverses and contradicts the attitude toward the land of the first (vv. 27, 32); while both reports note the power of the land's inhabitants, only the second asserts 'they are stronger than we are' (vv. 28, 31); only the second report claims that the entire population is of great size (v. 32), and that the giants are descendants of the Nephilim (v. 33); the 'seeing' motif in relation to the inhabitants appears once in the first report (v. 28), but twice in the second (vv. 32–33); the narrator's note that the scouts spread calumnies appears only in the second part (v. 32); and the scouts' self-perception and perception in the eyes of the inhabitants as grasshoppers appears only in the second part (v. 33). Opening with a fronted *hā'ănāšîm* (the men), the narrator underscores the scouts' status and influence over the people. There is some irony in the men's response for they are labelled the men 'who had ascended with him', but they claim 'We are not able to ascend.' 'We are not able' means 'YHWH is not able,' precisely the slander against YHWH's fame that Moses will seek to restrain among the nations in his intercession (see 14:15–16). Clearly, the scouts are faithless, making 'no reference to YHWH's promise to expel the inhabitants' (cf. 10:9, 35; Exod. 23:20–23, 29–31; Hausoul 2018: 81). While Moses had charged the men to 'strengthen yourselves' (*ḥāzaq*) and take the fruit of the land as a gesture of possessing the land (13:20), the scouts, on the contrary, reject the land, claiming that the people are 'stronger' (*ḥāzaq*). The contrast between Caleb and the faithless scouts is pointed: 'we are able' (*yākōl nûkal*, v. 30) versus 'we are not able' (*lō' nûkal*, v. 31). While fear of man may appear innocuous, its heinous root is a lack of the fear of YHWH.

If they had feared YHWH, they would not have feared the inhabitants in the land.

If Caleb had preempted the other scouts' negative report to Moses, the scouts now pre-empt Caleb's positive report to the people. After the rapid back and forth within the context of reporting to Moses, the scouts now delve into flagrant rebellion, usurping Moses' authority by spreading a 'bad report' (*dibbat*) of the land to the sons of Israel – the majority opinion is 'now leaked to the populace as a whole' (Magonet 1982: 15). In Genesis 37:2, Joseph had 'brought' (*bô'*) a bad report of his brothers to his father, which was true, whereas the ten scouts 'spread' (*yāṣā'*) a bad report, which is false and slanderous (13:32; 14:36, 37) and thus further dubbed 'evil' in 14:37 (cf. Nachmanides 1975: 131; Hirsch 2007a: 251–252). The narrator's description of the scouts' second report as *dibbat* functions to label it as false (cf. S. Schwartz 2020: 594). The damning sin was in their slandering 'the land' to God's people, for in reviling his long-awaited gift, they were despising the Giver, who had promised to bring his people into a 'good (*ṭôvāh*) land . . . flowing with milk and honey' (Exod. 3:8; cf. 3:17; 6:8; cf. Num. 10:29, 32). The faithless scouts 'surreptitiously spread an evil rumor among the sons of Israel' (13:32–33), as contrasted with 'Joshua and Caleb's open and public address' before the whole assembly of the sons of Israel (14:7) (Galbraith 2014: 38). While they had initially addressed their report to Moses, acknowledging his authority (v. 27), now they turn to the people and undermine his leadership. The scouts are insubordinate, defying and bypassing Moses' authority to foment a revolt (see Asher 1984). The nature of their slander is given in their description of the land as 'a land that devours its inhabitants'. Gray interprets this phrase as an idiom for the land's infertility, unable to produce enough to support its inhabitants (1903: 151), a manifest falsehood in the face of the cluster of grapes they brought back, but Noordtzij takes its meaning as referring to contested land, a battleground of nations (1983: 120), perpetually keeping its inhabitants at war, which resonates with Ezekiel 36:13–14 (Milgrom 1990: 106–107). The first scenario denies the good nature of the land as YHWH's gift, the second denies YHWH's promise to give them the land as a possession. Beyond Israel's inability to conquer the land's inhabitants (v. 31), now, lest any should muster up courage, they slander the land itself, in effect claiming that possessing the land would be useless since it was not fit for habitation. That the land 'devours its inhabitants' plays on the eating motif, reversing their own earlier testimony that the land indeed 'flows with milk and honey' (v. 27). This imagery is reinforced through the metaphor that the scouts 'were as grasshoppers'. Using the specific term 'grasshopper' (*ḥāgāb*) rather than 'locust' (*'arbeh*) is likely significant; while both are edible (see Lev. 11:22), the locust is regarded as a vexatious destroyer of crops (Exod. 10:12; Deut. 28:38; Judg. 6:5) – using grasshopper, then, focuses on the scouts' vulnerability alone (Markose 2015: 142; S. Schwartz 2020: 596). More broadly, the scouts' language of a devouring land employs cosmic imagery to portray the land as *Sheol*, which accords also with the mention of Nephilim (v. 33), mythic giants, which occur elsewhere only in the primeval era (Gen. 6:4). Rather than yielding abundant life-giving fruit like the garden of YHWH, the land is depicted as *Sheol*, swallowing up its inhabitants (cf. McEvenue 1971: 135–136). Whereas Zion's summit would be characterized as a new Eden, to which all the nations would be drawn to be taught of YHWH (Isa. 2:1–4), the scouts depict the land of God's holy mountain as its theologically extreme opposite: the watery deep that lies far below the cosmic mountain. Ironically, it will be in the wilderness (not the good land) where Israelites get swallowed up alive into *Sheol* (Num. 16:30–34). An earlier description by YHWH portrayed the land as vomiting out the Canaanites (Lev. 18:25). In sum the majority report has transitioned from 'the land is good, the people are bad', to 'the land is bad, the people are bad' – why battle giants for the sake of inhospitable lands?

The bad report includes the falsehood of hyperbole (contra Cruzer 2010): while some tall people were noted in one region, they declare that 'all the people' in the land were of 'great stature' (*middôt*). Not only so, but they saw there the Nephilim (lit. 'fallen ones'), legendary 'warriors' (*gibbôrîm*), created when the sons of God intermarried with daughters of men (Gen. 6:1–4). Genesis 6:4 and Numbers 13:33 are the only verses in Scripture that mention Nephilim, translated 'giants' (*gigantes*) in the Greek version. Hoping to escalate the people's fear, the ten scouts add mythological flavour to the children of Anak, first calling them Nephilim, then explaining that the sons of Anak derive from the Nephilim. Especially in the light of allusions to the patriarchal promises (e.g. 10:29; 11:12; 13:2), it may not be insignificant that the scouts make no mention of the tombs of the patriarchs, a history that 'is provocatively eclipsed as another continuity between the Nephilim and the inhabitants of Canaan is established' (Pardes 2000: 109).

The hyperbole escalates further as they describe themselves as mere grasshoppers by comparison to the giants, and, lest such an assessment be judged subjective, they claim an equal assessment through the eyes of the Nephilim themselves. Yet, only by contrast to YHWH God does humanity appear as mere grasshoppers (Isa. 40:22), and he was with Israel against the inhabitants. In summary, their slanderous report to the people spreads a view of the land as a violently open-mouthed grave, *Sheol*, inhabited by mighty giants so huge the Israelites are but grasshoppers by comparison. The expression their 'shade of defence' (*ṣillām*) likely refers to the protection of the people's gods and kings (Levine 1993: 364; E. W. Davies 1995b: 141).

Not only does their turning directly to the people, relying on their own status as leading men, undermine the leadership of Moses and Aaron, but their emphasis on being personal witnesses – note the twofold use of 'we saw' – does so as well. Their personal experience and testimony is set against YHWH's words to Moses, and Moses was *not* there – he had not seen the inhabitants. How will the people respond to this bad report? How will they weigh the words of these ten leaders, who have just returned from touring the land, against the long-standing promises of YHWH?

14:1–4. The scouts' undermining of Moses' leadership culminates with Israel's demand to replace the nation's leaders (cf. S. Schwartz 2020: 598), primarily a rejection of Moses in his prophetic office. Use of three different designations for the Israelites (vv. 1, 2) – 'the whole community' twice, 'the people', and 'the sons of Israel' – demonstrates that genera- tion's culpability, vindicating YHWH's ensuing judgement, but also underscores the overwhelming results of the heinous slander of the land by the ten scouts. Possibly, 'the whole community' lifting up their voices refers to the ongoing debate of the leaders at the courtyard gate, while 'the people' weeping refers to the rest of the Camp (v. 1), the two groups mentioned in chiastic reversal in verse 2 (Magonet 1982: 16). There is affinity between Israel's response to the report of the ten scouts here and their response to the gathered-rabble in Numbers 11. In both situations the people 'wept' (*wayyibkû*, 14:1; 11:4), decided that life in Egypt was 'good' (*ṭôb*, 14:3; 11:18), and 'despised' YHWH or the land (*mě'astem*, 14:31; 11:20). While the response is wholesale and widespread in both accounts, yet progression and escalation may be observed: whereas previ- ously, the people had sat and wept, here the people weep through the night; and previously the Israelites had decided that life had been good in Egypt, but here they determine that it would be good to return to Egypt – their despising of the land being a definitive rejection of God's plan for Israel. The crisis is emphasized by use of three verbs – 'lifted', 'put forth', 'wept' – and the description of the length of time, 'all that night', leading to 'the nation's desire to return to Egypt, symbolically turning back the clock on the Exodus and cancelling the covenant between the nation and God' (S. Schwartz 2020: 597). The bitter trajectory, ending with Israel's devastating failure of unbelief, may be traced from 11:18 through 14:3–4 – with reference to the people's backward glance to Egypt (on Egypt in the Pentateuch, see Greifenhagen 2002: 177–205). Even before the sea crossing, God had stated that if the people saw battle, they would have a change of heart and return to Egypt (Exod. 13:17; Levine 1993: 363), and then returning to Egypt became 'the essence' of the people's rebel- lions thereafter (Exod. 16:3; Num. 20:5; 21:5 ; Milgrom 1990: 88). Here, their words move from 'Egypt' to 'wilderness' to 'land', the trajectory of the exodus, and then back to 'Egypt' and 'Egypt' (see W. Brueggemann 1977: 36). Ironically, while they express the preference to have died first in Egypt and then in the wilderness, rather than dying in the land, God's faithful deliverance and protection of them both in Egypt and the wilderness prove his ability to grant them the land. The 'Egypt' inclusio, ending with a double referenced determination to 'return to Egypt', marks Israel's first generation (cf. Exod. 14:11–12) – though out of its geographical boundaries, they remained in Egyptian bondage inwardly.

The lifting and putting forth of the voice in weeping – throughout the night – describes an extreme form of wailing, manifesting the depths of Israel's despair over the bad report of the ten scouts, which they have weighed over YHWH's promise. Most often the formula recurs either as '*lifting up* the voice and weeping' with *nāśā'* (Gen. 21:16; 27:38; Judg. 2:4; 21:2; 1 Sam. 11:4; 24:16; 30:4; 2 Sam. 3:32; 13:36; Ruth 1:9, 14; Job 2:12), rarely as '*giving* one's voice to weeping' with *nātan* (Gen. 45:2), but here the remarkable use of both 'lift up' and 'give' (cf. Avishur 1999: 204). The heaped-up verbs ('lift up', 'give', 'weep') portray massive, widespread wailing, which 'appears to be tantamount to rebellion' (Knierim and Coats 2005: 187). The sons of Israel 'grumble' (*lûn*) against Moses and Aaron, something which they have done in the past (Exod. 15:24; 16:2, 7, 8, 9, 12; 17:3, 6), although this is the first of several instances in Numbers (14:2, 27, 29, 36; 16:11, 41; 17:5, 10) – six times in the present chapter. In verses 2–3, the whole community tells Moses and Aaron, through a variety of exclamations, that death would have been preferable to facing the onslaught of the land's inhabitants, and then that Egypt would be preferable to death. Worst of all, the people attribute evil motives to YHWH, claiming that he was bringing them into this land to slaughter them by the sword (Ashley 1993: 245), precisely the opposite of his desire to conquer their enemies, give them a land of abundance, and do them good. A mark of the unregenerate heart is a malicious view of God, expressing discontent in hateful speech aimed at maligning his character (cf. Gen. 3:4–5). After complaining, the people conspire together ('each man to his brother'), determining to appoint a 'head' (*rō'š*) for a return to Egypt – such yearning for Egypt being 'a symbol of Israel's apostasy' (Milgrom 1990: 108 cf. Isa. 30:1–7; 31:1–3; Jer. 2:18; Ezek. 17:15). YHWH had appointed Moses to deliver them out of Egypt; the Israelites want to appoint their own man to reverse the exodus. More recently, Moses had chosen twelve chieftains, 'heads' (*rā'šê*) of the sons of Israel (13:3), for the honoured task of claiming the land, each on behalf of his tribe; now the people seek to replace Moses with a head of their own choosing who will perform their desire. Their sentiments, heard by YHWH, will be turned into poetic judgements (vv. 28–31).

5–10. All the momentum and progress – Moses' deliverance as an infant (Exod. 2), his encounters with YHWH God at the flaming bush (Exod. 3, 6), his confrontations with Pharaoh (Exod. 5–10), the Passover redemption and death of the firstborn sons of Egypt (Exod. 11 – 13), the perilous sea crossing and jubilant praise of YHWH (Exod. 14 – 15), the thunderous Advent of YHWH at Mount Sinai and his gift of the Decalogue within a newly forged relationship (Exod. 19 – 24), Moses'

Herculean mediation after the golden calf apostasy (Exod. 32 – 34), and God's gift of his Dwelling (Exod. 25 – 31; 35 – 40) and the Levitical cult (Lev.), the Camp of Israel as a covenant community (Num. 1 – 10) – now comes to a chaotic halt on the verge of entering Canaan as the entire, colossal assembly of Israel revolts: 'Let us return to Egypt!' Moses, along with Aaron, thus fell 'before the whole assembly (qĕhal) of the community ('ădat) of the sons of Israel', a long description of the people, highlighting their relation to God in threefold manner. This prostration is somewhat ambiguous, understood alternately as expressing a fear of death (per de Vaulx 1972: 175), an attempt to propitiate the people or as an expression of helplessness and despair (per Milgrom 1990: 108), a gesture imploring the people to change their minds (per Galbraith 2014: 37), or an act of intercession (per Budd 1984: 156). Appointing a new leader (v. 4) may have involved a summary execution of the previous one(s). Moses' prostration before the people, however, rather than a fearful capitulation, was probably meant as a complete release of himself in submission to God. He had brought them all this way to the verge of the land, and they are ready to kill him – O YHWH, your will be done! E. W. Davies is close to this thought, seeing 'an act of contrition before God' (1995b: 141), which forms something of a parallel with Joshua and Caleb's rending of their garments – an expression of grief and terror over the heinousness of the people's sinful speech. Moses and Aaron's physical gesture shows their 'submission, not to the rebels, but to God' (Knierim and Coats 2005: 188). As a symbolic act, their prostration may hold multivalent significance, their submissive posture forming also an act of intercession – aware of both YHWH's presence in the midst of his people, and of the judgement that must ensue after the people's rebellious rupture of the covenant relationship.

With the threat of death looming over Moses his mentor, Joshua is now mentioned first (cf. Num. 11:28), joined by Caleb, as they rend their garments, an act that – typically used in the ANE to express bitter grief over tragedies, like the death of loved ones – demonstrates their repulsion and profound dismay over the people's rejection of YHWH's gift of land and his plans for Israel, and their vicious attack of Moses and Aaron. The opening vav, linked to the subjects, is disjunctive: 'Now' or 'But' – Joshua and Caleb interrupt the flow of action which was tending to violence against Moses and Aaron. The gloss that Joshua and Caleb 'were among those who searched out the land' adds gravity to their action for, having tasted the goodness and bounty of the land, they are horrified by the prospect of rejecting this divine gift. Their speech begins with an overturning of the other scouts' bad report of the land. In the first mention of Joshua and Caleb together, the houses of Ephraim and Judah, the northern and southern kingdoms, respectively, are represented. 'This means', writes Artus (2013: 373), 'that any Israelite, from the north or from the south, can identify himself with these exemplary characters within the narrative'. Within the purview of Israel's desire to choose a new leader, Joshua – who will be YHWH's chosen leader – steps forward, an adumbration of his later role (see 27:12–23).

If Caleb's original comments had inadvertently omitted God's power (13:30), it now becomes the focal point of Joshua and Caleb's response, both in relation to the land (14:8) and to its inhabitants (14:10) (Schwartz 2020: 599). Just as the description of the manna in 11:7–9 vindicated YHWH by vindicating his gift, so here in 14:7–9, the defence of the land's goodness serves to vindicate YHWH. Indeed, 'The-land' (*hā'āreṣ*) is their opening word. 'The land which we passed through', they say – for we, too, were there – 'is a good land (*ṭôbāh hā'āreṣ*) – very, very (*mě'ōd mě'ōd*)!' In Genesis 1:31, God looked at the pristine creation in all of its dawning beauty, every step 'good', and declared it to be 'very good' – adding *mě'od*. After searching out Canaan, Joshua and Caleb declare it to be 'very, very good'. They further say the land is 'flowing with milk and honey', a phrase linked to YHWH's own favoured description of the land (Exod. 3:8, 17; 13:5; 33:3; Lev. 20:24) and which returns to the original report (Num. 13:27). The thrust and central point of Joshua's exhortation is in verse 8: 'If YHWH delights (*ḥāpāṣ*) in us he will bring us into this land, and give it to us – a land flowing with milk and honey,' which may be retraced backward from the goodness of the land, to the land's being a gift of YHWH, to YHWH's bringing Israel into the land, and, finally, to the indispensable key: YHWH's favour – and what delights YHWH is faith, *trusting obedience to his word*. In Deuteronomy, Moses' references to the land for the second generation are regularly paired with the ascription 'good' (Deut. 1:25, 35; 3:25; 4:21–22; 6:18; 8:7, 10; 9:6; 11:17), Canaan's 'standard description' (Ashley 1993: 249).

The two faithful scouts come to the issue at hand: inheriting the land is contingent only – but surely – on YHWH's favour. In verse 9 rebellion against YHWH is equated with fearing the inhabitants of Canaan, a needless revolt since the inhabitants are unprotected:

9a **Do not rebel** against YHWH;
    9b **Do not fear** the people, ⤬ 9c their defence is turned away
       they are as bread   – **do not fear** them.

The words 'And you' (*wě'attem*) directly confront the people – you who have God Almighty dwelling in your midst and going before you in the strength of his might, should have no fear. Others may have cause to fear these nations, but not Israel (Milgrom 1990: 109). While fearing YHWH leads to courage before men; not fearing YHWH leads to the fear of man. By YHWH's help even the giants will be as Israel's bread – to be devoured in battle, for their shade of defence is turned away. Once more a metaphor of consumption is used, reversing the scouts' previous demagoguery, whereby the land would devour its inhabitants, and the

Canaanites would eat the grasshopper-like Israelites (13:32–33). The 'shade of defence' language utilizes a shadow metaphor, representing the protection of their gods, which functions to refute the scouts' mythological representation of the Anakites as Nephilim (S. Schwartz 2020: 600). The major contrast is: the Canaanites 'shade of defence has turned away' versus 'YHWH is with us', a point underscored in the epilogue when the people rebelliously attempt to ascend the mountain even though 'YHWH is not in your midst' (vv. 39–45). YHWH's presence with his people has been the issue at stake since the beginning (see Exod. 17:7). In Deuteronomy, Moses will remind the second generation of Israelites that, yes, there are mighty nations in Canaan, with powerful cities fortified up to heaven, and with descendants of the Anakim among its inhabitants, applying these realities to drive one application, the need to look to YHWH God who is invincible and promises to destroy their enemies (9:1–4). Moses also reminds them that Israel had rebelled against YHWH's commandment to take the land – 'you did not believe him or obey his voice' (Deut. 9:23; cf. Ps. 106:24–27). Similarly, the leading motif of Joshua and Caleb's impassioned plea is trust in YHWH and in his deliverance: 'If YHWH delights in us', 'Only do not rebel against YHWH', 'YHWH is with us'.

The whole community's response is 'to stone them'. There is some question as to who the referent of 'them' is here: Joshua and Caleb or Moses and Aaron. While Joshua and Caleb immediately precede this statement, the broader context favours Moses and Aaron as the referent. Joshua and Caleb, however, cannot be ruled out, and perhaps they were included in the threat to Moses and Aaron. In verses 4–5, the whole community called for appointing a replacement of Moses to lead them back to Egypt, and, in the face of mounting hostility, Moses and Aaron had fallen prostrate – so that even Joshua and Caleb's speech in verses 6–9 comes across as an attempt to shield Moses and Aaron from the people's threat as much as it is an effort to convince the people to possess the land. Their speech functioned within the 'trial' of Moses and Aaron, but the whole community nevertheless responded, 'Stone them!' Thus when Joshua and Caleb fail, and the whole community presses further to stone Moses and Aaron, YHWH himself intervenes (cf. *Num. Rab.* 16.21) – his glory appears at the Tent of Meeting 'to' or 'against' (*'el*) all the sons of Israel. YHWH, a consuming fire (Exod. 24:17; Deut. 4:24; 9:3; Isa. 33:14; Heb. 12:29), manifests his glory and the people's revolt is stayed. The 'glory of YHWH' (*kĕbôd yhwh*) appears in similar circumstances, either to protect Moses and Aaron or to help them (Exod. 16:10; Num. 17:7; 20:6; Kislev 2017: 48; cf. Boorer 2012: 56).

14:11–25. The ensuing dialogue between YHWH and Moses has been dubbed 'a highly sophisticated literary construction with deep theological motivations' and 'a striking example of Hebrew rhetorical technique' (Newing 1987: 212). YHWH first turns to Moses alone (vv.

11–25), engaging with his servant in his role as mediator of Israel's covenant relationship with YHWH. YHWH's judgement, proposed to Moses (vv. 11–12), is followed by Moses' intercession on Israel's behalf (vv. 13–19), and then by YHWH's relenting response to Moses by which both his justice and mercy will be upheld (vv. 20–25). Only after this deliberation with Moses, does YHWH then turn to both Moses and Aaron to make his settled pronouncement against the people (vv. 26–35).

11–12. How extraordinary Moses' role as mediator: YHWH's glory appears to the people but he does not address them; rather, he confides immediately with his favoured man, soliciting his counsel regarding Israel. The infinite, omniscient God poses two questions to his servant Moses, seeking, as it were, his 'help' in comprehending Israel's shameful obstinacy which has even exasperated the Almighty (cf. Isa. 7:13): 'How long (*'ad-'ānâ*) will this people spurn (*nā'aṣ*) me? How long will they not trust ('āman) in me, despite all the signs I have done in their midst?' The repetition of 'how long', as Widmer observes (2004: 287), occurs only in Psalm 13, where it is used four times in two verses to underscore the psalmist's excruciating lament. Sakenfeld points out that when *nā'aṣ* occurs in the piel as here it refers without exception to the despising of God or something sacred to him, an action 'regarded as tantamount to rejection of the whole covenant relationship', a complete abandonment and breaking of the covenant (cf. Deut. 31:20), evidenced in this case by the people's dual desire to replace the designated leader and to return to Egypt – and, as such, is an act that *cannot* go unpunished by God (1975: 321; cf. Coats 1968: 146). In the piel the term encompasses the notion of spurning, despising, rejecting, dishonouring, condemning and treating with contempt, as a blasphemer does of God (see Ruppert 1978). Hirsch defines this term as 'the highest degree of scorn and abuse', which 'does not consider the object worthy of any consideration whatsoever' (2007a: 256), a reality demonstrated both in their unwillingness to take the land with YHWH, and in their later effort to take it without him (vv. 40–45) – YHWH's presence is completely irrelevant to them. In verse 23, YHWH will, therefore, pronounce that 'all who spurned (*nā'aṣ*) will not see' the land. That YHWH is set to disinherit Israel, then, is expected, after the brazen nature of the nation's rejection of its covenant relationship with him (Sakenfeld 1975: 321–322). Indeed, this will be the focus of Moses' intercession. The two questions, which function as accusations (v. 11), are then followed by three terse statements of YHWH's intent, each with the first person singular prefix ('), understood best as cohortatives – 'let me . . .' – in the light of Moses' role as intercessor (Newing 1987: 213). Helpfully, Newing points to examples throughout Scripture whereby, in YHWH's condescension and deliberate invitation, the intercessory prayers of a prophetic mediator are effectual – so much so that Jeremiah, for example, is commanded not to pray for the people so that YHWH's judgement may come to pass (Jer. 7:16; 11:14; see also Gen. 18:17, 23–32;

Exod. 32:10–14; Amos 7:1–6, 7–9) (1987: 213–214). Milgrom similarly speaks of prophetic intercession being 'able' to block divine retribution, understood in the sense that YHWH was prompting Moses' intercession, even trying him (1990: 109–110).

YHWH's initial resolution swiftly reverses the situation: Israel is suddenly threatened with death, and Moses' life is safeguarded. The threat to 'strike down' (*nākāh*) the Israelites hearkens back to YHWH's smiting the firstborn of Egypt (Exod. 12:13; Num. 3:13; 8:17) and foreshadows the smiting of Israelites by the Amalekites and Canaanites with which this account ends (14:45). 'Pestilence' (*deber*) also resonates with the divine judgement on Egyptians (Exod. 5:3; 9:3), with Exodus 9:15 using both terms – fitting, since the people want to return to Egypt. The final threat of disinheriting Israel, using a form of *yāraš* (hiph.), the typical term for Israel's inheritance/possession of the land, marks the complete reversal of the exodus – an ironic judgement, acquiescing to the people's desire. Not for the first time, YHWH expresses his intention to annihilate Israel and make of Moses a replacement nation. After the golden calf apostasy, YHWH had said he would destroy Israel and make of Moses a 'great nation' (Exod. 32:10); here, he declares he will make of him a 'great and mighty nation' (cf. Deut. 9:1, 14). The allusion to YHWH's former response after the golden calf debacle is one of many connections, including the form of Moses' intercessory mediation, between Exodus 32 – 34 and Numbers 13 – 14 (cf. Horn 1993: 36–38). No idle threat, YHWH had already done as much in history, wiping out an entire generation of humanity, and starting over through Noah (Gen. 6 – 8). YHWH's purposes – his determined goal of being glorified among the nations – will stand, regardless of any delay (Ps. 90:42; Peter 3:8). Such statements from YHWH to Moses, however, are part of a dance between them observed throughout their relationship in the Pentateuch: YHWH solicits intercession from Moses, and Moses solicits intervention from YHWH. Here, YHWH tells him, 'I will . . .' awaiting Moses' response, whereas in verse 28 he tells Moses and Aaron, 'Say to them . . .' no longer soliciting engagement. The construction may express purpose or result, implying that the divine judgement is not yet settled and, further, provides an opening of the verdict to Moses' influence, as a king takes counsel with a most trusted advisor (Widmer 2004: 297). Such a statement from God at such a moment must surely have tested Moses to the core of his being.

13–19. It is in this moment that one may observe the greatness of Moses, as he pleads – in a 'most eloquent, passionate and persuasive defence' (J. M. Cohen 2000: 127) – for the lives and well-being of the very Israelites who had just doubted, despised, and rejected him and who were even calling for his public execution. And his greatness serves but to unveil an intimation of the infinite greatness and glory of YHWH God. Following Newing's analysis (1987: 215–223): Moses' intercession may be structured in two parts (vv. 13–16 and 17–19), with the central line of the first part, 'when you kill this people as one man' (15a), forming the protasis between apodosis I (vv. 13–14), focusing on theological motifs of exodus deliverance and divine presence, and apodosis II (vv. 15b–16), focusing on the motif of the land promise; the second part employs the theological motifs of the Sinai revelation (vv. 17–18) and of YHWH's providential care of Israel through the wilderness (v. 19b). In both parts of Moses' mediation there is a shift from YHWH's power and glory to his relationship with Israel. Moreover, whereas in 11:11–15, 21–22, Moses focused on his own favour in God's sight, using 'I' and 'me' terms, here where he focuses on YHWH's reputation, one finds many 'you' and 'your' terms – note the twofold use of 'you YHWH' (*'attā yhwh*, v. 14) – boldly pursuing Israel's life before the face of God with emphatic pleading. The fivefold use of 'this people' (*hā'ām hazzeh*; vv. 13, 14, 15, 16, 19), links Moses' response with YHWH's initial question 'How long will this people spurn me?' (v. 11). The name 'YHWH' also occurs five times (vv. 13–19) – plainly, Moses mediates between 'YHWH' and 'this people'. Ironically, Egypt's action among the nations, spreading defamatory speech about YHWH, mirrors the action of the ten scouts among the people of Israel. Moses will resolve the matter by referring YHWH to his own words about himself (Exod. 34:6–7; 20:5–6), which Moses had heard: 'just as you have spoken, saying . . .' (v. 17), and YHWH will respond by doing 'according to your [Moses'] word' (v. 20). Moses' original plea to behold a vision of YHWH's glory, leading to the Hebrew Scriptures' supreme revelation of YHWH's attributes had been aimed for precisely such a moment of mediation (Exod. 33:18).

Moses' mediation involves two main arguments, each feeding into the one major plea that YHWH should forgive Israel for the sake of his own glory – the glory of his own character and nature (cf. Balentine 1985: 68–69). First, YHWH's reputation among the nations is at stake: What will Egypt and the nations in Canaan think about his destruction of Israel in the wilderness – will they not decide that, after having delivered Israel out of Egypt, YHWH was not *able* (*yĕkōlet*) to overcome the inhabitants of Canaan and, by implication, their gods? Because YHWH's renown has reached the nations, and they know that he is among Israel daily, the nations will attribute Israel's destruction to YHWH but for the wrong reason – essentially publishing the blaspheming of God proclaimed by the faithless scouts ('we are not able', 13:31). These verses employ a fourfold use of 'to hear' (*šāma'*): the Egyptians 'will hear' (v. 13) and tell the inhabitants of the land, who 'have heard' of YHWH's dwelling amid his people (v. 14), for the nations 'have heard' of your 'fame' (v. 15; 'hearing-of-you', *šim'ăkā*) (Boorer 1992: 349). This significant wordplay underscores the heinous sin of the ten scouts who spread a bad report of the land to the rest of God's people; their 'we are not able to ascend' is a slander against YHWH, the same blaspheming of YHWH's Name

Moses wants to prevent Egypt from spreading to the nations. Those 'dwelling in this land' may have primary reference to the petty kings of Canaan (suggested by F. Andersen and N. Gottwald; cf. n. 13 in Newing 1987: 215). As part of his first argument, Moses mentions that YHWH had sworn to give the land to Israel (v. 16) – his character is at stake: will he fulfil his word in truth and faithfulness? Rhetorically, Moses describes YHWH's proposed action of 'smiting' the people (v. 12) as 'slaughtering' (*šāḥaṭ*) them, using a term more often used for killing beasts, either for food or in sacrifice (Gen. 37:31; Exod. 12:6; 29:11; Lev. 17:3; 22:28; etc.; BDB 1006). Third, Moses reminds YHWH that the true greatness of YHWH's character, the real strength of his glory, is his glory revealed in the magnificence of his mercy rather than in the perfection of his judgement. To be sure, God is glorified in judgement, and he will not be mocked (Gal. 6:7), but – *But!* – precisely against the backdrop of his righteous judgement, YHWH God is glorified in a greater way by his forbearance and loving-kindness, demonstrated in the forgiveness of his people's sin. His plea for YHWH's forbearance is buttressed by God's own proven nature in that he has already 'borne with this people from Egypt until now' (v. 19).

For his intercession after the golden calf apostasy, Moses had used the first two arguments. However, the first argument, related to YHWH's reputation, was restricted to Egypt, since Israel had not yet approached the nations with YHWH dwelling their midst, which also meant that YHWH would be accused of destroying Israel simply out of evil intent (Exod. 32:12), versus, as here, his 'inability' to bring them into the land (Num. 14:16) (Boorer 1992: 358). The second argument, God's promise to the patriarchs, was used in a more expanded form in Exodus 32:11–13. For his intercession after Israel's sin with the golden calf, Moses had even interposed his own life for Israel's sake (Exod. 32:32), and then YHWH proclaimed his Name to Moses and caused his goodness to pass before him by declaring his attributes – after which, Moses bowed and worshipped (Exod. 33:19–23; 34:5–8). Herein lies the difference between Moses' mediation in Exodus 32 and Numbers 14: Moses now pleads the glory of God revealed in Exodus 34:6–7 (see Exod. 20:5–6) – 'just as you have spoken', Moses says. The revelation of YHWH's attributes and character in Exodus 34, demonstrated throughout the ensuing history of Israel (see Pss 103:6–10; 145:7–9), is the highest unveiling of God until the Incarnation, and becomes the fountain for Moses' intercession. A significant difference, already noted, in relation to the first argument relates to God's intimate presence among the Israelites – indeed, in Exodus 32 – 34 Moses prays precisely for YHWH to fulfil his plan of setting his Dwelling and presence among his people. The Camp of Israel, the first historical expression and paradigm for the covenant community, and the fulfilment of Moses' mediation in Exodus 32 – 34, allows Moses to leverage YHWH's presence among them for the sake of sparing Israel. Moses' words in verse 14 reveal the nearly unspeakable, tremendous wonder of Israel's life in the Camp with YHWH: he dwells 'in the midst' of his people, he is seen 'eye to eye', his Cloud stands as a shield 'over them', and in the pillar of Cloud he 'is walking before them' by day, and in a pillar of fire by night. Whereas in 2 Samuel 7:6, YHWH says he walked in a Tent, here YHWH walks freely, as it were, outside his Tent, veiled within the pillar of Cloud (cf. Lev. 26:12).

The two parts in the second half of Moses' intercession (vv. 17–18, 19) follow a similar structure: petition (juss., imp.) followed by ('just as' *ka'ăšer*) supporting motif – first Sinai revelation, then wilderness protection (Newing 1987: 219–220). Moses had first stated that YHWH had delivered Israel from Egypt by his 'strength' (*kōaḥ*), by his deeds of power (v. 13), but now he pleads for YHWH to cause his 'strength' (*kōaḥ*) to grow ('be greater', *yigdal*) by demonstrating his attributes of being slow to anger, abundant in loving-kindness, forgiving guilt and transgression, bidding him to forgive according to the 'greatness' of his loving-kindness, his *rab-ḥesed*. YHWH's great 'strength' is in staying his hand of judgement, withholding the utter destruction of an exceedingly sinful people who have done nothing but challenge him to his face to devastate them with the blows of his fierce anger. The use of 'But now' (*wĕ'attā*) signals that the climax of the intercession has been reached (Newing 1987: 219). His first supporting argument is to quote YHWH back to him: 'just as you have spoken', referring to YHWH's self-revelation in Exodus 34:6. To display *ḥesed* is to be gracious and merciful and slow to anger; it is a forbearing loyalty aimed at *preserving* kindred relationships: the greatness of YHWH's *ḥesed* 'is evidenced by and concretized in his forgiveness of iniquity' – it is his '*surprising faithfulness*' (Sakenfeld 1975: 324–325, 329). Moses' goal is to preserve Israel's covenant with YHWH, to maintain the relationship through the inevitable judgement that *must* fall upon Israel's breach of covenant. In terms of relationships, then, *nā'aṣ* and *ḥesed* are opposing actions; the first spurns and abandons a relationship, while the other preserves and maintains it – in wondrously longsuffering mercy, YHWH's self-effacing *ḥesed* will prove stronger even than Israel's arrogant *nā'aṣ*. YHWH's forgiveness of Israel is a higher work, and manifests greater strength, than his judgement of Egypt. 'Rather than citing any redeeming qualities or redeemable quality of his miserable people, Moses clings to YHWH's own declaration of his character on Mount Sinai as the basis for hope' (Gane 2004: 612). Moses' intercession includes that God does not wholly clear the guilty, yet his emphasis remains on God's forbearance, which he has displayed to Israel from the first: 'Forgive, pray, the guilt of the people according to the greatness of your loving-kindness, just as you have borne (*nāśā'*) with this people from Egypt until now' (v. 19). To be clear, Moses is not pleading for YHWH to neglect justice or account-ability – the wicked will not escape judgement – but rather that YHWH would not utterly consume Israel 'as one man' and start over through Moses. God's forgiveness of Israel, based on his *ḥesed*, means 'the preservation of the community's relationship with God' (Sakenfeld 1975: 326). In YHWH's unsearchable wisdom, Israel will be brought into the land as a people (the second generation), even while he indeed brings judgement on the rebellious Israelites (the first generation) – again, he will not be mocked. How true for the second generation of Israelites in the wilderness, that they should '[c]onsider the kindness and severity of God: upon those who fell, severity, but toward you, kindness – if you remain in his kindness, otherwise you will be cut off' (Rom. 11:22). Rather than 'forgiveness' in the sense of erasing the first generation's accountability, Moses, seeking YHWH to be true to his own Name, calls upon him to show loyal solidarity with Israel, to remain faithful to the covenant relationship (Widmer 2004: 306–318). Noting that *ḥesed* is found in synonymous parallel with *bĕrît*, Widmer underscores the purpose of Moses' intercession as YHWH's maintenance of the covenant, his loyalty to Israel in continuing to uphold the relationship, along with the necessary forbearance to endure their ongoing obduracy and rebellious nature – a faithful relationship which 'does not preclude punishment of the guilty generation' (2004: 317).

What should not be missed is that YHWH's two speeches (14:11–12, 20–23) frame Moses' speech (14:13–19), tracing the astounding effort and effectual nature of Moses' mediation, for the 'difference in judgement which is the point towards which the whole text moves, comes about through Moses' intercession' (Boorer 1992: 346–348; also Balentine 1985: 71). The drama of Moses' intercession forms the key to unlocking the mysterious depths at the heart of the book's message, and even the heart of YHWH himself. Through Moses' mediation, the narrative unfolds the infinitely vast strength of the love of YHWH for Israel, a strength not only tested by Israel's waywardness, but unveiled precisely by Moses' plea for YHWH to forgive the people. Whereas as YHWH had suggested his making Moses into a 'great' nation, Moses pleads for him to make his forbearance 'great' (Milgrom 1990: 111). Out of profound humility, tenacious loyalty to Israel, and a fervent desire to uphold the glory of YHWH before the nations, Moses dismisses any suggestion of his own greatness, and pursues the divine agenda for history. YHWH's initial 'How long' questions over the apparent limitless of Israel's rebellion (v. 11) are transformed by Moses into a theological question of the strength of YHWH's longsuffering mercy – 'How long are you willing to be longsuffering to maintain your covenant with Israel?' The last two words of his plea in Hebrew, *'ad-hēnnâ* (until now), may even be read as an answer to YHWH's twofold 'How long?' (*'ad-'ānâ*) (Horn 1993: 41).

20. In a profound display of both the effectual nature of Moses' intimate relationship with YHWH and, more especially, of the majesty of YHWH himself, after threatening the annihilation of Israel, YHWH relents immediately with two Hebrew words: 'I-have-forgiven according-to-your-word (*sālaḥtî kidbārekā*).' Moses lives to guide Israel according to the *torah* of YHWH; here, YHWH condescends to say he has forgiven according to the word of Moses. Of course, Moses' word was saturated by the word and will – indeed, the ultimate redemptive purposes – of YHWH God. Again, 'forgive' here does not refer to ignoring or absolving the people's apostasy, but to maintaining the covenant relationship with Israel as a people, being reconciled to the nation and continuing his purposes to bring them into the land (Condie 2001: 133).

21. YHWH's declaration, far from out of place, responds to Moses' overarching point in verses 13–19; namely, YHWH's agenda to publish his glory throughout the earth, ultimately for the blessing of the nations (cf. Gen. 12:3; 22:18), an agenda confirmed by a solemn oath 'truly, as I live' (*ḥay-'ānî*), a rare expression in the Torah (Num. 14:21, 28; Deut. 32:40). YHWH's twofold response is framed by his divine oath – 'as I live' (14:21, 28), 'swear' (14:23), 'lift my hand (in oath)' (14:30) – which also serves to punctuate the punishment of the first generation, along with the seriousness of their sin (cf. Widmer 2004: 277, 312). Although many interpreters read this verse's second clause ('the whole earth . . .') in conjunction with the first clause (i.e. 'as the whole earth . . .'), subordinate to verse 22, yet, as Alter points out, Hebrew has no grammatical indication of such an 'as' structure and there are no precedents for God's swearing beyond merely his life, making it preferable 'to understand this clause as Ibn Ezra does, to point forward in time to God's unfolding historical plan' (2004: 752). 'As I live' is the divine version of what would become a familiar oath in Israel: 'As YHWH lives' (see 1 Sam. 26:10; 1 Kgs 2:24; Jer. 4:2; 5:2). YHWH is infinite life in himself, the wellspring of life, so that there cannot be anything surer than that he lives.

22–23. Now YHWH vindicates his honour in declaring judgement against those Israelites who have revolted against him, the men who have seen his glory and signs both in Egypt and in the wilderness. Aside from all else, the period from Egypt to Sinai and now on the cusp of Canaan has been marked by a display of God's glory and signs, and his people are accountable for responding with trust and obedience. These Israelite men are thus depicted as more recalcitrant than Pharaoh whose hardened heart would not bow to YHWH's glory in spite of all the signs and wonders he performed in Egypt. The root for 'to see' (*rā'āh*), occurring ten times in chapters 13–14, tells its own story: the scouts were commanded 'to see' the land (13:18); upon their return, they 'show' Moses and Aaron the fruit of the land (13:26), but tell them they 'saw' the children of Anak (13:28) and then they spread a bad report to the people saying (only) that they 'saw' men of great stature (13:32), and that they 'saw' the Nephilim (13:33) (see also Boorer 1992: 342). Fittingly, YHWH 'appears' before the people (14:10), Moses speaks of YHWH's being 'seen' face-to-face within the Camp (14:14), and YHWH's judgement is directed against those who have 'seen' his glory (14:22), their judgement being that they will not 'see' the land (14:23 [twice]) – clearly, their seeing YHWH's glory should have trumped their having seen the Canaanites, emboldening them to see the land within the sure hope of God's promise. Attempts have been made to enumerate the 'ten times' Israel has tested YHWH. Rashi cites the Babylonian Talmud (*Ar.* 15a–b) for the following ten tests: two at the sea (Exodus 14:11 and Ps. 106:7), two related to the manna (Exod. 16:19–20 and 16:27), two with the quail (Exod. 16:3 and Num. 11:4), two for lack of water (Exod. 15:23 and 17:2), the sin of the golden calf (Exod. 32), and, finally, the sin of the scouts here (1997: 4:166). The Mishnah teaches that the ten generations before the judgement of floodwaters, from Adam to Noah, serve to demonstrate the greatness of God's patience, since every one of those generations had provoked him to wrath (*m. Pirk. Av.* 5.2). Given the use of 'ten times' elsewhere (Job 19:3; Neh. 4:12), the phrase is likely idiomatic for 'many times', underscoring an inordinate amount. Schart (noted by M. Smith 1999: 185) observes that the number ten corresponds with the number of plagues in Egypt, and perhaps it is not irrelevant that this final testing of YHWH was through ten scouts. The 'testing' (*nāsāh*) of his people is a divine prerogative, meant to solicit or 'prove' faith and obedience (Gen. 22:1; Exod. 15:25; 16:4; 20:20), whereas the human testing of God stands as rebellious unbelief which 'tries' God's forbearance (Exod. 17:2, 7). The men have tested YHWH not only by not having 'heeded' (*šāma'*) his voice, but they have 'spurned' or 'contemned' (*nā'aṣ*) him (cf. 14:11). The Israelites, and especially the ten leaders who scouted the land, have treated YHWH and his word with contempt. That such will not 'see' (*rā'āh*) the land is given double emphasis, beginning and ending verse 23, a key term used ironically here inasmuch the scouts had been sent to 'see' the land (13:8). Since the land was 'sworn' (*šāba'*) 'to their fathers' (and not to this particular generation of Israelites), YHWH may withhold the land from the present generation without violating his oath – the second generation's inheritance of the land may fulfil his promise to bring in the descendants of the patriarchs. YHWH had long ago called Abram to 'a land that I will show (*rā'āh*) you' (Gen. 12:1), later bidding him to 'lift up your eyes and look (*rā'āh*) . . . for the land you are seeing (*rā'āh*) I will give to you and to your descendants for ever' (13:14–15). Because the ten scouts who saw the land brought a bad report of it, a malicious falsehood embraced by the Israelites, these descendants will by no means see the land. It is worth noting here that Moses himself is excluded from this judgement, for in Numbers 27:12–13 YHWH tells him to ascend Mount Abarim to 'see' the land he is giving the sons of Israel, and that after he has 'seen' it, he will be gathered to his people.

24. Entry into the land is by YHWH's sole prerogative, and Caleb now is singled out as an exception to his judgement. While the children of the first generation will inherit the land, Caleb himself will be brought

into the land and *then* bequeath it to his children (cf. Hirsch 2007a: 266). Rather than testing YHWH by not heeding his voice and spurning him, Caleb has fully 'followed-after' (*'aḥărāy*) him – this because he has a 'different' or 'another' (*'aḥeret*) spirit with him. Whereas the people 'turned away' (*šabtem*) from following-after YHWH (v. 43), Caleb has 'fully' (*mālē'*) followed after him. The word 'fully' is used typically for physically filling a space, whether the earth with life (Gen. 1:22, 28; 9:1; Exod. 1:7) or with violence, and so on (Gen. 6:11; Exod. 8:21; 10:6; Lev. 19:29), or filling a vessel with material, such as water or earth (Gen. 21:19; 24:16; 26:15; 42:25; Exod. 2:16), and is used metaphorically as 'fullness of days' (Gen. 25:24; 29:28: 50:30; Exod. 7:25) and for 'to consecrate' (Lev. 8:22, 28, 29, 31, 33; Num. 3:3). The term is also used for YHWH's 'filling' a person with the Spirit of God (Exod. 31:3; 35:31), and filling the Dwelling or earth with his glory (Exod. 40:34–35; Num. 14:21). Its use here – literally, 'he filled (*wayĕmallē'*) after me' – is an expression akin to being 'wholly devoted to YHWH', and is found mainly in connection with Caleb (Num. 14:24; 32:11, 12; Deut. 1:36; Josh. 14:8, 9, 14; cf. 1 Kgs 11:6) (see Weinfeld 1992: 78, 337). Given the association between 'fill' and 'spirit' (cf. Exod. 31:3; 35:31), the spread of YHWH's spirit that was upon Moses to seventy others (Num. 11), and the use of 'with him' (*'immô*), spirit here should likely be understood not as Caleb's having a different 'disposition' or 'psychological reality' than the other scouts, but rather that God's Spirit was with him. Most significantly, YHWH refers to Caleb as 'my servant', a designation of honour made only of Moses thus far: 'My servant Moses' (Num. 12:7, 8). Joshua, too, will be described as possessing *rûaḥ* (Num. 27:18; Deut. 34:9).

As with his judgement, YHWH's reward is fitting: Caleb will be 'brought' (*bô'*) into the land 'there where he entered (*bô'*)'. This point may also support the idea that the twelve scouts, princes of their tribes (13:2), may have been surveying the land more as a gesture of inheritance (like Abraham in Gen. 13:14–15), and that Caleb's purview had been Hebron specifically. The fulfilment of YHWH's word is recounted in Joshua 14:6–15: 'Give me this mountain' Caleb says, and Joshua blessed him and gave him 'Hebron for an inheritance'. Numbers 13 – 14 also highlights 'the mountain' (13:17, 29; 14:40, 44, 45), focusing on Hebron (13:22). A divine reward for Caleb's earlier urging of Israel to 'possess' (*yāraš*) the land (13:30), he is now ensured by YHWH that he and his descendants will 'possess' it.

Joshua will be noted with Caleb as exempt from divine judgement (vv. 30, 38), yet without any reason given. The distinction may be theological: Caleb will be brought in the land by YHWH for his fully following after him, while Joshua will bring Israel, including Caleb, in the land (Num. 27:17), as the protégé and successor of Moses (cf. Granot 2014b). In the Deuteronomy version of the scouts episode, Moses both includes Joshua with Caleb and separates him from Caleb within the space of four verses: Caleb is distinguished from the evil generation as one who will be given the land (1:35–36), while Joshua is distinguished from Moses as the one who will lead Israel to inherit the land (1:37–38). In Numbers as well, Joshua's identity as Moses' protégé and successor is primary (27:12–23; cf. Exod. 33:11; Num. 11:28), while Caleb is contrasted against the other scouts. The pattern of action, with Caleb's speaking (13:30) followed by that of Joshua and Caleb (14:6), is replicated in YHWH's response, referring first to Caleb (14:24) and then to both Caleb and Joshua (14:30); a summary statement then includes both (14:38). As mentored and groomed by Moses, Joshua will be Israel's next great leader, bringing the people into the land – this status, his being Moses' loyal assistant and the next shepherd of Israel, overshadows even his faithful testimony against the other scouts, although the latter is certainly noted. It is when the people sought to replace Moses with another leader to return to Egypt that Joshua is mentioned first in response (14:6; cf. 11:28). For Caleb, however, the exemplary stance against the other scouts is what exempts him from that generation's destruction and is, therefore, highlighted. Caleb, moreover, is associated with the tribe of Judah, which leads the eastward-oriented camp (2:3) and which will be the first tribe to ascend against the Canaanites (Judg. 1:1–2), so it is fitting to note his role especially.

In YHWH's three speeches, Moses alone is explicitly spared in the first (14:11–12), and then, after Moses' mediation, Caleb alone is spared in the second (14:20–25), and then both Caleb and Joshua are spared in the third (14:26–35; cf. v. 38). One major difference between YHWH's second and third speeches is their addressee: Moses alone in the second, but both Moses and Aaron in the third. If Moses already understood that Joshua would replace him in leading Israel into the land, then YHWH had no need to mention Joshua in his second speech – whereas the third speech was intended not as part of the personal dialogue between YHWH and his servant, but as a final verdict for Moses and Aaron to proclaim publicly. Intriguingly, in Moses' rehearsal of this narrative in Deuteronomy, he inserts God's judgement on himself for the people's sake (1:37) in between the divine announcements that Caleb would be given the land (1:36) and that Joshua would cause Israel to inherit the land (1:38) – preserving the distinct roles/perspectives of Caleb and Joshua, and presuming that, for the latter, his replacement of Moses was already inevitable. At the least, the sparing of Joshua functions to raise an obscurity that will be illuminated in 27:12–23. Caleb and Joshua, as representatives of the southern and northern kingdoms, respectively, perhaps also function as figures of hope – through their being spared, the roots of all Israel are also being spared. 'In other words', writes Widmer, the narrative 'gives the impression that the divine promise continues to be valid for people from all Israel' (2004: 280).

25. In 13:29, the scouts verbally blockaded Israel's entry into the land, beginning with the threats of Amalek and closing with that of the Canaanites; now YHWH lists these two threats – legitimate threats now that Israel has spurned YHWH – as a reason for Israel to turn away from possessing the land (Milgrom 1992: 113), a foreshadowing of the doom recounted in verses 40–45. Clearly YHWH's own presence and purpose singularly distinguishes whether the land's inhabitants are a real threat. Whereas earlier Joshua and Caleb had declared that the shade of defence had been removed from the people of the land (14:9), now Israel's protection has been removed.

YHWH's judgement poetically matches the rebellion of his people, giving them what they had wanted inasmuch as he is reversing the exodus movement: they are to turn and 'journey out' (nāsaʻ) into the wilderness – the very language of their journeys in the wilderness to the land, and this by way of the Sea of Suph (yam-sûp), recalling Israel's sea crossing (Exod. 13:8; 15:4, 22). Perhaps even the words 'for yourselves' (lākem) are a judgement, intended to recall the original command (13:2). For the first generation the exodus has indeed come undone.

26–28. Just as in his previous engagement with Moses (vv. 11–12), YHWH's speech, now to both Moses and Aaron as a formal proclamation, is in the form of question and answer (vv. 26–28). 'How long' (ʻad-mātay) is a slightly different expression from that used in verse 11 (ʻad-'ānāh), with the same basic meaning. How long for this evil community? How long can such deliberate rebellion in the face of YHWH go on before they are utterly consumed? The glorious Camp of Israel is now called 'this evil community' (ʻēdāh hārāʻāh) by YHWH himself who dwells in their midst. The people's rebellion is characterized by YHWH as 'grumbling' (lûn) against him, stated five times in this speech (three times in v. 27 alone, and then again in vv. 29, 36). All of Israel's unbelief and disobedience – maliciously stirring, boiling, fomenting in the heart – erupts into blasphemous words, grumbling, murmuring, against YHWH and thus serves as their summary sin. YHWH had given his Name to Israel that his people might call upon him in worship, warning them that no one who takes his Name up in vain will be held guiltless (Exod. 20:7, 24; Lev. 24:10–23; cf. Gen. 4:26; 12:8). Twice he says their grumbling is 'against me' (ʻālay). In 14:2 their grumbling had been directed against Moses and Aaron; although such grumbling against his servants is also against YHWH, nevertheless their grumbling has become more openly blatant against YHWH himself (v. 3). This grumbling against him, YHWH declares, 'I have heard', an integral element in the wilderness cycle of sin and punishment, occurring in verse 2 of the prologue (11:1–3), in verse 10 of the second cycle (11:4–35), in verse 2 of the third cycle (12:1–16), and now in the fourth cycle as well (chs. 13–14). Part of the message of Numbers 5 – 6 is that life in the Camp is lived before the face of YHWH, a reality with both blessings and dangers. Now, everything they spoke in his ears is to be brought back upon their heads.

YHWH directs Moses and Aaron to announce to the people their judgement in the clearest irrevocable terms: 'As I live'. The phrase 'utterance of YHWH' (nĕ'um-yhwh) designates a prophetic oracle, often expressing God's determined, unalterable will (e.g. Gen. 22:16; 1 Sam. 2:30; 2 Kgs 9:26; Amos 6:8; Zeph. 2:9). These firm assurances are capped, in the summary statement (v. 35), with 'I YHWH have spoken'. In a terrible instance of poetic justice, his retribution will be to render to the Israelites precisely what they had expressed in their grumbling: 'just as you have spoken in my ears, just so will I do to you'. Through divine wisdom and just wrath, Israel's grumbling becomes a self-fulfilling prophecy.

29–35. The poetic justice begins with YHWH's declaring that the people's carcasses will 'fall' (nāpal) in the wilderness – just as they had said 'if only we had died in this wilderness!' (v. 2), that YHWH was bringing them to the land 'to fall (nāpal) by the sword' (v. 3). The term 'fall' was also integral to the consequences for the strayed woman (5:21, 22, 27) and for the corpse-defiled Nazirite (6:12). That Israel's carcasses will fall/end in the wilderness is repeated three times (vv. 29, 32, 33), and then the summary statement in verse 35 repeats 'evil community' (from v. 27) and reiterates – the fourth time – that the first generation will die in the wilderness. Since Nephilim, literally 'fallen ones' (nĕpîlîm, 13:33) – perhaps 'the fallen gods . . . ejected from the celestial realm' (E. W. Davies 1995b: 140) – derives from the same root, this may be an instance of wordplay. The first mention of their carcasses falling in the wilderness (v. 29) is contrasted with Caleb, Joshua, and your little ones (vv. 30–31); the second and third mentions (vv. 32–33) sandwich the contrast, 'your sons'. The first generation is described as 'all of you who were appointed according to your whole number, from twenty years old and above' (v. 29), fixing their judgement within the theological paradigm of the Camp of Israel. Judgement in terms of the original census (chs. 1–2) accords with the focus of Numbers 11 – 15 on the outer camp of the twelve tribes – the Levites, who had not been counted (Num. 1:47–53), were also not represented among the twelve chieftains who scouted the land (13:1–15).

YHWH's threefold use of 'this wilderness' (bammidbor hazzê, vv. 29, 32, 35) echoes fiercely the only other use of the phrase in the chapter, Israel's murmuring, 'Would that we had died in this wilderness!' (v. 2). Other elements of divine poetic justice include YHWH's bringing in 'your little ones whom you said would be for spoil' (v. 31), referring to the people's complaint (v. 3), and the measure for measure allotment of forty years of wandering, one for each day of the scouts' forty-day mission to 'search out' the land (v. 34; 13:25). In Deuteronomy, Moses specifies the duration as thirty-eight years (2:14), so that 'forty years' in the wilderness, aside from being a round number (cf. McEvenue 1969), is understood as including Israel's whole time in the wilderness after the exodus out of Egypt (having encamped at Sinai until their second year).

Verse 30 marks the contrast between the rebellious generation of Israelites on the one hand, and Caleb and Joshua on the other. YHWH's lifting his hand (on oath) to bring his people into the land recalls Exodus 6:8, a striking and soberingly stark allusion, lending finality to YHWH's judgement – all the more since, within the context of Exodus 6, YHWH's words were intended to assure Israel's deliverance out of the bitter oppression of Egypt, and, more so, to seal their entry into the land. Now for the first generation the language is negated:

I will bring (*wĕhēbē'tî*) you into the land (*'el-hā'āreṣ*) of which I lifted my hand on oath (*'ăšer nāśā'tî 'et-yādî*) to give it to Abraham, to Isaac, and to Jacob. And I will give it to you for a possession – I am YHWH. (Exod. 6:8)

You will not be brought (*tābō'û*) into the land (*'el-hā'āreṣ*) of which I lifted my hand on oath (*'ăšer nāśā'tî 'et-yādî*) to have you dwell in it . . . (Num. 14:30)

Caleb is named before Joshua here as, again, the contrast is between those will not be brought in versus those who will; those who grumbled against YHWH versus those who stood for YHWH – while Joshua's role, as Moses' protégé, will be to bring the people into the land, continuing Moses' role as shepherd. A contrast is also made between the rebellious generation and their children: 'you will know (*yāda'*) my hostility' (v. 34) versus 'your little ones . . . will know (*yāda'*) the land' (v. 31) (cf. Ashley 1993: 267). YHWH's 'hostility' (*tĕnû'ātî* from *n-y-'*) has the sense of denial and negation, and may be understood as Israel's experiencing the result of denying God (Levine 1993: 370). The term for 'hostility' or 'opposition' (*tĕnû'ô*) occurs seven times in Numbers (14:34; 30:6 [twice], 9, 12; 32:7, 9) – only three times elsewhere (Job 33:10; Pss 33:10; 141:5).

'Your sons', YHWH declares, 'will be shepherding in the wilderness forty years' (v. 33); the term 'shepherding' (*rō'îm*) is not necessarily negative, although the context implies they are biding time until the first generation's carcasses come to an end in the wilderness. Moreover, that they will 'bear' (*nāśā'*) the whoredoms of the first generation does suggest the notion of enduring punishment – just as the first generation 'will bear your guilt' (v. 34). Designating the first generation's faithlessness as 'whoredoms' (*zĕnût*) may serve to demonstrate that Israel has chosen the path of the wayward woman (5:11–31), just as the second generation will do in Numbers 25 (see 5:11–31).

For the first generation, the forty years in the wilderness will be marked by the people's bearing their guilt, and knowing YHWH's hostility, his opposition as their enemy, until their carcasses finally fall in the wilderness – a sobering prospect followed by YHWH's affirmation, 'I YHWH have spoken.' The 'bearing' (*nāśā'*) of iniquities, forms the final of several uses of *nāśā'* in the exchange between Moses and YHWH, which artfully employs the full range of the word's significance, including to raise, to bear, and to forgive. As Horn explains, both of Moses' uses refer to YHWH's forgiving the people (vv. 18, 19), whereas YHWH uses the term for denying the land which he had 'raised' his hand on oath to give them (v. 30), to the children 'bearing' with the first generation's whoredoms (v. 33), and finally to the first generation's 'bearing' their iniquities for forty years (v. 34) (1993: 43). In the summary statement (v. 35), 'evil community' forms an inclusio with the same phrase in the opening line of verse 27, and 'come to an end' or 'completion' (*tāmam*) picks up the same term from verse 33. This evil community is further defined by YHWH as those 'who are gathered together against me', the same congregational conspiring against YHWH that will take place through Korah (16:11; 27:3). Rather than their being 'the community' (*hā'ēdāh*) who approach YHWH through the Tent of 'Meeting', Israel has become 'this evil community' who 'meets together' against him.

The 'land that you have despised (*mā'as*)' serves as something of a conclusion: the gift of YHWH, promised to the patriarchs centuries earlier, has been rejected by a faithless generation on the very cusp of possessing it. Again, the trajectory from Numbers 11, where the Israelites despised (*mā'as*) YHWH (v. 21), is discernable.

Against reading Moses' intercession as ineffective in the light of YHWH's judgement, it should be underscored that the continuity of Israel as people – and this through the children of those who had despised YHWH – is a profound wonder. It is not until one arrives at Numbers 26 and reads the divine assurance that these Israelites will inherit the land and, in so doing, preserve the 'name' of their fathers (cf. 27:1–11), that the greatness and remarkable accomplishment of Moses' intercession is really felt.

36–38. The story that opened with Moses sending men to search out the land by God's command (13:1–2) comes to an initial resolution here as the men die 'by the plague before YHWH'. The word 'plague' (*maggēpāh*) recalls God's judgements on the land of Egypt (e.g. Exod. 9:14), now directed against his own people. The root meaning is 'to strike', often used for sudden death inflicted by YHWH (Woods and Rogers 2006: 267). The sin of the ten scouts is twofold: they caused the whole community to grumble against Moses (and YHWH), and they did so by slandering the land (given double emphasis), leading the entire community to do so (cf. Lohfink 1994: 110–112). Chosen according to their political clout and influence, representing their respective tribes in the outer camp, they are severely accountable to YHWH and immediately executed. With such emphasis on the men who were sent to search out the land (vv. 36, 38), Joshua and Caleb are noted as exceptions – whereas the other men 'died' (*yāmutû*), 'they lived' (*ḥāyû*). Notably, then, there are two judgements for separate sins: the scouts who slandered the land were consumed in a divine plague, with Joshua and Caleb exempted (vv. 36–38), and the generation of Israel who, complaining against God, refused to possess the land were subject to a forty-year period of wandering and death in the wilderness (vv. 26–35) – even while Israel as a community and nation experience divine mercy.

39. Moses speaks YHWH's words to all the sons of Israel and they respond with mourning (*'ābal* in hith.), a term used for lamenting for the dead or over a severe calamity (BDB 5) – and this extreme expression of grief is described as done 'greatly' (*mĕ'ōd*). The community's response to the scouts' bad report, where they lifted their voice and 'wept' (*bākāh*) all night (14:1), now leads to their 'mourning greatly'.

40–45. After this second night of weeping, the people rise up early in the morning and, instead of following YHWH's command to journey out into the wilderness (v. 25), they ascend to the summit of the mountain. They try to justify their rebellion first by falsely describing their action as obedience to God's word ('the place that YHWH had said'), and secondly by disavowing their previous refusal with hollow piety ('for we sinned'). Their behaviour, including their mourning, was not the fruit of true repentance – for they are now wilfully disobeying YHWH's word (vv. 33–34). Their transgressing of YHWH's word may be understood from three angles: YHWH's command to 'turn and journey out for yourselves into the wilderness' (14:25); his declaration that 'you will not be brought into the land' (14:30; cf. v. 23); and his express prohibition, 'Do not ascend and do not fight, for I am not among you' (as recorded in Deut. 1:42–43) (cf. Samet 2014b: 185–186).

There is some ambiguity as to the precise root for the people's action in verse 44, *wayya'pilû* ('-p-l), which we have taken as 'they swelled up' (corresponding to the Arabic *'afala*), but which, alternatively, may derive from the Arabic root *gafala* meaning 'heedless' or 'reckless' (cf. Snaith 1967: 248). This new rebellion forms the mirror image of the first: To believe they can ascend and conquer without YHWH is as perverse as believing they cannot ascend and conquer with him – both scenarios were contrary to his word. Whereas before YHWH's promised presence with them against the Canaanites was irrelevant for possessing the land, due to their unbelief, now YHWH's declared absence from them is irrelevant – they neither heed his word nor trust in the power of his presence. Moses points out both matters: 'you are transgressing the commandment of YHWH', and 'YHWH is not in your midst'. He further forbids them to ascend 'lest you be struck by your enemies' and 'you will fall by sword', the latter expression ironically alluding to the people's original complaint in 14:3: 'Why did YHWH bring us to this land to fall by the sword?' Once more, their rebellion becomes a self-fulfilling prophecy. The resulting defeat is clearly explained by Moses:

'because you turned away from following after YHWH', a sharp contrast to Caleb who 'fully followed' after him (v. 24). Based on YHWH's own words referring to the Amalekites and Canaanites (v. 25), Moses sees the doomed nature of their ascent.

There is a reversal of Israel's original procession with the Ark of YHWH leading the hosts of Israel triumphantly, now with a special emphasis on YHWH's absence. The Ark, symbolizing YHWH's presence and leadership, was portrayed as setting forth from Sinai before the Camp (Num. 10:35), but now the Ark 'did not depart' – the people's attempt at taking possession of the land was an act of presumption, not a following of YHWH's leadership and voice. The narrative presentation is telling: YHWH did not abandon them, but they – who 'turned away from following after YHWH' – now break camp without him, an act contrary to the ideal of following after the Cloud. At best, they are testing him, forcing his hand, to follow them, which reverses the paradigm for the Camp's journeys. Earlier, the Israelites had been heedless to the admonition of Joshua and Caleb to take the land, for 'YHWH is with us' (14:9), and now, recklessly, they plunge onward even though 'YHWH is not with you.' Aside from the central issue of divine presence, the statement that the Ark and Moses did not depart with them also underscores that this campaign did not have God's approval or authority – by contrast with 13:1–2, this ascent was not sanctioned by Moses (cf. Levine 1993: 371). Predictably, then, the Amalekites and Canaanites struck down and crushed the people as far back as Hormah. When YHWH first called Abram out of Ur, and when he first called to Moses out of the burning bush, it was not for this hopeless destruction, for what de Vaux aptly dubbed 'an anti-Exodus' (1978: 2:520). Outside of Deuteronomy, the Ark's description as 'the Ark of the Covenant of YHWH' is found only here and in 10:33 (Milgrom 1990: 117), a literary feature forming an *inclusion* around chs. 11–14, capped by Numbers 15. The journey that had begun triumphantly, with YHWH's Ark leading the Camp of his earthly hosts, now ends with the Ark not departing from the Camp.

The designation 'Hormah', which means 'devoted to utter destruction', is actually given anachronistically, as a rhetorical device. The place of the second generation's first victory over their Canaanite enemies – after the forty years of judgement have passed – will be called 'Hormah' (see 21:3). Even while depicting the smiting and crushing of Israelites here, a glimmer of hope shines through: at the place of Israel's last defeat in rebellion against YHWH, at this very place, and in obedience to YHWH, they will taste triumph – because he will be with them. For now, though, 'Hormah' describes Israel's tragic routing.

In Moses' commentary on this event in Deuteronomy 1:41–45, he fills some gaps: It was YHWH who instructed Moses to tell the Israelites not to ascend or fight, lest they be defeated; the people are indicted in a threefold manner, for they 'would not listen', 'rebelled against the mouth of YHWH', and 'presumptuously ascended'; as a result 'the Amorites' (generic for Canaanites) crushed them 'from Seir to Hormah'; finally, Moses recounts that the people returned and 'wept' before YHWH, but he would not 'hear' their voice, nor give ear to them. In this way, the first generation in the wilderness, throughout their forty years of wandering, experiences YHWH's hostility as his absence or hiding, in a manner not unlike the threat of exile in Deuteronomy 32:20: 'I will hide my face from them; I will see what their end will be, for they are a perverse generation – children in whom there is no faith.'

THE OUTER CAMP'S FAILURE AND THE SIN OF ADAM AND WOMAN (GEN. 3)

The story of the outer camp of twelve tribes (chs. 11–15) was evidently conceived as a type of Adam and Woman's sin in relation to God's word and the Tree of the Knowledge of good and evil (see Y. Twersky 2007a: 1:25–37; 2007b: 2:144–160; also Curwin 2023: 85–91). The tribes' challenge throughout is also in relation to heeding the divine word through Moses' prophetic office (11:16–17, 24–30; 12:4–13). In Numbers 11, there are four uses of 'evil' (*ra'*, 11:1, 10, 11, 15) and an ironic use of 'good' (11:18), which should be 'evil', in contrast to the previous fivefold use of 'good' (*tôb*, 10:29, 32). As Israel's Camp embarks on the sojourn, Moses declares YHWH's promise to give the land to his people and to do them 'good', having spoken 'good' concerning Israel (10:29), whereas the people complain of 'evil' in the ears of YHWH and assert it was 'good' to be in Egypt (11:1, 18) – a clear example of exchanging good and evil (cf. Lev. 27:10, 13). The outer camp's story begins in chapter 11 by emphasizing the people's lusting (*hit'awwû ta'ăwâ*) dramatically (11:4, 34), recalling the root's first use in the garden when the woman saw the fruit forbidden by YHWH's command as 'good' and 'desirable' (*ta'ăwâ*, Gen. 3:6) – this precise form, *ta'ăwâ*, occurs in only these two accounts in the Torah (Y. Twersky 2007b: 2:150). By contrast, the people reject the provision of manna (11:6), associated with Eden ('as bdellium in the eyes', 11:7; cf. Gen. 2:12), and which functioned as a litmus for obedience to YHWH's word (see Exod. 16:4, 28; cf. Deut. 8:1–5, 16) – just as the primal couple were dissatisfied with YHWH's provision of food in the garden.

The motif of Moses' prophetic office, central to Numbers 11 (vv. 16–17, 24–30), continues into chapter 12 as Moses' prophetic office is diminished through slander. While reference to Moses' 'Cushite woman' (*hā'iššâ hakkušît*) remains an enigma (12:1), the Torah's first use of 'Cush' is for Eden's river (Gen. 2:13); this feature, along with use of 'the woman/wife' and 'the man/husband' (*hā'îš*) yields another link to the Eden narrative (Num. 12:1, 3). Indeed, Moses, 'the man/husband' (*hā'îš*), is compared with 'every *hā'ādom* on the face of the *hā'ădāmâ*' (12:3), language strikingly similar to that used for Adam in Eden (cf. Gen. 2:6–7). One may also wonder whether Miriam and Aaron do not in some way reflect Adam and Woman in their failure; apparently she had led him in transgression and then they are summoned and questioned by YHWH at the Tent of Meeting. After vindicating his word through Moses' prophetic office (12:5–8), Miriam is shut out of the Camp for seven days (12:14), an expulsion from YHWH's Edenic presence. The challenge to Moses' mediation of YHWH's word here augurs the outer camp's wholesale rejection of the divine promise of land in Numbers 13 – 14.

In scouting Canaan, Moses bids the chieftains to discern 'what the land is like . . . *hătôbâ* or *rā'â*' (good or evil), to see, literally, if there is 'a tree' (*'ēṣ*) there, and to embolden themselves to 'take the fruit' of the land (13:19–20), motifs echoing the garden of Eden narrative. In the entire Hebrew Scriptures, the phrase 'take of the fruit' occurs only in these stories (Gen. 3:6; Num. 13:20). Given the parallel with Noah's vineyard (Gen. 9:20–24), the possibility that the Tree of Knowledge was a grapevine yields a further connection with the cluster of grapes emphasized in the scouts narrative (13:20, 23–24; cf. Curwin 2023: 103–110). As made in God's image (Gen. 1:27–28), the primal couple was to judge what is 'good' in like manner to their Creator (cf. Gen. 1:4, 10, 12, etc.), according to his word rather than their own devices, and so failed precisely in grasping to 'be like god', in knowing 'good and evil', by transgressing his command (Gen. 2:16–17; 3:4–6). The tribal chieftains denied YHWH's good plans for Israel's life in the land, fail to assess the land as 'good', contradicting his word with an 'evil' report of the land (14:37; cf. 13:32; 14:36), although Joshua and Caleb passionately pronounced it 'an exceedingly good land' (*ṭôbâ hā'āreṣ mě'ōd mě'ōd*, 14:7). Ironically, Balaam, who cannot do either 'good or evil', will by the Spirit of God pronounce Israel's life with YHWH as 'good' (24:5, 13; cf. Bolger 1993: 223–224), in a vision that discerns the wonder of the Camp in terms of the nation's settlement in the land. Like the primal couple, the first generation's punishment is not immediate death, but life outside the land where they will eventually die in exile.

The outer camp of tribes was to follow the divine *qôl* (voice) through Moses' prophetic office, as YHWH spoke from between the cherubim in the holiest place, the cultic counterpart to the garden of Eden (Num. 7:89; for *qôl*, see Gen. 3:8, 10; for cherubim, Gen. 3:24). Israel's first generation lost life with YHWH in the good land of Canaan, just as Adam and Woman had done in paradise – both in relation to their lack of trust and obedience to God's word. YHWH declares the first generation of Israel will not see the land because 'they did not heed my voice' (*šom'û běqôlî*, Num. 14:22), just as Adam ignored the divine

command to heed the voice of his wife (Gen. 3:17). The outer camp's
sins relate to false speech (slandering, in turn, the manna, Moses, and the
land) and eating – transgressions of the mouth – and divine punishment
comes, accordingly, 'just as you have spoken in my ears' (14:28). Indeed,
there is an emphasis throughout these chapters on YHWH's hearing
the people's speech (11:1, 10, 20; 12:2; 14:28), and Moses' intercession
involves a balance between what the Egyptians and Canaanites hear
(14:13–14) and what YHWH himself has spoken (14:17–19).

In Deuteronomy, Y. Twersky insightfully observes (2007b: 2:158–159),
Moses declares that Israel 'rebelled against the command of YHWH
your God', and, distrusting him, did not 'heed his *qôl*' (Deut. 9:23; cf.
1:26, 43), so that no one of this 'evil' (*hāroʿ*) generation will see that
'good' (*haṭṭôbâ*) land (1:35) – and then, fascinatingly, describes the
second generation that will inherit the land as 'your little ones who today
have no knowledge of good and evil' (*lōʾ-yodʿû . . . ṭôb wāroʿ*, 1:39), a
lexical combination occurring elsewhere in the Torah only for the Tree
of Knowledge story (Gen. 2:9, 17; 3:5, 22; cf. Buber 1968). Deuteronomy
thus defines the first generation and its failure to enter the land as
having gained the knowledge of good and evil by disobeying YHWH's
command, meriting death (P. A. Barker 2004: 29; cf. Mann 1988: 161;
Sailhamer 1992: 424, 427, 474, 476; Bolger 1993: 227–232, 269–271;
Fretheim 1996: 49, 56–57; Leibtag 2012: 366–367; Sabato 2012: 440–441).
In deciding for themselves what was 'good' and 'evil', the sons of Israel
repeated the sin of the primal humans (Y. Twersky 2007b: 2:149), who
'pursued wisdom apart from obedience to God' (Bolger 1993: 160). As
the historical and literary contexts indicate, however, the scouts' transgression was the inverse of the first human beings: they failed to *enter* the
good land, even after taking of its fruit. Nevertheless, as Eden's garden
was forbidden Adam and Eve by the threat of a 'sword' (*hereb*, Gen.
3:24), so the land of Canaan was forbidden Israel by the threat of 'sword'
(*hereb*, Num. 14:43).

YHWH's response to the sin of the scouts and tribes is for Israelites
of the outer camp to wear *ṣîṣit* (tassels) on the wings of their garments.
Divine clothing, then, forms a response to both the sin of the Tree of
Knowledge (Gen. 3:21) and to the sin of the scouts (Num. 15:37–41).
The tassels, as Hirsch perceived (2007a: 116), were a remedy for the
sin of the Tree of Knowledge, by which YHWH challenged the primal
couple to discern good and evil through his command versus their carnal
desire: 'The woman saw that the tree was good for food, and that it was
desirable (*taʾăwâ*) for the eyes' (Gen. 3:6) is remedied by 'You will look
on it (the tassel) and remember all the commands of YHWH and do
them, and not scout after your hearts and your eyes, after which you
go whoring' (Num. 15:39). Profoundly, the *ṣîṣit* legislation deals not
only with Israel's immediate failure, but with its root of desire, encompassing the whole section (chs. 11–14), which begins with the mixed

multitude among them 'desiring a desire' and naming the place 'Graves of Desiring', where those who 'desired' were buried (11:4, 34).

Explanation

With its emphasis on the leadership of the covenant community, Numbers underscores the role of the scouts in the debacle of Israel's failure to possess the land: the selection of the chieftains by name, each representing one of the twelve tribes, begins the account ceremoniously (13:1–16), their role in giving a bad report of the land is the trigger for the people's despair and rebellion (13:31–33), and their own separate judgement – dying by plague before YHWH – is recorded (14:36–38). Each of these elements is missing from Moses' retelling in Deuteronomy, which focuses only on the people's accountability. The two faithful leaders among the scouts, Caleb and Joshua, are also singled out as exceptions to YHWH's judgement (14:24, 30). In the closing subsection of Numbers, which contains five speeches of YHWH (chs. 33–35), the central speech will designate new chieftains of the tribes among Israel's second generation, commissioning them to divide the land (34:16–29), a reversal of the first generation's failure. As the outer camp's challenge was to heed YHWH's word through Moses' prophetic office, the tribal failure involved sinful human speech, the 'evil tongue' (*lashon hara*): after Israelites slander the manna (ch. 11), and Miriam and Aaron slander Moses' prophetic office (ch. 12), ten chieftains slander YHWH's gift of the land (chs. 13–14; see *Tan., Shelach 5*).

The role of the chieftains as leaders of their tribes was fundamental to the nature of their scouting mission, which had not a military but a theological and political purpose; namely, to evaluate the divine gift of the land. They were expected to encourage their respective tribes with the goodness of God's gift. As Stubbs summarizes (2009: 128), 'The twelve are to be witnesses to the goodness of the land and the faithfulness of God (cf. Ps. 34:8). This would assure the people and give them the hope, courage, and trust in God needed for the final and potentially most dangerous part of their journey.' Moses would later give the second generation of Israel just such an expansive glimpse of the land's abundant goodness (Deut. 8:7–10). Occurring thirty-six times in Numbers 13 – 14, the motif of 'the land' is central to these chapters (also Boorer 2012: 47; for a theology of the land, see W. Brueggemann 1977; Habel 1995), and symbolizes the fulfilment of YHWH's promise to the patriarchs (Gen. 13:14–17; 15:7; 26:3; 28:4; etc.). The scouts' sin is portrayed with particular reference to defaming the land three times (Num. 13:32; 14:36, 37). Adding to their shame, it was after touring the same locale where Abraham was first promised the land, Hebron, that the faithless scouts rejected the gift of God. More deeply, the scouts and the people's rejection of the land is inseparable from a despising of YHWH himself:

Land: 'bad report' of the land (13:32), land you have 'rejected' (14:32), 'bad report' of the land (14:36), 'evil bad report' of the land (14:37)

YHWH: 'spurn me', 'not trust in me' (14:11), 'tested me', 'not heeded my voice' (14:22), 'spurned me' (14:23), 'who grumble against me' 'they grumble against me' (14:27), 'grumbled against me' (14:29), 'gathered together against me' (14:35), 'grumble against him' (14:36)

Life with YHWH God in the land was the goal of the exodus and the covenant at Sinai, for Israel's vocation among the nations. Even the Camp of Israel was merely the paradigm for the covenant community's life with God in the land. Yet, in utter faithlessness and outright rebellion, Israel rejected God's gift, and with it the entire history of his faithfulness and promises to their forefathers, and even their own reason for existence. They explicitly proclaim their desire to reverse the exodus (14:3–4). In Deuteronomy 28, the last verse to close a lengthy list of threats for Israel's enduring apostasy declares that YHWH would return them to Egypt (Deut. 28:68), yet this last conceivable option for YHWH is the first choice of the very Israelites who had experienced the bitter oppression of Egypt and his wondrous deliverance. The first generation of Israelites breached their covenant with YHWH, having spurned and forsaken him, and denied their vocation among the nations to be a 'priestly kingdom and holy nation' (Exod. 19:5–6). Appropriately, G. J. Wenham draws attention to Hebrews' application to the church (1981b: 139): 'Take care, brethren, lest there be in any of you an evil heart of unbelief, in departing (*apostēnai*) from the living God . . . For we are partakers of Christ if only we hold the beginning of our confidence steadfast to the end' (Heb. 3:12, 14).

While the twelve tribes, embodied by the twelve chieftains, represent all Israel, it is important to discern the narrative strategy of Numbers, which progresses according to the segments of Israel's Camp: first, the outer camp of twelve tribes (chs. 11–15), then the inner camp of Levites (chs. 16–18), and finally to the central camp of the *Shekhinah*, represented by Moses and Aaron (ch. 20). Levites, then, are nowhere implicated either in the offence or the judgement of Israel in the present story. Nothing could make this point more clearly than the pronouncement of YHWH's judgement in terms related to the establishment of the outer camp: 'In this wilderness your carcasses will fall, *even all of you who were appointed according to your whole number, from twenty years old and above*' (14:29; cf. Num. 1 – 2). As an analysis of the inner workings of the covenant community, and bringing in the subsection's twin themes of Moses' prophetic ministry and the twelve tribes (chs. 11–15), the message is: the tribal chieftains must lead their respective tribes in trusting YHWH's word and will, his *torah*, as conveyed through his chosen servant Moses. It is not incidental, then, that when the tribes fail, YHWH proposes not only to destroy Israel but to make of Moses a nation greater and mightier than they (14:12). Moses, however, uses his exclusive face-to-face relationship with YHWH rather to secure Israel's survival. Indeed, this first subunit of the wilderness section highlights Moses' intercession in every one of its four episodes (11:1–3; 11:4–35; 12:1–16; 13:1–14:45), so that it may be said justly that Israel progresses stage by stage through the wilderness by the prayers of YHWH's servant.

Not merely through Moses' intercession, but through YHWH's attribute of mercy as solicited by Moses (14:17–19; cf. Exod. 33:18–23; 34:5–9), Israel was not consumed – a second generation will arise to inherit the land. This transition to a renewed Israel was already foreshadowed both in the Nazirite law and in the second Passover legislation, whereby a new start is offered after cleansing from corpse pollution, a divine remedy applied in the transition from the first to the second generation of Israel in Numbers 19, which narrates the red heifer ritual for cleansing Israelites from corpse pollution.

In Deuteronomy, Moses will instruct the second generation in preparation for war, focusing on *the* deciding factor; namely, YHWH's presence with his people (20:1, 3–4). YHWH is 'with you', and this to 'save' (*hôšîa'*) you. 'Save' here is a form of Hoshea, Joshua's former name, changed by Moses to 'YHWH saves' (Num. 13:16), and he it was who, along with Caleb, encouraged the community not to fear the Canaanites because 'YHWH is with us' (14:9). Before God had vanquished the Egyptian hosts at the sea, Moses had urged the people to put away fear, for 'YHWH will fight for you' and then after their deliverance, he led Israel in singing 'YHWH is a Man of War – YHWH is his name!' (Exod. 14:14; 15:3). The lesson of YHWH's presence and salvation, however, had been neglected, and in their rebellion Israel forfeited his strength in battle: the account closes with Israelites being devastated at Hormah precisely because, as Moses declared, 'YHWH will not be with you', (14:44–45; cf. Deut. 20:1; 23:14). The Gospel of Matthew brings out these two themes, narrating how at his birth the Son of God was named both *Jesus* (Greek for 'Joshua'), because he would 'save' his people from their sins, and *Immanuel*, that is, 'God with us' (1:21, 23).

NUMBERS 15: YHWH'S RESPONSE TO THE TWELVE TRIBES OF THE OUTER CAMP

Translation

[1]Now YHWH spoke to Moses saying, [2]'Speak to the sons of Israel and say to them, "When you come to the land of your dwelling-places,

which I myself am giving to you, ³and you make a gift-by-fire to YHWH, a whole burnt offering or a sacrifice for a wondrous vow, or with a freewill offering, or in your appointed times, to make a restful aroma for YHWH from the herd or from the flock, ⁴then he who brings-near his near-offering for YHWH will bring-near a tribute offering of flour, a tenth measure mixed with a fourth measure of the hin of oil. ⁵And wine for a drink offering, a fourth of the hin you will make upon the whole burnt offering or for the sacrifice, for one lamb. ⁶Or for the ram, you will make a tribute offering of flour, two tenth measures mixed with the oil, a third of the hin. ⁷And wine for a drink offering, a third of the hin, and you will bring-near a restful aroma for YHWH. ⁸And when you make a bullock as a whole burnt offering or a sacrifice for a wondrous vow or peace offerings for YHWH, ⁹then he will bring-near with the bullock a tribute offering of flour, three-tenths of a measure mixed with oil, half the hin. ¹⁰And wine you will bring-near for a drink offering, half the hin, as a gift-by-fire, a restful aroma for YHWH. ¹¹Thus it will be done for one ox, or for one ram, or the lamb of the sheep or the goats. ¹²According to the number that you will do, thus you will do for each one according to their number. ¹³Every native will do these thus, to bring-near a gift-by-fire, a restful aroma for YHWH. ¹⁴And when a sojourner sojourns with you, or whoever is among you throughout your generations, and will make a gift-by-fire, a restful aroma for YHWH, just as you do just so he will do. ¹⁵The assembly will have one statute for you and for the sojourning sojourner, a perpetual statute throughout your generations, as you so will the sojourner be before YHWH. ¹⁶One teaching and one rule there will be for you and for the sojourner sojourning with you."'

¹⁷And YHWH spoke to Moses saying, ¹⁸'Speak to the sons of Israel and say to them: "When you come to the land, there where I myself am bringing you, ¹⁹then it will be when you eat from the bread of the land you will lift-up a contribution for YHWH. ²⁰The first of your dough, a cake you will lift-up as a contribution; just as a contribution of the threshing-floor, so you will lift it up. ²¹Of the first of your dough you will give for YHWH a contribution throughout your generations.

²²"And when you (all) err unintentionally and not do all these commands which YHWH spoke to Moses, ²³all that YHWH had commanded to you (all) by the hand of Moses from the day that YHWH commanded and henceforth throughout your generations, ²⁴then it will be if the unintentional error was done apart from the eyes of the community, all the community will do a bull – one bullock – for a whole burnt offering, for a restful aroma for YHWH, with its tribute offering and its drink offering according to the rule, one male of the goats for a purification offering. ²⁵And the priest will make atonement for the whole community of the sons of Israel, and it will be forgiven for them, for it was an unintentional error, and they brought their near-offering of the

gift-by-fire for YHWH, and their purification offering before YHWH for their unintentional error. ²⁶And it will be forgiven for the whole community of the sons of Israel and for the sojourner sojourning among you, for all the people were in unintentional error.

²⁷'"And if one soul sins by unintentional error and a she-goat is brought-near, a yearling for a purification offering, ²⁸then the priest will make atonement for the soul unintentionally erring in the sin of unintentional error before YHWH, to make atonement for him and it will be forgiven him. ²⁹For the native with the sons of Israel and for the sojourner sojourning among you, there will be one teaching for you for what to do with unintentional error. ³⁰But the soul that acts with a raised hand, whether native or sojourner, against YHWH he blasphemes, and that soul will be cut off from the midst of his people, ³¹for the word of YHWH he has despised, and his command he has broken – that soul will surely be cut off, his guilt is upon him."'

³²Now when the sons of Israel were in the wilderness, they found a man gathering sticks on the Sabbath day. ³³And they who found him gathering sticks brought him near to Moses and to Aaron and to the whole community. ³⁴And they rested him in the keep, for it was not discerned what should be done to him. ³⁵And YHWH said to Moses, 'The man must surely die; the whole community is to stone him with stones outside the camp.' ³⁶And the whole community brought him forth to outside the camp, and they stoned him with stones, and he died, just as YHWH had commanded Moses.

³⁷And YHWH said to Moses saying, ³⁸'Speak to the sons of Israel and say to them, "You will make for yourselves a tassel on the wings of your garments throughout your generations, and they will put on the tassel of the wing a cord of blue. ³⁹And it will be for you for a tassel, and you will see it and remember all the commands of YHWH and do them, so you will not search out after your heart and after your eyes, after which you go whoring, ⁴⁰in order for you to remember and do all my commands, and you will be holy to your God. ⁴¹I myself am YHWH your God who brought you out from the land of Egypt to be your God – I myself am YHWH your God."'

Notes on the text

15:4. 'a tenth measure': LXX adds 'of an ephah', the intended meaning.

5. 'one lamb': followed by 'for a soothing aroma' in LXX.

6. 'the ram': followed by 'when you make it for a whole burnt offering or for a sacrifice' in LXX.

9. 'he will bring near': *BHS* suggests 2nd m. sg., to match v. 8, but switching persons is not uncommon in legislation, and LXX also has 3rd m. sg.

15. 'the assembly': *haqqāhāl* is missing from Syr and Vg; LXX has *synagōgē*, but at the end of v. 14.
30. 'YHWH': LXX has 'God' (*ton theon*).
31. 'command': SamP, LXX, Syr and Tg have pl.
38–39. 'a tassel': SamP and LXX have pl. 'tassels', the latter likely interpreting the Hebr. as collective (cf. Wevers 1998: 255–257).

Form and structure

While Numbers 15 has long been deemed by scholars a jumbled repository of unrelated cultic laws (e.g. G. B. Gray 1903: 168; Holzinger 1903: 60; Noth 1968: 114), there has nevertheless been wide consensus among source critics that the contents derive from the Holiness school, given similarities with terminology (e.g. 'I am YHWH/your God', 'you will be holy', 'when you come into the land') and themes found in Leviticus 17 – 27, also assigned to the Holiness School (cf. Wright 2020: 46). The concern for community ethics and holiness, however, may be understood as flowing naturally out of the cult's sacrificial theology (Lev. 1 – 16; see Trevaskis 2011; Morales 2015: 213–220), and at least some H terminology is found within other purported sources (e.g. 'when you come into the land' in Deut. 17:4; 18:9; 26:1; etc.), with some denying the existence of H altogether (Blum 2009). Although the transition from Numbers 14 to these laws appears abrupt initially, and the laws seem to have little connection with one another, it is the relationship of Numbers 13 – 14 and 15 with *the land* that serves as the unifying factor: Israel in the former chapters slanders and rejects the land, but YHWH now reassures his gift of the land, albeit to the ensuing generation (Hausoul 2018: 82; cf. Budd 1984: 167). The basic outline of the chapter is as follows:

1. In the land: vow and freewill offerings	1–16	'YHWH spoke to Moses'
2. In the land: first-fruit offering of bread	17–21	'YHWH spoke to Moses'
3. Offering for unintentional sin	22–31	
by the community	22–26	
by an individual	27–31	
4. In the wilderness: Sabbath gatherer	32–36	'When the sons of Israel were in the wilderness'
5. Make tassel with blue cord	37–41	'YHWH said to Moses'

Formally, there is no new speech of YHWH to introduce verses 22–31 (although note 'which YHWH spoke to Moses' in v. 22) as a separate section from verses 17–21, in which case there would be four major sections instead of five, but since the topic has clearly switched, the present outline is justified. More difficult to discern in the light of this ambiguity, is whether the cultic legislation of section 3, 'Dealing with unintentional sin', is aimed at 'life in the land' (under section 2), or does it apply now, in the wilderness? As there is no formal break between sections 2 and 3, and the context does not shift until section 4, when we are told that the sons of Israel 'were in the wilderness', we will assume, with Milgrom (1990: 122), that section 3 forms a continuation of the previous context. Moreover, the tribute and drink offerings (v. 24) assume the content and context of YHWH's first speech (vv. 1–16), 'in the land', since they cannot be offered in the wilderness. Chapter 15 thus begins with three *future-oriented* sections for life in the land, then transitions to a *generically oriented* narrative in the wilderness period, in many ways symbolizing the first generation of Israel, and then closes with an application that is *present-oriented*, having especially the bringing up of the second generation who will inherit the land (according to sections 1 and 2) in its purview.

Attempts have been made to discern the links among these sections. For example, sections 1 (vv. 1–16) and 3 (vv. 22–31) are similar in content, and generally follow the pattern of Leviticus 1–5, which begins with freewill sacrifices (chs. 1–3), followed by sacrifices for sin (chs. 4–5) (Baden 2013b: 353; also Dillmann 1886: 83–84; see Gane 2010: 258–259 for similarities between Num. 15 and Lev. 23). The Sabbath gatherer of section 4 (vv. 32–36) is often seen as exemplary of the 'high handed' sin warned of in the previous section (v. 30), with the tassels law of the fifth section seen as a response to the Sabbath-gatherer narrative, aimed at keeping Israel from committing the same sort of defiant sin (vv. 37–41). Baden (2013b) has offered a unified reading of the last four sections of Numbers 15, drawing on parallels with the manna story of Exod. 16 – indeed, by claiming the manna story originally stood before the second section (Num. 15:17–21), which in turn severs any connection between verses 1–16 and 17–41, making their resemblance to Leviticus 1 – 5 'merely coincidental'. There are strong parallels not only between the Sabbath-gatherer episode (Num. 15:32–36) and the manna story (Exod. 16), but also with the blasphemer story of Leviticus 24:10–23, all three addressing Sabbath observance, and having an underlying Egypt motif. Just as Exodus, Leviticus and Numbers each recounts the inauguration of the Dwelling from a different angle (Exod. 40; Lev. 9; Num. 7), related to the special emphasis and particular theme of its book, so each book contains a Sabbath narrative. In the Pentateuch's final form, stories and laws have been organized according to an overarching scheme that sometimes prioritizes thematic coherence over chronology.

Rhetorically, Numbers 15 will be seen to function as a cap to chapters 11–14, bringing resolution to what has gone before, and allowing for something of a pause before moving into the rebellion of Korah in Numbers 16 – 17 (cf. e.g. Harrison 1990: 221). Ensuing comments will bring out some of the intertextuality between this chapter and 11–14, along with thematic connections, which also serve to unify the various sections of Numbers 15 together, and with a logical progression. The root *'āśāh* (to do, make) occurs twenty-one times (cf. Cole 2000: 243), in every section except the second (vv. 17–21), where 'lifting' and 'giving' a contribution is more appropriate; the phrase 'throughout your generations' occurs for all of the laws, five times: for the accompaniments (vv. 14, 15), bread contribution (v. 21), unintentional errors (v. 23), and for the tassels (v. 38); and uniform application for the 'sojourner', the root of which appears twelve times (*gûr, gēr*), recurs for the laws of accompaniments (vv. 14, 15, 16), the community's unintentional error (v. 26), the individual's unintentional error (v. 29), and for high-handed sin (v. 30). The sections may be divided into three major parts by context and genre:

> **Section One: laws for 'in the land' (vv. 1–31)**
>> 1. Tribute and drink offerings, a lamb (plus introduction, vv. 1–5)
>> 2. Tribute and drink offerings, a ram (vv. 6–7)
>> 3. Tribute and drink offerings, a bullock (plus conclusion, vv. 8–16)
>
> CENTRE → 4. Contribution of bread (vv. 17–21)
>> 5. Offerings for unintentional sin, the whole community (vv. 22–26) ◄────┐
>> 6. Offerings for unintentional sin, an individual (vv. 27–29)   'the whole
>> 7. Penalty for high handed sin (vv. 30–31)   community'
>
> **Section Two: a tale of high-handedness 'in the wilderness' (vv. 32–36)** ◄───┘
>
> **Section Three: application for Israelites now, blue-corded tassels (vv. 37–41)**

There are seven laws in section one, noted by Sailhamer (1992: 390), which appears to be a deliberate arrangement, having the fourth law, the contribution of bread (vv. 17–21), as the intended central focus. The first three laws are listed in ascending order of value (cf. Gane 2004: 620): from lamb, to ram, to bullock (chiastically reversed in the summary, v. 11); then the last three laws are listed in descending order: whole burnt and purification offerings for the whole community (a bullock and male goat), to a purification offering for an individual (a she-goat), to cutting off a defiant sinner (no offering) – with, perhaps, these last two individuals being contrasted. The fifth law alludes directly to the third law (v. 24), with its mention of the 'bullock' as well as 'its tribute offering and its drink offering according to the rule', framing the fourth law. As the central law, the contribution of bread forms the great reversal and remembrance of the heavenly gift of manna. Second, the phrase 'the whole community' occurs three times in the fifth law (vv. 22–26) and then three times again in section two's tale in the wilderness (vv. 32–36), linking them together and calling for comparison of the actions of 'the whole community'. Third, the first section, dealing with life in the land, ends solemnly with the prospect of one's being cut off from his people, even if he is a native ('arising from the soil'), a dreadful reality that is exemplified within the context of the wilderness by the tale in section two (vv. 32–36). The real possibility of being cut off from the Camp calls for the application that follows, that of making blue-corded tassels to prod Israel towards devoted obedience to YHWH's commands (section three, vv. 37–41). There is thus a logical flow throughout the chapter. Finally, the opening line of the first section, 'When you come to the land of your dwelling-places, which I myself am giving to you' (v. 2), has long been noted as functioning to provide divine assurance for Israel that, the righteous judgement on the first generation notwithstanding, YHWH still has good intentions for his people and will not renege on his promises of the land.

Comment

15:1–16. YHWH calls for tribute (grain) and drink offerings to accompany Israel's whole burnt and peace offerings (vv. 1–3), providing precise measures for when offering a lamb (vv. 4–5), a ram (vv. 6–7), and a bullock (vv. 8–10). After a summary (vv. 11–12), the requirement is enjoined equally on both native and sojourner (vv. 13–16). The prescribed tribute and drink offerings speak to the bountiful life awaiting Israel in the land, and the appropriate gratitude that should be expressed when living in YHWH's kingdom. In a manner, these instructions counter the slanderous false report of the land given by the ten faithless scouts: Moses had sent them to see the land, whether it was 'fat' or 'rich', literally oil-like (*šĕmēnāh*; 13:20), echoed now with the oil accompaniment, and the libations of wine point to the large cluster of grapes taken from Wadi Eshcol (13:23) (cf. Achenbach 2013: 206–209).

1–2. YHWH's speaking 'to Moses' for the sake of 'the sons of Israel' is noteworthy after Israel's failure in Numbers 13 – 14. Not only had the sons of Israel rejected YHWH's word in unbelief, but they had intended to replace Moses with another leader and to return to Egypt. The hierarchy is now divinely re-established. Indeed, the chapter reasserts Moses' role as singular mediator, through whom alone YHWH speaks, in a sevenfold manner (15:1, 17, 22, 23, 35, 36, 37). This opening speech from YHWH, moreover, stands as a divine assertion that confirms his earlier promise 'When you come to the land . . .' For the nation in the wilderness, needing to bear for forty years the harlotries of the generation that had rejected the land (14:33), this divine 'when' (*kî*) holds an ocean of consolation and hope (see R. J. Williams: 2007 § 445 for the temporal use of *kî*). The land is further defined as the 'land of your dwelling-places' (*môšĕbōtêkem*), the singular use of this ascription in the HB (cf. Hausoul 2018: 82), fostering the anticipation of God's gift, as if their homes were already prepared and waiting for their arrival. A similar expression, without 'land', is used in Exodus (35:3) regarding the prohibition of kindling a fire on the Sabbath, and three times in connection with the Sabbath and with festal Sabbaths in Leviticus (23:3, 21, 31); as the Sabbath will play a major role, its theology may underlie the whole chapter (15:32–36; 'your habitations' also appears in 35:29).

The last line uses the pronoun 'I' (*'ănî*) for emphasis and assurance, and the participle (am giving) rather than the imperfect ('will give'), making their entrance into the land part of YHWH's current, ongoing activity, a present reality. The language of Israel's 'coming' (*bô'*) into the 'land' (*'ereṣ*), introducing the first two laws (vv. 2, 18), connects the chapter to the scouts episode (13:27; 14:3, 8, 16, 24, 30, 31), reinforcing the land promise in the face of the first generation's condemnation to die in the wilderness (14:21–23, 26–35) (Gane 2010: 250). Further, the land 'I am giving you' (*nōtēn*, v. 2) forms an inclusio with the opening of the scouts episode (13:2), and, more broadly, with Israel's triumphant journeying out from Sinai for the land (10:29). By repetition of his original promise, YHWH confirms the ongoing validity of his gift of Canaan to Israel. These opening lines, then, characterize the whole chapter as a response to the catastrophe of Israel's failure to possess the land, Numbers 15 serving as a cap to chapters 11–14. The tribute and wine offerings that follow, entailing grain and grapes (unavailable in the wilderness), assume settled life in the land.

3. Milgrom explains that 'to make' (*'āśâ*) is 'a technical term in the cult that means "to sacrifice" in the sense of performing the entire sacrificial ritual' (1991: 266). The translation 'gift-by-fire' incorporates the two possible derivations of the Hebrew *'iššeh*, 'gift' and 'fire', and refers to the appropriation of the sacrificial gift to YHWH by having some portion of it burned on the altar (cf. Kurtz 1863: 150–151). Although Milgrom prefers 'gift', based on a possible Ugaritic (*itt*) or Arabic (*'atâtu*) root (1991: 162), Eberhart, following the Greek translations (along with BDB, *HALOT*), argues for 'fire' as the root (2004: 489–490; cf. 2002: 40–48). Milgrom further argues that some gifts may or may not be dubbed *'iššeh* irrespective of whether a portion has been burned on the altar (1991: 161–162); he was evidently mistaken, however, regarding the purification offering (cf. Num. 28:19, 22; Averbeck 1997), and the 'bread of the presence' *'iššeh* (Lev. 24:5–9) likely refers to the frankincense put on the loaves, part of which was indeed burned regularly in the cult (Lev. 2:1–2; 6:15, etc.). Here, 'gift-by-fire' refers specifically to the whole burnt offering and the peace offerings, with *zebaḥ* as shorthand for *zebaḥ šĕlāmîm* (see Exod. 24:5; 29:28; Lev. 3:1, 6; 7:18, 29, 32, 34; 10:14; etc.). The whole burnt offering was central to Israel's cult, and signified: (1) utter consecration to YHWH, inasmuch as the entire animal apart from its skin was offered on the altar; (2) atonement and propitiation, as the blameless, vicarious sacrifice was transformed by fire into a 'restful aroma', ascending to YHWH's heavenly abode, as its name *ʿōlāh* (ascending one) indicates (see Morales 2019a). 'Sacrifice' (*zebaḥ*) is also used of the Passover lamb (Exod. 12:27), which was a kind of peace offering, being eaten by the Israelite worshipper; as a verb, this root is repeatedly used in the Exodus narrative as a chief aim for releasing the Israelites (Exod. 3:18; 5:3, 8, 17; 8:4, 25, 26, 27, 28, 29; 10:25).

In Leviticus, the wondrous vow and freewill offering are two leading motives for the peace (7:16; 22:21) and whole burnt offerings (22:18) (Milgrom 1990: 118). Within Numbers, the terms in the phrase 'wondrous vow' (*pallē'-neder*) occur together only in this chapter and in 6:2 with reference to the Nazirite vow (*yapli' lindōr neder*). Cocco observes that this syntagma *pallē'-neder* 'recalls almost directly' Numbers 6:2 (2020: 180). Alluding to the vow likely functions to solicit a renewal of Israel's approach to the wilderness period after the consecrated manner of a Nazirite. The pattern of the Nazir vow is: a period of abstention followed by worship with sacrifices, including tribute and wine offerings. As a spiritual path set before Israel, the pattern is theologically expressed as: a period of abstention *during the sojourn through the wilderness*, followed by worship *in the land* with sacrifices, including tribute and wine offerings. Not only does Numbers 15 provide the richest instructions for drink offerings in the Torah, it should also be noted that the obligation to offer drink offerings is deferred until Israel's entrance into the land of Canaan (cf. Kurtz 1863: 300). The opening legislation of Numbers 15, then, does more than affirm YHWH's commitment to bringing Israel into the land; it also reaffirms the path of the Nazir originally set before Israel as the spiritually highest way of approaching the wilderness sojourn. Indeed, YHWH's first speech (vv. 1–16) is entirely taken up with the tribute and drink offerings that will accompany Israel's sacrificial worship. Chapter 15 ends, moreover, with the tassels law, reminding Israel to be 'holy to your God', reaffirming the nation's priestly vocation (cf. Exod. 19:6) – all of which resonates with the purpose of the Nazirite vow. More than this, since the scouts' expedition occurred in 'the days of the firstfruits of grapes' and they were commanded to 'take of the fruit of the land' (13:20), and the brief narrative spotlights the enormous cluster of grapes, for which the place was called Wadi of Eshcol (13:23–24), and since this affirmation of God's promise of a good land was virtually ignored by them (13:26–27), the wine libations – which are set within the context of YHWH's response to the events of chapters 13 – 14 – function as *tikkun*, a repair for the sin of the scouts (also Curwin 2023: 106).

The 'freewill offering' (*nĕdābāh*) is applied to gifts – the whole burnt or peace offering – 'presented out of the benevolence or religious impulse of heart of the giver, and not in fulfilment of any obligation, promise, or vow', and 'were made especially on great feast-days' (I. M. Price 1906: 506–507). The designation is first used with reference to the voluntary gifts given for the construction and service of the Dwelling, giving which, within the context of YHWH's steadfast love and mercy after Israel's apostasy with the golden calf, had demonstrated Israel's gratitude, loyalty and commitment to covenantal life with YHWH (Exod. 35 – 36) – Israelites gave so abundantly they needed to be restrained (Exod. 36:2–7). Within a similar context now of YHWH's forgiveness (Num. 14:17–20) and determined willingness to bring his people into the land, the heart characterized by the freewill offering was appropriate. The 'appointed times' are listed in Leviticus 23 and in Numbers 28 – 29, the former evincing calendric concerns while the latter displays emphasis on the particular offerings required throughout Israel's calendar (cf. Levine 1989: 153–154). 'Restful aroma' (*rêaḥ nîḥōaḥ*) is a technical designation, expressing one of the sacrificial cult's major aims, to propitiate divine wrath by atonement. Its first use occurs in the deluge account, when YHWH breathes-in the restful aroma of Noah's whole burnt offerings with the result that his heart is pacified and his divine wrath assuaged (Gen. 8:21; for ANE parallels, see Müller 1985; Morales 2012: 181–185). As the column of smoke ascended from the sacrifice to YHWH's heavenly abode, this anthropomorphic portrayal of his smelling the scent and being 'comforted' informed Israel's understanding of the cult's function, justifying translations of *rêaḥ nîḥōaḥ* as propitiating, pacifying and soothing savour (Kidner 1982: 123; Geller 1992: 100). The designation 'restful aroma' occurs six times in this chapter (vv. 3, 7, 10, 13, 14, 24), and the root occurs a seventh time (v. 34). Used primarily and foundationally in connection with the whole burnt offering, 'restful aroma' also occurs with the tribute, peace, and drink offerings – never with the reparation offering, and only once with the purification offering (Lev. 4:31) (Milgrom 1991: 162, 252). The burning rite (*hiqṭîr*) on the altar defines a sacrifice as an offering, transforming the material into a 'restful aroma' to YHWH (Eberhart 2004; Morales 2019a: 33–36).

4–12. Accompaniments for a lamb, ram, and bullock, either as a whole burnt offering or for the sacrifice (peace offering), are here explained. The accompaniments required for a lamb by the lay worshipper match precisely, in equal measure, the priesthood's offering of the *tāmîd* (continual, daily) lambs, morning and evening, in their daily service (Exod. 29:40–41). The *minḥāh* usually refers to a grain offering within the context of the cult (cf. G. A. Anderson 1987: 27–34), but translates literally as 'tribute' or 'gift'. In political contexts, *minḥāh* refers to the tribute given to a king (1 Sam. 10:27; 2 Sam. 8:2, 6; 1 Kgs 4:21; 10:25; 2 Kgs 8:9; 17:3, 4; 1 Chr. 18:2, 6; 2 Chr. 9:24; 17:5, 11; 26:8; 32:23; Pss 45:12; 72:10; Isa. 39:1; Hos. 10:6), which fits the narrative theology of Israel's cult: after the vicarious substitute ascends into YHWH's heavenly presence through the whole burnt offering's column of smoke ('ōlāh, 'ascending one'), the worshipper enters the King's presence with tribute (for the cultic journey as an ascent into God's presence, see Morales 2015: 124–141). The tribute offering so typically accompanied the whole burnt offering in the cult, sometimes only the whole burnt offering is mentioned although the tribute was also included (cf. Lev. 9:16–18, 22). Procedural requirements had already been established (Lev. 1:1–3:17; 6:8–23; 7:11–27), but in Table 23 the actual measures are given for the accompaniments (D. A. Brueggemann 2005: 318), listed in increasing order, matching the increasing value of the sacrificial animal.

The requirements testify to YHWH's own provision: life in the land will be marked by an abundance of grain, oil, and wine. A dry measure, an ephah equals a tenth of a homer (Ezek. 45:11); as a liquid measure, a hin is probably equivalent to a gallon (IDB, 107, 605). Verse 11's summary reverses the order, with 'ox' (šôr) standing for 'bullock' (ben-bāqār) (vv. 8–9; cf. Ps. 69:31). Psalm 104:15 captures the goodness of life in the land as comprised by the triad of wine, oil and bread (grain): 'Wine that gladdens the heart of man, oil to make his face shine, and bread that strengthens the heart of man.' Marking the three principal crops of the land, grain (first barley, and then wheat) was harvested April–June, grapes were pruned between mid-June and mid-August and gathered August–September (along with dates, figs and pomegranates), and olives began as early as September and ran through mid-November (Bimson 1988: 12–16). The emphasis on wine recalls the same motif within the context of the Nazirite vow (6:1–21). While the worshipper here is giving – rather than abstaining from – wine, nevertheless in both scenarios the person acknowledges the priority of God as the soul's highest joy (cf. Hirsch 2007a: 284–285). The wine motif is also connected with the grape cluster brought back from the land (13:23–27), a seal of the good life God had in store for his people if only they would be willing to forsake the comfort and pleasures of the world for a short, designated period of time in the wilderness. Moreover, as Olson noted, the sacrificial combination of animal, grain, and drink offerings for the consecration of Nazirites earlier in Numbers (6:14–17; as well as for the Feasts of Firstfruits and Weeks, Lev. 23:12–14, 18) has now been generalized for all Israelites whenever an offering by fire is made to YHWH from the herd or flock (1996: 92). Together with the tassels law, then, the chapter opens

Table 23: Accompaniment offerings

Animal	Grain	Oil	Wine
Lamb	1/10 ephah	1/4 hin	1/4 hin
Ram	2/10 ephah	1/3 hin	1/3 hin
Bullock	3/10 ephah	1/2 hin	1/2 hin

and closes with a call to holiness for all Israel, akin to that of the Nazirite whose holiness was comparable with the high priest.

In Numbers 18, YHWH will give all the 'best' (lit. 'fat') of the oil, and all the best of the new wine, and of the grain, their firstfruits, to his servants the priests, to Aaron and his house (v. 12; cf. Neh. 10:38; Ezek. 44:28–30).

13–16. The accompaniments section ends with emphasis placed on the uniformity of practice for the sojourner, and even the sojourner's equal standing with the native before YHWH – 'so will the sojourner be (*yihyeh*) before YHWH' (v. 15). The audience is spoken of indirectly: 'The native' (*hā'ezrāḥ*), one who springs from the soil, will do thus for an offering-by-fire, a restful aroma for YHWH (v. 13), then addressed directly as 'you (all)' when guided about the sojourner: The sojourner will do the same 'as you' for an offering-by-fire, a restful aroma for YHWH (v. 14). Verses 15 and 16 then state the principle: there is 'one statute', a 'perpetual statute', for both native and sojourner (v. 15), one 'teaching' and one 'rule' for you and the sojourner. 'Statute' (*ḥuqqā*) carries the notion of inscribing or cutting into stone, so that the law is fixed, here referring to a general obligation (see Ringgren 1986); *tôrāh* refers, in this context, to divine and authoritative teaching, and *mišpāṭ*, 'rule', often translated 'judgement', is also used for the 'pattern' or 'plan' of the Dwelling (Exod. 26:30), and here has the sense of process or practice.

Focus on the 'sojourner' (*gēr*), a term first used with reference to Abram's status within the land (Gen. 15:13; 17:8; 23:4), functions on a variety of levels (cf. 9:14). Since Israelites, also like Abraham, had been sojourners in Egypt (Gen. 12:10), they are to be mindful of the sojourner's place among them before YHWH. Israel's vocation is to bring blessing to the nations (Gen. 12:3; 22:18), and the sojourner would be a Gentile who has chosen to dwell among them and who desires to participate in the service of YHWH. Mention of sojourners also underscores the exceeding goodness of life with YHWH in the land, drawing sojourners to their midst. Finally, the issue of 'outsiders' and their influence has been highlighted since the beginning of Numbers 11 – 14 (see 11:1, 4; 12:1), and chapter 15 now brings some resolution with the prospect of Israelites and sojourners together offering sacrifices to YHWH out of the abundance of his land. A sojourner 'was not an Israelite by birth, but had been settled in the community for a considerable period, and in many respects was a member of it'; by contrast with a temporary visitor, the sojourner 'would probably have been circumcised, and was entitled to the care and protection of the community' (Budd 1984: 98). The distinction between sojourner and 'whoever is among you' remains ambiguous, perhaps referring to two kinds of sojourners: those who are 'sojourning' temporarily versus those who have more permanent residence.

Whereas previously it seems that foreigners were located at the periphery or fringes of the Camp (11:1, 4), these laws welcome the non-Israelite into the centre, to offer sacrifices and offerings to YHWH at the entrance of his Tent of Meeting, given equal status 'before YHWH' (cf. Olson 1996: 93). Along with the possibility of an Israelite's being cut off from the covenant community due to defiant sin (vv. 30–31), the message is clear: loyalty to YHWH, not ethnicity, marks a true member of YHWH's community. Medieval Jewish exegetes also interpreted the teaching on sojourners as concerning Caleb who, although absorbed into the tribe of Judah, was 'the son of Jephunneh, the Kenizzite' (Num. 32:12; cf. Gen. 15:19) (Staubli 1996: 256–257).

Double reference to 'your generations' (*lĕdōrōtêkem*), one of the unifying elements of the chapter (15:14, 15, 21, 23, 38), feeds into the overall message of comfort from YHWH to his people: not only will Israel surely be brought into the land, but the land will be a possession throughout their generations.

17–18. This law also begins with a reminder from YHWH through Moses that Israel will be brought into the land 'there where I myself (*'ănî*) am bringing you', reaffirming YHWH's promise (cf. 15:2), one of the major goals of this chapter.

19–21. The 'contribution' (*tĕrûmāh*) was a gift set aside 'to YHWH' (cf. 5:9; 8:10), built off the root *rûm* (high, exalted) and apparently part of the process of giving it to YHWH, hence: 'raise a contribution' (*tārîmû tĕrûmāh*, v. 20). Here the contribution of dough falls under the theology of firstfruits, whereby the 'first' (*rē'šît*), whether a firstborn as 'the first' of one's strength (Gen. 49:3), or of the firstfruits of the land (Exod. 23:19; 34:26; Lev. 2:12; 23:10), is given to YHWH in acknowledgement that the whole derives from and belongs to him. The meaning of *'ărîsāh*, 'ground meal' or 'dough', is uncertain, by context referring to the initial stage of bread-making (cf. also Neh. 10:37; Ezek. 44:30), which means the law is not limited to grain farmers – it is more about eating (when you eat . . .) than harvesting. The Mishnah (tractate *Hul.*) includes all five grains of the land within the compass of this law: wheat, barley, spelt, oats and rye. 'When (*bĕ*) you come into the land' is paralleled by 'when (*bĕ*) you eat from the bread of the land', linking the two thoughts to the manna in the wilderness, a divine provision that would cease once in the land. The phrase 'bread of the land' is unique (Levine 1993: 394), emphasizing that this bread will derive from the gift of the land (whereas the manna descended from the heavens). The 'cake' (*ḥallā*) of bread derived from 'the land' truly represented the fulfilment of YHWH's promise of the land, and his faithfulness in bringing his people to the journey's end out of the wilderness. He who had dependably rained down bread from heaven for Israel in the wilderness now has bread from the land lifted up to him by Israel throughout its generations, a token of thanksgiving.

The underlying thought of the contribution is brought out well in the firstfruits instructions given in Deuteronomy 26, where Israelites are told that 'when you enter the land . . . YHWH your God is giving you' they are to bring the first of the fruits of the land 'that YHWH your God is giving you' and confess, 'I have come to the land that YHWH swore to our fathers to give to us' (vv. 1–3). This statement is then followed by a recital of YHWH's saving acts:

> My father was a wandering Aramean, and he went down to Egypt and sojourned (yāgār) there . . . And YHWH brought us out from Egypt with a mighty hand and an outstretched arm, with great fearful deeds, with signs and wonders, and he brought us into this place and gave us this land, a land flowing with milk and honey. Now look! I bring the first of the fruit of the ground that you, O YHWH, have given me. (vv. 5–10)

The firstfruits, then, represent the culmination of everything YHWH had done for Israel, to raise them up to the place where they are now able to give back joyfully to him in worship. The first of the dough underscores more deeply the reversal of their plight in 'that great and terrible wilderness' (Deut. 1:19), where they had been utterly dependent on the heavenly manna. Whereas other laws have been understood to apply only after Israel had gained possession of the land, after the conquest, the bread contribution was required immediately upon entering the land, just as the manna ceased, as recounted in Joshua 5:10–12. As the 'contribution' of the Levites in Numbers 8 is given by YHWH for the priests, so here, as with the contribution of the threshing floor, the dough would be given to Levites and priests (see Num. 18:8–32).

22–29. These laws address 'unintentional error' (or 'inadvertent sin) by the community (vv. 22–26) and the individual (vv. 27–29). The issue of time (vv. 22–23), as Brin noted (1980), relates not to when the sin will be committed, but includes all the time from the giving of the law through Moses to succeeding generations. 'Unintentional error' (šĕgāgāh) – as a verb, 'to err' or 'go astray' (šāgāh, v. 22) – results from negligence or ignorance: 'Either the offender knows the law but accidentally violates it or he acts deliberately without knowing he did wrong' (Milgrom 1983b: 125). The root sh-g-h/sh-g-g occurs nine times within eight verses, demonstrating an emphasis on the unintended nature of sin, versus high-handed rebellion (Horn 1993: 46). In Numbers 35, killing someone by accident, such as by having thrown a stone without knowing anyone would be hit, is used as an example of an 'unintentional' (bišgāgāh) killing (vv. 11, 15, 22–23; Sklar 2012: 469). Leviticus had already established purification offerings for unintentional sin for the high priest, the assembly, a chieftain, and for the individual Israelite (4:1–35), as well as for non-defiant intentional sins (5:1; 6:1–7). By contrast, Numbers

15:22–31 legislates purification offerings for unintentional sin for the community and the individual (leaving out the high priest and chieftain), and addresses only the categories of unintentional and high-handed sins (leaving out non-defiant intentional sins). In Numbers 15, moreover, the purification offering for the community must be preceded by a whole burnt offering (v. 24), adding to the requirement in Leviticus 4:14. Modern scholars have explained these differences as due to independent traditions (Milgrom 1990: 404–405), or divergent sources, with Numbers 15 comprising a Holiness School (H) revision of Priestly Torah (P), Leviticus 4–5 (Knohl 1991; Wright 2020). Others, such as Ibn Ezra (so, too, Harrison 1990: 224; Woods and Rogers 2006: 272; Wright 2020: 47–49), approach Numbers 15 as covering sins of omission (violating performative commands), with Leviticus 4 covering sins of commission (violating prohibitive commands). An initial comparison between the language of Leviticus 4:2 and Numbers 15:22 would seem to support this view. Nachmanides thought the language of commission in 15:24 (*neʿeśtāh*) ruled out this overly subtle distinction, which does not, in any case, explain the absence of both priest and ruler in the present chapter. Gane (2010) satisfactorily explained how the differences in Numbers 15 all relate to the inclusion of the sojourner: (1) the high priest and chieftain cannot be sojourners, so they do not need to be readdressed, (2) the inclusion of foreigners justifies enlarging the purification offering for the community with the prefixed addition of a whole burnt offering, (3) while the purification offering for the individual remains the same as in Leviticus 4, it is mentioned again here as applying equally for the sojourner as well. Numbers 15 thus provides a needed expansion of Leviticus 4, in view of life in the land – a life that will inevitably include many more sojourners among them. Finally, of the three basic categories of sins – expiable unintentional sin, expiable non-defiant but deliberate sin, and inexpiable defiant (high-handed) sin – Numbers 15 deals only with expiable unintentional sin and inexpiable defiant sin. Again Gane clarifies that as an expansion of Leviticus, Numbers 15 does not intend to collapse or do away with expiation for non-defiant, deliberate sin (contra G. A. Anderson 1992a), but rather, by the polar contrast between the first and third categories, to underscore the seriousness of defiant sin – a strategy that also operates in Mesopotamian law collections (2010: 252–253).

24. As the verb *ʿāśāh* (to do, make) signals the procedural order of sacrifice rather than the administrative order, which typically lists sacrifices in order of value (see Rainey 1970), then it is clear that the whole burnt offering is offered up *before* the purification offering, which reverses the typical order – an occurrence also found in public feasts days of Numbers 28 – 29 (cf. Levine 1993: 396). When the whole burnt offering is prefixed to the purification offering, the effect is to make it a 'larger' purification offering, augmenting the quantity of expiation, expanded in this case for the inclusion of sojourners (Gane 2010: 254–257). This prefixed whole burnt offering is also subject to the new accompaniments law for the bullock (vv. 8–10), which underscores the accompaniments of grain, oil, and wine.

Reference to the 'community' (*'ēdāh*), occurring seven times in this chapter (vv. 24 [twice], 25, 26, 33, 35, 36), stresses the sort of obedience needed to avoid the community-wide failure of the scouts episode, where 'community' occurs ten times (13:26 [twice]; 14:1, 2, 5, 7, 10, 27, 35, 36).

25–26, 28–29. The emphasis of these laws for corporate and individual unintentional sin falls on two points. First, atonement (*kipper*, three times) and its consequent forgiveness (*sālaḥ*, three times), through the mediation of the priest (*hakkōhēn*) (vv. 25, 26, 28). Forgiveness is declared in the passive, as something granted by God alone, based on the priest's divinely ordained service. Especially after the looming judgement of Israel's destruction and Moses' plea for YHWH to 'forgive' (*sālaḥ*) them (14:19–20), the accent on forgiveness here is fitting. The second point of emphasis is on the inclusion of the sojourner, whether as part of the community (vv. 22–26) or as an individual (vv. 27–29).

30–31. By sharp contrast to the unintentional sin of the individual (vv. 27–29), the person (note the fronting of *wĕhannepeš*) – whether native or sojourner – who sins defiantly, with a 'raised hand', will not be provided atonement and forgiveness (on defiant sin, see Labuschagne 1982; Schenker 1983). We are reminded, therefore, that sacrificial atonement is 'a privilege granted by YHWH, not an inalienable right' (Gane 2005: 204). With good reason, commentators often make a correlation between 15:30–31 and the warning of Hebrews 10:26 (e.g. Attridge 1989: 292; Ellingworth 1993: 531), even seeing the former as the backdrop for the latter (Sklar 2008). Intentional but non-defiant sins could be forgiven, as addressed in Leviticus (5:1; 6:1–7). Milgrom suggested that high-handed sin refers to acts committed in open defiance of God – committed publicly, whereas non-public, even deliberate, sin could be commuted to the status of unintentional sin through repentance (Milgrom 1990: 125; 1991: 373–378). To sin with a 'raised hand' (*bĕyād rāmāh*) is further described as 'blaspheming' YHWH, 'despising' his word, and 'breaking' his command. All of these heinously rebellious acts are further under-scored as affronts to YHWH's face by fronting the objects (YHWH, his word, and his command) before the verb. The root *rûm* (high, exalted) occurs seven other times in this chapter, used for 'lifting up the contri-bution' of bread in verses 17–21 (*tārîmû tĕrûmāh*), the polar opposite of a 'high hand' against YHWH, idiomatic for 'defiance'. To 'blaspheme' (*gādap*) YHWH is connected with gross idolatry elsewhere (Ezek. 20:27–28); to 'despise' (*bāzāh*) YHWH defines the sin of Eli's household, which would be cut off and forbidden atonement (1 Sam. 2:30–33; 3:14), while despising his word defines the sin for which YHWH exiled Judah (2 Chr. 36:15–16); and 'breaking (*hēpar*) his commandment' is used in Ezra for a severe breach of covenant loyalty (9:14) – all of which terms help us understand 'high-handed' sin as a flagrant rejection of YHWH himself, a deliberately public act intended to express one's apostasy (Sklar 2012). Noting how the Israelites' refusal to enter Canaan was characterized as 'to rebel' (*mārad*, 14:9) and 'to despise' (*nāʾaṣ*, 14:11, 23), designating the breaking of covenant faith, Noonan rightly interprets the present law as functioning to characterize Israel's rebellion at Kadesh as high-handed sin (2020: 83–84).

Such high-handed sin, threefold in its heinousness, is met by threefold emphasis on its terrible judgement. That soul will be 'cut off from his people', even 'surely cut off' (*hikkārēt tikkārēt*), and his 'guilt' (*ʿăwōnāh*) remains on him – there is no sacrificial expiation provided to cleanse such a soul from guilt. The *kareth* penalty, a judgement that refers to permanent expulsion, including one's lineage, from the covenant community by way of death, either directly at the hands of YHWH or by judicial execution through the community (see Sklar 2005: 15–20; cf. Wold 1978; Hobson 2010), is concerned with the foundational distinctions of Israelite cosmology, including sacred time (Wold 1979; Frymer-Kensky 1983: 403–405; Gorman 1990: 191–192), as is the case here. As with the other laws, this fearful declaration applies equally to the native and the sojourner. Happy membership in the covenant community, along with the enjoyment of his good land, concerns loyalty to YHWH no less for ethnic Israel than for foreigners (cf. Bellinger 2001: 236). By contrasting high-handed sin with the unintentional sinner (vv. 27–29), the heinousness of rebellion against YHWH is underscored, a relevant focus given the narrative context of community-wide rebellions (Num. 14, 16). In some measure, these verses form a theodicy, justifying the divine judgement that fell on the first generation of Israelites in the wilderness, as well as his consequent judgements in Numbers 16 (cf. Olson 1985: 173–174; Artus 2008: 136–137; Gane 2010: 262) – as well as his judgement on the Sabbath gatherer in the little episode that follows. Even as Israel is being encouraged and comforted in YHWH's renewed commitment to bring his people into the land (15:1–29), this section, recalling Israel's rebellion and judgement at Kadesh (chs. 13–14), serves to guard against repeating the same high-handed sin, which would incur the same tragic judgement (cf. Noonan 2020: 86–87).

YHWH, whose nature and inclination is to show mercy, does prove able and willing to forgive his people's rebellion as a community, outside of the sacrificial system, typically through the intercession of an ordained mediator like Moses (e.g. Num. 14:13–20), although he may still require the death of the leading offender(s) (14:37; 25:4, 8, 11–13) (see Sklar 2012: 485–490). Nevertheless, even for the high-handed sin of Manasseh – the most wicked monarch of Judah, who shed innocent blood and promoted all sorts of debased occult practices – the God of all mercy proved willing to cleanse, forgive, and restore when he turned to YHWH in humility (2 Chr. 33:12–13), an atonement possible only through the eventual sacrifice of the Messiah, teaching us that a sinner need not despair of the infinite love of God for a world of sinners (John 3:16) (see Gane 2004: 626–628). Judaism teaches that a high-handed sinner's guilt only remains 'upon him' until he repents (*t. Shev.* 13a; see Rashi, Nachmanides, ad loc.).

15:32–36. While the Sabbath gatherer's act is nowhere dubbed 'high-handed sin', this tale has been widely received as serving to illustrate the previous threat against such an offence (cf. e.g. Knierim and Coats 2005: 201; Baden 2013b: 360). Similarly, while the phrase 'to cut off' is not stated explicitly, yet the judgement of taking the man 'outside the camp' for death by stoning would certainly fit being cut off from one's people (cf. Sklar 2005: 19). There is a deliberateness apparent in juxtaposing this story immediately after the warning against high-handed sin (vv. 30–31). Even as the high-handed law characterized Israel's rebellion at Kadesh as high-handed sin (chs. 13–14), Noonan demonstrates that the ensuing Sabbath-breaking story functions 'as an image of disinheriting the land', with the stick-gatherer serving 'as a microcosm of the generation that failed to enter Canaan' (2020: 87). G. Robinson's thorough study on the origin and development of the Sabbath in the Hebrew Scriptures concluded that 'the observance of the sabbath is always thought of in association with life in the promised land (cf. Lev. 26:34–35, 43; 2 Chr. 36:21)' and that the sabbath, as the sign of the covenant, was the 'central commandment', symbolizing submission to YHWH's sovereignty and so exemplified the fulfilment of the whole Torah (1988: 335, 342). Within its literary context, the Sabbath, observes Chavel (2009a: 50–51), is Janus-like, representative 'of any of God's laws, looking backwards at vv. 22–31, and equal to all of God's laws, looking forward to vv. 37–41'.

The high-handedness of the Sabbath gatherer becomes apparent on reflection that divine instruction about keeping the Sabbath Day holy had been given repeatedly (e.g. Exod. 16:23–30; 20:8–11; 35:2–3), and lay at the bedrock of Israel's theology (Gen. 2:1–3), with the Sabbath constituting *the* sign of Israel's covenant relationship with YHWH (Exod. 31:13–17):

And YHWH spoke to Moses, saying, You, speak to the sons of Israel, saying, Surely my Sabbaths you will keep, for it is a sign between me and you throughout your generations. You will keep the Sabbath, for it is holy to you. Whoever profanes it will surely be put to death – for whoever does any work on it, that soul will be cut off from among his people. For six days work will be done, but the seventh day is a Sabbath of rest, holy unto YHWH. Whoever does any work on the Sabbath Day will surely be put to death. Between me and the sons of Israel it is a sign for ever; for in six days YHWH made the heavens and the earth, but on the seventh day he rested and was refreshed.

Not keeping the Sabbath holy is already a breaking of the Decalogue (Exod. 20:8–11; Deut. 5:12–15), but to profane the Sabbath openly was tantamount to denying Israel's covenant relationship with YHWH, *which it signified* (Exod. 31:12–17; 35:1–3), a despising of the divine King who made humanity in his own image, giving him the Sabbath for the sake of enjoying communion and fellowship with their majestic Creator (see Morales 2015: 43–49). The Sabbath, as Noonan further explains (2020: 87–88), is connected with entrance into the land of Canaan, for the goal of the exodus out of Egypt was to enjoy life in the land with God (Exod. 3:7–8, 16–17; 6:6–8; Deut. 5:12–15), and numerous laws connect the Sabbath rest of the people with that of the land, whose owner is God (cf. Exod. 23:10–11; Lev. 25:1–7, 18–22; Deut. 15:1–6, 12–18). In this way, the Sabbath-breaker becomes emblematic of the Israelite generation that rejected the land in chapters 13–14. The 'rest' tradition in Scripture, closely connected to the concept of Sabbath, also aligns with entrance into the land (Noonan 2020: 88–89; see Ps. 95:8–11; Heb. 3:7 – 4:11). The penalty, being 'cut off' (*kārat*), paralleled with being 'put to death', is the severest form of excommunication: premature death, likely including the extirpation of one's lineage, at the hands of YHWH or by judicial execution through the community, usually by stoning (see Sklar 2005: 15–20).

Scholars disagree over what precisely was the nature of Moses' confusion – on what point did he need clarification from YHWH? Weingreen (1966) supposed the controversy was over the wood gatherer's *intent* to kindle a fire on the Sabbath (cf. Exod. 35:3). Phillips (1969) argued the Sabbath gatherer story was the priestly legislator's attempt to extend the scope of Sabbath law to include domestic activity, beyond 'occupational work'. T. Novick (2008) takes the enigma to be whether the Sabbath (or any) law still applied to Israel after their recent punishment (Num. 14), with the wood gatherer doubting the laws had continuing force. Burnside (2010) sees gathering sticks as sufficiently far enough removed from the paradigm case of Sabbath-breaking by way of gathering and processing manna, so as to raise doubts, which in turn called capital punishment into question. The text states that it was not 'discerned' (*pōraš*, 'distinctly declared') what should be 'done' (*'āśeh*) to him (v. 34), which most straightforwardly relates to the question of *how* the Sabbath-breaker was to be 'cut off', or the manner by which he was to be put to death (cf. Exod. 31:14; 35:2), and this is indeed the information YHWH supplies; namely, death by stoning outside the Camp (v. 35). Mode of execution was also the rabbinical understanding, and may be dubbed the 'traditional view' (*b. Sanh.* 78b; also Philo, *Moses* 2.217; *Sif. Emor* 14.5; *Sif. Num.* 114). While it may be argued that doubt as to 'what should be done' derived from confusion over whether the wood gatherer had actually broken the Sabbath, this approach fails to appreciate the context of chapter 15 whereby the gatherer's case has been juxtaposed with the person who sins with a high hand. Moreover, to dismiss the mode of execution as the central enigma by assuming previous cases that would have clarified the matter, fails to recognize the timeless character of the tale ('when the sons of Israel were in the wilderness') – in other words, this may well have been the first case, placed here after the law for high-handed sin for rhetorical purposes.

Numbers 15:32–36 is regularly grouped with three other stories sharing similar themes and vocabulary, with Moses seeking a word from YHWH to decide a matter in each case: the partly Egyptian son who blasphemed the Name of YHWH (Lev. 24:10–23), the second Passover (Num. 9:1–14), and the inheritance of land by the daughters of Zelophehad (Num. 27:1–11) (cf. Fishbane 1986: 98–104, 236–237; cf. also Chavel 2009b). One significant difference, however, is that whereas the other stories account for new and permanent legislation (see Lev. 24:15–16; Num. 9:10–14; 27:8–11), the story of the wood gatherer does not, perhaps a clue that its purpose is not to revise or expand Sabbath prohibitions. Rather, the tale uses Sabbath theology to buttress the warning against high-handed sin (vv. 30–31). The 'high handed' sin contrasts with the 'mighty hand' by which YHWH had delivered Israel out of Egypt, this for the sake of Sabbath fellowship and rest in the land (cf. Exod. 32:11; Deut. 5:15) (cf. Burnside 2010: 59).

32–34. Set 'in the wilderness', this story marks a contrast with the previous legislation not only in terms of genre but in relation to context, since the previous laws were set within the framework of life 'in the land' (15:2, 18). Nevertheless, the tale's Sabbath theology of 'rest' anticipates life in the land, and was likely placed here, after the judgement on the first generation (Num. 14), precisely as a dire threat against forsaking YHWH's promise to bring Israel into the land. Moreover, while some teachings will be implemented only after the Israelites are settled within their inheritance of the land, the Sabbath is to be observed always and in all places – even in the wilderness (cf. Exod. 16). 'The Sabbath is the basis of the whole of the sacral regulations in the Torah', writes Achenbach (2013: 227), 'and the Sabbath commandment is valid everywhere at every time (Gen. 2:2–3).'

Thematic parallels between Numbers 15:32–36 and Exodus 16, strengthen the connection between Sabbath and land, as Noonan observes (Noonan 2020: 88; see Exod. 16:35; Josh. 5:11–12): 'The cessation of manna on the Sabbath parallels the cessation of manna when Israel enters Canaan, linking the Sabbath with inheriting the land'. The word used for the man's 'gathering' of wood is *qāšaš*, a rare and different verb from the one used repeatedly for 'gathering' manna throughout Exodus 16, which is *lāqaṭ* (to glean, gather). Our story's word, *qāšaš*, is used in only one other context in the Torah, in Exodus 5, when the Israelites as slaves under Pharaoh's bitter bondage were scattered about gathering straw and stubble to make their quota of bricks (see vv. 5, 12). An Egyptian motif feeds into Sabbath theology in Deuteronomy as well: 'Keep (*šamar*) the Sabbath Day, to sanctify it . . . that your male servant and your female servant may rest (*nûaḥ*) as well as you. Now remember that you were a slave in the land of Egypt, but YHWH your God brought you forth from there with a mighty hand and outstretched arm, and, therefore, YHWH your God commanded you to observe the Sabbath Day' (5:12–15). YHWH had delivered his people from bondage in Egypt that they might enjoy his rest (*nûaḥ*, Exod. 20:11), that is, fellowship and communion with God in the land. As the sign of the covenant (Exod. 31:13, 17), the Sabbath signified Israel's embrace of the rest YHWH provides as opposed to the slavery of Pharaoh, so that the man's 'gathering' on the Sabbath day evoked Israel's bondage in Egypt – it was a rejection of YHWH as God, and a return to the tyrannical lordship of Pharaoh (Burnside 2010: 51, 53, 55). Similarly, T. Novick writes that to gather sticks on the Sabbath was to confirm the man's 'status as a slave to Pharaoh by denying himself the rest that he would be due as slave to God . . . the wood-gatherer symbolically turns backward to Egypt', just as the people had advocated upon hearing the scouts' report in Num. 14:2–4 (2008: 5). The term 'keep' or 'guard house' (*mišmār*, v. 34), occurs several times in the Joseph story (Gen. 40:4; 41:10; 42:17) (Levine 1993: 399), and may feed into the Egypt motif as well.

The story may be more about corporate Israel than the individual Sabbath-breaker. From this perspective, the message may be more positive than first appears, inasmuch the view of Israel as a unified community portrays them as vigilant over YHWH's Sabbath and obedient to his instructions through Moses. Just as dealing with the Midianites in chapter 31 functions as a rejection of the Baal Peor incident (ch. 25), so dealing with the Sabbath-breaker here functions as a rejection of the scouts incident (chs. 13–14).

That the man was 'found' is repeated (v. 32, *wayyimṣĕ'û*; v. 33, *hammōṣĕ'îm*), possibly forming wordplay with 'wood' (*'ēṣîm*, vv. 32, 33; perhaps with 'Egypt', *miṣrayim*, and 'his commandment', *miṣwātô*, v. 31, as well). Moreover, the verbs used for transporting the man vary, and are not the expected 'brought' (*bô'*): rather, he is 'brought-near' (*qārab*, v. 33), 'rested' (*nûaḥ*, v. 34), and 'brought-forth' (*yāṣā'*, v. 36). At least the use of 'rest' is ironic: the man who would not 'keep' (*šamar*) YHWH's 'rest' (*nûaḥ*) on the Sabbath (Deut. 5:12–15) is made to 'rest' (*nûaḥ*) in a 'keep' (*mišmār*). By contrast with the blasphemer story, where the sons of Israel bring the man to Moses alone (Lev. 24:11), here the sons of Israel bring the wood gatherer 'to Moses and to Aaron and to the whole community' (Num. 15:33), an echo of the previous story where the scouts came back 'to Moses and to Aaron and to the whole community of the sons of Israel' (13:26) – the 'sons of Israel' in the present story are the ones who find the wood gatherer, which explains the single difference. The story of the Sabbath gatherer, then, is more about the community and its response, than about the offender himself; here, the community *reverses* the rebellious response of the scouts episode. This is the only explicit instance where Israel obeys 'as YHWH had commanded Moses' within the entire wilderness section proper (Num. 11 – 25). The sons of Israel obediently wait upon YHWH's instruction through Moses, desirous to ensure that not one member among them remains brazenly rebellious.

35–36. YHWH says unequivocally that the man must 'surely die' (*môt yûmat*), just as he had said the high-handed sinner must 'surely be cut off' (v. 31). Not only is he to die by stoning, but this must be carried out by 'the whole community'. Just as with the expulsions in Numbers 5 – 6 to 'outside the Camp', a realm associated with uncleanness and death (G. J. Wenham 1979: 177; 1981b: 123), so here the execution of the man 'outside the camp' is significant theologically – his behaviour marks him as unfit for life in the Camp, for membership in the covenant community that has YHWH himself dwelling in its midst. Defying YHWH, the fountain of life, with an act that embodied an anti-Sabbath principle, with the Sabbath as the symbol, summary, and *telos* of all the laws of YHWH – indeed, of his salvation – the offender is himself steadily distanced from life: 'outside the camp . . . stoned with stones . . . and he died'. Having rejected the sign of belonging to YHWH's covenant community, the man is stoned to death outside the Camp, signifying his exclusion (Burnside 2010: 58). Given his judgement, the offender may well represent a microcosm of the first generation of Israel in the wilderness. In the Hebrew text, these verses form a palistrophe (Boys 1825: 40; Lund 1930: 107), not only bringing closure to the story, but centring on the community's obedience:

> And YHWH said to Moses
> > The man must surely die
> > > stone him with stones
> > > > the whole community outside the camp
> > > > > and they brought him
> > > > the whole community outside the camp
> > > stoned him with stones
> > and he died
> just as YHWH had commanded Moses.

The whole community's obedience to YHWH forms a response and reversal to their previous rebellion against him in the scouts narrative – again, the only such obedience reported for the whole community in the wilderness. That the whole community acted 'just as YHWH had commanded Moses' brings resolution, portraying ideal loyalty to YHWH and his word.

Finally, the Sabbath-breaker tale, in line with the chapter's literary function, serves as part of the divine response to the scouts' failure in Numbers 13 – 14. That the whole community 'stoned with stones' (*rāgôm 'ōtô bā'ăbānîm*) the man, an expression used twice (vv. 35, 36), recalls the only other use in the book, when the 'whole community' had urged 'to stone them with stones', wanting to execute Moses and Aaron (and/or Caleb and Joshua, 14:10).

37–38. As a response to the sobering law against high-handed sin (vv. 30–31) and the tale of the Sabbath gatherer (vv. 32–36), and, more deeply, to the sin of the whole community in the scouts narrative (Num. 13 – 14), YHWH, through Moses, commands the sons of Israel to implement reminders to obey his commands by making a 'tassel' (*ṣîṣit*) with a blue cord on the wings (extremities) of their garments. The *tzitzit* law is, in the words of Horn (1993: 43), 'a brilliant and subtle response to the causes of the failure of the spies and the community, and provides perfect closure to the entire episode'. He points out that key words in this law, such as 'to see' (*rā'ô*), 'to scout' (*tāturû*), 'your eyes' (*'ênêkem*) and 'whoring' (*zōnîm*), form deliberate echoes of the scouts episode (Horn 1993: 48; see 13:33; 14:33). The command is for the sons of Israel to make 'for yourselves' (*lāhem*), requiring the people's ownership, engagement and effort in the daily battle for obedience – and recalls YHWH's opening command in the scouts episode (13:2). Although 'the wing' (*hakkānāp*) of a garment is a plain enough term, within the book's theological context whereby Israel forms YHWH's earthly hosts (mirroring his heavenly host) and is called to be holy, that Israelites now have 'wings' is a propitious correlation. Horn writes (1993: 50):

A literal translation, 'the wings of your clothes', is more accurate and suggests a special intimacy between God and each of his people. The clothes of each lowly Israelite has wings, *kenafim*, like the . . . cherubim that define the exact site of God's presence in the Tabernacle. (See Exod. 25:20; 37:9.)

Jewish interpretation appropriately makes much of the correlation. Bachya, for example, likens the Israelites, when wearing *tzitzit*, to the four living creatures, each of which had four wings (*kĕnāpayim*, Ezek. 1:6), paralleling the four corners of the Israelite garment, and who support the divine chariot of YHWH in the celestial spheres, drawing on the analogy of Israel's Camp comprising YHWH's earthly hosts (see Bachya ben Asher 2003: 6:2071–2074). In the ANE East, the tassel was a mark of nobility, representing one's person and authority (even used for sealing documents), so that seizing the tassel of a god or man was a formal act of earnest petition (see Stephens 1931; Milgrom 1990: 410–411; cf. Bertman 1961; Sargent 2001). Focus on the community continues, in every Israelite's obedience in making the tassel. Moreover, it would not have been merely one's own tassels that reminded each Israelite to obey YHWH's word; the entire community being adorned and ornamented meant thousands of tassels served to remind each member of the loyalty due YHWH.

The word used for the high priest's golden 'diadem', inscribed with the words 'Holy unto YHWH', is *ṣîṣ* (see Exod. 28:36–38; 39:30–31), and makes the first part of the word 'tassel', *ṣîṣit*, which may be translated as 'little *tzitz*' (cf. Held 2017, 138). The diadem may have been shaped like a rosette, since *ṣîṣ* indicates a 'blossom' or 'flower' (*HALOT* 2:1023–1024; BDB 847, 851), used also of the carved cedar blossoms plated with gold that decorated the interior of Solomon's Temple amid other floral imagery (1 Kgs 6:18–29; Imes 2019: 35). Josephus refers to the high priest's gold diadem as a 'calyx' (*Ant.* 3.178; cf. *Ant.* 11.331), strengthening the floral association (Spoelstra 2019: 68). Calyxes were also fashioned on the golden Lampstand, which was a stylized almond tree, so that Aaron, donning his high priestly vestments, participated in the botanical beauty of the Dwelling as an architectural paradise. In the next section of Numbers (chs. 16–17), the staff of Aaron will 'bloom' (*wayyāṣēṣ*) with 'blossoms' (*ṣîṣ*), perhaps resembling his rosette diadem (17:8). Hirsch thus reads the command here as 'Let your garment sprout blossoms and flowers' (2007a: 116). The tassels, then, may have been rosette-shaped, as argued by Spoelstra (2019), who sees them as an extension of the high priest's rosette, and as having an apotropaic function. The significant point is the association of the tassel with the high priest's regalia. Structurally, with chapters 11–15 comprising a unit on the outer camp of the twelve tribes in relation to YHWH's prophetic word through Moses, and chapters 16–18 relating to the inner camp of Levites in relation to Aaron's high priesthood, both sections may be seen as being resolved through use of *ṣîṣ*: the 'tassels' (*ṣîṣit*) forms a prophetic response to the tribal failure, just as the 'blooming' (*wayyāṣēṣ*, 17:8) rod of Aaron forms a divine *cultic* sign for the Levite rebellion against the priesthood. Since, moreover, the gold *ṣîṣ* or diadem 'was the holiest item of the high priest's furnishings', inscribed with 'Holy unto YHWH' (Exod. 28:36), and dubbed 'holy crown' in the Torah (Exod. 39:30; Lev. 8:9) (Shamah 2011: 757), then the tassels should be seen as soliciting a Nazirite-like consecration of all Israel.

The 'blue' (*tĕkēlet*, 'violet', 'blue-purple') dye, being extracted in infinitesimal quantities from the gland of the murex snail found and gathered by hand in the shallow waters off the coast of Lebanon and ancient Phoenicia (some 12,000 snails per 1.4 grams of dye), was extremely valuable – so that, for example, blue wool was forty times more expensive than other colours in the sixth century BC – and enhanced the tassel's symbolism as a mark of nobility (Milgrom 1990: 411–412; cf. Ezek. 23:6; Esther 1:6). The significance of this colour is readily grasped by its use elsewhere. 'Blue', *tĕkēlet*, appears forty times in the Pentateuch. The thirty-four uses before Numbers pertain to the curtains of YHWH's Dwelling and the garments of the high priest. The ten curtains, decorated with heavenly cherubim, that lined the inside of the Dwelling were fashioned with blue (26:1, 4; 36:8, 11), including the Veil before the holiest place (26:31; 36:35), the screen into the holy place (26:36; 36:37), and the gate into the courtyard (27:16; 38:18). The high priest wore a robe entirely of blue (28:31; 39:22), his ephod and breastplate used blue (28:5, 6, 8, 15; 39:2, 3, 5, 8), and both the breastplate and the golden diadem were each attached with a 'blue cord' (*pĕtîl tĕkēlet*), the same language as the tassels' blue cord (Exod. 28:28, 37; 39:21, 31; cf. Num. 15:38) – making this requirement for the latter 'specifically related to the high priest' (Shamah 2011: 758). The remaining six uses of *tĕkēlet* occur in Numbers, five times in chapter four to describe the pure blue cloths used to cover the golden vessels of YHWH's Dwelling, the table of the presence, the candelabra, and the altar, along with their implements, vessels that were so threateningly holy they needed to be covered lest Levite transporters should gaze upon them and die (Num. 4:6, 7, 9, 11, 12) – a relevant connection to 15:39. Having associated the colour *tĕkēlet* with the royal holiness of YHWH's own Dwelling, furnishings, and high priest, the final and fortieth use of 'blue' is reserved for the 'blue cord' of the tassel all Israelites are to wear on the wings of their garments, a reminder of their calling to be 'a priestly kingdom and holy nation' (Exod. 19:6). Given the association of holy items with blue in the Torah, Ibn Ezra understood the blue colour itself as the memorial (cf. 1995: 78). Perhaps in a manner similar to the clothing of Adam and Eve after their sin (Gen. 3:21), YHWH here clothes his people *as a priesthood*, restoring and reinstating them in their calling as his covenant community (cf. Sargent 2001: 112–113; Hirsch 2007a: 325–328). Possibly, the blue cord was also a reminder that YHWH, the Holy One, dwelled in their midst. As noted above, the gold diadem of the high priest derives from *ṣîṣ* in Hebrew, so that use of both *tĕkēlet* and *ṣîṣit* for the tassels instruction forms a strong connection to what is arguably the holiest part of the high priest's clothing: the golden diadem inscribed with 'Holy unto YHWH', affixed to his turban with a blue cord. The tassels were a reminder to Israelites that, as a nation and as individuals, they had been redeemed out of Egypt, and now belonged to YHWH, called to be holy unto him. By the fifth century AD, although perhaps much earlier with the destruction of the Temple, it seems that *ṣîṣit* were no longer worn specifically with *tĕkēlet* blue, perhaps because the rich dye was no longer readily available (see Green and Kahn 2011; cf. Navon 2013). 'The *petil tekhelet*', Shamah writes (2011: 759), 'converts the everyday garment worn by non-priests into a counterpart to the high priest's holy crown with all that symbolizes.' Shamah also makes a further correlation to the Nazirite vow (2011: 759):

As Nazirite law provides non-priests a channel to holiness in the world outside the sanctuary, one based on laws pertaining to the high priest and his holy status, so does *ṣitṣit*. It provides a furnishing for non-priests to promote holiness in their lives . . . linked to the high priest's frontlet and *petil tekhelet* . . . In Israel, *tekhelet* of royalty is placed in service of promoting the goal of 'a kingdom of priests and a holy nation' (Exod. 19:6).

39–40. The tassel functions as a mnemonic device, a reminder for Israelites to obey all the commands of YHWH. To combat their wandering hearts, prone to stray into whoredom, he called Israelites to make for themselves reminders to 'delight in the *torah* of YHWH, meditating upon it day and night' (Ps. 1:2; cf. Deut. 6:6–9). Perhaps taking the masculine singular object of verse 39, translated 'it' (*ōtô*), as referring to God ('him'), one strand of Jewish tradition teaches that in observing the tassel law it is as if the Israelite has 'greeted the face of the *Shekhinah*, for *tekhelet* is the colour of the sea and the sea is like the sky and the sky is like the Divine Throne' (*Sif. Num.* 115; cf. *Men.* 43b; *Num. Rab.* 4.13). Likely, the referent is the 'ribbon, cord', which is masculine. More deeply, by using key terms and motifs from the scouts story (Num. 13 – 14), the tassel serves as a divine response and remedy for the first generation's failure in the wilderness (cf. Milgrom 1990: 127; T. Novick 2008: 3–4). The scouts' mission had been 'to search out' (*tûr*) the land (13:2, 16, 17, 21, 25, 32), where they 'saw' (*rā'āh*) the land (13:18) but also men of great stature, the Nephilim (13:32, 33), so that the scouts appeared 'in our own eyes' and 'in their eyes' (*'ayin*) as grass-hoppers (13:33) – and thus rebelled against YHWH, spreading an evil report of the land, leading to the 'whoredoms' (*zĕnût*) of the entire first generation of Israel (14:33). The tassel is now given by YHWH so the Israelites, when they 'see' (*rā'āh*) it, will not 'search out' (*tûr*) after your heart and after your eyes (*'ayin*), after which they go 'whoring' (*zĕnût*). To 'search out', *tûr*, was used twelve times in the scouts episode, and here as a reminder for Israelites *not* to 'search out' after their own heart and eyes, leading to whoredom. The root *zĕnût* (whoredom), typically a biblical metaphor for idolatry (see Exod. 34:15–16; Lev. 17:7; 20:5–6; Deut. 31:16), occurs three times in Numbers: the scouts episode (14:33), the tassel law (15:39) and for the second generation's apostasy with the daughters of Moab (25:1). With Numbers 15 serving as a cap to chapters 11–14, the tassels redress problems throughout this section, beyond the scouts episode. For example, earlier the sons of Israel had fallen into lusting after flesh, longing for their old life in Egypt, saying, We 'remember' (*zākar*) the fish and so on, and how there was now nothing except for this manna 'before our eyes' (*'ayin*), the manna being the 'colour' (*'ayin*) of bdellium in 'appearance' (*'ayin*) (11:4–6), and these terms may be intentionally evoked by the tassel law's use of *zākar* and *'ayin*. To be sure, following after one's eyes hearkens back to human-kind's first sin, which came about when the woman 'saw' (*rā'āh*) what was 'pleasant to the eyes ('*ayin*)' (Gen. 3:6).

Israel is to remember and do all YHWH's commands, for the sake of being 'holy (*qōdeš*) unto your God'. These words, as with the blue cord used to attach the gold plate to the high priest's turban, reading 'holy (*qōdeš*) unto YHWH' (Exod. 28:36–37), call Israel to be a holy nation of royal priests. Within the context of Israel's life and cult, when used of an object other than God himself, holiness means to belong utterly to YHWH. The tassel spurs Israel onward to live out the nation's identity and vocation as a special 'treasure' (*sĕgullā*) of YHWH (Exod. 19:5). YHWH could hardly have done anything more to demonstrate to his people that, even after their dismal failure and covenant-breaking throughout the wilderness journey, culminating in the scouts debacle (Num. 11 – 14), Israel still belonged to him as a treasured possession, and still possessed a priestly vocation among the nations of the earth, an ennobling privilege calling for spiritual maturity and loyalty, demon-strated in obedience to his wise and life-giving instructions. All that has been said, therefore, resonates remarkably well with the previous passage on the Sabbath-breaker (vv. 32–36), inasmuch as holiness is integral to the Sabbath in every respect (Gen. 2:1–3; Exod. 31:12–17).

The Midrash (*Sif. Num.* 115) and Babylonian Talmud (*Men.* 44a) recount the tale by Rabbi Nathan of a certain Jewish man who used 400 gold pieces to hire an extravagant harlot, the most beautiful woman he had ever seen. On approaching her, however, his four tassels happened to slap his face like four witnesses against him, so that he turned away from whoredom. As a result, the woman converted to Judaism, journeyed to the man's town and school, and sought him out in marriage. The tale conveys not only the function of the tassel, but also the underlying theology that, contrary to the false notions of our deceitful hearts, YHWH's commands lead to lasting joys (cf. Harvey 1986). Ortlund summarizes the idea, writing that the tassel law 'calls Israel both to deny what may seem right and expedient to oneself and to obey Yahweh even when the final outcome cannot be foreseen and assessed from a merely human perspective. Israel must trust Yahweh to be wiser than Israel in all the decrees of his law' (2002: 39–40). Ibn Ezra puts it penetratingly (1999: 124):

> The eye sees and the heart desires. The fringes thus serve as a sign and a mark that a person should not pursue the thoughts of his heart and all that his eyes desire. For one who follows his desires goes astray from the service of his God.

This is wisdom, for, 'There is a way that seems right to a man, but its end is the ways of death' (Prov. 14:12; 16:25).

The tassels command is repeated by Moses in Deuteronomy (22:12), and has been taken in Judaism as the highest command inasmuch as it aims at the remembrance and fulfilment of all commandments – the tassel 'signified the whole law' (Stephens 1931: 59). Many Jewish people therefore recite the tassel passage daily, morning and evening, as part of the Shema prayer (which includes Num. 15:37–41; Deut. 6:4–9; 11:13–21) (on the origins of the Shema recital, see Kohler 1919). The tassels law, especially as formulated in Deuteronomy 22:12 within the context of forbidden mixtures (vv. 9–11; cf. Lev. 19:19), has been understood as an exception to the prohibition against wearing garments of 'mixed material' (ša'aṭnēz), particularly wool and linen. 'The separation between the high priest and other priests and laypeople was maintained in part', writes Imes (2019: 38), 'by the prohibition of wool and linen blends in common clothing.' Since otherwise, ša'aṭnēz is used only for the garments and turban of the high priest and for the sanctuary, Milgrom contends that ša'aṭnēz refers to 'a holy mixture', explaining why it is normally forbidden for the rest of Israel, with the singular tassels exception serving to encourage all Israel to aspire to the high priest's holiness (1990: 413). Emphasizing the 'communalization' of the high priest's holiness, Spoelstra summarizes the parallels between the tassels and the high priest's rosette diadem (2019: 69–70). (See Table 24.)

The transformation of Israel is significant: before this legislative response by YHWH, the high priest was the only Israelite who wore tzit-accessories, and the only one donning the colour blue.

41. The verse begins and ends with the same declaration verbatim: 'I myself am YHWH your God', one part of the threefold covenant formula I will be your God, you will be my people, and I will dwell in your midst (cf. Morales 2015: 103–106). Echoing the prologue to the Decalogue (Exod. 20:2), the tassel law reinforces the appropriate response to his

Table 24: Israel's tassels and the high priest's diadem

Israel's tassels	High Priest's diadem (and vestments)
The tassels must have a blue cord (pĕtîl tĕkēlet), Num. 15:38	The rosette must be affixed to the turban with a blue cord (pĕtîl tĕkēlet), Exod. 28:37; 39:31
The ultimate purpose of the tassels is for Israel to be 'holy unto God' (qĕdōšîm lē'lōhêkem), Num. 15:40	The inscription on the golden rosette is 'holy unto YHWH' (qōdeš layhwh), Exod. 28:36; 39:30
The 'tassels' (ṣîṣit) may well resemble a rosette	The golden diadem was shaped as a rosette (ṣîṣ)
The tassel is sha'atnez, involving the mixture of wool and linen	The high priest's vestments involved the holy mixture of sha'atnez

glory-manifesting deliverance; namely, the first commandment: 'You shall have no other gods before me' (Exod. 20:3), as well as the comprehensive obedience to the whole Decalogue for which every Israelite should strive. But verse 41 also concludes the tassel law (and the outer camp section, chs. 11–15) on the note of YHWH's commitment to his people – 'I, who brought you out of Egypt in order to be your God, I myself am YHWH your God.' The affirmation is significant after the first generation's attempt to reverse the exodus and return to Egypt (cf. Olson 1996: 97). In the light of the prolonged judgement of God throughout the forty-year wilderness period, during which the first generation would know his hostility (14:34), Israel was assured that Moses' prayer had indeed been answered (14:13–19), that YHWH remained fully committed to Israel and to carrying out his agenda for the world through Abraham's seed. The original purpose of the exodus – 'to be your God' – continues, which means that Israel has been recommissioned as the covenant community of YHWH.

Explanation

Within the context of Israel's dismal failures and rebellions in the wilderness (chs. 11–14), especially of the scouts episode and YHWH's consequent judgement on the first generation (chs. 13–14), Numbers 15 functions as reassurance of God's intentions and of Israel's renewed calling. The various materials are unified at a deep level by this function, in three broad sections: (1) seven laws for life in the land (vv. 1–31), (2) a tale of warning in the wilderness (vv. 32–36), and (3) a practical law of application, encouraging Israel to pursue obedience and holiness (vv. 37–41). In the first part of the first section, YHWH, through Moses, designates the required accompaniments for whole burnt and peace offerings, giving Israel a message of hope and comfort that life in the land will indeed be attained, an abundant life marked by plentiful quantities of flour, oil and wine – along with many domesticated animals: sheep, rams and cattle (vv. 1–16). The wine libations function as a reversal of the sin of the scouts and a reaffirmation of the path of the Nazirite vow for Israel's journey through the wilderness. The central law on the bread contribution seals the end of the wilderness era marked by the provision of manna, when Israelites will be able to make bread for themselves from the land, acknowledging YHWH with thanksgiving (vv. 17–21). Through Moses, YHWH further comforts his people by reassuring them that their unintentional sins may be remedied through the cult and be forgiven freely (vv. 22–29), even as he also warns of high-handed rebellion, which will result in one's being cut off from among God's people and a failure to inherit the land (vv. 30–31).

In section two, the previous warning against high-handed sin is soberly and soundly upheld in the wilderness tale of the Sabbath wood-gatherer (vv. 32–36), who symbolizes the first generation of Israel that spurned YHWH's promise of rest in the land, preferring the straw-gathering oppression of Egypt instead. Lastly and by way of practical application, YHWH encourages Israel to pursue their high and holy calling as his people, ennobling and reminding them of their royal and priestly status, directing them to make for themselves tassels with a blue cord on the wings of their garments (vv. 37–41), an apparel feature which, thus far, has only been worn by the high priest. The tassel serves as a mnemonic device for remembering their priestly calling and privilege, resisting the wayward impulse of their hearts so as to follow YHWH closely, obeying his commandments in the pursuit of holiness. Both the community's obedient response to the Sabbath gatherer, and the community's charge to make a tassel 'for yourselves' rounds out the chapter with a focus on the whole community, rectifying the community's rebellion in the scouts episode. The ritual laws 'are directed *solely* to the people', as T. S. Clark observes (2014: 99–100), with the requirements calculated to enable them to 'respond to the disobedience manifested in Numbers 13–14'.

Throughout the section on the outer camp of twelve tribes (chs. 11–15), the primary focus and challenge remains in relation to the prophetic office of Moses, in heeding YHWH's *torah*. It is no surprise, then, that the present chapter is filled with admonitions to obey YHWH's commands, including provision for when you unintentionally 'do not do all these commands which YHWH spoke to Moses, all that YHWH had commanded you by the hand of Moses from the day that YHWH commanded and henceforth throughout your generations' (v. 22–23), a dreadful judgement on a soul 'for the word of YHWH he has despised, and his command he has broken' (31), a tale where 'the whole community' did 'just as YHWH had commanded Moses' (36), and the donning of tassels to help Israelites remember to 'do all my commands' (40). Through use of terms like 'search out' (*tûr*) and 'whoredom' (*zĕnût*), the tassel law evokes the scouts episode, *the* failure of the outer camp, supporting the law's intention for the tassel to serve as a remedy for preventing another such national disaster of faithless disobedience. Living according to YHWH's commands will enable Israel to function as a holy nation, knowing his blessings.

Taken together, the chapter's materials set before Israel two paths: attaining the abundant life in the land through loyalty to YHWH, or being cut off from the covenant community and life in the land through wilful rebellion against him. One reason 15:22–31 mentions only two categories of sin, either unintentional or defiant, is to make clear that there are only two paths (Sklar 2012: 485). These two paths are further juxtaposed with the Sabbath gatherer (vv. 32–36) and the tassel law (vv. 37–41). As with the paths of the wayward woman (5:11–31) versus the

Nazirite (6:1–21), set before Israel for the wilderness sojourn, so here two paths are set before Israel once more, now within the context of their forty year judgement in the wilderness: either disloyalty, marked by the Sabbath wood-gatherer (vv. 32–36) and 'whoredom' (v. 39), or loyalty, expressed through obedience and the pursuit of holiness (vv. 37–41). The essence of the gift of the Sabbath, a sign that it is YHWH who *sanctifies* Israel (Exod. 31:13), aligns with the purpose for making the tassel and placing it on the wings of the garment, and forms the antithesis to the Sabbath gatherer. Moreover, as the Nazirite law had set before all Israelites, whether male or female, the possibility of attaining holiness akin to that of the high priest himself, so the tassels function in a similar way now. The tassels' resemblance to the high priest's turban and other clothing, writes Milgrom (1990: 413), is not accidental, but results from a conscious attempt to encourage all Israel to aspire to a degree of holiness comparable to that of the priests, in accord with YHWH's repeated declarations 'You shall be holy, for I, YHWH your God, am holy' (Lev. 19:2; cf. 11:44: 20:26). Rather than straying after their hearts and eyes, to go 'whoring' (*zĕnût*) along the wayward path of the strayed woman, Israelites are called to belong to YHWH ever more deeply, growing in obedience and holiness, to delight in Sabbath communion and fellowship with YHWH, and so begin to fulfil their vocation to be a kingdom of priests and holy nation (Exod. 19:6). Wearing the tassels transforms Israel's clothing into uniforms of the royal priests of YHWH God (Milgrom 1990: 127). The wings of Jewish garments appear in Zechariah's prophecy whereby 'ten men from every language of the nations will grasp hold of the (garment) wing of Judean man, saying, "Let us go with you, for we have heard that God is with you"' (Zech. 8:23). In the Greek version, tassels are translated with *kraspedon*, which is used in the Gospels for Jesus' tassels: a woman with a twelve-year issue of blood grasped the tassel of his garment and was healed (Matt. 9:20–22; Luke 8:44). Many of the sick among the villages, cities, and countryside of Judea found deliverance by grasping our Saviour's tassel (Mark 6:56) – there was indeed healing in his wings (see Mal. 4:2).

Three aspects especially – the 'wings', 'blue cord' and 'be holy to your God' – form strong associations with the holiest place, objects and person of the cult, renewing Israel's call to embrace a Nazirite-like approach to the wilderness sojourn – a call that opens the chapter with the gift by fire offerings to YHWH (vv. 1–16), which allude to the Nazirite vow twice with *pallē'-neder* (15:3, 8; cf. 6:2). The sacrifices in the land, including the accompaniments of tribute (grain) and 'wine' or 'strong drink' (*yayin, nesek*), also portray the land at the end of the wilderness sojourn in a way that recalls the culmination of the Nazirite vow. The wilderness sojourn, as a time of probation and deprivation (chs. 11–25) is followed by a life of abundance in the land, marked by fire offerings with accompaniments of grain and wine and the fulfilment of vows (chs. 28–30) – this is the pattern for the Nazirite vow (6:13–18), including Israel's setback that required a cleansing from corpse pollution and a new start for the second generation (ch. 19; see 6:9–12).

Chapter 15 begins with YHWH's reaffirmation that he will bring his people into the land of Canaan, and ends with divine assurance that, despite the scouts episode and his judgement of the first generation, YHWH remains Israel's God. The laws confirm, therefore, that the *telos* of Israel's exodus out of Egypt; namely, the covenant relationship with YHWH God in the land as a dais for Israel's vocation among the nations, has been restored. YHWH remains committed to his people, and his people are encouraged to recommit themselves to him wholeheartedly, to embrace their calling to obey his commands and to be a holy people. Throughout the chapter, the role of sacrifice, the need for obedience to divine commands, and the status of the sojourner (or 'resident alien') among God's people in the land are underscored. The sojourner's place within YHWH's laws remind Israel of its purpose among the peoples to be a holy nation. In short, the path of the Nazirite vow is set before Israel – the outer camp of twelve tribes – once more.

NUMBERS 16 – 17: THE REBELLION AND JUDGEMENT OF THE INNER CAMP

Translation

[1]Now Korah, the son of Izhar the son of Kohath the son of Levi, took, and Dathan and Abiram, the sons of Eliab, and On, the son of Peleth, sons of Reuben, [2]and they rose up before Moses, with men from the sons of Israel, two hundred and fifty chieftains of the community, called ones of the appointed-council, men of name. [3]And they assembled against Moses and against Aaron, and said to them, 'Too much for yourselves! for all the community – every one of them – is holy, and YHWH is in the midst of them. Why do you lift up yourselves above the assembly of YHWH?'

[4]And Moses heard, and he fell upon his face. [5]And he spoke to Korah and to all his community, saying, 'In the morning YHWH will cause you to know who belongs to him and is holy and to be brought near to him, and him whom he chooses he will bring near to him. [6]Do this: take for yourselves censers, Korah and all his community, [7]and put fire in them and place incense on them before YHWH tomorrow; and it will be that the man whom YHWH chooses, he is the holy one. Too much for yourselves, sons of Levi!'

[8]And Moses said to Korah, 'Hear now sons of Levi, [9]Is it too small a thing for you that the God of Israel has separated you from the community of Israel to bring you near to himself to work in the labour

of the Dwelling of YHWH, and to stand before the community to minister to them? ¹⁰And he brought you near, and all of your brothers, the sons of Levi, with you – now you seek the priesthood also? ¹¹For thus you and all your community have met together against YHWH – and Aaron, what is he that you grumble against him?'

¹²And Moses sent to call for Dathan and for Abiram, the sons of Eliab, and they said, 'We will not ascend! ¹³Is it too small a thing that you have caused us to ascend out of a land that flows with milk and honey, in order to kill us in the wilderness, that you make yourself ruler over us to rule also? ¹⁴Indeed, to a land flowing with milk and honey you have not brought us, nor given us an inheritance of field and vineyard – will you gouge out the eyes of these men? We will not ascend!'

¹⁵And Moses was kindled greatly, and said to YHWH, 'Do not turn favorably to their tribute – not one donkey from them have I carried off, nor have I done evil to one of them!'

¹⁶And Moses said to Korah, 'You and all your community be before YHWH, you and they and Aaron, tomorrow. ¹⁷And take each man his censer and put incense on them, and bring near before YHWH each man his censer, two hundred and fifty censers, and you and Aaron, each man his censer.'

¹⁸And each man took his censer and put fire on them, placed incense on them, and stood at the door of the Tent of Meeting, with Moses and Aaron. ¹⁹And Korah assembled against them the whole community to the door of the Tent of Meeting, and the glory of YHWH appeared to all the community.

²⁰And YHWH spoke to Moses and to Aaron, saying, ²¹'Separate yourselves from the midst of this community – I will finish them in an instant.'

²²But they fell on their faces, and said, 'O El, God of the spirits of all flesh, will one man sin and you be angry with the whole community?'

²³And YHWH spoke to Moses, saying, ²⁴'Speak to the community, saying, "Ascend from around the dwelling of Korah, Dathan and Abiram."' ²

⁵And Moses arose and went to Dathan and Abiram, and the elders of Israel went after him. ²⁶And he spoke to the community, saying, 'Turn aside, now, from the tents of these wicked men, and do not touch anything that belongs to them, lest you be swept away with all their sins.'

²⁷And they ascended from the dwelling of Korah, Dathan and Abiram, from all around, but Dathan and Abiram came forth and stood at the door of their tents, and their wives, and their sons, and their little ones. ²⁸And Moses said, 'By this you will know that YHWH has sent me to do all these works, that it was not from my own heart. ²⁹If like the death of every human these die, or if what is appointed for every human is appointed for them, then it was not YHWH who sent me. ³⁰But if a new thing YHWH will create, and the ground opens her mouth and swallows

them up, with all that belongs to them, and they descend alive to *Sheol*, then you will know that these men have spurned YHWH.'

[31]And it happened when he finished to speak all these words, the ground that was under them cleaved open. [32]And the earth opened her mouth and swallowed them up, and their houses, and every human that belonged to Korah, and all the possessions. [33]And they and all that belonged to them descended alive to *Sheol*, and the earth covered over them, and they perished from the midst of the assembly. [34]And all Israel who were around them fled at their voice, for they said, 'Lest the earth swallow us up!' [35]Now a fire had come forth from YHWH, and consumed the two hundred and fifty, each man bringing near the incense.

[36]And YHWH spoke to Moses, saying, [37]'Say to Eleazar the son of Aaron the priest, that he raise up the censers from amid the burning, and scatter the fire away, for they are holy. [38]The censers of these sinners against their souls, they will make them hammered-out plates, a covering for the altar, for they brought them near before YHWH and (so) they are holy. Let them be for a sign for the sons of Israel.'

[39]And Eleazar the priest took the bronze censers that were brought near by the burned-up ones, and they were hammered out as a covering for the altar, [40]a memorial for the sons of Israel so that any stranger who is not of the seed of Aaron he will not come near to offer incense as smoke before YHWH, and he will not be like Korah and like his community, just as YHWH had spoken by the hand of Moses to him.

[41]But the whole community of the sons of Israel grumbled the next day against Moses and against Aaron, saying, 'You have killed the people of YHWH!'

[42]And it happened when the community assembled against Moses and against Aaron, and they turned to the Tent of Meeting – look! – the Cloud covered it, and the glory of YHWH appeared. [43]And Moses came, and Aaron, to the front of the Tent of Meeting. [44]Now YHWH spoke to Moses, saying, [45]'Arise from the midst of this community, and I will finish them in an instant.'

And they fell on their faces. [46]And Moses said to Aaron, 'Take the censer and put fire on it from the altar, and place incense, and go quickly to the community and make atonement for them, for the wrath from before YHWH has gone forth – the plague has begun!'

[47]And Aaron took just as Moses had spoken, and ran to the midst of the assembly, and – look! – the plague had begun among the people! And he put the incense and made atonement for the people. [48]And he stood between the dying and the living, and the plague was stayed. [49]Now those who died in the plague were fourteen thousand seven hundred, aside from those who died in the incident of Korah. [50]And Aaron returned to Moses to the door of the Tent of Meeting, but the plague was stayed.

^{17:1}Now YHWH spoke to Moses, saying, ²"Speak to the sons of Israel, and take from each of them a staff, a staff for the house of a father from all their chieftains, according to the house of their fathers, twelve staffs – each man's name you will write upon his staff. ³But the name of Aaron you will write upon the staff of Levi, for there will be one staff for the head of the house of their fathers. ⁴And you will rest them in the Tent of Meeting, before the Testimony, there where I will meet with you (all). ⁵And it will be that the man whom I choose, his staff will sprout; so I will cause to abate from me the grumblings of the sons of Israel whereby they are grumbling against you (all).'

⁶And Moses spoke to the sons of Israel, and all their chieftains gave to him a staff for every single chieftain, a staff for every single chieftain according to the house of their fathers, twelve staffs – but the staff of Aaron was in the midst of their staffs. ⁷And Moses rested the staffs before YHWH in the Tent of the Testimony. ⁸And it happened on the following day Moses went into the Tent of the Testimony, and – look! – the staff of Aaron for the house of Levi had sprouted, and brought forth flower-buds and bloomed blossoms and yielded almonds. ⁹And Moses brought forth all the staffs from before YHWH to all the sons of Israel, and they looked and took, each man his staff.   ¹⁰And YHWH said to Moses, 'Return the staff of Aaron before the Testimony, to be kept for a sign for the sons of rebellion, and let their grumblings finish against me, and they will not die.'

¹¹And Moses did so, just as YHWH had commanded him, just so he did.

¹²And the sons of Israel said to Moses, saying, 'Look! We perish! We are destroyed – all of us are destroyed! ¹³Whoever draws near – even draws near – to the Dwelling of YHWH will die! Are we to perish completely?'

Notes on the text

16:1. The ensuing absence of On prompts the suggestion that 'and On' should be dropped as dittography (Budd 1984: 180) – if so, it happened early since LXX includes 'and On'. 'Peleth' appears interchangeable with 'Pallu' (see 28:5, 8); 'sons of Reuben', pl. in MT, is sg. in SamP and LXX.

The opening verb 'took' (*wayyiqqaḥ*) has no object, a long-standing conundrum (see Richter 1921; Meek 1929: 167–168), probably a literary device (cf. 16:47). Many translations supply 'men', as proposed by Ibn Ezra (cf. 1999: 127), perhaps 'sons of Levi' (vv. 7, 8, 10). NIV has 'became insolent', based on a term that uses the same consonants, preferred by some (Snaith 1967: 255–256; Noth 1968: 122–123; Budd 1984: 180), but arguments based on Job 15:12 are unconvincing. LXX has 'and he spoke' (*elalēsan*), Syr and Tg have 'and he was divided', while *BHS* suggests emending to 'and he arose', matching v. 2 (for 'became rebellious', based on a Greek reading, see Meek 1929: 167–168). The verb 'to take' (*lāqaḥ*) recurs (16:1, 6, 17, 18, 39, 46, 47, etc.), which may be argued equally for retaining it here or for a copyist's mistake (cf. *BHS*).

3. 'lift up yourselves' (*titnaśśĕ'û*): in the hith., the term designates establishing oneself in the role of prince (GKC §54e; cf. 1 Kgs 1:5).

4. 'he fell upon his face': *BHS* suggests emending to 'his face fell' (cf. Gen. 4:5).

8. 'Hear now': LXX has 'listen to me' (*Eisakousate mou*).

15. 'their tribute': *BHS* suggests emending to 'groaning' or 'sighing'.

24. 'dwelling of Korah': *BHS* suggests emending to 'Dwelling of YHWH', missing the point that Korah has his own rival 'community' (*'ădātô*, v. 5) (cf. Budd 1984: 181), and the change would make the presence of 'Dathan and Abiram' unintelligible (cf. v. 27). LXX reads 'congregation' (*synagōgē*) here and in v. 27.

26. 'swept away' (*sāpāh*): reads as 'come to an end' (*sûp*) by LXX. If *sûp* were correct, it might function as an anti-exodus motif (Exod. 2:3, 5; 10:19; 13:18; 15:4, 22).

30. 'with all that belongs to them': LXX adds 'and their houses and their tents' before this phrase.

32. 'her mouth' (*pîhā*): missing from LXX, perhaps avoiding anthropomorphism.

39. 'Eleazar the priest': SamP and LXX also have 'son of Aaron' (as with v. 37).

44. LXX adds 'and Aaron' here and in vv. 23, 26, aligned with the pl. of the next verse (45) (on accentuating Aaron over Korah, see Findlay 2006).

17:2. 'twelve staffs': *BHS* suggests adding the final clause of the next verse ('for there will be one staff'), an unwarranted alteration.

4. 'meet with you (all)': four MT MSS, SamP, LXX and Vg read 'you' as singular (Exod. 25:22; 30:6, 36; but Exod. 29:42 has pl.).

6. Vg clarifies that Aaron's staff was counted separately from the twelve (*absque virga Aaron*).

10. 'finish': *BHS* suggests qal *tēkel*, a plausible if unnecessary change (cf. Exod. 39:32).

13. 'Whoever draws near': missing from LXX, Syr and Vg. MT seems redundant. *BHS* suggests a duplication (cf. Paterson 1900: 52).

Form and structure

The Masoretes marked 17:5, with its vindication of Aaron's priesthood, as the exact midpoint of Numbers. In the midst of the rebellion and death of the wilderness section proper (chs. 11–25), one finds a life-out-of-death sign – a branch blossoms and springs forth with almonds. *Chapters 16–18 particularly have the inner camp of Levites in focus,* their relationship both to the outer camp of twelve tribes and to the priesthood of Aaron's house, as divinely designed for the well-being of the covenant community, the Camp of Israel. Some argue that Numbers 16 – 17 forms the literary and theological centre of Numbers (see M. Douglas 2001: 118, 122, 130–135).

Numbers 16 – 17, writes Pyschny (2018: 117), 'is rightly considered one of the most puzzling murmuring stories of the Pentateuch'. Mainstream scholarship has long seen Numbers 16 and 17 as a composite work, integrating a political and Levitical revolt (cf. e.g. Kuenen 1878; G. B. Gray 1903: 186–187; Liver 1961; Gunneweg 1965: 175–177; Coats 1968: 156–162; Nicholson 1998: 17–19; Achenbach 2003b: 37–39; Knohl 2007: 73–85; Jeon 2015), typically read as ideological propaganda by post-exilic priests, reflecting the conflicts and power struggles that arose within the Jerusalem cult (e.g. Noth 1968: 196; Hutton 1992: 101; Levine 1993: 67; Jeon 2015), although Levites are never denigrated in Numbers. Chapter 16 presents two distinguishable revolts (and Num. 27:3 refers only to Korah and his company, while Deut. 11:6 refers only to Dathan and Abiram), yet it is an unwarranted leap to presume they derive from two independent traditions and that if only the one is mentioned elsewhere it is because the other was unknown (contra Baden 2013a), for the separate stories cannot stand alone (see Liver 1961: 194; G. J. Wenham 1981b: 157–159). The parallel plot heightens the story's rhetorical effect, increasing 'the complexity and the virulence of the conflict' (cf. Marguerat and Bourquin 1999: 54), and the two-front assault is inter-woven *logically* as well: Moses' divine authority is the basis for the consecration of Aaron's house as a priesthood, so Korah's contest for the priesthood requires the undermining of Moses' role by the sons of Reuben. Nevertheless, it is not without reason this section has been called a parade example of a difficult text (R. S. Briggs 2018: 129), and questions remain: What did Korah take? Who is On and where did he go? How many Levites were involved in Korah's rebellion? How did Korah die? Along with challenging features and ambiguities, however unresolved, the text also displays intentional artistry and unifying literary features, suggesting that some of the story's perplexities may be deliberate (cf. Alter 1981: 133–137; Taylor 2010: 209). Intriguingly, Moses' own ploy as a character 'seems to be to separate out the various groups who have banded together, and define their specific objections, the overt ones and the hidden ones' (Magonet 1982: 18) – perhaps, in detecting junctures and unravelling plotlines, the critic's sleuthing may be a tracing of Moses' experience, the intended effect of literary art.

Structurally, chapters 16 and 17 recount three episodes, all of which serve to vindicate the priesthood of Aaron (G. J. Wenham 1981b: 150; 1981a), along with its source, Moses' prophetic office. The first story vindicates Aaron in a twofold negative manner (16:1–35), demonstrating that others who approach YHWH with incense as priestly mediators will be consumed, *and* that those who challenge Moses' divine authority will be destroyed. The second story vindicates Aaron in a positive manner (16:36–50), demonstrating that through Aaron's own offering of incense before YHWH, Israel may be atoned and spared the wrath of God. The third story (17:1–13), involving a divinely orchestrated symbolic ritual whereby Aaron's rod buds and sprouts almonds, definitively closes the question of whom YHWH has chosen to draw near him as priest, for Israel's own sake. The three episodes are paralleled not only in theme, but also in structure, with each story taking place over the period of two days (G. J. Wenham 1981b: 150): the first two begin with the people's protest against Moses and Aaron, and conclude with a divine judgement that vindicates Aaron, while the third story reverses the order, beginning with YHWH's vindication of Aaron and concluding with the people's crying out to Moses. The rebellions are especially directed at Moses, since his authority is the basis for Aaron's role as high priest, and, as Moses points out (16:11), they are ultimately attacks on the person and character of YHWH himself who sent Moses. Seldom appreciated, the second story responds to the incense plot of the first story, while the third resolves the Dathan and Abiram storyline: Aaron's censer brings life, reversing the image of death through the hammered-out censers of the 250 princes; and Aaron's rod becomes a life-out-of-death symbol, reversing Dathan and Abiram's descending into *Sheol* alive (see Y. Twersky 2007b: 2:176–177). The first storyline underscores the efficacy of Aaron's priesthood, while the second demonstrates the divine authority of Aaron's priesthood, that Aaron's house was indeed chosen by YHWH through Moses.

Several key terms unite these chapters, often connecting chapters 16–20 as a whole.

Table 25: Key terms in Numbers 16 – 20

Terms	Numbers 16 – 20
lāqaḥ, 'to take'	16:1, 6, 17, 18, 39, 46, 47; 17:2, 9; 18:6, 26, 28; 19:2, 4, 6, 17, 18; 20:8, 9, 25
qādôš, 'holy'	16:3, 5, 7, 37, 38; 18:1, 3, 5, 8, 9 *four times*, 10 *three times*, 16, 17, 19, 29, 32; 19:20; 20:1, 12, 13, 14, 16, 22
qārab, 'draw near'	16:5 (twice), 9, 10, 17, 35, 38, 39, 40, 17:13 (twice); 18:2, 3, 4, 7, 9, 15, 22
bāḥar, 'to choose'	16:5, 7; 17:5
mût, 'to die'	16:13, 29 (twice), 41, 48, 49; 17:10, 13; 18:3, 7, 22, 32; 19:11, 13 (twice), 14, 16, 18; 20:1, 4, 26, 28
qāṣap, qeṣep, 'wrath'	16:22, 46; 18:5

Some of these terms are distributed regularly outside of chapters 16–20, but (draw near), for example, does not appear again until 24:17, while *qādôš* (holy), which appears five times in chapter 20, does not occur again until 27:14, and the root of *bāḥar* (choose) is found only once outside of chapters 16–17, in 11:28. The key words 'to take' and 'draw near' thematically develop the main storyline of Korah and his community, as they desire the priestly prerogative to draw near to YHWH. The narrative begins when Korah 'took', revolves around the cultic test of 'drawing near' to YHWH with censers (which they have 'taken'), which leads to their being consumed by YHWH's fire, and continues into the second episode where Aaron saves Israelites from a divine plague by 'taking' a censer, and culminates in the third episode with Israelites crying out that 'whoever draws near – even draws near – to the Dwelling of YHWH will die!' resolving the original presumption of Korah. The parallel rebellion of the sons of Reuben develops thematically through the key word 'ascend', not only in the complaint that Moses had caused them to 'ascend' out of Egypt with malicious intent, but also in their repeated defiance, 'We will not ascend!' The conflict resolves with their 'descending' alive into *Sheol*. One result of the interwoven plotline is that the emphasis of these chapters as a whole (chs. 16–19) remains focused on the priesthood, with chapter 20 then narrating the transition from the high priest of the first generation, Aaron, to the high priest for the second generation, Eleazar.

Several *hinnê* (look, behold) statements occur at key points in the material:

16:42: Look! The Cloud covered the Tent of Meeting and the glory of YHWH appeared!
16:47: Look! The plague began among the people!
17:8: Look! The staff of Aaron of the house of Levi sprouted!
17:12: Look! We perish!

18:6: Look! I have taken your brothers, the Levites.
18:8: Look! I have given you (Aaron) charge of my contribution offerings.
18:21: Look! I have given the sons of Levi all the tithe of Israel as an inheritance.

20:16: Look! We are in Kadesh!

The *hinnê* particle offers the audience a subjective view from the character's eyes, rather than the narrator's disconnected vantage, lending a sense of dramatic focus – 'the spectator's discovery and amazement are being introduced' (Fokkelman 1999: 140; cf. A. Berlin 1983: 62). Finally, seven rhetorical questions lend unity to chapters 16–17 (Taylor 2010: 132):

16:3: Why do you lift up yourselves against the assembly of YHWH?

16:9: Is it too small a thing for you that God as separated you (Korah) and the sons of Levi with you?

16:10: Do you seek the priesthood also?

16:11: Aaron – what is he that you grumble against him?

16:14: Will you gouge out the eyes of these men?

16:22: God of the spirits of all flesh, will one man sin and you be angry with the whole community?

17:13: Are we to perish completely?

The last question resolves the narrative inasmuch as the people are brought to the proper fear of YHWH and his holiness, ready now to receive what YHWH has established in order that his people not die in his presence; namely, the priesthood and Levites in their role as substitutes for firstborn sons of Israel. Thus, the answer to their final question is given in chapter 18.

The 'quinary scheme', which expands Aristotle's complication and denouement (*Poetics* 18) to exposition, complication, transforming action, denouement, and final situation (cf. Marguerat and Bourquin 1999: 43), will form the basis of my outline (with slight variation), as set forth by Taylor (2010: 210). (See Table 26.)

The first two plotlines are resolution in type, narrating the undoing of a conflict, while the last story's plot type is revelatory, expanding the reader's knowledge (Taylor 2010: 210; cf. Marguerat and Bourquin 1999: 56), forming a final resolution of conflict, making clear YHWH's choice of Aaron as high priest. Note that the Masoretes added a major paragraph break after 16:35, followed by 17:1 in MT rather than, as in English versions, 16:36. This feature leads us to link the denouement and final situation of the first story (16:36–40) more closely with the second story, as its contextual backdrop. Incorporating these verses into the second story also fits the pattern of two days for each of the accounts (16:41). We will follow the standard delineations for these stories – (1) 16:1–35, (2) 16:36–50, (3) 17:1–13 – while treating 16:36–40

Table 26: Quinary scheme for Numbers 16 – 17

Quinary scheme	Korah's rebellion	Israel's rebellion	Aaron's staff
Exposition	16:1–2	16:41	17:1–5
Complication	16:3–30	16:42–46	17:6–7
Transforming action	16:31–35	16:47	17:8–9
Denouement	16:36–38	16:48	17:10–11
Final situation	16:39–40	16:49–50	17:12–13
Plot type	Resolution	Resolution	Revelatory
Protagonist	Moses/YHWH	Aaron/YHWH	YHWH

as an overlapping section with dual functions, closing the first story and setting up the second.

Comment

16:1–35 Episode one: Korah's rebellion against Moses and Aaron

1–2. That four generations are traced out for Korah, signalling his prominence, cannot be without exegetical significance. In Exodus 6:14–25, the lines of Reuben, Simeon, and Levi are given, also tracing Izhar's line with detail. Magonet avers that Izhar's lineage functions to provide a 'cast list and essential background for the Korah rebellion' (1982: 5). Korah, the firstborn of Izhar, was first cousins with Aaron and Moses. The root of his name means something like 'baldhead' or 'bare' (see Lev. 13:40, 42, 43, 55; 21:5; Deut. 14:1; etc.). As a firstborn son, he likely lost his priestly privileges to Aaron's newly established priesthood. Moreover, given that the priesthood was led by Aaron (the firstborn son of Kohath's first son, Amram), it would have been natural for Levites to have been led by Korah (the firstborn son of Kohath's second son, Izhar), but, as we discover in 3:30, it was Elizaphan (the second son of Kohath's fourth son, Uzziel) who was put in charge over the Kohathite house. The construction of the inner camp (chs. 3–4) forms a key for interpreting its conflict and resolution (chs. 16–18). A long history of Jewish interpretation has thus seen Korah's rebellion as directly related to the replacement of the firstborn by Levites, intensified by the slight to him regarding the leadership of the Kohathite house: 'As for Amram the firstborn, his son Aaron attained to greatness (high priest) and Moses to royalty. Who then should rightly take the next office? . . . yet Moses appointed the son of Uzziel!' (*Num. Rab.* 18.2; for a reception history of Korah's rebellion, see B. P. Luther 2011; Biale 2016). Although he is singled out in the text, Korah never speaks for himself alone, but only as part of the gathering once (v. 3) – yet the story begins with his particular act, he took.

With the loss of firstborn rights in view it cannot come as a surprise to find Dathan and Abiram, and On in revolt, since they are 'sons of Reuben', firstborn son of Jacob, and would have felt the drastic change most deeply and could have demanded the priesthood on the broadest basis (Oehler 1950: 201), aside from political leadership, although this had already been denied by Jacob (Gen. 48:5; 49:3–4; 1 Chr.5:1). The 'leadership of Moses in itself', writes Liver (1961: 205), 'meant dispossession of Reuben from his time-honoured position'. Moreover, while the tribe of Reuben is listed first, as the firstborn son, in the opening census list (1:5), Judah was given the prominent place of encampment (2:3), a perceived slight. Not only are Korah and the sons of Reuben united by common cause, in the loss of firstborn privileges, but Numbers also places them together: the camp of Reuben was on the south side of the Dwelling (2:10), the same side, in the Levitical area, where the house of Kohath encamped (3:29). The ancient rabbis, picking up on these clues, portray the two groups united in rebellion after having fed on each other's discontent within the Camp (*Num. Rab.* 18.5). On, son of Peleth, does not appear again, either in this story or elsewhere in Scripture, presenting an enigma. The range of meaning for his name (*'wn*) includes 'sorrow', 'iniquity' and 'strength' or 'vigour'; the name of Judah's son, Onan, is similar (Gen. 38:4), as is Potipherah priest of On (Gen. 41:50), whose daughter Asenath Joseph married. Since he drops out as a character, the narrative emphasizes the complicity of Dathan and Abiram primarily. Jewish tradition fills the gap with a story of how On's wife prevented him from joining the rebellion any further, and that he lived up to his name, 'mourning' his original share in the revolt (*Num. Rab.* 18.20; *San.* 110a). The Midrash further identifies Dathan and Abiram with the two truculent Hebrews who even back in Egypt had challenged Moses' authority, saying, 'Who made you prince and judge over us?!' (Exod. 2:14; note use of *śar*). For ancient rabbis, Dathan and Abiram became pegs to hang every pair of hoodlums in Scripture: 'Whatever you can hang on this wicked pair, hang it!' (*Yalk. Shim.*, Exodus 167). When, for instance, after the scouts returned and brought back an evil report, so that 'each man said to his brother, "Let us return to Egypt,"' those two brothers were said to be Dathan and Abiram (Num. 14:4; *Exod. Rab.* 1.30), and they were also the 'some' who hoarded manna (Exod. 16:20; *Tan.*, *T'tzaveh* 11), and so on (Magonet 1982: 6–7). As a political challenge to the authority of Moses, the sons of Reuben may well have constituted a military faction staging a coup – the description of their emerging from their tents and 'taking their stand' (*niṣṣābîm*) in 16:27 might even imply taking up arms in military readiness (Nahmani 1964: 129–131; Magonet 1982: 8; cf. 1 Sam. 17:16). While we may distinguish the parallel lines of rebellion as 'religious' in character, in relation to Korah and his community, and as 'political', in relation to the sons of Reuben, ancient Israelites would not likely have acknowledged as sharp a distinction (see Liver 1961: 189–217). Nevertheless, and although Moses leads the response in both cases, the different locales for the narrative drama and the diverse judgements do distinguish between Korah's bid for priesthood, and the defiance of Moses' leadership by the sons of Reuben.

The third group of insurgents, 'men from the sons of Israel', are described elaborately as 'chieftains' (*nāśî'*) of the 'community' (*'ēdāh*), called ones of the 'appointed-council' (*mô'ēd*), and famous men – literally 'men of name'. They are leaders among the nation's representatives who would meet to make decisions related to the community; gifted political leaders from Israel's nobility, well-able to lead the nation. The designation 'called ones of the appointed-council' appears to be a variation on a similar title 'called ones of the community' (*qĕrû'ê hā'ēdāh*), given for the leaders who helped with the census (1:16), a title that applies also to Dathan and Abiram (see 26:9) (cf. Magonet 1982: 9). 'Called' probably refers to being 'summoned' for appointed meetings. Achenbach understands the phrase as 'dignitaries of the community who were responsible for the appointed festival-times' (2013: 217). The terms *'ēdāh* and *mô'ēd*, associating these leaders with the cult, begin the text's deliberate presentation of Korah's rebellion as forming a substitute cult, a pseudo covenant community – note use of *'ēdāh* in verses 5, 6, 11, 16 (cf. Noth 1968: 124). That these are 'men of name' reminds one of a similar expression in Genesis 6:4, *'anšê haššēm*, the infamous progeny of the sons of God and daughters of men whose wickedness incited God's judgement, bringing on the Deluge. That they were famous men will feed into the community's distraught response at their demise, leading to the second protest (16:41). In ancient Israel such prominence would normally be associated with firstborn sons among the clans. Ibn Ezra thus wrote (1999: 127):

> The princes of the congregation were firstborn. They offered the burnt offering. They therefore took the fire pans. The miracle of the staff, which demonstrated to all of Israel that God chose the Levites in place of the firstborn, is proof that this explanation is correct . . . Here is another rigorous proof: *seeing all the congregation are holy* (v. 3). The aforementioned alludes to the firstborn who are holy, for Scripture states, *Sanctify unto Me all the firstborn* (Exod. 13:2). The firstborn were the priests that *come near to the Lord* (Exod. 19:22). They were the most important ones of the congregation.

Such a view of the princes fits with the general context of the rebellion by Korah and the sons of Reuben as firstborn, also noted by Ibn Ezra, who suggested this revolt actually occurred earlier 'when the first-born were set aside [from serving as priests] and the Levites were placed in their stead . . . Dathan and Abiram rebelled because Moses removed the birthright from Reuben their forefather', and the Israelites were convinced that in these decisions 'Moses acted out of his own will' (1999: 126). The nobility of the first generation of Israel in the wilderness – among the Levites, Reubenites, and the princes of Israel – have risen up in defiant revolt against YHWH's designated leaders, Moses and Aaron. While the prerogatives of Aaron as high priest are the object of their envy, 'they rise up' (*wayyāqumû*) specifically 'before Moses' as the one who has established the new hierarchy – they slander him of power-mongering, denying his divine authority.

Korah is singled out at the start, including the singular form of *lāqaḥ* (he took), framing him as lead instigator and focusing the tension primarily around Aaron's role as high priest. The act *lāqaḥ* lacks a direct object, a gap typically filled with 'men' (Ibn Ezra; AV, ASV, ESV), more rarely as reflexive, 'he betook himself' (Rashi, Nachmanides; Fox 1995: 736). Supplying 'men' by ellipsis is 'highly improbable' (Meek 1929: 167; cf. Noth 1968: 195) and 'inadmissible' (R. P. Gordon 1991: 64). While the Greek version reads 'Korah spoke' (*elalēsen*), this is not followed by most interpreters. The term 'took' occurs seven times in the chapter (16:1, 6, 17, 18, 39, 46, 47), with every other instance referring to the bronze censers, with the last case, intriguingly mirroring 16:1 in its lack of a direct object (16:47, where 'the censer' is easily supplied by context) – so this possibility should not be ruled out for 16:1, and would fit well with the claim of holiness expressed (v. 3). On this reading, Korah's great ambition is 'to be the priest, and himself take the censer' (Magonet 1982: 22). The entire censer test, culminating with a devouring fire from YHWH, echoes the demise of Nadab and Abihu, whose story begins with the same verb – they 'took' (*lāqaḥ*) – and the object: 'each man his censer' (Lev. 10:1). Given the lack of object in 16:47, its lack in 16:1 was likely not the result of a scribal error, but a rhetorical touch, perhaps to add irony: the rebels castigate Moses and Aaron with 'Too much for yourselves!' (v. 3), the same expression thrown back in Moses' retort (v. 7), an idiom whereby *lāqaḥ* may be supplied ('you *take* too much for yourselves') – it is Korah who begins by 'taking' too much for himself, whereas it was YHWH who had 'taken' (*lāqaḥtî*) the Levites, giving them as a gift to Aaron's house, the priesthood (18:6). The lack of object allows for lingering focus on the verb itself, 'to take', and perhaps it is not irrelevant to recall that humanity's first sin involved one who 'took' (Gen. 3:6). Gane summarizes (2004: 633): 'So it appears that the lack in verse 1 is an intentional literary strategy to get the reader/listener thinking about what Korah wants to take, which we find out later is the censer of Aaron that represents his high priestly function'.

3. The root for 'they assembled' is used as a designation for God's community, the 'assembly' (*qāhal*) of YHWH, with which the verse ends, one of a variety of ways in which the rebellious cohort are shown as a pseudo-congregation, attempting to replace the covenant community – undoing Israel's Camp. The designation 'assembly' occurs again in verse 33, forming an inclusio with verse 3 – while 'community' (*'ēdāh*) occurs fourteen times (vv. 2, 3, 5, 6, 9 [twice], 11, 16, 19 [twice], 21, 22, 24, 26) (cf. Ashley 1993: 305). Since many of the chieftains were 'called ones of the appointed-council', this assembling together may have been an official gathering, albeit apart from Moses' authority. They assemble 'against' (*'al*) Moses and 'against' Aaron, but accuse them of exalting themselves 'above' or 'against' (*'al*) the assembly of YHWH. Aside from betraying their envy and ambition for power, the bookends of their complaint, 'Too much for yourselves!' and 'Why do you lift up yourselves above the assembly of YHWH', communicate the depth of their slander: that Moses has abused his authority for personal gain, unjustly privileged his brother Aaron (nepotism), and this, the implication, by deceptively claiming YHWH's warrant. The idiom 'Too much for yourselves!' expresses a severe criticism (cf. Deut. 1:6; 2:3; 3:19, 26; Ezek. 44:6; 45:9) (Levine 1993: 412), and will be redirected back to them by Moses (v. 7). The accusation of exalting (*nāśā'*) themselves uses the same root for chieftains (*nāśî'*, v. 2), who are making the charge – already having status, the princes covet the place of Moses and Aaron. Far from 'lifting up' himself, Moses will later declare he has not carried off ('lifted up' *nāśā'*) even one of their donkeys (v. 15). Sandwiched between their accusations, the gathered ones led by Korah assert the holiness of the community as an argument against hierarchy. The main focus, not only in this story, but in chapters 16–18, is on Aaron's priesthood, his prerogatives as high priest; Moses is attacked – his singular role and authority – as founder of the cult, the one who has orchestrated the new government and institutions of the nation since the people's arrival at Mount Sinai. Yet because of Moses' role as mediator, the attack on him strikes at the very foundation and underpinnings of the Sinai covenant; everything YHWH has revealed and given to Israel has been through Moses – to undermine his authority is to denigrate the Torah itself, to discard Israel's vocation, and to despise YHWH. Korah's rebellion, in short, threatens 'the very fabric of the Israelite community and its structure' (Magonet 1982: 16), for 'the stakes . . . concern Israel's organization, its recognition of YHWH, and its very survival' (Mirguet 2008: 312).

There is a long-recognized connection between the close of the previous chapter, where Israel is granted to don tassels with a blue cord, signifying a pursuit of the nation's priestly calling to be 'holy to your God' (15:37–41), and Korah's assertion that the whole community of Israel is holy (16:3) (cf. e.g. Held 2017: 136–140), a connection developed by the ancient rabbis who depict Korah approaching Moses with his cohort of 250 princes, all draped in prayer shawls entirely of blue (*Num. Rab.* 18.2; *Tan., Korah* 2; cf. Derrett 1993: 68–69). On the surface, their central declaration, that all the community is holy, appears merely as a democratizing wish, however violently asserted. The basis of their accusation against Moses and Aaron, then, is the reality of the Camp, with YHWH dwelling in the midst of his people, as well as the nation's vocation, for Israel had been separated to YHWH God to be a priestly kingdom and holy nation (Exod. 19:6), and charge, for they had been called to 'Be holy for I, YHWH your God, am holy' (Lev. 19:2). The rebel slogan is probably intended as an echo of Exodus 19:6, which closely associates 'priesthood' (*kōhănîm*) with 'holiness' (*qādôś*) (cf. Ashley 1993: 305; J. A. Davies 2004: 193). Whereas in the arrangement of the

Camp, YHWH had commanded that any 'stranger' (*zar*) who drew near the Dwelling would be put to death, Korah's position implies 'no line whatsoever between priest and *zar*, indeed, no such thing as a *zar*, at least among the Israelites' – it is not by accident, then, that the story resolves with a memorial that teaches 'no stranger, who is not the seed of Aaron, will draw near to offer incense before YHWH' (16:40) (Camp 2009: 207–208). Their argument fails to observe gradations of holiness – taking a general truth and neglecting distinctions – intrinsic to the threefold map of the Camp, a structure reasserted in Moses' response (vv. 9–10). 'Every one of the Israelites is holy', they assert, and the proof is their membership in the Camp that has YHWH in their midst – they can abide in the Camp without being destroyed by YHWH's holy presence. The statement points back to the theology of the Camp (chs. 1–6), and to a pressing question: How is it that any Israelite may abide in the presence of YHWH, that is, within the Camp, enjoying his blessed favour rather than incurring his wrathful judgement? Part of the answer is found in the cult of Aaron's priesthood: in its mediation and intercession, its shed blood of atonement and daily whole burnt offerings, its rites of cleansing, its upheld palms of blessing. Conjoined with this answer, Levites, who stand-in for firstborn sons of Israel, serve as a 'lightning rod to attract God's wrath' to themselves rather than on Israel (Milgrom 1990: 371), allowing for the tribes to dwell safely at a distance from YHWH's glory by interposing themselves between YHWH's Tent and the twelve tribes. Ironically, the language of YHWH's dwelling in the midst of his people may be traced to the statement in Exodus 29:45, 'And I will dwell among the sons of Israel, and I will be their God', a covenant formula built on YHWH's sanctification of Aaron and his sons to serve him as priests in the previous verse (44). Aaron's priesthood is linked inseparably with the Dwelling in a variety of ways, such as the similarity between his vestments, afforded a prominent place in the Sinai instructions, and the furnishings and curtains of the Dwelling (cf. Imes 2019) – *both* the priesthood *and* the Dwelling are needed together for YHWH to live among Israel. By abolishing the hierarchical – better, graded holiness – divisions within the Camp, Korah's rebellion would create a new separation: the Camp would be cut off from YHWH himself – for it is the Levitical inner camp, separating YHWH from the outer camp of the tribes, that allows the Camp to exist as a wholistic community, in spiritual unity with God in their midst.

Attacking the divinely ordained means by which the tribes were enabled to abide in YHWH's presence in the Camp, founded on the work of priestly mediation and entailing gradations of holiness, the rebels were undermining their own status within the Camp, along with its consequent benefits. They claim that rather than the Camp's having a threefold concentric division, there is really only one undivided encampment, twisting a partial truth into a falsehood. They claim a camp without separate encampments for priests and Levites. More especially, however, Korah is attacking the differences between Levites and priests, his own ambition driving him to grasp for the position of high priest. Finally, the attack comes from the south side of YHWH's Camp, the locale for both the Kohathites in their Levitical camp and the Reubenites in the tribal camp – the position of second-most honour in YHWH's community. In his grasp for greater status, Korah's revolt is archetypal, tracing the fall of Lucifer (Isa. 14:12–17; cf. Ezek. 28).

4–11. Moses' first response is to fall on his face, a gesture recalling the scouts episode (14:5). His prostration is an act of turning to YHWH, calling for his acknowledgement, although as a simple plea for help or as intercession is left ambiguous – the mounting action proceeds to Moses' address. Although Aaron was included in the address by Korah and company (v. 3), the original movement was that they 'rose up before Moses' (*lipnê mōšeh*, v. 2) specifically, and this account may be read as Moses' defence of Aaron in the latter's absence, until verse 20. Whereas 'he does not defend himself but leaves his defence to God (12:2–3; 16:4–5)', yet when 'Aaron is the target . . . Moses springs to his defence' (Milgrom 1990: 132). Aaron's office, the divinely-designated priesthood, is in focus while Aaron's own person as a character has faded into the background. By contrast Moses is active, demonstrating his God-given authority and leadership.

The argument of Korah and his community had neglected the specific role of priests and Levites as intermediaries, an omission that Mirguet sees as 'the cornerstone of Moses' argument' (2008: 330), his twofold response, first to Korah and his community (vv. 5–7) and then to Korah alone (vv. 8–11), focusing on YHWH's choice of high priest and then the separation of Levites, respectively. In Moses' first reply, moreover, he deals with the specific charges raised by Korah (vv. 5–7), while his second reply addresses the motive behind the charges, ingratitude and selfish ambition (vv. 8–11) (Ashley 1993: 306). A time-stamp is given twice: 'in the morning' (v. 5) and 'tomorrow' (v. 7), typically foreshadowing a decisive act by YHWH (Num. 11:18; 14:25; De Vries 1975; cf. v. 16).

Moses addresses Korah, as leader of the rebellion, and the rest of the group, the sons of Reuben and the 250 chieftains, are twice referred to as 'all his community' (vv. 5, 6), using *'ēdāh*, a designation for YHWH's community, indicting Korah as having created his own rival to the one ordained by YHWH through Moses (cf. de Vaulx 1972: 195; Artus 1997: 171–172). Since the question of the divine legitimacy of Moses' actions, especially in his installation of the Aaronide priesthood, is at issue, Moses sets up an ordeal whereby YHWH himself will make known whom he has chosen to draw near him, the one who is holy in the narrow, cultic sense, belonging utterly to YHWH. The narrative recalls the judgement of Nadab and Abihu, consumed by the fire of YHWH's glory, for approaching him with censers in an unauthorized manner even though they were sons of Aaron ordained to priesthood (Lev. 10:1–3) – a tragedy noted at the founding of the inner camp (Num. 3:4; cf. 26:61). Numerous parallels connect the Nadab and Abihu incident with Korah's rebellion, especially in their wider contexts (Lev. 9 – 10; Num. 16 – 18) (based on N. Cohen 2016). (See Table 27.)

Moses' authority is on display as he commands 'Do this', and they comply. The first act he commands recalls the account's opening word, *take*: Take censers (*maḥtôt*), put fire in them, and then – the crux of the test – put incense on them before YHWH. In Deuteronomy, Moses' blessing on the tribe of Levi includes the privilege of Aaron's house to 'put incense in your (YHWH's) nostrils' (33:10), and in First Samuel, YHWH declares he chose Aaron 'to burn incense' (2:28). As burning incense served as a self-contained offering (cf. Haran 1985: 244–245), like the soothing aroma of a burnt offering, and because burning incense was defining of priestly service, the censer serves well as a symbol for priesthood (for the non-ritual use of incense, see Nielsen 1986: 89–100). Rimon thus concludes 'that burning the incense is not a secondary service in the *Mishkan*, but rather a significant ritual bound up with the revelation of the Divine Presence' (2014: 247). The usurpers are to draw near to YHWH with incense as if they were legitimate divinely-ordained priests, as they have asserted. Perhaps, as a firstborn, Korah was able to recall a time when he had offered incense on behalf of his house, acceptable to YHWH, until that right was denied with the installation of Aaron's house as the official priesthood. The end result of the test is given as an inclusio around the instructions: 'him whom he (YHWH) chooses

Table 27: Korah's rebellion: parallels with Nadab and Abihu

Commonalities	Leviticus 9 – 10	Numbers 16 – 18
'took censers', put 'incense' and 'brought near' 'before YHWH'	10:1	16:6, 17
'a fire went out from (before) YHWH'	10:2	16:35
'strange fire' (*'ēš zārāh*) vs 'scatter fire' (*'ēš zĕrêh*) / 'strange man' (*'îš zār*) wordplay	10:1	16:37, 40
'holy', 'draw near'	10:3	16:5
Moses calls for removal after deaths by YHWH's fire	10:4–5	16:36–40
'glory of YHWH appeared to all the people/ community'	9:23	16:19, 42
'fell upon their faces'	9:24	16:4, 45
'wrath' (*qāṣap, qeṣep*)	10:6, 16	16:22, 46; 18:5
YHWH speaks directly to Aaron	10:8	18:1, 8, 20
Instructions for what priests may eat of offerings	10:14	18:18

(*bāḥar*) he will bring near (*qārab*) him' (5b), 'the man whom YHWH chooses, he will be the holy one' (7b). The psalmist would later exult in the happiness of 'the one you choose (*bāḥar*) and bring near (*qārab*), that he may dwell in your courts – we will be satisfied with the goodness of your house, even your holy Temple' (Ps. 65:4), but the story's drama focuses on the results for those *not* chosen (v. 35), a negative affirmation of Aaron's priesthood. In the second and third stories, a positive vindication of YHWH's 'choosing' of Aaron is given (16:48; 17:5).

Moses corrects the group's accusation, throwing it back on them, 'Too much for yourselves' (vv. 3, 7), dubbing them 'sons of Levi', although the 250 chieftains were from among all the tribes of Israel. It may be that, as a community that follows Korah ('all his community'), they are simply categorized under Korah's personal rebellion and thus called 'sons of Levi', or that, among the 250, Korah leads a group of Kohathites, the leading clan of the Levites responsible for the holy furnishings – or that Korah 'stands for all the rebellious Levites' (Milgrom 1990: 134). These men, along with Korah, are the ones who will take up censers at the entrance to the Tent of Meeting, while the drama of the sons of Reuben ensues at the locale of their own tents. The primary emphasis of the story, beyond nuanced distinctions, is to portray a Levitical revolt against the exclusive priesthood of Aaron's house.

Moses' second speech (vv. 8–11), while still addressing the community at large, is directed especially to Korah as an appeal, searching out his motives. Using the particle *nā'* (now, please) softens Moses' plea into a request and exhortation to listen (see GKC §105b, 110d), so that his ensuing argument, that Levites have been especially honoured among Israel in being given service at YHWH's Dwelling, should be read as an attempt to dissuade them from taking the priesthood, rather than as a heated attack (Magonet 1982: 18). The phrase 'too small a thing' is the semantic opposite of 'too much for yourselves' (vv. 3, 7), and it too will be repeated (vv. 9, 13) (cf. Milgrom 1990: 133, 419). The Levites have been greatly privileged already – but do you 'sons of Levi' count this as 'too small a thing'? The God of Israel – not Moses – had already 'separated' (*hibdîl*) them from the rest of the community, to 'bring them near' (*haqrîb*) to himself. There is a threefold division of holiness in Israel: the community of Israel had been separated from the nations and brought near to YHWH, enjoying life with his Dwelling in their midst; Levites had been separated from the community of Israel and brought nearer to YHWH for the sake of the tribes; the priests, although established before the role of Levites, may be thought of as being separated from them and brought nearer to YHWH, to make atonement, ensuring YHWH's presence among his people. The language of the Levites 'ministering' (*šārat*) to the congregation, as Ibn Ezra proposed (1999: 129; cf. Milgrom 1970a: 133), has reference to their assisting them with lay-aspects of preparing sacrifices. Levites find themselves in the middle gradation of holiness: as ingrates they had taken for granted their privilege above the rest of Israel, seeking the higher place of priests. This is Moses' point, going to the heart of Korah's ambition: YHWH 'brought you (sg.) near, and all of your brothers, the sons of Levi, with you – now you (pl.) seek the priesthood also?' The theology and drama of the revolt can be mapped out according to the Camp's design: Levites are privileged above the rest of the tribes, surround the Dwelling of YHWH, but they will not be satisfied until they have assumed the place of Moses and Aaron and the priesthood, who encamp on the east side, at the entrance to the Tent of Meeting – at the camp of the *Shekhinah*. Because the hierarchy and institutions were all established by YHWH, with Moses merely serving as a conduit for divine revelation, the Levitical rebellion is not 'against Moses and against Aaron' alone (v. 3), but 'against YHWH'. Moreover, Aaron has not taken the role of priesthood to himself – why grumble against him? Both Moses and Aaron are servants of YHWH; rather than honouring the positions, Levites have been envying the persons, rebelling against YHWH himself.

12–15. Moses, dealing with a multi-front attack, now 'sent to call' for Dathan and Abiram, who apparently had not gathered with Korah and the 250 princes at the Tent of Meeting, that he might appeal to them as well to relent from rebellion. The wording, that Moses 'sent' (*šālaḥ*) and they refused to 'ascend' ('*ālâ*), recounts the scouts fiasco *in nuce* (13:2, 3, 31), indicating Dathan and Abiram's narrative role: they continue the sin of the outer camp, rebelling against Moses' prophetic office, which in the broader story relates to YHWH's choice of Aaron through Moses. In an act of utter defiance, they flagrantly refuse to meet with Moses, an insolent gesture that summarizes their manifesto, that Moses is no legitimate leader sent from YHWH. Since Moses has set himself up as ruler, he has no authority, and they need not – *will not* – heed his summons. Psalm 106 explains that Dathan and Abiram 'were jealous' or 'envied' (*qānā'*) Moses in the Camp, and Aaron the holy one of YHWH (v. 16). They accuse him of self-aggrandizement and despotism, their speech forming a loose palistrophe (cf. similarly Wendland 2016: 9), having as its central focus the accusation that Moses 'made himself ruler' (*hiśtārēr*):

We will not ascend!
  Is it too small a thing?
      You caused us to ascend out of a land flowing with milk and honey, to kill us
          You make yourself ruler over us to rule also.
      You have not brought us to a land flowing with milk and honey, nor given inheritance
  Will you gouge out the eyes of these men?
We will not ascend!

The central claim (emphasized by use of hith. inf. abs.) is buttressed on either side with charges of treachery and failure, respectively. First, Moses had brought them *out* of a land flowing with milk and honey in order to kill them in the wilderness. They perversely twist Israel's deliverance from bitter bondage and death, into a forced migration out of paradise, and this by a vicious motive. A 'land flowing with milk and honey' is otherwise used exclusively with reference to YHWH's gift of Canaan (Num. 13:27; 14:8). Describing Egypt in these terms positions their complaint within the broader 'return to Egypt' motif (see Exod. 14:11–12; 16:3; 17:3; Num. 11:5, 18, 20; 14:2–4; 20:5). Second, they translate the divine promise of Canaan into merely a campaign slogan for Moses' political platform, a promise which he failed to bring to fruition – where is my inheritance of field and vineyard? The Midrash, noting their use of *'ap* ('indeed', 'also', v. 14), draws a comparison with the serpent's speech: 'Indeed (*'ap*), has God really said . . . ?', remarking that such *'ap* leads to YHWH's *'ap* ('wrath', see *Gen. Rab.* 19.2). Surprisingly, this is the first use of 'inheritance' (*naḥălâ*) in Numbers, which will show up again in clusters, six times in chapter 18 (nine times including verbal forms), and thirty-nine times throughout the final major division (chs. 26–36). The words 'field' and 'vineyard' are idiomatic for wealth and prosperity (see Exod. 22:4; Num. 20:17; 21:22; 1 Sam. 22:7). These charges are framed by questions – Is it too small a thing? Will you put out the eyes of these men? – that rhetorically unmask Moses as a charlatan, a fraud and deceiver. The reference to 'these men' may be a euphemistic self-designation ('us'), or may refer to 'the elders' who accompany Moses (see v. 25) (Milgrom 1990: 134; cf. G. B. Gray 1903: 201; R. P. Gordon 1991: 67). Their whole speech is framed with the declaration 'We will not ascend!' Their refusal to 'ascend' assumes special status, expressing 'the crux of their rebellion and its gravity' (Grossman 2014e: 230), with language of 'ascent' being rich in irony on multiple levels, related to the ascent out of Egypt and, especially, to the possession of the land, as a *key word* in the narrative of Numbers 13 – 14, used numerous times throughout the scouts episode (13:17 [twice], 18, 21, 22, 30 [twice], 31 [twice]; 14:9, 13, 40 [twice], 42, 44; cf., similarly, Widmer 2004: 255; Mirguet 2008: 325) – and indeed these sons of Reuben, under the first generation's judgement, will *not* ascend into the land. In cosmic geography, the Tent of Meeting as an architectural mountain of God is the high place of the Camp (see Morales 2012; cf. Keil 1869: 108; Grossman 2014e: 228–229), and *Sheol* forms the extreme antipode to the summit: the sons of Reuben, who had refused to 'ascend' to Moses, will end up 'descending' (*yārad*) into *Sheol* (v. 33). They who accused Moses of *killing* (*mût*) them in the wilderness, will descend *alive* (*ḥay*) into *Sheol*. In rebuffing the summons to Moses at the Tent of Meeting, moreover, they will not acknowledge what we might call the 'structural authority' of the centre of the Camp; instead, Moses will come to them, the new centre of gravity they have created and around which they have gathered a community as a rival camp (vv. 24–25). Pyschny (2018: 127), too, refers to 'the conceptualization of Dathan and Abiram's tents, which somehow present a (negative) counter-image to the tent of meeting'. Consistently, the imagery continues when YHWH commands for the community to 'ascend' from the dwelling of the sons of Reuben, and they comply by ascending from them (v. 24, 27). Notably, Dathan and Abiram make no mention of YHWH God, neither his signs and wonders in Egypt, nor his just judgement on the first generation of Israelites for their refusal to heed his word and take possession of the land. Moses is the only character who regularly acknowledges the presence of YHWH in the Camp, prostrating himself (v. 4), including YHWH in the discussion and bringing his activity to bear (vv. 5, 7, 9–10, 16–17), reminding Korah and his community that their rebellion is against YHWH himself (v. 11), and directly speaking to YHWH in the midst of the struggle (v. 15).

Taken metaphorically, their question 'Will you gouge out the eyes of these men' may accuse Moses of 'hoodwinking' Israel, deceiving them to such a degree they would need to be blind not to see his failed leadership. More literally, the idea would be that even under threat of punishment, Dathan and Abiram would not submit to Moses' leadership. Samet (2017a) observes that putting eyes out is a punishment found both in Scripture and throughout the ANE, an especially common practice against prisoners of war and slaves. Samson, a judge of Israel, had his eyes put out by Philistines, before being taken, bound, to Gaza to work a mill in the prison house (Judg. 16:21), and, after watching them slay his sons, Zedekiah, the last reigning king of Judah, had his eyes put out by Babylonians, before being taken, bound, to Babylon (2 Kgs 25:7). Nahash the Ammonite demanded, as terms for a treaty with the men of Jabesh, that he put out the right eye of each of their men (1 Sam. 11:2). Samet also quotes from a Hittite letter that reads (2017a): 'When you receive this letter, present yourself immediately; if not – your eyes will be put out,' and further explains that since masters could put out the eyes of their slaves for any cause mercilessly, putting out eyes became a symbol for slavery. Based on the parallelism between verses 13 and 14, he proposes understanding the question as 'Will you make us your slaves?' in parallel with 'Will you then lord over us?' – that is, 'You are not a prince over us, and we are not your servants!' (Samet 2017a):

You brought us up from a land flowing with milk and honey, to have
    us die in the wilderness;
    Will you then lord over us?
You have not brought us to a land flowing with milk and honey, nor
    given us an inheritance . . .
    Will you gouge out the eyes of these men?

Rhetorically, their words echo the recent tassel law, to 'not search . . . after your eyes' (15:39), intended as repair for the scouts' failure, indicating they 'would not accept the divinely mandated perspective – even if their own sight was physically taken from them!' (Y. Twersky 2007b: 2:173).

Belonging to the tribe of Jacob's firstborn son, Reuben, their refusal to acknowledge Moses' leadership – and worse, to undermine his integrity by accusing him of self-promotion by deceit in YHWH's Name – is an act that threatens revolution in the Camp. They accuse Moses of being a corrupt failure, tyrant, and deceiver. More, by undermining Moses' authority and legitimate role as prophet and mediator, they have undermined the foundation of Israel as a nation: the Sinai covenant, the Torah, the priesthood of Aaron's house, the organization of the covenant community with YHWH dwelling in the midst of Israel, all this has been mediated through Moses. The existence and vocation of Israel stands on the authenticity of Moses' ministry. YHWH's relationship with Moses is the basis for Israel's doctrine and theology, worldview and mission, for her cult and sacred calendar, for the ministry of all her subsequent prophets, the touchstone for all her decisions and judgements, and the wellspring of Messianic expectation.

Moses was 'kindled (ḥārāh) greatly' a phrase that up till now in Numbers has been associated only with YHWH's reaction to the people's sin, always coupled with the term 'fierce anger' ('ap), which is missing here (11:1, 10, 33; 12:9), and only once using the adverb 'greatly' (mĕ'ōd) as here (11:10). The only previous occasion for such a response from Moses was after Israel's apostasy with the golden calf – even there, lacking mĕ'ōd (Exod. 32:19). In his angered frustration, Moses demonstrates godliness, turning to YHWH with an imprecatory prayer. The Psalter is filled with divinely inspired psalms of imprecation, and their theology and application is relevant here: such prayers call for a vindication of God himself – his character and power, and for his reign to be established in justice, and, rather than attempting retribution for oneself, ultimate intervention and judgement is surrendered to the hands of God (see Zenger 1996; G. J. Wenham 2012: 167–179). 'Do not turn favourably to their tribute' he prays. 'Turn favourably' (from pānāh) has the idea of turning one's face to a person or object, which refers to favour (as in the priestly blessing, 6:25–26), whereas turning one's face away is a gesture of displeasure. The tribute offering (minḥāh), especially given its references in the previous chapter (15:4, 6, 9, 24), symbolized one's disposition of gratitude to YHWH, a joyful acknowledgement of his kingship, and probably represents the whole cultic approach to God (cf. Achenbach 2013: 213). In the hands of these rebels, the minḥāh would be a farce – to dishonour YHWH's servant is rather to court the vengeance of YHWH (cf. Num. 12:7–8). Moses' plea is a form of retributive justice, and keeps the issue of Aaron's priesthood within purview, for as high priest Aaron was consecrated to 'bear the iniquity of the holy things', making Israel's gifts acceptable before YHWH (Exod. 28:37–38; cf. B. Schwartz 1995: 16) – rejecting Aaron's role, their gifts will not be accepted favourably by YHWH. Disregarding their tribute suggests an open breach in Dathan and Abiram's relationship with YHWH. Moses' prayer also invalidates the accusations of Dathan and Abiram, demonstrating that he indeed shares an intimate relationship with YHWH, even able to influence a sacrifice's acceptance or rejection – in effect superseding the cult itself. Still, *minḥāh* seems to come out of nowhere, and likely functions to recall Cain's rejected *minḥāh* sacrifice (Gen. 4:5–6), the first such rejection by YHWH in history (Achenbach 2013: 210), a narrative echo that portrays Dathan and Abiram within a context of murderous envy over cult privileges.

In his defence to YHWH, Moses pleads that he has not taken one donkey, the use of which was likely well within his due and practical need (cf. Hirsch 2007a: 343), but the statement may also have been 'a conventional way of asserting one's honesty and integrity (cf. 1Sam. 12:3)' (E. W. Davies 1995b: 173), and he attests further that he has not done any ill to a single one of them. Although accused of 'lifting up' himself (v. 3), Moses has not 'lifted up' (*nāśā'*) even one of their donkeys. On the contrary, he has repeatedly interposed himself for their salvation from supremely warranted divine wrath. Far from self-promotion or love of money, Moses had forsaken the treasures of Egypt to suffer with God's people (Heb. 11:26–27). Moses, although exercising lordly functions, ruled among them as one who serves, becoming a paradigm for the suffering Servant of Isaiah (Morales 2020: 148–151).

16–22. Moses turns directly to Korah, addressing him and the members of his personal congregation – 'you and all your community (*'ēdāh*)' – instructing that he and they and Aaron are to place themselves (be before) in the presence of YHWH on the following day. As Magonet discerned, while the basic content of this speech mirrors Moses' previous speech (vv. 5–7), what is different here is that he addresses Korah personally, isolating him from his supporters and emphasizing his personal culpability (note the threefold use of *'attā*, 'you'), but also driving to the point at issue, 'you and Aaron, each man his censer' (1982: 19):

It is as if Korah who has hidden behind the various groups he leads is now being forced to step out into the public spotlight, and the issue that is really at stake, namely between him and Aaron, is finally exposed. What Korah really wants, says Moses, behind all his talk of the democracy of holiness, is to replace Aaron as the high priest; so let him stand there as he wishes beside Aaron, and let the Lord choose.

The thrice-repeated phrase 'each man his censer' stresses individual accountability for all the participants (cf. Magonet 1982: 19). What is of crucial importance for understanding the activity of Moses here and later with the sons of Reuben (vv. 28–30) is that both tests depend utterly on the will and action of YHWH: Moses neither asserts his own power in an authoritarian fashion nor directs the rebels to past precedent, but completely lays the matters open before YHWH God to demonstrate his will afresh.

Essentially, the narrative language as well as Moses' point of view portrays Korah as seeking to establish his own priesthood. Separate references to Korah and to 'his community' relate to more than his leadership in fomenting rebellion, but to his separate function among them: Korah is a pseudo high priest, and the 250 chieftains form his priestly house, mirroring Aaron and his house. The 250 censers are mentioned separately, and then 'you (Korah) and Aaron', bringing these two alongside each other as rivals. By aligning themselves with Korah, the 250 chieftains are 'sons of Levi', but elsewhere they are described as men 'from the sons of Israel' and 'chieftains of the community' (v. 2) – the rhetorical focus is on the Levitical nature of the grave rebellion. Their cultic claims are tested by a cultic ritual: Moses instructs Korah and his community to 'take' their censers, echoing Korah's original act of rebellion (v. 1). Putting incense on their censers, they are to 'bring near before YHWH' their censers, cultic language for approaching YHWH at the Tent of Meeting.

Verse 18 describes their follow-through obedience, adding that they 'put fire' on the incense, abbreviated in the previous verse's directions. One question that arises is whether verse 18 skips to the following day (assumed by most commentators), as per Moses' repeated instructions (vv. 7, 16), or whether Korah and his community, *immediately* gathered at the Tent of Meeting. Taking the latter scenario, then the second story, which happens on 'the next day' (v. 41), has Aaron taking his censer precisely when he was supposed to do so. The first story's repeated emphasis on Moses' instructions, along with the absence of any reference to Aaron taking his censer previously (or to the results of his original incense offering), make such a reading attractive. Tension rises with the notice that each man stood at the door of the Tent of Meeting. Before continuing the action, verse 19 recounts that Korah has further assembled 'the whole community' to the door of the Tent of Meeting as well, so that much of the Camp, along with the reader, will be witness to what transpires. This assembling (*qāhal*) of the community is 'against them' (Moses and Aaron), the revolt having swelled to encompass more of the Camp at the critical moment of drama. Korah's brazen and presumptuous mutiny is underscored by the locale, that he assembled all the community against them at the door of the Tent of Meeting, a strategic place: 'Assembling the people at the place where Moses serves as intermediary between YHWH and the people, where the investiture of the priests takes place, Korah positions himself as an alternative to the leadership of Moses and Aaron' (Mirguet 2008: 330; see Exod. 29:4;

Lev. 8:3). Now, at the midpoint of the story, YHWH appears in glory; the ensuing verses after this turning point forming an unravelling of the chaos created by Korah (vv. 20–40). Recounting YHWH's advent – 'the glory of YHWH appeared' – and this 'to all the community', the tension and anticipation begins to reach its climax. Verses 19 and 35 form an inclusion around the parallel rebellion of Dathan and Abiram (vv. 20–34), bringing the multifaceted insurrection under Korah as the main instigator.

While 'all the community' sees the glory of YHWH, his words are spoken to Moses and Aaron, a signal that already affirms what the rebels seek to undermine, the place of Moses and Aaron within the life of the community. The expected fiery judgement of God, we discover, is only delayed for the sake of Moses and Aaron's own safety: 'Separate yourselves from the midst of this community – I will finish them in an instant.' There is some irony in YHWH's language inasmuch as the rebels rail against separation and degrees of holiness, and because Moses and Aaron are to disassociate themselves from this false *'ēdāh* (community). To 'separate' (*bādal*) is one of the major actions of God in Creation (Gen. 1:4, 6, 7, 14, 18), as well as for the division within his Dwelling (Exod. 26:33), with the priesthood of Aaron being solemnly charged to separate between holy and profane, between clean and unclean (Lev. 10:10; 20:25), and all Israel being called to be separate from the nations (Lev. 20:24, 26). Earlier in Numbers, Levites had been 'separated' from Israel to YHWH (8:14), to which Moses had just alluded (16:9). As with Creation, these Camp divisions 'must be recognized and maintained if the created order is to continue to exist and not collapse into confusion and chaos' (Gorman 1990: 41). The rebels had denied divine separations, which led to chaos; YHWH creates cosmos by reasserting separations. Moses and Aaron, the objects of separation (16:21), become the divine means to re-establish the order of the Camp (cf. Mirguet 2008: 322). They are to separate themselves specifically 'from the midst of this community', a phrase that recalls the revolution slogan 'All the community is holy, and YHWH is *in the midst of them*' (v. 3) – he is indeed in their midst, and ready to destroy them. Like Lot and his house departing Sodom and Gomorrah before its fiery destruction (Gen. 19), Moses and Aaron are told to flee the community before the onset of YHWH's judgement. However, as on other occasions (Num. 14:11–20; cf. Gen. 18:16–33; Exod. 32:9–14), YHWH's declaration of judgement functions to solicit intercession.

All major translations read that YHWH will 'consume' them, presuming *'ākal*, but the Hebrew text actually uses *kālāh* (in the form *'akalleh*, which appears like *'ākal*): to 'cease', 'finish', here and in the parallel statement in verse 45 (see 16:21, 31, 45; 17:10). YHWH threatens to destroy 'this community' in an instant 'moment' (*rega'*). Moses and Aaron fall prostrate, and this time the prayer accompanying the gesture is disclosed, addressing YHWH as 'God, God of the spirits of all flesh', the Sovereign who alone is worthy of creating and destroy life – 'spirits' here as that which gives life to flesh (cf. 27:16). Akin to Abraham's intercession (Gen. 18:16–33), they plead in the form of a question: 'Will one man sin and you be angry with the whole community?' The phrase 'one man' is emphasized, fronting the verb. While a case for the community's culpability may certainly be made, the plea relates to the greater aggravation of sin on the part of those who lead. As an idiom, 'one man' refers to Korah, perhaps with Dathan and Abiram. Based upon YHWH's previous action, destroying by plague the ten scouts who had led the nation into unbelief and disobedience (14:36–37), as well as the recent legislation regarding high-handed sin and its consequences (15:30–36), the intercession of Moses and Aaron recognizes that, while the community may be spared, the leader must be punished (cf. 25:4, 7–13) – paralleling the uprisings of the outer and inner camps. Demonstrating the 'daring and persistent manner in which Moses carries on an intercessory dialogue with God' (P. D. Miller 1994: 272), he pleads for YHHW to spare the community while satisfying his justice on the one who has become an archetype of rebellion, Korah – for God will not be mocked.

There are seven occasions in Numbers where YHWH's theophanic presence arrives within the context of judgement, each involving some sort of intercession from Moses, and, with one exception (11:1–3), giving prominence to the Tent of Meeting. (See Table 28.)

23–27. YHWH responds only to Moses (cf. 16:43–44), although affirming the prayer of both Moses and Aaron, ready to wreak judgement upon the leaders of the rebellion. Rather than the previous call for Moses and Aaron to 'separate yourselves' from the community (v. 21), he now calls for the community to withdraw from the wicked leaders. The community is being called to disassociate with the core leaders of the revolt, and to reassociate as a community around YHWH's chosen leaders – this *ecclesiological* transfer expressing their realigned allegiance would protect them from the impending judgement of the insurgents. YHWH calls for the community specifically to 'ascend' from the leaders, a key word for the Dathan and Abiram line of the story. The very act the leaders, Dathan and Abiram, had refused, namely to 'ascend', YHWH now bids the community to perform against them, as an act of disassociation with their revolt. More positively, YHWH's command is a first step in reorganizing and establishing the original order of his Camp (Num. 1 – 6), an act of recreation out of chaos. The community is ordered to ascend specifically from around the 'dwelling' of Korah, Dathan and Abiram, a charge that has caused much scholarly consternation: previously, only Dathan and Abiram had been addressed as remaining behind – is Korah now among them? How can Korah's dwelling be with Dathan and Abiram's? While the dwelling of Korah is mentioned, the narrative

Table 28: Seven theophanies in Numbers

Numbers	Theophany	Moses' intercession	Tent of Meeting
11:1–3	'fire of YHWH', v. 1	'Moses prayed', v. 2	
11:4–35	'YHWH descended in a cloud', v. 25	'Moses said', vv. 11–15	Gather 70 elders 'around the Tent of Meeting', vv. 16, 24
12:1–16	'YHWH descended in a pillar of cloud', v. 5	'Moses cried', v. 13	'Come forth you three to the Tent of Meeting . . . YHWH stood at the door of the Tent', vv. 4, 5
14:1–38	'glory of YHWH appeared', v. 10	'Moses and Aaron fell on their faces', v. 5 'Moses said', vv. 13–19	The glory of YHWH appeared 'in the Tent of Meeting' before all the sons of Israel, v. 10
16:1–35	'glory of YHWH appeared', v. 19 'fire went forth from YHWH', v. 35	'they (Moses and Aaron) fell upon their faces and said', v. 22	Korah gathered all the congregation against them to the 'door of the Tent of Meeting', v. 19
16:41–50	'cloud covered it and the glory of YHWH appeared', v. 42	'they fell on their faces', v. 45	'they looked toward the Tent of Meeting', v. 42
20:1–13	'glory of YHWH appeared', v. 6	'they fell on their faces', v. 6	Moses and Aaron went 'to the door of the Tent of Meeting', v. 6

clues keep him at the Tent of Meeting; thus when Moses goes to deliver YHWH's message, he goes to 'Dathan and Abiram' but not to Korah (v. 25). More pressing, why is 'dwelling' in singular, as if Korah, Dathan and Abiram dwell within the same tent? Source critics propose emending the text to 'the dwelling of YHWH' (vv. 24), but this confounds the meaning of the text, as Moses restates YHWH's charge as, 'Turn aside, now, from the tents of these wicked men' (v. 26; cf. 'their houses', v. 32), and 'dwelling' may simply be a 'dwelling place' in general, so that the tents of Korah, Dathan and Abiram were pitched close together 'since they were plotting the revolt' (Liver 1961: 196–197). However, 'dwelling' in the singular is reserved for the Tabernacle (see Milgrom 1990: 136). Rather than a scribal error (cf. v. 27), 'the dwelling', as with references to Korah's 'community' and 'assembly', likely forms an ironic allusion to *the* Dwelling. Indeed, the phrase 'around the dwelling' (*sābîb lammiškān*) has occurred a few times already in Numbers to describe how Levites are to encamp 'around the Dwelling' of YHWH (1:50, 53), and this within the context of establishing the twelve tribes of Israel at a distance 'around' YHWH's Dwelling to form the Camp (2:2). So, we find once more that Korah's rebellion has created a pseudo-Camp, a rival 'community' gathered 'around the dwelling' of Korah, Dathan and Abiram. Shamah thus states the terminology 'seems to indicate that Korah . . . had set up a rival sanctuary district at his headquarters' (2011: 770), just as Y. Twersky writes of 'an alternative to the *Mishkan*' that attempts 'to usurp the meaning of the true camp' (2007b: 2:176). Mirguet similarly sees that the divinely-ordered encampment structure, organized by and around YHWH's central Dwelling, has been broken (2008: 326). While the Kohathites and Reubenites both dwelt in the south section of the Camp, they had been separated with the Levitical Kohathites encamped between YHWH's Dwelling and the tribe of Reuben. The depiction here may imply a blurring of boundaries, either that these sons of Reuben pitched their tents in Levitical space or vice versa – their cry after all had been that every member of the community was equally holy, undermining the foundations of the Camp's order and structure.

In response, Moses arose (recalling v. 2) and went to Dathan and Abiram. His doing so displays humility: whereas they would not deign to come to him publicly, he goes to them. The 'elders of Israel' are likely the same as the seventy empowered by the Spirit (cf. 11:30). The notice that the 'elders of Israel' followed after Moses not only underscores his leadership but demonstrates he is acting with legitimate authority – the revolt is not merely an interpersonal concern but a political revolution. Moses bids the community to 'turn aside, now, from the tents of these wicked men', adding that they not 'touch anything that belongs to them, lest you be swept away with all their sins', a command implied if not expressed directly by YHWH as a consistent principle in the theology of judgement (e.g. Josh. 6:18–19; 7:1, 20–26) and which reiterates Moses' innocence (see v. 15). The narrator's description of the people's compliance uses the language of YHWH, reporting that 'they ascended from the dwelling of Korah, Dathan and Abiram, from all around', signifying the undoing of Korah's pseudo-camp. Rather than ascending away themselves, we are told that Dathan and Abiram 'came forth and stood at the door of their tents, and their wives, and their sons, and their little ones', a lengthy description that adds narrative intensity with the prospect of their demise. The description of coming forth and standing or 'taking a stand' (*niṣṣābîm*), may imply military readiness (cf. 1 Sam. 17:4, 16), and foreshadows the opening up of the ground. However, their position closely echoes the situation in Exodus, after the golden calf apostasy (cf. also Cooper and Goldstein 1997: 211; Mirguet 2008: 328–329): YHWH had declared that he would 'not ascend' in 'the midst' of the people, lest he 'finish' them (33:3), so that Moses needed to pitch his tent far outside the encampment to meet with YHWH, while Israelites looked on, each man at the door of his tent (33:8). Allusions to the Exodus subtext, portray the current situation dismally, as that of a severed relationship: Israel has reverted back to the days before the construction of the covenant community (Num. 1 – 6) when, due to their apostasy, YHWH would not draw near in their midst lest he completely destroy them – which will be true enough for the leaders of the rebellion. Notably missing here is any mention of Korah himself, along with his family, again leaving the impression that while his community, and especially Dathan and Abiram, had gathered all around his 'dwelling', he himself remained with the 250 princes and their censers.

28–35. Moses' declaration goes to the heart of Dathan and Abiram's accusation, offering for the whole Camp to 'know that YHWH has sent' him to do all these works. Clearly, they had 'denied the divine mission of Moses' (Liver 1961: 195), and YHWH's impending act functions to vindicate his servant. The test Moses sets up is profound on several levels. First, it has a twofold accomplishment: the vindication of Moses' mediatorial ministry and the judgement of Dathan and Abiram for their revolt – the 'sign' of his having been sent by YHWH is in the rebels' own destruction, in how they will be judged. The same is true with the censer test, inasmuch as YHWH's judgement on the 250 princes is a negative vindication for Aaron. Second, the validation of Moses had already taken place within the context of the exodus out of Egypt (Exod. 3:12; 4:1–9). Every sign and wonder performed, their deliverance out of Egypt and crossing of the sea, hearing God's thunderous voice from Sinai, all these were further validations of Moses' divinely ordained office and calling – to question his divine authority now demonstrates the depths of the rebellion. Third, Moses' test should be understood as well within the context of the 'test of a true prophet', explained in Deuteronomy: 'When a prophet speaks in the name of YHWH, if the thing does not happen or does not come to pass, then that is a thing which YHWH has not spoken, but the prophet spoke it presumptuously – do not be afraid of him' (18:22). While a false prophet would seek an easy test, Moses, to validate his own ministry, chooses the most outlandishly improbable demonstration imaginable – something that had never before taken place: If the men die a normal death like all other humans, then YHWH has not sent Moses; but if YHWH will create a new thing, and the ground opens her mouth and swallows them up, with all that belongs to them, and they descend alive to *Sheol*, then Israel will know that these men have spurned YHWH. In Hebrew thought, *Sheol* is the abode of the dead, the underworld that is, in cosmic geography, the polar opposite of the heavens (cf. Amos 9:2; Isa. 7:11), likened to a watery pit of darkness (cf. Jon. 2:6; Ps. 88:3–7), and symbolizes the undoing of orderly cosmos, chaos (see Rudman 2001). Isaiah portrays a similar picture of judgement, as *Sheol* enlarges herself to 'open her mouth' without measure, so that all the glory, multitude, pomp, and rejoicing of God's people 'descend' into her (5:14). As with the censer test, this test hinges utterly on the reality, will, and action of YHWH (vs Hort 1959). Not even when young David stood armour-less before Goliath nor when Elijah poured twelve casks of water on the altar has such faith – such God-exalting confidence – in YHWH been shown. Fourth, Dathan and Abiram's judgement is an instance of measure for measure judgement: they who would not ascend in obedience, now descend in judgement. Moses, they claimed, had planned to kill them in the wilderness (v. 13), an obstinate response to YHWH's judgement on the first generation, so now they will indeed die in the wilderness. The poetic justice reaches back to the slander against Canaan, the evil report against the land brought by the ten scouts, who had said 'the land devours (*'ākal*) her inhabitants' (13:32), for now leaders of that faithless generation are swallowed up in the open mouth of the earth – and the fire of YHWH will 'consume' (*'ākal*) the 250 who offered incense (16:35). The imagery goes further back to Moses' song by the sea, where YHWH's victory over the Egyptian hosts is sung as 'You stretched out your hand, the earth swallowed (*bāla'*) them' (Exod. 15:12), the same term used here three times (vv. 30, 32, 34) and again when referring back to this judgement (26:10). Some have also connected the imagery of 'the ground' (*hā'ǎdāmāh*) 'opening' (*pāṣāh*) her 'mouth' (*peh*) with the story of Cain and Abel, when the ground opened her mouth to receive Abel's blood (Gen. 4:10–11; see Jørstad 2016) – a deep connection given Moses' reference to the *minḥāh* offering (16:15; Gen. 4:5).

Beyond vindicating himself, Moses' test aims to defend YHWH's honour. When Moses' word is fulfilled, it will become evident that these men, Korah, Dathan and Abiram, have spurned YHWH (v. 30), and the people will 'know' that YHWH had sent Moses indeed. Moses' own focus is on overturning the dishonour to YHWH, rather than on the vindication of himself, when the test proves true. To 'spurn' (*nā'aṣ*) has the idea of treating and regarding with contempt, and was used earlier, again with reference to the people's spurning of YHWH, in the scouts episode (14:11, 23). By treating YHWH's ordained servants and ordinances with contempt, their defiance was a war waged against YHWH. Later, the daughters of Zelophehad, representative of the second generation, will look back to Korah's community as having 'met together against YHWH' (27:3). As Moses 'finished' speaking – without pause for anticipation or wonder over whether Moses was a true prophet and his word would come true – the ground cleaved open under them. So fervently eager was he to commend and vindicate Moses, his faithful servant, YHWH had, as it were, to restrain himself even for Moses' speaking to end so that he might leap to the demonstration of his favour upon him. Use of 'finish' here echoes YHWH's earlier statement that he would 'finish' them in an instant (v. 21; cf. v. 45; 17:10).

Along with swallowing 'them and their houses', the text says the earth swallowed 'every human (*hā'ādām*) that belonged to Korah, and all the possessions'. If taken as a summary statement, then it refers to the previous line, describing Dathan and Abiram as those who belonged to Korah's faction; otherwise, it may refer to family members and – perhaps primarily – servants of Korah's house (cf. R. P. Gordon 1991: 68), or to a faction of Levites gathered by Korah (cf. Gane 2004: 636). Taking into account Deuteronomy, it was only Dathan and Abiram and their houses that endured this form of judgement as 'the earth opened its mouth and swallowed them up' (11:6), a scenario which reserves Korah's demise with the 250 men who were consumed by YHWH's fire for offering incense. In this case, 'belonged to Korah' implies 'had joined the rebellion led by Korah'. Although for now the focus is kept on the dreadful and admonitory judgement itself, later in Numbers we discover that at least 'the sons of Korah did not die' (26:11). Jewish tradition explains that they had repented and forsook rebellion (*Yalk.t Shim.*, Korah, 752). Their names are first given in Exodus 6:24: Assir, Elkanah, and Abiasaph ('to bind', 'God redeems', and 'my father gathers', respectively), and the 'sons of Korah' became musicians, singers, and gatekeepers in the Temple cult, associated with psalms marked by the theme of redemption from *Sheol* (cf. 1 Chr. 9:19, 31; 26:1, 19; 2 Chr. 20:19; Pss 42 – 49, 84 – 85, 87 – 88; see D. C. Mitchell 2006). Given their dangerous charge of transporting the holy furnishings of YHWH's Dwelling, the prospect of the demise of the Kohathites had been forewarned in a threefold manner (4:18–20): 'Do not allow the tribe of the clans of the Kohathites to be cut off from the midst of the Levites', YHWH had spoken, forbidding the Kohathites to approach and look, even for a moment, at the sacred vessels before the priests had covered them in blue drapes. Interestingly, 'even for a moment' is an idiom, '(as swift) as a swallow', that uses the same root (*bāla'*) for the earth's 'swallowing up' Korah's house (16:32). Significantly, the people did not simply 'perish' (*'ābad*), but 'perished from the midst of the assembly', exiled in a dreadful manner from YHWH's covenant community, once more underscoring that the uprising had struck to the foundation and nature of the Camp – it is an *ecclesiological* focus. Having 'spurned' (*nā'aṣ*) YHWH, they now perish – swallowed up into *Sheol* – from the midst of the assembly (cf. Cooper and Goldstein 1997: 211). The only other use of 'assembly' (*qāhāl*) was when the insurgents accused Moses and Aaron of having exalted themselves 'above the assembly of YHWH' (v. 3) – but now they themselves perish from the assembly of YHWH. More deeply, the 'dwelling' of Korah, Dathan and Abiram had become the centre of a new pseudo covenant community; YHWH, having dispersed the people from around it, now destroys the very epicenter of the false camp – demonstrating that, rather than connecting to heaven, their central dwelling led literally down to

Sheol. Psalm 1 also defines one's end communally, teaching that 'the way of the wicked will perish (*'ābad*)' (v. 6). That the earth covered or closed over them suggests the idea that the ground was left afterward appearing as if nothing had ever happened – one moment the insurgents and their houses were there, and the next moment they are gone. This was YHWH's doing, an immediate supernatural fulfilment of Moses' word. At the 'voice' or 'sound' (*qôl*) of the people's descent alive into *Sheol* – a gruesome detail – the Israelites fled, crying, 'Lest the earth swallow us up', perhaps demonstrating an awareness of their own guilt in the rebellion. Fear of YHWH is an appropriate response (cf. 17:13), and will lead to an appreciation of the hierarchy, along a graded system of holiness, that he has established (ch. 18). Driving to the theological heart of the passage, one seventeenth-century Jewish commentary, has the voices of the people's descent into *Sheol* screaming, 'Moses is King, Aaron is High Priest, and the Torah is True!' (*Yalk. Reuv.*, Num. 16:31). Later in Israel's history, David, perhaps reflecting on the demise of Korah's house, would utter an imprecatory prayer, calling on God to judge those who would deceptively and violently contend against YHWH's anointed king: 'May death seize them! May they descend alive into *Sheol*! For evil is in their dwelling place and in their midst' (Ps. 55:15).

In poetic justice for those who longed to return to Egypt, the demise of Dathan and Abiram and their households is orchestrated as a reversal of the exodus. Using language and motifs from the sea crossing (Exod. 14 – 15) their judgement is portrayed as a return to Egypt-as-*Sheol*. (See Table 29.)

The scene then flashes back to the Tent of Meeting conveying that simultaneously with the ground opening to swallow up Dathan and Abiram and their houses, a fire had gone forth from YHWH to devour the 250 men while they were bringing near their incense before him. The qatal form likely implies past perfect here, 'a fire had come forth' (cf. Samet 2014d: 219–220). YHWH was with Moses, vindicating him, by the tents of Dathan and Abiram, and YHWH was with Aaron, vindicating him, by the Tent of Meeting. Logically, the vindication of Moses' office as prophet and mediator precedes that of Aaron's office of high priest, the former being the basis for the latter – once Moses has been vindicated through YHWH's judgement on Dathan and Abiram, the fiery ruin of the 250 princes follows by necessity. The sons of Reuben who would not ascend, descend into *Sheol*; the 250 chieftains who grasped at the priesthood, presuming to draw near to YHWH, are consumed by his holy fire. Their judgement echoes the destruction of Nadab and Abihu, who were 'consumed' when 'fire went forth from YHWH' as they drew near him with their censers (Lev. 10:1–3; cf. Num. 3:4; 26:61). The opening prologue to the wilderness section (11:1–3), had narrated how the outskirts of the Camp had been 'consumed' by

Table 29: Dathan and Abiram's demise: parallels with the sea crossing

Sea crossing (Exodus 14 – 15)	Swallowed by the earth (Numbers 16)
'you took us to die (*mût*) in the wilderness . . . why did you deal with us this way, to bring us out of Egypt? . . . that we should die (*mût*) in the wilderness' (14:11–12)	'you have caused us to ascend out of a land flowing with milk and honey (Egypt) in order to kill (*mût*) us in the wilderness' (16:13)
'stretch out your hand over the sea and cleave it open (*bāqaʿ*) . . . and the waters were cleaved open (*bāqaʿ*)' (14:16, 21)	'the ground that was under them cleaved open (*bāqaʿ*)' (16:31)
'You stretched out your hand, the earth swallowed (*bālaʿ*) them up' (15:12)	'the ground opens her mouth and swallows (*bālaʿ*) them up . . . the earth opened her mouth and swallowed (*bālaʿ*) them up . . . Lest the earth swallow (*bālaʿ*) us up' (16:30, 32, 34; cf. 26:10)
'they descended (*yārad*) to the depths like a stone' (15:5)	'they descend (*yārad*) alive to *Sheol* . . . they and all that belonged to them descended (*yārad*) alive to *Sheol*' (16:30, 33)
'the waters returned and covered (*kāsāh*) the chariots . . . the depths of the sea covered (*kāsāh*) them . . . the sea covered (*kāsāh*) them' (14:28; 15:5, 10)	'the earth covered (*kāsāh*) over them' (16:33)
'The Egyptians said, "Let us flee (*nûs*) from the face of Israel, for YHWH fights for them against the Egyptians"' (14:25)	'all Israel who were around them fled (*nûs*) at their voice' (16:34)
'the Egyptians will know (*yādaʿ*) that I am YHWH (twice) . . . the people feared YHWH, and believed YHWH and his servant Moses' (14:4, 18, 31)	'you will know (*yādaʿ*) that YHWH has sent me . . . you will know (*yādaʿ*) these men have spurned YHWH' (16:28, 30)

'the fire of YHWH', so that the place was called 'Burning' (*Taberah*), a designation and lesson Korah and his community would have done well to remember. Similarly, the introduction to the Levitical camp's construction had narrated Nadab and Abihu's fiery demise, presaging the inner camp's failure and judgement (3:1–4).

What happened to Korah? The text is ambiguous: was Korah among the sons of Reuben who descended into *Sheol* or with the 250 who were consumed by fire? The Samaritan Pentateuch and Josephus assume Korah died by the fire of YHWH. Some ancient rabbis declare he died neither by being swallowed up nor by being burnt with fire, while others argue he died by both (*Sanh.* 110a; *Num. Rab.* 18.19;

Tan. Korah 23). Doré, in his engraving titled 'Death of Korah, Dathan and Abiram' (1865) had apparently opted for both, portraying Korah, dressed as a high priest with censer in hand, falling into the earth's cavern, with flames and smoke blazing up, ready to consume him. (See Fig. 12.)

The later notice in 26:10, moreover, is not conclusive, 'where the syntactically ambiguous phrase "and Korah" hovers uneasily between seismic convulsion and divine fire' (Alter 1981: 135), with some translations (GNT, JPS) favouring his fiery death in the second half of the verse (cf. Wendland 2016: 13–14). The Samaritan version of this verse reads: 'And the earth opened her mouth, and the earth swallowed them up, when the community died, when the fire devoured Korah and the 250 men', and Josephus promulgates a similar reading, that a 'terrible flame' destroyed 'all the company and Korah himself', and 'this so entirely, that their very bodies left no remains behind them' (*Ant.* 4.55–56; see Josephus 1987: 105). Perhaps, as with the survival of his sons (withheld until 26:11), the form of Korah's death is deliberately blurred, 'designed to heighten Korah's crime' by having him 'seemingly scorched to death in an inferno and also devoured alive by the ground' (Wendland 2016: 14). The application of the censers sign in verse 40 appears to assume that YHWH's fire was the manner by which Korah died (so, too, Milgrom 1990: 416). On this scenario, Korah dies by holy fire, even while his house (save his sons) and belongings were swallowed up into *Sheol*, so that in a manner he did suffer both judgements. Such a reading makes the most sense of the story's twofold plotline, and explains best its ambiguities – ensuring the message that, even though Korah died by fire individually for approaching YHWH with incense, judgement nevertheless fell on his house and belongings (while v. 24 mentions his dwelling, v. 27 does not mention Korah himself). When a similar fiery judgement had fallen on Nadab and Abihu, YHWH had declared: 'I will be sanctified (*q-d-š*) by those who draw near (*q-r-b*) me, and before all the people I will be glorified' (Lev. 10:3), a message relevant here as well. Aaron's role as high priest is vindicated negatively by the fiery destruction of those *not* ordained and anointed to draw near to YHWH. The usurpers lack of *status* is at issue (cf. Haran 1985: 232–233). In sum, 'while those who sought earthly power go down living into the earth, those who sought spiritual power go up as a burnt offering to heaven' (Magonet 1982: 21).

Mention of the 250 men in verse 35 provides a literary frame with verse 2 – the priestly cult 'has been tested and successfully defended' (Zeelander 2015: 333). The rebels had set themselves up as a 'self-styled rival Israel', but 'by means of the ordeal and its judgement (by the opening up of the earth and by fire), they are declared not to be holy, not to belong to YHWH, not to be his chosen intimates, in short, not to be Israel' (J. A. Davies 2004: 194–195).

Figure 12: Gustave Doré, *Death of Korah, Dathan and Abiram*

THE INNER CAMP'S FAILURE AND THE SIN OF CAIN (GEN. 4)

Transitioning from the outer camp (chs. 11–15) to the inner camp of Levites (chs. 16–18), the sub-text also appears to progress from the Adam and Eve story (Gen. 2 – 3) to that of Cain and Abel (Gen. 4), from Edenic life to matters of the cult – from prophecy to priesthood. Just as the expulsion from Eden's garden necessitated a sacrificial cult for life with God, so the twelve tribes, to abide with God as a covenant community, require the place and role of the Levitical cult. Y. Twersky presents a number of parallels between Numbers 16 – 18 and Genesis 4, which we expand (2007b: 2:172–182; also Curwin 2023: 171–176). (See Table 30.)

The verbal parallels, utterly unique regarding the ground opening her mouth (Gen. 4:11; Num. 30, 32), hint of deeper thematic links. Both stories portray brothers jealously striving after their lost firstborn status, as it relates to the cult – there is, as Y. Twersky writes (2007b: 2:175), 'tension between the firstborn and God's chosen one'. The connection is profound especially as the primordial cultic narratives function to prefigure the Levitical cult, a point that surfaces with numerous references to 'firstborn', 'tribute offering' and 'fat' when describing the priestly cult in Numbers 18:8–32, terms that together echo Abel's favourable worship. Tellingly, these parallels make sense of what is 'an

Table 30: Parallels between Numbers 16 – 18 and Genesis 4

Numbers 16–18	Genesis 4
'he fell (*wayyippōl*) on his face (*pānāyw*)' 16:4	'his face (*pānāyw*) fell (*wayyippĕlû*)' 4:5
'They rose up (*wayyāqumû*) before Moses' 16:2	'Cain rose up (*wayyāqom*) against Abel' 4:8
'the ground (*hā'ădāmâ*) opened (*ûpoṣtâ*) her mouth (*'et-pîhā*) and swallowed them up' 16:30, 32	'the ground (*hā'ădāmâ*) that has opened (*poṣtâ*) her mouth (*'et-pîhā*)' 4:11
'Moses was kindled greatly (*wayyihar lĕmōšê mĕ'ōd*) . . . Do not turn favorably to their tribute offering (*minhātom*)' 16:15	'But to Cain and to his tribute offering (*minhātô*) he did not gaze favorably, and Cain kindled greatly (*wayyihar lĕqayin mĕ'ōd*)' 4:5
'firstborn' (*bĕkôr*), 'tribute offering' (*minhâ*), 'fat' (*hēleb*), 18:8–32	'Abel, he also brought the firstborn (*bĕkōrôt*) of his flock, and of their fat (*hēleb*), and YHWH gazed favorably to Abel and his tribute offering (*minhātô*)' 4:4
'your brothers' (*'aḥekā*), 18:2, 6	'your brother' (*'aḥîkā*), 4:9 (cf. 4:2, 8, 9, 10, 11)

otherwise inscrutable detail' (Y. Twersky 2007b: 2:177), Moses' plea to YHWH: 'Do not turn favorably to their *minḥāh*!' (Num. 16:15). The only precedent of YHWH's disregarding a *minḥāh* that Moses could have in mind is Cain's offering.

The transition from Genesis 2–3, and the outer camp (chs. 11–15), to Genesis 4, and the inner camp (chs. 16–18), also involves a move from the Decalogue's first table to the second, where murder heads the list of sins against other humans. The Torah's first use of 'brother' (*'āḥ*) occurs in Genesis 4, naturally, since Cain and Abel are presented as the first brothers in history. Brotherliness, however, is indeed part of the story's message, with 8 uses of *'āḥ* in the chapter. Abel is consistently designated 'his brother', underscoring Cain's viciousness, that he rose up against Abel 'his brother' (4:8). Cain himself comes to the heart of the matter, asking, 'Am I my brother's keeper?' (4:9), and YHWH responds with 'the voice of your brother's blood cries out to me from the ground' (4:10) – not 'Abel's blood', but *your brother's* blood. Given the intense sibling rivalry pervading Korah's revolt, the accent on brotherly relations in YHWH's legislative response is explained in the light of Genesis 4. After a Cain-like rebellion, YHWH re-establishes brotherly relations between Aaron's house and the rest of Levi's tribe: 'And your brothers also of the tribe of Levi', 'And even I – look! – I have taken your brothers the Levites from the midst of the sons of Israel' (18:2, 6).

16:36–50 Episode two: Aaron's censer halts the plague

This second story resolves the censer plotline of the first story, dealing with the efficacy of Aaron's priesthood. The 250 princely would-be priests were consumed by fire, their censers becoming symbols of death; here, Aaron's censer becomes a symbol of life.

36–40 (17:1–5). This section serves as both epilogue, shifting focus to the meaning and application of the previous story for future generations of Israel, and prologue for the second episode: 'the people of YHWH' over whose death the people complain (v. 41) are the 250 princes. It begins with YHWH's instructions to Moses for Eleazar, and ends with a compliance report of Eleazar's obedience. The instructions (vv. 36–38) and compliance (vv. 39–40) are given in a panel construction with stylistic variation: whereas Eleazar is first called 'the son of Aaron', he is later referred to as 'the priest'; the censer bearers are first called 'these sinners against their souls', but are later dubbed 'the burned-up ones'; and what is first called a 'sign' is later termed a 'memorial'.

YHWH instructs Moses to direct Eleazar to 'raise up' (*qûm*) from amid the burning censers that had fallen to the ground with the incineration of their bearers, and to scatter the fire away. Possibly to spare Aaron as high priest contact with death, Eleazar performs the function of gathering up the censers which, in being offered to YHWH, had become holy, solely YHWH's possession (cf. Levine 1993: 418–419). Aside from sparing the high priest contact with death, Eleazar's role in collecting censers that will serve as a warning to the community is fitting, since he was in charge of the Levites responsible for guarding the Sanctuary (3:32; Gane 2004: 643). To 'scatter the fire' away, 'ēš zěrêh, forms a possible allusion to the 'strange fire' ('ēš zārāh) of the Nadab and Abihu incident (cf. 'strange man', v. 40), and the LXX uses the same designation, *pyr allotrion*, 'strange fire', for both texts. Evidently the fire continued burning, needing to be scattered. Those devoured by fire are described as having sinned against their own souls – they had approached YHWH at the cost of their lives, disregarding his warnings (see 1:51; 3:10, 38). They are also described grimly as 'the burned-up ones' (śěrupîm), a similar term from the same root used later for the 'fiery' (śěrāpîm) serpents (21:6). That the bronze censers were able to withstand fire contrasts with the 250 chieftains who were not able to withstand YHWH's holiness, for they had not been chosen and consecrated for the purpose, nor had yet attained as a nation such holiness in themselves (Exod. 3:2; Isa. 4:5; Zech. 2:5; cf. 1 Cor. 3:12–17). Some understand the censers account as an *aetiology*, explaining the origin of the altar's bronze overlay, although the instructions and construction of the bronze plating was already given in Exodus (27:2; 38:2) (see Liver 1961: 191). The LXX glosses Exodus with 'He made the brazen altar of the brazen censers, which belonged to the men engaged in sedition with the gathering of Korah' (Exod. 38:22; cf. Brenton 1986: 123). There is no reason, however, why the hammered-out censers could not simply have been added to the altar's original bronze plating, as the most natural place, presumably in a manner that distinguished the new construction. Justifiably, Haran suggests that 'the only possible way of disposing of them [the censers] was to add them to the bronze plating of the outer altar' (1985: 238). Ashley's suggestion that the plating may have been used for the golden incense altar cannot be maintained (1993: 325–326). Only gold is fitting for the holy place, so the bronze 'sign' would undermine its own message, and its function as a sign is precluded by such a locale.

Verse 38 opens with emphasis on the censers that will form a sign, beginning with the direct object 'the censers' ('ēt maḥtôt), and fronting the verb with their description in a five-word clause. The censers are to be made into 'hammered-out' (rāqaʿ) plates, the same term used for God's creation of the 'firmament' (Gen. 1:6, 7, 8, 14, 15, 17, 20), and refers here to thin sheets of metal. These bronze plate covers for the altar are to be a 'sign' ('ôt) for the sons of Israel, explained as a 'memorial' (zikkārôn): when they see the bronze plates they are to remember that no strange man ('îš zār) – defined as 'not of the seed of Aaron' – is to come near to offer incense before YHWH. The last reference to a 'sign' in the Torah was to the Sabbath, the sign of the Sinai covenant given for Israel to know that 'Even I, YHWH, am sanctifying you' (Exod. 31:13, 17). The reminding function of the sign is grounded in the reality of the bronze plating's grim history, signalling YHWH's fiery judgement to the worshipper. The altar, the central focus of Israel's worship, with its bronze plate covers thus becomes a warning sign so that Israelites and Levites will not end up 'like Korah and his community' by attempting to come near to YHWH. The hammered-out censers, relics of YHWH's consuming fire, thus serve as vivid reminders of his dreadful, unapproachable holiness, reinforcing the inner camp's nature and boundaries. Mention of Korah and his community (v. 40) brings closure to this episode. Camp points out the pattern of how establishing the Levites' special status is preceded by inappropriate cultic officiation (2009: 211–212): Nadab and Abihu's demise while using their censers (3:4) is followed by the Levites' special status (3:5–10), just as Korah and his community's demise while using their censers (Num. 16) is followed by the special status of Levites (Num. 18:1–7).

41–50 (17:6–15). The second episode parallels the first in several ways (see Grossman 1998): the sons of Israel 'assemble against Moses and against Aaron' (16:3; 16:41–42), accusing them of acting against the 'assembly of YHWH' or 'people of YHWH' (16:3; 16:41); Moses 'falls on his face' (16:4; 16:46, with Aaron); the glory of YHWH appears to the community at the Tent of Meeting (16:19; 16:42); YHWH bids Moses and Aaron to separate from 'the midst of this community', for 'I will finish them in an instant' (16:20–21; 16:44–45); and, including the third episode (17:1–13), there are two tests demonstrating Aaron to be YHWH's choice for the priesthood, each ending with a 'sign' for Israel (16:38; 17:10), and leading to the people's exclamation over death (16:34, 41; 17:12–13).

The story begins with the 'whole community of the sons of Israel' 'grumbling' (*lûn*) against Moses and Aaron, accusing them of killing the 'people of YHWH'. The pronoun 'you' (*'attem*, pl.) is emphatic, an unnecessary addition fronting the statement: 'You are the ones – not God – who have killed the people who belong to YHWH!' Moses had indeed set up the previous tests which, given his prophetic office, had made the people's demise certain (e.g. 2 Kgs 1:9–17) *unless* they would have turned away from their rebellion. With verses 36–40 serving as a backdrop, the death of the 250 princes are especially in view, men of renown who had been popular nobles among the tribes. Moreover, while we read of Israel's reaction to the ground opening up and swallowing the sons of Reuben and Korah's people into *Sheol* (v. 34), no such reaction was given for the fire that went forth from YHWH and consumed the 250 offering incense, until now. Perhaps they were not eye-witnesses to the censer test's results, or, alternatively, their grumbling may well derive from obstinate unbelief now chafing in the grief of death – 'Now they are dead! Could you not have devised a different test?' More treacherously, they may be proclaiming that Moses and Aaron put the chieftains to death in order to secure their authority. Whereas the original complaint in the first episode was that Moses and Aaron had exalted themselves over the assembly of YHWH (16:3), now they accuse Moses and Aaron of using their authority to destroy 'the people of YHWH' ('am yhwh) – their power-wielding leads to death. Soon, by divine design and wisdom, Moses and Aaron will use their offices for the life of Israel, making atonement and preserving them from death (vv. 46–49). The audacious use of 'the people of YHWH', along with previous uses of 'community', bend the narrative to a thematic question: 'Who are the *true* people of YHWH?' Such an ecclesiological focus is fitting after YHWH's wholesale judgement on the first generation of Israelites in the wilderness. Within the scope of chapters 16 and 17, the answer must include those who trustingly and gratefully embrace YHWH's established leadership, mapped out in the Camp's structure, in this case as related to the priesthood of Aaron's house, revealed through Moses.

The appearance of YHWH's glory is narrated dramatically, recounting how the assembled community turned to the Tent of Meeting and vividly describing the scene through their eyes with added intensity ('look', *hinnê*), as the Cloud covers the Tent and the glory of YHWH appears. The threat was so great against his servants, YHWH appears immediately, even before Moses can respond to their grumbling. It may be the community had gathered about the tents of Moses and Aaron, east of the Tent of Meeting, for we read that Moses and Aaron came 'to the front of the Tent of Meeting' after YHWH's appearance. Although his instruction is for both Moses and Aaron, YHWH addresses Moses alone, asserting his established hierarchy. For the second time (cf. 16:20–21), YHWH bids them to arise from the midst of the community, that he might finish them in an instant, perhaps a play on 'consume' (v. 35). Moses and Aaron fall on their faces, a posture of supplication and intercession on the people's behalf, but we are given no words and much less any dialogue with YHWH – and, to be sure, Moses cannot plead for the sparing of the innocent as before (16:22), since now it is not chieftains but the 'whole community' that is in rebellion (cf. Olson 1996: 106). The scene cuts quickly to Moses' instructions for Aaron, which end with the intense report: 'the plague has begun!' Among the most urgent words of Moses recorded, he bids Aaron to 'Take the censer . . . and go quickly to the community and make atonement for them'. Nevertheless, his instructions are precise, listed in methodical steps, exemplifying how the utterly dangerous holiness of YHWH's presence may be approached only by divine warrant, and with care.

Atonement is central to the message of this story, and to Numbers as a whole (cf. Brodie 2008). That 'the wrath (*qeṣep*) of YHWH has gone forth' was a prospect for which Israel had already been warned and provided: 'But the Levites will camp around the Dwelling of the

Testimony, lest there be wrath (*qeṣep*) upon the community of the sons of Israel – the Levites will keep the charge of the Dwelling of the Testimony' (1:53). As Mirguet explains (2008: 324–325):

> Since the spatial organization of the people, with its reflections in its rituals and hierarchy, is the very condition for the presence of YHWH among the congregation, the divine anger appears as a consequence of the geographic, political, and religious confusion. The assembly has lost its centre – YHWH's Dwelling – and, with it, its own distinctiveness, which is the condition of its very existence.

This passage is much like the central passage of Leviticus, the Day of Atonement (Lev. 16): in both, Aaron is instructed to take a censer, putting on it (burning coals of) fire from the altar and incense, for the sake of making atonement for the people of YHWH (see Lev. 16:12). Leviticus, which pertains to the cultic approach to YHWH, focuses on Aaron's role in the holy of holies, while Numbers, which pertains to the Camp of Israel, centres on Aaron's role for the covenant community's survival in the wilderness.

Moreover, as with the term 'wrath', so 'plague' (*negep*) is linked to the early chapters of Numbers and the role of Levites:

> And I give the Levites – wholly given – to Aaron and to his sons from the midst of the sons of Israel to serve the service of the sons of Israel in the Tent of Meeting, and to make atonement for the sons of Israel, so that there will be no plague (*negep*) on the sons of Israel when the sons of Israel approach the Sanctuary. (8:19)

The message is clear: the very Camp structure which Korah had challenged was YHWH's provision for their safety from the dangers of his holiness, a structure YHWH would reassert after his judgements (18:5). 'So both these terms, the wrath of God (*qeṣep*) and the plague (*negep*), which come together as a consequence of the Korah episode have their explanation and their first mention here in these early chapters of Numbers' (Magonet 1982: 11). Moses and Aaron had only recently fallen on their faces praying that YHWH would not be 'wrathful' against the whole community (v. 22), but now Aaron the high priest must run into the midst of that wrath, to face 'the plague' (*hannāgep*) with censer and incense – and the object of his labour is also spelled out, to 'make atonement' (*kipper*) for the people. Intentionally, Aaron is called to perform precisely what had led to the fiery demise of the 250 princes, to offer incense to YHWH. Connected to the 'pleasing aroma' sent up to God through the atoning sacrifices on the altar, incense offering functions as the sacrificial system in microcosm, resonating with notions of intercessory prayer (cf. Ps. 141:2) and atonement (see Van Dam 1991).

Amid the rebellion of the people against YHWH and his chosen leaders, threatening the community with disorder and chaos, atonement reconciles, it reorders, restructures, and reunifies life with YHWH among the tribes, maintaining the divinely organized Camp. The exceptional act of offering incense *outside* the precincts of the Tent of Meeting, among the people, vividly displays the role of the priesthood for the sake of the rest of the Camp, underscoring the connection between priestly service and the community's well-being, especially by making atonement.

Complementing Moses' precise instructions, Aaron's obedience in taking the censer is described as 'just as Moses had spoken', affirming Moses' authority as the basis for Aaron's role as high priest, along with the benefit of these for the community's well-being. As with the opening verse (16:1), there is no object here for the verb 'took', although context makes 'the censer' obvious (16:47). Aaron's taking of his censer, resulting in the halt of the plague, is a legitimating act, an antithesis to Korah's illegitimate taking in 16:1 (J. A. Davies 2004: 191). The urgency of Moses continues with Aaron who 'ran' (*rûṣ*) to the midst of the assembly, rushing, that more souls might be spared from death. As with the original Camp structure, which had begun to come undone, the high priest is now in the midst of the 'assembly' (*qāhāl*), and Aaron's act will demonstrate just why YHWH had so ordered the community, to preserve Israel alive. With another 'look!' (*hinnê*) we view the assembly of people from Aaron's vantage point and we see that 'the plague had begun among the people!' The story uses both forms of 'plague', *negep* (17:11, 12) and *maggēpāh* (17:13, 14, 15), the latter of which also occurs four times in Numbers 25, when YHWH plagues Israel after their apostasy with the women of Moab; the terms were also used in Exodus for YHWH's judgements on the Egyptians (e.g. 9:14; 12:13) – rather than enjoy his covenant benefits in loyalty, they are experiencing his plagues in rebellion. What such a sight of plague entailed perhaps only the original audience could appreciate, but clearly people were being struck down in some fashion by the outpoured wrath of YHWH.

Aaron puts the incense on the flame of his censer and makes atonement. Atonement through priestly mediation is a major theme in Numbers (see Brodie 2008), and at the heart of the Torah's message (Lev. 16; cf. Morales 2015). While Leviticus underscores the role of priestly atonement in drawing near to YHWH in worship through the cult, Numbers, as the current narrative exemplifies, focuses on the necessity of priestly atonement for the sake of Israel's survival as a nation (cf. Num. 25:7–9). In an iconic description of the priesthood, of their role and vocation as mediators between earth and heaven, humanity and God, Aaron 'stood between the dying and the living, and the plague was stayed'. 'What a moving scene,' writes Van Dam (1991: 193); 'There was the high priest of Israel standing in the midst of a dying people interceding with incense, the incense offering that spoke of atonement and that also spoke of prayer.'

As priest of Israel Aaron's role is to demarcate, maintain, and guard the divinely established boundary between life and death, holy and profane, instructing Israel in the same (cf. Lev. 10:10), which he does here in a way that vividly communicates the theology of the cult. Whereas the censers of the 250 chieftains had provoked the fiery, devouring wrath of YHWH, leading to their deaths, Aaron's censer propitiates and stays his wrath, saving all Israel from certain destruction. Here is priestly mediation: the high priest interposing himself between death and life, courageously, obediently, holding up his censer, aflame by the sacred altar, with plumes of divinely formulated incense sending clouds of fragrance heavenward so that the wave of YHWH's fury, tumbling thousands into its sea of death, suddenly halts, heaped up against the clouds of atoning incense like the waters of the sea crossing – with thousands of Israelites finding refuge behind the chosen mediator, Aaron the high priest. 'The theme of incense integrates the two chapters (Num. 16 – 17),' writes Jenson (1992: 111), 'and the successful atonement by the legitimate High Priest through an incense offering (Num. 17:11) confirms his legitimacy in the same terms in which it was challenged.' In the gifts for the Tabernacle's dedication, given by the princes of the tribes in Numbers 7, twelve verses – describing the same gifts by each of the twelve tribes – end with 'full of incense' (7:14, 20 26, 32, 38, 44, 50, 56, 62, 68, 74, 78; cf. 7:86). The only previous reference to incense was to the priesthood's charge over it (4:16). In the present episode, the divine wisdom comes to fruition as the high priest intercedes for the tribes with the incense they had supplied.

A formal report of the death toll is given, 14,700, with the notice that these casualties were aside from 'those who died in the incident of Korah', linking this story to the previous episode. Having been sent out by Moses, Aaron now returns to him at the door of the Tent of Meeting, the locale of their divine sanction, 'but', we are told, 'the plague was stayed', ensuring that his return was only after he had secured Israel's salvation. The dramatic action is narrated with symmetry, moving out from and then returning to the centre:

16:46: Moses sends Aaron with censer and incense to make atonement, wrath goes out from YHWH, the plague has begun.

16:48: Aaron stands between the living and the dead, the plague is stayed.

16:50: Aaron returned to Moses to door of the Tent of Meeting, but the plague was stayed.

Both judgement, in the form of a plague of divine wrath, and mercy, in the form of a divinely appointed priest to make atonement, go forth from the Tent of Meeting.

LEVITES: THE FIRSTBORN BACKSTORY TO NUMBERS

Rivalry between brothers is a recurring theme in Genesis, a conflict which, more particularly, revolves around the rights of the firstborn son. As a result of his failure to honour YHWH through his offering, Cain had lost his firstborn privileges to Abel, who had brought of the 'firstborn' (*bĕkōrôt*) of his flock for sacrifice (Gen. 4:4). Though Cain slayed his brother, Seth was raised up in his place to serve as Adam's firstborn (see the genealogy of Gen. 5:3). The rights and blessings of the firstborn are integral as well to the stories of Noah's sons, Ishmael and Isaac, Jacob and Esau, and of Jacob's twelve sons. Attempting to claim his rights early, Reuben (Jacob's firstborn) had taken his father's concubine, Bilhah (Gen. 35:22), an act that resulted in the transfer of his blessing to Joseph's sons (Gen. 48:1 – 49:4; 1 Chr. 5:1). While the birthright went to Joseph (firstborn by Rachel), kingship eventually passed to Judah, and the priesthood to Aaron's house, of the tribe of Levi. Later, the tribe of Levi was conferred the status of lay ministers at the Tabernacle (Exod. 32:25–29; Num. 3). These last transfers become a source of tension throughout Numbers.

Considering the relationship between the firstborn and the priesthood in ancient Israel, it is a fair deduction from Scripture – fully assumed in Jewish tradition – that, before the inauguration of the Levitical priesthood, cultic duties were the charge of a household's firstborn son, a commonplace practice in the ANE. Some of the Targums such as Onqelos, translate the MT's 'young men of the sons of Israel' who offered up burnt offerings (Exod. 24:5) as the 'firstborn sons' of Israel (also *TgPs-J*; *b. Zeb.* 115b). Shamah writes (2011: 691): 'Prior to establishment of the Tabernacle, although the Torah does not state so explicitly, it is likely that the firstborn males served as the exclusive priests, as stated in the Mishnah (*m. Zebaḥ* 14:4).' The Targum on 1 Chronicles (attributed to Rabbi Joseph) proposes that sons from the tribe of Reuben, the firstborn of Jacob, led the cult as high priests until the consecration of Aaron's house (see Tg; 1 Chr. 5:1–2): 'the high priesthood was taken away from the sons of Reuben and, because of them, from all their first-born, and given to Aaron and his sons, the sacred service (was given) to the Levites' (Beattie and McIvor 1994: 64). Perhaps in accord with the picture that emerges with Hannah's consecration of Samuel, her firstborn, to serve in the sanctuary at Shiloh (1 Sam. 1 – 2), Israel's firstborn sons were to be consecrated for service to YHWH (Sweeney 2012: 128). In the Passover legislation of Exodus 13, YHWH had said, 'Consecrate (*qaddēš*) to me all the firstborn' (v. 2), and again in Exodus 22:29 he declared, 'The firstborn of your sons you shall give to me.' In Numbers, however, YHWH takes the Levites 'instead of every firstborn' so that 'Levites shall be mine' to serve in place of the former (3:12–13;

also 8:14–18). This commission was part of the blessing Levites received for standing with Moses in zeal for YHWH, being willing to oppose any brother or son who had committed idolatry with the golden calf (Exod. 32:26–29; see Deut. 33:8–9), presumably not having committed apostasy themselves. We may deduce, then, that the Tabernacle duties given to Levites would otherwise have been rendered by Israel's firstborn sons. 'The sons of Aaron are set aside as the priests of Israel, but the rest of Israel is represented in the Levites. The sons of Levi stand in for the firstborn of Israel' (Thomas 2011: 78). Originally, then, Israel's firstborn sons were to serve in a lay-priestly role (alongside Aaron's house once the latter were designated by YHWH), but were replaced by Levites.

The progress to this lay-priestly status of Levites may be traced in the following manner, beginning with the significance of firstborn sons of Israel (also Brin 1994: 221–237). Exodus provides three statements on the consecration of the firstborn (Exod. 13:1–16; 22:28–29; 34:10–27), and Numbers gives three statements on the replacement of the firstborn by Levites (Num. 3:5–13; 3:40–43, 44–51; 8:13–19). Exodus 13:1–16 is set within the larger context of Passover legislation and begins with YHWH's command to consecrate to himself all the firstborn males of the womb, both human and animal, as belonging to him and, thereby, requiring that firstborn sons be redeemed. Exodus 34:10–29, paralleling the previous Passover legislation, further combines the consecration of the firstborn in Exodus 22:28–29 with the annual feasts legislation of Exodus 23:14–19 so that the consecration of Israel's firstborn sons is set within the overall theology of firstfruits (particularly Feasts of Weeks and Ingathering). Turning to the passages in Numbers, each of the three texts has a specific function (Sweeney 2015): Numbers 3:5–13 states the principle that Levites will replace the firstborn and therefore provide Aaron and his sons assistance in their Tabernacle duties; Num. 3:40–43, 44–51 establishes the redemption price paid to Aaron's house for firstborn sons in excess of Levites; Num. 8:13–19 explains that Levites function as a *tĕnûpāh* ('wave' or 'elevation') offering in place of the firstborn for Aaron's house. This latter text, in particular, fills in the theology of Levitical service. The *tĕnûpāh* offerings were those portions set aside specifically for the support of the priesthood; Israelites were thereby giving Aaron's priesthood the tribe of Levi in place of their own firstborn sons for the purpose of assisting the priesthood with their sacred duties. By God's direction, Levites become an offering and then a gift: an offering from Israel both owed and yielded to God (who claimed the firstborn as his own), and which God himself then gave as a gift (*nĕtunîm*) to Aaron's priesthood, precisely the dynamic of *tĕnûpāh* offerings: from Israel to God to the priests – or, from Israel to the priests through God.

Further, Numbers 8:19 states that Levites perform Tabernacle work on behalf of the sons of Israel at the Tent of Meeting, and make atonement for them so they will not be plagued when drawing near the sanctuary. Levites serve as a buffer zone between YHWH and Israel, a lightning rod, as Milgrom put it (1990: 371), attracting God's wrath on themselves whenever an Israelite encroached sancta. We may fill in this theology of Levites by returning to what appears to be the focal point of their election by God, in the aftermath of Israel's apostasy with the golden calf (Exod. 32:26–29). The Levites had aligned themselves decisively with YHWH and Moses, separating themselves from the other tribes of Israel to carry out the divine wrath. Upon this demonstration of zeal for YHWH's honour, they were called by Moses to consecrate themselves for YHWH to bestow a blessing on them, unfulfilled until Numbers. Its zeal for the worship of YHWH God fitted the tribe of Levi to function as the firstborn sons of Israel, to become representatives of all Israel, not only before God and the nations, but before all Israel, modelling the goal of consecration to YHWH.

While the change from Israel's firstborn sons to the Levites is often taken for granted readily from the vantage point of subsequent history, it would be difficult to overemphasize the radical nature of such a shift. Numbers records the (quite negative) initial response among the tribes of Israel, the self-assertion and jealousy that recall the firstborn rivalry stories in Genesis. Presumably, the inauguration of the Levitical priesthood would have affected the tribe of Reuben in particular. The Targum of First Chronicles is telling on this point. Amid the genealogy of Reuben found in 1 Chronicles 5:1–3, the following comment (Beattie and McIvor 1994: 64) is included:

> As for Levi, he was a godly man, and (the Levites) did not act sinfully in the affair of 'The Calf', so the high priesthood was taken away from the sons of Reuben and, because of them, from all their firstborn, and given to Aaron and his sons, the sacred service (was given) to the Levites.

The import of this reading becomes apparent when turning to the rebellion of Korah (chs. 16–17). Ibn Ezra suggested Korah's rebellion had occurred as a direct consequence of the replacement of the firstborn by Levites, following the events of the golden calf (1999: 26). Korah, a firstborn himself (Exod. 6:25), claimed that in transferring priestly duties Moses had acted without God's approval; he was unwilling, therefore, to accept a secondary role in the sanctuary service and approached the censer-incense test with the confidence of long-standing tribal tradition (Y. Green 1985). Moses' response accords with this reading: 'you shall know YHWH sent me to do all these works, because I have not done them of my own will' (16:28). Korah and his band of rebels argued, further, that 'all the congregation is holy (qĕdōšîm)', a point not only resonating with YHWH's declaration that 'Israel is my firstborn son'

(Exod. 4:22) but especially relevant to firstborn sons of Israel, whom YHWH had consecrated (*qaddeš*) to himself (Exod. 13:2). Clearly, Korah was 'seeking the priesthood' (Num. 16:10). It cannot be super-fluous, then, that Korah is introduced as 'the son of Izhar, the son of Kohath, the son of Levi' (16:1). Nor is it likely a coincidence that in the same verse the other named rebels, Dathan, Abiram, and On, are introduced as 'sons of Reuben', descendants of Jacob's firstborn. As Oehler observed, it is 'especially the princes of the tribe of the firstborn, Reuben, who demand a priesthood on the broadest basis' (1950: 201). As for the 250 sons of Israel, designated 'princes (*nĕśî'ê*) of the congregation, called ones of the assembly, men of name' (Num. 16:2), Ibn Ezra surmised they were also firstborn who had formerly offered the whole burnt offering, and who used to carry the censers (1999: 127).

In retrospect, information offered in Numbers 3 – 4, as well as earlier in the Torah, can be understood as preparation for reading the Korah narrative. Along with Korah's lengthy pedigree (16:1), scholars have noted the highly selective genealogy found in Exodus 6:14–25, which begins with Reuben and Simeon but remains with and develops Levi's line alone. Childs questioned why Izhar's line is traced with such detail (2004: 117), and Magonet provides the clearest answer: the lineage functions first and foremost to give the relation of Korah to Aaron and Moses – they are first cousins – in order to provide a 'cast list and essential background for the Korah rebellion' (1982: 5). We also discover in Numbers 3:30 that leadership of the Kohathites had fallen to Elizaphan the son of Uzziel (Kohath's fourth son). Given that Aaron the son of Amram (Kohath's first son) led the priesthood, it would have been natural for leadership of Levites to go to Korah (Kohath's second son). For this reason, rabbinical tradition detected Elizaphan's leadership of Levites as a slight on Korah, deepening his motive for rebellion. More broadly, the first ten chapters of Numbers offer several foreshadowings of chapter 16 (Magonet 1982: 10–13): 'wrath' (*qeṣep*, 1:53 with 16:22, 46; 18:5), 'plague' (*negep*, 8:19 with 16:46). Understanding the displacement of firstborn by Levites enables one to appreciate more deeply the drama of the wilderness narratives. Upon resolution of the inner camp's rebellion, YHWH reaffirms his will: 'No longer will the sons of Israel draw near the Tent of Meeting, lest they bear sin and die. But the Levites are the ones who will serve in the service of the Tent of Meeting; they are the ones who will bear their guilt' (18:22–23).

17:1–13 Episode three: YHWH's vindication of Aaron as high priest

YHWH's two speeches (vv. 1–5 and 10) direct the action, with Moses' obedience following each speech (vv. 6–9, 11), and the divinely intended result – the people's fear of YHWH and his holiness, embracing their need of the priesthood of Aaron – closes the story (vv. 12–13). From the cultic object of a censer used in the first two stories, this last account shifts focus to the staff, an object of authority that was integral in the exodus out of Egypt and the dividing of the sea (Exod. 4:2–4, 17, 20; 7:15–20; 9:23; 14:16; etc.), in fighting against the Amalekites (Exod. 17:9), and in bringing forth water from the rock (Exod. 17:1–6) (Taylor 2010: 235). Intriguingly similar to the divine test of staffs, Exodus 7:8–12 records a divinely orchestrated contest among staffs, between Aaron's staff and those of the Egyptian magicians of Pharaoh's court, aimed at validating Moses and Aaron's mission.

While the first two stories vindicated Aaron as high priest by demonstrating the vast separation of the priesthood from Levites and the rest of the tribes, in this story Levites are associated more closely with Aaron's house (e.g. Bick 2014a), as separated from the twelve tribes even while remaining under the priests, restoring the Camp's original structure (Num. 1 – 4). The second plotline of the first story, involving Dathan and Abiram regarding Moses' divine authority to appoint Aaron's house as priesthood, is here resolved. The descent of Dathan and Abiram alive into *Sheol* had vindicated YHWH's choice of Aaron, through his messenger Moses, in a negative manner; here, a life-out-of-death symbol vindicates YHWH's choice of Aaron, through Moses, in a positive manner. YHWH's orchestration of *Moses'* actions is not an incidental part of the lesson: he has chosen Aaron through Moses.

1–7. YHWH initiates a decisive test aimed at bringing closure to the people's lingering doubts and rebellion over his choice of man ('îš), causing their grumbling against Moses and Aaron to subside. The episode shares terminology with the opening census of the book, perhaps a clue that by this cultic revelation YHWH is re-establishing the order of his Camp, beginning with the role and *place* of the priesthood. The census had entailed 'a man for every tribe', twelve 'chieftains', each 'a head of the house of their fathers', each of the men designated by 'name' (1:1–19), just as the cultic test entails 'a staff for every single chieftain', 'twelve staffs', according to 'the head of the house of their fathers', each man's 'name' written on his staff. Moses is told to 'take' (cf. 16:1, 47; 20:8), taking from each of the tribes a staff belonging to the chieftain who is the head of that tribe's ancestral house. In a twofold manner the symbolism of each staff, as representing one of the twelve tribes, is forged: first, the word for 'staff', *maṭṭê*, also means 'tribe', and, second, the name of each tribe's chieftain is written on the staff. The word *maṭṭê* is found some 120 times in Numbers, most often referring to the tribes (e.g. 1:21). A key word in this story, *maṭṭê*, is used sixteen times, alternating its meaning between 'staff' and 'tribe'. The staff 'was a common symbol of power and authority in the ancient Near East' (Amy-Dressler 1986: 26), closely linked to its owner, being made unique by some design so as to serve as a form of identification (see Gen. 38:18, 25). Perhaps these staffs had been passed down from the twelve patriarchs. Although Aaron was the head of the house of Kohath, Levi's second son, YHWH appoints him chieftain of the tribe of Levi, so that his name is written on the Levite's staff (cf. J. A. Davies 2004: 190). The test will also exalt the tribe 'of Levi' (vv. 3, 8), not the house of Aaron only – when the staff of Aaron blossoms, it confirms YHWH's election of his house to serve as priests, but also that of the whole tribe of Levi to serve alongside priests. In the next chapter, Aaron will be told to 'bring near your brothers, the tribe of Levi, the tribe of your father' (18:7).

There is ambiguity over whether the total number of staffs is twelve or thirteen. Assuming the tribal division of the Camp, then Levi's staff is the thirteenth: verse 2 covers the tribes of the outer camp, 'twelve staffs', with verse 3 adding Aaron and the tribe of Levi; verse 6 is structured similarly, moving from 'twelve staffs' to the notice that Aaron's staff, the thirteenth, was placed 'in the midst' of the others (see Dillmann 1886: 97; G. B. Gray 1903: 214–215; Holzinger 1903: 70; McNeile 1911: 93; Heinisch 1936: 69; Noordtzij 1983: 157; G. J. Wenham 1981b: 156; Ashley 1993: 332). The language of the staff of Aaron and the tribe of Levi being 'in the midst of' the staffs of the twelve tribes recalls the structure of the Camp (Num. 1 – 4); given the alternative reading of *maṭṭê*, the end of verse 6 could read, 'but the tribe of Aaron was in the midst of their tribes'. This is a contest, then, between Aaron and twelve leading chieftains from among the tribes, with YHWH's solution re-establishing the hierarchy that structures the Camp. Hirsch comments that the tribes are called *maṭṭôt* (lit. 'branches') 'because they branch from one common stem'; namely, Jacob (2007a: 356). Given this organic imagery, of Israel as a tree, it may be that the culmination of the test, with Aaron's staff springing forth into life, serves to identify his house, the office of priesthood, as the vine for the tree: apart from relating to God through the ordained priesthood and its work of atonement, each tribe remains a dead branch, fit to be thrown into fire (cf. John 15:1–8).

Moses is to deposit – literally, to 'rest' (*nûaḥ*) – the staffs 'in the Tent of Meeting, before the Testimony, there where I will meet with you', that is, they are brought into the holy presence of YHWH, where he appears in a cloud of glory (see Lev. 16:2). 'The Testimony' (*hā'ēdût*) refers to the Decalogue deposited within the Ark, its notions of enduring divine witness and warning a fitting emphasis for the test: the result will serve as a divine witness and warning regarding the priest whom YHWH has chosen. The 'you' of verse 4 is plural, a rare instance in this context. The only other time YHWH says he 'will meet with you (all)' is with reference to the door of the Tent of Meeting (Exod. 29:45); for the other occasions, which relate to the atonement lid of the Ark of the Testimony, the 'you' is singular, referring to Moses (Exod. 25:22; 30:6, 36; cf. 7:89). The symbolism of the staffs in mind, it is as if the twelve tribes have been ushered into the most holy presence of YHWH – he will meet with them. That their staffs would eventually come away from his presence as dead wood justifies their terror-stricken response 'We perish, we are destroyed! – all of us are destroyed! Whoever draws near – even draws near – to the Dwelling of YHWH will die – are we to perish completely?' Aaron, however, as high priest, had already been admitted into the holiest, with carefully precise instructions, for the Day of Atonement, to cleanse YHWH's house and people by the blood of purification offerings (Lev. 16). Within its original context, the Day of Atonement ritual was revealed as a response to the deaths of Nadab and Abihu (cf. Lev. 10:1–3; 16:1–2). Both Numbers 17 and Leviticus 16 unveil Aaron's sole access to the holiest as Israel's high priest, and serve as divine responses to deaths by YHWH's consuming fire for incense-burning.

The result and point of the test is made clear: 'the man whom I choose, his staff will sprout', as if it were yet a living branch. YHWH is the fountain and wellspring of life. Holiness is abundant life; the unclean – whatever is polluted with or smacks of death – cannot enter absolute life without being obliterated. By the same token, whatever is enabled to be brought into the presence of life, through cleansing and consecration, has access to greater, fuller life. The staff that sprouts confirms whom YHWH has chosen to draw near to himself. Because the sons of Israel had been questioning and challenging YHWH's established choice of Aaron's house to serve as priests, this demonstration is not merely a revelation, but a verdict against their rebellion and a putting away of their grumbling. Moses and the sons of Israel's obedience is reported in two verses (vv. 6–7), closing with the resting of staffs 'before YHWH' in the Tent of the Testimony.

8–13. Moses' role is noteworthy, described almost casually: 'on the following day Moses entered into the Tent of the Testimony'. Readers are then given a view through Moses' eyes – 'look', *hinnê* – within the Tent: 'the staff of Aaron of the house of Levi had sprouted'! The first word after *hinnê* is 'sprouted' (*pārah*), fronting the phrase 'the staff of Aaron of the house of Levi', lending emphasis to the fulfilment of YHWH's word (v. 5), confirming his choice of Aaron. Yet in an excessively abundant demonstration, dispelling any doubt, Aaron's staff not only sprouts, but produces a fantastic display of abundant life and vitality. The three actions – 'brought forth' flower-buds, 'bloomed' blossoms, 'yielded' almonds – use wayyiqtol verbs, typically narrating consecutive action, so that the idea seems to be that readers discover the sprouted staff with Moses and then before our very eyes the sprouted staff brings forth flower-buds, and continues, blooming blossoms, and, growing further, yields almonds (cf. Rashbam, Bekhor Shor, ad loc.). What is the significance of almonds? While there is a ring of truth in some associations made by interpreters (e.g. G. J. Wenham 1981a: 281; Hirsch 2007a: 359), the leading link within the Torah, surprisingly absent in the majority of commentaries, is with the golden lampstand, the *mĕnôrāh*, which was a stylized almond tree set within the holy place, representing Eden's Tree of Life (see Meyers 1976), its light symbolizing the light of YHWH's blessing. Quoting one reference is sufficient to discern the manifest parallels:

> Three bowls shaped as almonds (*mĕšuqqādîm*), with a calyx and a flower (*peraḥ*) in one branch, and three bowls shaped as almonds (*mĕšuqqādîm*), with a calyx and a flower (*peraḥ*) in the other branch, just so for the six branches that are brought forth (*yāṣā'*) from the *mĕnôrāh*. (Exod. 25:33)

The word 'almond' (*šĕqēdîm*) occurs eight times in the Torah: here (Num. 17:8) and six times with reference to the lampstand (Exod. 25:33, 34; 37:19, 20; the other use is in Gen. 43:11). In Numbers 17:8, 'sprouted' (*pāraḥ*) and 'flower-buds' (*peraḥ*) recall the flowers of the lampstand, the noun 'flower' occurring nine times in the Torah for the flowers of the *mĕnôrāh* (Exod. 25:31, 33 [twice], 34; 37:17, 19 [twice], 20; Num. 8:4). Even use of the word 'brought forth' (*yāṣā'*), a common enough term, is also used of the lampstand. The root of the words 'bloomed' (*yāṣēṣ*) and 'blossoms' (or 'flowers', *ṣîṣ*) occurs eight times in the Torah, arguably associated with the priesthood in every case, used three times for the golden rosette that adorned Aaron's priestly headdress, inscribed with 'Holy unto YHWH' (Exod. 28:36; 39:40; Lev. 8:9), three times more for the 'fringes' or 'rosettes' of Israel's tassels, meant to remind them of their priestly calling as a nation (Num. 15:38, 39), and twice here to describe the Levitical staff of Aaron, YHWH's chosen high priest for Israel. Chapters 11–15 comprising a unit on the outer camp of the twelve tribes in relation to YHWH's prophetic word through Moses, and chapters 16–18 relating to the inner camp of Levites in relation to Aaron's high priesthood, both sections find resolution through use of *ṣîṣ*: the 'tassels' (*ṣîṣit*) form a prophetic response to the tribal failure, just as the 'blooming' (*wayyāṣēṣ*, 17:8) rod of Aaron forms a divine *cultic* sign for the Levite rebellion against the priesthood. While all Israel is called to be 'holy', as solicited by their dawning of *ṣîṣit*-tassels, the high priest's holiness, vindicated through his 'blooming' branch, surpasses Israel in holiness for the sake of their sanctification. Returning to the question of almonds, then: that Aaron's staff supernaturally budded with almonds portrays his staff as a branch that flows with the sap of the heavenly tree, as if the branch had been grafted onto the *mĕnôrāh*, not the golden copy but grafted onto the heavenly reality. With a golden rosette (*ṣîṣ*) on his brow and a blossoming staff in hand, fruitful with almonds, the high priest is portrayed 'as a sort of sacred (almond) tree' (Spoelstra 2019: 77, 78–79), of a piece with the golden lampstand. YHWH's vitalizing power – his Spirit, bringing forth life out of death – and all of its fruitfulness may be channelled for the sake of Israel through the divinely chosen conduit and mediator, the high priest of the house of Aaron. Here, at the heart of Numbers is a sign and demonstration of resurrection life in the wilderness. YHWH God, the infinite and inexhaustible fountain of life, is able to grant Israel life through the mediation of his chosen high priest. Waxman writes that what apparently could not be accomplished by terrifying miracles, yielding death, is finally resolved by a flowering piece of wood, whereby death gives way to life (2014b: 269).

Moses returns from within YHWH's Tent bringing forth all the staffs 'from before YHWH' to all the sons of Israel. The other staffs show no signs of life, their deadness symbolizing 'the death that will overtake these tribes if they attempt to enter God's presence' (G. J. Wenham 1981a: 281). Succinctly, with four words in Hebrew, the text reads 'they looked, and they took each man his staff', their ultimate reaction being kept for the close of the story, its finale.

YHWH now directs Moses to 'return' (*šûb*) the staff of Aaron before the Testimony to be kept as a 'sign' (*'ôt*) for the 'sons of rebellion' (*běnê-merî*) – the only such designation of Israelites in the HB (G. B. Gray 1903: 217). An underlying notion may be that, as kept in YHWH's life-giving presence, the staff will continue to 'live', rather than dry out in death, so that its life may continue to serve as a sign (when brought out before Israel – cf. 20:8–9). As symbolizing YHWH's choice of Aaron's house for the priesthood, the staff becomes an admonitory sign, warning rebels off from challenging YHWH's authority in grumbling against his designated leaders. While all the staffs had been brought into YHWH's presence, only one will 'return', as one that belongs inside the Tent of Meeting before the Testimony: like Aaron, his rod, may enter the holiest, while the others must remain outside (cf. Frevel 2013b: 151). Returning Aaron's staff to a permanent place in the divine presence, given the parallel between staff and person/tribe, emphatically marks out Aaron's house and the tribe of Levi as set apart to YHWH. After the censer test, all the censers had been claimed by YHWH – having been offered to him, they had become holy, belonging to him (16:37–38). The staffs, however, had not been 'offered' in this way; rather, representing the tribes, they were 'brought near' before YHWH, more akin to the 250 chieftains themselves who had drawn near and wound up consumed by holy fire. The parallel was not lost on the tribes, who cry out (vv. 12–13):

> Look! We perish!
>> We are destroyed – all of us are destroyed!
>> Whoever draws near – even draws near – to the Dwelling of YHWH will die!
> Are we to perish completely?

The opening three verbs of verse 12, which serves as a culminating conclusion to the stories of Numbers 16 – 17, are 'prophetic perfects', expressing a reality so imminent it is spoken of as already accomplished (GCK § 106n) – it is with this cliff-hanger expectation of certain doom that the narrative ends. 'Any suggestion that the people of God are immune from divine displeasure as a consequence of their 'consecrated' status is quickly dispelled, and the need for mediation, clearly evident in the Sinai pericope, is reinforced' (J. A. Davies 2004: 189). Their lament is notable, however, in that they have turned to Moses, their mediator with YHWH, for help. The cry begins and ends with 'perish', and repeats 'destroyed' and 'draws near' in the centre, culminating with the verdict that they 'will die' (cf. also Sherwood 2002: 168; Zeelander 2015: 337). Connecting this third story with the Dathan and Abiram plotline of the first brings the people's response here (17:12–13) into parallel with their previous dread over Dathan and Abiram's destruction: 'All Israel fled at their voice, for they said, Lest the earth swallow us up!' (16:34, whereas the response to failed censers is given separately in vv. 41–42).

The people's proclamation of dread is precisely the wanted denouement: their dismay and unwillingness to approach YHWH's Tent means 'the need for mediation is established and the priestly prerogatives of the Aaronides is vindicated' (J. A. Davies 2004: 190). Such fear of approaching YHWH is entirely appropriate, and the last words of YHWH's last speech were that the people 'will not die' (v. 10), given they cease their grumblings and embrace the very priesthood he had established to grant them life in his presence, safeguarding them from the threat of his holiness. Knowing that drawing near to YHWH's Dwelling leads to death, they ask, 'Are we to perish completely?' Having a renewed sense of dread over YHWH's holiness and of their own sinfulness and need for atonement, they cry out over their need for mediation, ready now to receive humbly and heartily what YHWH had already established for the Camp; namely, the service of the priesthood (Exod. 29; Lev. 8) and Levites (Num. 3 – 4, 8). Reaffirming the role of the priests and Levites within the life of Israel is thus taken up directly in the next chapter. Indeed, YHWH's charge to the priesthood forms a sure response to the people's fears (18:5): 'And you will keep the charge of the Sanctuary, and the charge of the altar, so there will no longer be wrath against the sons of Israel.' Although the rebellion against Aaron's role as high priest and against the authority of Moses as its basis had attacked the very foundations of the Camp, YHWH's vindication of Aaron has reasserted that foundation – it is only the priesthood of Aaron that allows for YHWH to dwell in the midst of Israel, marking the community as a priestly kingdom and holy nation. Note the link in Exodus 29 between Aaron's priesthood and YHWH's dwelling among Israel:

I will consecrate the Tent of Meeting and the altar, and Aaron and his sons I will consecrate to serve me as priests. Then I will dwell among the sons of Israel and be their God. And they will know that even I am YHWH their God, who brought them out of the land of Egypt so that I may dwell among them – I am YHWH their God. (vv. 44–46)

To be 'their God' and to 'dwell among' Israel is nothing less than the essence of the covenant relationship, embodied paradigmatically by the structure of the Camp – without the priesthood of Aaron's house, chosen and consecrated by YHWH, there can be no covenant community, no relationship with YHWH God.

Explanation

The subsection of chapters 16–20, ending with Aaron's death and the transition of the high priest's office to his son Eleazar, is primarily about the priesthood. Even the rebellion of Reuben's sons may be linked thematically to the priesthood inasmuch as the status of firstborn appears to have entailed priestly duties. Numbers 16 – 17 narrates three stories whereby Aaron's role as high priest of Israel is vindicated by YHWH. In the first double-plotted story (16:1–40), the Levite Korah gathers a cohort among the nobility of the tribes, along with a faction of Levites, and leads a rebellion against Moses and Aaron. The narrative alternates between Korah and the 250 princes at the Tent of Meeting, who attempting to approach YHWH with censers end up consumed by his fire, and Dathan and Abiram, sons of Reuben, at their tents in the Camp, who defying Moses' authority descend alive into *Sheol* as the ground beneath them opens and swallows them up. The first plotline, involving censers, relates to the efficacy of Aaron's priesthood, while the second relates to the divine authority of his priesthood, as chosen by YHWH through Moses. Korah, driven by ambition, had grasped for Aaron's exclusive privileges as high priest, and the 250 chieftains for his priesthood, while the sons of Reuben had attacked Moses' authority and divine mission, undermining the priesthood of Aaron's house. Destruction by fire and earthquake reinforce the divine sanction of Aaron's role as high priest negatively, by punishing those who would usurp his position or attack its divine basis.

In the second story (16:36–50), developing the censers plotline of the first story, the community of the sons of Israel murmur against Moses and Aaron, accusing them of having put to death the chieftains of Israel, 'the people of YHWH' who had approached him with censers. When YHWH responds with a devastating plague among the people, Aaron offers incense in their midst, standing between the dead and the living, and makes atonement, halting the plague, so that his priestly office is vindicated positively.

In the third story (17:1–13), resolving the Dathan and Abiram plotline of the first story, YHWH orchestrates a test of staffs through Moses, intending to put away any further question or grumbling against his choice of Aaron as high priest, through Moses. After an evening in YHWH's presence before the Testimony, the staffs of the twelve tribes remain dead wood, while Aaron's staff sprouts, blossoms, and yields ripe almonds, thus vindicating Aaron as high priest both negatively, inasmuch as the other staffs remained dead and dry, and positively, inasmuch as his own staff became supernaturally living and fruitful. There is, then, 'a complete theology of priesthood that is to be found in these chapters: its divine origin, its sacred character, its cultic role, but above all its expiatory function, for the theologies of sin and priesthood are intimately linked' (de Vaulx 1972: 189; quoted in G. J. Wenham 1981b: 150). The stories of earthquake, holy fire, and raging plague give way to two signs, signs of remembrance and admonition: bronze plating for the outer altar, and Aaron's budded staff, kept before the Testimony. The stories contrast two paths: whereas revolting against Aaron's priesthood as established by Moses' divine authority leads to death in judgement, approaching YHWH through Aaron, the priestly house he has chosen through Moses, leads to supernaturally abundant life.

A major issue addressed by these stories is Israel's need for a priesthood to deal with the threat of annihilation at the hands of YHWH and confirmation of the choice of Aaron's house to be that priesthood against rival claims, either from the tribe of Levi or from other tribes (J. A. Davies 2004: 190). Within this context, there is also a focus on the relationship of Aaron's priesthood to the tribe of Levites. Although the divine choice of Aaron and his family for the priesthood had already been set forth (Exod. 28 – 29; Lev. 8 – 10), along with the difference between priests and Levites (Num. 3:5–10; 8), evidently the priesthood's role and position was not attained without struggle (Ashley 1993: 296). Israel needed to learn that one takes the priesthood to himself only at the cost of his own life (16:35). But while the first story marks the vast separation between Aaron's house and Levites, the third story shows their organic relationship even while preserving the former's sacred status: Aaron is the chieftain and leader of the tribe of Levites. The second and third stories demonstrate that Aaron's role as high priest is ordained by YHWH God through Moses for the sake of Israel, not only to counter the divine threat of death (16:47–48), but to channel YHWH's life-giving power to Israel for their fruitful blessedness. Holiness is equivalent to abundant life: the same dreadful reality that consumes those not qualified to access YHWH's presence, yields abundant, paradisal life through his chosen conduit.

Delving more deeply into the theological heart of these chapters, *the threefold narrative concerns the structure of the Camp* – that is, the foundation of the covenant community itself. Budd remarks that the sin of the community of chapters 13–14, in rejecting the land, provides a structural balance to Numbers 1 – 2, with its arrangement of the twelve tribes in the Camp, and the sin of chapters 16–17, in rejecting the new priestly hierarchy, corresponds to Numbers 3 – 4, with its constitution of the priestly hierarchy (1984: 188). M. Douglas makes a similar observation within the compass of chapters 16–17, relating the threefold rebellion to the three categories of people set out in Numbers 1 – 4: the Levites, the chieftains, and the whole congregation, meet with the corresponding punishments of fire, earthquake and plague (2001: 128). As recognized by Mirguet, the spatial organization of the Dwelling – that is, the structure of the Camp – is directly reflected in the hierarchy of the congregation (2008: 322; cf. Jenson 1992: 115–148; George 2009). In the early chapters of Numbers, various passages closely linked with the role of Levites and their protective encampment around the Dwelling of the Testimony contain references to 'wrath', 'plague', and even to preventing the dying out of the Kohathites from among the tribe of Levi (1:53; 3:4; 4:15–20; 8:19), all foreshadowing the crisis and theology of Korah's revolt. It can be no coincidence that the term 'wrath' appears three times in this section, the final reference aimed at preventing 'plague' among the sons of Israel (16:22, 46; 18:5). After Israel experiences the dreadful consequences of undermining the divine provision of Aaron's house to serve as priests (16:22; 16:46), YHWH re-establishes the Camp structure and the dual role of Aaron's priesthood and Levites (18:5).

Just as with the book's opening, these central chapters work along the concentric organization of the Camp, steadily moving toward YHWH's Tent, into the Holiest place where, through the eyes of Moses, we watch the sprouted staff of Aaron the high priest of the tribe of Levi as it blossoms and shoots forth almonds. The issue of Israel's need for a priesthood, then, reaches beyond the threat of annihilation in the midst of YHWH's presence, but relates profoundly to the bedrock foundation of the covenant community itself – there can be no Camp of Israel, no covenant relationship, no City of God with YHWH dwelling in the midst of his people, apart from a divinely chosen and consecrated priesthood. In this context, Korah's revolt may be seen as an act of anti-creation, threatening the orderly cosmos established in the book's opening chapters, in fulfilment of the Sinai covenant. Numbers 16 – 17 thus serve as an exposition of *how* the Camp functions as a divine institution, that is, how the reality of life before the face of YHWH, with the majestic, transcendent King of all creation dwelling in the midst of his people, is possible. Such a life with God can only happen through the mediation and atonement work of a divinely chosen and consecrated priesthood, along with the shielding role of Levites, establishing a system of graded holiness. With the cry, 'We perish! Are we to perish completely?' the people have begun finally to appreciate the wonder that is the Camp, life lived *with* God, and thus their dire need for priestly mediation between the utterly holy, sovereign Creator and creatures prone to impurity and defiance.

The Levitical focus of these chapters serves another function as well. As Levites had not been noted as taking part in any of the previous rebellions in the wilderness, the reader may well wonder whether they have been excluded from YHWH's judgement on the first generation – especially since they had also not been counted in the original census, and YHWH's judgement was pronounced in terms of the census (cf. 14:29). Now, with Korah's rebellion, we see that they were pulled 'into the powerful vortex of the whirlpool of rebellion and revolt', and have joined 'the old wilderness generation in dying outside the promised land' (Olson 1996: 101). In many ways these are chapters of death, especially so within the larger unit of Numbers 16 – 20 (see Mann 1987): the death of Korah, Dathan and Abiram, along with their houses, as the leaders of the revolt; the death of 250 chieftains in rebellion, men of prominence among the twelve tribes of Israel; the death of masses of Israelites, 14,700; and, finally, the death of Aaron himself. Images of the earth opening to swallow up into *Sheol*, a consuming fire, a raging plague, charred censers hammered out as a bronze covering for the altar, and the concluding desperate cry (We perish!), all convey the ruin of the covenant community under the shadow of death. Each image stands also as a symbol for the real and threatening presence of YHWH among his people, a dreadfully dangerous reality that must lead to death within an organic community that is polluted by sin and rebellion. But, thankfully, there are other images to be found in the midst of death: Aaron the high priest, swaying his golden censer, columns of aromatic smoke ascending to the heavens, as he stands between the dead and the living, halting the plague; and then a staff – of Aaron the high priest – sprouting forth with blossoms and almonds. These images stand as symbols for the peace and the abundant life of YHWH, the fountain and source of all life, that may be experienced in his presence within the Camp, through the mediation of his designated high priest (cf. Spoelstra 2019: 79). The forces of death within the Camp, the people's sin and impurities, may be countered by the work of atonement and cleansing, by Aaron's priesthood. Israel's divinely chosen and consecrated high priest is a conduit of life and cleansing for the whole Camp, and it is this underlying message that justifies these images of death, for this message of at-one-ment and life with YHWH God becomes the hope and life-line of the second generation of Israel, and of every ensuing generation.

Two signs remain to catechize future generations of Israel about both the dreadful threat and the life-yielding promise of YHWH God's holy presence, and about the role of the cult in mediating between death and life, profane and holy: the bronze plating warns against death and cover the altar, appropriately, since Israelites may not approach the altar or any space beyond it; and the budded staff of Aaron, kept within the holy of holies, demonstrates that YHWH, the fountain of life, pours forth his life-giving blessing only through the sieve of his chosen and consecrated high priest, of the house of Aaron. Olson contrasts the two images (1996: 112): the bronze plating is a 'cold, metallic, and lifeless reminder of death', of the princes who 'died in a fiery holocaust', while the 'budding, blossoming, fruit-bearing staff of Aaron' signifies God's blessings of powerful life among his people conveyed through the Aaronic priesthood. Within a subsection dealing with holiness and death, chapters 16–20 (see Mann 1987), where the holiness of YHWH stands as a pervasive threat of death, Aaron's budded staff, upheld before the people, signifies an alternative dynamic, that of holiness and life – it proclaims that holiness, YHWH himself, is the source and substance, the context and conduit, of life. YHWH's central Tent of Meeting was divinely instituted to be the wellspring and fountain of life for Israel's Camp in the wilderness (cf. 6:22–27). By following closely YHWH's established sacrificial way of approach, including through his chosen and consecrated mediator, the high priest, Israel's Camp may drink from the abundant supply of the waters of life, experiencing God's goodness, bounty and fruitfulness. The threatening impasse of death in the presence of the Holy One, may finally yield to life – abundant, fruitful life – when sin and rebellion are forsaken, and a humble surrender to YHWH's cult, his designated way of connecting his people to himself, is embraced. This is the whole purpose in presenting Leviticus before the organization of the tribes around his Tent of Meeting – only through the cult may such an architectural and spiritual union with YHWH be achieved, in a manner that yields life rather than death for God's people.

Jewish tradition says that Aaron's staff had originally belonged to Judah (Gen. 38:8: 'your staff that is in your hand'), and then was held by every king of Judah until the destruction of the Temple, when it was divinely hidden away, destined to be wielded by the hand of King Messiah, as it is written, 'The staff (*maṭṭê*) of your strength YHWH will send out of Zion: rule in the midst of your enemies' (Ps. 110:2; see *Num. Rab.* 18.23). Early Christian commentators, who saw Aaron's staff as a type of Messiah's resurrection life after the crucifixion, also joined the budded staff to the Davidic Messiah, the sprouting stump of Jesse in Isaiah 11:2 (Olson 1996: 112; cf. Calvin 2003b: 4:127). In contrast with Korah, Jesus did not 'grasp' for his own exaltation, but abased himself, humbly and obediently embracing the Cross of death

(Phil. 2:5–11). The author of Hebrews teaches that just as Aaron did not take to himself the honour of priesthood, but was called of God, so Messiah did not glorify himself in becoming high priest, but was appointed by God who said to him, 'You are my son, today I have begotten you' (Heb. 5:4–5; Ps. 2:7).

As the high priest is the only person designated 'anointed' (*hakkōhēn hammāšîaḥ*, 'the anointed priest', Lev. 4:3, 5, 16, 6:22) or 'Messiah' in the Torah, Korah's revolt was a gathering together against YHWH's Anointed, an archetypal rebellion akin to that set forth against the Messianic King in Psalm 2. The vindication of Aaron, then, was a vindication of YHWH's Anointed: drawing near to God through Aaron would lead to life; doing so apart from this messiah would lead to death: 'We perish, we are destroyed – all of us are destroyed!' (17:12–13). With the Advent of the Son of God, the symbolic worship of the Tent of Meeting has given way to the heavenly reality: people draw near to God through the rent flesh and shed blood of the Messiah, the great high priest 'who loved us and gave himself up for us, an offering of pleasing aroma and sacrifice to God' (Eph. 5:2). His Resurrection, like Aaron's budding staff, is a life-out-of-death sign, God's vindication of Jesus' mediatorial work: any approach to God apart from the Messiah, his designated high priest, is rebellion and must end in death (John 14:6; Acts 4:12; 17:31). Yet having such a high priest, an all-sufficient Shepherd who laid down his life for his sheep, God's people may draw near with full – and joyful – assurance (Heb. 10:19–22).

The divine vindications of Aaron and Moses are parallel in their movements from death to life. To vindicate Aaron, the censer imagery transforms from the fiery death of 250 princes to the iconic portrayal of Aaron standing between the dead and the living, halting the plague and yielding life for Israel. To vindicate Moses as the basis for Aaron's priesthood, the image of Dathan and Abiram's descent alive into *Sheol* is replaced by a life-out-of-death symbol as a dead staff of wood sprouts living blossoms and produces almonds. Without question the negative vindication of Moses, with the earth opening her mouth to swallow up his antagonists, was, as the text expresses, an uncommon 'new thing', by far the most outstanding supernatural event of vindication within the bounds of the HB – and perhaps one that prefigured the 'great earthquake' that accompanied the resurrection of the Lord Jesus Christ, wherein saints walked out of *Sheol* (Matt. 27:51–53; 28:2). Jesus' dead body, resurrected, became like Aaron's staff a living testimony of God, the vindication of the Son whose resurrection forms testimony that he has been appointed Judge of the world (see Acts 17:31). New creation life is found at the centre of Numbers, blossoms and the sprouting of almonds within a wilderness of death.

NUMBERS 18 – 19: YHWH'S RESPONSE TO THE INNER CAMP, AND THE TRANSITION OF GENERATIONS

Translation

[18:1]And YHWH said to Aaron, 'You and your sons, and the house of your father with you, will bear the guilt of the Sanctuary, and you and your sons with you will bear the guilt of your priesthood. [2]And your brothers, also, the tribe of Levi, the tribe of your father, you will draw near with you – let them be levied unto you and let them minister unto you, but you and your sons with you are to be before the Tent of the Testimony. [3]And they will guard your charge and the charge of all the Tent – only to the vessels of the Sanctuary and to the altar they will not draw near, so they will not die, neither they nor you. [4]And they will be levied unto you, and keep the guard duty of the Tent of Meeting, for all the labour of the Tent; but the stranger must not draw near to you (all). [5]And you (all) will guard the charge of the Sanctuary, and the charge of the altar, so there will no longer be wrath against the sons of Israel. [6]Even I – look! – I have taken your brothers the Levites from the midst of the sons of Israel; as a gift for you (all) they are given for YHWH, to work the labour of the Tent of Meeting. [7]Now you and your sons with you will guard your priesthood for every matter of the altar and for within the veil, and you will serve; as a gift of service I give your priesthood, but the stranger who draws near will be put to death.'

[8]And YHWH spoke to Aaron, 'Even I – look! – I give you charge of my contributions, for all the holy things of the sons of Israel, to you I give them as a share and for your sons, for a perpetual due. [9]This will be for you from the most holy things from the fire: all their near-offerings, for all their tribute offerings and for all their purification offerings and for all their reparation offerings, which they return to me; they are most holy things for you and for your sons. [10]In the most holy environs you will eat it, every male will eat it – holy it will be for you. [11]And this is for you: the contribution of their gift, for all the elevation offerings of the sons of Israel, to you I give them, and to your sons and to your daughters with you, for a perpetual due, all who are clean within your house will eat it. [12]All the fat of the oil, and all the fat of the new wine and the grain, the firstfruits of them which they will give to YHWH, to you I give them. [13]The firstfruits of all that is in their land which they will bring to YHWH, for you it will be – all who are clean in your house will eat it. [14]Every devoted thing in Israel, for you it will be. [15]Everything that opens the womb, for all flesh which they bring near for YHWH, among humans or among beast, will be for you; only you will surely redeem the firstborn of the human, and the firstborn of the unclean beast you will redeem. [16]And its redemption from a month old you will redeem by

your valuation, five shekels of silver, by the shekel of the Sanctuary it is twelve gerahs. ¹⁷Only the firstborn of an ox or the firstborn of a sheep or the firstborn of a goat you will not redeem; they are holy – their blood you will dash against the altar and their fat you will turn to smoke, a fire offering for a restful aroma unto YHWH. ¹⁸And their flesh will be for you, as the breast of the elevation offering and as the right thigh, for you it will be. ¹⁹All the contributions of the holy things which the sons of Israel will lift for YHWH, I give to you and to your sons and to your daughters with you, for a perpetual due; it is a covenant of salt perpetually before YHWH, to you and to your seed with you.'

²⁰And YHWH said to Aaron, 'In their land you will not inherit, and there will be no portion for you in their midst – I myself am your portion and your inheritance amid the sons of Israel. ²¹And to the sons of Levi – look! – I have given all the tithe in Israel for an inheritance in exchange for their service which they are serving, the service of the Tent of Meeting. ²²The sons of Israel will no longer draw near to the Tent of Meeting, to bear sin to die. ²³But the Levite, he will serve the service of the Tent of Meeting, and they will bear their guilt, a perpetual statute throughout your generations, and in the midst of the sons of Israel they will not inherit an inheritance. ²⁴For the tithe of the sons of Israel which they lift for YHWH as a contribution, I give to the Levites for an inheritance; therefore, I have said to them, in the midst of the sons of Israel they will not inherit an inheritance.'

²⁵Now YHWH spoke to Moses, saying, ²⁶'To the Levites you will speak and say to them, "When you take from the sons of Israel the tithe which I have given to you from them as your inheritance, you will lift up from it a contribution for YHWH, a tithe from the tithe. ²⁷It will be accounted for you as your contribution, as the grain from the threshing floor and as the fullness of the winepress. ²⁸Just so you also will lift up a contribution for YHWH from all your tithes which you will take from the sons of Israel, and you will give from it the contribution for YHWH to Aaron the priest. ²⁹From all your gifts you will lift up all the contribution for YHWH, from all the fat of it, even from its holy part." ³⁰And you will say to them, "When you have lifted up the fat from it, then it will be accounted for the Levites as the harvest of the threshing floor and as the harvest of the winepress. ³¹And you will eat it in every place, you and your house, for it is wages for you in exchange for your service at the Tent of Meeting. ³²And you will not bear sin by it, when you contribute the fat from it, and the holy things of the sons of Israel you will not profane and you will not die."'

^{19:1}And YHWH spoke to Moses and to Aaron, saying, ²'This is a statute of the law which YHWH has commanded, saying, "Speak to the sons of Israel that they are to take to you a blameless red heifer wherein there is no blemish, and over which has never ascended a yoke. ³And you will

give her to Eleazar the priest, and he will bring her forth to outside the Camp, and he will slaughter her before it (the Camp). ⁴And Eleazar the priest will take of her blood with his finger, and sprinkle toward the front of the Tent of Meeting seven times. ⁵And one will burn the heifer before his eyes – her skin, and her flesh, and her blood, with her offal, one will burn. ⁶And the priest will take wood of cedar and hyssop and a scarlet thread, and cast (them) into the midst of the burning of the heifer. ⁷Then the priest will wash his garments, and will bathe his flesh in water, and afterward he will come into the Camp, and the priest will be unclean until the evening. ⁸And the one who burned her will wash his garments in water, and will bathe his flesh in water, and he will be unclean until the evening. ⁹And a man who is clean will gather the ashes of the heifer, and he will rest them outside the Camp in a clean place, and it will be for the community of the sons of Israel kept for waters of separation – it is a purification offering. ¹⁰And the one who gathered the ashes of the heifer will wash his garments and be unclean until the evening; and it will be for the sons of Israel and for the sojourner sojourning among them, for a perpetual statute.

¹¹“Whoever touches a dead body of any human will be unclean for seven days. ¹²He will undergo purification on the third day, and on the seventh day he will be clean, but if he does not undergo purification on the third day then on the seventh day he will not be clean. ¹³And all who touch the dead body of a human who has died, and does not undergo purification the Dwelling of YHWH he defiles, and that soul will be cut off from Israel, for the waters of separation were not dashed upon him – he will be unclean, his uncleanness is upon him.

¹⁴“This is the law when a human dies in a tent: all who come into the tent and all who are in the tent will be unclean seven days. ¹⁵And every open vessel which has no cover corded upon it, it is unclean. ¹⁶And all who touch one who is slain in the open field, or one who has died, or the bone of a human, or a grave, will be unclean seven days.

¹⁷“And for the unclean, they will take from the ashes of the burnt purification offering and one will pour living water upon it in a vessel. ¹⁸And a clean man will take hyssop and dip it into the water, and sprinkle it upon the tent and upon all the vessels and upon the souls who were there, and upon the one who touched a bone, or a slain one, or one who died, or a grave. ¹⁹And a clean person will sprinkle the unclean on the third day and on the seventh day, and he will purify him on the seventh day, and he will wash his garments and bathe in waters, and he will be clean in the evening. ²⁰But the man who is unclean and does not undergo purification, that soul will be cut off from the midst of the assembly, for the Sanctuary of YHWH he has defiled – the waters of separation were not dashed upon him; he is unclean. ²¹And it will be for them a perpetual statute, and the one who sprinkles the waters of separation will wash his garments, and he who touches the waters of separation will be unclean

until the evening. ²²And all the unclean person touches will be unclean, and the soul who touches will be unclean until the evening.'"

Notes on the text

18:6. 'for you (all)': missing from LXX, Syr and Vg; MT preserves the more complex reality.

7. 'as a gift of service I give your priesthood': is intelligible, making *BHS* deletion unnecessary.

9. 'from the fire': *BHS* proposes 'fire offering', and LXX reads *tōn karpōmatōn*, favoured by Snaith (1967).

'they return': SamP constructs the word as 'they offend', perhaps by dittography from previous 'reparation offering' (*'ăšām*).

10–11. 'you': LXX has pl.

23. 'the Levite': sg. in MT and LXX; pl. in Syr, Tg and Vg.

29. 'its holy part': MT has 'its sanctuary' (*miqdĕšô*).

19:1. 'and to Aaron': lacking from some MSS; 'speak' and 'to you' in v. 2 are both sg., making Aaron's inclusion here dubious. The verb in v. 3, however, is pl. (LXX and Vg have sg.).

2. 'statute of the law': *BHS* proposes emending to 'statute of the heifer', but there is no MS support, and the phrase occurs again in Num. 31:21 (cf. Num. 27:11; 35:29).

3. 'he will slaughter . . . before it (the Camp)': alternatives include understanding 'before him (YHWH)' (de Vaulx 1972: 214), or rendering the verb passive ('the heifer will be slaughtered', ESV, NET); LXX and Vg have pl. verbs here and in v. 5, apparently attempts at clarification; *TgPs.-J.* glosses the subjects of vv. 3 and 5 as other priests who assist Eleazar.

'outside the Camp': LXX adds 'in a pure place' (*eis topon katharon*).

9. 'it is a purification offering': the K reads 3rd m. sg. pronoun, indicating the ash, while the Q has 3rd f. sg. pronoun, referring to the cow.

12. 'he will be clean': SamP, LXX, Syr and Vg have 'and so be clean'. MT's *yitḥār* parallels the closing clause, but could have been a duplication.

14. 'a tent': LXX has 'a house' (*oikia*) throughout vv. 14 and 18.

16. Noam (2009) proposed emending to include 'by blood' of a corpse as one of the defilements, based on a presumed reception in the Temple Scroll 11Q19 50.4–7, the War Scroll 1QM 9.7–9a and a Geniza fragment of Midrash *Sifre Zuta* on Num. 19:11.

17. 'one will pour': MT verb is sg.; SamP, LXX, Syr and Vg read pl.; for *nātan* as 'pour', see van Dijk (1968) and Reif (1970).

18. 'all the vessels': missing from some MT MSS.

19. 'and he will be clean in the evening': LXX and Vg read 'he will be unclean until the evening'; likely changed for consistency (see vv. 7–8).

21. 'for them': SamP, LXX, Syr and *TgPs-J* have 2nd m. pl. here but, given the context of vv. 1–2, MT is acceptable.

Form and structure

Source critics have for the most part considered chapters 18 and 19 as isolated texts, derived from the priestly source, noting the presence of earlier layers of P (cf. Baentsch 1903: 555–564; G. B. Gray 1903: 218–219, 241–44; Holzinger 1903: 71–72, 78–79; Noth 1968: 133–134, 139–141; Budd 1984: 201–204, 209–212). The material readily divides according to YHWH's five speeches: the first three to Aaron alone (18:1–7, 8–19, 20–24), the fourth to Moses (18:25–32), and the last comprising one long speech by YHWH to both Moses and Aaron (19:1–22). The designation *ḥāq* or *ḥuqqat 'ôlām* occurs six times (18:8, 11, 19, 23; 19:10, 21), linking the chapters together, as does the notion of 'guarding' or 'keeping' (*mišmeret*): while priests keep guard of the Sanctuary and altar (18:5), and Levites keep guard over the Tent and its service (18:3–4), the ashes of the red heifer are kept outside of the Camp for, and possibly by, the community of the sons of Israel (19:9). Framed within the narrative setting of Numbers, chapter 18 reads like a legal document, granting Aaron's house the priesthood, along with its revenues, and granting Levites the tithes of Israel, for generations to come (Porten 1993; Taggar-Cohen 1998; see *Sif.*, Num. 117).

The Red Heifer ceremony of chapter 19 has been the subject of much speculation since the time of the rabbinic sages, who were fascinated by the conundrum of how the ashes of the Red Heifer can purify those who are defiled *and* defile those who are pure (see *Num. Rab.* 19.1, 5; *PesRK* 4.6; *Par.* IV 4.4). Stories abound of Solomon's plea for the greater wisdom needed to penetrate into this insoluble mystery, and of the Holy One himself busy in the study of the ceremony, enthralled with the means of purifying Israel (see *Num. Rab.* 19.3–5; *PesRK* 4.3–7; *PesRab.* 12–13; Blau 1967). Modern scholars, too, consider the law of the red heifer 'one of the most puzzling' and 'anomalous' passages in Numbers (J. S. Ackerman 1987: 85). The Mishnah and Tosefta include a tractate on the Red Heifer (*Par.*) which clarifies gaps in the text, such as the suitable age of the cow. Beyond the rite's central paradox, several other difficulties present themselves (H. P. Smith 1909: 208; Humann 2011: 5): Why was the regulation placed where it is rather than being grouped together with other purification laws? Why is this purification offering alone slaughtered and burned outside the Camp rather than being sacrificed at the altar? Why must the animal be female, why red, and why are scarlet material, cedar, and hyssop also burnt? E. W. Davies, who views Numbers as 'probably the product of various literary sources stemming from different historical periods', offers the red heifer ritual as an example of the book's incoherent structure, stating that 'no convincing explanation has yet been provided as to why chap. 19 with its unsystematically arranged collection of laws has been inserted at this particular point in the narrative' (2015: 14–15). Given such puzzling features, it is no surprise that allegorical and typological approaches to the Red Heifer ritual have been common throughout history, with Jewish exegetes seeing the red heifer as a figure for Israel being led away to Babylonian captivity, and Christian commentators finding a type of Christ (H. P. Smith 1909; see Philo, *Spec. Laws* 1.267–269; *Barn.* 8; Augustine, *Quaest. in Num.*, No. 33).

Critical scholarship has approached Numbers 19 largely in isolation from its narrative context (cf. e.g. G. B. Gray 1903: 241) and in terms of comparative studies, assuming that taboos and rituals of cleansing belonged to primitive societies marked by superstition and magic, with Israel retaining vestiges of such practices while reinterpreting their significance (e.g. J. Spencer 1685; G. B. Gray 1903: 241–256; Holzinger 1903: 78–80; Bewer 1905b; H. P. Smith 1908; Scheftelowitz 1921; Robertson Smith 1927; Noth 1968: 138–143; Sturdy 1976: 137; Seebass 1993: 2:249–251). Two levels of disparate material are typically discerned: vv. 1–13 and vv. 14–22, the latter section being a supplementary addition (e.g. Wellhausen 1889: 178; G. B. Gray 1903: 254; Holzinger 1903: 78–79; cf. McNeile 1911: 101). Other diachronic studies have detected three separate sections: vv. 1–10, 11–13, and 14–22 (see Noth 1968: 139–143; Noordtzij 1983: 167), and Wefing develops her own approach to the text's historical development, suggesting that two separate rituals have been combined, a communal sacrifice of a red cow and purification from corpse pollution, linked together in the final redaction by the waters of purification (1981; cf. Budd 1984: 210–211). Often the various addressees – from Moses and Aaron, to Eleazar, the priest, and unnamed individuals (who appear exclusively from verse 8 onward) – are taken as evidence of a complex history of development (de Vaulx 1972: 214–216). Many such discrepancies and supposed fissures in the text, however, are more apparent than real, and the participants of the ritual, whether priest or layman, may be accounted for readily (see Humann 2011: 78–174).

Although Milgrom understands Numbers 19 to contain vestiges of pre-Israelite paganism (1981b: 65–66, 68–72), he also sees the chapter's final form as an ideological and structural unity, citing the observation of ancient rabbis that the text contains seven subjects mentioned seven times (heifer, burning, sprinkling, washing, uncleanness, cleanness, priests; see *Num. Rab.* 19.2; *PesRK* 4.2; *PesRab.* 14.6), and offers a panel structure outline (Milgrom 1990: 437–438). (See Table 31.)

In Milgrom's scheme, differences in phraseology may be explained as stylistic: 'Dwelling' (v. 13) versus 'Sanctuary' (v. 20), 'cut off from Israel' (v. 13) versus 'cut off from the midst of the assembly' (v. 20) (1990: 438). Arguably, *lāqaḥ* (to take) is a key word in chapter 19 (vv. 2, 4, 6, 17, 18; cf.

Table 31: Numbers 19 panel outline

Panel A	Panel B
'This is the ritual law' (2a)	'This is the ritual' (14a)
Preparation of ashes renders impure (2b–10)	Touching corpse or derivatives renders impure (14–16)
Purification procedure (11–12)	Purification procedure (17–19)
Penalty for non-purification (13)	Penalty for non-purification (20) / 'Law for all time' (21a)
	(Addition [21b–22])

Cole 2000: 302), as it is in chapters 16–17. The five speeches of YHWH form the broad outline of chapters 18–19, with further subdivisions given in the comments:

YHWH's speeches to Aaron

18:1–7: Duties and responsibilities of priests and Levites for guarding the Sanctuary
18:8–19: Contributions for priests and Levites
18:20–24: Inheritance of priests and Levites

YHWH's speech to Moses

18:25–32: Levitical tithes

YHWH's speech to both Moses and Aaron

19:1–22: Cleansing from death pollution, through priests

That YHWH speaks directly to Aaron alone in chapter 18 is exceedingly rare and highly significant. The only other occasion where he does so, in Leviticus 10:8–11 (cf. Exod. 4:27), proves programmatic for the rest of the book, addressing the distinctions between holy and profane (Lev. 17 – 25) and clean and unclean (Lev. 11 – 16) (see Morales 2015: 150–151), and which, as with Numbers 18, comes as a response to fiery judgement within the context of the cult (Lev. 10:1–5). Do the three speeches directed exclusively to the high priest in Numbers 18 display a similarly special function? A good case can be made that they do play a pivotal role, in terms of the book's structure and content. YHWH's first speech to Aaron recalls the first major division of Numbers, focused on the structure of the Camp (18:1–7, chs. 1–10). His second speech underscores one of the central messages of the book's central section (18:8–19, chs. 16–17), and the third divine speech to Aaron, related to tithes and inheritance, foreshadows the third major section of Numbers (18:20–24, chs. 26–36). As chapter 15 formed a divine response and cap for the section on the outer camp of twelve tribes (chs. 11–15), so chapter 18 forms a divine response and cap for the inner camp section (chs. 16–18), and chapter 19 functions as a transition from the old to the new generation of Israel.

Comment

18:1–7: Duties of Priests and Levites for guarding the Sanctuary

The first speech to Aaron designates the guarding responsibilities of priests and Levites. YHWH's Dwelling or its vessels, the sacred space and objects of their guarding, are noted thirteen times: Sanctuary (vv. 1, 3, 5), Tent (vv. 3, 4), Tent of Meeting (vv. 4, 6), Tent of the Testimony (v. 2), Altar (vv. 3, 5, 7); Veil (v. 7), vessels (v. 3); and the root for 'guarding' (*šamar*) occurs nine times (vv. 3 [three times], 4 [twice], 5 [three times], 7). In a loose palistrophe, the paragraph begins and ends with the priestly responsibilities of Aaron (vv. 1, 7), continues with two statements about Levites serving with Aaron as 'brothers' (vv. 2, 6), and two explanations that priests alone have access to the 'Sanctuary' and the 'altar' (vv. 3, 5), and has as its central focus the summary statement that Levites are 'levied' to the priests and given charge of the Tent, versus any other Israelites (v. 4) (cf. Leveen 2013: 253–255; P. Schmidt 2020: 70–73). Generally, these verses address the responsibilities of Levites, with three exceptions related to priests interspersed: 'but you and your sons' (v. 2), 'only the vessels of the Sanctuary' (v. 3), 'And you (priests) will guard' (v. 5). Warnings or threats of death for drawing near occur no less than four times: 'so they (Levites) will not die, neither they nor you (priests)' (v. 3), 'but the stranger (any Israelite) must not draw near to you' (v. 4), 'so there will no longer be wrath against the sons of Israel' (v. 5), 'but the stranger (Levite or Israelite) who draws near will be put to death' (v. 7). The last threat concludes YHWH's first speech soberly, underscoring the weighty role of priests and Levites in preventing the threat of YHWH's wrath on the rest of the Camp, as displayed in chapters 16–17.

The tribe of Levi, including Aaron's house of priests, will now bear the penalty of divine wrath, along with the actual culprit(s), for any unauthorized encroachments of the Sanctuary, this culpability in place of the community of Israel. While Levites had already been given guard duty earlier (1:53), that had been to prevent outbreaks of divine wrath from falling on the entire people, 'but now their incentive to stop a violator literally dead in his tracks (cf. 1:51) is to protect themselves' (Gane 2004: 652). More narrowly, priests will bear the penalty for any encroachments of priestly prerogatives, including their service at the outer altar and within the veil, either by disqualified priests of Aaron's house or by any non-priests, whether Levites or Israelites (18:3, 7), a duty that had also been charged earlier (3:10, 38), but returns, again, with the new condition that priests will bear the culpability to protect the entire community from YHWH's wrath. This chapter, as Shamah discerns (2011: 775), presents a 'major demand' on priests and Levites, increasing their earlier charge, but one that 'relieves the people of their fears', since it transfers the punishment of encroachment 'to the guardians' themselves.

1. YHWH speaks directly to Aaron alone, his address beginning with an emphatic 'you' (*'attā*). Having been vindicated three times in Numbers 16 – 17, Aaron now receives the highest approbation, divine revelation, addressed directly three times by YHWH in a manner usually reserved for Moses, the personal message also underscoring the weighty responsibilities communicated. This verse likely refers *only* to Aaron's priestly house. As P. Schmidt argues (2020), 'your father's house' should be understood as Aaron's 'family', the two lines of verse 1 forming a parallelism, whereas Levites are not in view until verse 2. Otherwise, 'you and your sons' refers to the priesthood, while 'the house of your father' would include the Kohathites – Aaron's ancestral line – in charge of transporting the holy vessels (4:1–20). To 'bear the guilt' (*tiś'û 'et-'āwōn*) means to bear the consequences of YHWH's wrath for violations of encroachment on his sacred space, whether his Dwelling or its vessels. While individual violators themselves must be put to death (v. 7), the priests' bearing of the guilt helps ensure that YHWH's wrath does not break out against the whole community. 'Sanctuary' here may also be read as 'holy objects' (cf. Milgrom 1970b: 1:23–24 n. 78). In either case, 'Sanctuary' includes its holy vessels – *sancta* – with priests bearing the penalty, including for encroachments by other priests who are blemished (Lev. 21:23), drunk (Lev. 10:9), unwashed (Exod. 30:20) or improperly dressed (Exod. 28:43) (Milgrom 1990: 146). The strong opening emphasis on Aaron and his sons serves as a key for the rest of the chapter (Leveen 2013: 255).

2. The Levites are now levied to the priests as Aaron is bidden by YHWH to bring them near with himself, so they may be joined to him. Our translation 'levied' (*lāwāh*), following Alter (2004: 774), captures the Hebrew play on 'Levi', from which his name derives: Leah had hoped that with the birth of this third son, her husband Jacob would finally be more 'attached' to her (Gen. 29:34), but in divine wisdom the name is fulfilled by her son's descendants being attached to the priesthood, joined more closely to God. A significant emphasis dawns with this divine speech, the close relationship of Aaron (and the priesthood) with the tribe of Levites. Milgrom notes that 'levied unto (*'āl*) you' implies subordination, whereas 'with' (*'im*) you is an attachment of equals (1990: 147) – the Levites, joined to Aaron, are subordinate to his house, the priesthood. In previous

accounts concerning Levites (3:5–9; 8:5–14, 16–19), there had been no hint that Aaron and Levites were related in a familial or tribal manner (see Bick 2014a), presumably because they were each elected to service independently: Aaron's priesthood is essentially assumed in the Torah, perhaps based on his role in the exodus out of Egypt (Exod. 28:1), while the Levites' role was a fitting reward for their faithfulness in the incident of the golden calf (Exod. 32:25–29) (see Morales 2019b). But beginning in the previous chapter, with Aaron's staff symbolizing the tribe of Levi (17:3, 8), and now here, as Aaron himself, as an act of his own volition, is to draw them near with himself, Levites are designated with familial terms alongside the priests: the Levites are 'your brothers' (cf. v. 6) and 'the tribe of your father'. Bick further notes that the Netziv explains the symbolism of Aaron's staff with the blossoms representing the Levites and the almonds representing the priesthood, so that there is now a single, organic continuum, with Aaron serving as priest because the priesthood is the nobility of the divinely elected tribe of Levi (2014a: 238–239). The present passage prioritizes Aaron the priest who 'levies' the Levites to himself, but the basic point stands: YHWH's solution to the rivalries of ambition between Levites and priests is to underscore more deeply their brotherly and familial bond. They are not to see themselves as utterly separate, distinct entities, but as organically related in a mutual service.

Yet, while they are joined together, the hierarchy and its related duties must be maintained. Clearly delineating their separate roles, YHWH pronounces that Levites are to 'minister' (šārat) to Aaron, but the priesthood – an emphatic 'you' ('attā) and your sons – are to be before the Tent of the Testimony.

3–5. These verses form three generally parallel statements, each containing at least two of three elements: (1) description of the Levites' duty to guard the Tent, (2) a priestly exception, and (3) a warning or threat for encroaching sacred space and/or objects. Verse 4 is the focus of YHWH's speech, the centre of its concentric structure. Levites, attached to the priests, will guard the Tent from the approach of any Israelites, but they themselves must not approach the sacred vessels of the Sanctuary or the Altar, lest they die. Priests guard both the Tent and the Altar from any encroachers, including Levites. Within the cult, 'stranger' (zār) refers to anyone not authorized to approach sacred space, here a non-Levite – an 'unauthorized encroacher' (Milgrom 1990: 424), one who 'tries to claim the priesthood's right, even though he has no legal right, for he does not belong to the family' (Taggar-Cohen 1998: 80). The Levitical guard duty includes putting to death the one who encroaches. Since YHWH's wrath for encroachment would vent on the negligent Levite guard, rather than against the sons of Israel (v. 5), the Levite's execution of the encroacher may include a measure of self-defence (so Milgrom 1990: 424). More fundamentally, the encroacher dies justly for defying YHWH and transgressing both his law and sacred space. YHWH's consoling response to the people's despair of approaching his Dwelling (17:13) is to limit his wrath to the Levitical guards, including priests. Such a grave role on behalf of the covenant community will be rewarded, however, as Levites are granted an abundant share of Israel's tithes (18:21–24, 31). Milgrom's chart, which includes verses 22–23, offers a helpful summary of the respective guard duties of priests and Levites (1990: 424). (See Table 32.)

Milgrom's scheme needs some nuance: as noted already, verse 1 likely relates only to Aaron's family, and even Kohathite duties remained under the charge of Aaron's sons (3:32; 4:16–20) – priests did not escape accountability when sacred objects were 'in transit'.

Within its literary context, the sacral hierarchy established by YHWH may now be received more readily as a welcomed gift for the sake of the entire Camp: 'so they (Levites) will not die' (v. 3) recalls the death of Korah and his community, and 'so there will no longer be wrath (*qeṣep*) against the sons of Israel' (v. 5) recalls the devastating plague that had 'struck down' thousands of Israelites (17:11–15), a term used earlier in Moses and Aaron's prayer in 16:22 (*tiqṣōp*). YHWH's response serves to allay the people's fears, expressed after Korah's rebellion. Note the progress from 1:53, where the Levitical encampment around the Dwelling was so that wrath will *not* fall on the sons of Israel, to 18:5, where guarding sacred space is so that wrath will *no longer* fall on the sons of Israel (Mirguet 2008: 324) – now that Israel has tasted the wrath of YHWH, the Levites' role and geographical position within the Camp's hierarchical structure is reaffirmed and embraced: access to YHWH's Tent 'will be regulated according to concentric circles of authority, moving from the congregation as a whole, to the Levites, to the priests' (Mann 1987: 184). More than a reaffirmation, YHWH's speech may be an act of reorganization of the Camp's structure, given the chaos it had apparently become through Korah's rebellion. What is really at stake in YHWH's speech 'is the proper guarding of boundaries' (Leveen 2013: 256), with priests charged to guard all that is within the Sanctuary (plus the altar), and Levites charged to guard outside of the Sanctuary.

6–7. Mason recognized the *wa'ănî hinnê/ wĕ'attā* (And I – look! / And you) structure as formulaic in the Pentateuch for an eternal covenant, stipulating the conditions of both parties – YHWH (Even I – look!) and

Table 32: Priestly and Levitical duties

Verse	Sacral class	Responsible for	Encroachment of
1b, 5a, 7a	Priests	Most sacred objects	Disqualified priests
3	Priests and Levites	Most sacred objects (at rest)	Levites
1a	Kohathites	Most sacred objects (in transit)	Israelites
22, 23	Levites	The tabernacle (as a whole)	Israelites

Aaron's house (Now you and your sons with you') – with these verses bridging the first two speeches (note the occurrence of 'Even I – look!' in v. 8; 2008: 194–195). With an emphatic 'I' (*'ănî*), underscored further with 'look!' (*hinnê*), the election of Levites is defined within the framework of YHWH's sovereign gift to the priesthood. The phrase *wa'ănî hinnê lāqaḥtî* appears verbatim in 3:12 with reference to Levites, here inserting 'your brothers' (*'ăḥêkem*) before 'the Levites', highlighting their organic unity. As in the Camp structure, the Levites are taken 'from the midst of the sons of Israel' (see 3:9, 12; 8:19). As 'given' (*nĕtunîm*) for YHWH (cf. 3:11–13; 8:16), the Levites are his 'gift' (*mattānāh*) for the priests, 'to work the labour' of the Tent of Meeting, understood as the Tent's dismantling, reassembling and portage (Milgrom 1983b: 18–46; cf. Noth 1968: 135). Forms of 'to give' occur twelve times in the chapter, and 'gift', using the same root, another four times, reversing the previous key word for chapter 16, 'take' (16:1, etc.; cf. Y. Twersky 2007b: 2:180–181). It is YHWH who has 'taken your brothers the Levites'. By comparison to the *tidennūtu* documents of Nuzi whereby a *tidennu*-person, who was always a family member, enters a creditor's household for work as a familial legal transaction, Taggar-Cohen notes that Levites are taken by YHWH as *ntwnym* (v. 6) to work at his house in place of the firstborn sons of Israel; while supervised by priests who are in charge of his house, and given to them for this purpose, nevertheless Levites work for the sake of God, their master, and as a familial transaction on behalf of the sons of Israel (1998: 87–90). She further underscores how Numbers 3 – 4 emphasized the goal of their work as the reason Levites were given to Aaron, while Numbers 8 highlighted their function as protectors of Israel (1998: 79); likely both aspects of their role are in view here (S. D. Mason 2008: 196 n. 21).

The priestly office is also a divine gift (*mattānāh*), and for the sake of service (for 'gift of service' as an unresolved crux, see Milgrom 1990: 315 n. 17). As with the gift of Levitical help, these priestly duties given to Aaron's house are royal grants from YHWH (Taggar-Cohen 1998: 77; cf. J. A. Davies 2004: 185), and anticipate the reward of gifts (or 'dues') given to the priesthood for their labour in verses 8–19. More deeply, the *wĕ'attā* (and you) language points to the conditions of 'the covenant of salt perpetually' (v. 19) on the part of Aaron's line: 'By the use of *wĕ'attā*, Aaron and his sons are commissioned to perform the duties of the inner sancta. This includes seeing that an encroacher is put to death (*yûmāt*)' (S. D. Mason 2008: 197). Ashley is likely correct in understanding 'guard' (or 'keep) as the priests' guard duty, concerning sacred objects, and 'serve' (or 'work') as referring to their 'dangerous tasks of dismantling, covering, and, in due course, unpacking the holy objects (4:5–15)' (1993: 344). Aaron and his sons are admonished to guard especially the outer altar and within the veil – any encroachment permitted on these areas will result in their bearing the guilt and consequent divine wrath. The 'veil' (*pārōket*) refers to the inner veil, before the holy of holies and ark of the covenant, whereas *māsak* is used for all other screens and veils (e.g. Exod. 26:36–36; 38:18): the outer altar and inner sanctum form a merism, referring to the entire priestly domain by its outermost and innermost extremes (Gane 2004: 653).

Use of the terms 'service' or 'labour' (*'ăbōdāh*) and 'guard' (*šamar*) for both priests (v. 7) and Levites (vv. 5–6) throughout this section, underscoring the need to guard the Sanctuary, recalls Adam's duties 'to serve and to obey' (*lĕ'obdāh ûlĕšomrāh*) within the garden of Eden (Gen. 2:15), the original sanctuary of the cosmos (see Morales 2012: 99–100; G. J. Wenham 2014: 163). The parallel between Adam's duties in the garden sanctuary and that of priests and Levites at YHWH's Tent portrays the reality of the Camp's spiritual dynamic: the twelve tribes of Israel, with YHWH's Dwelling in their midst, have access to the Edenic paradise of God – mediated by Aaron's house, and guarded by both priests and Levites.

YHWH's first speech to Aaron closes with a sobering reality, that for the sake of sparing the nation and protecting many thousands of Israelites, priests must stand ready to put to death anyone who encroaches upon YHWH's sacred space, to 'execute discriminate bloodshed' (S. D. Mason 2008: 203). Unauthorized approach – by a 'stranger' (*zār*) – threatens the purity of the Sanctuary (cf. Levine 1974: 76), and relates not only to disqualified priests, but also to any Levites and Israelites. The priests and Levites' bearing of guilt for encroachment is divinely aimed to allay Israel's fears (cf. Knohl 2007: 80), opening the prospect of fellowship with YHWH once more, with peace and joy. Since 'illicit contact with the sacred incurs divine wrath or plague', which may destroy the entire community, the Levitical cordon is empowered to strike down the encroacher, but also held fully responsible in the event any encroachment occurs, which means Levites rather than all Israel actually bear the divine judgement – so 'the Israelites need not worry that God will punish the entire community' (Milgrom 1997: 243). It is possible to read the Levites' bearing of the divine penalty as only a renewed emphasis, instead of new legislation (see Hirsch 2007a: 363–365); even in this case, YHWH's speech *now* serves to allay the people's fears, reminding Israelites 'that God has already provided what they are crying out for' (G. J. Wenham 1981b: 159). Israel may now 'serve God acceptably with reverence and awed caution – for our God is a consuming fire' (Heb. 12:28–29). The execution of an encroacher, as Milgrom points out (1997: 244), is not to be confused with the legal category of capital punishment; rather than a just payment for a particular crime, the execution of an encroacher is about defence (against incurring God's unbounded wrath), not justice. The sobering close of YHWH's first speech to Aaron not only looks back to the thousands who died under divine judgement in chapters 16 and 17, but looks forward, grimly foreshadowing the execution of Zimri, a chieftain of the tribe of Simeon, along with his Midianite consort, by Phinehas the priest (Num. 25).

18:8–19: YHWH gives his contributions to Aaron and his house, the priesthood

This second speech by YHWH to Aaron begins and ends with summary statements that YHWH's 'contributions' are 'given' to Aaron and his priestly house 'for a perpetual statute' (8, 19), and then specifies the sorts of contributions and what they entail under two broad headings: 'most holy' (vv. 9–10) and 'holy' (vv. 11–19). Modifying Gane's delineation (2004: 653–654), and taking verse 19 as a summary frame with verse 8, the priestly gifts include the following:

Summary statement (18:8)

Most holy gifts (18:9–10)

    (1) threefold gift of portions of the most holy sacrifices (18:9–10; cf. Lev. 6–7):
        tribute offerings
        purification offerings
        reparation offerings

Holy gifts (18:11–18)

    (2) dedicated portions of sacred gifts (18:11; cf. Lev. 7:30–36), possibly a summary of vv. 12–18;
    (3) the threefold gift of firstfruits offerings (18:12–13):
        oil
        new wine
        grain
    (4) every devoted thing (18:14; cf. Lev. 27:21, 28);
    (5) threefold gift of the meat of firstborn animal sacrifices (18:15–18):
        ox
        sheep
        goat
    (6) redemption price for firstborn sons and non-sacrificial animals (18:16).

Summary statement (18:19)

YHWH's fourth speech, to Moses (18:25–32)

    (7) a tithe of the tithes received by Levites (18:25–32).

Forms of 'give' (*nātan*) occur seven times and 'for you' (*lĕkā*), including for your sons or daughters, occurs twenty-one times in the section, underlining YHWH's benevolence to the priesthood. The second, central speech by YHWH to Aaron alone encompasses the focus at the centre of the wilderness section (chs. 11–25), on Aaron and his priestly house (chs. 16–20).

8. With similar phraseology to verse 6, 'Even I – look!' (*'ănî hinnê*), YHWH declares that he has 'given' (*nātattî*) to Aaron charge of 'my teruma' (*tĕrûmōtāy*). The two gifts, giving Aaron's line the Levites (v. 6) and the priestly due of contributions (v. 8), form YHWH's responsibilities in 'the covenant of salt perpetually' (v. 19), as Aaron and his sons fulfil their condition, their priestly guardianship and duties (vv. 1, 7). The word *tĕrûmāh* means literally 'lifted off, separated' (cf. 8:8–13). While traditionally rendered 'heave offering' this is a general term for any gift that goes to the priests by way of dedication to YHWH, and is always offered 'to YHWH' rather than 'before YHWH' (Milgrom 1983b: 159–172). The 'holy things of the sons of Israel' refers to what is offered to YHWH, set apart to belong to him. They are given as a 'share' (*môšḥāh*), the root of which carries the idea of 'oil' and 'anoint', implying a portion that has been consecrated (see BDB 602–603). The share is for you (Aaron) and for 'your sons', although the summary statement in verse 19 will include 'your daughters with you', a difference that appreciates the distinction among the three sorts of contributions – only the elevation offerings may be eaten by all who are clean within the priestly house, including daughters (v. 11). The priestly charge over YHWH's contribution is a 'perpetual due' (*ḥāq-'ôlām*), 'technical terms for the sacrificial offerings assigned to the priests as their legal portion' (Ringgren 1986: 144; Milgrom 1991: 435, 618–619), binding for all generations. In the ANE, priestly revenues were the subject of grants and royal bestowals, as here by Israel's divine King (see Weinfeld 1970: 201–202; as with vv. 19, 21).

Gifts of the most holy things from the fire

9–10. The 'most holy things' (*qōdeš haqqŏdāšîm*) refers to offerings 'brought by the people that were taken over into the Holy Place (the Court of the Priests) and therefore never came back again out of the Holy Place', eaten 'by the priests themselves and not by their households also' (see Lev. 6:18; Snaith 1973: 373). Designation of the most holy things that will be for Aaron stipulates three kinds of offerings from all 'near-offerings' (*qorbān*) of Israel: tribute, purification and reparation offerings. The whole burnt offering is left out since it is given completely and wholly to YHWH, the entire animal apart from its skin consumed on the altar. The fourfold repetition of 'all' (*kol*) underscores the lavishness of YHWH's gift. The clause 'which they return (*šûb*)' to YHWH is linked with the reparation offering (see 5:7–8; Milgrom 1990:

150). Verse 9 concludes with a summary repetition of its opening words, 'they are most holy things for you and your sons', signalling closure of the primary statement. The next verse details where and who may eat: in 'most holy environs' (*qōdeš haqqŏdāšîm*), referring to the courtyard (cf. Lev. 6:9, 19; 7:6), and 'every male' of Aaron's house (i.e. priests). Such shares of the near-offerings are to be regarded as 'holy' by Aaron's house – being given to them does not lessen their sacred status, being obtained from among YHWH's possessions.

Gifts of the elevation offerings

11–13. This section (vv. 11–19) begins with *zeh-lĕkā* (this is for you), similar to the beginning of the last section (*zeh-yihyeh lĕkā*, v. 9). From general to specific, the designation for the gift moves from 'the contribution of their gift' to 'all the elevation (*tĕnûpāh*) offerings of the sons of Israel' (cf. 8:8–13). Since the elevation offerings are not portions from the 'most holy things from the fire', their consumption is not reserved for authorized priests as a ritual act, but may be consumed by all who are 'clean' (*ṭāhôr*), including sons and daughters, within the priest's house (vs the 'most holy environs' of v. 10) – this being a 'perpetual due' (cf. v. 8). Inclusion of 'and his daughters' (18:11, 19), as Frevel points out (2013b: 147), moves beyond the circle of Aaron and his four sons, towards 'a class of priests', a 'family affair'. The elevation offerings are detailed as the 'fat' (*ḥēleb*), the richest and best part, of oil, new wine, and grain, a common triad of 'firstfruits' (*rēʾšît*), although usually listed in reverse order (e.g. Deut. 7:13; 11:14; 12:17; 14:23; 18:4; 28:51; Speier 1946: 315). As the major crops of Canaan, oil, wine and grain may be a metonym for all the produce of the land (Milgrom 1990: 435). Two words are translated 'firstfruits' in this passage: *rēʾšît* (v. 12) and *bikkûrîm* (v. 13). While *bikkûrîm* refers to the firstfruits of crops, 'first ripe', the designation *rēʾšît* encompasses foods 'first processed' from crops; as the first issue of life from the womb or the soil, firstfruits were considered intrinsically holy (belonging to God), and transferred to God while seeking his blessing on the rest of the crop (Milgrom 1990: 427). Of all that he requires of his people, he freely and graciously gives back: 'the firstfruits of them which they will give to YHWH, to you I give them', the 'firstfruits of all that is in their land which they will bring to YHWH, for you it will be' – what is *layhwh* (for YHWH) becomes *lĕkā* (for you). Deuteronomy lists seven crops of the land: wheat, barley, grape, fig, pomegranate, olive oil and (date) honey, ancient rabbis limiting the priestly perquisites to these (*m. Bek.* 1.3; Milgrom 1990: 151). The detailed explanation (vv. 12–13) ends the same way as the general summary (v. 11), with the notice that 'all who are clean' within the priest's house may eat of the elevation offerings, able to enjoy

YHWH's abundant provision through his people. In God's design there is a reciprocal relationship of interdependence established between the priesthood and Israel: the priests shield the people from the threat of YHWH's wrath, given his absolute holiness, even while opening the cultic way of approaching his sanctifying presence in worship, and being the conduits of his blessing on them; the people, in turn, return to YHWH the first portions of their abundant provisions, the fruit of his blessing, from which priests derive their livelihood.

Gifts of the devoted things, and firstfruits of the womb

14–18. The summary statement of the third class of gifts (devoted things) is brief, fronting 'Every devoted thing (*ḥērem*)' for emphasis, while the detailed delineation of the fourth class (firstfruits of the womb) is lengthy since rules of redemption need to be addressed (vv. 15–18). M. Greenberg defines *ḥērem* as 'the status of that which is separated from common use or contact either because it is proscribed as an abomination to God or because it is consecrated to Him' (1971: 10) – it is, as Milgrom put it (1990: 428), 'the ultimate in dedication', often designating spoils of war. In Leviticus, YHWH warns that 'a devoted thing which a man will devote unto YHWH from all that belongs to him, whether of human or beast or inherited field, will neither be sold nor redeemed – every devoted thing, holy of holies it is unto YHWH' (27:28). This means devoted things become the possession of YHWH for Sanctuary use by priests, or it must be destroyed. Use of *ḥērem* looks forward to the conquest of the land (see Josh. 6:17, 18, 21, etc.), a foretaste of which comes later in Numbers (see 21:2, 3; 31:25–54). So, while inheriting no land themselves, priests receive both the spoils of conquering the land and the choice firstfruits of the land – these being YHWH's own share, which he grants them.

Whereas the previous section concerned the firstfruits of harvest, which become elevation offerings (vv. 11–13), here the focus is on first-fruits 'of flesh', that is, 'everything that opens the womb' among humans and beasts which 'they bring near' (*yaqrîbû*) for YHWH – these, too, are 'for you' (*lĕkā*). To say of the firstborn 'they are holy' (*qōdeš hēm*) means the same as 'they are mine (YHWH's)', which is why they must be sacrificed (cf. Brin 1994: 180–195, 218–219). Since, however, human sacrifice is an abomination to YHWH (Lev. 18:21–23; 20:1–6; Deut. 12:30–32; 18:9–12; cf. Jer. 7:31), the 'firstborn' (*bĕkôr*) of any human (i.e., who 'opens the womb') must be redeemed, and because unclean animals may not be offered to YHWH, these need to be redeemed as well – note the greater stress upon redeeming humans, which is mandatory: 'you will *surely* redeem' (*pādōh tipdeh*), versus 'unclean animals' (*tipdeh*), which may be redeemed or simply given to the priesthood for their use instead (see Lev. 27:27). The word translated 'redeem' is *pādāh*, and carries the idea of ransoming from death for an assessed price (see BDB 804). By contrast with *gā'al* (redemption), which implies a buying back what belonged to one originally, *pādah* refers to buying what was not one's own, for all the firstborn belong inherently to YHWH, 'offered' to him, not 'given' (Milgrom 1990: 152). The redemption is to occur when the child is a month old ('a son of a month'), when the child's survival seems secure, and the redemption price is set at five shekels of silver (twelve gerahs per shekel; see Lev. 27:6; Num. 3:47), which goes to the priests.

Having provided for the exceptions that need to be redeemed, YHWH safeguards against any inclination by priests to allow the redemption of clean animals (and collecting the money), which would be robbery against YHWH: 'Only' (*'ak*) the firstborn of oxen, sheep or goats you will not redeem – that is, you will not allow them to be redeemed, you will not accept a redemption price for them. These are 'holy', meaning they belong to YHWH. Therefore, priests must sacrifice them, dashing their blood on the altar and turning their fat into smoke on the altar fire, a soothing aroma to YHWH. Not only is this portion YHWH's due, but the 'restful aroma' designates the propitiating influence on YHWH of such fire offerings (see Morales 2019a: 28–31), part of the priestly ministry to him which was also for the well-being and prosperity of his people. The flesh of these devoted things 'will be for you (*lāk*, f. sg.) . . . for you (*lĕkā*, m. sg.) it will be'. They are to be regarded as the breast of the elevation offering and as the right thigh, which means the firstborn of oxen, sheep, and goats are sacrificed as peace offerings, granting the offeror – in this case the priest, who owns the firstborn on behalf of YHWH – a share of the flesh as a feast (cf. Exod. 29:27–28; Lev. 10:14–15; Milgrom 1990: 153).

19. This verse, parallel with verse 8, summarizes the previous legislation that YHWH gives all the 'contributions' (*tĕrûmōt*), which the sons of Israel 'lift' (*yārîmû*) for YHWH, to Aaron's house, you and your sons and your daughters. Note that daughters are again included as the summary refers to 'the holy things', not 'the most holy things' (vv. 9–10). Again, what is given to YHWH, as his due possession, he in turn gives to the priests, for the well-being of their households, to Aaron and his 'descendants' (*zera'*) with him. That these gifts are a 'perpetual due' is repeated (cf. v. 8), this time encompassing that due within the broader 'covenant of salt perpetually' (*bĕrît melaḥ 'ôlām*) before YHWH. Comparing Leviticus 24 with Numbers 18, the only two passages in the HB employing 'eternal covenant', 'eternal due', and 'eternal statute' within a single chapter, S. D. Mason affirms that perpetual due is not equivalent to eternal or perpetual covenant: the statute refers only to the rewards or due bestowed on priests, and is encompassed by the broader two-sided covenant arrangement, which includes the duties of priests (2008: 200). Of the five uses of *bĕrît* in Numbers, three involve the phrase *bĕrît 'ôlām*, found here in 18:19 and in 25:12–13, two passages further connected by their topics of high priesthood and atonement (cf. 10:33; 14:44; S. D. Mason 2008: 189–190). Likely an idiom for 'enduring' or 'lasting', used also of YHWH's covenant with David (2 Chr. 13:5; cf. Lev. 2:13), 'salt' (*melaḥ*) may refer to a bond of peace between two parties who have shared a meal formally (so that 'there is salt between us'), applied in the Hebrew cult through the mingling of salt with sacrifices (G. B. Gray 1903: 232; Robertson Smith 1927: 252), or simply, and perhaps more originally, because salt has since ancient times been widely understood as a symbol of permanence (Milgrom 1990: 154). The everlasting nature of the 'covenant of salt perpetually' should not, however, be construed in terms of unconditionality, that is, as opposed to breakability – within the enduring covenant relationship, every generation in the lineage of Aaron is accountable for the conditions set forth, for the proper stewardship of their priestly responsibilities (see S. D. Mason 2008: 201, 206). As a response to the people's cry 'Are we all to perish?' (17:27–28), YHWH's definitive 'No' through the reaffirmation of the consecrated priesthood of Aaron's house is substantiated profoundly in being formally arranged as an eternal covenant, the nature of which encompasses the entirety of chapter 18 (cf. S. D. Mason 2008: 193, 197). As such the covenant has the nation's survival within its purview. By contrast with Leviticus, which presents priests as necessary mediators for Israel's worship of YHWH at the Tent of Meeting, in Numbers the priesthood is set forth as the divine means of Israel's survival in the wilderness, protected from his wrath through the work of atonement.

S. D. Mason compares the perpetual covenant of salt for Aaron's house (Num. 18) with the perpetual covenant (*bĕrît 'ôlām*) granted Abraham in Genesis 17 (esp. vv. 17–18): both passages speak of an eternal covenant and concern a special relationship with God and land inheritance 'for your seed' (*ûlĕzar'ăkā*) – but in Numbers 18, 'for bearing the responsibility of serving in the presence of God at the Tabernacle, the priests *and their seed* receive the fruits *of the land* rather than the land itself' (2008: 201–202; emphasis original). In this sense, the priesthood does not need land, for they receive the choicest benefits of the land from YHWH's hand through the people's contributions (vv. 8–19) and tithes (vv. 20–32). Such an understanding manifests the remarkable nature of the twin gifts of YHWH for the priesthood, people and land: Levites represent the firstborn *seed* of Israel, and the dues and tithes represent the choice bounty of *the land* (cf. S. D. Mason 2008: 204). Therefore, even while functioning to allay the nation's concern for protection from divine wrath, through priestly service, Numbers 18 also functions for the priesthood somewhat like the census in Numbers 26 for the rest of the tribes, as a promissory foretaste of life in the land.

18:20–24: Inheritance of Priests and Levites

The third and final direct speech by YHWH to Aaron alone relates to inheritance, its root (*nāḥal*, *naḥălāh*) occurring eight times (and once more in v. 26). As the subject of inheritance occurs again beginning with chapter 26, the root found some fifty-one times throughout Numbers 26 – 36, this divine speech may be seen as foreshadowing the prospect of inheritance within Canaan that serves as a major theme in the final section of the book. Further support comes from the use of the root for 'apportion' or 'portion' (*ḥālaq*, *ḥēleq*) in verse 20, which surfaces again five times in Numbers 26 in relation to land inheritance (26:30 [twice], 53, 55, 56). The words 'not inherit' and 'amid the sons of Israel' recur in the beginning, middle, and end of the paragraph (vv. 20, 23d, 24c), and the notion of YHWH's giving frames the central message ('I have given', v. 21; 'I give', 24b), with the heart of YHWH's speech found in verses 22–23. Although Masoretes placed a samek paragraph break after verse 20, apparently understanding the verse as relating only to priests while verses 21–24 relate to Levites, yet verses 20–24 form one speech of YHWH, unified both thematically and lexically. Nevertheless, the paragraph break does point to the central place and significant function of verse 20, brought out by Leveen's division (2013: 252), slightly modified:

Unit 1–7:   Focus on Priests and Levites

Unit 8–19:   Focus on Priests (12 verses)
X   20:   God as Aaron's portion and inheritance
Unit 21–32: Focus on Levites (12 verses)

20. This final address to Aaron alone, the last such instance in the Torah, is further underscored since the previous two also concerned Aaron's sons ('and your sons', vv. 1, 8), while here the speech mentions only Aaron ('you', *lĕkā*) (Milgrom 1990: 154). 'In their land' (*bĕ'arṣām*) fronts the verb with emphasis. Canaan is 'their' land, the land of the sons of Israel, but not of Aaron for there will be no 'portion' (*ḥēleq*) for him among 'them'. The reason is that YHWH himself – 'I' (*'ănî*) – is both the portion and inheritance of Aaron's house, so that verse 20 provides the 'theological grounding' of verse 19 (Budd 1984: 203; cf. S. D. Mason 2008: 202). As demonstrated by the three divine speeches, spoken singly to Aaron (vv. 1, 8, 20), the gift of the priesthood to Aaron's house does not merely concern duties, but is first and foremost the gift of a special relationship with YHWH, to whom priests have unique access by their sacred office (cf. Olson 1996: 114) – and with YHWH as their portion and inheritance, Aaron's house also receives YHWH's due of firstborn sons (firstfruits of the womb, by way of the Levites) and of the firstfruits of the land. The verse makes two parallel statements that repeat 'inherit' and 'portion' in reverse and end with Aaron's place (or lack of place) 'in the midst' of the Israelites. In Leviticus, it is clear that priests receive the sacrifices as their due (Lev. 7:34) (Taggar-Cohen 1998: 82), but the emphasis here is on the priesthood's close connection with YHWH. Possessing him, they also have what belongs to him, the tithes of Israel, as a divine gift. Noting that this third divine address to Aaron is not restricted to 'you and your sons' (as with vv. 1, 8), Milgrom suggests that Aaron is addressed here not as priest but as chieftain of the tribe of Levi, the statement applying to Levites as well as priests, and that this verse stands as the antecedent of 'therefore I have said' in verse 24 (1990: 154). While, positively, Milgrom's construction explains the function of verse 20 in relation to verses 21–24, unifying the speech, yet the more obvious antecedent of verse 24 is verse 23, which matches both the language (in the midst of the sons of Israel) and context ('I have said *to them*' vs 'to you') more closely. Nevertheless, Milgrom's reading finds support in Deuteronomy as YHWH is said to be the inheritance of the whole tribe of Levi, not of the priests only (cf. Deut. 18:1–2). While not receiving land as their allotted entitlement, 'Levites receive a higher portion', YHWH is their inheritance (Deut. 10:8–9; Habel 1995: 49).

21, 24. For Levites particularly YHWH begins with what they will inherit, all the tithe of Israel, before pronouncing that in the midst of the sons of Israel they will not inherit an inheritance, a tribal allotment of land. Tithing first appears in Genesis as an assumed practice by Abraham (Gen. 14:18–20). Here the emphasis (look!) is upon the abundance of YHWH's provision, in giving them all the tithe, that it is a divine gift ('I have given'; 'I give'), and such an inheritance of the tithe is in exchange (*ḥēlep*; see v. 31) for the service of the Tent of Meeting. In Leviticus 'all the tithe of the land' is said to belong to YHWH, and holy unto YHWH (27:30); now, in return for their service, YHWH grants the tithes to Levites. As noted above, the closing statement of verse 24 begins with 'therefore I have said to them', referring to YHWH's previous statement in verse 23 as its explanation: 'in the midst of the sons of Israel they will not inherit an inheritance'. YHWH himself is the portion and inheritance of Aaron (perhaps including his tribe) in verse 20; here the tithes of Israel are underscored as the inheritance of Levites. In this way, Levites are connected more closely with the sons of Israel (mentioned four times in verses 21–24), whose firstborn sons they have replaced, while priests are separated completely unto YHWH. Levitical replacement of firstborn sons was at the heart of the rebellions recounted in Numbers 16 but now becomes the answer to the people's cry at the end of Numbers 17 – 'Are we all to perish completely?' The later assignment of cities and their surrounding pasture to Levites (35:1–8) and to priests (Josh. 21:13–19) does not contradict the prohibition against their owning land, since the tribal allotment involved agricultural land only (Milgrom 1990: 154).

22–23. At the close of Numbers 17, the 'sons of Israel', full of terror, had exclaimed that whoever 'draws near – even draws near – to the Dwelling of YHWH will die!' Part of YHWH's response is that the 'sons of Israel' will no longer 'draw near' to the Tent of Meeting, so as to bear sin and, therefore, 'die'. As with the Camp structure itself, the Levites' service allows the tribes to keep a safe distance from the Tent of Meeting. Whether this statement is merely a needed reaffirmation of YHWH's original organization of the Camp or a truly novel change is a matter of debate. In Numbers 7, the chieftains of the tribes are portrayed as making offerings (see 7:3, 10–11, 12, 18, etc.), but it is difficult to know precisely their level of participation – interestingly, priests are nowhere mentioned in that chapter. What is clearer is that henceforth Levites will bear the penalty of YHWH's wrath on themselves, in place of Israelites: the Levite – 'he' (hû'), not the sons of Israel – will serve at the Tent of Meeting, and the Levites – 'they' (hēm), not the sons of Israel – will bear their (the Israelites') guilt, the penalty for encroachment. This new practice is binding as a 'perpetual statute' for generations. Verse 23 ends with the statement that 'in the midst of the sons of Israel they (Levites) will not inherit an inheritance', a remark explained in verse 24, which itself marks a return to the substance of verse 21, that Levites receive all the tithe of the sons of Israel as their inheritance. 'Aaron's role as representative of the Levites, as a whole, becomes evident', S. D. Mason observes (2008: 202), 'as v. 23 applies the "no land" principle to the entire tribe of Levi'.

These central verses underscore the dangerous role intrinsic to the Levitical labour of guard duty, fully justifying their reception of Israel's tithes from YHWH. Whereas previously Levites were presented as a buffer between the holy presence of YHWH and the rest of the Camp, they have now indeed become a 'lightning rod', to use Milgrom's phrase (1990: 371), attracting YHWH's wrath on themselves for any Israelite encroachment on sancta. To be sure, the previous plague was a result of the people's rebellion (16:41–50), to which they would still be susceptible (see Num. 25), and the consuming of the 250 princes for approaching YHWH's presence would still be the inevitable response to any encroachers – but YHWH would no longer intend to destroy the whole people for such encroachments (cf. 16:20), for his wrath would fall on the priests and Levites in their place.

18:25–32: Levitical contribution from the tithe

While the third speech had underscored similarities between Aaron's house and the tribe of Levi, in that both will not inherit land (vv. 20–24), the fourth speech reiterates the distinction and hierarchical relationship between them. As the focus shifts to what Levites are to provide 'to Aaron the priest', YHWH's speech is now addressed to Moses instead of Aaron. Rather than having Aaron himself call the Levites to give to his priestly house, Levites will be directed to do so by Moses. The divine speech has two major parts ('say to them', v. 25; 'say to them', v. 30): the first calling Levites to tithe 'for YHWH' and 'to Aaron the priest' from the tithes they collect from the sons of Israel, which Levites receive as part of their inheritance (vv. 25–29), and the second dealing with further details about consuming the tithes and not bearing sin from them (vv. 30–32). Clearly, Levites are subordinate to priests. Harmonizing Israel's tithing legislation here with Deuteronomy is a challenge (12:17–19; 14:22–29; 26:12–14), although Milgrom points out that Numbers refers to an obligatory tithe while Deuteronomy refers to true charity (1990: 432–436). The New Testament upholds the principle that those who derive spiritual benefit from ministers should give to support their well-being (Matt. 10:9–10; Rom. 15:27; 1 Cor. 9:2–18; 1 Tim. 5:17–18; cf. 1 Cor. 16:1–2).

25–29. In the first part of the speech, verses 26–28 are arranged concentrically with 'take from the sons of Israel' and 'I have given to you from them'/'you will give from [them] for YHWH to Aaron' occurring at the front of verse 26 and end of verse 28; 'you will lift up a contribution for YHWH' and 'a tithe from the tithe'/'from all your tithes' occurring at the end of verse 26 and beginning of verse 28. These verses frame verse 27 as the central focus: the Levitical tithe will be accounted as their contribution for YHWH, as the grain of the threshing floor and the fullness of the winepress. That Levites are to 'take' (*lāqaḥ*) the tithe from the sons of Israel demonstrates that tithing was not voluntary. Verse 29 offers a restatement by way of emphasis. The phrase 'for YHWH' occurs four times – Levites are tithing to YHWH, even though it will go ultimately to Aaron the priest, as YHWH's gift to the priests. YHWH reminds the Levites that when they 'take' from the sons of Israel their tithe, they take that which YHWH has 'given' to Levites; as they have received from YHWH, so now they themselves also tithe back to him from their inheritance. Three parallel statements define the Levitical contribution as 'a tithe from the tithe', 'from all your tithes', and 'from all the fat of it, even from its holy part', as the tithe is understood not merely as 10% of a whole, but the best portion of the whole – its cream or fat. The tithe is of a piece with the understanding of the firstborn or firstfruits as being the strength of the rest of the house or crop (Gen. 49:3; cf. Rom. 11:16; 1 Cor. 15:20), belonging to YHWH and designated 'holy'. The hierarchical structure of the Camp, around YHWH's central presence, is evident: the sons of Israel tithe for YHWH to the Levites, the Levites tithe for YHWH to Aaron the priest.

30–32. The second part of what Moses is 'to say to them [Levites]' begins with a summary of the previous section: contributing (lifting up) the fat of their inheritance for YHWH counts as a yielding of the firstfruits of the harvests of threshing floor and winepress from Levites.

After lifting up the tithe, Levites retain the majority of their inheritance to enjoy, concerning which YHWH provides four relevant details: (1) Levites may eat of it in 'every place', (2) with their entire household, (3) the inheritance of the tithes of the sons of Israel counts as 'wages' (*śākār*) in 'exchange' (*ḥēlep*) for their service at the Tent of Meeting, and (4) Levites will not bear sin by their consumption of this inheritance so long as they have contributed the tithe – its holy part, the fat of it – to YHWH. Otherwise, Levites and their houses would be eating the holy part even though they had not been consecrated as priests, a threatening scenario. In Leviticus, the tithe had been designated as belonging to YHWH and therefore as 'holy unto YHWH' (see Lev. 27:30–33) – now, it is the tithe of the tithe that is holy. Their eating of YHWH's holy tithe, therefore, would result in profaning sancta, incurring YHWH's wrath on them – they would 'die'. Contributing the fat, the holy things of the sons of Israel, will ensure that Levites do not bear sin; they will not profane YHWH's possession and will not die. Again, the hierarchy is reaffirmed: Levites themselves are not priests and must tithe the fat of their inheritance for YHWH to Aaron the priest; but those closest to YHWH serve for the sake of the rest – the divine structure is for the sake of all, so 'you will not die'.

19:1–22: The red heifer ritual

As a ritual provision intended to cleanse from corpse pollution, YHWH's instructions concerning the red heifer stress the nature of the Camp, with YHWH dwelling among the tribes of Israel, as both clean and life-yielding. Movements 'outside the Camp' (vv. 3, 9) and 'into the Camp' (v. 7) are noted, underscoring the Camp's boundary line, and the preparation of the ashes takes place 'before' the Camp (v. 3). Leveen observes that, taking chapters 18 and 19 together spatially, 'the Tabernacle, all of the camp, and outside the camp are covered' (2013: 265). The root for 'unclean' (*ṭāmē'*) occurs nineteen times (vv. 7, 8, 10, 11, 13 [three times], 14, 15, 16, 17, 19, 20 [three times], 21, 22 [three times]), more than in the previous sections on the Camp's purity combined (thirteen times in Num. 5 – 6; three times in Num. 9; once in 35:31 related to the land), and the term 'clean' occurs seven times (9 [twice], 12 [twice], 18, 19 [twice]), as does the root for 'purification' (9, 12 [twice], 13, 17, 19, 20). While 'the priest' oversees the preparation of the ashes (5 times: vv. 3, 4, 6, 7 [twice]), a 'clean' person assists him (v. 9), and may perform the actual cleansing ceremony (vv. 18, 19). The 'waters of separation' (*mê niddā*, five times: vv. 9, 13, 20, 21 [twice]), comprising living water and the prepared ashes of the red heifer, are used to purify a person defiled by death, enabling that person's passage from the wilderness into the Camp. Although the red heifer is not offered up to YHWH on his altar, and its burning uses the word for common incineration, *śārap*, rather than the cultic designation *hiqṭîr*, used for turning offerings into smoke on the altar, nevertheless, the prepared ashes are designated a 'purification offering' (*ḥaṭṭā't hiw'*, v. 9) in prospect of its use with living water as 'waters of separation', and may thus be thought of as a 'portable purification offering' that functions as an *entrance rite*, back into the Camp. Within the narrative context, the red heifer ritual serves to cleanse the second generation from the pollution of death caused by the first generation who, for their faithless rebellions against YHWH, were judged to die in the wilderness. Not by accident, the next chapter opens with the time-stamp 'in the first month' (of the fortieth year), signifying the new era of the second generation. While the role of priests is significant, Levites are not mentioned whatsoever, and the divine speech is addressed to 'the sons of Israel', features which make chapter 19 remarkably similar to the previous purity laws (Num. 5 – 6).

19:1–13: Preparing ashes of a red heifer for the waters of separation

The first half of the chapter, dealing with the preparation of ashes to be used later for the waters of separation, focuses on death, on the incineration of the red heifer.

1–2. YHWH's fifth speech is addressed to Moses and Aaron both, introduced as 'a statute of the law' (*ḥuqqat hattôrāh*), which is 'commanded' (*ṣiwwā*) by YHWH. The designation 'statute of the law' appears only twice in the HB, both in Numbers with reference to the waters of separation (19:2; 31:21), leading to the possibility that the phrase stands as a technical label for this specific legislation. After the battle with the Midianites, Eleazar, referring to Numbers 19, calls the Israelite fighters, along with their spoils of war, to undergo cleansing by the waters of purification, after which they may enter the Camp on the seventh day (31:21–24), since anyone who had killed a person or had touched any slain were to remain outside the Camp until being cleansed on the third and seventh days (31:19). Moses and Aaron are to convey the statute to the 'sons of Israel' as it pertains to the life and purity of the whole Camp.

The sons of Israel are to take a heifer to Moses, a communal act for the sake of the community's purification. Although translated as 'heifer' (a female that has never had a calf) by custom, the term *pārāh* only means cow, fully grown (see *m. Par.* 1.1). While there is some debate in Jewish tradition (*m. Par.* 2.1), it has been a longstanding deduction that the cow is a heifer, understanding the requirement 'over which has never ascended a yoke' as including that no male has mounted her – so taken in *TgPs-J* (see Hayward 1992: 11–13), with the Greek translation, employing *damalis*. The cow must be 'blameless' or 'whole' (*tammîm*), a typical designation for sacrificial animals, signifying no broken or missing body parts physically, but also pointing to the prerequisite character for anyone who would approach YHWH (see Ps. 15:2; cf. Gen. 6:9). Ancient rabbis connected *tammîm* with 'red', so that the cow had to be 'completely' or 'wholly' red – with even two discoloured hairs disqualifying the animal (*m. Par.* 2.5). That a female bovine is required is best explained by Milgrom (1981b: 65): although brought by the community for the whole community's use, the red cow's ashes are applied to individual Israelites, and individuals may only bring a female of the flock for a purification offering (Lev. 4:22–35; Num. 15:27–29); wanting, however, a maximum amount of ashes (for many individuals) a bovine is required, while avoiding use of a bull, which is the purification offering reserved for either the high priest (Lev. 4:1–12; 16:11) or the community as a whole (Lev. 4:13–21). Some strands of Jewish tradition relate the cow to the golden calf (cf. Hayward 1992; M. A. Greenberg 1997). In Deuteronomy, to put away the guilt of innocent blood when someone is found slain in the land and the murderer is unknown, the 'neck of a heifer' (*'eglat bāqār*) is to be broken and the city's elders are to wash their hands over it, confessing their innocence and ignorance of the matter – these are the only two ritual uses of a cow for Israel. The cow is to be 'red' (*'ădummā*), a term that in other contexts may refer to the colour of blood (Isa. 63:2), crimson (Isa. 1:18), or of wine (Prov. 23:31), but when used of an animal's hide basically means 'brown' (Brenner 1982: 58–80). Given that the heifer's 'blood' (*dāmāh*) is to be burned (v. 5), along with cedar (wood with a reddish hue) and a scarlet thread (v. 6), the cow's redness likely serves to emphasize the blood aspect of the ashes, especially since blood is the main agent of cleansing in all other purification offerings – it increases symbolically 'the amount of blood in the ashes' (Milgrom 1990: 158). There is, moreover, a paronomasia link formed between the words 'red' (*'ădummā*) and 'blood' (*dām*) (Humann 2011: 108–109). In Genesis, 'the man' (*hā'ādām*) is formed from the 'dust' (*'āpār*) of the 'the ground' (*hā'ădāmāh*) (2:7), judged to return to 'the ground' (*hā'ădāmāh*), from 'dust' to 'dust' (*'āpār*) (3:19), and warned that whoever sheds the 'blood' (*dām*) of 'the man' (*hā'ādām*), by 'man' (*'ādām*) his 'blood' (*dām*) will be shed (9:6) – all three texts employing paronomasia. Humann, therefore, suggests that the 'red cow' (*pārāh 'ădummā*) which is reduced to 'ashes' (*'ēper*) is symbolically linked with the primeval story of man, with the heifer's incineration likely being an elaborate symbol of human mortality (2011: 109): 'What is depicted in the ceremony is the reversal of the creation of man, a return to the dust of the earth.' Given the theme of exile (Gen. 4:16), use of 'blood' and 'ground' (Gen. 4:10–11), the first occurrence of *ḥaṭṭā't* (Gen. 4:7; Num. 19:9, 17), and possible wordplay with 'wander' (*nûd, nādad*, Gen. 4:12, 14, 16) and *niddâ* ('separation', 'impurity', Num. 19:9), it may be Cain's murder forms a subtext as it does elsewhere in relation to the Levitical camp (Num. 16; cf. 35:9–34) – here in the form of resolution.

The cow, further, is to have no 'blemish' or 'defect' (*mûm*), another basic requirement for sacrificial animals (see Lev. 22:20–25), which together with 'blameless' (*tammîm*) may form a redundancy for added emphasis (Milgrom 1990: 158). Leviticus lists a variety of defects that would disqualify animals from being offered, such as 'those that are blind or broken or maimed, or have an abscess or festering eruption or scabs' (see 22:20–25). Finally, the cow must not have had a yoke on it, she must not have been used already for agrarian labour, and perhaps, as noted above, encompasses the idea that the cow must be a heifer. The general intention is that to be sacrificed, the cow must not have already been dedicated to profane use (cf. *m. Par.* 2.3; see Deut. 21:3). Building on other allusions to the Eden narrative (Gen. 2–3), Humann compares the cow's not having had any yoke upon her to Adam in the garden *before* the punishment of 'tilling the ground' was laid upon him (2011: 259–260).

3–6. Moses and Aaron, who received the red cow from the sons of Israel, now give her to Eleazar the priest. While passing the task to Eleazar may be understood as sparing Aaron, as high priest, any defilement outside the Camp, yet the shift also portends the transition from the first generation of Israelites in the wilderness to the second. By contrast to multiple ambiguous subjects, 'Eleazar's status as priest is emphasized by repetition of his title' (Gilders 2006: 7). Eleazar then brings her forth to outside the Camp (or this is done by an unspecified person; cf. Licht 1991: 2:187), moving eastward from the courtyard entrance of the Tent of Meeting, where animals were typically presented. The movement to outside the Camp is significant, not only as the nexus for the ritual's abnormalities, but because the context of the waters of separation is the need for cleansing by those who are barred from the Camp through death's pollution, relegated to the wilderness space 'outside the Camp' (see 5:1–3), and thus underscoring the nature of the Camp itself as a pure place of life lived before the central, holy presence of YHWH. Just as Adam (*hā'ādām*) was formed from the dust of 'the ground' (*hā'ădāmāh*) outside and brought inside the garden of Eden, but was then banished eastward of the garden, doomed to return to 'dust' (*'āpār*) (Gen. 2:7–8, 15; 3:19, 24), so the 'red' (*'ădummā*) heifer is incinerated into 'dust' (*'āpār*) outside the Camp, eastward of YHWH's Dwelling, so that through the waters of separation banished Israelites, defiled by human corpse pollution, may re-enter the Camp (see Humann 2011: 253–260).

The subject at the end of verse 3, which simply reads 'he will slaughter', is debated even though it is most naturally understood as Eleazar. The phrase is often adjusted in translation to read 'and one will slaughter' for two reasons. First, because a similar scenario occurs in verse 5, where someone other than Eleazar must be meant since that one is addressed separately as needing to wash in verse 8. Second, the end of verse 3 reads *lĕpānāyw*, 'before him (or it)', leading to the idea that someone else slaughters the cow before Eleazar (v. 5). While these are strong points, there is no indication in the rest of the text that someone other than Eleazar has performed the slaughter rite, and, for example, was rendered unclean, needing to bathe, as would be expected, a gap readily explained if Eleazar is the subject, since he is instructed to undergo washing (v. 7). Besides, both 'before him' and 'before his eyes' may refer to YHWH inasmuch as the ritual is performed in view of the Tent of Meeting (cf. de Vaulx 1972: 214). A similar understanding informs my own translation, marking 'Camp' as the antecedent, 'before it, the Camp', since 'Camp' is the last object mentioned, and because *spatial orientation* is a highly significant interpretative facet of the ceremony: the red heifer is led outside the Camp, slaughtered before the Camp, her blood sprinkled toward the front (lit. 'face', *pĕnê*) of the Tent of Meeting, indicating the 'place of sacred, ritual activity' (Gorman 1990: 205). Humann, affirming NEB, explains how Numbers begins with a lengthy description of the orientation of the Camp of Israel, with the 'front' of the Camp referring to the eastern side, the entrance to YHWH's Dwelling where the houses of both Moses and Aaron were stationed, 'encamped before (*lipnê*) the Dwelling on the east, before (*lipnê*) the Tent of Meeting eastward' (3:38), and states (2011: 113–117): 'Thus the ceremony of the Red Heifer is, narratively speaking, oriented spatially in a two-fold manner; it occurs not only outside the camp, but also to the east of the camp.' Even with taking the slaughter rite as performed before the Camp, it may still be that someone else, assisting Eleazar, performed the slaughter rite, enabling Eleazar to collect the blood for sprinkling (the basic format for sacrifices, see Lev. 4:4–5).

That the cow is 'slaughtered' (*šāḥaṭ*) is consistent with other sacrifices, including purification offerings (see Lev. 1:5; 3:2; 4:4, 15, 24), and the sevenfold sprinkling of blood (or some blood manipulation with the priest's finger) is a regular feature of the purification offering (Lev. 4:6, 17, 25), in which blood manipulation is the rite of central focus (see Morales 2015: 130–132). No explanation is given for the act of sprinkling the blood toward the Tent of Meeting, and commentators are divided: either the Sanctuary consecrates the blood, along with the heifer, for ritual use (Vriezen 1950; Milgrom 1981b; Gorman 1990: 205), or the blood guards the Sanctuary from future defilement of death's pollution (Levine 1974: 75; 1993: 462; Kiuchi 1987: 56:123). Against the first position, that sprinkling toward the Sanctuary consecrates the blood, Gilders maintains there is not a single explicit instance where sprinkling blood is unequivocally explained as consecrating the blood, and that, unlike oil, blood does not need to be consecrated since it has inherent power, being the life of the animal (2006: 9–10). Against the second position, such proleptic safeguarding (rather than actual purification) is not in accord with other purification scenarios. Rather, sprinkling the waters of separation (containing the ashes of the cow, including its blood) is the truer parallel to other scenarios where an object receives the application of blood. Amid the ambiguities, two definitive, if more basic, points can be made: first, the blood sprinkling, an essential and exclusive rite of the purification offering, establishes the red heifer ritual as a purification offering (Humann 2011: 122), identified as such explicitly in verse 9; and sprinkling the blood toward the Sanctuary establishes a link between the two – as an indexical sign, the blood-sprinkling *indicates* the Sanctuary and places the ritual and its participants into a relationship with the Sanctuary, associating the red heifer ritual with the other rituals that take place there, underscoring the pivotal role of the priesthood (Gilders 2006: 13). At a basic level, then, the blood-sprinkling toward the Sanctuary, establishing symbolic interaction between them, communicates that the procedure is a sacrificial one (Gane 2004: 660). Beyond this we may add that orienting the ritual toward the Sanctuary keeps the *telos* of the ashes' later use in focus: purifying people and objects from death's pollution is performed lest the 'Dwelling of YHWH', his 'Sanctuary', be defiled (9:13, 20). At least indirectly, then, the blood-sprinkling, in the light of the whole ritual, may be said to purify the Sanctuary (see Gane 2005: 185–191), perhaps having an *analeptic* function, when the waters of separation are used. The red heifer ritual acknowledges and reverently affirms YHWH's Dwelling as the pillar and foundation of the Camp as covenant community, a focus that accords with the aftermath of Korah's revolt, which also centred on the relationship between death and YHWH's Dwelling (cf. 17:13). The red heifer ceremony is another way in which YHWH facilitates life in his holy presence within the wonder that is the Camp, through the mediation of his chosen priesthood.

Rather than being drained, the blood, as 'the ritual detergent *par excellence*' (Milgrom 1990: 159), will be burned with the heifer, incinerated as part of the ashes, endowing them with atoning power (see Keil and Delitzsch 1973: 3:124; Gorman 1990: 206). That the law stipulates a heifer of red colour, the inclusion of blood in the burning, along with the addition of cedar wood and scarlet thread, functions to magnify the blood aspect of the resulting ashes, stored as a portable purification offering (see Milgrom 1990: 158, 440; Olson 1996: 121). Leviticus 17:11 underlies the way blood represents the 'soul' – or, rather, the 'life' – of the flesh, offered up sacrificially soul-for-soul, life-for-life, on behalf of the worshipper needing purification. As with water, blood holds a dual symbolism, pertaining to both death (when shed) and life (when offered), here used ritually in a rite of passage, not only purifying Israelites from the pollution of human death, but, as a result of that cleansing, conveying them from the wilderness/outside the Camp to inside the Camp/covenant community of YHWH. The blood in the 'waters of impurity', writes Gorman, 'functions to cleanse *and* restore to life the corpse-contaminated', not only purifying but communicating life, enabling the passage not merely from unclean to clean, 'but from death to life' (1990: 193, 206; cf. 202–203), precisely the transition from the first generation of Israel to the second.

Assuming that 'before his eyes' refers to Eleazar the priest (v. 5), then the burning rite is being authorized and validated by Aaron's house, the priesthood, perhaps a necessary precaution since the actual purification of the defiled, the sprinkling of the ashes mixed with living water, may be accomplished by lay-Israelites. The term for 'burn' here is *śārap*, used for common and complete incineration, and within the cult for that which is left over after a sacrificial meal or for the disposal of portions not used in sacrifice (cf. Lev. 4:12, 21; 6:30; 8:17; 9:11; 10:16; 16:27) (Rüttersworden 2004: 219), whereas the burning that takes place on YHWH's altar uses *hiqṭîr* (turn into smoke) consistently. The cow's skin, flesh, blood and offal, are burned together, with *śārap* forming an inclusion around verse 5 (cf. Sherwood 2002: 170). Even for whole burnt offerings, the skin was not included as it is here (Lev. 1:6). Offal (or 'entrails', *pereš*) does not necessarily imply excrement, only what is left within the intestines (cf. Budd 1984: 208). Typically for purification offerings, after the fat portions of the animal are offered to YHWH, 'burned' (*hiqṭîr*) on the altar, then the animal's remains (including its hide and entrails) are taken outside the Camp to a clean place and 'burned' (*śārap*) (see Lev. 4:11–12, 21), while here the whole animal is burned (*śārap*) outside the Camp – the only such case in the Pentateuch (Sakenfeld 1995: 108) – since the goal is to have *ashes* for purification, rather than an offering to YHWH. Nevertheless, Humann notes a variety of parallels particularly with the purification offerings of bull and goat on the Day of Atonement (2011: 124–125): after their blood is brought into the holy place, the bull and the goat are taken 'outside the Camp', where their hides, flesh and dung are burned in fire (Lev. 16:27); the one who burns the bull and goat is also to bathe and wash his garments before entering the Camp (16:28). The Day of Atonement and the Red Heifer ceremony, moreover, are both *entrance rites*: the former entailing the high priest's entrance into the innermost holy place, the centre of the Camp and throne room of YHWH, while the latter enables an Israelite to enter within the Camp. Both the Day of Atonement and red heifer ceremony reveal a close link between YHWH's Dwelling and his people: in Leviticus 16, sprinkling the Tent and its furnishings not only cleanses YHWH's Dwelling but also Israel (16:30); in Numbers 19 sprinkling Israelites keeps the Dwelling from defilement (19:13, 20).

Into the midst of the burning cow, the priest, understood as Eleazar, adds cedar wood, hyssop and a scarlet thread ('scarlet of a worm'). As noted, the cedar wood, a 'branch' in this context, and scarlet thread appear to further the symbolism of blood. The rabbis also noted a practical purpose: by adding large quantities of cedar and hyssop branches, the amount of ashes was increased (e.g. *TgPs-J* 19.6; *Tos. Par.* 4.10; *Sif. Num.* 124). 'Scarlet thread' (*šĕnî tôlāʿat*) occurs, in reverse order (*tôlaʿat šānî*), as part of the scarlet material used for YHWH's Dwelling, the sacred garments of the high priest, and the covering for the most holy vessels (e.g. Exod. 25:4; 39:1; Num. 4:4), and may serve here to 'indicate the person of the high priest and his ministration in the holy Tabernacle' (Humann 2011: 128). 'Hyssop' (*ʾēzôb*), derived from the Greek *hyssōpos* although not native to the region, is generally taken as referring either to *Origanum syriacum* or to *Capparis spinosa*, with the idea that the plant would have some sponge-like feature able to hold and spatter blood, but ambiguity remains (see Baldensperger and Crowfoot 1931; Harrison 1954; *Fauna and Flora of the Bible* 1980: 129–130). Even as used in verse 18 for sprinkling the waters of separation, hyssop is associated with cleansing (cf. also Exod. 12:22; Lev. 14:4; Ps. 51:7), and Ibn Ezra similarly noted the cleansing-by-hyssop connection among the regulations concerning Passover, skin disease ('leprosy'), and corpse pollution (see Ibn Ezra 2004: 3:105). Arguably, then, Eleazar's actions focus on the blood aspect of the ritual: leaving aside those actions where the subject is ambiguous, Eleazar receives Israel's cow from Moses and Aaron, sprinkles her blood seven times toward the front of the Tent of Meeting, and adds the cedar wood, hyssop and scarlet thread to the heifer's burning, while others perform the burning and the gathering and storing of the ashes. Passover, Israel's deliverance from Egypt as *Sheol* through a blood rite and use of hyssop, forms a theological undercurrent for the transition from death in the wilderness to life in the Camp. Intriguingly, the same three items – cedar wood, hyssop and a scarlet thread – are also used, and mentioned repeatedly, for the cleansing of lepers and their houses (Lev. 14:4, 6, 49, 51, 52). There are a variety parallels between the cleansing of lepers, a disease experienced as 'a living death' (G. J. Wenham 1979: 201; see Milgrom 1990: 97, 310; J. W. Kleinig 2003: 286), and the red heifer ritual, which cleanses from death's pollution. The cleansing of lepers in Leviticus also involved: a seven-day process (13:5), locating the defiled outside the Camp (13:46), the priest going outside the Camp (14:3), use of cedar wood, scarlet thread, and hyssop (14:4), use of living water (14:5), sprinkling a concoction (14:7), the goal of entering the Camp, tracing the rite of passage from death to life (14:8; on this last point, see Milgrom 1991: 889). Just as there appears to be a symbolic association of the red heifer ritual with the narrative of primeval man, so G. J. Wenham compared the leper's excommunication from the Camp, which experienced God's blessing, to the expulsion of Adam and Eve from Eden (1979: 201). Whether because the waters for leprosy are not a purification offering (per Milgrom 1990: 440), or, perhaps more likely, because the triad of cedar, hyssop and scarlet thread has not been incinerated and reduced to ash in 'a process of elimination which defiles' (per Humann 2011: 132), the leprosy cleansing ritual does not defile the manipulator, while the red heifer ceremony does.

The focus of the first half of the red heifer ceremony is on the burning into ashes of the cow, its blood, flesh and entrails, along with cedar wood, hyssop and a scarlet thread, all reduced to ashes and dust. The burning symbolizes a 'total annihilation of life, an orchestration of death' (Hieke 2009: 58).

7–10. The priest's entrance 'into the Camp' (*'el-hammaḥăneh*) under-scores the spatial dimension at work in the ritual. Because Eleazar's work renders him unclean, he is required to wash his garments and bathe his flesh in water before entering the Camp, remaining in an unclean status until evening. During this brief period of impurity, he must refrain from consuming holy meat from sacrifices, approaching the altar, or entering the Tent of Meeting. The same stipulations for washing, almost verbatim, are given for the one who burned the cow and the 'clean man' (*'îš ṭāhôr*) who gathers the ashes to a 'clean place' (*māqôm ṭāhôr*) outside the Camp except the latter must *only* wash his clothes and be unclean until evening – there is no direction to bathe as with the priest (v. 7) and the one who burned the heifer (v. 8). The difference may be that the priest and the one who burns the heifer had contact with the blood whereas the man who gathers the ashes did not (so Kiuchi 1987: 56:139); more likely, it is assumed that the gatherer of ashes will also bathe himself (cf. v. 21), this part of the instruction absent by *ellipsis*. The threefold notice of uncleanness at least indirectly calls attention to this facet of the ritual, that those involved in cleansing others from death's pollution cannot help becoming defiled themselves, albeit a relatively low level of uncleanness. The requirement to wash clothes and bathe oneself is similar to other single-day impurities (cf. Lev. 15:5, 6, 7, 8, 10, 16, 17, 18), except that here the person must remain outside the Camp until washing (cf. Milgrom 1990: 159).

Verse 9 is definitive for the ritual. The ashes are to be gathered by a clean man and 'rested' (*nûaḥ*) in a clean place outside the Camp, to be 'kept' (*mišmeret*) for the community of the sons of Israel for 'waters of separation' (*mê niddā*) – it is a 'purification offering' (*ḥaṭṭā't*). The verb 'rest' likely connotes that the storage of ashes is to be a regular, ongoing practice for the wilderness Camp. The ashes form a portable purification offering, able to be stored for use as need arose, and to which one may simply add living water to purify those defiled by human death. The six uses of *mê niddā* in this chapter (vv. 9, 13, 20, and twice as *mê hanniddā* in v. 21), along with its occurrence in 31:23, directly referring to chapter 19, are the only occurrences of this phrase – although the Nazirite's seventh day cleansing refers to this rite (6:9), and the cleansing of Levites includes *mê ḥaṭṭā't*, 'waters of purification' (8:7). The phrase *mê niddā* is regularly translated 'waters of impurity', understood as 'waters for impurity' (and thus 'waters of purification'). The word *niddā* is used primarily for women's flow of blood (Lev. 12:2, 5; 15:19–33; cf. Ezek. 18:6; 22:10; 36:17), coming to signify the 'impurity' of menstruation and so used for other impurities as well, its meaning including filthiness and separation. Its root derives either from *nādad*, referring to fleeing, retreating, or departing away, or *nādāh* (in pi.), used for thrusting away or excluding (see M. Greenberg 1995), the two roots perhaps being synonymous and basically meaning to chase or drive away – expulsion or exclusion (Milgrom and Wright 1998). However, rather than understanding 'waters of expulsion (of impurity)', Greenberg, who favours the double ayin root *nādad*, underscores the idea of the exclusion or separation of women socially during their time menstrual impurity (1995: 75), and Humann, who follows Greenberg's reading, translates the phrase as 'waters of separation (from defilement, the impurity of death)' (2011: 135–136; cf. Gorman 1990: 197), which I have used (cf. AV). If the notion of a woman's impurity, as addressed in Leviticus, is allowed to influence our understanding of the red heifer ritual, then perhaps Israel is being cleansed as 'the bride of Yahweh', from the 'whoring' of the first generation (cf. 14:33; 15:39).

There is some discussion on whether the 'it' in 'it is a purification offering' should be rendered masculine (K), pertaining to the ashes (Milgrom 1981b: 67), or feminine, pertaining to the cow (Gilders 2006: 7–8), although even the ashes themselves may be considered the whole cow incinerated. The ordinance is a perpetual statute (*ḥuqqat ʿôlām*) (cf. 10:8) for both the sons of Israel and for the sojourner (*gēr*) sojourning among them.

11–13. The first part of the regulation closes with general conditions requiring the waters of separation, along with the penalty for failing to be cleansed. The expression 'dead (*mēt*) body of any human (*nepeš ʾādām*)' (vv. 11, 13; cf. Gen. 9:5), observed already in Numbers 9:6, requires some comment, especially in relation to the odd use of *nepeš*, which often refers to a living being, yet presumed by some to be a euphemism for 'corpse' (e.g. Wolff 1974; cf. Westermann 1997), an interpretation dismissed as groundless by others (Michel 1994). One also finds the expression *nepeš mēt* (Lev. 21:11; Num. 6:6), which in contrast with *nepeš ḥayyā* (living person) in Genesis 2:7, would simply mean 'dead person'. As a general designation suitable for casuistic law, *nepeš* is used four other times in this chapter with the sense of 'person' or 'someone' (vv. 13, 18, 20, 22; Westermann 1997: 755), making the two uses in question as 'corpse' unlikely (Humann 2011: 139). Some scholars, appropriately noting that any person or open container present within the tent of one who dies is rendered unclean, posit a departing life-force or even malevolent ghost, a notion that accords conveniently with the theory that the red cow ritual betrays vestiges of an ancient pagan cult of the dead (see Seligson 1951; Michel 1994). More recently, however, serious doubts have emerged about the antiquity of the red cow ritual (e.g. MacDonald 2012b; Achenbach 2003b: 505–508, 525–528), arguing against any hidden agenda, whether against a cult of the dead or as a transformed sort of exorcism to ward off the effects of ghosts (see Frevel 2012: 213–222). Maccoby (1997), moreover, maintains that death's pollution should not be viewed as any material 'substance that crept around rooms', gas-like or otherwise, explaining that defilement resulted simply from the situation of being together with a corpse in a certain kind of area. While questions remain, four observations may be made about the usage of *nepeš* here and in related passages (Humann 2011: 137–144; Frevel 2013c: 391–400). First, all such references to *nepeš* occur in priestly legislation concerned with the contraction of impurity. Second, within the Torah, *nepeš* is used particularly regarding dead humans by contrast to the carcasses of animals, for which *něbēlāh* is used – Numbers 19 thus supplements the purity laws of Leviticus 11, which had dealt only with defilement from animal carcasses. Third, use of *nepeš* points to the unique composition of human beings: the 'living soul' is comprised from both the dust of the ground and YHWH's breath of life (Gen. 2:7; cf. 9:5), and death undoes this union. The dead body should not be confused with a living person – just as the body and soul are separate (cf. Hirsch 2007a: 409–412). Fourth, the death of 'the human' (*hā'ādām*, v. 13), made in the image of God, and this within the context of the life-giving cult of YHWH and its purity regulations that were based on the opposition between YHWH's life and death as the wages of sin, is more seriously defiling than the carcasses of animals for which one need merely wash one's clothes and remain unclean until evening, necessitating no 'waters of separation'. In sum, as allusions to the creation account of humanity, the terminology of Numbers 19:11 and 13 'communicates the Priestly conception of the nature of man, and the tragedy of his death' – the 'undoing of the image of God' (Humann 2011: 144, 246).

The major defilement of human death must be cleansed away from God's people before their entry into the Camp, lest they defile the Sanctuary. The purification process takes seven days, as it does for both the Nazirite who comes into contact with a human corpse (6:9) and for those with leprosy (Lev. 13:5; 14:9; 15:13). Cleansing by way of sprinkling with the waters of separation occurs on the third and seventh days, days arguably representing new life and completeness, respectively (cf. Gen. 1:11–13; 2:1–3) – with the eighth day signifying new creation status. Similarly, Humann observes (2011: 244–245):

The application of the waters on the third day has its analogue in the third day of creation – when the separation of the waters brought forth the dry land from out of the primordial abyss. The seventh day represents the fullness and completion of this renewal of creation.

He further notes that the symbolic use of 'seven' is found throughout many of the other ritual prescriptions, all of which pertain to the Sanctuary and are designated a 'perpetual statute' (ḥuqqat ʿôlām) (2011: 97–98). Moreover, the third day is the first day of organic life, and the seventh day represents the spiritual *telos* of humanity to which the entire cosmos is directed under its divine dominion, even fellowship with God (see Hirsch 2007a: 434; cf. 2007b: 25).

The term for 'dash' (zōraq) here (v. 13) and in verse 20 is different than for 'sprinkle' (hizzâ), used in verses 18 and 19, which has led some to suppose different sources. Cole, however, is correct to point out two features that mark the change as intentionally rhetorical (2000: 313): the chiastic distribution of usage in verses 13, 18, 19, 20 (zōraq, hizzâ, hizzâ, zōraq), and that zōraq is used for the sprinkling process in the exclusionary cases because of noncompliance, whereas hizzâ is used in the case of active sprinkling for purification. Use of zōraq, which is more general in nature, is fitting for the summary statements in verses 13, 20 (cf. Ganzel 2020: 234–235). Failure to undergo this purification means the person 'will not be clean' (v. 11), he 'will be unclean, his uncleanness is upon him' (v. 13). The form of purification here, yithattā' (vv. 12 [twice], 13, 20) in hithpael, signifies 'to undergo purification' rather than 'to purify oneself' (Humann 2011: 164–165). The central problem for the one who contracts corpse pollution and does not undergo cleansing on the third and seventh days, remaining in a state of major impurity, is that such a person defiles the Dwelling of YHWH, a problem so serious it is punished with that soul being '*cut off* from Israel' – the dreadful *kareth* penalty. The basis and essence of the covenant community is having YHWH's Dwelling in the midst of his people (cf. Exod. 29:45–46), the fountain of life and blessing at the Camp's centre, and this foundational core, pure and holy, must be kept separate from the defilements of sin and the pollution of death. At the end of the purity laws in Leviticus (chs. 11–15), YHWH declared that by such legislation Moses and Aaron were to 'separate' (nāzar) the sons of Israel from their 'uncleanness' (ṭum'āh), so they will not die in their 'uncleanness' (ṭum'āh) by 'defiling' (ṭāmē') 'my Dwelling that is in their midst' (15:31), and the cleansing from corpse pollution here has the same object in mind. A corpse, the dead body of a human being made in the image of God, was considered the ultimate source of impurity in the rabbinic system, dubbed 'father of fathers of impurity' (Rashi on *b. Pes.* 5.14b, 17a; *m. Kel.* 1.1–4; cf. Harrington 1993: 147–150), which in the priestly system would form the polar opposite of YHWH God, the fountain of life. A person stained by the pollution of a human corpse, merely by his or her presence within the Camp, would defile YHWH's Dwelling (Büchler 1967: 265). Stained by death, a person belongs to the realm of *Sheol* – thus unfit to partake of the Camp which has the pure life of God as its basis (cf. Frymer-Kensky 1983: 399–400, 404–405). Nevertheless, the text stresses especially the wanton sin of failing to purify oneself, bringing death into the realm of life (Wold 1978: 18; Humann 2011: 151–153). If one will not take the divinely proffered gift of the red heifer's death and annihilation in one's place, then such a person will endure that judgement for oneself.

The *kareth* penalty of being *cut off* refers to severe excommunication from membership in Israel by way of destruction, either directly at the hands of God or by judicial execution at the hands of the covenant community, so that one's name and lineage are eradicated, a judgement threatened for wilful transgression of the boundary between holiness and impurity, involving sacred space, status, or time (Wold 1979; Horbury 1985; Sklar 2005: 15–20). As such, the kareth penalty, as Gorman observes, 'is concerned with the most basic categorical distinctions of Israelite cosmology' (1990: 191–192; cf. Frymer-Kensky 1983: 403–405) – the Camp is being restored as a microcosm. Holiness and life are nearly synonymous with reference to YHWH their source and wellspring. The divine Camp, in the transition from the first generation to the second, is being cleansed from the death-stain of the former and being renewed in life to abide with YHWH God. Within the context of the red heifer ceremony, excommunication 'from Israel' (v. 13) and 'from the midst of the assembly' (v. 20) is emphasized – the privilege of being part of the covenant community, the Camp of Israel. Humann makes two helpful observations (2011: 157): As the only purification ritual in the Pentateuch that threatens the *kareth* penalty, the severity of human corpse pollution is underscored, which in turn brings into focus the utter purity of the Camp having the absolute life of YHWH as its structural core. The penalty, furthermore, is *spatially oriented* along the axis of the Camp, as excommunication from the covenant community, so that the red heifer ceremony may be understood clearly as a *rite of passage*, transferring the individual spatially from the wilderness into the gathering of Israel around YHWH. Failure to undergo purification is to despise membership within the covenant community, rejecting the prospect of life with YHWH in the land; such a failure aligns a person with the rebellious old generation, which preferred to appoint a leader and return to Egypt (see Num. 11:5, 18–20; 14:3–4).

While the unclean person is instructed to 'purify himself' on the third and seventh days, warned that otherwise he will remain unclean, and threatened that such a failure to undergo purification defiles YHWH's Dwelling and will result in the terrible *kareth* judgement, yet it is not until verse 13 that the 'waters of separation' are mentioned. Even the section on the preparation of the red heifer's ashes (vv. 1–10), which has had these cleansing waters in view, gives no hint as to their use, reserving the explanation until verses 17–19.

19:14–22: Detailed circumstances for applying the waters of separation

Beginning with 'This is the law (or "the teaching", *hattôrāh*)', this section forms a second panel in the chapter's literary structure, covering detailed circumstances for applying the waters of separation. While making the ashes required priestly supervision, the application of the ashes mixed with living water, may be performed by 'a clean man'. The priesthood is not mentioned at all in this section but, given the scenario described after the battle with Midianites in Numbers 31:19–24, even the cleansing by waters of separation was regulated by the priesthood, especially as the priests, along with Levites, were charged with guarding the Sanctuary from defilement (Num. 18:1). As the first half of the chapter focused on death, by way of the incineration of the red heifer (vv. 1–13), the second half focuses on life, on being cleansed from death's pollution by 'living' waters and restored to life-giving fellowship with God and his people within the Camp.

14–16. The introductory formula is used to introduce ritual instruction, in this case related to purity matters (Gorman 1990: 194; citing Begrich 1936). These verses comprise detailed circumstances, added to the general ones listed in verses 11–13, for which the waters of separation must be applied on the third and seventh days. There are two basic situations that result in impurity by way of a human corpse (Humann 2011: 159): 'contact, direct or indirect, with a corpse within a domestic dwelling (vv. 14–15), and direct contact with a corpse out in the open (v. 16)'. For the first situation, when a human dies within a tent, 'contact' is established by being inside (or entering) the tent with the corpse – that is, by proximity to the corpse within an enclosed space. As the impurity is 'trapped within the covered, enclosed structure' (Levine 1993: 466), being inside the tent establishes (indirect) contact. The same is true also for any open vessels within the tent, vessels that have no 'cover (*ṣāmîd*) corded (*pātîl*)' upon them – likely referring to a lid attached to the vessel by cords that passed through holes in the lid and through the vessel's handles (Milgrom 1990: 161; cf. *m. Kel.* 10.1–8). By contrast, corpses encountered 'in the open field', that is, *not* within an enclosed structure, defile only by direct contact – by 'touching' (*nāga‘*). The detailed listing may be oriented to time, beginning with the (recently) slain and ending with the grave – in any case, the level of defilement remains the same. This teaching, especially regarding the slain, will be implemented after war with the Midianites (31:19–24), war being a scenario in which defilement is inescapable. Frevel offers a useful arrangement of the four cases that expands the temporal dimension of defilement from the time of death to the existence in the grave, an enduring 'abode' (2013c: 395). (See Table 33.)

As with the defilement of a corpse within a tent, the period for uncleanness upon contact with the dead out in the open, whether by

Table 33: Temporal dimensions of corpse defilement

Matter	Time	Space
One who has been slain by sword	Between slaughter and burial	Any space
One who has died	After death until burial and beginning of decomposition	Any open or enclosed space
A human bone or skeleton	During and after decomposition of the body	Any open but usually enclosed space
A grave	Utilization phase	A defined enclosed space

touching a slain person or a single human bone, is seven days – presuming a third- and seventh-day purification by the waters of separation.

17–19. The making and application of the waters of separation are explained in these verses. Underscoring this process is the fact that human corpse pollution is so intense, 'peculiarly strong and difficult to remove', that 'washing with mere water was not sufficient' (Kurtz 1863: 424). For the unclean person 'they will take', implying a communal concern for the purity of each individual. They will take 'from' (*min*) the ashes – while the heifer was given on behalf of the community and for sake of making a large quantity of ashes, the application, as a purification offering, is per individual (although some scenarios will involve many individuals and objects, as with Num. 31). The word translated 'ashes', *'ăpar*, also means 'dust', and is different from the more standard term for ashes in verses 9 and 10, which is *'ēper*. Within Numbers, one recalls the 'dust' (*'ăpar*) of the Tabernacle floor that is put into water to make the 'bitter waters' a strayed woman is to drink (5:17). Within the Torah's context, the echo sounds the creation of man by YHWH God who formed him from the 'dust' (*'ăpar*) of the ground and breathed into his nostrils the breath of life so that he became a living soul (Gen. 2:7), a subtext for the red cow rite. Equally relevant, the divine curse for Adam's transgression was death: 'for you are dust (*'ăpar*), and to dust (*'ăpar*) you will return' (Gen. 3:19). Humann, building on Levine (1993: 468), further explains that in some passages both *'ēper* and *'ăpar* are used as an idiom – 'dust and ashes' (Gen. 18:27; Job 30:19) – that underscores the *mortality* of human nature, 'dust' being a mark of humiliation, the domain of death to which mortals return (2011: 162–163; cf. Habel 1985: 420, 582). He suggests a wordplay, serving as 'an allusion to the narrative of man's creation, punishment and inevitable mortality' (Humann 2011: 163). The ashes are of 'the burnt purification offering' or of 'the burning (*śĕrēpat*) of the purification offering (*haḥaṭṭā't*)' (cf. Milgrom 1990: 441); they function as a portable purification offering. Hieke, similarly, refers to an 'instant-*ḥaṭṭā't*' (2009: 59; cf. G. J. Wenham 1981b: 164; Philip 1987: 216). One then pours 'living water' (*mayim ḥayyîm*), running water fresh from a spring or stream, on the ashes in a vessel, which in combination with the blood-infused ashes creates a 'solution of life' (Rudman 2003: 76), the focus of the second half of the legislation being on cleansing, life, and re-entry into the Camp. Just as the human person is dual, formed from the dust of the earth and the breath of YHWH (Gen. 2:7), so the ashes, representing man's mortality, are combined with living waters, which point ultimately to YHWH himself, 'the fountain of living waters' (*měqôr mayim ḥayyîm*, Jer. 2:13; 17:13).

As the one who prepared the waters of separation, having handled the ashes, was himself rendered unclean thereby, verses 18 and 19 call for a 'clean man' to sprinkle the waters, underscoring that it is a 'clean person' who must sprinkle the 'unclean', setting forth a vision of the covenant community whereby God's people serve and cleanse one another (see John 13:1–17; Phil. 2:1–11; 1 John 3:16–23; Jude 22–23). Using a hyssop branch to sprinkle the waters, the pollution caused by death is cleansed away from the tent, vessels, and persons. Hyssop was first used for applying blood to the doorframe of Israelite homes in Egypt, signifying the cleansing of the household within, a purification that guarded them from the death-threat looming over all the firstborn in Egypt (Exod. 12:22), redeeming Israel, God's firstborn son, from the land of death (see Morales 2020: 50–54). Similarly, the rite of cleansing from leprosy – a disease likened to death – involved the application of blood by a hyssop branch (see Lev. 14:4, 6, 49, 51, 52). Hyssop, then, is used in the transition from impurity to purity, from death to life, and its ritual significance may encompass its foundational use in the exodus. The rite of passage from death to life marks the transition between the generations – the first had died in the wilderness, the second would inherit life in the land – perhaps as an exodus experience for the latter.

20–22. While verse 13 stipulates the *kareth* penalty, being cut off, 'for' (*kî*) failing to be dashed with the waters of separation, verse 20 says it is 'for' (*kî*) defiling YHWH's sanctuary (cf. Ashley 1993: 373–374), a rhetorical device that unites cause and effect into a single reality for which one would be cut off. There is, moreover, a parallel between God's people and his earthly Dwelling, the defilement of one leading to that of the other – a mystery unveiled more fully in the New Testament (see 2 Cor. 6:16; Eph. 2:19–22; 1 Peter 2:4–10). Stylistic variation among the two panels is seen with the reference to 'the Dwelling of YHWH' (v. 13) and 'the Sanctuary of YHWH' (v. 20), and in being cut off 'from Israel' (v. 13) and 'from the midst of the assembly' (v. 20). The latter part of verse 19, along with verses 20–21, refers to the one who sprinkled the waters. This person contracts secondary impurity, a minor form which does not require undergoing purification by the waters of separation. Rather, the person simply needs to wash his garments (and bathe himself, taken for granted here by ellipsis) in order to be clean the evening of the same day he sprinkled the unclean person. However, for one who merely touches the waters of separation – not having sprinkled them – it seems no washing of clothes or bathing is necessary, but only a waiting until evening. Becoming unclean until evening presents the shortest duration of ritual impurity (Budd 1984: 213). By contrast, one who has been defiled by a human corpse not only requires seven days and a twofold purification by waters of separation, but during this time he or she becomes a source of secondary defilement to others, making corpse-defilement the most severe of all ritual impurities – death being the greatest defilement (Humann 2011: 167–168). Part of the paradox of the red heifer ritual is that its waters cleanse the defiled even while defiling the clean: the one who sprinkles the waters of separation or even touches the waters will be unclean until evening, just as anyone touched by the person defiled by a human corpse becomes unclean until evening. Rudman suggests that the waters of separation, which cause a relatively minor form of impurity, function by diluting the power of death's pollution, and so enabling the cleansing of those defiled by human corpse even while defiling those who are clean (2003), a reading similar to that of R. T. Harris who suggested *mê niddā* should be understood as 'waters of menstrual impurity' (1998). These studies perceive something of the false dilemma involved in the paradox, inasmuch as different sorts of impurity are involved: the waters do not defile nearly as severely as the human corpse pollution which they cleanse. Milgrom's explanation of the paradox through the fact that the ashes of the red cow function as a purification offering is likely closer to the mark (1981b: 67–68; cf. Frick 2002: 229). Even this explanation, however, requires that the ashes defile prospectively, before being used for purification (Wright 1992a: 116), a point Baumgarten sees as a major flaw, preferring instead to view the required cleansing from contact with the ashes or waters of separation in terms of de-sanctification (1993). Capping the chapter, the ritual is once more labelled a 'perpetual statute'.

Explanation

In the aftermath of Korah's rebellion and YHWH's threefold vindication of Aaron as high priest, and the great death toll by divine earthquake, fire and plague, the sons of Israel turned to Moses, crying out, 'We perish!' and asking, 'Are we to perish completely?' The focus of their fears was the reality of YHWH's presence in their midst: 'Whoever draws near – even draws near – to the Dwelling of YHWH will die' (17:27–28). Numbers 18 – 19, with their attention to the roles of the priesthood and Levites, who will bear responsibility for encroachment of YHWH's Tent so his wrath does not fall on Israel en masse, and the remedy for cleansing from death's pollution, function as the answer to the people's cry. Although chapter 18 reaffirms YHWH's original Camp structure and the place and responsibilities of priests and Levites within it (Num. 1:50–53; 3:10–15, 38; 8), the legislation also establishes new practice and contains new emphases – and, after the challenges to the priesthood (chs. 16–17), substantiates and seals the status and function of the priesthood by way of an eternal covenant (18:19; see S. D. Mason 2008: 189–206). Verbal and nominal forms of 'to give' (*nātan*) occur sixteen times in chapter 18, underscoring the gift nature of YHWH's remedy. Numbers 18 reasserts the social spheres and hierarchical relationships that had been divinely established for God's people (cf. T. S. Clark 2014: 101–112), embodied by the structure of the Camp, and chapter 19 focuses on the cleansing from death's pollution needed for re-entering the Camp out of the wilderness, underscoring the purity of life with YHWH in the Camp (cf. Num. 5 – 6), and marks the second generation's transition and cleansing from the first generation's judgement. While Numbers 18 reaffirms the inner boundaries of the Camp, then, Numbers 19 reaffirms the outer boundary, that between the wilderness and entrance into the Camp. Accordingly, while Numbers 18 emphasized the work of priests and Levites, chapter 19 highlights the responsibility of average Israelites not only to undergo purification but to cleanse one another, as a kingdom of priests (cf. Stubbs 2009: 155). In this way, chapters 18–19 present the guarding of the purity of YHWH's sacred Dwelling by all three divisions of people in the Camp – the priests, Levites, and Israelites.

YHWH delivers four speeches, the first three, significantly, addressed to Aaron alone and seemingly paralleling the threefold division of Numbers thematically. The first speech reiterates material from earlier in the book (1:50–53; 3:10–15, 38; 4:1–20; 8:5–26), with two added points of emphasis: first, the priests and Levites are brothers, organically related; second, the priests and Levites will now shield the tribes of Israel from the wrath of YHWH, bearing the penalty for encroachment themselves. The divine resolution, however, does not dissolve the differences between priests and Levites, but reinforces the hierarchy – as with Aaron's budding staff, Aaron and his priestly house form the aristocracy, as it were, of the tribe of Levi, its leadership. Reinforcing the hierarchy means that YHWH's resolution includes not only the people's protection from divine wrath, but also addresses the rebellion of Korah who, as a Levite, sought to usurp priestly prerogatives (cf. Mann 1987: 184–185). Using terminology from the Eden narrative (Gen. 2 – 3), the Levitical and priestly duty of guarding the Sanctuary recalls the role of Adam, the archetypal high priest within the garden (Morales 2015: 51–53; cf. Humann 2011: 251–252), a hint that life with God in the Camp is a spiritual paradise (cf. Num. 24:5–7), a microcosm of the divine intention for the whole cosmos. The first speech thereby forms an innovative summary of the *first major section of the book*, Numbers 1 – 10.

YHWH's second speech to Aaron grants the priesthood a share of his holy things of the sons of Israel as a perpetual statute. Aaron and his house are given from the most holy things from the fire, out of Israel's tribute, purification and reparation offerings, which any son of Aaron – any clean priest – may eat in holy environs. They are also given from the holy things, which may be eaten by any clean member of Aaron's house, both sons and daughters. These gifts include elevation offerings, the best of Israel's oil, wine and grain, their firstfruits, devoted things and firstborn (or redemption price) of humans and animals. With this bountiful display of divine approbation, the priesthood is exalted before all Israel. Through 'the covenant of salt perpetually', Aaron's house is granted by YHWH both people and the benefits of the land, that is, Levites and contributions and firstfruits of the land, this because YHWH himself is their portion and inheritance, and these gifts belong to him. The covenantal conditions for priests include their regular service of cultic mediation, protecting the inner sancta and altar, and putting the encroacher to death. On this score, S. D. Mason has well argued that *'Phinehas' 'righteous' act in Numbers 25 fulfils Aaron's eternal covenant of Numbers 18 and ensures that it will be promulgated through his particular line'* (2008: 190; emphasis original). The second speech underscores one of the *central messages of the book*, found in its central section (chs. 16–20), the pivotal role of YHWH's ordained priesthood in the survival of Israel as a covenant community having YHWH God dwelling in their midst.

YHWH's third and final speech addressed to Aaron alone grants the tithes of Israel to Levites as an inheritance for their dangerous labour of guarding the Tent of Meeting, bearing the penalty for any unauthorized encroachments. This third speech, focused on the subject of inheritance, adumbrates *the final major section of Numbers*, with its setting of Israel's expectation of inheriting the land (chs. 26–36). In this way, just as with YHWH's previous divine speech addressed to Aaron alone in Leviticus (10:8–11), which was programmatic for the rest of the book, YHWH's three speeches to Aaron here offer a glimpse of the three major sections of Numbers, and their underlying emphasis on the priesthood of Aaron.

YHWH's fourth speech is addressed to Moses, although on Aaron's behalf, instructing that Levites, out of the abundance of Israel's tithes they receive as YHWH's gift, will lift up a contribution for YHWH, a tithe from the tithe, which YHWH in turn gives to Aaron's house, the priests. Once more, the divine legislation assumes and asserts a clear hierarchy, *mapped according to the structure of the Camp*: Israel gives to Levites, and Levites give to the priests – with YHWH's intervening, both receiving and giving, at each juncture. The speeches of YHWH in chapter 18 create a divinely oriented centripetal force within the Camp, whereby Israel acknowledges its debt to YHWH by bringing in tithes and offerings toward the centre: the Israelites tithe for the Levites, and then Levites tithe for the priests. Not only is this inward movement a proper response to the outward movement from the centre, of priestly protection and blessing (cf. Num. 6:22–27), but it forms a corrective to the deviant inward movement of previous chapters whereby Korah and his community had approached the Tent of Meeting to usurp the priestly prerogatives of Aaron's house.

Moreover, the abundance of provisions delineated for the well-being of the priests and Levites, out of the surplus of the tribes of Israel as they enjoy a life of blessedness in the land, serves to foster hope and comfort among God's people in the wilderness. Just as chapter 15 functions as YHWH's response to the concerns of the outer camp of twelve tribes (chs. 11–14), which had lost and regained the land, so chapter 18 functions as YHWH's response to the concerns of the inner camp of Levites (chs. 16–17), which had lost and regained its status. The proliferation of 'inheritance' (*naḥălâ*) throughout this chapter may function as a response to the only previous use: Dathan and Abiram's complaint that Moses had not 'given us an inheritance of fields and vineyards' (16:14).

In chapter 19, YHWH speaks to both Moses and Aaron (his fifth and last speech in Num. 18 – 19), legislating a cleansing ritual to maintain the purity of the Camp from human corpse defilement. The foundational basis for the ritual purity system of ancient Israel was the dichotomy between life, as the realm of God, and death, as the realm of creation plagued by sin (see Morales 2015: 153–167). The red heifer ritual, whose waters of separation cleanse from the serious contamination of human corpses, aims at re-entry into the Camp for life with God and his people, while keeping his Sanctuary clear of defilement. The ashes, including blood as 'the most potent cleansing and sanctifying agent in the Bible' along with 'other traditional cleansing agents' like cedar wood, hyssop and scarlet stuff (G. J. Wenham 1981b: 164), form a portable or instant purification offering which may be added to living water as needed for the cleansing rite. While priests were necessary for preparing the ashes, lay Israelites could apply the mixture of ashes and living water, sprinkling the waters of separation (on the third and seventh days), for the cleansing of those defiled by human corpses. In this way, the ritual, which took place outside the Camp, relieved a twofold problem: for the impure person could not approach the Sanctuary within the Camp to offer a purification offering (Num. 5:1–4), and priests needed to avoid corpse contamination (Lev. 21:1–4, 11) (Gane 2004: 659). The red heifer ceremony was an *entrance rite*, conveying people from the realm of death, through contact with a human corpse, to the realm of life, within the Camp of YHWH's people gathered about his Dwelling.

Although attention has already been drawn in the Pentateuch to the defilement caused by human corpses (Lev. 21:1–4, 10; 22:4–7; Num. 5:2; 6:6–13; 9:6), legislation of the divine remedy for purification was not revealed – textually – until the red heifer ritual of Numbers 19. Why place the purification ritual here rather than elsewhere? Some connect the ritual with the immediate context of chapters 16–18, either in the similar aim of guarding the Sanctuary from defilement (19:13, 20) (Milgrom 1990: 157; cf. G. J. Wenham 1981b: 145–146), or as cleansing from the many deaths recounted in Numbers 16 – 17 (Budd 1984: 211; Ashley 1993: 361–362). Josephus noted the contextual relation to the death of Miriam in chapter 20 (see *Ant.* 4.78–84). On these rationales, however, it remains unclear why *this context* should trump others in the book (whether Num. 6:9–12, 9:1–14, or 31:12–24). Rather, the rite of purification through the waters of separation is connected with the book's transition from the first generation to the second: the second generation of Israel that emerges in Numbers 20 has been cleansed from the defilement of the first generation that had been sentenced to die throughout the forty years of wandering in the wilderness. While it is correct to understand the purification ritual as an urgent response to all the death involved in chapters 11–17 (Olson 1996: 119), the red heifer ceremony's placement here rather than in chapter 25, so as to incorporate the deaths at Baal Peor, is explained only by the transition of generations. In other words, the cleansing from death's pollution with its consequent re-entry into life with God in the Camp represents the new start for Israel's second generation. *Numbers 19 signals the transition from the first to the second generation of Israel.*

Scholars have understood Israel's deliverance out of Egypt, journey through the wilderness and entry into Canaan according to the threefold paradigm of rites of passage (*separation* from Egypt, *liminality* in the wilderness and *reincorporation* in the land) (e.g. Vogels 2000), a passage that comes into focus with the death of the first generation and birth of the second. In the wilderness Israel must die and be reborn (Cohn 1981: 10–13, 16), a passage which may be summarized by the transition from the wilderness to re-entry within the Camp entailed in the red heifer ritual. As Humann writes (2011: 228; emphasis original): 'The placement of Num. 19 within the narrative is thus highly significant. It is the *final liturgical law given during the era of the Sinai generation* and itself thematizes purification and separation from death and the wilderness'. Moreover, the refusal to undergo purification for re-entry into the Camp is analogous to the old generation's refusal to enter the land, appropriately subject to the *kareth* penalty, akin to the divine judgement of death in the wilderness (cf. Humann 2011: 229–230). Lichtenstein, aptly, divides Numbers into two sections (2014b: 286–287): the first half dealing with the first generation, chapters 1–18, and the second half, dealing with the second generation's preparation to settle the land, chapters 20–36, with the red heifer ritual marking the transition point between the generations. Such a context is weighted theologically, with the rite of cleansing from death pollution functioning to set forth the risen, second generation as cleansed from the shadow of the first generation's faults and judgement (cf. Hattin 2012: 280). As Samet (1997) writes:

> With the conclusion of this process of distinction between the two generations [in the death of the first generation in the wilderness], we reach the stage of purification from the impurity of death, in preparation for the new and pure life that awaits the generation about to enter the land of Canaan.

More than this, *Israel is being portrayed in terms of the Nazirite vow*, which had centred on an initial setback within the period of deprivation that called for cleansing and a new start (6:9–12). Just as the Nazir defiled by death, needed to undergo waters of purification, so as to begin the period of consecration afresh, so there is now a new beginning for Israel as the second generation is cleansed from the defilement of the first. Within the Nazirite paradigm, which entailed an undefined period of abstention followed by the vow's fulfilment with sacrifices in the land, the actual cleansing remedy for defilement by corpse pollution was withheld until now, an editorial strategy aimed at portraying Israel's wilderness sojourn to the land in terms of the Nazirite vow.

Considering the structure of Numbers 19, with the first half focusing on death, in the incineration of the red heifer to ashes (vv. 1–13), and the second half focusing on life, with cleansing from death's pollution through the living waters of separation (vv. 14–22), the symbolism of Israel's death and rebirth is a natural application, especially within the ritual's narrative placement on the cusp of the transition from Israel's first generation, doomed to die in the wilderness, and the second generation, destined for life with God in the land:

> The heifer, as a symbol of the old generation Israel, is reduced to dust in the wilderness; by means of the ashes of the heifer and living water the one contaminated by death is restored to a living relationship with God, even as the new generation is transferred from the wilderness to the land of promise. (Humann 2011: 228–229)

Given the substitutionary facet of the cultic system, whereby the sacrificial animal takes the place of and, further, *represents* the worshipper, identifying the red heifer with Israel has an exegetical basis. Jewish commentary incorporates both the heifer-as-Israel symbolism and the movement of death and rebirth, from outside to inside the Camp, to apply the ritual to Israel's experience of exile and return. Riskin, for example, writes of the ritual's inherent symbolism of historic Israel, nursing humanity with the milk of God's word, who although she is destined to be slaughtered for the sake of fulfilling her mission learns that 'only God can ultimately redeem us from death', and offers an application related to the survival of the Jewish people after Auschwitz (2009: 156–159). He ends his meditation by quoting from the prophet Ezekiel:

Thus says the Lord your God . . . I will open your graves and cause you to come up out of your graves and bring you into the Land of Israel . . . And I shall put my Spirit in you and you shall live and I shall place you in your land. (37:13–14)

Elsewhere in Ezekiel the sprinkled waters of purification point to the cleansing work of the Holy Spirit (36:25–29), linked to the restoration or 'resurrection' of Israel (ch. 37). Ganzel points out how the cleansing of the nation of Israel in Ezekiel 36:25 parallels the cleansing of Israelites from corpse pollution in Numbers 19 (2020: 234–237), an insight in accord with the literary function of the red heifer ritual as signifying the cleansing of *the nation*, the second generation, from the death and defilement of the first. Ezekiel's ensuing vision of the nation's cleansing as Israel's resurrection from the dead (ch. 37), invites a similar perspective in Numbers: Israel is not only defiled and cleansed on the wilderness sojourn, but dies and is resurrected. Christian interpretation, understanding the red heifer as a type of Jesus (cf. Hebrews 9:13–14; 13:10–13; *Barn.* 8.1–2), is not far removed from the Jewish viewpoint, inasmuch as Jesus stands as a representative of all Israel: his sacrificial death and resurrection as a new creation is set forth in the New Testament as the definitive exile and restoration unto God. Just as the red heifer ritual moves from blood to water, from a sacrifice that had already taken place to its present application through the sprinkling of water, so Jesus' once-for-all sacrifice is subsequently applied by pouring out the Spirit on his people (see John 1:32–34; 4:13–14; 7:37–39; 19:33–35; 20:22; Acts 1 – 2). To the Ezekiel reference, one may add Zechariah which, as noted by Milgrom (1990: 160), uses the designations of both the purification offering and the waters of separation: 'In that day, a fountain will be opened for the house of David and for the inhabitants of Jerusalem for purification (*ḥaṭṭaʾt*) and for cleansing (*niddā*)' (13:1).

The red heifer ceremony, then, signifies the destruction – by being reduced to ashes – of Israel in the wilderness, the judgement upon the first generation of rebels, and, through the waters of separation, the rebirth of Israel, cleansed and returned to life with YHWH in the Camp. Not without justification, Brodie claims these chapters (Num. 18 – 19) as 'the centre of the drama' focusing on atonement, which 'counters the forces of death', and purity, which 'brings vitality, in effect a form of blessedness' (2008: 456, 467). Not only absolutely necessary for the nation's survival in the wilderness (chs. 16–17, 25), the priesthood, chosen and consecrated by YHWH, is *the* means that enables a transition from the old generation to the new, *the way* YHWH has provided for giving Israel a fresh start, cleansed from the defilement of death and rebellion. As an entrance rite into the purity of the Camp, where YHWH's Dwelling forms the centre of life among his people, one gets a faint foreshadowing of the final realization of the covenant community, the New Jerusalem as set forth in Revelation. In this the consummate entrance rite, we read 'there will by no means enter it anything that defiles' (21:27). How then can anyone hope to enter this City and abide before the face of God? Thankfully, the Apocalypse opens with the answer: All may enter who belong to the Lamb 'who loved us and washed us from our sins in his own blood' (1:5).

www.ingramcontent.com/pod-product-compliance
Lightning Source LLC
Chambersburg PA
CBHW060424100426

42812CB00030B/3301/J